THIRD EDITION

History of the Dance in Art and Education

Richard Kraus
Sarah Chapman Hilsendager
Brenda Dixon

Temple University

PRENTICE HALL, Englewood Cliffs, New Jersey 07632

Library of Congress Cataloging-in-Publication Data

KRAUS, RICHARD G.
 History of the dance in art and education / Richard Kraus, Sarah
Chapman Hilsendager, and Brenda Dixon.—3rd ed.
  p. cm.
  Includes bibliographical references.
  ISBN 0-13-389362-6
  1. Dancing—History. 2. Dancing—Study and teaching.
I. Hilsendager, Sarah Chapman. II. Dixon, Brenda. III. Title.
GV1601.K7 1991
375'.7928'09—dc20
       90-32573
       CIP

Editorial/production supervision
 and interior design: F. Hubert

Cover design: Patricia Kelly

Manufacturing buyer: Herb Klein

©1991, 1981, 1969 by Prentice-Hall, Inc.
A Division of Simon & Schuster
Englewood Cliffs, New Jersey 07632

Printed in the United States of America

10 9 8 7 6 5 4 3 2 1

ISBN 0-13-389362-6

PRENTICE-HALL INTERNATIONAL (UK) LIMITED, *London*
PRENTICE-HALL OF AUSTRALIA PTY. LIMITED, *Sydney*
PRENTICE-HALL CANADA INC., *Toronto*
PRENTICE-HALL HISPANOAMERICANA, S.A., *Mexico*
PRENTICE-HALL OF INDIA PRIVATE LIMITED, *New Delhi*
PRENTICE-HALL OF JAPAN, INC., *Tokyo*
SIMON & SCHUSTER ASIA PTE. LTD., *Singapore*
EDITORA PRENTICE-HALL DO BRASIL, LTDA., *Rio de Janeiro*

Contents

CHAPTER 8
Age of Innovation in Ballet 141

CHAPTER 9
Ballet Today 159

CHAPTER 10
Modern Dance Today 195

CHAPTER 11
Black Dance in America 241

Preface

THIS TEXT IS THE THIRD EDITION of a book that was first published in 1969, authored solely by Dr. Richard Kraus, formerly coordinator of the dance curriculum at Teachers College, Columbia University. In the second edition, published in 1981, Dr. Kraus was joined by coauthor Dr. Sarah Chapman Hilsendager of the Temple University dance faculty. In the third edition, another coauthor has been added— Dr. Brenda Dixon, also of Temple University.

Through the combined efforts of these authors, the book has been brought fully up to date, with numerous references describing trends in dance as a major art form and education medium, through the late 1980s. As in the previous editions, the book's two primary emphases are: (a) a conceptual and historical examination of dance in human society, including its changing role as a form of theatrical entertainment in the United States and abroad; and (b) its growing acceptance on several levels of education, in elementary and secondary schools, and in both undergraduate and graduate curricula in hundreds of colleges and universities. As growing numbers of dance scholars in the fields of history, philosophy, anthropology, and related disciplines study dance, dance becomes the focus of increased research and publication— and *History of the Dance in Art and Education* seeks to reflect this development.

However, the authors are not concerned with dance solely from an academic point of view, or strictly as an educational medium. Instead, they examine dance as a *public* art—that is, in terms of its societal role, its degree of economic support, and its relationship to other aesthetic and cultural forms.

In revising the book, four important new chapters have been added: "Black Dance in America"; "Dance as a Public Art: Prospects and Strategies"; "Dance Research and Criticism"; and "Careers in Dance Today." The authors are convinced that these new chapters add relevance and timeliness to the text, and will make it increasingly valuable to dance faculty members, students, and professional dancers.

As part of the revision, a number of changes have been made in the book's terminology. For example, the use of the term *primitive* to describe nonwhite and non-Western societies has been changed, and the term *lineage-based societies* has been substituted—not as a mere cosmetic change, but one which reflects a profound rethinking of the identity and roles of different world cultural groups. Actual practices and trends in both ballet and modern dance are examined in detail, with shifts in avant-garde dance through the 1970s and 1980s presented clearly. The emergence of a number of important national organizations that promote and enrich dance in education and facilitate its growth as a popular performing art is also described.

Numerous sources have been consulted in researching this third edition. The writings of several dance critics have been used extensively, including Anna Kisselgoff, Jack Anderson, and Barry Laine of the *New York Times*, and Nancy Goldner of the *Philadelphia Inquirer*. Among contemporary scholar-critics, several references have been drawn from the writings of Judith Lynne Hanna. The dance publications that have been consulted for useful sources include *Dance Magazine*, *Dance Teacher Now*, and *Ballet News*, along with issues of the *Journal of Physical Education, Recreation and Dance*, and other publications dealing with dance in education. Numerous citations have been drawn from *American Dance*, published by the American Dance Guild, and the *Dance Research Journal*, published by the Congress on Research in Dance. Other publications of the National Dance Association, the National Association of Schools of Dance, and other organizations concerned with such specialized interests as dance therapy, dance notation, and similar concerns, have also been consulted for useful material.

A number of colleges and universities were also helpful in providing materials regarding their dance curricula. These include, among others, departments or programs in dance and dance education at the following: Florida State University; the University of Northern Colorado; Texas Christian University; Teachers College, Columbia; the University of California at Los Angeles; New York University; Ohio State University; University of Utah; University of Illinois; Goucher College; and Stockton State College in New Jersey.

The assistance of Lisa Kraus in editing sections of the book on contemporary dance is gratefully acknowledged. We also thank prepublication reviewers Linda H. Swiniuch, State University of New York at Buffalo, and Natalie W. Duffy. It is not possible to name all of the other organizations and individuals who contributed to the book in one form or another, but their help was invaluable.

Given the rapid rate of change in the performing arts world, the perceptive reader will recognize that, although the text's details are current at the time of publication, changes may occur shortly after publication with respect to company affiliations, the careers of individual dancers or choreographers, and college dance programs.

The authors were fortunate in being able to share some distinctly different areas of personal experience in their joint effort. Sarah Chapman Hilsendager has become widely known over the past fifteen years as a writer and editor of dance publications, and as an officer in several important national and regional dance education organizations. Brenda Dixon has been an active dancer and choreographer in the United States and abroad, as a member of the Mary Anthony Dance Company and the Open Theater, but she is best known as a critic and lecturer on dance from a sociological and anthropological perspective. Richard Kraus's long interest in leisure and cultural development, as reflected in a number of leading textbooks he has written, complemented the contributions of his coauthors.

Given these varied resources, the authors sought to compile a rich, interesting text. Some may feel that they have done too much, in combining a comprehensive history of dance, an appraisal of the current dance scene, an overview of dance in education, and an introduction to dance as a career field. However, it is the authors' belief that these elements are all closely linked, and that they all represent subjects that dance students should be exposed to. Although this third edition of *History of Dance in Art and Education* may contain almost *too much* information, professors who use it as a text have the option of focusing on one section or another, based on the goals of a particular course.

The authors hope that they have helped to enrich the understanding and career development of students of dance, and that this book will serve as a valuable and enjoyable resource for everyone interested in the varied aspects of dance in society.

RICHARD KRAUS

SARAH CHAPMAN HILSENDAGER

BRENDA DIXON

CHAPTER 1

Dance in American Society

... dance education (was weak) as the country entered the 1970s. Then a curious phenomenon occurred. During the 70s a new and vital lifeblood flowed through dance across this country. Older, established companies were revitalized. New and experimental dance groups emerged, sometimes in the most unlikely locales. An audience for dance appeared. A new interest in dance classes, beginning with aerobic dance and expanding to jazz and modern, occurred. American choreography established itself and competed on equal footing with Russian ballet, which had long been recognized as leading the dance field.... This strong national interest in dance meant a new interest in dance in the schools.[1]

ONE OF THE MOST STRIKING ASPECTS OF THE CULTURAL SCENE in the United States today—and throughout the Western world—has been the rapid growth of dance, both as a performing art and as a form of creative education. This book depicts that growth in detail, and presents an accurate picture of dance in American culture today. In so doing, it examines the history and current status of dance as a performing art, and also its other important functions in human society. Interwoven with this analysis is a review of the past and present role of dance education in schools and colleges.

Recent Perspectives on Dance in Popular Culture

To begin, it is helpful to review the changes that occurred with respect to dance's place in American society over the past three decades, particularly in terms of ballet and modern dance. During the 1960s and 1970s in the United States, both forms of dance found new audiences by the millions. Hundreds of new performing companies were established in communities that had never seen ballet or modern dance before. In the United States, as in other Western nations, federal and state governments moved vigorously to support the arts. Dance companies received subsidies to support new choreography, employment of professional dancers, and performance on various levels—including touring on a wide scale.

Other forms of dance, such as musical theater or jazz dance, became increasingly popular, and movies and television featured leading dancers and choreographers. Folk and square dance, clog and tap dance, disco and break dancing, and aerobic dance and Jazzercise all gained the public's interest.

Growth of Interest in the Arts

Numerous factors were responsible for the dramatic upsurge of interest in dance. With increased leisure time and affluence and growing numbers of individuals attending colleges and universities, popular taste swung sharply toward the arts. After World War II, there was enormous growth in the number of symphony orchestras, operas, art galleries, theaters, drama companies, and community art centers throughout the United States. The 1970s, in particular, were marked by expansion of the arts in general, and especially of dance. Von Obenauer pointed out:

> In the last ten years, the number of professional American dance companies with budgets over $100,000 has risen from fewer than ten to over 50. Just three years ago, 70% of America's dance audience was to be found in New York City. Today, 70% of America's dance audience is spread over the country. . . .[2]

In the late 1960s, the national audience for dance was 1.5 million; by the late 1970s, it was estimated at 15 million. By 1978, some 350 regional and resident dance companies had joined the American Association of Dance Companies—50 in one year alone! What did all these statistics mean? Desmond summarized them in a report in *Performing Arts Review:*

> Dance is the fastest-growing art form in America. . . . Within the last 15 years, due to increased funding, greater media exposure, the build-up of superstars (whoever thought that a modern dancer would make the cover of the New York Times Magazine?), and the slow, begrudged granting of its legitimacy as an art form by academia, dance has reached out to a wider audience than ever before.[3]

Expansion of Dance Education

Accompanying the growth of dance on the American cultural scene was the expansion of dance education in varied forms. In 1978, *Time Magazine* reported that there were thousands of ballet schools, from small studios with a single proprietor-instructor to complex organizations affiliated with the major professional companies. Typically, the American Ballet Theater school had 1,000 students, a 25 percent increase over the previous five years. Schools run by the San Francisco Ballet (587 students), the Minnesota Dance Theater (950), and the Ballet West in Salt Lake City (1,000) all had doubled in enrollment.[4]

More and more specialized programs of dance education were established on the secondary school level, with some states or cities sponsoring public high schools of performing arts. Dozens of colleges initiated bachelor's and master's degree programs leading to performing and teaching specializations, and several universities offered doctoral programs emphasizing advanced scholarship and research in dance.

Trends in the 1980s

Interest in dance continued to grow steadily, supported by new organizations, councils, and regional associations that promoted dance both as a cultural art form and as a significant medium of education. However, in the late 1970s and early 1980s, fiscal pressures compelled a cutback in government funding for the arts, eliminating the National Endowment for the Arts touring program, which had assisted numerous performing groups and college dance curricula.[5] With increased costs for many performing arts organizations, the pressure to seek grants led to the use of professional strategists and fund-raising campaigns. Nielsen wrote:

> Devotees of the arts . . . now find themselves increasingly pursued by indefatigable fund-raisers. At every turn—at the museum door, between the acts at the ballet, even at home in the mail and on public TV—the cup is rattled, the hat is passed. More than annoying, this solicitation raises deep questions about the sustenance and even survival of some of our finest cultural institutions.[6]

In summary, the early 1980s were a time of severe financial stringency for the arts, including dance companies. Beverly D'Anne, director of the dance program of the New York State Council for the Arts, commented in 1982 that the "miserly" climate of shrinking funds and redirected priorities was particularly unfortunate at a time when there had been a ". . . huge proliferation of dance companies. . . . No one in the arts field feels private or corporate funding will fill the gap the government is leaving."[7]

Despite such problems, dance continued to thrive in the 1980s. As later chapters show more fully, many dance companies were able to achieve a more stable base of financial support. A renewed effort was made to draw major corporations into the arts field, with growing success during the decade. Regional dance associations and performing arts sponsors developed local alliances and often began networking with similar groups around the country to facilitate performances by touring companies.

In 1983, Frank Hodson, Chairman of the National Endowment for the Arts and Humanities, urged that steps be taken to put arts organizations on a more stable, long-term financial footing. He wrote:

> Basically, we want to encourage cultural institutions to become more effective, taking on some of the best aspects of business in handling their operations. . . . The artistic content has to be from the head of Zeus, but the management that gets the work produced and promoted should not be very different from other businesses. People have to pay more attention to that.[8]

Arts organizations began to sponsor management workshops, and universities established degree programs in arts management. More and more, dancers and choreographers recognized that it was becoming increasingly necessary to rely on sophisticated methods of promotion to attract audiences. For example, Jennifer Dunning wrote that when the Paul Taylor company first advertised a season opening, twenty years before, they would just mimeograph and mail announcements to several hundred people on a list—staying up all night licking stamps.

But, in April 1986, when the Taylor company opened a four-week season at City Center, at the same time that the Joffrey Ballet and Murray Louis Dance Company were both beginning three-week seasons, the process was much more complicated: ". . . at the official start of the spring dance season, the theater-going public will have been bombarded by posters, advertisements, computerized subscription lists and sophisticated brochures laden with color photographs and rapturous critics' quotes."[9]

Promotional Strategies

New efforts were made to enlist corporate support of the arts in the 1980s. For example, 200 American corporations joined together through the National Corporate Fund for Dance, to provide support for leading dance companies. In some cases, such assistance was mobilized on a regional basis. The Minneapolis-based Dayton-Hudson Corporation formed an association of forty-five of the area's leading companies, including General Mills, Honeywell, and Pillsbury, to raise over $11 million a year for philanthropy. Of this, almost 40 percent went to the arts, much of it to dance.[10]

Other corporations have contributed to individual dance companies. Philip Morris, for example, has given substantial sums to the Alvin Ailey American Dance Theater and the Joffrey Ballet for domestic and European tours, and also has helped fund the Dance Theater of Harlem. In 1988, the New York Telephone Company provided funds to assist the New York City Ballet in its annual presentation of *The Nutcracker,* and American Express sponsored performances of Jerome Robbins's *Broadway,* a re-creation of show-stopping dance numbers from *The King and I, West Side Story, Fiddler on the Roof,* and other famous musicals.

New Dance Company Linkages

Traditionally, most dance companies were isolated in their struggle for artistic survival. Over the past two decades, this pattern has been reversed, as more and more companies combined their resources in planning dance seasons, tours, festivals, and similar projects.

In some cases, such efforts have been carried out by organizations devoted to promoting the performing arts in general. For example, since its nonprofit incorporation in Wisconsin in 1966, Affiliate Artists has become a leading producer of performing arts residencies—including dance—in the United States. By the early 1980s, this organization had raised over $18.5 million to place performers in more than 1,000 communities in forty-six states, Puerto Rico, and Canada. In New York

City, Dance Theater Workshop (DTW), since its founding in 1965, became a magnet for hundreds of independent choreographers and small companies and, in the mid-1980s, formed the National Performance Network to circulate new work around the country. Sponsoring 250 or more performances every year, DTW has served as a launching pad for hundreds of nonmainstream artists who have since achieved national recognition.[11]

In some cities, a single charismatic individual has been responsible for forming such dance alliances. For example, Julie McLeod, a dance teacher, critic, choreographer, and activist, was the moving force behind the Santa Barbara, California, Dance Warehouse—a vigorous group that has thirty-five choreographers and eighty dancers in its membership.[12]

In an effort to promote financial stability and strengthen themselves artistically, two leading ballet companies, the Pennsylvania and Milwaukee ballets, joined forces formally in 1987. It was anticipated that this arrangement would permit the new combined group to maintain a more complete repertoire of dances and to attract more outstanding young dancers at a time when competition for them is intense.[13]

Other Flourishing Companies

Other dance companies have been successful in obtaining a high level of community support. For example, the Houston Ballet expanded its company and built a major new facility during the 1980s, and has maintained a nine-week, fifty-five-performance domestic tour in addition to extended European and Asian trips. Under its British-trained director, Ben Stevenson, the company moved from a virtual rent-a-corps status to a gifted forty-four-member ensemble with a hefty $6.3 million budget. As Barry Laine wrote:

> In a time of general economic retrenchment, the company continues to grow. This year it has opened a spacious new $5.6 million administrative, rehearsal and school facility, and plans are laid for both an expanded performance schedule and a larger roster of dancers upon completion of Houston's promising arts complex, the Wortham Theater Center. . . .[14]

Similarly, in 1988 the Boston Ballet announced plans for a $4.6 million expansion of the company's home and school. When the company's director, Bruce Marks, arrived in 1985 from Ballet West in Salt Lake City, the Boston Ballet had a $1 million debt. Since then, it has raised $11.6 million, brought in new dancers and choreographers, strengthened the corps, and, in cooperation with the city's largest producer of modern dance, Dance Umbrella/Boston, sponsored a Discovery Festival for young performers.[15]

Dance Festivals and Regional Companies

On other levels, dance has been thriving, with solid public support. In all regions of the country, major summer dance festivals have presented a rich mixture of dance forms, often in combination with music and other performing arts. Conducted in cooperation with a major dance company or college dance department serving as host, festivals include performances for the general public, master classes, workshops, lectures, and symposiums. Anderson wrote:

> No limitations exist as to genre. The regional ballet association defines "ballet" broadly enough to encompass all forms of theatrical dance and, even though American colleges have long been bastions of modern dance, the college association welcomes jazz and classical ballet.[16]

International Trends in Dance

A final important trend in theatrical dance during the 1980s was the growing internationalization of both modern dance and ballet. Many young American dancers are performing with European companies, and many ballet and modern dance companies from England, France, the Soviet Union, West Germany, and other European nations, as well as China, Japan, and other Asian nations have toured the United States. Instrumental in this process has been the International Choreographers Workshop which, funded by the U.S. Information Agency, has enabled choreographers from around the world to study and exchange views at the American Dance Festival in Durham, North Carolina, since 1984.

Growth of Other Dance Forms

Although the primary emphasis thus far in this chapter has been on theatrical dance forms—modern dance and ballet—there also has been a striking expansion of other forms of dance. As this text discusses in detail, there are at least eight different types of dance which the public may experience on one level or another today. These dance forms may be categorized briefly as follows:

1. *Ballet.* The highly disciplined and codified stage art of ballet is based on a centuries-old tradition of movement skills. It has a repertoire today that is drawn from classical performance side by side with the most contemporary themes and choreographic approaches.

2. *Modern Dance.* Often referred to as contemporary dance, this highly individualistic and diverse form of artistic expression began as a rejection of what its advocates condemned as the formalism and sterility of traditional ballet. Today, it still emphasizes the artistic expression of the individual performer or choreographer, although an increasing number of companies are performing works by earlier modern dance pioneers. Its practitioners range from those who accept ballet as an indispensable form of training, or those who actually choreograph for ballet companies, to those avant-garde practitioners who, in performance at least, appear to be concerned with nondance.

3. *Musical Stage Dance.* This hybrid form, found on the Broadway stage, in movies, or on television, usually combines elements of ballet and modern dance, jazz, tap and clog, and even ethnic dance. It tends to be a bright and highly polished form of glamorous entertainment, visually pleasing to a broad audience. Many of the

stage works by choreographers such as Jerome Robbins and Agnes de Mille have been recognized as important dance creations.

4. *Ballroom Dance.* The most widespread form of participating dance, ballroom dance ranges from the familiar social dances which were popular in past decades, such as the fox trot, waltz, tango, rumba, or other Latin-American steps, to the pulsating and physically exciting rock-and-roll or discotheque dances.

5. *Other Recreational Dance Forms.* Many individuals today enjoy performing the traditional folk dances of other countries, either because of their own national heritage or because they are part of an international folk dance movement. Similarly, American square and round dancing are practiced by many thousands of enthusiasts in urban and suburban adult clubs. While these forms of dance—when done originally by the common people—were quite simple, today they are often extremely complicated, with new dances constantly being invented and introduced.

6. *Ethnic Dance.* This refers to the type of dance performed by specialized ethnic groups—usually of non-European origins. Such dances tend to be highly traditional, linked directly to social customs or religious practices, and stylized in their movement and presentation. While the common people may perform such dances in their own countries, when we see them in the United States they are usually presented by trained touring companies as a form of spectacular entertainment.

7. *Exercise Dance.* This includes several forms of dance which are commonly performed for fitness purposes but which contain elements that are distinctly dance-like. Examples are Jazzercise and aerobics. Exercise dance also may be done in swimming pools, particularly as a therapeutic activity.

8. *Allied Movement Forms.* Several other types of movement activity that are choreographed and performed before audiences, such as ice dancing, aerial dancing, gymnastic floor exercise, and water ballet or synchronized swimming have become increasingly accepted as forms of dance. So-called martial arts, such as aikido or t'ai chi chuan, or relaxation disciplines, such as yoga, also fit in this category.

Chapter 12 describes a number of these dance forms in more detail. At this point, it is enough to say that each specialized type of dance has gained increasing public interest in recent years. For example, ballroom dancing has been greatly popularized through the efforts of the United States Dance Foundation, which works with both amateur dancers and professionals to improve ballroom dance education and performance. A number of performing companies have designed popular theatrical presentations based on ballroom dance, and ballroom dance participation appears to be reaching a much broader age span than in the past.[17]

Continued Growth of Dance Education

Accompanying these trends, the decade of the 1980s saw a steady growth in dance education. On elementary and secondary school levels, new standards and guidelines for educational dance as a discipline-based art form were developed by state curriculum experts and dance education associations. College and university dance programs continued to expand both in numbers and quality. Chapman summarized some of the new directions in dance education:

Dance in American public and private education is positioned on a new threshold, one which challenges stereotypes . . . both inside and out of the studio/classroom/ gymnasium. Having long been considered the forgotten art in arts education circles dominated by musicians and visual artists, and often being lost within programs of physical education, dance educators have begun to analyze, theorize, and publicize their work in ever more revealing and powerful ways. Professional preparation courses in colleges and universities nationwide have begun to examine the meaning of the dance experience within the current, diverse society.[18]

An important aspect of this growth has been the recognition of dance-related research as a valid form of academic scholarship. Sponsored by such organizations as the Congress on Research in Dance (CORD), the Society for Dance History Scholars, and the Dance Critic's Association, there has been a steady increase in the number of research conferences, symposiums and workshops, and publications devoted to the presentation of dance scholarship. Greater numbers of historians, anthropologists, and philosophers have entered this field, with impressive findings regarding dance's role as an artistic and cultural force.

Revitalization of Dance

During the mid-1980s, some concern was expressed that dance had lost the surge and enthusiasm that had characterized its rapid growth during the preceding decades. Anna Kisselgoff, dance critic of the *New York Times,* asked, "Has the dance boom run its course?"

Some critics felt that the death of George Balanchine, a giant figure in American ballet, had left a gap that could not be filled. Others argued that dance had reached the end of an era—that choreographers like Frederick Ashton and Antony Tudor, or great stars like Rudolf Nureyev, who had lent glamour to ballet and attracted huge new audiences, were no longer contributing significantly. Yet the history of dance has shown that, as one generation of choreographers and dancers leaves the stage, new creative geniuses take their place.

Despite fears that dance would suffer dramatically because of the decline in government or foundation funding, it has developed an array of new presenting organizations and networking groups, which are described more fully in Chapter 13. Indeed, Kisselgoff pointed out that it is a misconception to believe that government funding created the dance boom. The reality is that federal and state grants-in-aid programs were a response to the vitality of the arts in America. And, Kisselgoff concluded, dance has certain qualities that other stage arts do not have: "Unlike theater, which exists mainly in a commercial context, dance rarely tried simply to please an audience. The paradox is that it has pleased so many in the process."[19]

The long-term growth of American dance over the period from the early 1970s to the mid-1980s is illustrated by statistics gathered by Dance/USA, the national service organization for professional dance companies. By comparing nine leading ballet companies that had been examined in 1971 by a Ford Foundation study of the performing arts with their status in 1983–1984, it was found that their total income had risen from $14.2 million to $63.4 million—an increase of 360 percent. Similarly, the increase for the eight modern dance companies examined in both studies was 360 percent. Today, the fifty-nine largest American companies have a total income of approximately $110 million. The same companies today earn 66 percent of their income at the box office, with 34 percent coming from contributions—an earned income ratio bettered only by the professional theater.[20]

Careers in Dance

The relatively healthy state of dance as it enters the 1990s is particularly important for those young people who are considering a career in it. Typically, many young men and women who study in private studios, company-connected academies, or degree-granting curricula, look forward to dancing or choreographing professionally. At the outset, they must realize that the challenges facing all creative artists—and particularly performing artists—are severe.

Like those in other performing arts, the dancer must struggle for the relatively few openings that occur in established companies each year or must gain a foothold in new performing groups and settings. Unless he or she is remarkably gifted, the battle is often protracted and difficult. In the mid-1980s, Lappe pointed out:

> The United States Office of Labor reveals that at any given time in 1980, an average of 6500 individuals worked as professional dancers in this country. Professional dancing careers and the relatively small number of job openings have resulted in keen competition, and employment predictions do not suggest a noticeable increase in performance opportunities for dancers in the next decade.[21]

However, there are numerous other kinds of career possibilities for young people interested in dance, including many positions as teachers in schools and colleges, private studios, or community arts centers. There are also opportunities in dance therapy, recreational dance, fitness programs, or jobs in the business or management end of dance production. For those interested in a more academic approach to dance, criticism and research have expanded in terms of career possibilities. For the determined young dance artist, all such work can be combined with dance performance and beginning choreographic work.

Minton pointed out that many who graduate from dance programs each year will need to seek out such opportunities. She wrote: "Many will have to become the entrepreneurs of the dance world. They will have to apply their training in creative ways, make new connections outside the dance community, and organize professional opportunities by themselves."[22]

In later chapters of this book, a number of such strategies are discussed, along with methods that successful dance companies use to gain public interest and support. But first, we explore the meaning of dance itself, its history throughout the ages, and the role it plays in contemporary society.

Notes

1 John McLaughlin, "A Stepchild Comes of Age," *Journal of Physical Education, Recreation and Dance,* November/December 1988, p. 58.

2 Heidi von Obenauer, *Dance Magazine*, March 1976, p. 98.

3 Jane Desmond, *Performing Arts Review*, vol. 7, no. 2, 1977.

4 "Boom at the Box Office," *Time*, May 1, 1978, p. 88.

5 See Anna Kisselgoff, "Has the Dance Boom Run Its Course?", *New York Times*, March 3, 1985, p. H-32.

6 Waldemar A. Nielsen, "Needy Arts: Where Have All the Patrons Gone?" *New York Times*, October 26, 1980, p. D-1.

7 Beverly D'Anne, cited in Ginger Danto, "Dance Troupes Tighten Belts," *New York Times*, September 19, 1982, p. H-20.

8 Frank Hodsoll, "The Arts Must Take on the Best Aspects of Business," *U.S. News and World Report*, January 17, 1983, p. 63.

9 Jennifer Dunning, "Dance as Big Business, May Pose a Threat to Dance as Art," *New York Times*, March 30, 1986, p. H-1.

10 Sandra Salmans, "Big Business Tightens Its Arts Budget," *New York Times*, February 20, 1983, p. 2-27.

11 Sali Ann Kriegsman, "Networking," *Ballet News*, May 1985, p. 26.

12 Joan Crowder, "Julie McLeod: Dance Teacher, Critic, Choreographer and Activist," *Dance Teacher Now*, October 1986, p. 10.

13 Nancy Goldner, "Penna and Milwaukee Ballets Plan Joint Venture," *Philadelphia Inquirer*, January 30, 1987, p. 7-C.

14 Barry Laine, "Houston Ballet: Growing Fast and Flourishing," *New York Times*, October 13, 1985, p. 8-H.

15 Susan Diesenhouse, "Ballet in Boston Unveils Plans for a Larger Home," *New York Times*, April 10, 1988, p. 44.

16 Jack Anderson, "No Stars, But Lots of Verve at the Regional Festivals," *New York Times*, August 18, 1985, p. F-8.

17 Susan Wershing, "David Key and the United States Dance Foundation," *Dance Teacher Now*, April 1986, pp. 12–16.

18 Sarah Chapman, "Dance Dynamics: Shaping a New Vision," *Journal of Physical Education, Recreation and Dance*, November/December 1988, p. 57.

19 Anna Kisselgoff, "Art for the Artist's Sake Still Applies to Dance," *New York Times*, November 18, 1984, p. H-8.

20 Donald A. Moore, Director of Dance/USA, national service organization for professional dance companies, in *New York Times*, March 10, 1985, p. H-19.

21 Mary Martha Lappe, "Dance Careers for the Next Decade," *Journal of Physical Education, Recreation and Dance*, May/June 1984, p. 76.

22 Sandra Minton, "An Entrepreneur's Opportunity in Dance," *Journal of Physical Education, Recreation and Dance*, February 1987, p. 74.

CHAPTER 2

The Meaning of Dance: Basic Concepts

Dance is a nearly universal behavior with a history probably as old as humanity itself. Since antiquity, paintings, friezes, sculpture, myths, oral expression, and then literature attest to the existence of dance. Dance is embedded in our being. Even when not physically manifest, the concept and vision of dance emerge in our thinking. The dynamics of dance, culture, and society are inseparable.[1]

To comprehend fully the powerful appeal of dance and the reasons for its growth as a cultural activity in modern society, one must understand the nature of dance itself. Rather than simply relying on labels like *ballet, modern dance,* or *ballroom dance,* this chapter explores the basic concept of dance as an art form and means of human expression. So varied are the forms of dance, and so complex are the motivations for carrying them on, that it is difficult to offer a single definition that encompasses all forms of dance.

Dance may range from social pastime to theatrical performance, or from religious rite to fitness-related activity. In one form or another, it appeals to all social classes and widely ranging levels of artistic taste. Some dances are centuries old; others were evolved only yesterday. Dance has become an important part of our cultural, recreational, and educational experience. But what *is* dance? Why does it continue to have such a strong appeal on all these levels, for both spectator and participant? What, essentially, is the meaning and purpose of dance in human society?

Ways of Viewing Dance

One might consider the meaning and purpose of dance from several viewpoints—in terms of the etymological source of the word; or through historical examinations of how dance was viewed in earlier societies; or through the eyes of the philosopher, the psychologist, the anthropologist, the dance critic, or the dancer. All of these viewpoints will be helpful in framing a definition.

To begin with, we examine the word itself. According to Lincoln Kirstein, the English word *dance* is related to the French *danse,* which is believed to have been derived from the ancient high German word *danson,* meaning to stretch or drag. Each of these terms, along with other European variants (*dands, danca, danza, tanz*) is based on the root combination of letters *tan,* found in the original Sanskrit, meaning tension, or stretching.[2] However, in a number of definitions dating from the time in which dance was gaining popularity in the courts of Europe, emphasis was given to its spectacular qualities, its social values, or its use as a form of communication.

For example, in Arbeau's famous *Orchesographie* (1583), the author wrote:

Dancing . . . is to jump, to hop, to prance, to sway, to tread, to tip-toe, and to move the feet, hands and body in certain rhythms, measures, and movements consisting of jumps, bendings of the body, straddlings, limpings, bendings of the knees, risings on tip-toe, throwings-forward of the feet, changes and other movements. . . .

Dancing or saltation is an art both pleasing and profitable which confers and preserves health, is adapted for the youthful, agreeable to the aged and very suitable for all. . . . [it] depends on music because, without the virtue of rhythm, dancing would be meaningless and confused, so much so that it is necessary that the gestures of the limbs should keep time with the musical instruments. . . .[3]

Other authorities stressed dance's elegance, grace, and beauty. John Weaver wrote in 1721: "Dance is an elegant, and regular movement, harmoniously composed of beautiful attitudes, and contrasted graceful posture of the body, and parts thereof."[4] Jean Georges Noverre, in 1760, described dance as follows:

Dancing, according to the accepted definition of the word, is the art of composing steps with grace, precision, and facility to the time and bars given in the music, just as music itself is simply the art of combining sounds and modulations so that they afford pleasure to the ear.[5]

Another early definition that stressed order, precision, and graceful movement to the accompaniment of music was found in Diderot's *Encyclopedia* (ca. 1772): "[Dancing is] ordered movements of the body, leaps, and measured steps made to the accompaniment of musical instruments or the voice. . . ."[6]

Clearly, these definitions were based on the kinds of ballroom or theatrical dance which were common in Europe during the eighteenth century. Dance was chiefly thought of as the graceful, formal, and highly stylized couple or set dances performed by members of the court, or as the equally stylized ballet of the period, performed as entertainment and narrative in its effect. One famed historian of the dance, Gaston Vuillier, made it clear that only these forms were regarded as dance; indeed, among earlier or less developed cultures, he conjectured, there was no dance:

> Like poetry and music, to which it is closely allied . . . the choreographic art . . . was probably unknown to the earlier ages of humanity. Savage man, wandering in forests, devouring the quivering flesh of his spoils, can have known nothing of those rhythmic postures which reflect sweet and caressing sensations entirely alien to his moods. The nearest approach to such must have been the leaps and bounds, the incoherent gestures, by which he expressed the joys and furies of his brutal life.[7]

But a true definition of dance must recognize that prehistoric humans *did* dance; indeed, that this was a highly important part of life, and was the ancestor of dance as we know it today. Sheldon Cheney, a distinguished historian of the drama, pointed out the significance of dance as an ancient form of artistic expression:

> Man dances. After the activities that secure to primitive peoples the material necessities, food and shelter, the dance comes first. It is the earliest outlet for emotion and the beginning of the arts. . . .
>
> Not only did drama as such—the art of which *action* is a pivotal material—arise out of primitive dance. . . . Music, too, which can hardly be dissociated from the theatre's beginnings, traces its ancestry to the sounds made to accentuate the primitive dance rhythm, the stamping of feet and clapping of hands, the shaking of rattles, the beating of drums and sticks. Dance, then, is the great mother of the arts.[8]

Numerous American and European historians, anthropologists, and other social scientists have used the term *primitive* to denote preindustrial tribal cultures with limited technology and without written language. However, the word also has been used in a pejorative way to identify non–Western, nonwhite cultures and has frequently implied that such societies exist at a savage, almost subhuman level. Obviously, the term is culture-specific—almost like the ancient Greeks who described all foreigners as barbarians. For this reason, *primitive* is not used throughout this text, other than in quotations from other, earlier authors.

Instead, the term *lineage-based societies* is used to describe those cultural groups which, contrary to the stereotype implied by *primitive,* often have highly complex social structures, religious practices, and art forms. According to Dr. Lynda Shaffer, professor of history at Tufts University, a majority of African, Native American (including North and South American and Alaskan cultures), and aboriginal cultures are lineage-based societies. These groups are characterized by ancestor worship, oral transmission of customs and tradition, and allegiance to specific geographical landmarks.

Dance as Artistic Expression

Two philosophers, James K. Feibleman and Thomas Munro, have attempted to analyze dance systematically, as a form of artistic experience.

Feibleman suggested that there are seven traditionally accepted fine arts: sculpture, dance, painting, architecture, poetry, drama, and music. Each of these has a basic concern, and a medium through which it finds expression. Thus, drama is the art which deals with the human social relations of life situations. Painting is the art which deals with the colors and qualities of two-dimensional space. Music is concerned with time, making use of sound vibrations in a temporal relationship. Feibleman defined dance as simply "that art which deals with the motions of the human body."[9]

Accepting this as a concise statement which distinguishes dance from other art forms, one must then explore the nature of art. Here one enters the domain of aesthetic philosophy, a battleground of ideas where it is difficult to find agreement. The term *aesthetic* itself has been variously defined as "of or pertaining to the beautiful, as distinguished from the merely pleasing, the moral, or the useful," as "the science of cognition through the senses," and as being "responsive to the beautiful in art or nature." In some definitions, it is used to refer to standards of beauty, correct form, and good taste. Similarly, the word *aesthetics* refers to the branch of philosophy dealing with beauty and the beautiful and ways of judging them, especially in the fine arts.[10]

The philosopher Monroe Beardsley argued that "a work of art (in the broad sense) is any perceptual or intentional object that is deliberately regarded from the aesthetic point of view."[11] Carrying the analysis a step further, Beardsley suggested that the aesthetic value of an object is the value it possesses in terms of its ability to provide aesthetic gratification. This, in turn, may depend *either* on the inherent qualities of the object or art expression, in terms of certain commonly accepted principles (such as formal unity), *or* on how people perceive it, which is highly subjective.

Some viewers or critics, in judging an art object, base their reactions on what Meyer Schapiro described as ". . . the fascination of the image, its marvelous likeness to physical reality, and the artist's wonderful skill. . . ."[12]

While the ability of a painter or sculptor to depict objects or people realistically is often used as the basis for judging his or her competence as an artist (particularly by art critics with a representational bias), it is doubtful whether it can be applied at all to arts such as dance, music, or architecture. Certainly much modern art and poetry (to name only two examples) has become totally nonobjective. Nelson Goodman, in an essay on representationalism in art, commented that "Art is not a copy of the real world. One of the damn things is enough."[13]

A common way of approaching the idea of aesthetic worth is to use such terms as *balanced, somber, dynamic, vivid, moving, trite, sentimental, tragic,* or, of course, *beautiful,* in describing or assessing the artistic value of objects. However, these tend to be subjective in their application, and it is unlikely that the same set of adjectives could apply to Michelangelo's ceiling fresco in the Sistine Chapel and to Picasso's *Guernica,* a highly stylized depiction of a brutal bombing during the Spanish Civil War. Frank Sibley concluded that although aesthetic concepts and terms are used widely in identifying or analyzing the worth of art objects, it is not possible to develop a set of rules or standards for their use that will be generally acceptable.[14]

Thomas Munro suggested that there are many levels of art, ranging from what might simply be a skill, or product of human manipulation, to the liberal arts, the fine arts, and the performing arts. Different types of art have different characteristics, in terms of how they are perceived, what their subject matter is, and whether or not they are directly functional. Munro suggested that there are:

> Arts of simultaneous perception, such as architecture, sculpture, or painting, where we see all that is there to see, at once.
>
> Arts of successive perception, which continue in time, changing form, such as music, dance, poetry, and drama.
>
> Arts of space; some art forms are stationary, such as sculpture or painting. Others, like theater, or dance, are movable.
>
> Arts that are imitative or nonimitative. Munro suggested that sculpture and painting are imitative, and that music and architecture are nonimitative. This distinction is not as useful today as in the past; however, if it is applied, dance may be both imitative and nonimitative.
>
> Arts that are serviceable or nonserviceable; architecture and crafts are generally seen as serviceable in that they perform a "useful" function. Dancing, while less so, may perform a service, just as music or art may.

Munro discussed dance at length, pointing out that it is partly a theater art, partly a ballroom art, and partly a religious art. Finally, he stated:

> Dance is an art of rhythmic bodily movement, presenting to the observer an ordered sequence of moving visual patterns of line, solid shape, and color. The postures and gestures of which these are made suggest kinesthetic experiences of tension, relaxation, etc., and emotional moods and attitudes associated with them. They may also represent imaginary characters, actions, and stories. Dances are performed by one person or by two or more in mutual coordination; some animals can be trained to do simple dances. The movements are usually synchronized with, and partly aided by, musical or other rhythmic sounds. . . .[15]

Munro's analysis tends to be a description rather than a definition. We need a clarification of *why* dance is done. Susanne Langer suggested that ". . . the dancer expresses in gesture what he feels as the emotional content of music. . . ." The implication that the music must be the basis for dance performance, and the goal of the dancer merely to reflect what he or she feels to be the mood or emotional content of the music, is not satisfactory. Many choreographers would reject this view, pointing out that the idea of the dance may come first, and that the music may then be composed to accompany the dance. Other, more avant-garde choreographers may take the position that dance does not need music at all. Again, Langer referred to dance as a "plastic art, a spectacle of shifting patterns of created design. . . ."[16] It is an illusion, a vivid representation, created, organized, formal—the play of power made visible. The use of the word *dance* to convey the idea of a play of power or shifting pattern of opposing forces is illustrated in the headlines of news articles dealing with nuclear arms negotiations ("The Superpower Tango") or with design in space ("Warplanes Join in Soaring Ballet for Refueling").

Phenomenological Analysis of Dance

This way of conceptualizing dance has been extended by a number of philosophers using the phenomenological approach to aesthetics. Phenomenology is a form of philosophical analysis which seeks to eliminate preexisting biases and assumptions in an attempt to get a pure and unencumbered vision of what a thing essentially is. One analyst, Maxine Sheets-Johnston, pointed out that to describe dance as a *force* in *time* and *space* (a frequently heard construct) does not convey its meaning as a lived experience, but instead suggests a number of separate objective factors with no unifying center or wholeness. Instead, dance must be conceived, in her terms, as *forcetimespace,* an art form which involves both expression on the part of the performer and evocation of feeling on the part of the audience. Sheets-Johnston wrote:

> The dance, as it is formed and performed by the dancers, is a unity of succession, a cohesive moving form, and so it is to the audience. . . . Dance is not only a kinetic phenomenon which appears, which gives itself to consciousness; it is also a living, vital human experience . . . for both dancer and audience. . . . [17]

Dance as Emotional Expression

The view that emotional expression is at the heart of dance has been expressed by a number of writers in this field. John Martin, an influential dance critic and author during the early years of dance's growth on the American scene, suggested that no matter what the nature of dance activity and despite many variations in outward appearances, all dance is essentially the same. Dance, according to Martin, emerges when the dancer

> . . . allows each of these impulses to express itself in movements which he deliberately remembers and develops in order to be able to convey to others something of his own intuitive reaction which is too deep for words. Thus, at the root of all these varied manifestations of dancing . . . lies the common impulse to resort to movement to externalize states which we cannot externalize by rational means. This is basic dance. . . . [18]

This concept was supported and amplified by the statements of two outstanding modern dance pioneers, Martha Graham and Doris Humphrey. Graham wrote:

> I am a dancer. My experience has been with dance as an art. Each art has an instrument and a medium. The instrument of dance is the human body; the medium is movement. . . . It has not been my aim to evolve or discover a new method of dance training, but rather to dance significantly. To dance significantly means "through the medium of discipline and by means of a sensitive, strong instrument, to bring into focus unhackneyed movement, a human being. . . ."[19]

Humphrey's view of the underlying purpose of dance was expressed in the following statement:

My dance is an art concerned with human values. It upholds only those values which make for harmony and opposes all forces inimical to those values. In part, its movement may be used for decoration, entertainment, emotional release, or technical display; but primarily it is composed as an expression of American life as I see it today. . . . I believe that the dancer belongs to his time and place and that he can only express that which passes through or close to his experience.[20]

More recently, in a discussion of dance as education, Fowler expressed the following view:

Dance is a way to feel what it is to be human and to be alive. In that sense it is celebration. It makes something special out of life. It is revelation; some would say, "illumination." Because it involves the self, it *reveals* self. It communicates what one knows of one's own body feeling. Like all the other arts, dance is a code—in this case a structuring of gestures and motions that captures and conveys subjective inner experience. The elements that make up this code are sound, movement, line, pattern, form, space, shape, rhythm, time, and energy.[21]

Fetters made the same point in suggesting that dance is a form of aesthetic experience in which the moving body is at the same time the instrument of creation and the means through which the artist perceives and responds to other stimuli or images. Thus, the body becomes a sensuous, intensely felt, and expressive means of aesthetic creation. Fetters wrote:

The performer's body demonstrates at once one's objective and subjective orders of being. It is . . . quantitative and visible, but it is also a subject who sees and feels and is sensitive to the world. Thus the aesthetic experience of the body by the performer is particularly unique and distinct from the aesthetic experience of other art objects.[22]

Nonverbal Communication

Judith Lynne Hanna agreed that dance becomes a physical instrument or symbol for feeling and/or thought and may provide a more effective means of communication than verbal language. She wrote:

As an anthropologist attempting to understand all human forms of dance . . . I conceptualize dance in this way: human behavior composed—from the dancer's point of view—of purposeful, intentionally rhythmical, and culturally patterned sequences of extraordinary nonverbal body movements that have inherent and "aesthetic" values, that is, appropriateness and competency.[23]

In a more detailed and technical discussion of dance as nonverbal communication, Hanna added:

Dance is a whole complex of communication symbols, a vehicle for conceptualization. It may be a paralanguage, a semiotic system, like articulate speech, made up of signifiers that refer to things other than themselves. . . . Obviously, dance may not communicate in the same way to everyone. Within a culture, differential understandings of symbols may be based on, and sometimes be exclusive to, the dancer's age, sex, association, occupation, political status groups, and so on.[24]

Does this concept apply to all forms of dance? The view that all dance has as its fundamental purpose the dancer's expression of personal emotions or feelings about life experience would be meaningful if all dance were intended as communicative expression. Clearly, however, it is not. Much dance is simply ritual, practiced again and again as a matter of tribal or societal custom. Other dance involves social interaction, pastime, or simply a display of physical agility and grace. Even in dance that is intended as an artistic or theatrical presentation, there is great variety. Anderson wrote:

> Dance is movement that has been organized so that it is rewarding to behold, and the craft of making and arranging dances is called choreography. Out of all the possible movement combinations that exist, the choreographer selects, edits, heightens, and sharpens those he thinks are suitable for his specific purposes. The gestures in some dances may refer to specific emotional states and their sequence may tell a story. Other dances tell no story, but instead present beautiful images of people in motion, the choreographer believing that pure movement in itself is worthy of attention.[25]

The anthropologist Gertrude Kurath argued that it is difficult to distinguish between dance and other forms of movement, like working or walking, which use the same physical equipment and are subject to the same physical laws of weight, balance, and dynamics. Ultimately, Kurath defined dance in terms that exclude any mention of communicative purpose:

> . . . rhythmic movement having as its aim the creation of visual designs by a series of poses and tracing of patterns through space in the course of measured units of time, the two components, static and kinetic, receiving varying emphases . . . and being executed by different parts of the body in accordance with temperament, artistic precepts, and purpose.[26]

Societal Role of Dance

Since dance takes so many forms and may stem from so many motivations, how can one probe for its essential meaning? Sociologists have pointed out that in many cultures, dance is seen as being far more than graceful movement. Instead, it is a profoundly important social experience—a powerful rite shared by all members of the culture, and essential to its well-being. Margaret Mead commented about her anthropological studies in Samoa that "Dancing is the only activity in which almost all ages and both sexes participate, and it therefore offers a unique opportunity for an analysis of education."[27]

A cultural historian, Curt Sachs, has written that in lineage-based societies and in ancient civilizations, few experiences or communal functions approach the dance in importance. Dance is not viewed as an activity that is external to survival; indeed, Sachs wrote, it "provides bread and everything else that is needed to sustain life." Sachs continued:

It is not a sin proscribed by the priest or at best merely accepted by him, but rather a sacred act and priestly office; not a pastime to be tolerated only, but a very serious activity of the entire tribe. On no occasion in the life of primitive peoples could the dance be dispensed with. Birth, circumcision, and the consecration of maidens, marriage and death, planting and harvest, the celebration of chieftains, hunting, war, and feasts, the changes of the moon and sickness—for all of these the dance is needed.[28]

So important to the life of men and women in lineage-based cultures was dance, that it became a primary means of social identification. According to Havelock Ellis, when a man belonging to one branch of the African Bantu tribe met a Bantu of another branch, he would ask, "What do you dance?" The great power of dance for establishing a sense of tribal unity is vividly described in the following passage by anthropologist Ruth Benedict. She wrote of the Zuni tribe in the American Southwest:

> The dance, like their ritual poetry, is a monotonous compulsion of natural forces by reiteration. The tireless pounding of their feet draws together the mist in the sky and heaps it into the piled rainclouds. It forces out the rain upon the earth. They are bent not at all upon an ecstatic experience, but upon so thorough-going an identification with nature that the forces of nature will swing to their purposes. This intent dictates the form and spirit of Pueblo dances. There is nothing wild about them. It is the cumulative force of the rhythm, the perfection of forty men moving as one, that makes them effective. . . .[29]

Among lineage-based cultures, then, one of the great purposes of dance has been to establish social unity and provide a means of collective strength and purpose. Closely linked to this is the function of religious celebration or worship, in which dance is used as a means of communication with the forces of nature—for becoming one with the gods. A number of examples of dance as religious worship are illustrated in chapter 3.

The Collective Unconscious

One theory of the origins of art concerns what Walter Abell called the "collective unconscious."[30] In this sense, art—rather than simply representing beautiful designs or melodic musical structures—grows out of the history, traditions, myths, and primordial images of a people. It stems both from cultural realities, social relationships, historical events, and from the full range of folklore, myths, legends, fairy tales, heroes, and ogres that appeared in a nation's past and that often continue, although apparently submerged, to influence human behavior.

To understand a society's culture, Abell wrote, it is necessary to apply a psychohistorical method of uncovering the "collective dream in art." This approach would apply equally well to examining works of classical ballet, which are based on ancient myths or folk tales, and to much more cryptic or expressionist works of contemporary dance. As a simple example, even the traditional folk games, songs, and dances that have been passed down from generation to generation through the centuries as forms of children's play may have their origin in religious practice, social custom, or historical events of the past.

Dance, then, although it may apparently be based on purely contemporary themes or artistic impulses, is also an expression of deeper, hidden psychological impulses and cultural influences. Sometimes, like other art forms, it may express these in somewhat poetic or spiritual terms. Panayotis Michelis described the general function of art experience:

> Art materializes ideas or at least expresses the deeper spiritual anguish of man and his highest ideals in eternal symbols. . . . [it] fascinates man and releases him from immediate practical concerns, transports him into the peaceful environment of a transcendental vision and fills his soul with joy. . . .[31]

However, art may also be used to express more immediate and concrete human concerns; typically, it may take the form of political propaganda or social protests. While some may argue that this is an inappropriate function of art, throughout history the artist has expressed the visions, crises, and needs of each period, as commentator or propagandist. For example, a number of modern dance works during the late 1930s were concerned with anti-Fascist themes, or with other forms of social oppression. In Communist societies such as the Soviet Union and China, ballet has been used to celebrate revolutionary triumph and promote nationalist zeal.

Human Movement and Dance

A unique aspect of dance is that, of all the arts, it is most dependent on human movement. A powerful motivation for dance has been the pervasive need to express oneself physically through rhythmic play and through exploration of one's bodily powers and physical environment. Ted Shawn wrote, in *Dance We Must*:

> We know that body movement is life itself—our movement begins in the womb before our birth and the new-born infant's need for movement is imperative and continuous. When we sleep there is constant movement, our hearts beat, our intestines work; in fact as long as there is life there is movement, and to move is hence to satisfy a basic and external need. . . .[32]

Clearly, dance is *physical* behavior; the head, body, and limbs move through space, stretching, flexing, turning, contracting and releasing, leaping, rising, falling, and gesturing. When one compares dance with sport, work activities, or other forms of exercise, many of the movements are similar. But Thomas pointed out that, although the mechanics of movement may be similar, their intent places them within a particular movement category:

> . . . the leap of a dancer and the leap of a wide receiver in football may be mechanically identical and require basically the same energy demands. In one instance, however, the leap may be a stylized expression classifying it as a dance movement. The functional and goal-directed leap of the football player to catch a ball makes style or expression irrelevant and places it in a sport/athletic mode.[33]

So it is not enough simply to classify dance as a form of movement. Instead, the intent and quality of the movement experience are crucial. And dance has the capacity to promote a special kind of feeling—a sense of heightening of life, of exhilaration, or joy. It blends the physical and emotional aspects of our being in an integrated expression. The ability to release one's feelings in this way is a deeply therapeutic and healthful function. A distinguished psychoanalyst, Joost Meerloo, suggested that dance is such a widespread form of human expression and emotional release that those who cannot dance are "imprisoned in their own ego" and have lost the "tune of life." He described such people as "deeply repressed" and "forlorn." According to Meerloo, through the ages,

> . . . sorrow, pleasure and ecstasy have been expressed by ritualized, festive dances. The rhythm of life brings the dance, and the dance brings the *saltatio,* jump, and the *ludus,* the playful activity. Every dance transforms man's innate passive rhythm—the mechanical beat in him—into the active rhythm of personal music. Dancing promotes man's vital pulsations, it changes mechanical repetitiveness into passionate and ebullient life. It lets man rediscover his body as a tool of expression.[34]

Fred Schroeder compared dance to other forms of ritualized and disciplined display, such as team games or even such events as bullfighting or professional wrestling, which in many ways represent choreographed movement. Although such activities may have a common aesthetic with dance, based on physical ability, strength, bodily control, or precision, Schroeder suggested that dance is a *cultivated art form,* marked by "design, meaning, and creativity," and that these elements separate it from other forms of athletic display or movement.[35]

Some experimental modern dance companies have developed works that appear to bridge the gap between dance and these other forms of physical display. For example, Stephanie Evanitsky's Multigravitational Aerodance Group performs in the air, thanks to scaffolding, cables, and other equipment. John Curry's Ice Dancing Company performs on skates, but its works are carefully and artistically composed, in some instances by noted choreographers.

At the same time, some avant-garde dancers restrict their movements to casual walking, skipping, or other familiar motions that unsophisticated audiences may have difficulty accepting as dance. As new movement forms emerge, we will need to reexamine and reshape our understanding of dance as movement, in terms of distinguishing it from other forms of physical activity.

Functions of Dance

Thus far, we have examined the functions of dance from several perspectives, seeing it as emotional experience, nonverbal communication, a means of establishing social unity, an expression of the collective unconscious of a society, and a form of movement. What other purposes does dance serve?

A commonly cited function is its role in courtship between the sexes. It is an expression of sexual drive, a means of displaying one's vigor or beauty, and part of the complicated ritual surrounding the entrance into adulthood and the act of courtship. Dancing provides socially accepted physical contact and is a direct means of expressing sexual attractiveness; indeed, many social dances performed today are frankly sexual and derived from movements that were related to fertility symbolism. But this is true only of some dances, and there are many forms in which courtship or sexual attraction plays no part.

It is a mistake, then, to assume that *all* forms of dance have a common core or purpose or meaning. Instead, dance may have many functions, but these vary, according to the society, the class, the age or sex, the religious structure, and similar factors about those who dance. Within varied kinds of societies, past and present, one might find any or all of the following purposes for dance:

1. It is an art form, an outlet for self-expressiveness and personal creativity. Within the mainstream of cultural inheritance, it may be the source of great works which are performed as part of a continuing tradition, or a basis for continuing artistic experimentation.

2. It may also be a form of popular entertainment, appealing to a broader audience than when it represents an art form with a high level of aesthetic worth.

3. It is a form of social affirmation, a means of expressing national or tribal loyalty and strength.

4. It is a means of religious worship, as a form of ritual and direct means of communicating with the gods.

5. It serves as a means of expressing physical exuberance, strength, and agility.

6. It offers an important social and recreational outlet, both as a means of restoring oneself physically, and of finding social acceptance within group participation.

7. It provides a medium through which courtship can be carried on.

8. It serves as a means of education, in the sense that it is taught to achieve the specific purposes of education within a given society, just as art, music, or theater are taught as cultural forms.

9. It serves as an occupation; in increasing numbers, it offers a means of livelihood to performers and teachers.

10. Finally, dance serves as therapy; for many it offers a form of physical and emotional release and rehabilitation; therefore, it is provided, along with other therapies, in many treatment centers.

Characteristics of Dance

Recognizing that dance may be performed for many reasons that influence its form and manner of presentation, are there some common elements that can be used to develop a definition of dance? The following seem to be universal characteristics of all types of dance:

1. *Use of the Human Body.* Here we are concerned only with those forms of dance which involve people in performance. While, as Langer pointed out, one might refer to the dancing of gnats in the air as a kind of dance motif or patterned

movement, and while animals or birds frequently carry on dance-like and even ritualistic movements, in this context we will not consider these forms as dance.

2. *Extends through Time*. Dance is not a frozen tableau, or a single gesture or picture of movement; instead, it is a continuing sequence of activity, extending through time, and may comprise a few moments, or may last for several hours or days.

3. *Exists in Space*. Dance is three-dimensional; it exists in the general space of a ballroom floor, on a stage, or in a village square; it exists in the personal space (*kinesphere*) of the person dancing.

4. *Exists in Force (Weight)*. Dance is a result of energy expenditure; it is viewed as a greater or lesser degree of muscular energy used to articulate movement.

5. *Exists in Flow*. The amount of energy which is restricted within or gathered toward the physical center of movement, or released away from that center, is reflected as *flow* in dance.

6. *Accompanied by Rhythm*. Most dance is rhythmically patterned; it is performed either to the accompaniment of music, chanting, hand-clapping, or percussive beating. Even those dances which may be performed silently, or to the accompaniment of speech or arbitrarily devised or selected sound effects, usually have a rhythmic structure.

7. *Serves to Communicate*. Most dance has communicative intent, ranging from the literal characterization or story-telling of pantomimic dance or traditional ballet, to the expression of personal emotion or physical exuberance. Even dances which are intended as abstract, nonliteral forms convey a kind of meaning to the onlooker—depending on his or her ability to perceive or respond to the movement in personal terms.

8. *Has Movement Style and Form*. Unlike a child's aimless and play-like exploration of movement, most dance has a characteristic movement style and has a structure or form.

Spectator and Participant Dance Forms

One final distinction may be made. It has been suggested that there are two types of dance—the kind which is performed by people, usually as a mass activity, without an audience (or in which the idea of performance is secondary to the idea of doing the dance for oneself), and the kind of dance which is *meant* to be performed for an audience. John Martin phrased it in this way:

> Dance falls naturally into two major categories: that which is done for the emotional release of the individual dancers, without regard to the possible interest of a spectator; and that, on the other hand, which is done for the enjoyment of a spectator either as an exhibition of skill, the telling of a story, the presentation of pleasurable designs, or the communication of emotional experience. . . .[36]

According to this view, most dances were originally of the first type and were meant to be performed as communal activity; the second type is considered to have descended from the first. Ballet and modern dance are essentially meant to be performed before an audience of spectators. On the other hand, such forms as social, folk, or square dance are primarily participant forms.

However, this distinction does not always hold. In ethnic dances performed for ritual purposes or as a matter of community tradition, it is not uncommon to have a large group of dancers taking part in what is clearly a communal form of participant dance. However, they are likely to be surrounded by many other nondancers who, while not taking part in the dance actively, clearly share its emotional experience and symbolic impact. In some avant-garde dance works today, the audience is expected to interact with the performers, and thus the distinction between the two groups is erased.

Ballet and modern dance are regarded as concert or theatrical forms of dance rather than participant activities. Yet many children and adults study them in schools, colleges, or private studios because of the pleasure or physical benefit they derive—without ever taking part in a performance, other than perhaps a recital at the end of the year. Similarly, folk, square, and ballroom dance, which are essentially participant dance forms, are often done on a highly skilled level, and may provide the basis for performances or exhibitions. Rather than dividing dance rigidly into spectator and participant forms, dance may range from the simple to the complex and may, under one circumstance or another, have as its primary purpose either performance or participation.

Definition of Dance

Based on all these considerations, and using the word *art* in its broadest sense (that of involving human skill), we arrive at the following definition:

> Dance is an art performed by individuals or groups of human beings, existing in time, space, force, and flow, in which the human body is the instrument, and movement is the medium. The movement is stylized, and the entire dance work is characterized by form and structure. Dance is commonly performed to musical or other rhythmic accompaniment, and has as a primary purpose the expression of inner feelings and emotions, although it is often performed for social, ritual, entertainment, or other purposes.

Societal Acceptance and Support of Dance

Although the number of performing dance companies and dance events during each year has grown tremendously, and although dance is more widely accepted now in schools and colleges than in the past, it still tends to enjoy less public recognition than other art forms. For example, there are fewer recognized ballet and modern dance companies today than there are symphony orchestras. Frequently, in government statistics or other reports on the performing arts, dance is included as a subcategory of music or theater. Perhaps the reason for this is the stereotype of classical ballet as it was performed in the past, or the image of modern dance when it was known as interpretive dance—as a perplexing, murkily symbolic group of long-haired dancers with flowers in their teeth performing incomprehensible gymnastics.

Certainly, today there is much greater comprehension of dance and more openness to its varied forms than in the past. Yet, with the exception of several major ballet companies, and particularly the exception of a limited number of ballet superstars who can command huge fees, most dance companies and artists have difficulty supporting themselves and must rely heavily on teaching or other forms of income, or on grants and subsidies, in order to carry on their work.

The economic struggle that must be carried on to support dance as a creative art form, as well as the stereotypes that surround it as a career field, can best be understood in the light of history. Therefore, before presenting a contemporary analysis of dance as a cultural art form or a significant medium of modern education, we examine its past.

Notes

1 Judith Lynne Hanna, *The Performer-Audience Connection: Emotion to Metaphor in Dance and Society* (Austin, Tex.: University of Texas Press, 1983), p. 3.

2 Lincoln Kirstein, *Dance: A Short History of Classic Theatrical Dancing* (New York: G. P. Putnam's Sons, 1935), p. 1.

3 Thoinot Arbeau, *Orchesographie: A Treatise in the Form of a Dialogue* (New York: Dance Horizons, Inc.), pp. 20, 23.

4 Cited in Anatole Chujoy, *The Dance Encyclopedia* (New York: A. S. Barnes, Inc., 1948), p. 125.

5 Ibid.

6 Ibid.

7 Gaston Vuillier, *A History of Dance* (New York: D. Appleton and Co., 1897), p. ix.

8 Sheldon Cheney, *Three Thousand Years of Drama, Acting and Stagecraft* (New York: Tudor Publishing Co., 1929), pp. 11–12.

9 James K. Feibleman, *Aesthetics: A Study of the Fine Arts in Theory and Practice* (New York: Duell, Sloan and Pearce, 1949), p. 302.

10 *Webster's New International Dictionary* (Springfield, Mass.: G. and C. Merriam Co., 1956), p. 42.

11 Monroe Beardsley, "The Aesthetic Point of View," in Joseph Margolis, ed., *Philosophy Looks at the Arts* (Philadelphia: Temple University Press, 1987), pp. 10–26.

12 Meyer Schapiro, cited in Beardsley, "Aesthetic Point of View," p. 22.

13 Quotation from Nelson Goodman, "Reality Remade," in Margolis, p. 283. Original source unknown.

14 Frank Sibley, "Aesthetic Concepts," in Margolis, pp. 29–50.

15 Thomas Munro, *The Arts and Their Interrelationships* (New York: The Liberal Arts Press, 1951), p. 496.

16 Susanne Langer, *Feeling and Form* (New York: Charles Scribner's Sons, 1953), pp. 2–3.

17 Maxine Sheets-Johnston, in Myron H. Nadel and Constance G. Nadel, *The Dance Experience* (New York: Praeger Books, 1970), p. 46.

18 John Martin, *John Martin's Book of the Dance* (New York: Tudor Publishing Co., 1963), p. 8.

19 Martha Graham, "A Modern Dancer's Primer for Action," in Frederick Rand Rogers, *Dance: A Basic Educational Technique* (New York: Macmillan Co., 1941), p. 178.

20 Doris Humphrey, in Rogers, p. 188.

21 Charles B. Fowler and Araminta Little, *Dance in Education* (Washington, D.C.: National Dance Association and Alliance for Arts Education, 1977), p. 2.

22 See Jan Fetters, "An Experiential Body Aesthetic," in Carolyn E. Thomas, ed., *Aesthetics and Dance* (Reston, Va.: National Dance Association, 1980), p. 8.

23 Judith Lynne Hanna, "Dance and Ritual," *Journal of Physical Education, Recreation and Dance,* November/December 1988, p. 40.

24 Judith Lynne Hanna, *To Dance is Human: A Theory of Non-Verbal Communication* (Austin, Tex.: University of Texas Press, 1979), p. 26.

25 Jack Anderson, *Dance* (New York: Newsweek Books, 1974), p. 9.

26 Gertrude Kurath, cited in Hanna, *To Dance is Human,* p. 21.

27 Margaret Mead, *From the South Seas* (New York: William Morrow and Co., 1939), p. 110.

28 Curt Sachs, *World History of the Dance* (New York: W. W. Norton and Co., 1937), p. 4.

29 Ruth Benedict, *Patterns of Culture* (New York: Mentor Books, 1946), pp. 84–85.

30 Walter Abell, *The Collective Dream in Art: A Psychohistorical Theory of Culture* (New York: Schocken Books, 1966), p. 45.

31 Panayotis Michelis, *Aesthetikos* (Detroit: Wayne State University Press, 1977), p. 46.

32 Ted Shawn, *Dance We Must* (London: Dennis Dobson Ltd., 1946), p. 9.

33 Carolyn Thomas, *Sport in a Philosophic Context* (Philadelphia: Lea and Febiger, 1982), p. 12.

34 Joost Meerloo, *The Dance* (New York: Chilton Book Co., 1960), pp. 39–40.

35 Fred E. Schroeder, *Outlaw Aesthetics: Arts and the Public Mind* (Bowling Green, Ohio: Bowling Green University Press, 1977), pp. 44–47.

36 Martin, *Book of the Dance,* p. 20.

CHAPTER 3

The Roots of Dance: Lineage-Based Societies and Pre-Christian Forms

I saw so many of their different varieties of dance amongst the Sioux that I should be disposed to denominate them the "dancing Indians." It would seem as if they had dances for everything. And in so large a village, there was scarcely an hour in any day or night, but what the beat of the drum could somewhere be heard. These dances are almost as various and different in their character as they are numerous—some of them so exceedingly grotesque and laughable, as to keep the bystander in an irresistible roar of laughter—others are calculated to excite his pity, and forcibly appeal to his sympathies, whilst others disgust, and yet others terrify and alarm him with their frightful threats and contortions.[1]

IN EXAMINING THE EARLY HISTORY OF DANCE, it is reasonable to assume that prehistoric peoples danced; indeed, we have records of what appear to be war dances and shaman dances in cave paintings that date back tens of thousands of years. However, because of the limited number of examples, little is known of these dances.

This chapter, therefore, begins with an analysis of dance as it has been observed in a number of lineage-based societies over the past several centuries, recorded by explorers and, more recently, anthropologists and other social scientists or scholars. Clearly, it is impossible to draw a conclusive, direct parallel between such cultures and more ancient societies. Nonetheless, some have speculated that the customs, religious practices, and art forms observed among Native Americans, Africans, and South Pacific islanders in the relatively recent past yield clues to the lives of more ancient peoples.

Dance in Lineage-Based Societies

Within lineage-based cultures past and present, dance has been a major form of religious ritual and social expression—a utilitarian and omnipresent art. Pearl Primus, a black American dancer who went to Africa to study the dance of her forebears, wrote with the trained eye of an anthropologist:

> The role of the professional dancer was of tremendous importance in Africa. He was necessary to all ceremonies, all feasts, all occasions which involved the health and well-being of the tribe. In return for his services the tribe fed and clothed him and provided for him in his every need. He was left free to dance. . . . Is it any wonder then that dance stands with music and art at the very top of the list of cultural contributions of the African to the world? Is it any wonder that the dancer developed to such an extent that he could spin his head on his neck so rapidly that the onlooker saw nothing but blur . . . or that he could leap from the ground with feet outstretched in a wide sitting position and land on his buttocks only to spring into the air again unhurt? Is it any wonder that a group of fifty warriors could dance their spear dances and not one finger be out of place?[2]

Why has dance been so important to lineage-based societies? Essentially, its functions have been similar to those discussed in chapter 2: Dance was used as a means of worship, a way of expressing and reinforcing tribal unity and strength, a framework for courtship or mating, a means of communication, and a therapeutic experience.

It is likely that the use of dance as a means of aesthetic expression, with only a few skilled artists performing for large audiences, would rarely be found among early lineage-based cultures. Instead of forming the audiences for such performances, the people danced themselves. Certainly in such cultures there were numerous harvest, victory, and other celebratory feasts with music, dancing games, and other play-like experiences that were thoroughly integrated with the productive life of the tribe.

Origins of Early Dance

How did dance begin among early lineage-based cultures? Douglas Kennedy suggested that the religious aspect of dance generally was used for communication with the unseen forces which provided food, promoted fertility, regulated the weather, gave good fortune in warfare—and thus controlled tribal welfare and human survival. People danced originally to supplicate the gods on all important occasions of life. Kennedy wrote:

> As the faith behind such primitive religious impulses weakens, the dances which express it are not immediately abandoned, but they gradually change their character. The form of the ritual remains, but some of the magical content departs. The dancer becomes less and less of a medicine-maker and more and more a performing artist. In fact, the ritual changes imperceptibly into art. It was in some such manner that the folk dances in different parts of Europe grew out of old pagan rites as the pagans themselves were converted to Christianity and gradually lost

their primitive beliefs. . . . in industrialized . . . England, there are still a few ancient rituals directly descended from the pre-Christian era, and retaining, to a surprising degree, their aura of primitive magic.[3]

Dance as a Gift of the Gods

Among existing lineage-based cultures, the aborigines, or first inhabitants of Australia, represent a society that has remained relatively aloof from Western European influences and that continues to use dance as an integral part of daily life. A spokesperson for a group of aborigines that toured America in the early 1980s explained, "We are instructed to tell you these dances were established in the beginning and handed down from father to son." The traditional tribal dances of the aborigines are believed to have been given to them by the spirit world at the time of creation, which they call the *Dreaming* or *Dreamtime*. At that time, spirits shaped the land and created human life, then living in both humans and animals, and even the landscape. Kisselgoff noted that in the aborigines' totemic culture, each clan has its own animal totem or totem ancestor and its own mythic tales and songs about the past.

> It was made clear . . . that each dance was "owned" by those who executed it. The animal life or natural features inhabited by the spirit hero-ancestors link their descendants with the "Dreamtime." In this view of nature at one with all living things, a dancer who dances about birds and animals is, in a sense, dancing about himself in union with the divine.[4]

Linkages to Nature:
The Dance of Birds and Animals

One of the important sources of inspiration for dance in many cultures has been the movements of birds and animals. Early humans were undoubtedly acutely aware of the living things around them. They hunted them for food and clothing, they fought them for survival, and they knew well their courage, their beauty, and their cunning. Most such peoples had an animist religion, in which they believed in animals possessing souls and being much like people. Indeed, among many tribes, the ideas of reincarnation and of transmigration of souls between humans and animals were completely accepted. All this was woven in with a sense of mystery about the natural phenomena that surrounded them—the sun, the moon, the stars, night, day, the seasons of the year, life, and death. As part of this, early humans observed animals closely, felt at one with them, painted and sculpted them, and undoubtedly attributed great powers to them. They also danced like them.

Without question, the dance-like movements of other living creatures were one of the inspirations for the dances of early humans. It is true that many insects, birds, animals, and even fish carry out ritualized movement patterns that appear to be much like our conception of dance.

George Wald, a professor of biology at Harvard, noted that many human behavior patterns have evolved from those of animals. He suggested that fear and rage, for example, grew out of the need to prepare the body for sudden, strenuous action—either to fight or to flee. He described, too, how certain movement patterns are used by bees as part of their total social behavior and as a means of communication and decision making. His analysis is based on the work of an Austrian investigator, Karl von Frisch, who found that, by certain dance-like routines, a bee can tell other bees where it has found a rich store of nectar. Now, another researcher

> . . . has discovered that dances are also used in searching for a site for a new hive. Worker bees fan out in this hunt. When they find a likely place, they return and dance before the swarm. The better the spot, the more prolonged and intense the dance. Other workers, told of the site through the dance pattern, go out to investigate and in turn give their opinion by a dance. . . . In this way the swarm achieves a consensus and flies out to build its new home. . . .[5]

Joost Meerloo described dancing movements among fish, particularly the astonishing breeding behavior and courtship of the Cichlids, whose slow dancing movements, together with their extremely vivid color, provide what Meerloo called a "slow motion waltz." Meerloo also referred to the unusual mass behavior of ants, in which they march in complicated and elaborate patterns and formations.[6]

Sachs has described the dance of an unusual stork-like bird, the stilt bird of Cape York in northeastern Australia, only one of many birds which have been observed to fly or move around the ground in rhythmic and graceful patterns which resemble dance. These birds have been observed assembling by the hundreds in a secluded swamp area. In a quadrille-like formation, they move rhythmically and gracefully in unison:

> In groups of a score or more they advanced and retreated, lifting high their long legs and standing on their toes, now and then bowing gracefully one to another, now and then one pair encircling with prancing daintiness a group whose heads moved downwards and sidewide to the stepping of the pair. . . .[7]

Perhaps most dance-like of all are the play forms, almost approaching dance, which are carried on by chimpanzees. A German investigator, Kohler, observed a number of these large apes over a period of time, and described them as having a variety of behaviors to which newcomers joining their group were introduced. They used instruments and implements for reaching or climbing; carried on a "sort of rhythmic play or dance," and made a variety of murmurs, wails, and rejoicing sounds. Two of the apes in particular, Tschego and Grande, developed a game of spinning round and round like dervishes in a spirit of friendly play, which the other apes enjoyed greatly. The resemblance to human dance became striking when one ape stretched out her arm horizontally as she spun around or revolved slowly. The group of chimpanzees sometimes trotted around a post, marking a rough rhythm by accenting the movement of one foot.[8]

Wild apes have even been observed to join hands and move around rhythmically in a circle or weaving line, sometimes bedecking themselves with leaves and boughs. Observing the movements of animals carrying on such dance-like activities, it is natural that early humans would imitate them. They may have believed that by impersonating, they would gain their strength or cunning. Their purpose may have been to imitate the animal as part of storytelling, or for amusement, or to recount adventures. In any case, just as animals are personified within folk myths and appear again and again in folk art, so many dances in lineage-based societies are based on specific animal themes.

Religious Role of Dance

Probably one of the first uses of dance among early lineage-based cultures was as a meaningful gesture in order to communicate. Susanne Langer wrote at length on the development of language and symbolic gesture, showing how humans developed certain stylized ways of expressing thoughts. Gradually, hand and body movements, facial expressions, and guttural sounds were combined in the process of communication. Thus, dance was used as a means of telling a story or giving information. Because of the lack of a developed vocabulary, the prehistoric hunter or warrior was probably compelled to use recognizable gestures, often supplementing the movement with the cries of animals or other natural sounds, or with whatever basic words he or she had developed. The elaborate East Indian *mudras,* or hand language used in dance, and the sign language of the American Indian, are both examples of this kind of gesture communication, elaborately systematized.

Gradually, during performance ritual, simpler imitative movements or gesture language became transformed into a more elaborate structure of symbolic arts, combining dance, acting, singing, and speech, all surrounded by complicated conventions and undergirded by an unquestioning belief in the efficacy of ceremony. All nature was embraced by such rites. Langer wrote:

> The apparently misguided efforts . . . to induce rain by dancing and drumming are not practical mistakes at all; they are rites in which the rain has a part. White observers of Indian rain dances have often commented on the fact that in an extraordinary number of instances the downpour really "results." Others of a more cynical turn remark that the leaders of the dance know the weather so well that they time their dance to meet its approaching changes and simulate "rainmaking." This may well be the case; yet it is not a pure imposture. A "magic" effect is one which completes a rite . . . he dances *with* the rain; he invites the elements to do their part. . . . if heaven and earth do not answer him, the rite is simply unconsummated. . . .[9]

Courtship and Procreation Themes

A great concern of lineage-based societies has been the "magical" act of perpetuating the species. Thus, many dance rituals are concerned with fertility and are performed at ceremonies concerning entrance into adolescence, courtship, marriage, and birth. Tore Hakansson wrote that such art

> . . . is representational, conventional, and intended to be understood by the audience for which the artist creates. He decorates houses and equipment and he

composes ceremonies concerned with birth, puberty rites, marriage, ancestors, hunting, harvestings, the seasons, and war. The primitive artist is really a craftsman. He is well integrated with the community in which he works. Whereas in our civilization the artist is a specialist and an outsider, a rebel against the conventions of his society, in the primitive community art is a necessity, not merely a form of entertainment. . . . art . . . produces an esthetic effect that is both gratifying and vital, and is a useful social phenomenon, leading to participation of the artist-craftsman with the fellow members of his community in the use of his work—generally in dancing, rituals, and feasts.[10]

Hakansson pointed out that often art portrays dances and rituals which are part of initiation, clearly phallic in nature. Sex and sexual functions are expressed naturally, with a degree of distortion, or abstractly; often abstract decorations of art objects are really stylized sex symbols and are recognized as such by the tribe that uses them.

Types of Dance Movement

Typical movements found in dances of lineage-based societies include whirling, leaping, vibrating, rolling of the pelvis, striding, and stamping. In some societies, dances tend to have a much narrower range of movement, and the movement itself may be much more subtle. Such dances frequently are performed on a limited base, with swinging, swaying, and suspension, and with gesture language of the hands and arms. In certain dances on Pacific islands, particularly in the Marshall Archipelago, women sit on their heels; in others they sit cross-legged.

Early Spanish explorers described Chamorro dancing in the Marshalls in considerable detail. It often involved social rituals and celebrations, with the sexes playing distinctly separate roles. Father Gobien wrote:

> . . . they meet often together, to regale on fish, fruit, and a certain liquor, made of rice and grated Cocoas, and then exercise themselves in dancing, running, leaping, and wrestling. They recite the heroic deeds of their ancestors, and repeat the work of their poets, which are full of fable and extravagance.[11]

Often, dancers in the South Pacific islands were elaborately decorated. Another observer, in the Carolines, described how young people gathered around their chief's house in the evening to sing and dance:

> The men are placed opposite to the women, and move their heads, arms, and legs, in exact cadence. On these occasions they are dressed in all their finery. On their heads they have crowns of feathers, aromatic flowers hanging from their nostrils, and palm leaves from their ears. Their arms, hands, and feet are also ornamented.[12]

Agnes de Mille commented that rhythmic, complex foot movements are often stressed rather than elaborate or extended body movements. In some societies, because of the tribesman's nakedness and vulnerability, he bends close to the ground to protect his vitals. Those who must hunt barefoot, unprotected by armor or weapons for killing at a distance, ". . . have certain characteristics in common. They stamp out rhythms. They run crouched low in imitation of animals or of the precautionary attitudes adopted when stalking prey or an enemy."[13]

In another analysis of dance movement in lineage-based societies, Curt Sachs concluded that dances were essentially of two types: those out of harmony with the body and those in harmony.[14] In general, in a dance that is out of harmony, the dancers work themselves into extreme nervous excitement. The song is panted out; movements are jerky and uncontrolled. The action is wild, ecstatic. Dancers may actually go into a trance corresponding to a medical description of clonic convulsion—a state of forceful flexion and relaxation of the muscles which may lead to a throwing about of the body in wild paroxyms. (While Sachs has been regarded as a respected authority on dance, his conclusion that certain dances are out of harmony with the body, or that they mortify or degrade it, is essentially subjective. There is no evidence that such dances are harmful, or that dancers who are in a state of possession do not recover rapidly and fully.)

In Sach's terms, the dance that is in harmony with the body does not mortify or degrade the body, but exalts it. Through repeated movement, the dancer achieves exhilaration. The dance is powerful, with strong motor reactions, every muscle stretched taut; it brings about a release from gravity with buoyant movements forward and upward. Actions involve leaping, lifting, slapping, stamping, striding, and lunging. Such dances are bold and positive.

Dance in some religious rituals provides a means of autosuggestion or autointoxication, through which the dancer may surrender himself or herself temporarily to a supernatural being or force. In an altered state of consciousness, phenomena may occur that are difficult to explain rationally. A dervish who dances for twelve or fifteen hours, whirling steadily without faltering, exhibits a degree of endurance and self-control that is almost beyond belief. Trance dancers in Indonesia repeatedly thrust sharp daggers against their bare chests so forcefully that the weapons are bent; yet they are not injured. In contemporary Western society, we see numerous examples of worshippers in evangelical or charismatic Protestant sects who speak in tongues and dance wildly in a state of religious possession.

Themes and Examples of Dance in Lineage-Based Societies

There are many themes of dance in lineage-based societies. As indicated, many are animal dances, often with masks which give the dancer the god-like or magic power of the animal portrayed. Sometimes skins or horns are worn. Such dances are performed as a prelude to hunting, or sometimes as part of fertility rituals. War dances are found in tribes throughout the world; often these are weapon dances, in which the motions of warfare are used and in which dancers may work themselves up to a pitch of hysteria or trance. In many cultures, ancient myths are acted out—often with the essential theme of the battle between good and evil, life and death, reenacted.

Dance of Native Americans

Among the American Plains Indians, the dancing ground frequently was laid out so that it had four sacred places, each named in honor of the deities who presided over the four cardinal points of the compass. Among the Cherokees, these points were known as the Sun Land (east), the Frigid Land (north), the Darkening Land (west), and Wahala (south). Each of these had a color assigned to it, and each color had symbolic meaning. White and red spirits were usually invoked for peace and health, red alone for success of an undertaking, blue for defeating a cunning enemy, and black for causing an enemy's death.

One of the most famous dances of the Plains Indians was the Sun Dance. Radin described it, as performed by the Oglala Dakota. Basically, it is interpreted as a dance concerned with supplication to the deities for power and success in warfare, and it represents the cruelest kind of testing of the braves who took part in it. It was usually carried out by a warrior in fulfillment of a vow made at a crucial moment in his life when the help of the gods was needed. After a number of secret rites were carried out to purify and prepare the initiate, there was a ceremonial search for a center-pole for the dance. When the proper tree was found, it was felled, brought to the camp, and erected. There was a period of fasting, prayer, chanting, and offerings to the gods for several days and nights.

The Sun Dance itself involved a dramatic climax of self-inflicted torture. Medicine men would take up as much of the skin of the breast under the nipple of each dancer as could be held between the thumb and forefinger. A cut would be made and a skewer inserted through the flesh. The skewer would then be tethered to the center-pole and fastened by long ropes of woven hair or thongs. The warriors then danced, straining back against the thongs and staring up into the blinding white sun, until finally the flesh of their chest had torn loose and the thongs and skewers were pulled through. Radin wrote:

> . . . as they dance, they hold eagle pipes in their mouths, this being a term for flutes made from one of the bones in an eaglet's wing. They had to be sounded throughout the time the young man was dancing. The dancing was done in the manner of a buck jump, the body and legs being stiff and all movements being upon the tips of the toes. The dancers kept looking at the sun, and either dropped the hands to the sides in the military position of "attention" with the palms to the front, or else held them upward and outward at an angle of 45 degrees, with the fingers spread apart and inclined toward the sun. . . .[15]

This ordeal frequently continued for many hours, until the warrior had proved his manhood by completing the ritual successfully. To understand such a dance, it is necessary to recognize that it is part of a total religious belief, a symbolic representation, a prayer which in many cases is hundreds of years old. In a sense, it is part of an elaborate drama which embraces all the arts and which is performed with the strictest adherence to authentic detail. Fergusson wrote:

> Most of the Indian ceremonials are extremely elaborate, lasting for days and ending on the last day or night with the dance. Outsiders are usually permitted to see only the dance. The secret ceremonies take place in the kiva or medicine lodge and are open only to clan members or to the dancers. Sometimes they are historical or legendary in character, presenting the life of the whole people or of a certain hero. Often elaborate altars are erected and painted with symbolic decorations, sand

paintings are made and destroyed at specified hours and, with meticulous care for detail, costumes are prepared for the dance, masks are painted and decorated with feathers, prayer sticks are made. The dancers must be purified by means of fasting and medication, bathing the body, and washing the hair. Everything is done under the direction of the cacique or medicine-man, whose duty it is to see that nothing goes wrong, as the slightest slip may ruin the effect of the entire ceremony.[16]

An impressive example of the use of dance is found in the religious rituals of the Aztec Indians of Central America, before their conquest by Spanish conquistadors in the early sixteenth century. The invading soldiers and priests found the Aztec culture rich in complex ceremonies for every occasion of a political, religious, or commercial nature, or to mark such events as births, weddings, and death. Gertrude Kurath pointed out that the Aztecs dedicated ceremonies to their gods for rain, fruitfulness of the crops, victory in war, success in the hunt, and the tribal dead, with an annual succession of eighteen ceremonies based on the ecological calendar. A later observer concluded that the Aztecs believed dance to be meritorious, like deeds of charity or penance:

> In these religious festivals and their dances, they not only called on and honored and praised their gods with songs but also with the heart and with the movements of the body. In order to do this properly, they . . . used many patterns, not only in the movements of the head, of the arms, and of the feet but with all their body . . . and this they called *maceualiztli,* penance and good deed.[17]

There were several uniquely different styles of dance, as well as certain dances which were extremely spectacular, or which were carried on in connection with ritual sacrifices of animals or humans, held by the priesthood and the nobility. Among these, Kurath described the *Volador* (flying pole, in which participants swung out widely, suspended by ropes from a high pole), and the *Comelagotoazte,* or small ferris wheel; these ceremonies were associated with shooting arrows at a crucified victim. In contrast, dances of the early Mayan cultures tended to be "artful, gay, and festive . . . part of all public and private festivities. . . ."[18]

African Dance

So varied are the dances of African nations and tribes that it is difficult to characterize or classify them meaningfully. They embrace all the themes and motivations described earlier; war, the hunt, fertility, courtship, marriage, harvest, birth, initiation into adolescence or adulthood, and burial. Typically, many African dances are derived from motions performed during work. Rhythm also pervades their labor; by singing and moving in unison, such tasks as rowing, carrying heavy burdens, or felling trees are made easier.

Although a number of the functions of dance in African societies have declined as Western cultural forms have been introduced and urbanization has increased, often traditional dance forms continue to be practiced as a matter of custom and pride. Today, they may no longer be based on original religious beliefs, but instead may be viewed as talismans of good fortune or as expressions of patriotic unity.

Typically, in the dry, grassy plains of Mali, south of the Sahara desert in West Africa, Bambara tribe members have retained many of their historic dances, which are performed with animal masks. These are done as part of elaborate annual festivals, in which different groups compete against each other for tribal acclaim. What was once done as part of a secret ritual is now open to all and is essentially a form of social entertainment. However, the historic dances remain an important aspect of tribal life, with much time spent preparing costumes and masks and choreographing the dance performances.

In a number of African nations, a strong effort is made to retain traditional folk customs—particularly the dance. In 1966, King Sobhuza II, the Ngwenyama, or Lion of Swaziland, joined thousands of his people in a ceremonial six-day *incwala,* a central ritual in the life of Swaziland, symbolic of the renewal of the people, land, and king.

> The Ngwenyama, who wears three-piece suits when he addresses Parliament or dedicates factories, was dressed like his warriors. That is, he wore a head-dress of fancy plumage, a leopard-skin girdle, and a mantle of ox tails. He danced barefoot on the earth of the royal cattle corral, where the ceremony took place. Many sophisticated young Swazis, European educated, took part. One university graduate said: "I used to shy away from these ceremonies. But there has been a remarkable change of late. We all realize now that this is our national land. It's something we've got to support and be proud of. . . ."[19]

Ritual Dances in Western Nations

In other countries, even in the Western world, where ritual dances of earlier centuries have all but disappeared, there is a deliberate effort to retain and revive these forms as evidences of the historical past. One example is England, where the efforts of Cecil Sharp led to the development of the English Folk Dance and Song Society, which has been instrumental in a widespread revival of English country, Morris, and sword dancing. Of the dances done by clubs and teams throughout England, some are directly suggestive of early rituals which continued to be practiced long after the conversion of rural populations to Christianity. Thus, even in a heavily industrialized nation, such traditional dance forms continue to be practiced. In other European countries where village life, simple handicrafts, and agricultural pursuits have remained reasonably intact, similar early dance-and-drama forms still exist and hold much of their ancient appeal for the peasantry—although the original magical belief that prompted them has largely disappeared.

An example of how non-Christian folk practices have survived is found in mid-twentieth-century Poland. Sula Benet described the cyclical nature of farm life, the peasant's calendar fitted to the recurrent tasks of planting, tending the crops, and reaping, and each season's own cluster of holidays and observances. Benet pointed out that the holidays are not an interruption of the agricultural task, but rather are essential to it. Although they consist primarily of worship and religious ritual, they also provide rest and recreation for peasants and their families. Benet wrote:

[The holidays] are rich too in magical rites and observances carried over from pre-Christian days and mingling comfortably with Roman Catholic ritual and precept. All the important holidays that the peasant observes are linked with agricultural festivals initiated by his remote ancestors.[20]

As an example, the Shrovetide festivals that begin the Easter holidays and end after Holy Week are marked by varied dramatizations and celebrations of winter's death and the return of spring. These include symbolic representations of spring by beautiful young maidens, customs which ridicule young unmarried men, and carnival-like parades in which many animal and human masks and costumes appear. Typical of the many unique dances with symbolic meaning that have become a social form of amusement is a Shrove Tuesday dance done by married women, originally intended to make the hemp crop grow tall. Benet wrote:

The women gather in the tavern and when they begin to feel the liquor they dance around a barrel on which stands a *koziolek,* or 'little ram'—a small figure made of wood and pieces of cloth. During the dance they try to leap as high as possible, to make the hemp grow higher. The men spur them on, as each woman tries to outdo the others, and the serious purpose of the dance is buried under waves of merriment.[21]

In other countries which have become more heavily industrialized or in which the folklore roots of culture have largely disappeared, the relation of dance to religion is less clear. However, the examples that have been cited here clearly indicate how dance has been inextricably intertwined with ritual and social custom from the earliest periods of human development. This is made explicit as one reviews the major historical eras of our past, beginning with the pre-Christian civilizations that arose in the Mediterranean region of Europe, the Middle East, and North Africa.

Dance in Pre-Christian Civilizations

As suggested at the beginning of this chapter, our knowledge of dance among prehistoric peoples is extremely limited. Our first real knowledge of dance in early human history comes with the Mediterranean and Middle Eastern civilizations that preceded the Christian era.

The early Sumerians had a vigorous musical culture; in the third millennium B.C. they developed lyres, pipes, harps, and drums, some of which they passed on to succeeding Babylonians and Assyrians. In Sumer, a sacred dance was practiced in various forms. In one, a procession of singers moved soberly, perhaps around an altar, to liturgies played on flutes. In another, dancers prostrated themselves before an altar or other sacred objects, as part of religious worship.

In ancient Assyria, many depictions of dancing men and women have been found, suggesting that dance was both part of religious practice and part of the social life of the time. In Babylon, too, the occurrence of temple dancing has been confirmed; in the text of the Assurbanipal, it is stated that at a religious festival the performers danced a ring-dance to musical accompaniment around the idol of the god who was being worshipped.[22]

Dance in Ancient Egypt

However, it was in ancient Egypt, a civilization which lasted for 4,000 years, that dance for the first time reached a full flowering and was richly recorded, in wall paintings and reliefs, and in the literary record of the hieroglyphs. The Egyptian culture was complex, and it achieved an advanced understanding of astronomy and geometry, sculpture, architecture, and engineering, and initiated the use of paper and weaving processes. It also developed for the first time a varied class structure, with royal families, workers and peasants, slaves, a powerful priesthood, and, in later dynasties, troupes of professional entertainers.

Ted Shawn wrote that in Egypt, where the priesthood was all-powerful, dance was the chief medium of religious expression. The secret doctrines and mysteries of the Egyptian mythology, based primarily on the annual rise and fall of the River Nile (resulting in a legend of resurrection and belief in human survival) were portrayed through symbolic dance dramas. In these, the central theme of the Egyptian religion—that of Osiris being slain and dismembered, with the parts of his body hidden throughout the earth, followed by the search of his sister-wife, Isis, to find and bury the body of the god—all this "was re-enacted constantly within the temples in dramatic dance form, and the young people were thus given their religious education. . . ."[23]

There was a complex and highly ritualized system of worship in ancient Egypt, concerned chiefly with death and rebirth, and attached to certain holy cities

Egyptian dancing girls and a musician. From a tombstone fresco at Karnak, about 1420 B.C.

associated with the cult. As part of this system, there began to appear trained dancers who performed regularly as part of religious services. Chiefly, these services were connected to rituals of planting and harvest. Lincoln Kirstein pointed out that annually a mystery play or tragedy was produced at Abydos; in the ritual, the priest, or first dancer, became the personification of the entire enacted legend. He was aided by a larger group of dancers, performing en masse.[24]

Other religious dances included a traditional festival performed in honor of the bull Apis, one of the most powerful of Egyptian gods. To carry on this ceremonial, a special bull was selected and raised; in his quarters, the Apeum, the priests or priestesses who attended him would perform secret dances, retelling the adventures of the god of whom the bull Apis was the living image.

Since they were so preoccupied with themes of life and death and sought to conquer death by making the body of the buried nobleman immortal, funeral ceremonies were extremely important to the ancient Egyptians. On the occasion of the burial of important personages, a man skilled as a mimic was dressed in the dead man's garments and, having his face covered with a mask as nearly as possible resembling the face of the deceased, he immediately preceded the hearse. As the procession moved slowly along to the sound of solemn music, he performed a pantomimic dance to show the remarkable deeds achieved during the lifetime of the man being borne to his tomb.

But such themes were not the sole preoccupation of dance among the Egyptians. They enjoyed sports, acrobatics, and various forms of entertainment, and they had complex orchestras, including copper cymbals, tambourines, bone clackers, drums, pipes, castanets, whistles, and other stringed and percussive instruments. Bands of female performers were attached to temples, and the royal houses also owned troupes of entertainers who performed on both sacred and social occasions. Slaves were taught both dancing and music, and in the later dynasties there developed a class of professional performers who were independent, in that they were neither owned by the nobility nor attached to temples. Alexander Bland pointed out that the Pharaoh himself took part in sacred dance rituals; ancient paintings show him first sitting on a throne and then removing his robe to dance four times around a field in a short garment.[25]

Kirstein cited several examples of Egyptian dancing at various periods of history:

> As far back as the first Dynasty (ca. 3000 B.C.), a wooden relief shows King Semti dancing rhythmically to instrumental music.
>
> An official of King Assa (ca. 2400 B.C.) brought from a distant land a Pygmy dancer who was believed to have come from the spirit world. Such dancers, who performed in a buffoon-like and grotesque style, were prized; there is an ivory statuette of a dancing Pygmy in the Metropolitan Museum in New York, dated about 1950 B.C.
>
> Wall reliefs at Gizeh (ca. 1580–1150 B.C.) show "girls posturing with tambourines, clacking castanets curved and carved to form conventionalized fingers."[26]

Gradually, the practice developed of having dance as professional entertainment at private dinner parties. Although the upper classes had once danced, they gradually relinquished this practice to slaves or highly skilled paid performers.

In a physical sense, what was the dance of ancient Egypt like? Because of the stylized treatment of figures in all reliefs and paintings, it is difficult to tell whether the poses and movements that are shown give a realistic picture of the actual dances that were done. However, the movement seems to have ranged from quiet, dignified walking steps, with arms outstretched, to difficult acrobatic positions, such as the famous "bridge" position, or handstands. In some cases, vigorous striding, leaping, or running movements are shown. Other acrobatic actions, such as tumbling, somersaults, and splits, were also common.

Dancers often performed as soloists, or in groups of two or three; sometimes they formed larger groups of performers. One such group work was described in a later period (fourth century B.C.) as an entertainment seen in the city of Memphis:

> Then came forward a group of dancers who jumped about in all directions, gathered together again, climbed on top of each other with incredible dexterity, mounting on shoulders and heads, forming pyramids reaching to the ceiling of the hall, then descended suddenly one after the other to perform new jumps and admirable somersaults. Without stopping, they danced on their hands, paired off, one placed his head between his legs and his partner then lifted him in turn and returned to the original position, each of them alternately being lifted and, as he fell, lifted his partner up.[27]

What was the influence of Egypt, then, in terms of the development of dance? Certainly part of its influence was that dance found a formal place in religious practice, as well as in popular or courtly entertainment. The scope and variety of dance movement, as well as the development of a professional class of dancers within the increasingly differentiated Egyptian social structure, were additional important developments. Without question, Egypt was influential in terms of spreading its cultural forms throughout the Mediterranean world. Even beyond the Mediterranean, at Cadiz, dancing that was essentially Egyptian in character was established. Havelock Ellis wrote: "The Nile and Cadiz were thus the two great centers of ancient dancing, and Martial mentions them both together, for each supplied its dancers to Rome."[28]

Dance among the Ancient Hebrews

While there are no wall reliefs or paintings to tell of dance as performed by the ancient Hebrews, there are abundant references to this practice in the Old Testament. Numerous Biblical allusions show that dance was highly respected and was particularly used on occasions of celebration and triumph:

> "And David danced before the Lord with all his might" (2 Samuel 6:14)
>
> "Then shall the virgin rejoice in the dance" (Jeremiah 31:13)
>
> "Let them praise his name in the dance: let them sing praises unto him with the timbrel and harp" (Psalms 149 1:3)
>
> "A time to mourn, and a time to dance" (Ecclesiastes 3:4)

Throughout the Bible, there are such references. When the prodigal son returned home, he was welcomed with music and dancing, to signify reconciliation and joy. When David slew Goliath, the passage reads, "Is not this David the king of the land? Did they not sing to one another of him in dances, saying—Saul hath slain his thousands, but David his ten thousands?" Exodus tells of the dance of celebration by Miriam and the other women, with the timbrel in hand, after the crossing of the Red Sea.

What were the types of dances performed by the ancient Jews? Several forms are described in the Old Testament. A circular, or ring dance, is the dance around the Golden Calf portrayed in Exodus 32:6,19. In other passages, we are told how David took the Ark to David's City in a processional march. Along the way, he stopped from time to time to prepare sacrifices and to dance with all his strength before the Lord and his Ark.

Other dances are described as hopping dances or whirling dances, usually carried on in celebration. And still other passages refer to use of the dance in divine service, although no formal provision was made in the Mosaic law for music or dance in the service of the Lord. Alfred Sendrey and Mildred Norton wrote:

> In both religions, processional dances were used in ritual ceremonies. National festivals alike include popular dancing. The harvest festival was celebrated by both people with fertility dancing, the husbandman of Israel rejoicing, like the Egyptian, with palm and willow branches. . . . Even the Egyptian belief that their gods themselves indulged in dancing had its parallel in a conception of the Hebrews. . . .[29]

Indeed, Hanna pointed out that the Talmud, ancient Rabbinic writings that provide a complex set of laws underlying traditional Judaism, refers to dancing as the principal function of the angels.[30]

As evidence that the ancient Hebrews must have danced on every possible occasion, both in daily life and for special occasions and ceremonies, Sendrey and Norton pointed out that biblical Hebrew has no less than twelve verbs to express the act of dancing. The Hebrew word most frequently used is *hul,* or *hil,* meaning "to whirl." Sachs interpreted this as "to turn," a word used both for a sword swung in a circle and for the whirlwind. From this is derived the word for dance, *mahol* (the source of the girl's name Mahelah, or, today, Mahalia). At least two psalms have in their headings the instruction *al mahalath,* suggesting that they were meant to be performed with some kind of dance. Another interesting term is the word *pasah,* which has two meanings: "to pass over," or "to spare" (thus *Pesah,* the Feast of the Passover), and "to limp," or "to dance in a limping fashion."

In addition to ritual processions or circle dances, or dances of celebration, dances were performed on certain other occasions; some of these have lingered as customs throughout the history of the Jews. Wedding dances were performed in ancient times; centuries later, during the Middle Ages, it was the custom for the bridal party to dance all the way to the house of the wedding. Dignified rabbis were not above dancing before the bridal couple with myrtle and olive branches. Although mixed dancing was common in the earlier pagan cultures, men and women were customarily separated in religious dances. The rabbis of the Middle Ages only permitted those who were closely related (husband and wife, brother and sister, or father and daughter) to dance together. In Eastern Europe during this period, the extremely orthodox Hasidic Jews made a practice of having only the men dance certain ritual dances during religious worship.

Thus, we see that among the ancient Hebrews there was great interest in and respect for the dance. However, certain prohibitions began to appear. Dance is not mentioned formally in the Mosaic code. Men and women were not permitted to take part together in certain dances. And, finally, a distinction was made between those dances which are of a sacred or holy nature and those which resemble pagan ceremonies—such as dancing around the Golden Calf, a form of idolatry. This distinction made by the early Jews, whose faith was the first of the great monotheistic religions, was to be made even more sharply by the Christians in the centuries that followed.

Dance in Ancient Greece

Just as among the early Egyptians and Hebrews, dance was held in great esteem by the ancient Greeks. They speculated on its antiquity and saw it as divinely inspired. It seemed to them that the stars and planets in the sky were doing some sort of cosmic dance; indeed, Urania, the patroness of astronomy, was also a Muse and a patroness of the dance. In the *Laws,* Plato suggested that dance arose from the natural desire of all young creatures to move their bodies in order to express emotions—especially joy. But, he went on, the sense of harmony and rhythm which actually makes dances out of natural and instinctive movements is the specific gift of the gods and the Muses.

The Greeks did not really think of dance as a separate entity. Instead, it was closely linked with other kinds of experiences. Thus, the word *orcheisthai,* which was translated in English "to dance," actually suggests rhythmical movements of many sorts—the feet, hands, head, eyes, or entire body. It might even describe marching, the playing of games, juggling, or tumbling, just as in Egypt professional dancers were also acrobats. Another Greek word was *mousiké,* the "art of the Muses"; this embraced music, poetry, and the dance, which, to the ancient Greeks, were all interconnected.

The sources of information about Greek dance are many. Among the literary sources are the words of songs written for dance, lines of poetry (including the great Homeric epics), the writings of philosophers, and many other forms of literature, including the work of later Roman historians and essayists. Archaeological sources, such as statues, wall reliefs, carvings, and paintings on walls or pottery, all frequently provide actual pictures of dancing.

The earliest references to dance within the region of the Aegean Sea are to the dances performed on the island of Crete from about 3000 to 1400 B.C. Archaeological excavations at Knossos and elsewhere on the island show the Cretans performing a variety of games, sports, dancing, and musical activities during this period. So renowned for their dancing skill and agility were the men of Crete that in Homer's *Iliad,* Aeneas says to one of them, "Even though you are a dancer, I might have stopped you with my spear."[31]

One of the oldest of the dances was that of the Curetes, a wild, leaping men's dance, with much shouting and clashing of weapons. Other war-like dances were performed, as well as simple circle dances, patterned dances for women, dances with animal masks or heads, and fertility dances which involved "front and back somersaults, flying leaps and rapid kicks, standing on their heads, standing and walking on their hands or forearms, or bending far backward like wheels."

Dance in ancient Crete was clearly a form of entertainment and display, as well as religious ritual or military training. Sappho described the "Cretan woman dancing in rhythm around the altar with her delicate feet, treading the soft smooth flowers of the meadow," and paintings of this period show female dancers with elaborate make-up and hair styles, as well as lavish ornaments and display of the body.

The colorful and spectacular dance of Crete was said to have inspired the dance of the Mycenaean Greeks, who came into being during the Bronze Age on the mainland of Greece. These vigorous and talented warriors fortified their steep hills into impregnable fortresses and sallied forth to conquer the Cretan cities, as well as other neighboring powers—such as the Trojans, in Asia Minor. Theirs was the civilization which Homer celebrated in the epic poems of the *Iliad* and the *Odyssey*.

A vivid picture of dance is given in the eighteenth book of the *Iliad,* where Homer describes the armor of Achilles. Three dances are depicted on the shield. One of these portrays a place where young men and maidens danced, holding their hands on one another's wrists:

> The maidens had soft linen garments, and the youths wore well-woven chitons, faintly glistening with oil. The maidens had fair garlands, and the youths had golden daggers hanging from silver belts. And now they ran around with skillful feet, very lightly, as when a potter, sitting by his wheel, which fits in his hands, tries it to see if it runs. And then again, they would run in lines to meet one another. And a great throng stood around the colorful dancing floor, enjoying the sight; and among them an inspired musician was singing and playing on his lyre, and through their midst, leading the measure, two tumblers whirled. . . .[32]

As Greece moved into its classical period, the Greeks worshipped a number of deities cast in the shape of men and women. Many myths surrounded these gods and goddesses, each of whom had special attributes, powers, and cults. Thus, fertility rites were often offered to Dionysus, the god of fertility and wine; indeed, the term *tragedy* is believed to have originated with the bacchic rites that were offered in his honor. Some of the mythological companions of Dionysus were believed to be satyrs, or "goatmen"; when dancers performed these roles at festivals, they wore goat costumes and footwear. The Greek word for "goat" is *tragos,* and goat-dancing contests carried on during the sixth century B.C. came to be known as competitions in *tragoedia,* or "goat song." Again, the term *orchestra* originally meant the circular dancing place of the theater.[33]

Among the other deities who had dances and festivals performed in their honor were Apollo and his sister Artemis at Delphi on the island of Delos in the Aegean; indeed, Apollo was said to have dictated the laws of choreography. Similarly, Athena, Hecate, Demeter, and Persephone all were worshipped by their own special cults at different holidays during the year.

One of the most common uses of dance in ancient Greece was in education. The leading Greek philosophers strongly supported this art as an ideal integration of the body and spirit. Aristotle defined education as a blend of music and gymnastics, and Socrates urged that it be taught more widely, saying that those who honor the gods most beautifully in dances are best in war. Plato wrote, "to sing well and to dance well is to be well educated," and he devoted a great deal of attention to the importance of dance in education in his treatise on the *Laws.* He emphasized that there are two kinds of dance and music—the *noble,* concerned with what is fine and honorable; and the *ignoble,* imitating what is mean or ugly:

> He would have all children, boys and girls alike, instructed from an early age in noble music and dancing, and would spur them on with contests. . . . He would give to officials absolute power to exclude from the schools and from public performances all unworthy rhythms and harmonies, steps and gestures. Music and dancing should be consecrated to the gods . . . inasmuch as the gods themselves dance and create dance. . . . Noble dances should confer on the student not only health and agility and beauty of the body, but also goodness of the soul and a well-balanced mind. . . .[34]

Hanna pointed out that Plato approved of slaves and noncitizens performing comic and bacchanal dances because these could be state-regulated. Beyond this, Hanna wrote: "Considering dance to be identical with education as a whole, Plato deemed the uneducated man *achoreutos* or danceless; the educated one, *kechoreukos,* endowed with dance."[35]

Aristotle considered dance to be an important means of moral training and to be useful in helping to purge a youth's soul of undesirable emotions. In this sense, it was similar to the other arts, like theater, which helped to bring the audience to an emotional catharsis of sad or frightening feelings.

The Greeks learned to dance at an early age, with most of the instruction apparently at the hands of private teachers. They practiced a variety of physical disciplines; they were extremely athletic, and their movements were full and vigorous. Particularly among the boys, dancing was taught as an aid to military education in Athens and Sparta. In the *palaestra* (wrestling school) and *gymnasium,* they took part in Pyrrhic dances and others designed to prepare them to execute battle motions. The dances fell into several categories:

Podism: quick, shifting movements of the feet, to train the warrior for hand-to-hand combat.

Xiphism: mock battle, in which groups of youths would practice the arts of warfare in dance-like form.

Homos: high leaps and vaults, to prepare youths for leaping over high logs and boulders, or for scaling walls and fortresses.

Tetracomos: stately group formations, in which soldiers would advance on the enemy en masse or protect themselves through interlocked shields.

Not only were these dances learned, as in Sparta, at training schools for boys, but they also were performed regularly at the Panathenaic Festivals and were carried on regularly as part of the continuing training of soldiers. Shawn wrote: "We have records today of some 18 named Pyrrhic dances—solo, duet, and ensemble—which were mimetic warfare dances, by which the soldier attained the mind-body coordinations, the muscular strength, the discipline, which made him supreme on the field of battle."[36]

So esteemed was dance that it was accepted practice for statesmen, generals, philosophers, and other outstanding Greeks of the Periclean Age to perform solo dances before audiences of many thousands on important public occasions or on return from a military campaign or victory.

The Greek satirist, Lucian (who lived in a later era in Rome), remarked that the Greeks valued dancing to such an extent that ". . . the most noble and greatest personages in every city are the dancers, and so little are they ashamed of it, that they applaud themselves more upon their dexterity in that species of talent, than on their nobility, their posts of honor, and the dignities of their forefathers."[37]

There were specific types of dances in Greek drama:

Emmeleia: This was a grave, serious type of dance, typically used for tragic themes; it embodied a code of symbolic gestures through which the dancer could tell the entire story of a dramatic work without speaking.

Kordax: This was the characteristic dance of comedy and has been described as obscene and ignoble; it involved suggestive rotations of the body, kicking one's buttocks, slapping one's chest and thighs, and similar movements.

Sikinnis: This was the dance typical of the Greek satyr plays during the sixth century B.C. It was lively, vigorous, and disrespectful, with much horseplay and acrobatic movement; often it involved satirical reenactment of mythological themes.

Not only was dance featured in the Greek theater; it also was an essential element in the entertainment of guests, known as *Komos,* or *Komoi.* It was the practice to have afterdinner entertainment of singing, juggling, playing musical instruments, and dancing. At first, this was done by the host or guests. Gradually, however, a class of professional dancers developed—and these performers displaced the amateurs. By the fifth and fourth centuries B.C., such performers were widely found and had developed a high degree of specialized skill. In some cases, slaves were trained as dancers and then performed for pay.

Following the conquests of Alexander and his return with Eastern captives, Greek dance began to show Asiatic influences, with gesture language used increasingly. During the Hellenistic and Greco-Roman periods, the *pantomimus,* or pantomimic dancer, became highly popular. A solo dancer, wearing different costumes and masks, would make use of flamboyant gesture and mimicry to tell a story in several scenes, each episode being separated by musical interludes. This form of entertainment was found most widely in Rome during its peak of power.

In Greece, we see a civilization in which dance began as an essential element in religion and an important and respected means of military training. Gradually, it became part of the developing Greek theater and then part of popular entertainment. Always, the Greeks respected dance; one of their seven Muses, on an equal plane with the Muses of epic poetry and music, was Terpsichore, the Muse of Dancing. But the respect held for dance was based on the total philosophy of the Greeks during the age of Pericles—their belief in the integrity of mind, spirit, and body and their keen interest in all the arts as essential expressions of humankind's spirit.

Dance in Ancient Rome

Dancing was much less important to the Romans than to the Greeks, from whom they borrowed much of their culture. The educated Romans looked on Greece as the source of culture and civilization; Roman aristocrats spoke Greek, employed Greek tutors, and copied Greek arts and literature. Early Roman art was vigorous, simple, and well proportioned. However, as the nation grew wealthy and powerful, it ceased to value such qualities in art; indeed, war and lust for conquest brought thousands of captives and great wealth to Rome.

Shawn commented that while the Romans were great organizers, military conquerors, and lawmakers, within the arts they were only borrowers. Ultimately, they debased all they touched. So it was, he said, with the dance: "Here in Imperial Rome we find the dance first completely theatricalized—then commercialized; and as the religious life of Rome gradually decayed and became orgiastic, so the religious dances became occasions for unbridled licentiousness and sensuality. . . ."[38]

How did it all begin?

During the earliest period of recorded history in what was to become Rome, the men of certain corporations, or societies, were grouped together under the name of *Salii,* which some have interpreted as derived from *saltio,* the Latin word for "dance," and *saltantes,* the word for "dancers." The *Salii,* who included sowing priests who purified the fields, warriors who performed weapon dances, and the priests of Mars (god of war), carried on spring processionals which had a somewhat dance-like character. During this period, other choral dances were done, with choruses of older and younger men who marched around in a circle to the rhythmic beating of their shields. Other feasts and holidays throughout the year were celebrated, with dancing that was apparently of a dignified and restrained nature: ". . . at the Palilia, or festival of Pales, solemn and magnificent dances were performed in the fields by shepherds, who during the night formed circles around blazing fires of straw and stubble. The Floralia, or festival of Flora, gave rise to the May Day customs still surviving in parts of England. . . ."[39]

These customs continued for centuries. A Roman writer, Suetonius, commented at a much later date on the processionals of the *Salii,* held as a three-week ritual in March and October. Clad in embroidered tunics and high conical caps, armed and bearing shields, they trooped through the public places of the city, dancing and singing sacred songs.

Other customs included the religious festivals of the *Lupercalia,* the *Saturnalia,* and the *Ludiones.* The *Lupercalia* were held during the Kalends of March, in honor of the god Pan. The priests of this cult, the *Luperci,* danced naked through the streets of Rome, armed with whips, with which they were said to have struck at the crowds of spectators. The *Saturnalia* was a great feast, held in mid-December, in honor of

Saturn. It was a time for revelry, feasting, drunkenness, dancing in the streets, and for class distinctions to be set aside. Kirstein commented that this pagan holiday was adopted by Roman Christians for Christ's Mass, or Christmas, and that it became, in ensuing centuries, the occasion for many dramatic dances.[40]

As an example of the more excessive forms that religious dance took at this time, Chadwick described the festival of *Cybele* and *Attis,* in which the *Archigallas,* or high priest, stabbed his arms and presented his blood as an offering to the gods:

> Stirred by the wild barbaric music of clashing cymbals . . . and screaming flutes, the inferior clergy whirled about in the dance with waggling heads and streaming hair; until, rapt in a frenzy of excitement and insensible to pain, they gashed their bodies with potsherds or slashed them with knives in order to bespatter the altar and the sacred tree with their flowing blood.[41]

Dance in the Roman Theater. Dance also played a part in the early Roman theater, although much of this was the work of imported Greek performers or players from Istria who were brought to Rome in the middle of the fourth century B.C. to placate the gods with entertainment and to distract a population that had been racked by plague. The dancers and pantomimists from Istria were known as *istriones;* their name was the source of the modern word *histrionic.* They wore goatskin shepherd's cloaks; the name for these, *saturae,* is said to be the source of the term *satire* or satirical. Their performances were farcical enactments which parodied the lives of gods, heroes, or everyday men, often in rustic settings. They were carried on usually without speaking, relying on gesture to tell the story. Kirstein commented that dance, in the form of the *choros,* had little place in the Roman theater. Romans preferred the excitement and color of mass spectacles, which were performed in huge circuses and arenas, to the thoughtful and literary works that were found on the Greek stage.

Since this was the case, the stage became unattractive as a profession; actors and dancers in performing companies tended to be Greek or south Italian slaves formerly owned by rich noblemen and now rented out to theatrical managers. For a long time, no women appeared on the stage; their parts were taken by young men. Later, women, who among the Greeks were not even permitted to take part in tragedy or comedy, appeared in Rome in pantomime.

For a period of time beginning at about 200 B.C., it became fashionable for Roman patricians to dance. Etruscan and Greek choreographers taught private dancing classes, attended by the sons and daughters of the nobility. Dance became an important social grace. Later, dance was inveighed against as a softening of the fiber of Roman citizenry; indeed, one emperor, Scipio Africanus, closed the dancing schools by edict in about 150 B.C. However, it was hardly necessary; the Romans had little real inclination or aptitude for dancing. The only real popularity of dance over a period of time was extended to the pantomimic dance, which developed as an independent stage form under Caesar Augustus about 22 B.C.

Romans enjoyed the lively spectacle of pantomime dance. By the time of Caesar Augustus, Rome was filled with a huge, heterogeneous population of varied origins. They spoke not only Latin, but Greek, Syrian, Gallic, Teutonic, and many other languages. It was impossible to present spoken dramas that could be understood by all these varied spectators, particularly in huge theaters with poor acoustics. Therefore, the pantomime developed to an extremely fine degree and achieved immense popularity.

This dance form was much like an early stage of Greek tragedy, in which one actor, with the aid of varying costumes and masks, portrayed a number of characters in a single tale. Instead of speaking or chanting, the pantomimic dancer performed with dance and gestures alone. The typical costume for the pantomime performer was full and heavy, with elaborate embellishments and masks for almost all roles. Feet and legs were apparently used chiefly for taking dramatic poses and marking rhythm, while the trunk of the body was gracefully twisted, and the hands and arms were used expressively to convey meaning. Lawler commented that the effect on the public was tremendous:

> . . . spectators sometimes sat in the theaters for whole days, watching the dancers almost as if hypnotized; they thought of the dancers as virtually divine, and Seneca calls the craze for their performance 'a disease'—*morbus*. Women swooned, high officials of the state hung on every move, and Roman emperors summoned the dancers for command performances. . . .[42]

Vuillier wrote:

> We can form but a faint idea of the perfection to which the art of pantomime attained among the Romans. It ranged over the whole domain of fable, poetry, and history. Roman actors translated the most subtle sensations by gestures of extraordinary precision and mobility, and their audience understood every turn of this language, which conveyed far more to them than declamation. . . . the strength, the infinite gradations of this mute expression, made the dancing of the ancients a great art. . . .[43]

Public opinion was divided about pantomime artists; some emperors favored them while others opposed or banned them. Marcus Aurelius put a limit on the wages they might be paid and on their production expenses. The developing Christian Church kept up an unremitting attack on them, and yet at one time, when Rome was suffering from famine and even orators and teachers were banished, three thousand dancers were allowed to remain in the city—so vital was this entertainment considered to be. Yet, more and more, moralists spoke out against the pantomime. Lucian, in the second century A.D., had one of his characters, Crato, ask in a dialogue: "[How can anyone] sit still and listen to the sounds of a flute, and watch the antics of an effeminate creature got up in soft raiment to sing lascivious songs and mimic the passions of prehistoric strumpets to the accompaniment of twanging string and shrilling pipe and clattering heel?"[44]

The controversy continued, but gradually the popularity of the pantomimists declined, and many of them were forced to withdraw from the cities and to perform in smaller towns. Probably their last performances were in the late fourth and early fifth centuries A.D. By this time, dance was criticized more and more and was attacked by many of Rome's leading citizens and writers. "I let myself be taken to a dancing class," said Scipio in the second century, "and there, by God, I saw over 50 girls and boys, including a youth of less than 12 years old . . . who was performing . . . a dance of which any wretched slave would be ashamed." Increasingly, dance came to be seen as corrupt, immoral, and inappropriate for a person of good society. Sallust wrote of a noblewoman, "She played and danced more gracefully than a respectable woman should," and Cicero wrote the following condemnation of an art which had declined from the lofty stature it had held in Greek civilization:

> Cato calls Lucius Muena a dancer. If this be imputed to him truly, it is the reproach of a violent accuser; but if falsely, it is the abuse of a scurrilous railer. . . . For no man, one may almost say, ever dances when sober, unless perhaps he be a madman; nor in solitude, nor in a moderate and sober party; dancing is the last companion of prolonged feasting, of luxurious situation, and of many refinements.[45]

In essence, dance suffered from the sickness that had seized the entire Roman empire. The sturdy, simple patriotism of the Roman citizen had given way to a decadence that demanded "bread and circuses." Tremendous public spectacles were staged, featuring the torture and slaughter of thousands of captives and slaves taken during Roman conquests. A variety of performers offered their talents—singers, dancers, jugglers, musicians, animal trainers, acrobats—but most of all the Roman citizens demanded violent and sadistic spectacles. There were chariot races; gladiatorial contests pitting captives of war, condemned prisoners, and professional fighters together; cleverly staged "sea-fights" with slave-manned galleys in flooded ditches; and a variety of other brutal spectacles. These were carried on in huge arenas. The Circus Maximus was said to have held at one time 350,000 spectators.

Two emperors, in particular, were identified with these monstrous games: Caligula, who was extremely fond of singing and dancing and who frequently performed in the circuses; and Nero, under whom the persecution of Christians was unrelenting. Tacitus wrote that many Christians ". . . were dressed in the skins of wild beasts, and exposed to be torn to pieces by dogs in the public games, that they were crucified, or condemned to be burnt; and at nightfall serve in place of lamps to lighten the darkness, Nero's own gardens being used for the spectacle."[46]

Dance itself was often used for gruesome purposes. The historian Plutarch recorded that condemned criminals, clothed in rich garments and wearing wreaths, often were compelled to dance in the crowded arena until their clothing, which had been treated with some secret chemical, suddenly burst into flames and they died agonizingly.[47]

Because of all it represented, the Roman way of life was bitterly condemned by the early Christians, who suffered under it, yet survived it. And, because dance was so integral a part of the corruption of the Romans in their later days of empire, dance too was condemned by the Church Fathers. But this relationship, after the fall of Rome and through the Dark and Middle Ages, was strangely contradictory.

Dance became linked to the Christian Church in many ways and at the same time was violently condemned by it as centuries passed.

Notes

1 George Catlin, cited in Karen Lynn Smith, "Religion and Ritual Dance of the Plains Indians," in *Focus on Dance X,* eds. Dennis Fallon and Mary Jane Wolbers (Reston, Va.: National Dance Association, 1982), p. 21.

2 Pearl Primus, "Out of Africa," in Walter Sorell, *The Dance Has Many Faces* (New York: World Publishing Co., 1951), pp. 256–57.

3 Douglas Kennedy, *England's Dances* (London: G. Bell & Sons, Ltd., 1950), pp. 31–32.

4 Anna Kisselgoff, "Were Men Really Dancing 40,000 Years Ago?" *New York Times,* August 2, 1981, p. 6-D.

5 *The New York Times,* March 15, 1966, p. 40.

6 Joost Meerloo, *The Dance* (New York: Chilton Book Co., 1960), pp. 45–46.

7 Curt Sachs, *World History of the Dance* (New York: W. W. Norton & Co., 1937), p. 9.

8 See Susanne Langer, *Philosophy in a New Key: A Study in the Symbolism of Reason, Rite, and Art* (New York: The New American Library, 1951), p. 114.

9 Ibid., pp. 138–39.

10 Tore Hakansson, "Sex in Primitive Art and Dance," in *The Encyclopedia of Sexual Behavior,* eds. Albert Ellis and Albert Abarbanel (New York: Hawthorn Books, Inc., 1961), pp. 154–60.

11 See Mary Browning, "Micronesian Heritage," in *Dance Perspectives,* no. 43 (Autumn 1970), p. 9.

12 Ibid.

13 Agnes de Mille, *The Book of the Dance* (New York: Golden Press, 1963), pp. 32–33.

14 Sachs, *World History,* p. 157.

15 Paul Radin, *The Story of the American Indian* (New York: Garden City Publishing Co., 1937), p. 313.

16 Erna Fergusson, *Indian Ceremonials of New Mexico and Arizona* (Albuquerque, N. Mex.: University of New Mexico Press, 1951), p. xviii.

17 Samuel Merti and Gertrude Kurath, *Dances of Anáhuac* (Chicago: Aldine Publishing Co., and Wenner-Gren Foundation, 1964), p. 25.

18 Ibid., p. 26.

19 *The New York Times,* January 13, 1966, p. L-9.

20 Sula Benet, *Song, Dance and Customs of Peasant Poland* (London: Dennis Dobson Ltd., 1951), p. 36.

21 Ibid., p. 47.

22 E. Louis Backman, *Religious Dances* (London: George Allen and Unwin Ltd., 1952), pp. 2–3.

23 Ted Shawn, *Dance We Must* (London: Dennis Dobson Ltd., 1946), p. 16.

24 Lincoln Kirstein, *Dance: A Short History of Classic Theatrical Dancing* (New York: G. P. Putnam's Sons, 1935), p. 7.

25 Alexander Bland, *A History of Ballet and Dance in the Western World* (New York: Praeger Book Co., 1976), p. 14.

26 Kirstein, *Dance: A Short History,* pp. 11–12.

27 Bland, *A History of Ballet,* p. 14.

28 Havelock Ellis, *The Dance of Life* (Boston: Houghton Mifflin Co., 1923), p. 54.

29 Alfred Sendrey and Mildred Norton, *David's Harp: The Story of Music in Biblical Times* (New York: The New American Library, 1964), p. 207.

30 Judith Lynne Hanna, *The Performer-Audience Connection: Emotion to Metaphor in Dance and Society* (Austin, Tex.: University of Texas Press, 1983), p. 29.

31 Bland, *A History of Ballet,* p. 21.

32 Lillian B. Lawler, *The Dance in Ancient Greece* (Middletown, Conn.: Wesleyan University Press, 1964), p. 14.

33 Ibid., pp. 76–81.

34 Ibid., p. 124.

35 Hanna, *Performer-Audience Connection,* p. 29.

36 Shawn, *Dance We Must,* p. 18.

37 Ethel L. Urlin, *Dancing, Ancient and Modern* (New York: D. Appleton and Co., 1914), pp. 29–30.

38 Shawn, *Dance We Must,* p. 17.

39 Urlin, *Dancing,* p. 35.

40 Kirstein, *Dance: A Short History,* p. 46.

41 Ida F. Chadwick, "Dance: An Agent of 'Ekstasis'," in *Focus on Dance X,* Fallon and Wolbers, eds., p. 5.

42 Lawler, *Dance in Ancient Greece,* p. 140.

43 Gaston Vuillier, *A History of Dance* (New York: D. Appleton and Co., 1987), p. 39.

44 Kirstein, *Dance: A Short History,* p. 50.

45 Ibid., p. 45.

46 Ibid., p. 57.

47 Lawler, *Dance in Ancient Greece,* p. 142.

CHAPTER 4

Dance in the Middle Ages and Renaissance

There were boisterous dances as well where the dancers even limped in time, as well as hopped and skipped. In the *Hoppelvogel*, bird-hops, the *Firlefanz*, fiddle-faddle, and *Krummen Reihen* (crooked rows), the German ladies shrieked, while their cavaliers yelled back. There were also such pantomimic dances as described in the *Ruodlieb* of the first half of the eleventh century, when a young man parodied the flight of a falcon, his lady the pursued swallow.

Early German Gothic dancing was habitually performed in rows or circles. When the personal physical contact of dancing in pairs came in, there was the same sort of scandal which rocked Europe at the entrance of the waltz six hundred years later. The town council of Ulm at once prohibited the public performance of paired dances. Then the noblemen in the free cities of the Holy Roman Empire built themselves private ballrooms.[1]

THE HISTORY OF DANCE—AS OF ALL THE ARTS—following the fall of Rome is closely linked with the development of the Catholic Church in Europe. The early Church founders were filled with bitter antagonism toward the Roman way of life and all its excesses. By religious conviction, they rejected this hedonistic philosophy and instead moved toward a fanatical asceticism.

After the fall of the Roman Empire, Europe was overrun with warring tribes and shifting forces. The organized power of Rome, which had built roads, extended commerce, and given protection to the arts and the centers of learning, was at an end. Within this vacuum, during the Dark Ages, the Christian Church offered a unity and form of universal citizenship in Europe. The Church and the feudal lords who emerged, each controlling his own fiefdom, were the sources of authority in this era. They were closely interlocked, and it was the church that was the sole custodian of learning and education and the source of morals. Margaret H'Doubler suggested that the characteristic feature of early Christian thought was its other-worldliness, placing a sharp emphasis on the reward to be gained after death and condemning all carnality and hedonism:

> The paramount consideration of all living was to save the soul. Consequently, the body was looked upon as a hindrance. To exalt the soul the body was ignored, punished, and bruised. Anything that expressed the livelier feelings of instinctive human nature or in any way suggested former pagan ways and ideals of living, was banished into the realm of wickedness. . . .[2]

Theatrical entertainment in particular was prohibited. As early as 300 A.D., with the coming of the first Christian emperors, a council at Elvira decided that the rite of baptism could not be extended to those connected with the circus or pantomime. In 398, at the Council of Carthage, an edict excommunicated those who attended the theater on holy days. So poor was public regard for stage performers that it was almost assumed that female artists would become prostitutes. Kirstein pointed out that, after the Lombard invasion of 568, shows and games were rarely mentioned in Rome itself. For two or three hundred years, they are reported to have been carried on in the Eastern Empire, and isolated professional entertainers probably wandered through the countryside, but the great spectacles and organized shows of Imperial Rome were over.

Yet there is clear evidence that dance was performed from the very beginning of Christianity and under the most unlikely of auspices—within the Church itself. How could the Church founders approve of dance? First, beginning with the early Hebrews, a distinction was made between prayerful dance that propitiates God and immoral or sensual, unrestrained dance. Second, Christianity grew out of earlier pagan religions, and many of its rites and customs necessarily borrowed from these earlier practices or were influenced by them. Despite their historic condemnation of the body as a source of immoral pleasure, Hanna suggested that Christians have had a love-hate view of the human body. She pointed out, "Christ was flesh, God's creation. Christians call the church the 'body of Christ'." In the Revised Standard Version of the Bible, we read, "Do you know that your body is a temple of the Holy Spirit within you, which you have from God? . . . Glorify God in your Body." Hanna continued:

> The Bible recognizes body communication. For example, "A worthless person, a wicked man, goes about with crooked speech, winks with his eyes, scrapes with his feet, points with his finger" (Proverbs, 6:12,13).
> Yet flesh was scorned as inferior, animal-like, and decaying. It was the root of all evil, forbidden but desired and attractive. The ubiquitous body was to be transcended. In St. Paul's view, it was to be mortified.[3]

Examples of Early Christian Dance

What form did dance take within the Christian Church? The earliest examples are described by the Catholic Father Héliot in his history of religious orders of monks. A number of Christian sects, the Therapeutae, withdrew into the wilderness in order to avoid persecution, assembling on Sundays and other holy days in groves of oases to dance ring dances and sing psalms and hymns. The Therapeutae had a highly developed cult dance, according to Backman:

> Following a night watch (*vigilium*), the participants grouped themselves into two facing choral groups, one of men and one of women. Each group had a leader. During the alternate singing of songs, the singers sometimes remained stationary, sometimes they moved forward, sometimes backward, sometimes to right and sometimes to left, as circumstances required. Then they united in a single chorus. . . .[4]

Dating from about the year 160, there exists a remarkable hymn, known as the *Acts of John,* quoted in the Catholic Dictionary as being known to Augustine. It offers a version of the Lord's Supper in which Christ, taking leave of his disciples, instituted the custom of Holy Communion. However, instead of the traditional symbolic acts of breaking bread and sipping wine, Jesus is described as having his disciples surround him with hands joined, singing and circling around.

Chadwick argued that when they realized that converts to Christianity would not accept a religion without rituals, the early Church founders included in their services some of the ritualistic elements to which the converts had been accustomed. Dance was one of these. Chadwick quoted a passage of Clement of Alexandria (150 to 216 A.D.) illustrating the use of dance in religious celebration:

> This is the mountain beloved of God. On it rejoice God's daughters, the most beautiful lambs, which reveal the reverent festivals of the Word to the accompaniment of constantly repeated choral dancing. By righteousness man may take part in them. Whilst torches are borne before me, I perceive the heavens and God. I am led into the service of God. Thou, also, if thou wishest, mayest let thyself be led. Then shalt thou dance in a ring, together with the angels.[5]

Epiphanius, who was made Bishop of Salamis on Cyprus in 367, gave a sermon on Palm Sunday on the entry of Christ into Jerusalem. The festival of celebration is described in these words: "Rejoice in the highest, Daughter of Zion! Rejoice, be glad and leap boisterously thou all-embracing Church. For behold, once again the King approaches . . . once again perform the choral dances . . . leap wildly, ye Heavens; sing Hymns, ye Angels; ye who dwell in Zion, dance ring dances. . . ."[6]

Those who have interpreted this work conclude that it describes not only the spirit of the ceremony, but also literal dances done within the Church. This view is supported by the writings of Basilius, Bishop of Caesarea, who lived between 344 and 407. Basilius wrote frequently of the existence of the dance in the time of early Christianity, including one passage which suggested that pagan rites such as dawn ceremonies, which greeted the sunrise, were also found in the early Catholic Church: "Could there be anything more blessed than to imitate on earth the ring-dance of the angels and at dawn to raise our voices in prayer and by hymns and songs glorify the rising Creator?"[7]

In many other ways, the Catholic Church based its practices on the rituals of earlier religions. When the heathen tribes of Europe and Asia Minor were converted, the missionaries (most of whom were Roman) built their churches on existing shrines or temple sites. Often, they established the Christian holy days at the same times as earlier pagan festivals. Such implements of Catholic ritual as the bell, candles, incense, singing, and dancing had all been found in heathen faiths. Thus, it was natural that dance would be included in the services.

Ambrose, Bishop of Milan in the late fourth century, wrote profusely in support of church dance, taking his text from Luke 7:32, "We have piped unto you and ye have not danced." However, he also warned against being snared by the appeal of indecent dances and the stage:

> . . . No, the dance should be conducted as did David when he danced before the Ark of the Lord, for everything is right which springs from the fear of God. Let us not be ashamed of a show of reverence which will enrich the cult and deepen the adoration of God. For this reason the dance must in no wise be regarded as a mark of reverence for vanity and luxury, but as something which uplifts every living body instead of allowing the limbs to rest motionless upon the ground or the slow feet to become numb. St. Paul danced in this spirit when he exerted himself for us. . . .[8]

Chadwick pointed out that such warnings were not enough, and that often worshippers recaptured the pagan spirit of earlier rituals. Basilius condemned the excessive dancing at the celebration of the Resurrection:

> . . . despising God and his angels, they [the women] shamelessly attract the attention of every man. With unkempt hair, clothed in bodices and hopping about, they dance with lustful eyes and loud laughter; as if seized by a kind of frenzy they excite the lusts of youths. They execute ringdances in the churches of the Martyrs and at their graves instead of in the public buildings, transforming the Holy places into the scene of their lewdness.[9]

Thus, dance, when it expressed vice and luxury, was condemned. When it was virtuous and performed in honor of God, it was praised. St. Gregory of Nazianzus, an eminent theologian of the fourth century who became Bishop of Constantinople, delivered a stern exhortation to the Emperor Julian, which has frequently been quoted:

> . . . if you wish to dance in devotion . . . then dance, but not the shameless dance of the daughter of Herod, which accompanied the execution of the Baptist, but the Dance of David to the true refreshment of the Ark, which I consider to be the approach to God, the swift encircling steps in the manner of the mysteries. . . .[10]

Many other illustrations support the view of Curt Sachs that dance continued to be practiced widely by those Europeans who had been converted to Christianity but who retained many of their earlier pagan customs:

> Even with Christianity the theme and content scarcely change their outer garb. The charms for fertility still occupy the central position; with undiminished power they dominate at Shrovetide, the first of May, and at weddings, at midsummer, and at funeral ceremonies. . . . Maypole and fire dances, sword dances, mask dances. . . .[11]

As the Dark Ages drew to a close, there was continuing confirmation of the use of dance in Christian worship. A hymn which dates from the tenth century, for early morning Mass during the celebration of Easter at the Monastery of Moissac in France, states:

> His [Christ's] life, His speech and miracle,
> His wondrous death prove it.
> The congregation adorns the sanctity,
> Come and behold the host of ring-dances!

Dance Customs in the Middle Ages

A second form of religious dance was to be found in certain church festivals which were carried on in the latter part of the Dark Ages and apparently through the Middle Ages. These were particularly popular with the lower clergy—the monks, choirboys, and younger priests and subdeacons—and often they were highly disrespectful of the upper clergy. Just as in earlier religions, these festivals included various forms of acting, singing, dancing, and the playing of games. John Beleth, who lived in the twelfth century and was Rector of the University of Paris, described four kinds of dance in use at church festivals: the Deacons' Festival dance on St. Stephen's Day, the Priests' on St. John's Day, the choirboys' on Innocents' Day, and the subdeacons' on the Feast of the Circumcision.

Other ceremonies which were of a dramatic or dance-like nature were carried on outside of the formal service of the church but with a greater degree of approval by the authorities. A Children's Festival, or Festival of the Choristers, at which a child bishop was elected, was celebrated usually on Innocent's Day, December 28; this custom is believed to have begun in the twelfth century. At the Cathedral of Auxerres, during the thirteenth century, a religious mystery play was carried out which made use of a ball game played on a labyrinth design on the cathedral nave's floor. This custom was based on pre-Christian ceremonies in early Greece, and it illustrates that games, as well as dance, were sometimes part of pagan religious worship.

Dance Processions

Particularly in France and Germany, great processions were carried out to ward off distress or bring relief from pain or epidemics. These were recorded as having taken place regularly in the ninth and tenth centuries, and from the twelfth to the sixteenth centuries. As they marched, the worshippers often carried relics of saints and martyrs, crosses and banners, and images of the Holy Virgin. The movement involved rhythmic steps, with the procession stopping at certain stations and performing sacral dances: ceremonial greetings, bows, turns, advancing, and retiring. Backman described this ceremony as a

> . . . moving chorus advancing in harmony and with a sort of cadence through the various parts of the church. The processions passing through the choir and aisles,

swinging the censer, do so to measured movements prescribed in the ritual . . . representing by their symbolical movements and figures holy and mystical dances.[12]

Another source, from the ninth century, used the phrase, ". . . the holy relics were borne amidst happy dancing." Because they marched with crosses, banners, and relics, and because of their reverence, those taking part in these processions were not condemned by the church.

With the beginning of the Middle Ages and extending until about 1400, a variety of dramatic activities was carried on with religious themes, but not as a formal part of religious service. These included mystery plays, which dealt with events found in both the Old and New Testaments; these striking displays were staged in church squares or public marketplaces. So-called miracle plays tended to be portrayals of the lives of the saints and martyrs. Somewhat later appeared the morality plays, which were concerned with depicting the truths of moral behavior; essentially, they were allegorical representations of the struggle between good and evil, virtue and vice.

All of these apparently stemmed from earlier pagan sources, although their themes were Christian. Kennedy suggested that the yearly cycle of miracle and morality plays helped to convert many ignorant and illiterate peasants to Christianity:

> . . . outside the control of the Church popular custom continued to practice one relic of the old religion in the form of a midwinter drama/dance performance, in which was portrayed by the actor/dancers a contest between life and death. The European folk dances performed during the winter season . . . all include some scraps of this old drama of life and death . . . acted on or near Christmas Day, it is a symbolic death and resurrection. This death and revival drama, performed at the turn of the year, is known in every European country. As one would expect, it is found most complete among the primitive peasantry in Eastern Europe.[13]

Even today, such "mummer's plays" are performed by traditional English dance and song groups in the British Isles and America at several major holidays during the year.

The Dance of Death

Certain phenomena, however, which were carried on outside the control of the Church, and which involved dance, aroused more serious condemnation by religious authorities. One of these was the Dance of Death, or *Toten Tanz*. This was a custom believed to have originated in France, which then filtered into Germany, Italy, Spain, and England. It was carried on throughout the Middle Ages, and apparently it was at its peak during the fourteenth and fifteenth centuries, when many references to it appear in songs, poems, and dramas, or are depicted on murals in cemeteries, churches, cloisters, and vaults.

The Dance of Death reveals the great preoccupation with death during this period. Backman pointed out that among primitive peoples, the dead often were regarded as dangerous and hostile to the living. Legends of vampires, werewolves, and ghosts were found throughout Europe during the Dark Ages, and many customs had been devised to prevent the dead from returning. These included binding together the feet of the dead, driving nails into their feet, carrying on a death watch—and, in many instances, singing and performing games and dances during wakes or after the grave had received the corpse.

Particularly in northern European countries, it was customary for such rites to include music and dancing. Backman suggested that the belief was that music exorcised the dead, forced them into compliance at being taken to the grave, and prevented them from walking the earth again: Church bells were thought to drive demons away and to comfort and protect the dead. In addition, there was a widespread folk belief that the dead themselves liked to dance in churchyards and cemeteries in a sort of *danse macabre*. According to this superstition, they attempted to entice the living into the ranks of their ghostly dancing; however, those who danced with them would then die within the year. The Dance of Death, then, suggests that the living themselves dance toward their own deaths; death is a wedding dance, and one dances in death toward the bridegroom.

Henri Stegmaier pointed out that, in its earliest form: ". . . the Dance of Death is actually a Dance of the Dead . . . in which the dead bodies lure the living from the various ranks of society in their midnight frolic. Later, the dead are conceived of no longer as corpses, but each as the personified figure of death himself."[14]

Death appears in the ritual, and in the many songs, poems, and pictures of the Dance of Death, as a dancer. He compels people of every station and age, however reluctant, to dance with him. Each in turn is taken, according to a graduated social scale—saints and sinners, rich and poor, young and old. A document in the archives of the church at Caudbec, France, described a dramatic dance held in 1393, in which actors represented the various ranks and professions and in which, after each repetition of the dance, one of the dancers withdrew and disappeared. In essence, this was a parable, depicting Death as the universal leveler. It says, "Death avenges all wrong, and all, no matter how powerful in the living world, must at last yield to him."

The Dance of Death has been interpreted as a form of social and religious satire and the healthy reaction of the people against the strict asceticism of the Church. It is also seen as evidence of the awakening spirit of democracy in the dying Middle Ages, in that it protested against the tremendous power and wealth of the ruling classes as well as the miserable lives led by the common folk. In essence, it was "a desperate statement of the common man's disillusionment with the entire social, political, and religious scheme under which he lived; Death leveled all ranks and stations and proved them ultimately vain. . . ."[15]

The Church was well aware of this symbolic meaning. From the fourth century well into the eighteenth century, there were many prohibitions against dancing for the dead in graveyards, particularly against dances which were ribald and indecent or which involved drinking and feasting. The Roman Synod under Leo IV ordered at the beginning of the ninth century that: "In witness of the true and living God, the devilish songs which are heard at night on the graves of the dead are to cease, as well as the noise which accompanies them." And a later resolution says: "Whoever buries the dead should do so with fear, trembling and decency. No one shall be permitted to sing devil songs and perform games and dances which are inspired by the devil and have been invented by the heathen."[16]

However, these and later prohibitions failed to put an end to the Dance of Death. As late as the 1930s, Backman reported a *Bal de La Mort* carried on in certain regions of Catalonia as part of the church processions during Holy Week. This took the form of a quadrille, performed by twelve men and three women wearing black clothes on which white skeletons had been painted:

> Their faces were covered with masks representing skulls. One of the dancers carries a scythe, another a pendulum clock, and a third a banner. The musician, with only a drum, is clad in armour, enveloped in a black mantle. They follow the Corpus Christi procession and therefore are a part of the popular church dance. The one who carries the scythe must not take part in the dance, but just swings his scythe toward the bystanders. The others dance and hop. . . .[17]

A number of similar phenomena appeared during the Middle Ages, reflecting belief in witchcraft, religious fanaticism, and the lingering influence of heathen superstition. In a sense, they represented the common people's primitive fear of death in the midst of famine, war, and plagues.

Witch dances, carried on at night, paid homage to the devil with wild bacchanals, accompanied by grotesque costumes and masks, sacrifices, and sexual excesses (just as angels were thought to dance heavenly ring dances in honor of God). The *Witches' Sabbath,* carried on during the night of April 30, was a traditional time for such rites, which took place in dark and lonely places. Another craze which spread over Europe from the eleventh to the fourteenth centuries was *St. Vitus's Dance,* or, as it was sometimes known, *St. John's Dance,* named after the patron saint who was supposed to protect the afflicted. Here, men, women, and children danced in wild delirium; they performed frenzied leaps and turns, writhing as if suffering from epileptic seizures, screaming out uncontrollably, and foaming at the mouth. Similar to this was *tarantism,* a form of seizure-like dance which was thought at first to be the result of the bite of the tarantula spider, and which was later deliberately performed in order to avert the effects of the tarantula's poison. Eventually, as the superstitious belief in this "remedy" diminished, it was continued as a traditional folk dance appearing in many Italian provinces—the *Tarantella*.

Danseomania

The most striking and unusual dance expression of the Middle Ages and early Renaissance was the so-called *danseomania,* or dancing mania, which flourished throughout Europe from the eleventh to the fourteenth centuries. John Martin commented that the people of Europe had been so affected by a succession of natural calamities (wars, plagues, fires) that they sought an outlet for emotional strain in the dancing manias: "Whole communities of people . . . were stricken with a kind of madness that sent them dancing and gyrating through the streets and from village to village for days at a time until they died in agonized exhaustion. . . ."[18]

Kirstein referred to the dancing mania as a form of pathological aberration which was widely documented by writings of the thirteenth and fourteenth centuries, particularly in Germany and the Low Countries. Sometimes it affected children, sometimes large numbers of adults. In 1237, a party of German children danced from Erfurt to Arnstadt, many dying along the way. In 1278, a bridge at Marburg collapsed beneath a company of dancers, and all were drowned. In 1347, several hundred men and women danced from Aix-la-Chapelle to Metz, despite the efforts of priests to break the spell that had seized them. There were accounts of men and women who began to sing and dance suddenly in the churchyard, disrupting divine service. In some cases, when they refused to stop, they were cursed by the priest to dance the whole year through, until the ban was withdrawn by a higher church official. A twelfth-century writer, Giraldus Cambrensis, described such an outburst:

> You may see men or girls, now in the churchyard, now in the dance, which is led round the churchyard with a song, on a sudden falling on the ground as in a trance, then jumping up as in a frenzy, and representing with their hands and feet, before the people, whatever work they have unlawfully done on feast days. . . .[19]

The height of the dancing manias came about when the Black Plague, or bubonic plague, raged over Europe, killing thousands and wiping out entire villages and cities. This occurred in the year 1349, and in the decades following, it became customary for huge crowds to wander through the countryside, particularly in Germany and the Low Countries. They danced as if bewitched, and all the rites of exorcism that were tried failed to drive out the mysterious demons which had possessed them. Petrus de Herenthal, a fourteenth-century monk, described such dances carried on during the year 1374. There came to Aachen, he said, a curious sect of men and women from various regions of Germany:

> Persons of both sexes were so tormented by the devil that in markets and churches, as well as in their own homes, they danced, held each others' hands and leaped high in the air. While they danced their minds were no longer clear, and they paid no heed to modesty though bystanders looked on . . . they cried out names of demons . . . and that they were dying. . . .[20]

Those possessed, who were sometimes called choreomaniacs, were frequently accused of being heretics and of flaunting the devil willfully. The fact that they were forced to *dance* uncontrollably as part of the spell that had been cast over them confirmed the essential paganism of dance in the eyes of many Church founders.

The dance epidemics continued well into the seventeenth century, although they appear to have reached their peak of virulence during the fourteenth and fifteenth centuries. At a later stage, they were almost taken for granted as a fairly mild, recurrent illness from which certain people suffered, or as a practice carried on regularly as part of community tradition. The legend of the Pied Piper is believed to have been based on the dance epidemics of the late Middle Ages.

Continued Attempts to Prohibit Dance

As suggested earlier, secular forms of dance had from the very beginning of Christianity been the subject of opposition by the Church founders. Gradually, even the dances that were done in the church came under increasing attack during the Dark and Middle Ages. The Council of Toledo, held in 539, urged that dancing and singing at saints' festivals and processions be rooted out of Spain. The Council of Auxerres, 573–702, forbade the public to dance in choir dances or nuns to sing in them. Again, the Council of Toledo, in 633, attacked the Festival of Fools, with its singing, dancing, and feasting in churches. At the beginning of the tenth century, Patriarch John III threatened to excommunicate women who visited graves to play music and dance. The Council of Avignon decreed in 1209 that, in night watches for the saints, "there shall not be performed in churches play-acting, hopping dances, indecent gestures, ring-dance, neither shall there be sung love songs or ditties. . . ."

In 1667, there was a decree of the Parliament of Paris forbidding religious dances in general and particularly the public dances of January 1 and May 1, the torch dances of the first Sunday in Lent, and those which were held around bonfires on the Vigil of St. John. But one reason why dancing managed to survive was that the clergy, who sold dancing indulgences and who therefore derived much income from these fees, resented these prohibitions and refused to enforce them.

In Spain, there were concerted attempts to end religious dance, including a royal decree in Madrid in 1777, which attempted to end all dancing on holy days in churches or churchyards, or before images of the saints. Backman concluded that, while these attempts were ultimately successful in ending dancing by the clergy, they were never able to suppress popular church dances in which the communicants participated. To this day, such religious dances are still held in Spain, particularly on saints' days and other important holidays. And, until comparatively recently, similar ritual forms have been presented in the Rhône region of France and in Brittany. Ethel Urlin wrote:

> Dancing still forms an important part of the Breton Pardons. After the bells have been tolled, Mass said, and the statues of the Saints decorated and clad in national dress, and after offerings have been made to them of corn, flax, sheepskins and cakes, dancing is inaugurated to the sound of the national *binyou* around a moss-grown dolmen.[21]

Dance as Popular Pastime

Although the Church had condemned dance as entertainment early on, there continued to be wandering entertainers during the Dark and early Middle Ages. These performers, who were apparently combinations of singers, dancers, poets, musicians, actors, and jugglers, wandered through the countryside performing in village squares. Sachs pointed out that such an entertainer was known in Germany as *spielmann,* which is derived from *spielen,* "to dance." Another name was *joculator,*

Peasant dances at the May feasts.
From a 15th-century prayer book min-
iature in the Bibliotheque Nationale,
Paris.

which later became *jongleur,* or "juggler." Sometimes they were known as
minnesingers, and sometimes as *troubadors.* Increasingly, during the later Middle
Ages, as the restrictions of the Catholic Church were less strongly enforced, these
entertainers were welcomed in the castles and chateaus of feudal lords.

In addition to the performances of professional entertainers, the common
people amused themselves by doing dances that were essentially social in character.
There were two basic types of medieval dancing performed by peasants—the round
dance and the couple dance. The round dance, or *Reigen,* was the more popular
form. Sometimes called the *Chorea,* or *Carole,* this was usually performed by a long
chain of dancers holding each other by the hand and moving about in an open or
closed circle, or in an extended line. Early German dancing, for example, is reported
to have been habitually performed in rows or circles. Couple dances were less
common and did not become widely popular until the fifteenth century—partly
because they were considered somewhat scandalous at first.

Sachs distinguished between the two dance forms—the couple dance is
pantomimic in character, whereas the round dance is not. As an example of the
former, Nettl cited a poem written in southern Germany, about the year 1000. It

describes a dance passage between a young man and a young lady to the music of a harp player; the action is quite suggestive of the Bavarian folk dance, the *Laendler,* as performed today:

> Now the young man gets up, and then the maiden, and then a chasing and hunting begins, sometimes with loud, then with soft music. They fly hither and thither, as when the falcon hunts the dove in the air. He has reached her, the hunt is finished,—but no,—she escapes again, and the game begins anew. Truly their art would fascinate the critics, so skillfully do the dancers master the dance, the leaping, the gesture of the hands.[22]

The dances performed by peasants were extremely boisterous and robust, often frank in their sexuality and earthiness. Their names and brief descriptions suggest this character:

> *Hoppaldei:* peasants rushing around like wild boars, moving in couples as though they wanted to fly; arms waving, shoulders heaving and rolling.
>
> *Ahselrotten:* a shoulder–rolling dance, lively, flirtatious, erotic.
>
> *Springeltanz:* a wild dance in which the performers hopped and leaped about.
>
> *Houbetschotten:* a shrugging of shoulders while sliding along the floor, shaking the head.
>
> *Gimpel-Gampel:* described both as a boisterous leaping dance and as a skipping dance.

Beginnings of Court Dance

Peasant dances were copied by the nobility, but in more refined and courtly form. Court dances were part of the chivalric way of life, and they stressed coquetry, with much posturing and preening. Because of the heavy, long gowns and trains of the noblewomen, and their elaborate headdresses and jewelry, the ladies of the court were not able to move freely. Indeed, their dance steps at first tended to be little more than gliding, curtseying, and posing. Most of the dances done at first were known as *basse* dances, which meant that the action was low; close to the floor.

Nettl cited two courtly dances, as described by poets of the German *minnesinger* period, about the thirteenth century:

> The women carried their trains . . . in their hands and smiled . . . and with their eyes signalled with love-sick and secret glances . . . the knight walked between two ladies, holding each by the hand and the page walked between two maids. The fiddlers stood close at hand. [The dance] is performed slowly with solemn steps, in long peaked shoes. All the dancers advanced like this in a long row with dragging steps, and two fiddlers play the music.[23]

In addition to their robust spirit, the peasant dances tended to have large movements and wide-stepping figures. In part, this may have been because of their costume, as well as because they danced on grass or on the beaten earth of the town square. In contrast, when the court danced in a ballroom (the first of these is reported to have been built at Frankfurt-am-Main in 1350), the smooth floor of wood or polished marble made it possible for dancers to do graceful gliding or turning steps, while maintaining contact with the floor. As an additional contrast, while peasant dances tended to be performed either in couples or rather free formations of both sexes, the courtly dances were precisely defined in group formations.

Gradually, the severe asceticism and preoccupation with spiritual concerns which had characterized the early Middle Ages gave way to the more worldly minded spirit of the Renaissance. The gradual rise of a capitalist class produced patrons of learning and art—within a world which was increasingly secularized. No longer did art have to justify itself through religious content.

Within this context, and with a breaking down of the old restraints, the dance which had once been banned by the Church was now wholly accepted. The *minnesingers,* jugglers, and jesters now became valuable adjuncts to the courts of Italy and France in particular. A special profession developed—that of the dancing master. Nettl wrote of the dancing master:

> He accompanied the prince or the count to whose court he was attached on all journeys, and, in fact, he occupied a position of trust and confidence in his patron's household. He was at the same time an arbiter of etiquette, where the instruction given the young men and women of noble family was considered an essential part of their education.[24]

Thus, history had come full circle. After a period in which the arts, learning, music, and dance had been submerged beneath the fanatic asceticism of the Church, there was again an atmosphere in which they could flourish and in which music, drama, and dance, in particular, could reach new heights of artistic development and popularity. This was to be the Renaissance.

Influence of the Renaissance

Historians generally view the first half of the Middle Ages (roughly from A.D. 400 to 1000) as the Dark Ages, and about the next four to five hundred years as high (later) Middle Ages. The Renaissance is said to have begun in Italy about A.D. 1350, in France about 1450, and in England about 1500. It marked a transition between the medieval world and the modern age. The term *renaissance* means "rebirth," and it describes the revived interest in the scholarship, philosophy, and arts of ancient Greece and Rome which occurred at this time. More broadly, it also includes a new freedom of thought and expression, a more rational and scientific view of life, and the expansion of commerce and travel throughout Europe.

With the coming of the Renaissance, most notably in fifteenth-century Italy and France, all the arts enjoyed a rebirth of interest and artistic experimentation. The old restraints were loosened during the Renaissance, and learning, literature, the stage arts, and all creative expressions of the human spirit were no longer dominated by clerical ideals and purposes. Instead, they were to serve the secular goals of the wealthy and powerful kings and queens who had emerged throughout Europe—

along with the luxury-loving members of their courts. The revival of interest in classical scholarship and in the arts of ancient Greece and Rome led to a fresh interest in mythology, ancient history, and the great heroes of past centuries. With the invention of printing, it became possible to distribute widely printed dance music; at one stroke, there was a flood of music published for such instruments as lutes, guitars, organs, and others. The character of music itself changed abruptly. As Louis Horst pointed out, the pale, austere, rhythmically irregular music of the medieval period—as exemplified by the Gregorian chants—shifted to more brilliant and spirited music with pronounced rhythm and a single strong melodic line.[25]

Court Dances of the Renaissance

What were the court dances of the Renaissance that preceded and led to the development of ballet as a performing art?

At the outset, they had been divided into two broad categories—the *Basse Danse,* in which the feet did not leave the floor, and the *Haute Danse,* in which there were higher skips and jumps. However, both of these were broad types, with no precisely designed steps or floor patterns. The term *branle,* which later described a separate dance, was at first only a step sideways with balancing of the body, or swaying. A number of extremely simple dances were described as having been performed during the fifteenth century by aristocrats of the French, Italian, Spanish, and German courts. Often, they were known by one name in one country and another name elsewhere. For example, one of the best known early dances was the *Saltarello,* called *Alta Danza* in Spain and *Pas de Brebant* in France.

Other dances of the period were the *Piva, Saltarello Tedesco,* and *Calata;* however, none of these apparently had prescribed forms. Neither their descriptions nor the music to which they were danced were recorded for history. It was not until the end of the sixteenth century that rules were formulated for the proper steps for each dance and for the appropriate dance music to be played. This meant that, in terms of progress in dance, a whole system of movement and a vocabulary of steps and patterns were developed. In terms of music, the need for contrast in rhythm and musical form meant that each dance soon had its characteristic accompaniment; the composers of the period grouped the selections that were played in a certain order, giving birth to the musical suite—which ultimately became the sonata form.

The most famous dances of the period were the *Pavane,* the *Galliard,* the *Allemande,* the *Courante,* the *Sarabande,* the *Gigue,* and the *Minuet.*

Pavane. This was a dance of ceremonious splendor and great dignity, which is said to have originated in the court of Spain during the Inquisition. Its mood was solemn and religious (the name is derived from the Latin *pavo,* or "peacock"), and it suggests this stately and pompous fowl. The Pavane was apparently used on some religious occasions; Thoinot Arbeau wrote in 1588, in his *Orchesographie:*

> Our musicians play it when a damsel of good family is taken to Holy Church to be married, or when musicians head a religious procession of the chaplains, masters and brethren of some notable guild. . . . It is used by kings, princes and

great lords, to display themselves on some day of solemn festival with their fine mantles and robes of ceremony; and then the queens and princesses and great ladies accompany them with the long trains of their dresses let down and trailing behind them. These Pavanes are also used in masquerades (or ballets) where there is a procession of triumphant chariots of gods and goddesses. . . .[26]

The Pavane was a *Basse Danse,* involving a simple walking step performed by one or more couples, advancing and retreating. It was done in a slow tempo, and one source described it as a "grave kind of dance borrowed from the Spaniards, wherein the performers make a kind of wheel or tail before each other, like that of a peacock." The Pavane continued to be popular from about 1530 to about 1670; it was used as the opening dance of great festive balls, usually being followed by the spirited Galliard.

Galliard. Arbeau described the Galliard as a blithe and lively dance, of which there were at least twenty different versions. Its source was said to be Italy, where it was also called the *Romanesca.* It included a number of leaping, kicking, and leg-thrusting steps, and it was most popular from the last quarter of the sixteenth century to about the middle of the seventeenth. Sometimes the Galliard was considered to be immodest; one author referred to it as an "invention of the devil, full of shameful and obscene gestures."

When the Pavane, in 4/4 time, was followed by the lively Galliard, in 3/4 time, as a customary sequence at court balls, the first musical suite was born. Many musical compositions were composed with this contrasting structure.

Allemande. This dance eventually replaced the Pavane as the first part of what was to become the four-part classic suite. The Allemande is considered to have been a very ancient German dance, simple and grave in demeanor. One writer, in 1584, described it as "knights in armour, treading a warlike almain."

After it was introduced at the French court, the Allemande gained rather flowing and sentimental characteristics; it was usually danced in 4/4 time, played in a slow and dignified tempo. Its unique aspect was that it required partners to keep their hands joined throughout the entire dance, as they turned and performed various patterns; after it was no longer performed as a separate dance, this action was still perpetuated in folk and country dancing. In square dancing today, to turn one's partner or corner by the hand is called an allemande.

Courante. Destined to become the second dance of the four-part classic suite, the Courante was said to have originated both in Italy and France. The first phase of the Courante came from Italy and was brought to France by Catherine de Medici. Played with running passages of eighth notes in quick 3/4 time, it was colorfully described: "It is danced with short passages of coming and going, and has a very pliant movement of the knees, which recalls that of a fish when it plunges lightly through the water and returns suddenly to the surface."[27]

The second form originated in France and was the more popular version of the Courante. It was apparently a pantomime dance; as described by Arbeau, it was danced by three couples in a row, showing gestures of courtship and flirtation.

Movements included running and gliding, and as the dance continued to be performed through the years, it gradually became more solemn and noble in its attitudes. The Courante was a great favorite for about two centuries, from 1550 to 1750.

Sarabande. Eventually to become the third dance of the four-part suite, the Sarabande, like the Pavane, was of Spanish ancestry and was a solemn dance which was widely used in religious processions and Masses. It appears to have been performed as early as the twelfth century, although it was not introduced at the French court until about 1588. The dance was like a grave and proud *Minuet,* involving much advancing and retreating, with couples passing between lines of other dancers almost as a processional. Some thought that it originated first with the Moors in Spain, and it was often performed with castanets. The Sarabande was played in two parts, in 3/4 time, in a slow tempo.

Gigue. The fourth dance of the four-part classic suite was the Gigue—a lively and exciting dance which apparently was found in varying forms in many countries of Europe. The earliest form recorded was in Italy, where the name was derived from the *giga,* a small stringed instrument. Horst pointed out that the German name for fiddle was *geige,* and traditionally the Gigue, or Jig, has always been performed to spirited fiddle music, played in 3/8, 6/8, 9/8, or 12/8 time. The Gigue was most popular in the sixteenth and seventeenth centuries, although it continued to be done in later centuries as a sort of individual folk dance step, or a music hall turn.

Other dances described by Horst as being performed during the preclassic period of the sixteenth and seventeenth centuries were the *Minuet* (which continued to be widely performed as late as the nineteenth century); the *Gavotte,* originally a lively and flirtatious peasant dance; the *Bourrée,* an earthy and vigorous dance, also of peasant origin; and the *Rigaudon,* a light, gay dance with running, hopping, and turning steps.

As court music became more complex and the courtiers more skilled dancers, the original two-part suite of the Pavane and Galliard was replaced, about 1620, by the four-part suite of the Allemande, Courante, Sarabande, and Gigue. Many great composers of the seventeenth, eighteenth, and nineteenth centuries wrote in one or another of these forms, including Purcell, Bach, Handel, Couperin, and Lully; among later composers who derived inspiration from them were Satie, Ravel, Schoenberg, Debussy, and Prokofieff.

The Court Entertainments

The court entertainments did not suddenly spring into life as a form of extravagant display. Throughout the Middle Ages, there had been customs and performances which held in them the seed of the Renaissance spectacles. Under religious auspices, there had been festivals, miracle and mystery plays, and a variety of other celebrations, many of which were theatrical in character. Banquets in the homes of great nobles increasingly relied on entertainments by the resident troubador or dancing master and members of the court themselves; often these were elaborately

Equestrian ballet, *Guerra d'Amore*, in honor of Cosimo de Medici, Grand Duke of Tuscany. Engraving by Jacques Callot, published in 1615. Reprinted with permission of the Dance Collection of the Library and Museum of the Performing Arts at Lincoln Center in New York City.

costumed and provided colorful displays. Even the trade guilds of the later Middle Ages had developed the practice of performing allegorical plays which involved singing, dancing, and acting.

Thus, out of the life of the Middle Ages came both inspiration and a readiness for new forms of artistic performance. These took the form of great banquets in the Italian and French courts, usually at times of weddings, as homage to visiting royalty, or in celebration of the coronation of kings. Each of these banquets featured elaborate spectacles, with singing, dancing, and acting, richly costumed and sometimes with specially designed and built stage sets. Sometimes they were held in the castle itself, in the banquet hall, and sometimes at the city gates or at a bridge leading to the city. Their themes were diverse, including the acting out of stories from Greek mythology and fables, stories of the Crusades, tales of Roman history, Christian ceremonials, and episodes from the Old Testament.

Among the leading dance spectacles of the later Middle Ages and early Renaissance were the following:

1. Charles V of France presented a major spectacle to the German Emperor Charles

IV in 1377. Like many other entertainments, it portrayed a major episode of the Crusades. Two heavily armed wagons drove up to the banquet table. One represented the city of Jerusalem, held by Saracen defenders, and the other a galley holding soldiers of Godfrey of Bouillon. After a long, stylized combat, the crusaders successfully stormed the city. Similar pageants were held in England, when Henry V returned from victory at Agincourt in 1415, and when Henry VI and his French wife Catherine returned in 1432 from their coronation as King and Queen of France and England.

2. In 1462, King René of Provence put on an entertainment that was both religious and social, on the eve of Corpus Christi. Lacking any single theme or plot, it offered tributes to the royalty of the day and also portrayed, in a series of separate dramatic episodes, the Roman gods Mars and Minerva, Pan, Pluto, and Proserpine; fauns, dryads, and tritons; King Herod persecuted by devils; ancient Jews dancing around a Golden Calf; Christ and the Apostles; Death with a scythe, and the Magi following a star.

One of the most popular themes of such entertainments was the *Moresca,* or *Moresche,* which depicted the battles between the Moors, or Saracens, and the Crusaders. This was found both as a form of popular folk ritual and as a subject for court displays. Other aspects of the same theme included the reoccupation of Spain by the Christians and the attack on Jerusalem by the Crusader Godfrey. For example, at the celebration of the conquest of Granada in 1493, a pantomimic pageant with triumphal arches, a procession of Spanish royalty, Moorish dances, and bullfights was performed. Usually in these performances, the Moors were depicted as black people, and there may have been a connection between the *Moresca* and the Morris Dance—a traditional English folk dance in which it was the custom for certain of the dancers to blacken their faces.

Throughout all of these pageants, dance served as a means of pantomiming the action. In many of the entrees, or interludes, other dances which had become popular during the Renaissance were performed. These were the so-called court dances, or preclassic dances, which were described in the preceding section of this chapter. They were typically performed in couples or small group formations and covered a wide range of music, mood, and movement styles. They differed from the dances done during the entertainments in that they were essentially social forms of dance, not intended to tell a story.

Dancing gradually became an everyday adjunct to court life in all of the palaces of the Renaissance. Queen Elizabeth of England was said to have made Sir Christopher Hatton her Lord Chancellor not because of his wisdom in the law, but because "he wore green bows on his shoes and danced the pavane to perfection. . . ." During the Middle Ages, dancing had become widely accepted in the courts throughout Europe, and training in it was now viewed as indispensable to the education of a nobleman. Agnes de Mille pointed out that the invention of firearms meant that whereas at one time brute strength and endurance had been prize qualities for a courtier who also was a soldier, now intelligence and alertness counted for more. Just as the giant Percheron warhorses (to bear the lords clad in weighty armor) were replaced by lighter and more graceful Arabian thoroughbreds, so during the Renaissance, "clothes became lighter, manners daintier, dueling more expert and dancing more skilled. . . ."

The First Ballets

Dance historians usually assign the date of the first ballet to 1581, when the so-called *Ballet Comique de la Reine* was produced at the court of Henry III of France, at Fontainebleau. It was a tremendously elaborate and expensive spectacle, produced by the queen mother, Catherine de Medici, who, when she came to France to wed Henry II, had brought with her a company of highly trained musicians and dancers from the city of Florence. The *Ballet Comique* was produced in honor of the queen's daughter-in-law; it was the work of Catherine's *valet de chambre,* Balthasar de Beaujoyeux, an Italian. It was a mixture of Old Testament tales and Greek and Roman mythology; basically, its theme was the legend of Circe, the Greek enchantress. Original music, poetry, and songs were composed by professionals of the court, and elaborate sets and scenic devices, including fountains and aquatic machines, accompanied the performance. Over ten thousand spectators saw the performance, which lasted from ten in the evening until four in the morning, and which cost between three and five million francs to produce.

Although the quality of performance and the splendor of the entire work far exceeded any court entertainment that had been produced before, it was chiefly because the *Ballet Comique* attempted to confine itself to a single major dramatic theme that it is regarded as the first real ballet to have been presented in Europe. The performance was regarded as a major artistic success; copies of its poetry and music were printed and sent to all the courts of Europe. After the *Ballet Comique,* France was viewed as the center of the development of ballet, while Italy served as the home of the developing opera of the Renaissance.

The term *ballet* was derived from the Italian *ballare,* meaning "to dance," and from the word *ballo,* referring to dances as performed in a ballroom. *Ballate* were songs used to accompany dancing in Tuscany in the thirteenth and fourteenth centuries; and Chujoy pointed out that during the later years of the Renaissance the Medici princes wrote *canzone a ballo,* or dance songs. The word *balleti* was the diminutive of *ballo* and is the direct source of the word *ballet.* At first it meant performances of patterned dances and had no specific theatrical meaning. Balthasar de Beaujoyeux, choreographer of the *Ballet Comique,* defined ballet as "a geometric combination of several persons dancing together."

Similarly, in 1641, Saint-Hubert wrote of ballet as an essentially nondramatic work requiring "subject, airs, dancing, costumes, machines, and organization." About the same time, Marolles emphasized its spectacular character, asking:

> But what is a Ballet of the type today among us? It seems to me that it is a dance of many masked persons dressed in dazzling clothes, composed of diverse entrées or parts which can be distributed into several acts and which relate agreeably to a whole, with some different airs to represent an invented subject where the pleasing, the unusual and the marvelous are not forgotten.[28]

Gradually, the term *ballet* came to mean a form of theatrical storytelling through dance. The *Encyclopedia* of Diderot, published in France about 1772, says, "Ballet is action explained by a dance . . . specifically theatrical, spectacular, and done to be seen. . . ." Another eighteenth-century conception was, "The stage is, as it were, the canvas, on which the composer (choreographer) renders his ideas; the choice of music, scenery and costumes are his colors; the choreographer is the painter."

In addition to considering ballet in terms of its outward form, one might also view it historically, as the traditional concert dance form of the Western world. Conceived in Italy, it came to life in France in the court of Louis XIV in the latter part of the seventeenth century. It developed through the contributions of individual dancers, choreographers, and teachers in the centuries that followed, reaching a peak of creativity and popular appeal during a so-called Golden Age in the 1830s and 1840s. In this period, a complex system of movement and floor patterns was developed, as well as a teaching system that allowed ballet to be taught with relative exactitude in the courts, opera houses, and academies of Europe, and fundamental concepts of form and style which distinguished it from other dance forms.

Following the *Ballet Comique* in 1581, a number of other outstanding court entertainments were presented, none of comparable scope or artistic excellence. One of these was performed in the Salle de Bourbon, in 1615, to celebrate a royal marriage in France. Gaston Vuillier described it:

> Thirty genii [being the chamber and chapel musicians of the King], suspended in the air, heralded the coming of Minerva, the Queen of Spain. This goddess, surrounded by fourteen nymphs, her companions, appeared in a mighty gilded car drawn by two Cupids. A band of Amazons accompanied the car and made a concord of lutes. . . . Forty persons were on the stage at once, thirty high in the sky, and six suspended in mid-air; all of these dancing and singing at the same time.[29]

Over eighty such ballets were performed at the French Court of Henry IV (whose reign was from 1589 to 1610), in addition to numerous balls and masquerades. Such works were known in France as *Masques,* since all the dancers wore masks—a custom that was not abolished in ballet until as late as 1773.

Louis XIII, who followed Henry IV, was another great patron of the dance. Under his reign, many ballets were performed; the king himself played a leading role in *La Délivrance de Renault* in 1617, and he composed dance music for other works. A fairly typical work of this period was the *Mountain Ballet,* an allegorical entertainment in which the scenery consisted of five great mountains—the Windy, the Resounding, the Luminous, the Shadowy, and the Alps. In the midst was a Field of Glory, which the inhabitants of the mountains wished to capture:

> Fame opened the ballet and explained its subject. Disguised as an old woman, she rode an ass and carried a wooden trumpet. Then the mountains opened their sides, and quadrilles of dancers came out, in flesh-colored attire, having bellows in their hands, by the nymph Echo, wearing bells for head-dresses, and on their bodies lesser bells, and carrying drums. Falsehood hobbled forward on a wooden leg, with masks hung over his coat, and a dark lantern in his hand. . . .[30]

Such works usually consisted of a series of dances, ranging in number from about ten to about thirty, by different groups of dancers who dramatized related phases of a common theme. At the end, general dancing was held, in which all the members of the court participated along with those who had performed in the entertainment. With the exception of those few professionals who were attached to the court as dancing masters, musicians, and composers, all were amateurs. John Martin pointed out that during the reign of Louis XIII, a single performance in an evening often was not enough; the king and his fellow dancers trooped from the royal palace to other mansions of the nobility, repeating the performance. Frequently the evening was brought to a close with a final performance on a platform erected in front of the City Hall, with townspeople as spectators. Thus, ballet was not an elite or exclusive dance form; commoners were able to enter the royal palace to see the court ballets, and court ballets were sometimes performed in the provinces. Wealthy private citizens sometimes staged ballets in their own homes, and even Jesuits had ballets performed in their colleges.

Noblewomen did not customarily dance in the formal court ballets. Instead, the roles of girls and women were usually taken by boys and slender youths wearing elaborate wigs and masks. However, Kisselgoff pointed out that women did dance in certain roles. Much of the dance at this time was of a satirical and grotesque nature, with numerous burlesque roles. Louis XIII often played burlesque figures— "fantastic creatures or ordinary folk and tradesmen depicted in exaggerated form."[31]

John Baron commented that the court ballet was significant because it represented the most spectacular and often the most artistically successful entertainment at one of the most powerful courts of Europe for almost a century. Its multimedia elements of mask, costume, music, and dance, taken from the court entertainment tradition in both France and Italy's Renaissance past, influenced French dramatic and musical art, including opera, for centuries to follow. Baron wrote: "The influence of the ballet de cour on the English masque and on international ballet extends the importance of this art form well beyond French borders."[32]

Louis XIV, the Sun King

Ballet progressed a great deal during the reign of Louis XIV, the Sun King, who was probably as enthusiastic and helpful a patron as dance has ever known. The king was an excellent dancer as a young man and delighted in performing. He took daily lessons from his dancing master, Pierre Beauchamps, for over twenty years, and only when he was too heavy to dance gracefully, in middle age, did he stop performing.

Because of his great interest in ballet, Louis employed a number of outstanding musicians and dancing masters, among them Jean-Baptiste Lully, an Italian-born musician and dancer who ultimately became the director of the Royal Academy of Music and Dance. Another key figure was Beauchamps, a brilliant dancer who formulated many of the beginning principles of ballet and became *maître de ballet* at the Royal Academy.

Louis XIV in the Ballet Royal de la Nuit, 1653. Reprinted with permission of the Dance Collection of the Library and Museum of the Performing Arts at Lincoln Center in New York City.

Beginning in 1651, when he was thirteen, Louis XIV danced in public in the *Masque of Cassandra*. He continued until 1670 as a leading performer, dancing in twenty-six grand ballets, not to mention the intermezzi of numerous lyrical tragedies and comedy ballets. Throughout his reign, many ballets were danced at the Tuilleries and at the Louvre, at Versailles, and at Fontainebleau. One performance, the *Ballet du Carrousel,* was held on a large open space in front of the Tuilleries in 1662; in this ballet Louis XIV danced at the head of the Roman armies while his brother led the Persians, the Prince de Condé commanded the Turks, and the Duc de Guise commanded the Americans. In addition to these separate ballets, a number of ballets were danced in the operas of Lully and other musicians of the period.

Dancing until this time had been an amateur art and was usually performed within the ballroom. Typically, the king and his household sat at the end of the hall on a dais. Along the other sides of the room, spectators sat in long galleries on the edge of the floor. There was no stage, and the dancers were close to the audience. The dance movement was fairly simple, based in large degree on the preclassic court dances of the period. The dancers were encumbered by extremely heavy wigs, masks, and costumes; some of these weighed as much as 150 pounds. For amateurs, the noblemen of the court were excellent dancers. Every courtier could dance; de Mille commented that their style was always noble and controlled—the demeanor of a king. Gestures were symmetrical and harmonious, all opening from a central axis, based on the turned-out leg and *port de bras* (fencing position).

The nobleman, in de Mille's words, "danced as he was used to moving in all court procedures . . . [with] movement characterized by arrogant confidence, affected yet elegant, ornate, swift and commanding, highly disciplined; with erect posture, lightness, strength, brilliance, and catlike use of the foot. . . ."[33]

But, in the Sun King's view, this was not enough. Realizing that from a technical standpoint ballet could be developed much more fully, in 1661 Louis XIV asked his ballet master, Beauchamps, to establish rules for ballet, to describe the foot and arm positions and all the known patterns of movement. This Beauchamps did, thus establishing the basis for ballet technique that was to develop through the centuries. In addition, in 1661, the king granted a charter to the Royal Academy of Dance, which was to provide a home for professional instruction in the art of dancing. This art, according to the letters patent founding the Academy:

> . . . has ever been acknowledged to be one of the most suitable and necessary arts for physical development and for affording the primary and most natural preparation for all bodily exercises, and, among others, those concerning the use of weapons, and consequently it is one of the most valuable and useful arts for nobles and others who have the honor to enter our presence not only in time of war in our armies, but even in time of peace in our ballets.[34]

Professionalization of Ballet: Lully and Beauchamps

In 1671, Lully obtained the charter of the Royal Academy of Music and combined it with the Academy of Dance to form a single strong organization. Within two years, the new academy which joined both arts was given the use of the theater in the Palais Royal, built about thirty years before by Cardinal Richelieu and occupied until the death of Molière by that famous playwright and his company. This magnificent theater was built in the recently developed manner of the new Italian theater; it had an elevated stage on which the action took place at one end of the hall beneath a proscenium arch. All the spectators sat in front, rather than on three sides of the dancer, as in the past.

The use of Richelieu's theater had two important effects on the development of ballet as a professional art at this time. First, since the dancer only had to be concerned with how he would look from one direction, it became necessary to think of the audience, *in front,* as a focus. When moving from side to side across the stage, the best way to do this while facing the audience was to turn the hip and knee out, so the feet pointed to the side instead of straight forward. Gradually, the turnout became more and more pronounced and became the basis of the five positions of the foot in classic ballet, which Beauchamps recorded about 1700 and which are essential to all ballet technique today.

A second important effect of the new theater and its stage was that for the first time the performers were markedly separated from their audience. No longer did dance represent a somewhat casual, social activity in which members of the court might intermingle freely with professionals. Performance became the domain of the professional dancers, who were trained in the Royal Academy and who developed an increasingly high level of skill that separated them, more and more, from the amateur performers in the nobility.

In *The Triumph of Love,* women for the first time performed on the professional stage. Lully succeeded in persuading some of the greatest ladies of the court, including the Dauphiness and a number of princesses, to dance professionally— still wearing masks, of course.

The ballet became increasingly professional. Much of the technique was derived from the court dances performed during the preclassic period. However, gradually it moved from *danse terre à terre* (close to the earth) to *danse haute,* with leaps, springing steps, and such actions as the *entrechat.* The design of movement became vertical, rather than horizontal. Based on the five fundamental positions of the feet and the twelve positions of the arm which Beauchamps had formulated, a wide variety of steps was developed and named; these became the basis of ballet technique and the *danse d'école*—or education in ballet.

Lully, who directed the new company that performed in the Palais Royal, felt that the Paris audience which now was permitted to attend performances in the new theater would enjoy plays that combined both dancing and singing. Thus, in the early days of the Royal Academy, its company performed in so-called lyric dramas. In these, while the dance may have slowed the dramatic action, it served to carry the plot along. Gradually, however, in the early and middle eighteenth century, the so-called Opera Ballet came into being. This included both dancing and orchestral music; it dealt with many kinds of subject matter within a single work, and often the content of one act was not related to that of the following act. In essence, the dramatic action almost disappeared, and the stage work became a vehicle for singers and dancers to display their talents. Gradually, as the plot became less important, dancers tended to perform movement that was increasingly decorative and abstract— rather than storytelling in nature.

In a sense, this reflected a change in the times. Vuillier wrote:

> The art of the new era inclined to artificiality . . . painters sought inspiration in love and joy, in sylvan delights, in dainty idylls . . . great financiers began to patronise dawning talent, and to encourage the growth of a luxurious elegance. It was a reign of daintiness and of taste . . . perhaps a little mincing and affected. Pictorial art lacked energy and deep feeling—lacked greatness, in a word; but it was pretty, it was seductive.[35]

It was at this time that a pattern developed with respect to the role of the sexes in dance that has often been repeated since. The leading *organizers* of dance—the teachers, innovators, choreographers, theoreticians—were men such as Lully and Beauchamps. Lully was a musician and a dancer, but far more than this, a clever politician, wise in the ways of the court, who was able to mobilize the efforts of the king in his behalf. Further, he produced many works and composed operas and ballets. Beauchamps, while a brilliant performer who had introduced much technique and was known for his elevations, turns, *pirouettes,* and *tours en l'air,* was also a leading codifier of the dance. His system of dance shorthand, or notation, was the first of its kind, and it was his analysis of the fundamentals of ballet movement that laid the groundwork for the development of this art.

Early Stars of the Ballet

While men monopolized organizational roles, women began to assume the roles of stars—glamorous and brilliant dancers who won the acclaim of growing audiences. They no longer came from the nobility. Instead, they tended to come from poorer families and to have learned their craft in the Academy. They performed on the stage of the Palais Royal before an audience that was still aristocratic for the most part, although with a sprinkling of wealthy bourgeois. Among these talented performers were Camargo, Sallé, and Prévost.

Marie Anne de Camargo, who lived between 1710 and 1770, is reputed to have been the outstanding French dancer of the eighteenth century. Her style was gay and light, her movements lusty and vigorous with strong contrasts. Camargo was considered an extremely expressive dancer; she made ballet a vehicle of interpretation. She had a particular ability for elevation and was able to cross and recross her feet in the air rapidly (*entrechat*), and this gave her the courage to modify the traditional ballet costume. At this point, women wore stiff-hooped skirts that were heavily panniered and reached the floor, as well as elaborate, heavy headdresses, masks, coats, and heeled shoes. In order to give her legs greater freedom and to permit her ingenious improvisations to be seen, Camargo adopted a much shorter skirt than was the custom and an undergarment which was the predecessor of ballet tights. In addition, she wore soft slippers which were the forerunners of ballet slippers.

Another great female star of the eighteenth century was Marie Sallé. Unlike Camargo, her style was not that of a brilliant virtuoso. Instead, she brought to ballet a dramatic realism and a natural expressiveness in movement. She, too, sought to abandon the traditional ballet costume and introduced flowing draperies modeled after Greek sculpture. In fact, it was her intent to abandon the set uniform of ballet entirely and to dress each character in its appropriate national style, or in terms of its place in the plot—a reform that has been suggested again and again by ballet innovators. So popular was Sallé, who lived from 1707 to 1756, that Vuillier wrote of her:

> She was idolised. The huge crowds that pressed about the doors of the theater fought for a sight of her. Enthusiastic spectators, who had paid great sums for seats, had to make their way in with their fists. Upon her benefit appearance in London, at the close of the piece, purses filled with guineas and jewels were showered on the stage at her feet. . . . On this memorable night, Mademoiselle Sallé received more than two hundred thousand francs, an enormous sum for that time.[36]

Another leading performer during this period was Françoise Prévost, who danced during the early 1700s and who was known for her lightness and precision as well as for her dramatic ability. In addition, there were a number of leading male dancers, such as Louis Pécours, who starred in many of Lully's and Beauchamps's ballets, choreographed a number of works for the Palais Royal, and taught in the Academy. However, without question, it was the brilliant female stars who attracted the most fervently enthusiastic audiences.

It was at this time that rulers in Italy, Austria, Russia, England, and Scandinavia established royal opera houses and theaters, to which ballet companies became promptly attached. This meant that the companies were established in permanent residence and guaranteed continuity and protection. All are still functioning as the ornaments of the state and repositories of great national works and technical styles. Among the famous theaters and opera houses which were established at this time were: The King's Theater, in Haymarket, London, 1705; the Royal Danish Ballet, in the National Theater, Copenhagen, 1726; the Royal Opera, in Covent Garden, London, 1732; and numerous others in Naples, 1737; Vienna, 1748; Stuttgart, 1750; Munich, 1752; Moscow, 1776; Milan, 1778; and St. Petersburg, 1783.

In some cases, ballet was founded as a separate company, under royal subsidy and protection; in others, it was a valued component of a major opera company. In each instance, support was assured so that a high level of training and performance could be maintained; ballet had gained status that was to assure its continuity through the centuries.

In a sense, this represented a threat to the continuing creative development of ballet. Just as in any art form which becomes attached to the establishment, its ways became fixed and stereotyped. The choreographers of the early and middle 1700s made no attempt to reform the existing Opera Ballet practices. Every opera had *Passepieds* in its prologue, followed by *Musettes* in the first act, by *Tambourins* in the second, and by *Chaconnes* and *Passepieds* in the acts following (these were dances popular during the period). According to Vuillier, no one dared to violate this formula:

> . . . in every opera, each leading character had to dance his special dance, and the best dancer always concluded. It was by this law, and not by the action of the poem, that the dancing was governed. And what intensified the mischief was that poets, musicians, costumiers, decorators, never consulted one another. Each had his prescriptive routine; each pursued his own old path, indifferent as to whether he arrived at the same goal as his neighbor. To reform all this was a Herculean task. No single individual could diverge from the beaten track until all abandoned it. . . .[37]

Few tried. Famous performers or choreographers of the middle and late eighteenth century such as Gaetano Vestris, distinguished member of a great ballet family; Jean Dauberval, a French dancer and choreographer who composed the famed *La Fille Mal Gardée;* Madeleine Guimard, a leading female dancer toward the end of the century who was extremely popular with royalty and conducted a leading salon; Charles Didelot, a dancer and choreographer in Sweden and at the Paris Opéra; and Salvatore Vigano, a leading Italian dancer and choreographer—all of these were generally content with their lot. It remained for one person, Jean Georges Noverre, to propose a set of sweeping reforms in ballet that ultimately changed this theatrical art in a number of radical ways.

The Reforms of Noverre

Noverre, who lived from 1727 to 1810, made his debut as a dancer at the age of sixteen in the Opéra Comique and was appointed ballet master four years later. Ultimately, he became a leading choreographer, critic, writer, and reformer of ballet. He was the first to fully envision ballet's artistic possibilities and to eliminate the conventionalized movements, gestures, and stage traditions. Noverre's book, *Letters on Dancing and Ballet,* published in 1760, stressed that dancing should not only be physical virtuosity, but also a means for dramatic expression and communication. Ballet had become a collection of miscellaneous short dances which tended to be thrown together to casually written music. These were presented at random in operas, with no relation to the action or plot, chiefly because they permitted the stars to show off their special abilities before the large audiences which only a performance of opera could obtain.

Noverre's philosophy (one which he presented so vigorously that ultimately he was compelled to leave Paris and to seek posts elsewhere, in England, Vienna, and Stuttgart) comprised the following ideas:

1. Balletic movement should not only be technically brilliant, but should move the audience emotionally through its dramatic expressiveness.
2. The plots of ballets should be unified in design, with logical and understandable stories that contribute to a central theme, and with all solos or other dance sequences that do not relate to the plot eliminated.
3. The scenery, the music, and the plot should all be unified; a reform of costumes was necessary so that they would be appropriate to the theme of the dance; and music should be specially written so as to be suitable for the dance as well.
4. Pantomime, which had become increasingly conventionalized and meaningless, needed to be made simpler and more understandable.

These and many other suggestions were summed up in Noverre's writings on the *ballet d'action*—that is, ballet in which the dance actually promotes the dramatic representation instead of interrupting it for meaningless displays of virtuosity. In his own work, Noverre collaborated with musicians closely. He sought appropriate subject matter first, worked out a libretto or poem, developed dance movements to express the content of the poem, and then explained the plot to the composer and asked that music be composed to fit this work specifically—rather than just setting a dance to existing music.

Noverre wrote: "A well-composed ballet is a living picture of the passions, manners, habits, ceremonies, and customs of all nations of the globe . . . if it be devoid of expression, of striking pictures, or strong situations, it becomes a cold and dreary spectacle. . . ."[38]

Gradually, Noverre's ideas gained influence. When he urged dancers to ". . . break hideous masks, to bury ridiculous perukes, to suppress clumsy panniers, to do away with still more inconvenient hip pads. . . ." he lent courage to leading performers who had long wished that costumes might be reformed. Thus, in 1772, when *Castor and Pollux,* an opera by Rameau, was performed, Gaetano Vestris was scheduled to perform as Apollo, wearing a traditional enormous black wig, a mask, and a big gilded copper sun on his chest. Unable to appear, Vestris's role was taken by Maximilien Gardel, who was determined to let the audience know that *he* was playing the role of the Sun God, rather than Vestris. He refused to wear the wig, the mask, and the copper sun. The public approved the change, and from this time on the use of the mask was abandoned by leading dancers.

Noverre never completely succeeded in his wish to make ballet a completely independent theater art rather than a decorative adjunct to opera. Nonetheless, he represented a force for the revitalization of ballet that was not to be duplicated until Michel Fokine left Russia for Paris, over a century later.

The next major influence to touch and modify ballet was the French Revolution. The immediate effect of this violent overthrow of the French monarchy was to challenge the place of ballet in public life as a form of entertainment that was essentially an aristocratic art and was identified with the pastimes of the very royalty that had fled the country in terror, or had been executed on the guillotine. However, dancers, as always, were adaptable. Before long, the Paris Opéra figured in the forefront of a number of fetes of the Republic; there were patriotic spectacles in which the performers were supported by large choirs singing patriotic hymns and cantatas. In one such fete, the Marseillaise was danced as a great public spectacle. In another, during the second year of the Revolution, a festival titled "Festival of the Supreme Being" dealt with revolutionary themes; it was designed by David, conducted by Robespierre, and presented by decree of the National Convention.

While the Revolution caused a temporary cessation to some forms of dance, it did not quench the French passion for this activity as a social art. According to Vuillier, scarcely was the ruthless execution of great numbers of Parisians (known as the Terror) at an end, than twenty-three theaters and 1,800 dancing schools were open every evening in Paris. Mercier, a writer of the period, described the scene:

> . . . dancing is universal; they dance at the Carmelites, between the massacres; they dance at the Jesuits' Seminary; at the Convent of Carmelites du Marais; at the seminary of Saint-Sulpice; at the Filles de Sainte-Marie; they dance in three ruined churches of my section, and upon the stones of all the tombs which have not been destroyed. They dance in every tavern on the Boulevards, in the Champs Elysées, and along the quays. They dance at Ruggieri's, Lucquet's, Mauduit's, Wenzel's, and Montausier's. There are balls for all classes. Dancing, perhaps, is a means of forgetfulness. . . .[39]

Parisians had much to forget. Strangely, one festivity was instituted—a so-called *Victim Ball*—to which were admitted only relatives of those who had died on the scaffold as part of the persecution during the Revolution. Mercier asked:

> Will posterity believe that people, whose relatives had died on the scaffold, inaugurated, not days of solemn general grief when assembled in mourning garb, that they might bear witness to their sorrow at the cruel losses so recently incurred, but days of dancing, drinking, and feasting? For admission to one of these banquets and dances, it is necessary to show a certificate of the loss of a father, a mother, a husband, a wife, a brother or a sister under the knife of the guillotine.[40]

When the Revolution came to an end, ballet, which had been suspended except for the sort of patriotic spectacles mentioned earlier, resumed. Now, however, under the Republic, its themes were quite different. There were ballets dealing with the *sans-culottes* of the Revolution. Other works commemorated the American Revolution, and some ballets were choreographed which criticized religion and the Catholic Church—reflecting the viewpoint of the new government. All this represented not only an accommodation to the existing powers, but also the first breaths of a new idea—political and social democracy. It was linked to a concern with contemporaneous thought, and with the first stirrings of another sort of revolution—the Romantic Revolution. With poetry, music, painting, and literature, the ballet was to be a vital part of this new artistic movement. And, as it reached its height during the nineteenth century, ballet entered what has been called its Golden Age.

Notes

1 Thoinot Arbeau, *Orchesographie: A Treatise in the Form of a Dialogue* (1588), (New York: Dance Horizons, Inc., 1925), p. 103.

2 Margaret H'Doubler, *Dance: A Creative Art Experience* (New York: F. S. Crofts and Co., 1940), p. 13.

3 Judith Lynne Hanna, *The Performer-Audience Connection: Emotion to Metaphor in Dance and Society* (Austin, Tex.: University of Texas Press, 1983), p. 30.

4 E. Louis Backman, *Religious Dances* (London: George Allen and Unwin Ltd., 1952) p. 11.

5 Ida F. Chadwick, "Dance: An Agent of 'Ekstasis'," in *Focus on Dance X,* eds. Dennis Fallon and Mary Jane Wolbers (Reston, Va.: National Dance Association, 1982), p. 6.

6 Backman, *Religious Dances,* p. 24.

7 Ibid., p. 25.

8 Ibid., p. 26.

9 Chadwick, "Dance," p. 6.

10 Backman, *Religious Dances,* p. 31.

11 Curt Sachs, *World History of the Dance* (New York: W. W. Norton and Co., 1937), pp. 248–49.

12 Backman, *Religious Dances,* p. 85.

13 Douglas Kennedy, *England's Dances* (London: G. Bell and Sons, Ltd., 1950), p. 36.

14 Henri Stegmaier, *The Dance of Death in Folk Song* (Chicago: University of Chicago Libraries, 1939), p. 6.

15 John Martin, *John Martin's Book of the Dance* (New York: Tudor Publishing Co., 1963), p. 22.

16 Paul Nettl, *The Story of Dance Music* (New York: Philosophical Library, 1947), p. 44.

17 Backman, *Religious Dances,* p. 153.

18 Martin, *Book of the Dance,* p. 22.

19 Sachs, *World History,* pp. 253–54.

20 Backman, *Religious Dances,* p. 191.

21 Ethel L. Urlin, *Dancing, Ancient and Modern* (New York: D. Appleton and Co., 1914), p. 41.

22 Nettl, *Story of Dance Music,* p. 51.

23 Ibid., p. 56.

24 Ibid., p. 71.

25 Louis Horst, *Pre-Classic Dance Forms* (New York: Kamin Dance Publishers, 1953), pp. 1–2.

26 Thoinot Arbeau, *Orchesographie,* quoted in Horst, *Pre-Classic Dance,* p. 7.

27 Horst, *Pre-Classic Dance,* p. 35.

28 John Baron, "History of the Ballet de Cour and the Court of Louis XIII," *Dance Perspectives,* 16, no. 66 (Summer 1975), 4.

29 Pere Menestrier, quoted in Gaston Vuillier, *A History of Dance* (New York: D. Appleton and Co., 1897), p. 90.

30 Vuillier, *History of Dance,* p. 87.

31 Anna Kisselgoff, "Early Court Ballet in France Was Varied and Lively," *New York Times,* November 23, 1986, p. H-9.

32 Baron, "History of the Ballet," p. 4.

33 Agnes de Mille, *The Book of the Dance* (New York: Golden Press, 1963), p. 81.

34 Ibid., p. 90.

35 Vuillier, *History of Dance,* pp. 138–39.

36 Ibid., p. 142.

37 Ibid., p. 153.

38 Jean Georges Noverre, *Letters on Dancing and Ballet,* trans. Cyril Beaumont (published originally in 1760, republished by Dance Horizons, Inc., New York, 1966), p. 16.

39 Henry Fourment, *Paris During the Revolution,* quoted in Vuillier, *History of Dance,* p. 197.

40 Vuillier, *History of Dance,* p. 196.

CHAPTER 5

The Golden Age
of Ballet

In the eighteenth century, the lines of battle were drawn between virtuosity and expression: dance as display, epitomized in the moribund conventions of opera-ballet, and dance as a mirror held up to reality, representing the full range of human experience—Noverre's *ballet d'action*.

In the early decades of the nineteenth century . . . romanticism asserted an aesthetic warmed by passion and a yearning to transcend earthly bounds. The romantic era marked the apogee of the Opera, as ballet masters vied for the privilege of creating for its stage. Their numerous works elaborated the iconography of romanticism—moonlit glades, spectral maidens, chaste manners—wedding this to a vision of etherealized femininity that to this day shapes the popular perception of ballet.[1]

IN THE DECADES FOLLOWING THE FRENCH REVOLUTION, ballet continued to change radically in terms of its aesthetic content and format, technical style, and vocabulary. Instrumental in this development were three leading figures: Salvatore Vigano, Carlo Blasis, and Théophile Gautier.

Vigano, who lived from 1769 to 1821, had been a disciple of Noverre and of the famed ballet master Dauberval. He attempted to carry out Noverre's theories of unity of form and dramatic expression, and he contributed much to the development of pantomime to replace the conventionalized gestures that were widely used to develop plot. He attempted to develop what he called the *choreodrame;* this made use of groups of dancers who were treated in a plastic, almost sculptural way. He composed many of the leading ballets of his era as ballet master at La Scala and at other leading opera houses in Vienna, Venice, and other European cities.

Blasis (1787–1878) was, without question, one of the towering figures of ballet history. He was an Italian dancer, choreographer, and teacher who had been strongly influenced by both Noverre and Vigano. He had danced and composed in both France and England, and he returned to La Scala in Milan as the outstanding ballet master of his time. He developed a comprehensive system for practicing and teaching the art of ballet; his method of education is still widely influential today. He developed major theories involving the laws of equilibrium and balance and geometric schemes governing the body's movement in ballet exercises. In 1830, he published his famous *Code of Terpsichore,* which contained a fundamental system of ballet instruction, a model that every ballet school since has used. In the Imperial Academy of Dancing and Pantomime in Milan, of which Blasis became director in 1837, the following practices were instituted: Pupils were not admitted before the age of eight, or after the age of twelve (fourteen in the case of boys). They had to be medically sound, and of "good stock." Their training was fully mapped out: three hours of practice a day and one hour of mime. They were attached to the school for eight years, and after that their careers as performers were assured by an ascending scale of salaries.

Without question, Blasis was the key figure in the development of the *danse d'école* during the early nineteenth century. It remained for Théophile Gautier to provide the inspiration that helped to plunge ballet into the thick of the Romantic movement in Europe.

Gautier was a poet, journalist, and dramatic critic of the Romantic era in France, with a great passion for the ballet. He took an active part in the development of this art during its so-called Golden Age. As an extremely influential critic, Gautier helped to shape public taste and enthusiasm and influenced the entire course of ballet in the Romantic age.

Romanticism in Ballet

What was Romanticism? Essentially, it was a revolutionary movement in art which overthrew the rigid forms that had been established by the academic schools that had dominated artistic activity in the eighteenth century. The Romantic poets, artists, and composers were concerned with the occult and the supernatural; they depicted humankind's pursuit of the unattainable, exemplified in the hopeless love of a mortal for an unworldly being.

During the twenty years that followed the end of the Napoleonic era in 1815, Romanticism conquered all the arts in France and spread throughout Europe. Earlier conventions were disregarded, and new works were produced with meaning and emotional content that appealed to a fresh new audience. In a sense, Romanticism represented an attempt to escape the realities of life as it was. People had suffered badly during the wars of the previous decade; and the developing Industrial Revolution, with its mines and factories, was now bringing new suffering and wretchedness to millions of underprivileged people throughout Europe. Thus, the Romantic movement, which offered color, fantasy, fairy tales, and folk legends—

romantic love and beautiful dreams—offered a protest against the sordid quality of real life.

In ballet, this contrast between the bitter reality of life and the yearning for fantastic possibilities meant that a new kind of subject matter was to be used. Supernatural creatures fell in love with mortal men; dead maidens rose from the grave to haunt unfaithful lovers; there were moral victories of aerial and spiritual creatures over earthy and sensual beings.[2] Perhaps most typical of all ballets of this era was *La Sylphide,* choreographed by Philippe Taglioni for his daughter, Marie, one of the great ballerinas of this era. *Sylphide* depicted a woodland creature of supernatural origin who fell in love with a Scotsman; the ballet is the tale of their tragic romance. For this work, a new costume was devised for the ballerina—full but filmy white skirts that reached halfway down to the ankles. Ballets of this type, which filled the stage with white-clad dancers, were called *ballets blancs,* or white ballets, because of the shimmering effect they created.

As part of the yearning for the unattainable, dance itself became increasingly elevated. More and more, the ballerina defied gravity by soaring through the air and dancing *sur les pointes* (on the tips of her toes). In some ballets, female dancers actually flew above the stage by being suspended from wires so that they could glide along overhead. Such devices were useful not only because of the ethereal roles they made possible, but as a symbol of the spiritual and exalted role which the Romantic ballet gave to women. Indeed, the ballerina was raised to a new height of glamour and popular favor, while the male dancer's role was reduced to being little more than a support for her brilliant solos. Even as partners, their roles were diminished and, with few exceptions, all solos were given to the ballerina. The male dancer became little more than a background for her.[3]

Ballet Becomes a Female Art

The predominant tone of the ballet was female, and the critics themselves ridiculed men who performed as dancers. One writer, Jules Janin, summed up the view of his fellows:

> You know perhaps that we are hardly a supporter of what are called the grand danseurs. The grand danseur appears to us so sad and so heavy! . . . He responds to nothing, he represents nothing, he is nothing. Speak to us of a pretty dancing girl who displays the grace of her features and the elegance of her figure. . . . Thank God, I understand that perfectly. . . . But a man, a frightful man, as ugly as you and I, a wretched fellow who leaps about without knowing why, a creature specially made to carry a musket and a sword and to wear a uniform. That this fellow should dance as a woman does—impossible![4]

Even more cruel in his attacks was Gautier, who despised the male dancer almost as much as he worshipped the ballerina. According to Gautier, a ballet without men is the height of good taste, "for nothing is more abominable than a man who displays his red neck, his great muscular arms, his legs with calves like church beadles', his whole heavily masculine frame, shaken with leaps and pirouettes. . . ." The criticism was often inconsistent. On the one hand, Gautier criticized men for their masculine clumsiness; however, when they were too graceful, he attacked them also: "The dancers at the Opéra are of a nature to encourage the opinion which will only allow women in ballet [for they affect] that false grace, those ambiguous and revolting mincing manners which have sickened the public of male dancing. . . ." And finally, Gautier wrote: "For us a male dancer is something monstrous and indecent which we cannot conceive. . . . Strength is the only grace permissible to men."[5]

By the middle of the 1840s, so strong was the feeling against male dancers that they were eliminated from the corps de ballet whenever a justification could be found. The device of the *danseuse en travesti* (female dancers in male costumes) was then discovered, and women began to play the roles of sailor boys, hussars, and toreadors ". . . even as they displaced real men as romantic leads. Until well into the twentieth century, the female dancer who donned the mufti of a cavalier was a commonplace of European ballet."[6]

Garafola commented that this shifting of sex roles reflected the change of ballet from a courtly, aristocratic art to a form of popular entertainment geared to the marketplace and to the tastes of a new bourgeois public. In Russia and in Copenhagen, leading male dancers continued to perform, but in France and England they tended to be limited to character roles which demanded skills as actors and mimes and could be performed by those long past their prime. However, the romantic male leads were often performed by women, and it was inevitable that the style of masculine dancing would then become feminized in the Romantic ballet.

Although talented male dancers continued to appear in Paris, the standard of their work gradually declined, and fewer and fewer young boys entered the Paris Opéra's School of Dance. Dance was a career that had little appeal for them.

Ballerinas of the Golden Age

The great stars of this period were five ballerinas who flourished during the Golden Age of ballet, the 1830s and 1840s, when ballet was at its creative heights in terms of artistic inspiration and an expanding body of technique and brilliant choreography.

Marie Taglioni (1804–1884) was considered by many the greatest dancer of the century. She danced in Vienna, Italy, Germany, and France and later in her life became a star of the St. Petersburg Imperial Theater. Her outstanding work was *La Sylphide,* which was a sensation throughout Europe and was considered to be the first great Romantic ballet. Taglioni was the first ballerina to develop the art of *pointe* dancing; she was extremely light, almost floating, and had great elevation. She represented the mystical side of Romanticism; her technique was superb—fragile and exquisite.

Taglioni's greatest rival was Fanny Elssler, who lived between 1810 and 1884. She was a Viennese dancer who symbolized the earthy side of Romanticism and was viewed as a pagan dancer; the stage image she conveyed was far more passionate than spiritual. Her movement was closer to the earth than Taglioni's but had great style and precision. She perfected character dances of other lands—such as Hungary,

Pas de Quatre, danced in 1845 in London by Marie Taglioni, Carlotta Grisi, Fanny Cerrito, and Lucile Grahn. Color lithograph by John Brandard, in Cia Fornaroli Collection.

Poland, and Spain. When she toured America in 1840, she was a tremendous sensation.

Fanny Cerrito (1821–1899) was a famous Italian ballerina and choreographer of the Romantic period who danced in Naples, Vienna, London, and Paris. She was a spirited and beautiful dancer with great technical skill whose popularity was close to that of Taglioni and Elssler. Lucile Grahn (1821–1907) was a famous Danish ballerina who studied first in Copenhagen and then performed in Paris at the Opéra in *La Sylphide,* competing with Taglioni. She was considered the greatest classic technician of her time and was noted for a quality of dreamy grace and abandon. Her teacher and choreographer was the renowned August Bournonville; his versions of *Giselle* and *La Sylphide* were among her great roles. Carlotta Grisi (1821–1899) was an eminent Italian ballerina of the Romantic period who created the role of *Giselle* and was a protégé of Théophile Gautier.

Gradually, the creative inspiration that had enabled ballet to reach its height in the 1830s and 1840s declined. Innovations were perpetuated as custom, and the great variety of new technical achievements that had been developed served chiefly as a means of displaying acrobatic brilliance. There were no great male dancers; and with the decline of the great ballerinas of the period, interest in ballet itself declined in Italy, France, and England.

The typical ballet of the middle and later nineteenth century was a romance of ancient days or a fairy tale. It usually lasted for the entire evening, with three or four acts and intermissions that often lasted as long as forty-five minutes each. The plot was told through sign language of the hands, which often was not intelligible to the audience; dance numbers interrupted the ballet from time to time, with little relation to the drama itself. Uninspired music was turned out in a perfunctory fashion by staff composers and artists; the whole point of the performance was to demonstrate the technical skill and beauty of the ballerina.[7]

Ballroom dancing in mid-19th-century Paris. Lithograph of the Bal Mabille by A. Provost, about 1850. Reprinted with permission of the Dance Collection of the Library and Museum of the Performing Arts at Lincoln Center in New York City.

Small wonder that public tastes declined and that audiences became apathetic. Haskell commented that "two hundred years after the founding of the Academy, ballet in the country of its birth was artistically bankrupt . . . merely a prelude to flirtation. . . ."[8] In England, matters grew even worse. Ballet became a popular routine on music hall programs, with poor music, decor, and choreography. In Paris, it hung on as part of operatic performance, although, according to Shawn:

> . . . the "Golden Age" of the ballet was a period when the dancers were the supreme stars of the stage, and a bored public walked out into the foyer while the singing of the opera was proceeding. . . . At the beginning of this present century, the ballet was at a very low ebb indeed. Sterile, artificial, distinguished neither by greatness of execution nor of idea, written down to by the opera composers, it was now during the ballet that the audience preferred to walk about in the foyer, rather than watch the mechanical, lifeless performances. . . .[9]

Bournonville and the Danish Ballet

Despite the decline of ballet in Paris, it flourished in other settings. One of these was Denmark, where August Bournonville was a leading dancer and choreographer for over fifty years. Bournonville had studied at Copenhagen's Royal Ballet School as a boy and then had gone to Paris to work under Auguste Vestris. Returning to Denmark, he was given the title of Royal Dancer and filled leading solo roles. He studied and danced again at the Paris Opéra for six years, and after a tour of European capitals he returned to Copenhagen as a choreographer with the Royal Theater and as dancing master to the Court. From 1829 to 1877, he choreographed over forty outstanding ballets; during this period, he was recognized by knighthood and became a member of the Danish nobility. Many leading dancers developed under his tutelage, and the Royal Danish Ballet developed a style and founded a tradition that continues to this day.

Ballet in Czarist Russia

However, only in Russia did ballet maintain its full popularity and prestige during the second half of the nineteenth century. It remained firmly entrenched as a cherished ornament of the aristocratic regime, with a widespread audience that remained unquestioningly loyal to it.

Ballet in Russia had a long and respected tradition. As early as the time of Louis XIV of France, traveling Muscovites had visited his court to observe the court ballets. At the time of Peter the Great (1672–1725), it became government policy to westernize Russia, which had been sealed off from the rest of Europe for centuries. Peter the Great resolved to break down social customs which had kept his nation behind the times. Therefore, he decreed that the boyars (wealthy landowners) must shave their beards and give up their "dignified and cumbersome robes," and that women might join men in social dances and assemblies which had heretofore been unknown. As in France and Italy, an interest in ballet as a stage art soon followed this introduction of social dance in the court. Almost from the beginning, however, it became a professional art, with the importation of distinguished foreign teachers and choreographers and the training of skilled, paid performers. Arnold Haskell wrote:

> The Empress Anne (1693–1740) founded the Academy, which survives today under a different regime, importing a Frenchman, Lande, to direct it, and thinking it of sufficient importance to include dancing in the curriculum of the cadets. . . . The most intense development took place with Catherine the Great (1762–1796) who imported a Frenchman, Le Picq, and the great Italian, Angiolini, to her court . . . enthusiasm and knowledge [of ballet] spread. . . .[10]

In Russia, where there were vast estates, courtiers had to provide their own amusements and cultural activities. Thus, when Catherine the Great favored ballet, the nobility followed suit, forming ballet troupes of their own and spreading a great interest in ballet throughout the land. Gradually, these separate companies became merged in the two great ballet organizations in St. Petersburg and Moscow. The dancers who joined these companies were given their freedom long before the serfs at large. Haskell commented that ballet became the most cherished possession of the Russian Czars, with huge sums expended to support its performance and to import foreign dancers, choreographers, and teachers.

Charles Louis Didelot (1767–1837), an outstanding French dancer, choreographer, and teacher, was one of the greatest imported to Russia. Though born in Stockholm, he had an extensive career at the Paris Opéra and in London, where he choreographed a number of major works. He was brought to St. Petersburg by Czar Paul as ballet master of the Imperial Theater and continued at this post into the regime of Alexander I. From 1801 to 1811, and then again after 1816, he remained in St. Petersburg where he choreographed over fifty ballets.

Other foreign performers who influenced the Russian ballet during the nineteenth century included Marie Taglioni, Jules Perrot, Christian Johannsen, Charles Saint-Léon, Enrico Cecchetti, and Marius Petipa.

Following the debut of Fanny Elssler at the Paris Opéra, Taglioni left France to accept a profitable three-year contract at the St. Petersburg Imperial Theater, from 1837 to 1839. While there, she performed in many of the ballets then being done in Western Europe and so introduced them to Russian audiences.

Jules Perrot (1810–1892), a leading French dancer and choreographer who had had an outstanding career dancing with the great Romantic ballerinas at the Paris Opéra, went to St. Petersburg in 1848. He was a leading dancer and choreographer there until 1859, producing nearly twenty ballets in that time—many of these based on realistic themes, with strong dramatic plots.

Christian Johannsen (1817–1903), a Swedish dancer and teacher who had studied under Bournonville in Copenhagen, went to Russia to perform in the St. Petersburg ballet in 1841. He became the leading male dancer there, remaining a *premier danseur* until 1869, when he devoted himself exclusively to teaching at the ballet school. In the decades that followed, he taught all of the great Russian dancers who developed in this period.

Charles Saint-Léon, who lived from about 1815 to 1870, was another leading French choreographer, dancer, and musician who became ballet master of the Imperial Ballet in St. Petersburg in 1859. While there, he produced a number of original works, including the first ballet based on Russian themes.

Enrico Cecchetti, an Italian dancer and ballet master who lived from 1850 to 1928, starred at La Scala in Milan, in London, and was with the first major Italian ballet company to tour the United States. He came to Russia in 1887, where he made his debut at the Maryinsky Theater in St. Petersburg and shortly became the second ballet master at the Imperial Theater and instructor at the Imperial school. He taught many of the great stars of the Russian ballet and became the private instructor of Anna Pavlova. As official instructor for the Diaghileff company, he taught such outstanding performers of the twentieth century as Leonid Massine, Adolph Bolm, Ninette de Valois, Alexandra Danilova, Anton Dolin, Serge Lifar, and others.

Through the contributions of all these foreigners, the lavishly supported and prestigious Russian ballet gradually gained world eminence. It blended the distinctive styles of the French and Russian dancers into a system of balanced training and performance. In a history of the Russian ballet, one of its leading dancers, Nicholas Legat, wrote:

> The secret of the development of Russian dancing lay in the fact that we learned from everybody and adapted what we learnt to ourselves. We copied, borrowed from, and emulated every source that gave us inspiration, and then, working on our acquired knowledge and lending it the stamp of the Russian national genius, we moulded it into the eclectic art of the Russian ballet. . . .[11]

Without question, the most influential of all the foreign artists who came to Russia was Marius Petipa.

Marius Petipa

Petipa (1822–1910) was best known as a choreographer of the Imperial Ballet in St. Petersburg and has often been referred to as the "father of the classic ballet." He studied in France and made his debut at the Paris Opéra opposite Fanny Elssler in 1841. He was regarded as an excellent dancer, with particular strength in the art of partnering. However, it is chiefly for his choreography and direction of the St. Petersburg ballet that he is known. Joining the Imperial Ballet in 1847, he remained active for over fifty years, during which time he became the dominant force in Russian ballet. He choreographed over sixty full-length ballets (which usually had four or five acts and lasted for the entire evening) and many shorter ballets and divertissements. Among his best known works were *Don Quixote, La Bayadère, The Sleeping Beauty,* and *Bluebeard.* He also restaged many great ballets which had originally been performed elsewhere.

In addition to his gift for choreography, Petipa was noted for his detailed research and planning for each ballet he produced. He worked intensively with the composers and set designers who were attached to the Imperial Theater, but he placed choreography high above all the other arts which contributed to the ballet.

Thus, even in working with a composer of Tchaikovsky's stature, Petipa rigidly dictated the kind of music he wanted—the style, mood, length, beat, tempo, and dynamics. He developed a format for his full-length ballets which he applied consistently through the years: These patterns always involved three repeats of the same technical action and a fourth variant of it to complete the sequence. In the second half of the nineteenth century, his dominance was unquestioned in Russia, and indeed throughout Europe, for many of the leading dancers throughout the Continent came to study and dance with him.

During this period, a class of spectators emerged who came to be known as *balletomanes*. These were the enthusiastic and knowledgeable audiences that packed the Bolshoi and Maryinsky Imperial Theaters in Moscow and St. Petersburg and other ballet houses throughout Russia. Ballet was cherished by the powerful and wealthy, as well as by intellectuals, students, young officers, and all classes that could afford to attend. With the exception of those seats reserved for the royal family and high public officials, all other seats in the orchestra and boxes and loges, as well as some in the balcony, were sold by subscription. These were highly valued and would often remain in the same family for generations; occasionally one would be sold at a very high price. Thus, the dominant audience for the ballet constituted an exclusive circle that knew the mechanics and tradition of ballet thoroughly and was essentially highly conservative and refused to accept change.

Through the 1880s and 1890s, ballet in Russia became increasingly stodgy and stereotyped—following the same format that had been in effect for the previous three decades. Pantomimic sign language, which often was incomprehensible to the dancers as well as to the audience, was still used. The *corps de ballet* was usually used for purely decorative interludes that had no relation to the theme of the ballet itself. Costumes, music, and decor were all composed in a perfunctory way that contributed to the sterility of the performance and had little vitality or originality.

Finally, reform was not welcomed or even possible under Petipa. Thus, when two great Russians of the early twentieth century, Diaghileff and Fokine, broke through the traditions of the past, it was not in St. Petersburg or Moscow, but in Paris.

Notes

1 Lynn Garafola, "Cradle of Classicism," *Dance Magazine,* July 1986, p. 52.

2 John Martin, *John Martin's Book of the Dance* (New York: Tudor Publishing Co., 1963), p. 34.

3 Lincoln Kirstein, *Dance: A Short History of Classic Theatrical Dancing* (New York: G. P. Putnam's Sons, 1935), p. 253.

4 Jules Janin, quoted in Ivor Guest, *The Romantic Ballet in Paris* (Middletown, Conn.: Wesleyan University Press, 1966), p. 2.

5 Théophile Gautier, quoted in Deidre Priddin, *The Art of the Dance in French Literature* (London: A. and C. Black, Ltd., 1952), p. 41.

6 Lynn Garafola, "The Travesty Dance in Nineteenth Century Ballet," *Dance Research Journal,* vol. 17, no. 2/vol. 18, no. 1 (1985–1986), p. 35.

7 Martin, *Book of the Dance,* pp. 38–39.

8 Arnold Haskell, *Ballet* (Middlesex, England: Penguin Books, 1951), p. 30.

9 Ted Shawn, *Dance We Must* (London: Dennis Dobson, Ltd., 1946), pp. 21–22.

10 Haskell, *Ballet,* p. 32.

11 Nicholas Legat, quoted in Anatole Chujoy, *The Dance Encyclopedia* (New York: A. S. Barnes and Co., 1949), p. 411.

CHAPTER 6

Dance in America: Colonial Period and Nineteenth Century

It is surely of note that a male dancer like George Washington Smith had a long and successful career. He taught ballet and ballroom dancing in Philadelphia after 1881, and when he died in 1899 he was about eighty years old. He . . . became the first of the American choreographers and its very first *premier danseur noble*. As such, Smith danced in the best of company . . . the Ronzani company . . . the Cecchetti family . . . ballerinas Giovanna Ciocca and Giuseppina Morlacchi; a famous Spaniard Pepita Soto; and the infamous Lola Montez. . . .

An astute seer . . . might have beheld the strong nucleus of an American ballet. The evidences of native talent were there. Maywood alone testified to a prodigious strength and quickness, the very same qualities on which Balanchine would base his development of the American classical technician in the next century.[1]

MEANWHILE, WHAT WAS THE DEVELOPMENT OF DANCE on the North American continent? Certainly, what happened in the American colonies prior to the American Revolution could not be considered out of context with what one historian called the Atlantic Civilization. Those who settled in New England, in the Mid-Atlantic colonies, and in the coastal region of the South were all Europeans—and they brought with them many of the attitudes and customs of their homelands. There was a steady flow of traffic back and forth, of colonists, journalists, performers, and publications. Clearly, a stone cast at the French court, or in London, spread ripples abroad.

Yet there were certain distinct features in the New World that made life here very different—and particularly so for those concerned with the dance as art or recreation. One factor was the distance and danger of the ocean journey; this tended to reduce communication, and it prevented vogues in the arts from being seized on as rapidly in the American colonies as they were throughout Europe. Another factor was the difficulty of living on the North American continent—the first need of all was to survive. One had to plant crops, to cut down forests and clear fields, to build shelters, and to protect oneself against the winter, against hunger, disease, and the sometimes hostile Indians who surrounded the colonies. In such a situation, it was difficult to justify amusements and public entertainment. This was a democratic society; there was no royalty that would view dance, theater, or other arts as a means of amusing itself or enhancing its own prestige and that would therefore subsidize and protect performing companies.

Then there was the matter of religious attitude.

Puritan Disapproval of Dance

During the seventeenth century, there was a widespread condemnation of idleness and casual amusement. Foster Dulles pointed out that in Puritan New England, where the stern rule of Calvinism prohibited any sort of play, the tradition was that life should be wholly devoted to work. There was no place for an "idle drone" in such a society.[2]

The Puritans had come to the New World in order to set up a society based on a Calvinistic interpretation of the Bible. They believed that they were a chosen people; the early government of Massachusetts, for example, was a theocracy, run by Puritan ministers, who thought that the Bible was the disclosed word of God and that its meaning and intention on every subject had been made plain and explicit to them. Not all colonists in New England were Puritans, of course, but they were the dominant group, and those who resisted them were often punished or banished. Typically, Massachusetts and Connecticut banned dice, cards, quoits, bowls, ninepins, "or any other unlawful game in house, yard, garden or backside. . . ." The theater was completely prohibited in a number of colonies; Connecticut adjudged as common rogues and served fifteen lashes on the bare back of anyone foolish enough to "set up and practice common plays, interludes, or other crafty science."

In particular, the early Puritans forbade mixed dancing (between men and women), dancing in taverns, Maypole dancing (which they saw as an expression of paganism), or dancing accompanied by feasting and drinking.

A group of Puritan ministers in Boston issued a tract against dancing in 1684, titled *An Arrow Against Profane and Promiscuous Dancing, drawn out of the quiver of the Scriptures*. Yet, even as they condemned "mixt or promiscuous dancing," they indicated that dance could be a means of teaching "due poyse and Composure of Body," and that if a parent wished to have his children learn it, he should send them "to a grave person who will teach them decency of behaviour, and each sex by themselves."[3]

The truth is that, despite the reputation of the Puritans for being opposed to any form of dance, they had themselves come out of an English tradition which valued poetry and literature and in which music and dance formed part of the education of every cultivated person. While in England, Joy van Cleef pointed out, many of the Puritans, like other members of their social class, had studied dance as a basic skill of the society and a widely accepted pastime. However, it was generally regarded as a private matter to be enjoyed in the home and family circle rather than in public spectacles and performances.

The same distinctions that had been made by the Church founders during the Dark and Middle Ages in Europe were again made in eighteenth-century America. The Reverend John Cotton, who was to come to New England in 1633 and become the leading minister of Boston and New England, said while still in England in 1625:

> Dancing (yea though mixt) I would not simply condem. For I see two sorts of mixt dancings in use with God's people in the Old Testament, the one religious, Exod. XV, 20, 21, the other civil, tending to the praise of conquerers, as the former of God, I Sam. XVII, 6, 7. Only lascivious dancing, and amorous gestures and wanton dalliances, especially after feasts, I would bear witness against, as a great *flabella libidinis.*[4]

Others were less liberal than Cotton, and the court records during the seventeenth century, particularly in New England, frequently mention severe punishment for mixed dancing, dancing in taverns, and similar offenses. Yet, in spite of condemnation and punishment, settlers in communities large and small throughout the colonies of the North continued to dance. Beginning in the 1670s, dancing masters began to appear in the New England towns, and people of quality began to give balls. Polite society, particularly members of the less strict Anglican faith, accepted dance wholeheartedly as a form of social custom. Indeed, many ministers sanctioned dancing schools provided that they were conducted by "grave persons" and did not teach "mixt" dancing. The dances that were most frequently taught were drawn from the newly published English work, John Playford's *Dancing-Master.* While these country dances had both men and women dancing together, they were in sets, or formations, and did not involve couple dancing as such. Since they taught good manners and were desired by the more influential people in the community, they were accepted by ministers.

Van Cleef described these dances, explaining why they were approved by the Puritans while other forms were frowned on:

> . . . though popular at court, the country dances were not dances of self-presentation like those ordinarily performed by one couple at a time while the rest of the company watched, dancers taking the floor in the order of their rank and position. They were not "show-off" dances. Nor were they extravagant or spectacular like the galliard, nor bold and indecorous like the volta, which required the man to lift . . . his partner into the air while executing rapid turns. . . . The country dance was a democratic affair in which a number of people danced together. Its interest lay in the figures, or patterns—sometimes extremely intricate [requiring] a team effort on the part of the whole group, or set, in order to succeed.[5]

Dance in the Southern Colonies

Further to the South, members of the ruling class in Virginia had closer ties with England and were of a higher social class in general than the Puritans who had settled New England. They had both wealth and leisure because of the nature of the land they settled and the large plantations which were worked by indentured servants and slaves. Thus, they were more inclined toward aristocratic forms of amusement and were able to indulge their inclinations. While the laws of the colony, applied by Governor Argall in 1618, "strictly banned any Sabbath-day dancing, fiddling, card-playing, hunting or fishing," these laws gradually fell into abeyance. In any case, dancing was permitted on other occasions and even justified as an important aspect of education.

> Dance served an even more important role than that of social amusement. It was believed to be one of the accomplishments proper for a gentleman, and not having a knowledge of dance showed a lack of the proper education. Writers on aristocratic education expected a gentleman to dance well, but not to become so proficient that he rival the dancing master.[6]

For gentlemen, both dancing and fencing were seen as "ornaments to grace and accomplishment," and for young ladies, it was thought that "to lead a dance gracefully" was a commendable quality. Thus, by the end of the 1600s, Virginia was well supplied with dancing masters as part of the life of its plantation owners, which was closely modeled after that of country squires in the mother country.

During the eighteenth century, an increasing number of dancing teachers were found in the colonies of both the North and South. Marks cited many examples of such masters advertising to the public: In 1712, George Brownell offered the young ladies of Boston "Writing, cyphering, dancing, treble violin, flute, spinet, etc." Samuel Perpoint advertised in the *Pennsylvania Mercury* in 1728 and later in 1729 that he gave instruction in dancing and small sword. In Williamsburg, Virginia, Mrs. Neil stated that she was opening a boarding school of young ladies on the English plan, and that "The best Masters will attend to teaching Dancing and writing." Marks wrote: "Dancing masters, like preachers, doctors, lawyers, peddlers and many other trades and professions during the eighteenth and early nineteenth centuries, traveled from town to town, often advertising ahead that they planned to open a dancing school 'if there be sufficient inducement'."[7]

Dance was seen as contributing to the ends of education. A book on education in Philadelphia in 1792 made clear that ornamental accomplishments were not an end in themselves: ". . . though the well-bred woman should learn to dance, sing, recite, and draw; the end of a good education is not that they may become singers, dancers, players, or painters; its real object is, to make them good daughters, good wives, good mistresses, good members of society and good christians."[8]

Toward the end of the century, an increasing number of balls and assemblies were held, particularly in the larger cities. It is probable that the colonists performed both the country dances, jigs, and cotillions which became popular during this period, and also such dances as the Minuet, Courante, Galliard, Rigadoon, and Gavotte. All appeared in Rameau's text, *The Dancing Master,* which was found in libraries throughout the colonies.

Both George Washington and Thomas Jefferson were known as zealous and enthusiastic dancers who frequently attended concerts and the theater. Washington Irving, in his *Life of George Washington,* told how the "young ladies of Maryland rode to the assembly at Annapolis in scarlet riding-habits thrown over their satin ball dresses, kerchiefs drawn about the great masses of their puffed and pomaded hair, and after dancing through the night rode home again in the shadowy dawn." The young John Quincy Adams, in Newburyport, described going to a dancing hall with his friends during the 1780s and dancing continually from seven at night to three or four in the morning.

Clearly, dance as recreation had taken hold in the colonies by the time of the American Revolution. But meanwhile, what of dance as theater? Here there was less to report.

Beginning Theatrical Dance

From the beginning, stage performers—whether they were actors, singers, dancers, or acrobats—were viewed with suspicion in the colonies, especially in the North. Gradually, however, as the early bans against theater were relaxed and a leisure class began to develop, professional performances began to be offered. At first, these were given by amateur or semiprofessional groups, or dancing masters themselves, who seized on the opportunity to earn additional income as well as to enhance their reputation by dancing before an audience. In time, the first truly professional troupes appeared on American stages; they came from Europe.

The first of these was an English company, headed by Lewis Hallam, which toured the colonies during the mid-1700s to perform Harlequinades, spectacles, and incidental dances. Shortly thereafter, in 1767, the John Street Theater opened in New York and became the center of week-long performances of drama, pantomime, opera, and ballet spectacles by various visiting companies. These were imported intermittently from Europe and probably visited other cities, performing wherever they could find a hall and a sponsor. There was a cessation of theatrical activity during the American Revolution, due first to a prohibition of theater by the first Continental Congress in 1774, and then to an antitheater law passed by Congress in 1787. However, this law was repealed, and now an increasing number of foreign troupes visited the new United States.

Baltimore was the scene of the first major revival of American theater after the Revolution, with a new theater built in 1781 that was to boast of having the first resident stock company of professional actors in America. Numerous dance attractions appeared on its stage. In 1787, the Baltimorean Boy, the first black theatrical artist to appear in that city, did a number of "slack-rope tricks" called "Strength of the Knee—Mermaid—Skinning the Eel—and Sleeping on the Cord." Also known as the Incomparable African, he also exhibited "curious Attitudes in jumping and Tumbling on the Floor . . . [balanced] himself with his Hand upon a Chair . . . [played] four different instruments . . . [and concluded] with walking on the Ladder, and acting the Clown."[9]

In 1792, Alexandre Placide, his wife, and a well-trained company presented operettas and ballets. Patriotric spectacles had briefly come into vogue during the Revolution, and Placide's company presented a number of these during the 1790s. Performances were diverse, including such unusual elements as specialty dancers, acrobats, tightrope walkers, and similar features.

Perhaps the best example of this was John Durang, who gained in reputation during the 1790s and in fact established himself as the head of a famous dancing and theatrical dynasty—the first in the new land. While Durang was known chiefly as a dancer, he was also an "actor, singer, tightrope performer, acrobat, designer and scene painter, puppeteer, circus clown, and author." When he performed individually, he often did specialty numbers like an *Alamande,* or the *Hornpipe,* for which he was most noted.

The first ballet to be regarded as a serious work in the United States was a performance of *La Forêt Noire,* in the New Chestnut Theater in Philadelphia, in 1794. This featured a well-known French dancer, Madame Gardie; Durang danced in the leading male role as her partner and also performed in a variety of specialty numbers and character dances including his famous *Hornpipe.*

Dance in the Nineteenth Century: Visitors and Native Dancers

By the turn of the century, an increasing number of European companies had visited the United States, and American audiences had become more knowledgeable and demanding in terms of the dance art. However, there was no real center of theatrical art in the country such as existed in European opera houses, where ballet had become firmly established. Nor was there any academy for the teaching of dance. The few Americans who established a reputation in this field usually received their training in a fragmentary way, from the European stars who came here to perform.

In the early decades of the nineteenth century, the leading centers of drama and dance were New York and Philadelphia; by 1830 there were three theaters in the latter city. In Richmond, Virginia, in 1819, a new theater, the Richmond, was built. It was an impressive structure with a dome that was 120 feet in circumference and that was "said to exceed in beauty the elegant dome of the National Theater in New York."

French performers began to dominate ballet in America. One of the first of the foreign visitors who captivated American audiences was the ballerina Francisque Hutin, who showed them the first *pointe* footwork, in multiple pirouettes, that had been seen here. Other French artists, including Charles and Ronzi Vestris, and the Ravels, a family of acrobats and ballet dancers, toured the country during the 1820s. Gradually, terminology like *pas de deux* and *corps de ballet* began to enter the language; Americans were becoming somewhat knowledgeable in this new art.

The greatest European visitor of the century was Fanny Elssler, who arrived in 1840 and toured the country for two years. Elssler was the inspiration of almost hysterical acclaim. She was a prodigious success wherever she went:

> Champagne was drunk out of her slippers and red carpets were laid at her feet. Congress adjourned because so many of its members were absent, paying homage to the adorable Fanny. President Van Buren received her at the White House and the government treated her like a visiting dignitary. When she went out driving in

her carriage infatuated young gentlemen took the horses from the shafts and harnessed themselves in their places. In the theater, Elssler had only to appear to receive an ovation. . . .[10]

Others who visited included the Paul Taglionis (he was the brother of Marie Taglioni); Jean Antoine Petipa and his son, the eighteen-year-old Marius, who was to become the dominant figure in Russian ballet; and even Enrico Cecchetti, who, traveling with his family, made his debut in 1857 at the Philadelphia Academy of Music at the age of seven. While the tours of these outstanding European visitors did not succeed in creating an American dance tradition, they helped develop high quality in a number of leading American ballet performers.

Mary Ann Lee was known as the first American to achieve nationwide fame as a performer of the classic ballet. Born in Philadelphia about 1823, she made her debut as a dancer at the Chestnut Street Theater in 1837 as Fatima in *The Maid of Cashmere,* the English version of a French opera. Later, her appearances ranged from Shakespeare to burlesque, from *La Sylphide* and *Giselle* to the *Sailor's Hornpipe.* Both Mary Ann Lee and Augusta Maywood, one of her early rivals, had received training in Philadelphia from the French performer P. H. Hazard. They danced together and competed for public favor until Maywood left for Europe in 1838, where she was to spend the rest of her career. After performing in such works as *La Bayadère* and *La Sylphide* (most of the ballets performed at this time were copies of European successes), Lee herself went to Europe in 1844. She studied for a year in the ballet school of the Paris Opéra. When she returned to the United States, she was not only much improved as a performer, but she brought with her a number of other European works to introduce for the first time in America.

Julia Turnbull was Mary Ann Lee's strongest rival during the major period of her career. The two dancers starred in an original ballet, *The Sisters,* in 1839. Turnbull was soloist with the Fanny Elssler company during her tour of the United States, and she performed principal roles in such works as *Nathalie, La Bayadère, Esmerelda,* and *Giselle.*

Augusta Maywood, born in 1825, was regarded as America's first great prima ballerina. She was an expatriate who spent the major part of her career in Europe, where she was ranked as being close in ability to the greatest dancers of the Golden Age. After a brilliant early career in New York and Philadelphia, she went to Europe. In 1839 she made her debut at the Paris Opéra. Regarded as an infant prodigy, she received the acclaim of Théophile Gautier. She toured widely, performing in Paris, Vienna, Lisbon, and ultimately, La Scala, in Milan. Forming her own touring company, she remained in Europe throughout her performing career, and particularly in Italy, where she was regarded as the leading ballerina of the era.

After Durang, who retired from the stage in 1819, the next widely known American male dancer was George Washington Smith. Smith's career encompassed almost two-thirds of the nineteenth century, since he first danced in public in 1838 and was still a teacher of dancing at the time of his death in 1899. Smith danced in everything from classical ballet works and opera to the circus. He partnered almost every one of the great ballerinas who visited this country, including Elssler, and he staged and performed in many of the great Romantic ballets, including *Giselle, La Fille du Danube,* and *La Jolie Fille de Gand.* He learned much of his classical ballet technique from Sylvain, Elssler's ballet master, and from Jules Perrot, in New York and Boston.

In the latter part of the nineteenth century, no dancers emerged on the American scene to equal these four. Indeed, ballet itself underwent a decline in the late 1850s. While other foreign performers toured the United States, including the company of Dominico Ronzani (who was later to become the leading choreographer at La Scala), ballet never took root here or flourished. America lacked major theaters and houses of opera, state-supported schools, and government patronage. Public taste was willing to support occasional foreign stars and touring groups, but did not value native American performers. Indeed, the major dance phenomenon of the latter part of the nineteenth century was *The Black Crook,* an elaborate and immensely popular musical play of questionable artistic merit.[11]

The Black Crook

The Black Crook was performed for the first time at Niblo's Garden in New York in September, 1866. It was based on a melodrama with a trivial plot which nonetheless provided the basis for a spectacular production, using props and decor from another performance whose theater had burned down. The plot included a remarkable hodgepodge of sorcery, demonism, and wickedness, with such characters as an alchemist, the Devil, fairies, demons, and baronial servants. The great feature of the musical was a Great Parisienne Ballet Troupe, featuring Marie Bonfanti, star of the Paris Opéra and Covent Garden Theater in London; the cast included many other leading dancers, with a company of eighty dancers in all. Part of the attraction of *The Black Crook* was its impressive stage sets and effects. Another appealing aspect was the ballet success of "the 'witching Pas de Demons,' in which the demons, who wear no clothes to speak of, so gracefully and prettily disported as to draw forth thunders of applause." The show ran continuously for sixteen months to overflow houses, making almost a million dollars. It continued to be performed with added embellishments for forty years in various forms throughout the country.

Although other popular extravaganzas continued to be performed, with lavish productions and dancing girls, the quality of the dancing was low caliber. Maynard commented that dancers were poorly paid and socially ostracized:

> The American dancing girls of the period had the worst of reputations, especially as the management believed in advertising them as Parisians, and had them masquerade under Gallic names, with the supposed Gallic reputation for amorousness. They were required not only to dance but often to sing, act, and support comedians, trained animal acts, or starred singers, in variety shows. . . . How the performers endured the fatigue of their profession is a wonder. Many of them worked in factories by day and danced in the *corps de ballet* at night. Most of them were waitresses on the side. . . .[12]

During the nineteenth century, other dance forms, in addition to theatrical dance, enriched the cultural scene. Three of these are worthy of mention here: the continuing popularity of social dancing, the gradual development of a black dance art that was to make major contributions to entertainment in America, and that strange phenomenon of religious dance carried out by the Shakers in New England.

Popularity of Social Dancing

At the beginning of the nineteenth century, social dancing had become widely popular and accepted throughout the young United States. In both the North and South, religious objections to it had largely diminished, although as new provocations appeared, resistance from the pulpit continued to be voiced from time to time. A contemporary historian wrote that dancing had become "the principal and favorite amusement in New England; and of this the young people of both sexes are extremely fond."[13]

In the cities, where dancing masters conducted regular classes and where education in dance had become a mark of aristocratic upbringing, instruction was formal and disciplined.

But on the frontier and in rural areas, where life was rougher, there were few dancing masters and no formal cotillions or rules of etiquette. Girls and women were scarce, and often the action was rough and ready. Dulles quoted a description of the time: "None of your straddling, mincing, sadying," wrote Davy Crockett, "but a regular sifter, cut-the-buckle, chicken flutter set-to. It is a good wholesome exercise; and when one of our boys puts his arm around his partner, it's a good hug, and no harm in it."[14]

Dancing was carried on at country fairs, logrollings, quilting parties, and at special holiday celebrations. After dinner and sports or games, the climax of every gathering was a dance. The men and women of the frontier loved to dance, doing Virginia Reels, country jigs, and shakedowns. It was a favorite form of entertainment everywhere, commented on with surprise by traveler after traveler amazed to find such rollicking gaiety in frontier settlements.

Gradually, new forms of dancing emerged, arousing new condemnation from the moralist leaders. In the 1830s, the waltz and polka became popular on the European scene and soon were enthusiastically adopted on the dance floors of the New World. These whirling, giddy dances were shocking because they involved dancing in a facing, closed-couple position. Ministers preached vehemently against "the abomination of permitting a man who was neither your lover nor your husband to encircle you with his arms, and slightly press the contour of your waist." Nonetheless, the exciting new importations won their way into society: "The *New York Herald* raved about 'the indecency of the polka as danced at Saratoga and Newport. . . . It even outstrips the most disgraceful exhibitions of the lowest haunts of Paris and London.' But the floor would be crowded on a Saturday night. . . ."[15]

Opposition to dance at this time stemmed from a general religious disapproval of many forms of play. One leading preacher of the period, Henry Ward Beecher, attacked racing, the theater, the circus, and "promiscuous balls . . . night-revelling,

Bacchanalian feasts, and other similar indulgences." To such attractions, he explained, "resort all the idle, the dissipated, the rogues, the licentious, the epicures, the gluttons, the artful jades, the immodest prudes, the joyous, the worthless, the refuse."[16] However, even Beecher did not object to dancing in the form of private dancing parties, or dancing at home.

Gradually, some voices spoke up in favor of dance. One woman editor of a widely read magazine, the famous *Saturday Visitor,* pointed out that no page of scripture either directly or indirectly condemned dance. She went on to describe it as a "good, right, proper" exercise, "well calculated to promote the harmonious development of mind and body" and opposed to the money-loving, hard-crusted spirit of the time. Another leading public figure, Dr. Sylvester Graham, wrote in a progressive journal, the *Regenerator:*

> Dancing, when properly regulated, is one of the most salutary kinds of social enjoyment, ever practiced in civic life; and every enlightened philanthropist must regret to see it give way to any other kind of amusement. The religious prejudice against dance is altogether illfounded; for it is entirely certain that this kind of social enjoyment, when properly regulated, is more favorable to good health, sound morality, and true religion, than perhaps any known in society.[17]

The upper social class had formal assemblies and cotillions; to match these, public balls, with admissions ranging from twenty-five cents to a dollar, came into being. For the lower classes, there were less respectable dance halls, cheap variety shows, concert saloons, and beer gardens—"branches of Satan's den" as those of Puritan conviction named them. In cattle towns and mining camps in the West, there were "hurdy-gurdy houses," where drinking, gambling, prostitution, and dancing might all be found together.

In the latter part of the nineteenth century, there were huge society balls for those of wealth and prestige in New York, Chicago, San Francisco, and the major society resorts. Dancing was a universal social pastime for those of the middle and upper classes; trade, professional, and fraternal organizations all gave annual balls. It was accepted that businessmen and their wives would attend dancing classes through the year, which would usually terminate in a *German,* or *Assembly.* Dulles cited a typical program of one such event: *The Lancers, Waltz, Polka, Military March, Quadrille, York, Portland Fancy, Caledonia,* and the *Virginia Reel.* Most of these were set or line dances, with the exception of the waltz or polka. On a grander scale, Ward McAllister wrote in 1890 of a great society ball; the ostentation had begun to approach that of the royal courts of the Baroque era in Europe:

> For one ball the host built a special addition to his home providing a magnificent Louis XIV ballroom which would accommodate twelve hundred. . . . At a reception given at the Metropolitan Opera House, twelve hundred guests danced the Sir Roger de Coverly on a floor built over stage and auditorium, and were then served supper at small tables by three hundred liveried servants. It was a world of jewels and satins, of terrapin and canvasbacks, of Chateau Lafite and imported champagne. . . .[18]

To teach the dances, and to act as arbiters of social taste, there were many successful dancing masters. The best known and most successful of these was Allen Dodworth, who, since childhood, had been a member of his family's fashionable band and orchestra. Dodworth was an accepted member of society himself, as founder and first treasurer of the New York Philharmonic Society and one of its first violinists. He had entrée into the leading ballrooms and private parties of the best society, and he operated a fashionable dance academy that catered to the most exclusive and socially ambitious families in New York.

"The dancing school," as Dodworth saw it, "is not a place of amusement. . . ." Instead, it was a place where dance was taught in a rigorous and precise way; Dodworth was the author of a widely respected text on social dancing published in 1885. The precise foot positions, the carriage of the body, and the whole ritual of social behavior were taught inflexibly by Dodworth, who ". . . battled with the world on the issue of dancing as a medium of education and cultured behavior, including health, morals, and manners. He demanded good teaching and not merely coaching in the transitory fads of the ballroom, and he strongly advocated the setting up of a standard practice."[19]

By 1900, there were many other influential and successful teachers, and the private dancing academy was well established as one of the channels through which social-climbing families might pry their way into accepted society.

Emergence of Black Dance

Another quite different aspect of dance during the nineteenth century was the emergence of black dance and music on the North American continent. When African slaves were brought to America, they carried with them their folklore and religious traditions. Although they were converted to Christianity, many of their dances continued to be performed for reasons of custom and social entertainment and also as a tenacious and deep-seated cultural retention of past religious beliefs and practices. Herbert Asbury commented that one term attached to such practice was *Voodoo* or *Vodun,* and he explained the unique permission that was given to slaves to dance publicly in early nineteenth-century New Orleans:

> The Sunday dances of the slaves in Congo Square, legalized by the Municipal Council of New Orleans, were an attempt of the "city authorities to combat Voodooism." They were supposed to act as a kind of safety valve to keep the slaves contented. The dances also became a remunerative tourist attraction at which Voodoo music happened to be played. . . .[20]

Public performances of these black dances were held in a large empty lot known as Congo Square, off and on from 1817 to 1885. Asbury described the early days of such performances:

> At a signal from a police official, the slaves were summoned to the center of the square by the prolonged rattling of two huge beef bones upon the head of a cask, out of which had been fashioned a sort of drum or tambourine called the bamboula. . . . The favorite dances of the slaves were the Calinda, a variation of

which was also used in the Voodoo ceremonies, and the Dance of the Bamboula, both of which were primarily based on the primitive dances of the African jungle. . . . The entire square was an almost solid mass of black bodies stamping and swaying to the rhythmic beat of the bones on the cask, the frenzied chanting of the women, and the clanging of pieces of metal which dangled from the ankles of the men.[21]

In a somewhat similar custom, slaves on the British-owned Caribbean island of Jamaica were permitted to take part freely in Christmas festivities in the homes of their masters during the eighteenth and early nineteenth centuries. Robert Dirks described a scene of the period in which an English lady lustily played the piano while her slaves "skipped and pranced around her parlor. . . . Indeed, things often became boisterous, with slaves joining in satirical songs aimed at their hosts or boldly offering free advice concerning plantation affairs. . . . In the evening, the slaves left to dance in their own quarters."[22]

In a related Jamaican holiday custom believed to have derived from traditional African practice, masked characters known as *John Canoes* were impersonated by male black slaves. Wearing terrifying masks with boars' tusks protruding from the mouth and ox horns sprouting from the head, and swinging wooden swords, John Canoes roamed entire neighborhoods, stopping at every home to dance. Other slaves took the part of Koo-Koo, or Actor-boy, a Christmas character unique to Jamaica, or engaged in other singing and dancing festivities. There are many accounts of black slaves acting as musicians and dancers on southern plantations during the eighteenth and nineteenth centuries. In many areas, an adapted form of white people's dance was the only kind of dance permitted. As Marian Winter points out, that black music making and dancing survived at all is remarkable when one considers the Slave Laws of 1740, which remained among the basic regulations for black slaves for a century and a quarter. These laws were instituted after a slave insurrection in South Carolina in 1739:

> A group of slaves attempted an escape to Florida . . . and were captured in a bloody charge. They had marched "with colors flying and drums beating." The laws of 1740 stringently prohibited any Negro from "beating drums, blowing horns or the like" which might on occasion be used to arouse slaves to insurrectionary activity. . . .[23]

When drums were forbidden, black slaves devised substitutes; they used bone clappers like castanets, and other artifacts to provide rhythm: jawbones, black-smiths' iron rasps—and handclapping and foot beating. The latter, with increasingly intricate heel and toe beats, was based on traditional African step dances.

Early Black Entertainers

One of these step dances, the *juba* dance, resembled an elaborately varied jig; it was found wherever blacks settled in the New World. *Juba* and *Jube* were slave names traditionally associated with dancers and musicians. Ultimately, *Juba* was to become the sobriquet of the most famous of all black stage dancers.

Black dance routines had long been known (either as originals, or as white men in blackface) on the American stage. Winter commented that by 1810, the singing and dancing "Negro Boy" was established with the traditional clown as a dance-hall or circus character. This role was played by impersonators who performed English or Irish jig or clog steps to the accompaniment of popular songs which had allusions to blacks in their lyrics. Only rarely did a genuine black appear. Indeed, the original Jim Crow, known as a famous black performer in the early nineteenth century, was a white entertainer, Daddy Rice, who tried to use fairly authentic source materials in his act.

The first actual black to achieve distinction as a performer on the stage was Juba, who was born, probably free, under the name of William Henry Lane in about 1825. Juba began performing professionally at about the age of fifteen, having learned much from an older black jig and reel dancer, Uncle Jim Lowe, who had not appeared in the regular theaters of the day. By 1845, Winter wrote, it was widely accepted by professional entertainers that Juba was "beyond question the very greatest of all dancers. He was possessed not only of wonderful and unique execution, but also of unsurpassed grace and endurance."[24]

Winter described Juba's routine as imitating all the well-known dancers of the day and their special steps, and then going through his original specialties, including a comic "walkaround," in which he impersonated a number of different styles and characters. By 1845, Juba's position was so secure that he was able to tour with four white minstrel players and receive top billing as "Master Juba! The Greatest Dancer in the World." In 1848, he went to London, where he drew immense audiences and such praise as ". . . the dancing of Juba exceeded anything ever witnessed in Europe. . . . The style as well as the execution is unlike anything ever witnessed in this country. . . ."[25]

At least partly due to Juba's influence, the traditional role of the Gay Negro Boy was adopted in British, French, and German circuses, and blackface clowns appeared in circuses and fairs. Because his material was essentially faithful to black dance steps and rhythms as seen on Southern plantations, many white minstrel-show performers imitated him and other black dancers—thus keeping a measure of authenticity in minstrel-show dancing. By contrast, minstrel-show music had little relation to its original source.

Although the American black continued to be the source of inspiration of music hall performances, blacks themselves found it increasingly difficult to find employment on the stage. Winter commented that increasingly, the black was forced into playing a caricature of a superstitious, vain, ignorant, and child-like creature (often wearing a fright wig, which could be made to stand suddenly on end at moments of shock). When he was allowed to appear at all as a musical or dancing performer, he was usually forced to play the role of the happy lazy plantation black indulging in childish pranks. Sometimes, he was cast as a foreign performer; Zouave dancers and drill teams, or "Koo-i-baba, the Hindoo baritone," were examples of such exotic types that permitted the talented black performer to find a place on the stage.

Christy's Minstrels in *Skedaddle*, the celebrated "walk-around." Lithograph by H. C. Maguire. Reprinted with permission of the Dance Collection of the Library and Museum of the Performing Arts at Lincoln Center in New York City.

The final irony, as America moved toward the close of the nineteenth century, was that blacks were no longer permitted to share the stage with white performers. Racial segregation became increasingly widespread, and it might happen that a black performing group would appear on stage during the afternoon, and a white group, in blackface, would appear at night (at this time, all minstrel-show performers, white or black, customarily used blackface). However, despite Juba's fame and the unquestioned ability of many black dancers, singers, and musicians, there was little opportunity for such performers until several decades had passed.

Shaker Dance

A final aspect of dance in nineteenth-century America relates to a unique phenomenon that joined dancing and religion. This was the appearance in New England, and as far west as Ohio and Kentucky, of an unusual Protestant sect called the Shaking Quakers, or Shakers. Descended from a group called the United Society of Believers in Christ's Second Appearance, which appeared in Manchester and Bolton, England, as early as 1747, the Shakers actually traced their spiritual lineage far back to "an ancient heretical tradition for dancing as part of the adoration of

Shaker dancing near Lebanon, N.Y. Lithograph, about 1825. Reprinted with permission of the Dance Collection of the Library and Museum of the Performing Arts at Lincoln Center in New York City.

God," as seen in early Christian sects. E. D. Andrews commented that: "The worship of many spiritual sects was similar: the early Quakers and Baptists, the French Prophets, the Merry Dancers of England, the Kentucky Revivalists, the Girlingites or Shakers of the New Forest, the Shaker Indians of Puget Sound. . . ."[26]

The small band of English colonists who came to be known as Shaking Quakers first made their appearance in this country in the region of Albany, New York, at about the time of the Revolutionary War. They had an extremely strict code; founding a religious order that was separate from the world, they rejected a corrupt society, and forswore marriage and all carnal practices.

The Shakers expanded their order rapidly, developing eleven communities by 1792, with meetinghouses that had spacious halls for expanded ceremonies, and with seats along the walls for outsiders. The dance of the Shakers seems to have been very similar to some of the religious dances that were carried on during the Middle Ages in Europe. Apparently, Shakers were convinced that Judgment Day was close at hand and that salvation could be obtained only by confessing and forsaking all fleshly practices. Dance was, for them, a way of entering into a state of religious possession, "the ecstasy of a chosen and exalted people." Andrews wrote: "The first Believers were seized by such ecstasy of spirit that, like leaves in the wind, they were moved into the most disordered exercises: running about the room, jumping, shaking, whirling, reeling, and at the same time shouting, laughing or singing snatches of song. No form existed. . . ."[27]

Gradually, their dance changed to a more organized and structured form, including the square-order shuffle, which was patterned on a vision of angels dancing around the throne of God. Recognizing that a lively worship ceremony was impressive to onlookers and would help in conversion, the Eastern leaders of the Shakers began to encourage the composition and performance of lively songs and dances. These included various formations, in circles, lines, and weaving patterns. Pantomime became increasingly used; "gestures, such as bowing, stamping, whirling, acting out 'signs' . . . were incorporated into the structure of worship, assuming, to a lesser or greater degree, symbolic meaning. . . ."[28]

Sometimes, the ceremony involved acting out chasing the Devil, in which true believers would surround a backslider, pointing their fingers at him and shouting, "Woe, Woe, damn his devil," and attempting in other ways to save him for the Lord.

During the 1820s, the Shakers choreographed specific dances, with names such as the *Continuous Ring Dance* or the *Union Dance*. Damro described these as follows:

> The *"Continuous Ring Dance"* consisted of the brethren forming four lines, or ranks, facing in opposite directions, as the sisters did the same. Then all marched forward singing, while turning from one line to the other. The *"Union Dance"* was devised to promote union of the followers and to make the worshipers conscious of the everlasting fellowship they shared. . . . brethren and sisters lined up in two rows facing each other. While the brethren went down [their] line greeting each individual by grasping hands and singing, the sisters were giving the same greeting in their lines.[29]

During the 1840s, there was a great revival of religious belief, and the Shakers developed increasingly complex and elaborate dance forms as part of worship. Andrews pointed out that a variety of formation dances were used during the Great Revival—lines, crosses, squares, stars, and other patterns. But now the dances took on new symbolic meaning:

> The devotees felt that they were indeed marching heavenward, that the circle was the perfect emblem of their union. The "wheel-within-a-wheel," three or more concentric circles turning in alternate directions around a central chorus, became a figure of the all-inclusiveness of their gospel; the outer ring the ultimate circle of truth, the Shaker dispensation; the singers, the harmony and perfection of God that were at the heart of life. In another exercise, "The Narrow Path," a single file of dancers, with heads bowed, placed one foot before the other as they trod the narrow way to salvation. . . .[30]

Gradually, the Shaker communities that had flourished throughout the Northeast and Midwest declined; the songs and dances that were performed as an attempt to reach an ideal communion with God were abandoned early in this century. In retrospect, the Shakers represented one extreme of religious practice—the use of dance in worship that was typical of pre-Christian or early Christian worship.

Divided Religious Views of Dance

In 1894, the *New York Times* conducted a survey of the attitudes of churchmen:

> Among the clergymen the division is as marked and as profound as it is among the laity. There are clergymen of the liberal school who not merely attend balls given by their parishioners but who applaud the waltz and the polka, and deny the responsibility of harm being inherent in either of them.
>
> On the other hand, many clergymen, both of New York and Brooklyn, make no effort to conceal their opposition to all forms and varieties of public dancing, and especially the dances [waltz and polka] so vehemently denounced at the Brooklyn revival.[31]

Among the more liberal clergymen, it was considered acceptable to sponsor dancing in the church gymnasium, and one minister in Jersey City considered opening a dancing school for young people. It was his view that if young people were going to dance, it should be in desirable surroundings; he approved of dance as wholesome exercise and a means of promoting graceful movement and carriage of the body.

Dance at Century's End

At the end of the nineteenth century in America, social dancing had become extremely popular on all class levels, and the dance in education had begun to gain broad acceptance. In terms of theatrical dance, however, and particularly ballet, the situation was at a low ebb. There was no continuous development or sustained tradition for ballet in America, in contrast to Europe, where the ballet:

> . . . was a venerated art and a formal institution, affiliated with permanent opera companies, amply supported by official or private means and assured of a supply of well-trained dancers from their schools. In America the ballet was entirely left to private initiative, to enterprising impresarios or theatre owners or to the choreographers and dancers themselves. There was little opportunity for aspiring artists to study classic dancing and even less to see good performances.[32]

In America, there was comparatively little ballet as such, and what there was was poor. De Mille wrote that the performers were pitied and scorned, and dance gained an unsavory name in the United States. No longer could it command respect as an artistic or theatrical enterprise.[33] On the music hall stage, varied forms of dance were shown, ranging from acrobatics to toe dancing to variations of the "Little Egypt belly-dancer" theme, or the skirt-dancing and scarf-twirling effects of performers like Loie Fuller. In Europe, while ballet remained an established state institution, the art had declined markedly both in inspiration and its appeal for audiences.

To this sad state at the turn of the century, two pioneers addressed themselves. One was a European—Michel Fokine, and the other an American—Isadora Duncan. Between them, they changed the face of dance for the twentieth century.

Notes

1 Olga Maynard, *The American Ballet* (Philadelphia: Macrae Smith Co., 1959), p. 21.

2 Foster Rhea Dulles, *A History of Recreation* (New York: Appleton Century Crofts, 1965), p. 5.

3 Joseph E. Marks, *America Learns to Dance* (New York: Exposition Press, 1957), pp. 20–21.

4 John Cotton, quoted in Marks, *America Learns*, p. 15.

5 Joy Van Cleef, "Rural Felicity: Social Dance in 18th Century Connecticut," *Dance Perspectives*, 17, no. 65 (Spring 1976), 7–8.

6 Marks, *America Learns*, pp. 25–26.

7 Ibid., p. 40.

8 Ibid., p. 47.

9 Chrystelle T. Bond, "A Chronicle of Dance in Baltimore," *Dance Perspectives*, 17, no. 66 (Summer 1976), 5.

10 Maynard, *American Ballet*, p. 18.

11 George Freedley, "The Black Crook and the White Fawn," in *Chronicles of the American Dance*, ed. Paul Magriel (New York: Henry Holt and Co., 1948), pp. 65–79.

12 Maynard, *American Ballet*, p. 24.

13 Dulles, *History of Recreation*, p. 37.

14 Ibid., pp. 76–77.

15 Ibid., pp. 151–52.

16 Henry Ward Beecher, cited in Arthur C. Cole, "The Puritan and Fair Terpsichore," *Mississippi Valley Historical Review*, June, 1942, reprinted by Dance Horizons, Inc., New York, n.d., p. 10.

17 Ibid., p. 11.

18 Ward McAllister, *Society as I Have Found It*, quoted in Dulles, *History of Recreation*, p. 232.

19 Rosetta O'Neill, "The Dodworth Family and Ballroom Dancing in New York," in Magriel, *Chronicles*, p. 81.

20 Marshall W. Stearns, *The Story of Jazz* (New York: Oxford University Press, 1956), pp. 44–45.

21 Herbert Asbury, *The French Quarter* (New York: Alfred A. Knopf, 1936), p. 243.

22 Robert Dirks, "Slaves' Holiday," *Natural History*, December, 1975, p. 86.

23 Marian Hannah Winter, "Juba and American Minstrelsy," in Magriel, *Chronicles*, pp. 39–40.

24 Ibid., p. 39.

25 Ibid., p. 50.

26 E. D. Andrews, "The Dance in Shaker Ritual," in Magriel, *Chronicles*, p. 4.

27 See Judith Lynne Hanna, *To Dance is Human: A Theory of Non-Verbal Communication* (Austin, Tex.: University of Texas Press, 1979), p. 53.

28 Andrews, "Dance in Shaker Ritual," p. 8.

29 Dianne Damro, "Dance of the Shakers," *Journal of Physical Education and Recreation,* May, 1977, p. 47.

30 Andrews, "Dance in Shaker Ritual," p. 10.

31 *The New York Times,* February 18, 1894, p. 12.

32 George Amberg, *Ballet in America* (New York: Duell, Sloan and Pearce, 1949), p. 9.

33 Agnes de Mille, *Book of the Dance* (New York: Golden Press, 1963), p. 128.

CHAPTER 7

Modern Dance: The Beginning Years

I have often been asked whether it is not painful to me to experience the evanescence of my own dance works. Well, after all, I can look back on an impressive number of self-composed and successfully performed solo dances, dance cycles, group dances, choreographies for stage and choric dance works, but I must admit that I have never really mourned their loss. They simply became part of the past! Their fleeting uniqueness, which they received in the process of creation—their transience, so basic to the dance itself—have always seemed to me to have been conditioned and dictated by its nature. For instance, I would never have wanted to perform the dances of my youth again later in life and probably would never have been able to do so, because different and more essential things have taken their places in the various seasons of my life ...[1]

THE DANCE FORM THAT WAS TO APPEAR IN AMERICA during the twentieth century, and that was to have a profound effect on dance education, was modern dance. Beginning with Isadora Duncan, who broke away from the classical ballet and urged a new use of dance as a powerful medium of personal expression, the foundation was laid. Ruth St. Denis and Ted Shawn followed by providing a generation of Americans with their first awareness of dance as an exciting theater art. But it was the small group of dancers and choreographers who burst on the scene in the late 1920s and early 1930s who were the first modern dancers. These were the great early figures—Martha Graham, Doris Humphrey and Charles Weidman, Helen Tamiris, and the German dance pioneer, Mary Wigman.

How is modern dance defined? At the outset, many viewed it chiefly as a form of dance which rebelled against the formalism, decadence, stereotyped choreography, and productions of classical ballet. They welcomed a form of dance which responded to modern concerns and was an American—rather than imported—art form.

In rejecting the vocabulary of ballet movements and the artificiality of its traditional forms and themes, modern dance was viewed as a true expression of contemporary life—alive, vital, and constantly changing. It was based on natural, expressive, basic movement, through which the dancer was able to express a broad range of feeling—rather than only the decorative, romantic, or pseudotragic emotions of the classical ballet. John Martin wrote that the prime purpose of modern dance was not spectacle, but to communicate emotional experiences, intuitive perceptions, and elusive truths.

Selma Jean Cohen suggested that, although the first modern dancers did not set out to shock their audiences, they had to be extreme to make their point:

> They simply had to discard all the trappings of the familiar traditions to make their audience see with fresh eyes. By eliminating the decorative, the superficial, the glib polish, they aimed to dig down to the essence of significant movement; movement that had long been disguised by distortion and ornament; movement that—when laid bare—would be recognized as the symbol of long-hidden realities.[2]

Since there was no universally accepted system of movement, each of the leading choreographers of this early period sought to explore and develop his or her own vocabulary of dance. Martha Graham based her fundamental idea of contraction and release of energy on the basic breathing rhythm of the body and the effect of inhaling and exhaling breath. Doris Humphrey saw all human movement as existing in a transitional state between equilibrium and disequilibrium, calling the process "fall and recovery." In each case, a language of dance was developed to suit individual creative needs.

Rejection of Ballet

The specific skills of ballet, as well as the emphasis on performing extremely difficult feats with an air of perfect aplomb and gracious ease, were rejected. Instead, the movement of modern dance tended to reveal the performer, rather than to mask him or her. A wide variety of nondiscursive gestures was developed; movement that was harsh, forceful, percussive—often primitive in quality—was developed. Instead of involving highly controlled leaps, turns, and other springing movements in the air, or dancing on the *pointes,* or holding the arms and feet in rigidly preordained poses, the body and limbs became flexible; they were held in any pose; they were wracked, torn, twisted, to suit the purposes of the dance.

Similarly, the traditional ballet hierarchy of leading dancers—the ballerina and the *premier danseur*—secondary dancers, and the corps, all performing in a ritualized sequence in which they played separate and largely unrelated roles, was discarded. Instead, modern dancers almost lost identity in their roles; the group itself was fluid and treated as a sculptural whole. Don McDonagh commented that even though there were stars, or leading dancers, in modern dance's basically egalitarian structure, it was common practice to "treat each of the members of a particular company as being equal and liable to be given individual variations to dance in the course of a piece. The company was considered an ensemble basically, in contrast to the traditional ballet company, which was as hierarchically arranged as an army or a king's court."[3]

In every way, through its stark and simple costumes, its simple and sculptural decor, and its music composed by leading contemporary composers in most cases, modern dance was an expression of the contemporary scene. Typically, during one period in the 1930s, the titles of works performed on the modern dance stage included: *Strike, Heretic, Traditions, Stock Exchange, Lynch Town, Work and Play,* and *American Provincials*. But, like modern art, such preoccupations were cyclic; at other points, and in the hands of other choreographers, the themes of modern dance works might encompass Greek mythology; ancient or modern poetry or other literary works; American folklore and legendry; major social issues; interpersonal relationships approached psychoanalytically; historical events; or, simply, abstract and lyrical works that had no theme or story line.

One element which has always characterized modern dance is *freedom*. Modern dance's primary value has always stressed permitting the individual choreographer to develop his or her own art, without regard to preexisting forms and traditions. This does not suggest, as some have concluded, that modern dance has no discipline. Merce Cunningham wrote:

> Since he works with the body—the strongest and, at the same instant, the most fragile of instruments—the necessity to organize and understand its way of moving is of great urgency for the dancer. Technique is the disciplining of one's energies through physical action in order to free that energy at any desired instant in its highest possible physical and spiritual form. . . . The most essential thing in dance discipline is devotion, the steadfast and willing devotion to the labor that makes the classwork not a gymnastic hour and a half, or at the lowest level, a daily drudgery, but a devotion that allows the classroom discipline to be moments of dancing too. . . .[4]

Isadora Duncan is usually referred to as the liberating spirit who gave expression to modern dance. Actually, there were a number of other rebels and pioneers who preceded her and who helped to shape the form of dance that was to emerge. Among these were François Delsarte, Émile Jaques-Dalcroze, and Loie Fuller.

Delsarte, Dalcroze, and Fuller

François Delsarte, a French teacher of music and acting who lived from 1811 to 1871, had a remarkable influence not only on the actors of his time whom he taught but also on Ruth St. Denis, Ted Shawn, and a generation of twentieth-century German and Central European dancers. Delsarte sought to develop a logical system of expressive movement and gesture; in so doing he spent his life observing people in a variety of circumstances, particularly under stress:

He even visited morgues and mines, after an explosion, to watch . . . how the bereaved betrayed their grief. From behind bushes in parks he studied children at play and . . . analyzed the differences in movement behavior between the attendants who loved children and those who did not . . . with cold scientific detachment he peered at humanity unconsciously registering its emotions and made copious notes. . . .[5]

Some of the great actors of his day were disciples of Delsarte. He developed a complex system of gesture based on three zones of the body and of human expression. These were: *mental,* or *intellectual* (head and neck); *emotional* and *spiritual* (torso and arms); and *physical* (lower trunk and legs). In turn, each of these zones had three subdivisions, which were further divided in terms of function. The Delsartian method had nine fundamental laws of gesture on which were based exercises to develop freedom and relaxation of every part of the body and to serve as a discipline for learning gesture and pantomime.

Delsarte also developed a system of dividing movement into three major orders, or types. These were *oppositions, parallelisms,* and *successions,* terms which were widely used in modern dance vocabulary many decades later, as they had been transmitted to German modern dancers by Rudolf von Laban, who studied with a pupil of Delsarte. In addition, Ruth St. Denis and Ted Shawn made use of the Delsarte system by having one of his disciples teach in their school.

It was Shawn's view that Delsarte's teaching was the first to reveal what modern dancers call tension and relaxation or contraction and release; thus, it was Shawn who laid the foundation for the German modern dance which, in turn, strongly influenced the American modern dance.[6]

Émile Jaques-Dalcroze, a Swiss music teacher and composer who was born in 1865 and continued to have a major influence on the teaching of music and dance from the late nineteenth century well into the twentieth century, was a professor of harmony at Geneva. Concerned over the lack of expressiveness of many music students, he determined to make use of physical movements to accentuate rhythmic awareness and musical creativity. He created a system of bodily exercises and approaches to the teaching of music and movement which strongly influenced many dancers and choreographers.

In 1910, a college for instruction in the Dalcroze method was built in Hellerau, Germany. One of Dalcroze's pupils, Miriam Rambach, who later became known in England as Marie Rambert, was assigned to teach the members of Diaghileff's ballet company; in particular, Vaslav Nijinsky was much influenced by the Dalcroze approach and revealed its effect in his own dancing and choreography. Hanya Holm, Kurt Jooss, Ruth St. Denis, and Mary Wigman were among many other influential dancers who learned through his personal teaching or through his disciples and writing. Many of the 3,000 pupils he graduated scattered throughout the world and taught the Dalcroze method in America, England, France, Sweden, and other lands—usually under the name *eurhythmics.* Stated simply, his technique provided a basis for strengthening the dancer's or musician's sense of rhythmic and harmonic structure through a progressive system of music visualization and other exercises.

Of the many other dancers who performed in the years preceding Isadora Duncan and who were not within the mainstream of the ballet idiom, one of the most unusual was an American performer, Loie Fuller, who lived from 1862 to 1928.

There were a number of popular dancers (known as skirt dancers) in this period, who performed in American and English music halls where variety performances were presented. Skirt dancing consisted of graceful, somewhat balletic steps, without dancing on *pointe* or executing lifts; the performers rustled extremely full skirts. Loie Fuller's contribution at the outset was to swath herself in yards of luminous veils; gradually she extended this to dance with 100 yards or more of diaphanous fabric which she manipulated with sticks under the play of colored lights. By the time she was well embarked on her career, electric lights had been invented, and she experimented widely with the use of moving lanterns of colored glass.

Although Fuller was said to be a mediocre dancer who had had less than half a dozen dancing lessons in her life, the effect she created was spectacular. One description from a writer of the time tells how one could see

> . . . at the back of the darkened stage, the indistinct form of a woman clad in a confused mass of drapery. Suddenly, a stream of light issued apparently from the woman herself, while around her the folds of gauze rose and fell in phosphorescent waves, which seemed to have assumed, one knows not how, a subtle materiality, taking the form of a golden drinking cup, a magnificent lily, or a huge glistening moth. . . .[7]

Isadora Duncan met Fuller in Berlin and was much impressed by the magic that had been wrought with the help of colored lights, fabrics, glass mirrors, luminescent cloth, and skilled electricians: "Before our very eyes she turned to many colored, shining orchids, to a wavering, flowing sea flower, and at length to a spiral-like lily, all magic of Merlin, the sorcery of light, color, flowing form. What an extraordinary genius."[8]

Perhaps the lesson that Loie Fuller taught was that a single person dancing on the stage could create an image capable of gripping and moving a huge audience—and this without reliance on the traditional classic dance technique that heretofore was the weapon of star ballerinas who captured the public's adoration. Isadora Duncan was to demonstrate the same effect—but she accomplished it without the aid of the brilliant stage effects that Fuller used. Her only instruments were her body and the magnetism of her expressive personality.

Isadora Duncan

Isadora Duncan was born in San Francisco, California. Her family was artistic; her mother taught music, and young Isadora studied ballet. However, she soon broke away from the classic dance form, which did not suit her spirit. Years later, she was to write about what she felt was the artificial idiom of ballet:

> The whole tendency of this training seems to be to separate the gymnastic movements of the body completely from the mind. The mind, on the contrary, can only suffer in aloofness from this rigorous muscular discipline. This is just the

opposite from all the theories on which I founded my school, by which the body becomes transparent and is a medium for the mind and spirit.[9]

At an early age, Isadora began to give dancing lessons. At the age of eighteen, she left for Chicago; then she gave concerts in New York at the Carnegie Hall Studios. In 1899, she danced in London and Paris and began to develop an interest in Greek vases and statuary. Her fame began to spread; she danced in Budapest, Berlin, Italy, Greece, and then Russia, where she met Diaghileff and Stanislavsky and visited the Imperial Ballet School. Her first appearance in Russia, in 1905, stimulated a controversy between the traditional balletomanes and critics and those who proposed reform of the ballet.

There was nothing theatrical about her performance in the sense of characterization, telling a story, or exhibiting brilliant dance technique. Instead, it was an art of personal expression in which Isadora threw away the conventional corsets, ballet slippers, and tutus of the period and danced barefooted and barelegged in a filmy, short Greek tunic. She performed moderate lifts and leaps, ran, and skipped. Her arms were often extended in an upsoaring gesture, never held in a fixed or formalized way; her neck and face were mobile and expressive. Overall, her movement was simple, but heroic:

> She reclined rather than fell; she kneeled to rise again; her movements were mainly upspringing. Although she vitalized the dance, gave it new weight and force, it did not have the dynamic range or accent of today's. It was more a harmonious plasticity, swinging, swaying, flowing rhythms, with no marked dissonances, no little vibratory movements. . . .[10]

The quality of Isadora's dance is well described in her own writing. She had a personal vision of America dancing, in which she saw ". . . great strides, leaps and bounds, lifted forehead and farflung arms, dancing the language of our pioneers, the fortitude of our heroes, the justice, kindness, purity of our women and through it all the inspired love and tenderness of our mothers, that will be America dancing. . . ."[11]

She danced to the accompaniment of great musical works of the time and of earlier periods—including many selections which had never been considered suitable for dance. For over twenty-five years, she danced to music by Chopin—Mazurkas, Preludes, and Nocturnes, Ballades, Valses, and Polonaises. She used the operas of Gluck: *Orpheus et Euridice* and *Iphigenia in Aulis.* In 1904, she danced the Bachannal in Wagner's *Tannhauser* at Bayreuth; later, she was to perform to such powerful pieces as Wagner's *Forest Murmurs, Funeral March,* and *Ride of the Valkyrie.* She danced to three movements of Beethoven's *Seventh Symphony* and to major works by Berlioz, Bach, Mozart, Scriabin, Rachmaninoff, Schubert, and Tchaikovsky.

She never did exactly the same work twice, and she often improvised on the stage, as in her famous performances of *March Slav* and the *Marseillaise* at the time of World War I. Indeed, she had no system of dance as such and no steps that she taught her own classes. Basically, she disapproved of schools and would not teach her pupils to imitate her own dancing. Instead, she wanted to help them develop movements that reflected their individual styles and preferences.

Isadora continued to dance throughout North and South America and in Europe during the 1920s until she was killed in an automobile accident in Nice in 1927. Her life was marked by a number of tragedies and unhappy romances; indeed, she rejected the common morality of the time and led an unorthodox life.

Isadora's contribution to dance was not in terms of technique or of a conscious system of dance. For several decades after her death, those who had performed in her group or studied with her called themselves Duncan dancers. However, Lincoln Kirstein, a leading patron and organizer of American ballet and a respected dance historian, described these "pitiful, aspiring devotees" of her art as giving recitals "which were only shadows of her violent impulse." More recently, in the 1970s and 1980s, a number of dancers, including Annabelle Gamson, have reconstructed Duncan's art and given performances which have been enthusiastically acclaimed by critics and public alike. However, support of such revivals tends to stem both from interest in their historical meaning and appreciation of Duncan's genius—rather than from Isadora's continuing influence on contemporary dance forms. Certainly, the

Isadora Duncan in *La Marseillaise*. Photograph by Arnold Genthe, 1916. Reprinted with permission of the Dance Collection of the Library and Museum of the Performing Arts at Lincoln Center in New York City.

interpretive dancing that flooded the United States in the early 1900s was due partly to her influence; however, it was also linked to the so-called aesthetic dance popular in the preceding decades, for which she was not responsible.

Despite his scorn for Duncan's dance and that of her followers, Kirstein recognized the impact that Duncan had on dance's place in the world of culture. Sharing Walt Whitman's democratic vistas, he wrote, she claimed fervently that anybody and everybody could and should dance. As America became a world power, Duncan cast herself in the liberated role of a "Statue of Possibility." In love with culture, music, and museums, she felt that everyone could dance as she did. Beyond that, Kirstein argued:

> . . . Isadora filled a theatrical vacuum . . . She animated dead stone, was drawn by Rodin, Bourdelle and Walkowitz. Paris claimed her as . . . "Victory" on the Arc de Triomphe; she wrapped herself in the Tricolor to dance "La Marseillaise." In her prime, ballet in France, Italy and Denmark was starved for that advance-guard activity in arts and letters which for half a century had disrupted moribund academies . . .[12]

In retrospect, probably Isadora's foremost achievement was to cast dance in a new light. It was now seen primarily as a means of personal expression, as a powerful and emotional stage art, and as something which might be freed from the rigid classical technique and stereotyped performance found in traditional ballet. While she had no direct successors, she set the stage for the next great dance artists who were to emerge—Ruth St. Denis and Ted Shawn.

Denishawn

Born in New Jersey in 1877, Ruth St. Denis had little early dance training. It is said that she took only three lessons from Madame Bonfanti, the Italian ballerina who had been a star of *The Black Crook* decades before. However, she was greatly interested in the theater, and after touring as an actress, skirt dancer, and toe dancer, she began in 1904 to take an interest in Egyptian dance art. She created what was first an Egyptian, and then a Hindu dance production—the ballet *Radha*—in 1906. Like her other works in this vein, it was authentically costumed, and set to music that was composed with an Oriental flavor but played with Western instruments. *Radha* was instantly popular, and St. Denis toured with it on the vaudeville circuit in the United States, the British Isles, and Europe. Gradually, she composed other numbers, all based on exotic themes: *The Nautch Dance; The Yogi;* and *O-Mika,* based on the Japanese Noh drama form. Audiences appreciated the colorful theatricality of her work, which she attributed in part to Loie Fuller, saying: "She brought appurtenances—lights and veils—to dance and where would I be, pray, without my lights? where would Isadora have been without her simple lighting effects? where would the theatre dancers of today find themselves without Loie's magnificent contributions?"[13]

She was greatly influenced, too, by the great spiritual quality and emotional force of Isadora Duncan, whom she had seen dance in London about 1900. Later, she was to refer to Duncan as having a divine inheritance from ancient Greece and as being "the embodiment of cosmic rhythm."

In 1914, Ruth St. Denis married Ted Shawn, who became her partner, and thus Denishawn was founded. Shawn was born in Kansas City, Missouri, in 1891 and grew up in Denver, where he entered college to study for the ministry. He was struck by diphtheria, was slightly paralyzed, and took up the study of dance as remedial exercise. Entering the field professionally, he studied ballet, opened a dancing school in Los Angeles, and made an early motion picture of dance. While touring the country he met Ruth St. Denis, and their marriage followed shortly.

These two great individualists remained together as a team until 1932. In that time, they organized thirteen major tours of the country, helping to bring about a recognition of American dance as an independent art form and, in effect, creating a new audience for dance among middle class theatergoers who heretofore had seen only the pioneering Diaghileff tours. In addition to their tours, St. Denis and Shawn founded schools, first in Los Angeles and then in New York; there were a number of other branches and teachers of the Denishawn method in smaller cities throughout the country.

After they separated, Shawn formed his famous men's group which toured the United States in the mid- to late 1930s. In addition, he founded and was director for many years of the Jacob's Pillow School of Dance in Lee, Massachusetts (Norman Walker held this position after Shawn's death). Ruth St. Denis, who had by this time become known as the First Lady of American Dance, continued to run Denishawn

Ruth St. Denis (center) in *Egypta*. Photograph by Sarony, New York, 1910. Denishawn Collection. Reprinted with permission of the Dance Collection of the Library and Museum of the Performing Arts at Lincoln Center in New York.

Ruth St. Denis and Ted Shawn in *Siamese Ballet*.
Photograph by Lou Goodale Bigelow, 1918-19.
Denishawn Collection.

House in New York City for a number of years. Later, in semiretirement, she continued to experiment with works based on a linkage of dance and other related arts with religious service; typically, at lecture-demonstrations, she would perform Psalms using the Indian *mudras,* or gesture language.

St. Denis and Ted Shawn made major contributions to modern dance. First, St. Denis's dance was filled with theatrical appeal; she made great use of color, lighting, scenery, and exotic (and often abbreviated) costuming. Although her dance movement in ethnic-based works was not truly authentic, nonetheless it gave a more accurate picture of authentic dance styles of exotic lands than ballet had ever done. However, St. Denis's movement skills were not highly developed; her technique tended to be largely a matter of "plastiques and poses, of manipulation of scarves and draperies, in decorative costumes, all very pictorial, and all done with an air."[14]

St. Denis had a very personal gift for movement and a facility for improvisation. She also developed a choreographic technique of music visualization, under which each dancer followed a specific instrument in an orchestral score—as Dalcroze had done years before.

Ted Shawn, in contrast, was less mystic and more analytical. He had a considerable respect for technical training in dance and included various elements in the system that was presented in the Denishawn school—a barefoot adaptation of classical ballet instruction, ethnic and folk dance steps and styles, Dalcroze training, and even beginning German modern dance. In 1930, the first course in Wigman dance technique was sponsored in America by Denishawn. All of this was combined in an eclectic but vigorous and impressive style, most visible in Shawn's company and then at Jacob's Pillow.

In addition to his concept of dance training, Shawn made the following important contributions:

He focused on the need to develop male dancers and fought to obtain recognition for dancing as a worthy art for men on the concert stage and in colleges and universities.

He began the practice of commissioning music especially for his original dance works; composers such as Charles Wakefield Cadman, Deems Taylor, and Vaughan Williams were among the contemporary musicians with whom he worked. In addition, Shawn was among the first to make use of such composers as Debussy, Scriabin, and Satie.

He made widespread use of themes related to Americana—the early pioneers, the Indians, the American black, and the Spanish Conquistador. *Xochitl,* Shawn's production on an Aztec theme, showed movement that was stylized in the manner of figures seen on ancient Mexican reliefs; both he and St. Denis did intensive research in preparation for their dances. Other compositions of Shawn's were less literal; two of his works, *Labor Symphony* and *Kinetic Molpai,* were vigorous, abstract representations of primitive forces and masculine vigor.

Ted Shawn and his male dancers in *Kinetic Molpai.* Photograph by Shapiro, Pittsfield, Mass., 1936. Reprinted with permission of the Dance Collection of the Library and Museum of the Performing Arts at Lincoln Center in New York City.

Shawn was a great crusader for dance. He wrote a number of widely read books, including *Fundamentals of a Dance Education* and *Dance We Must,* and taught at a number of colleges, including Springfield College and Peabody—thus helping to gain recognition for creative dance as an educative medium.

Before Denishawn, America had largely been a wilderness of dance art and dance appreciation, consisting of hoofers, skirt dancers, acrobatic dancers, and vaudevillians. The only seriously regarded dance was European, and the greatest of the American dancers, like Augusta Maywood or Isadora Duncan, spent the major part of their careers in Europe. Denishawn exerted a tremendous influence on the youth of America; it has been said that it converted as many to this form of dance as Pavlova did to ballet.

A final major contribution of Denishawn was that it provided a training ground for the great modern dancers who were to follow. In Martin's view, modern dance was not so much an outgrowth of Denishawn as a rebellion against it. Martha Graham, Doris Humphrey, and Charles Weidman were all leading Denishawn dancers and were deeply influenced by the training and theatrical experience they received in the company. However, when their original ideas for choreography and their drive to create independently were stifled within the Denishawn framework, they declared their independence. Thus, in the 1920s, modern dance as such came into being.

Martha Graham

Generally accepted as the greatest single figure in American modern dance, and the symbol of it in the popular mind, Martha Graham has been described by the ballet choreographer Agnes de Mille, her close personal friend, as probably the greatest American choreographer and an international cultural influence in fields extending beyond her own. Particularly, she has been one of the few persons to create new forms of movement.

> Her invention is prodigious. Like Picasso's, her art has changed deeply in style and technique many times during her career. For every new work, there was not only a new design in steps, but a new concept in technique and dynamics, a restudying of the basis of movement. . . .[15]

A tenth-generation American of New England stock, Martha Graham was born in Pennsylvania in about 1898 and was raised in California. As a teenager, she saw Ruth St. Denis dance and was impressed by her; in 1916, she entered the Denishawn School as a student and studied intensively with Shawn. Three years later, she joined the company, taking the leading female role in *Xochitl*. For several years, she performed with Denishawn both in the United States and abroad. Then, in 1923, she separated from the company, dancing in the Greenwich Village Follies and then teaching dance at the Eastman School of Music in Rochester.

In 1926, when she offered her first dance concert in New York City, she embarked on a career of choreography and performance that has been unmatched. During the period between 1926 and 1949, she composed over one hundred dances, many of them full-scale theater pieces. She explored an extensive range of themes in her dances, frequently becoming preoccupied with one concept until she exhausted its creative potential. Some of the themes dealt with in her earlier years include the following: American Indian and primitive ritual, American pioneers, tragicomedy, Greek mythology, and both narrative and abstract works dealing with psychological insights and conflicts.

None of her dances can truthfully be assigned to just one thematic category; they are all extremely complex in terms of symbolic meaning, psychological implications, and literary illusion. As a creator of dance, Graham has been unfailingly experimental, uncompromising, often disturbing, and, to the uninitiated audience, frequently the source of bewilderment and angry resistance.

Yet, with it all, critics and fellow choreographers deny that she is deliberately seeking to puzzle or to horrify the audience. Terry suggested that she is concerned with the universality of human emotions and behavior and with the revelation of human character. He wrote:

> Her dance purpose is to give physical substance to things felt, to lamentation, to celebration, to hate, to passion, to the experience of "frontier," to bigotry, to . . . underlying passions, dreams, fears and tragedies. . . . Far from being a cultist or an obscurist, she endeavors to remove the clock of obscurity from the purposes and aspects of human behavior and to reveal in solid dance architecture the architecture of the inner man.[16]

While Graham continued to explore new forms of movement throughout her creative life, her dance was characterized by certain movement principles and sequential techniques which were codified and recorded in the film *A Dancer's World*—the basic forty-five-minute warm-up used in Graham classes. These principles and techniques rejected the serene and smooth control characteristic of classic ballet, in which all the strain, effort, or uncertainty of the body is hidden. Instead, in Graham's technique, the "engineering, the effort" are revealed. "She threw aside all the traditional steps and techniques of ballet, the straight long leg, the pointed toe, the quiet, even hips, the flexed foot, the relaxed hand; she stressed continuous unfolding movement from a central core . . . but added spasm and resistance . . . she made the floor a part of gesture; invented many beautiful falls and recoveries from the ground; she discovered a whole technique of balancing on bent knees, with her thighs as a hinge and the spine cantilevered and suspended . . . she invented turns with a changing and swinging axis. . . ."[17]

Graham commissioned many of the leading modern composers, including, in an early period, pieces by Louis Horst, Lehman Engel, and Wallingford Riegger, and, in a somewhat later period, Samuel Barber, Gian Carlo Menotti, Norman Dello Joio, and Carlos Surinach. She also danced to classical works by Cesar Franck, Debussy, Bach, and Handel, among many others. In addition to using orchestral music, she danced just to the spoken word and to a variety of forms of accompaniment in between. Many of the musical works composed for Graham's dances have been recognized as outstanding contemporary compositions in their own right, such as Copland's "Appalachian Spring."

Martha Graham in *Letter to the World*.
Photograph by Barbara Morgan.

Similarly, Graham set a whole fashion with respect to stage design and costuming through her own brilliantly imaginative costume designs and those of Edythe Gilfond, as well as by having leading modern artists and sculptors, such as Rouben Ter-Arutunian, Isamu Noguchi, Jean Rosenthal, Oliver Smith, and Arch Lauterer, design her sets for her. Graham introduced a number of staging techniques that are now widely used: symbolic props and sets; the use of mobile scenery; and the use of sculpturally designed props as a fully integrated part of the movement design of the dance work.

Most of the leading modern dancers of the 1930s and 1940s were members of the Graham company—Erick Hawkins, Merce Cunningham, Jane Dudley, Sophie Maslow, May O'Donnell, Jean Erdman, Dorothy Bird, Mark Ryder, and many others. In later years, the leading roles were taken by Bertram Ross, Helen McGehee, Ethel Winter, Matt Turney, Linda Hodes, Yuriko, Mary Hinkson, Robert Cohan, David Wood—all of them superb dancers of outstanding physical presence—many of them gifted teachers or choreographers as well. One of Martha Graham's great contributions to American modern dance was that she was the first to use blacks and Orientals regularly in her company, in contrast to earlier companies, which had established a rigid color line.

Through the 1950s and 1960s, Graham continued to compose and present a number of major works of the American dance theatre—*Judith* (1950), *The Triumph of Saint Joan* (1951), both inspired solo performances; *Seraphic Dialogue* (a 1955 larger version of *The Triumph of Saint Joan*); *Embattled Garden* (1958); *Phaedra* (1962), and too many other critical triumphs to enumerate. Through this period, she continued to operate her school in New York City, to offer special short-term courses for teachers, to present master courses at Connecticut College, and to tour both the United States and Europe to overwhelming acclaim.

In the 1970s and 1980s, with the energy and vitality of choreographers half her age, Graham continued both to revive past classics with striking new productions and to create well-received new works. Among her new dances in the latter period were: *The Rite of Spring* (1984) and *Tangled Night* and *Temptations of the Moon* (1986). In her earlier years a controversial figure, Martha Graham became so widely known and accepted that, if anything, she was regarded by many as traditional—part of the establishment. Nonetheless, it would be difficult to conceive of a more vital influence than she continued to be. Emily Coleman summarized her impact:

> How is one to say how many dancers, choreographers, actors and directors, have reflected in their own work the impact of Miss Graham's incandescent intensity on the stage? The precise degree of coloration may be impossible to gauge, but it is assuredly present. "Martha Graham is not only a great dancer," says Katharine Cornell. "She is also a great actress. She is one of the two or three great American creative artists in all fields."[18]

Doris Humphrey

During the 1930s and 1940s, the other American modern dancer whose work was regarded as comparable to that of Martha Graham was Doris Humphrey. Born in 1895 and, like Graham, of New England ancestry, Doris Humphrey attended the Francis Parker School in Chicago. There, she received early training from Mary Wood Hinman in ballroom, clog, folk, and aesthetic dance. Later, she studied ballet and began to perform semi-professionally as well as to teach dance at summer workshops and in classes that she organized herself in Oak Park. In 1917, she went to Los Angeles to study with Ruth St. Denis at Denishawn. Shortly after, she joined the Denishawn company and danced in many of its leading roles in tours throughout the United States and a number of Oriental countries. In 1928, she and Charles Weidman left Denishawn and founded a school and small performing company in New York.

From that time until 1945, when she retired as a dancer because of arthritis of the hip, Humphrey was active as a dancer, choreographer, and teacher who was extremely influential in the development of dance in education in the United States. She created a distinct technique to express her choreographic ideas, toured extensively with the Humphrey-Weidman company, appeared as guest teacher and lecturer, and wrote articles, all of which helped to establish modern dance as a new art form. She is considered to have been one of the greatest teachers of choreography as a fine art; she had the gift of releasing, rather than cramping, creativity.[19]

Humphrey-Weidman group in *The Shakers*. Photograph by Barbara Morgan, about 1941.

Her major works, some of which have been revived in recent years, include: *Air for the G String* (1928); *Drama of Motion* (1930); *Dance of the Chosen* (later named *The Shakers*) (1931); *New Dance Trilogy—New Dance, Theater Piece, With My Red Fires* (1935–36); *Passacaglia in C Minor* (1938); *Song of the West* (1940); *El Salon Mexico* (1943); and *Inquest* (1944). Retiring as a dancer in 1945, she continued to choreograph a number of major works for José Limón and his company, including *The Story of Mankind* and *Lament for Ignacio Sánchez Mejías* (1946); *Night Spell* (1951); and *Ritmo Jondo* (1953). During this period, while serving as artistic director of the José Limón Company, she also served on the faculty of the Connecticut College School of Dance and the Dance Department of the Juilliard School of Music in New York. A number of other major compositions were commissioned especially for the American Dance Festival in New London and the Juilliard Dance Theater. In 1958 she died, leaving a final unfinished dance work, *Brandenburg Concerto No. 4*, to be completed by Ruth Currier, and a book on choreography, *The Art of Making Dances*, published posthumously in 1959.

While Doris Humphrey's work was often highly moving, she tended to be less concerned with dramatic representation than with an abstract evocation of mood. She studied movement intensely for years and developed a personal theory of dance movement as representing an arc between the pull of gravity and equilibrium—between fall and recovery.

She was gifted as a choreographer both in small groupings and in working with large-scale companies; her work ranged from a satirical comment on humanity and its foibles in *Theater Piece* or *Race of Life* to a serene and abstract design in *Passacaglia.* Both through her own work and as choreographer and artistic director for José Limón, Doris Humphrey made a major contribution to the American dance theater.

Charles Weidman

Closely allied to Doris Humphrey during much of her career was Charles Weidman. Born in Lincoln, Nebraska, in 1901, he joined the Denishawn school and company in 1920; Doris Humphrey was his first teacher, and soon they became co-performers. His gift for pantomime was evident, and he became recognized as the leading male dance comic and satirist of his day. Weidman's most famous works were *The Happy Hypocrite, Candide, Atavisms, Flickers, And Daddy Was a Fireman,* and *House Divided,* in which he depicted Abraham Lincoln during the Civil War.

Weidman staged the dances for a number of major Broadway musical shows, as well as separate dance revues. He taught at Bennington and a number of other colleges, was influential in training many dance educators, and numbered among his pupils such well-known performers as José Limón, Sybil Shearer, Jack Cole, and Peter Hamilton. His greatest gift was for narrative pantomime. Extremely inventive, he created movement that was fragmentary, mercurial, comic—making use of abrupt changes of tempo, rhythm, and dynamics. Lloyd wrote:

> He jested in stroke and curlicue, lampooning right and left with his pencil-slim body, making jokes with his fingers and witty observations with his bare toes. . . . He could always be counted on to do the unexpected thing. The movement was choppy on the surface, but underneath flowed the current of human feeling; sometimes the surface, too, was smooth with serious intent.[20]

In such a work as *Lynchtown,* his group choreography had dramatic strength and a charged atmosphere that created a powerful effect; however, most of his work tended to be light, humorous, and entertaining rather than deeply moving. Following his twenty years spent as a collaborator with Doris Humphrey, Weidman continued to perform with his own small company and to teach at a number of universities. In the mid-1960s he established, with Mikhail Santaro, in New York City, the Expression of Two Arts Theater, which gave periodic performances demonstrating the linkage of the graphic and performing arts. He continued to perform with a small modern dance company until his death in 1975. That year, Alvin Ailey had dedicated his company's season to Weidman as one of the "extraordinary papas of American dance." Ten years later, his life and work were celebrated in a three-day tribute of film, performance, and panel discussions at the American Dance Festival in Durham, North Carolina.[21]

Rudolf von Laban

Rudolf von Laban was a Hungarian-born scholar who had studied painting in Munich and dancing in Paris but whose major contribution was as a theoretician of dance and human movement. Beginning in the first years of the twentieth century, he worked on experiments exploring the nature of human movement and on a systematic analysis of so-called plastic rhythm. As early as 1910, in Munich, his first movement-choirs performed dancing for recreation. He was successful in developing huge civic festivals; throughout his life, he was concerned with the nature of work movements and the effective utilization of effort in labor. After directing his own dance company, which performed a number of experimental works, Laban became Ballet Master of the State Theater in Berlin during the 1920s. However, his most notable work was not in choreography, but in terms of his analysis of the physical laws governing dance movement and the approach to dance training that he developed with his pupil and collaborator, Kurt Jooss.

According to his theory of *eukinetics,* all movement may be divided into two major categories: outgoing and incoming. Laban developed a number of theories relating to *centrifugal* movement (movement originating in the center of the body and radiating or spreading out to the periphery) and *peripheral* movement (beginning with the extremities and moving to the center of the body). He carefully analyzed movement as to intensity, speed, and direction, making use of the object known as the *icosahedron,* the twenty-faced geometrical form which is a midpoint between a cube and a sphere. The essential concept of the icosahedron was that people's movements are both spherical and related to the three dimensions of space which are represented by the cube. Thus, movement takes place in three dimensions and also on diagonals and inclines, limited only by the anatomical possibilities of the body; Laban used the imaginary points in space dictated by the icosahedron to develop a complicated movement scale that provided a systematic basis for dance training.

Laban also was known for his development of the movement-choir, a form of mass gymnastics somewhat similar to Dalcroze's music visualization but with a greater degree of aesthetic purpose and emotional content. Following the Nazi takeover of Germany, Laban went to England, where he began an Art of Movement Guild. There, he had a major impact on the theory and practice of elementary education and physical education. Bruce wrote:

> . . . his philosophy has impregnated the teaching of physical education, particularly as far as women are concerned. Laban's work has been taken most directly into the teaching of modern educational dance or free dance and dance drama as we see it in many schools and training colleges. Indirectly, his theories have become the basis of schemes of physical education, and have replaced to a great extent, in women's work especially, the anatomical and physiological approach which existed previously.[22]

Laban's major contribution to dance performance was his system of dance notation, called originally *kinetographie,* and now known as *Labanotation.* Of the many types of notation that have been proposed, this is today the best known and most widely used throughout the world.

Kurt Jooss, a German choreographer and dancer who studied in Paris and Vienna and under Laban at the National Theater in Mannheim in 1921, later became his assistant and principal dancer. Jooss was supervisor of the dance group in the Essen Opera House and other German companies and later founded his own Jooss

Ballet. However, having worked closely with Laban, Jooss had a concept of ballet that was far from the traditional classic style; in such experimental works as his famous *The Green Table,* the quality of the movement and choreography was very much like that of the beginning modern dance of the period.

Mary Wigman

The most influential of Laban's pupils and co-workers, however, was the German dancer, choreographer, and teacher, Mary Wigman. She is widely regarded as having been one of the great germinal forces underlying the development of modern dance in the 1920s. Although all her teaching was done in Europe, she exerted tremendous influence through her three tours of the United States in the early 1930s and through the many American dancers who came to study with her in Dresden— as well as through the work of her disciples.

Wigman, who was born in 1886 and who continued to teach in Germany when she was well into her seventies, studied with Dalcroze at Hellerau and absorbed much of his teaching, although she rejected his primary emphasis on musical elements. She next studied under Laban and was his teaching assistant in Zurich, Switzerland, during World War I. While she absorbed much of his intellectual viewpoint toward movement, her own approach was less systematic and more emotional. Like Laban, she rejected the vocabulary of movement as well as the total artistic viewpoint of classic ballet; her approach to dance, in her first performances in 1919, was almost acrobatic. In part, this was an outcome of the environment in which she worked. Germany had never had as strong a ballet movement as other European countries and was receptive to new forms of art that were revolutionary

Mary Wigman in *Dance of Silence* from the dance cycle *Autumnal Dances.* Photograph by S. Enkelman, Berlin-Charlottenburg, 1937. Reprinted with permission of the Dance Collection of the Library and Museum of the Performing Arts at Lincoln Center in New York City.

in their approach in the tortured years of inflation and political and spiritual turmoil following World War I. In such a setting, Wigman's radical new approach to dance found a welcome audience.

By 1926, she had formed a major school in Dresden, as well as lesser schools elsewhere, and had developed a performing group which became widely known. Her choreography tended toward full-length works, or dance cycles, that were concerned with fundamental human emotions, superstitions, or relationships. When she performed in the United States in 1931 and 1932, she showed fragments of these larger works performed by herself alone, without scenery and often without music. They had such titles as *Summer Dance, Witch Dance, Storm Song, Dream Image, Dance of Sorrow, Dance for the Earth, Lament, Death Call,* and *Dance into Death.* These were drawn from larger cycles, including *Visions, Sacrifice,* and *The Way.* In 1933, she appeared in the United States with her twelve-member company (all women), and American audiences had a fuller look at her art.

Her other works included a major antiwar statement in *Totenmal,* performed in Munich in 1930, and such later suites or cycles as *Woman Dances, Autumnal Dances, Bright Queen,* and *Dark Queen.* During World War II, Wigman's career was suspended; however, after 1945 she resumed her teaching and choreography on a reduced scale in Leipzig. There, she produced Gluck's *Orpheus* as a dance–drama in 1947. In the years that followed, she taught in Leipzig and in West Berlin and choreographed for the Municipal Opera in Berlin and the National Theater in Mannheim.

What was the essence of Wigman's dance? First, in terms of the content of her works, she was deeply concerned with primitive and symbolic themes treated in a mystical and often grotesque manner; she is said to have had a preoccupation with death and to have used it constantly as a symbol in her dances. Her general orientation was to deal not with intensely individual problems, but rather with the universal elements of life. Lloyd wrote:

> . . . it was something primordial, something that dug deep into forgotten roots, an almost atavistic approach to man in relation to his universe, a return to the primitive through layers of civilization. It was something that stirred distant reverberations of things long past, something inexplicable, truly unutterable in words. . . .[23]

In movement, the use of music, and staging, Wigman's approach was unique for her time. Her actions were described as "predominantly low-keyed." She tended to kneel, crouch, crawl, and creep; her head was often downcast, and her arms were rarely lifted high. She avoided all balletic movements and never danced on her toes, although she did use the turned-out knee and foot for the sake of balance.

In a film of several of her shorter solo dances which was assembled by Professor Allegra Fuller Snyder of the Dance Department of the University of California at Los Angeles and shown in the mid–1970s, a somewhat different mood is displayed. Such works as *Seraphic Song, Pastoral, Festive Rhythm,* and *Dance of Summer* show Wigman's less familiar, joyous, and lyrical side.

Mary Wigman Dance Group in *Der Weg*, about 1932. Hanya Holm Collection. Reprinted with permission of the Dance Collection of the Library and Museum of the Performing Arts at Lincoln Center in New York City.

In general, the visual effect of Wigman's dance was stark, harsh, and gloomy. Many saw it as ugly and disturbing. Critics referred to her costuming as distressing, but original, and certainly successful in conveying the mood she sought. Costumes were simple, somewhat Asian or primitive in appearance, and usually made from dark, rough fabrics. She used platforms as part of her staging; her lighting was simple, and stage effects had little importance for her. Far more crucial was her sense of space as a vital element in staging and performance. Space, to Wigman, was not simply a vacuum to be filled or an area in which the dancer moved. Instead, it was a force that was tangible—almost like water, through which the dancer must swim.

Wigman's approach to music differed radically from that of Isadora Duncan's, in that Duncan had used music as a primary source of inspiration, whereas Wigman often danced without music, or with a simple melodic line of a woodwind instrument, or with primitive percussion accompaniment. She made much use of such Oriental instruments as Hindu drums and Balinese gongs, sometimes held in the dancer's hand. Dance and accompaniment were not composed separately but developed together in an organic fashion.

Many critics and audiences did not readily accept Wigman's viewpoint. Kirstein commented that although her influence on contemporary dancers was powerful, she had little to offer those who were primarily interested in theatrical dancing or who wished to demonstrate dramatic ideas "larger than their own frustration." Describing her instructional system as basic and semiacrobatic, he sharply criticized her custom of releasing students in the studio to improvise freely movements such as joy, terror, or grief, to percussive accompaniment. Finally, Kirstein suggested that Wigman's dance was based on the era's "loose thinking" on progressive education and adolescent self-expression.[24]

Nonetheless, Wigman's impact was a major one. She broadened the scope of dance concern and represented a major influence on beginning modern dancers in America, who were operating in an educational and intellectual climate which *did* stress a growing concern with self-expression and a psychologically oriented creativity. In her work with such European dancers as Kurt Jooss and Harald Kreutzberg, a brilliant mime, she strongly influenced a number of performers and choreographers who were essentially balletic. Through her major disciple, Hanya Holm, she exercised a strong effect on the American dance scene, including choreography for the musical stage. Second- and third-generation descendants of Wigman also included Helmut Fricke-Gottschild and Pina Bausch (see chapter 10).

Other Early Modern Dancers

A number of other outstanding modern dancers and choreographers emerged during the 1930s and 1940s and influenced this new art form. Among the most important ones were Hanya Holm, José Limón, Helen Tamiris, and the Dudley-Maslow-Bales Trio.

Hanya Holm

Hanya Holm came to the United States in 1931 to open a branch of the Wigman School. Originally, she had studied at the Dalcroze Institute and had been a leading dancer with Wigman's original dance company during the 1920s. Later, she headed the faculty of the Wigman School in Dresden and acted as assistant director and a leading dancer in Wigman's major work, *Totenmal*.

Holm remained in the United States, fusing Wigman's original theories with her own creative impulses to develop a new dance art that was uniquely American in outlook. Her major compositions included *Trend, Dance Sonata, What Dreams May Come, Tragic Exodus,* and *The Golden Fleece,* which was filmed in 1941. As a choreographer, she was extremely gifted; her works had a remarkable plastic quality and were marked by originality of staging and much technical excitement. Music was extremely important in her work, and such modern composers as Norman Lloyd, John Cage, and Roy Harris wrote for her.

While never an outstanding dancer herself, Holm was an unusually gifted teacher who exposed her students to a logical and detailed development of technique and to working in various planes, directions, dimensions, and extensions that reflected Laban's original thinking. She stressed the centrality of the body that makes possible unified and integrated movement. At Bennington, Juilliard, at her own school in New York City (in 1936, the original name of Wigman School was changed to the Hanya Holm School of Dance), and especially at Colorado College, where she was in charge of a summer dance workshop for many years, Hanya Holm had a strong influence on American dance educators. She was also one of the

Hanya Holm Dance Group in *Dance of Work and Play*. Performed at Bennington College. Photograph by Barbara Morgan, 1938.

comparatively few modern dancers who have been successful on the Broadway stage; two of her best known shows were *Kiss Me, Kate,* and *My Fair Lady*.

José Limón

José Limón, born in Mexico and brought up in California, was without question a towering figure in American modern dance. John Martin called him "the greatest American male dancer in his field," and Walter Terry referred to him as "without peer in his generation of men dancers."

From an early interest in painting and music, Limón turned to dance in 1928. He performed and choreographed during the 1930s, mostly for small groups. He joined the Humphrey–Weidman Company, becoming the leading male dancer, save Weidman himself. After World War II he formed his own company, with Doris Humphrey, who had just retired from active dancing, as his artistic director. The company was well received, presenting a number of major works to critical acclaim and traveling on several tours of Europe and South America sponsored by the State Department. Limón's work includes the retelling of an ancient legend of the

José Limón as the Moor in *The Moor's Pavane*. Photograph by Walter Strate.
Reprinted with permission of the Dance Collection of the Library and Museum of
the Performing Arts at Lincoln Center in New York City.

conquest of Mexico by Spain, *Malinche,* with music by Norman Lloyd; *The Moor's Pavane,* the story of Othello, set to music by Purcell; and *Missa Brevis,* to music by Kodály. His own dancing was somber, powerful, and majestic; even when past the age of highest capability, he always commanded respect.

Limón's company originally included Dorothy Bird and Beatrice Seckler; later dancers were Lucas Hoving, Betty Jones, Ruth Currier, and Pauline Koner, all of them outstanding choreographers and heading their own companies as well. In addition to performing, José Limón was a gifted teacher at the Connecticut Summer School of the Dance, at his own studio in New York, and at the Juilliard School of the Dance.

Helen Tamiris

Helen Tamiris was another leading modern dance figure during the 1930s and 1940s. Born of Russian parents on New York's East Side, she studied at the Henry Street

Settlement House under Irene Lewisohn; in addition to interpretive dance, she had ballet training at the Metropolitan Opera Ballet school. She learned Italian ballet from Rosina Galli and Russian ballet from Michel Fokine. She danced for a period of time in Broadway revues and night clubs, and with the Metropolitan Opera as well, including performances abroad in Berlin and Paris. Then, in 1927, she began a career as a concert dancer. Her aim was to be a dancer of her age and country, and she felt that ballet, ethnic dance, or even Duncan dance could not help her do this. Modern dance could, and this, to her, was one of its purposes—to deal meaningfully with modern problems and motivate audiences to a stage of concern and readiness for action.

Thus, most of her choreography dealt with vital social themes; the works had titles such as *Revolutionary March; Dance of the City; How Long Brethren; Songs of Protest;* and *Adelante,* based on the Spanish Civil War. They were dances of camaraderie, protest, and affirmation, closely linked to the strong left-wing movement of the time. Black spirituals and Caribbean ceremonials were also an important part of her customary concert program. Tamiris was an effective organizer; she brought together a Dance Repertory Company in 1930 which included Martha Graham, Doris Humphrey, Charles Weidman, and, in the following year, Agnes de Mille. While its program was successful and well received, the Repertory Company did not continue. Instead, Tamiris danced independently and later, in the early 1960s, formed the Tamiris–Nagrin Dance Company with her husband, Daniel Nagrin, who had been a featured dancer with her in concerts and night-clubs and a leading performer on the Broadway musical stage and on television. Tamiris, too, was active on the Broadway stage during her career; among the shows that she choreographed were *Annie Get Your Gun, Show Boat, Up in Central Park,* and *Inside U.S.A.*

In addition to her gifts as a dancer and choreographer, Tamiris was a strong force for the promotion of modern dance. She was one of the main organizers of the First National Dance Congress, first president of the American Dance Association, and influential in having dance made part of the Federal Theater Program of the Works Progress Administration during the late 1930s.

Dudley, Maslow, and Bales

Jane Dudley had been a pupil of Hanya Holm and was a featured dancer in the Graham Company; one of her best-known roles was in *Letter to the World.* Like Tamiris, much of her choreography was based on social themes; she also had a strong concern with folklore and jazz rhythms. Her best-known works include *Harmonica Breakdown, Adolescence, Short Story, American Morning, Swing Your Lady,* and *New World A-Coming.* There was much comedy and sheer animal spirit in her work. Like most of the dancers of her generation, she continued to teach, at Teachers College, Columbia University, Bennington College, the New Dance Group in New York, in Israel, and most recently in Great Britain.

Sophie Maslow studied at the Neighborhood Playhouse and with Irene Lewisohn at the Manhattan Opera Ballet School. One of her best-known works was

Folksay, done to verses from Carl Sandburg's "The People, Yes," interspersed with folk ballads and stories. She also composed *Inheritance, Partisan Journey, Champion,* and *Festival,* the last of which was later developed into a full-length work, *The Village I Knew.* All her dances are lyrical and expressive of human drives and conflicts but are not sharply partisan as many of the earlier social protest dances were. She continued to choreograph major works for public festival programs in New York City and to teach extensively.

Bill Bales, the third member of what came to be known as the Dudley-Maslow-Bales Trio, which was closely associated with the New Dance Group in New York, attended the Carnegie Tech Drama School and studied ballet and Dalcroze eurhythmics. He danced in the Humphrey-Weidman Company and taught on the faculty at Bennington until 1967. He was a guest artist with Hanya Holm and choreographed many solo works, as well as featured roles in the major New Dance Group presentations. Most of his choreography was based on Spanish, Mexican, and black themes. During the early and mid-1970s, Bales served as Dean of Dance at the State University College at Purchase, New York, as part of that newly established institution's strong emphasis on the performing arts.

There were many other dancers in the period prior to mid–century, including such figures as Jean Erdman, Eve Gentry, Nona Schurman, May O'Donnell, Pearl Lang, Pauline Koner, Lester Horton, Ruth Currier, Katherine Litz, Eleanor King, Talley Beatty, Katherine Dunham, Pearl Primus, Sybil Shearer, and many others. It is not possible to describe all of their careers even in brief, other than to say that in most cases they continued to teach, choreograph, and perform throughout the 1960s, 1970s, and in some cases the 1980s. A number of them will therefore be discussed in chapter 10, which deals with the more recent modern dance scene.

Modern Dance at Mid-Century

After half a century of development, what was the state of modern dance in the early 1950s? First, it was clear that it was an American art. The impulses that had given birth to Mary Wigman and other European experimenters were spent, and now the United States was the scene of contemporary dance activity. Those Europeans who wished to study modern dance came here, to the studios of the major modern dancers or to the colleges that offered specialized dance programs.

What had begun as the creative expression of a few gifted individuals, who operated independently but were able to reach fairly large audiences through their tours and theater presentations, had changed considerably. Now there were many choreographers and many small companies throughout the country—located chiefly in the large cities where the cultural arts tended to find a sympathetic audience, and also in many university communities. Particularly during the 1930s and 1940s, modern dance had swept through colleges and universities, exciting the interest not only of physical education departments—which usually placed dance in the hands of educators who had a special interest but often a limited background in dance—but also of others in the arts.

However, the great surge of creativity and popular enthusiasm for modern dance was over. It was apparent that, although probably hundreds of thousands of college students—mostly women—had been exposed to modern dance over a period of three decades, this had not succeeded in building a large, literate, and supportive audience for modern dance. To the contrary: During the 1940s and 1950s, many performers found that it had become increasingly difficult to schedule and finance company tours throughout the country or to have successful performances, extending beyond a day or two, in theaters in the large cities. Partly, this was the inevitable outcome of the growing costs of production. It was also because the audience for modern dance proved to be limited in terms of taste.

One of the problems was that, like all modern arts—modern poetry, painting, and theater—modern dance was hard to understand, and people did not know how to receive it. Too few artists, and too few educators, had been successful in achieving a sense of how to view, or be open to, these pioneering, avant-garde forms. And, in dance, one of the great problems was its diversity. There was no single method or technique. In the hundreds of tiny groups that performed around the country (for anyone was entitled to call himself or herself a performer or a choreographer), the quality of both composition and performance ranged from the most abysmally weak to an extremely high level of competence. Viewing this range, too many audiences, already insecure in terms of understanding and appreciating dance, had quick reactions that rejected compositions that were, to them, pretentious, confusing, or silly, or that shocked or disturbed them. No longer did the notion that one needed only to express one's feelings to make a stage work worthwhile have any meaning—if it ever did.

McDonagh commented that many of the pioneer modern dancers thought of themselves as constituting a movement and, at times, even a crusade. They were opposed to decorative prettiness, superficial or silly themes, ornate settings and costumes, and wary of the commercial theater. McDonagh pointed out that:

> The act of courage for these dancer/choreographers was to abandon commercial success in pursuit of artistic expression. [They were] brave in asserting that dance was a serious mode of expression or could be, when the prevailing theater world did not believe it to be so. The forerunners strove to demonstrate their belief to the existent audience; the new generation looked for a new audience. . . .[25]

Clearly, the pioneers of the 1930s and 1940s had been successful in gaining critical and intellectual appreciation for dance as a significant art form. But their followers, after mid-century, were ready to abandon the harsh, stark tenets of the early modern dance and to move out into a greater range of themes and theatrical approaches. Indeed, the very rationale that led to the development of modern dance was under challenge. Originally, it had been developed to provide an alternative to ballet. One of its major premises was that ballet technique was outdated, arbitrary, and uncreative, and that the artistic works of ballet companies also were archaic and meaningless in a modern world. Thus, the early modern dancers tended to avoid balletic training in their studios (although many of them had had at least a modicum of such training); they dealt with thematic materials, and used choreographic approaches that were completely unlike those of the classic ballet. In a sense, it was this freshness of modern dance, its contemporary significance, its ability to say things that were personal and immediately meaningful to an audience, that captured its first fresh audiences—and that the audiences found lacking in ballet.

But, over a fifty-year period, ballet too had changed. It was no longer the same art form that had been tired and stereotyped at the end of the nineteenth century. Instead, it was now a fresh and vital art that had gained tremendous new audiences and that, indeed, owed much of its spirit and contemporary outlook to the influence of modern dance.

What were the steps that led to the revival and enrichment of ballet and to its recapture of public interest? The first of them took place in Russia and in France in the early part of this century.

Notes

1 Mary Wigman, *The Language of Dance,* trans. Walter Sorell (Middletown, Conn.: Wesleyan University Press, 1966), p. 16.

2 Selma Jean Cohen, *The Modern Dance: Seven Statements of Belief* (Middletown, Conn.: Wesleyan University Press, 1965), p. 7.

3 Don McDonagh, *Complete Guide to Modern Dance* (New York: Popular Library, 1977), p. 18.

4 Merce Cunningham, "The Function of a Technique for Dance," in *The Dance Has Many Faces,* ed. Walter Sorell (New York: World Publishing Co., 1951), pp. 250–51.

5 Margaret Lloyd, *The Borzoi Book of Modern Dance* (New York: Alfred A. Knopf, 1949), p. 29.

6 Ted Shawn, *Dance We Must* (London: Dennis Dobson, Ltd., 1946), pp. 48–49.

7 Clare de Morinni, "Loie Fuller, The Fairy of Light," in *Chronicles of the American Dance,* ed. Paul Magriel (New York: Henry Holt and Co., 1948), p. 209.

8 Isadora Duncan, quoted in Lincoln Kirstein, *Dance: A Short History of Classic Theatrical Dancing* (New York: G. P. Putnam's Sons, 1935), p. 268.

9 Ibid., p. 271.

10 Lloyd, *Borzoi Book,* p. 4.

11 Isadora Duncan, quoted in Walter Terry, *The Dance in America* (New York: Harper and Row, 1956), p. 40.

12 Lincoln Kirstein, "Dance and the Curse of Isadora," *New York Times,* November 23, 1986, p. H-28.

13 Walter Terry, "The Legacy of Isadora Duncan and Ruth St. Denis," in *Dance Perspectives,* no. 5 (1959), p. 30.

14 Lloyd, *Borzoi Book,* p. 25.

15 Agnes de Mille, *The Book of the Dance* (New York: Golden Press, 1962), p. 157.

16 Walter Terry, "Martha Graham," in *The Dance Encyclopedia,* ed. Anatole Chujoy (New York: A. S. Barnes and Co., 1949), p. 216.

17 de Mille, *Book of the Dance,* pp. 157–58.

18 Emily Coleman, "Martha Graham Still Leaps Forward," *New York Times Magazine,* April 9, 1961, p. 44.

19 de Mille, *Book of the Dance,* p. 162.

20 Lloyd, *Borzoi Book,* p. 89.

21 For a discussion of Laban's influence on Wigman, see Lincoln Kirstein, *Dance: a Short History of Classic Theatrical Dancing* (New York: G. P. Putnam's Sons, 1935), pp. 303–5.

22 V. Bruce, *Dance and Dance Drama in Education* (London: Pergamon Press, 1965), p. 4.

23 Lloyd, *Borzoi Book,* p. 15.

24 Kirstein, pp. 306–7.

25 McDonagh, *Complete Guide,* pp. 69–70.

CHAPTER 8

Age of Innovation in Ballet

The opening bars of Igor Stravinsky's dissonant score must have convinced Parisians in 1913 that "Sacre" (as dancers call the ballet for short) would be extraordinary. Vaslav Nijinsky's choreography owed little to traditional balletic ideals of grace in its depiction of the ceremonies of a prehistoric Slavic tribe.... Nicholas Roerich's designs looked barbaric, and the entire production seemed an assault on eye and ear. Catcalls arose. So did cheers. That opening night performance was, quite literally, a riot.[1]

BALLET IN EUROPE REACHED A LOW EBB AT THE END of the nineteenth century and in the early twentieth century. Hanya Holm told of her choice to join the Wigman company: "At that time, there was nothing but ballet. And ballet was not in good standing. It was at its lowest."[2] Only in Russia had ballet retained a measure of its former grandeur, and even there, under the artistic despotism of Petipa, it had become stereotyped and lacking in inspiration. Paradoxically, it would be two Russians, Michel Fokine and Serge Diaghileff, who would make radical reforms that would embark the ballet on a journey of innovation that would restore its stature. And it would be a third Russian, George Balanchine, who would provide brilliant leadership to the ballet movement in the United States through the middle decades of the twentieth century.

Michel Fokine

Michel Fokine was born in St. Petersburg in 1880; he entered the Imperial School of Ballet in 1889. Graduating nine years later, he entered the Maryinsky Theater ballet company as a soloist instead of a member of the corps. He was a brilliant dancer but ultimately became known as a choreographer and teacher rather than a *premier danseur.* Fokine was much disturbed by the rigidity and sterility of Russian ballet, which he criticized in his writings. He described the nature of a typical *pas de deux* of his early years as a performer, commenting that each dance was little more than an exhibition of agility and physical virtuosity. There was little conscious choreography involved:

> We did whatever we felt we could do best. I did high jumps and Pavlova pirouettes. There was no connection whatsoever between our "number" and the ballet into which it was inserted. Neither was there any connection with the music. We began our adagio when the music began and finished when the music came to an end.[3]

Gradually, Fokine began to teach and to assume responsibility for choreographing student performances. In 1904, he submitted a plan for the ballet *Daphnis and Chloe,* which revealed his philosophy for the first time. It was much like that of Noverre, stressing the need for unifying ballet as a meaningful dramatic enterprise and for fusing its major elements of dance, music, and painting. This proposal was rejected, but three years later Fokine's first major ballet, *Le Pavillon d'Armide,* was produced featuring two brilliant young performers, Vaslav Nijinsky and Anna Pavlova. However, Fokine had little opportunity to put his ideas for reform into practice; typically, when he attempted to have dancers playing the role of Greeks dance with bare feet, the force of tradition was so strong that he was compelled to have them wear pink tights with toes painted on them. Shortly after, Fokine was impressed by Isadora Duncan on her visit to Russia, and when the opportunity came to travel to Paris to stage several ballets for the Russian company that was going to perform there in the summer of 1909 with Serge Diaghileff as impresario, he seized it.

It was in Paris, during the years between 1909 and 1914, that Fokine rapidly achieved success as a choreographer. In that period, he staged a number of major works, including: *Prince Igor* (1909); *Les Sylphides* (1909); *Carnaval* (1910); *Firebird* (1910); *Le Spectre de la Rose* (1911); *Petrouchka* (1911); and *Le Coq D'Or* (1914). It was there, too, that his philosophy of ballet matured. His views were fully expressed in a famous letter to *The London Times* in 1914, in which he outlined five major principles which should govern the choreography and production of ballet:

1. It is necessary to create for each dance new forms of movement, suitable to the subject matter, period, or country of the ballet, and appropriate to the music, rather than to use ready-made movements straight from the classic tradition.

2. The dramatic action of the ballet should be continuously developed by means of movement, rather than using sections of pantomime to relate the story alternating with dance numbers that had no dramatic or narrative significance.

3. The traditional gesture-language, or pantomime, which often was unintelligible to the audience and even sometimes to the dancers, should be abandoned; instead, in its place, the entire body of the dancer should be used to communicate ideas and feelings.

4. Similarly, the entire group of dancers should be used to develop the theme of the

ballet and should be part of the plot, rather than having the corps de ballet provide decorative interludes that had no significance.

5. Ballet should reflect an active and equal cooperation of all the arts involved in it; music, scenery, dancing, costuming all are crucial to a unified creative effort. Specifically, music should no longer be a series of separate and unrelated numbers but should be a unified composition dramatically integrated with the plot.[4]

Fokine's concern was to make the ballet a fully expressive art that mirrored life. For the period, his ideas were revolutionary, and the Paris audiences were immensely enthusiastic. In part, this was because the French ballet had become so lackluster, particularly in terms of male dancing. When the brilliant Russian dancers appeared on stage in Fokine's colorful and dynamic ballets, disregarding the rigid conventions of past choreography, and dancing in a manner that involved real characterization, the audiences went wild. Fokine wrote of their excitement: "After the Polovetzian Dances, the audience rushed forward and actually tore off the orchestra rail in the Chatelet Theater. The success was absolutely unbelievable."[5]

De Mille commented that in these early years in Paris, and in four years in England during World War I, ballet was transformed from a pretty entertainment to a major form of theater. Fokine based the choreography of his ballets on the locale and period in which they were laid. The music, too, was closely integrated with these elements. The style of the dances and their manner of execution were a sharp break from previous models; the classic technique was expanded to include freer and fuller arm and leg movements and a more supple back. The former rigid positions for the head and arm were now loosened, and the movement generally was more free-flowing and emotional. Costumes suited the period and plot; the old classic costumes were abandoned for these new works.

In 1912, Diaghileff replaced Fokine, with Nijinsky as choreographer. Although he continued to create a few ballets for the company, Fokine left in 1914 and worked intermittently with opera-ballet companies in Copenhagen, Paris, Buenos Aires, and with his own company in New York. Fokine died in America in 1942; it was unfortunate that for over two decades, while he was at the height of his creative powers, he had not been associated with a major company of stability for which he could have continued to choreograph his brilliant ballets.

Serge Diaghileff

Serge Diaghileff, who lived from 1872 to 1929, was born a member of the Russian nobility. He studied both law and music, became interested in ballet and opera, and was given a supervisory post at the Maryinsky Theater. Because of his independence, he found it difficult to work there and resigned shortly. He staged art exhibitions in St. Petersburg and Paris and, in 1908, became a theatrical impresario. It was in this role that he made his great contribution to dance. In 1909, he assembled a group of the leading Russian dancers of the Imperial Ballet and arranged to present a season in Paris during the summer vacation. His dancers for this first season included Michel Fokine, Anna Pavlova, Tamara Karsavina, Vaslav Nijinsky, and Mikhail Mordkin; the ballets were mostly the work of Fokine.

The next summer, Diaghileff's company appeared at the Paris Opéra, and such new works or revivals as *Scheherazade, Firebird,* and *Giselle* were added to the repertoire. In 1911, Nijinsky resigned from the St. Petersburg Company, and Diaghileff decided to establish his company on a permanent basis rather than have it continue as an informal offshoot of the Imperial Russian Ballet.

In 1911, the company played a season in Rome, Monte Carlo, Paris, and London; in the following year it also appeared in Berlin, Vienna, and Budapest; after that in South America, and, in 1916, in the United States. There it created a sensation and spurred American interest in the ballet. Diaghileff's company toured steadily from 1916 to 1929, during what had become an international period for ballet—but one in which increasingly the art came to be considered almost exclusively Russian. In 1923, Diaghileff signed a contract with the principality of Monaco to become the official ballet of the Monte Carlo Ballet; its name was changed to Les Ballets Russes de Monte Carlo.

During all this time, although Diaghileff used different choreographers, including Fokine, Nijinsky, Massine, Nijinska, and Balanchine, as well as a host of leading dancers, the Diaghileff company was preeminent in world ballet. What was the gift that accounted for Diaghileff's leadership? He had remarkable ability as a manager and organizer and, while not a dancer himself, had great artistic taste and judgment. Like Fokine, he recognized that ballet was a combination of choreography, painting, and music; he was able to get great artists in each of these areas to collaborate fully with each other. Always, he encouraged the new and different; it is said that his most frequent command was, "Astonish me."

In addition to the aforementioned choreographers, most of whom also were among his leading dancers, Diaghileff's stars included Tamara Karsavina, Anna Pavlova, Adolph Bolm, Alicia Markova, Anton Dolin, and Alexandra Danilova. He was part of the total revolutionary movement in modern art and knew well the many painters and composers who were working, particularly in France, during this period. Among the composers whom he used for his ballets were Stravinsky, Ravel, Glazounov, Prokofieff, Debussy, Satie, and Milhaud. Similarly, among painters, such leading artists as Bakst, Benois, Picasso, Tchelitcheff, Chirico, and Cocteau designed for his productions. Without question, his contribution was tremendous; he influenced every aspect of art in his era and brought together the great creative artists of his time in a "hotbed of collaboration."[6]

Gradually, through the 1920s, the great generation that had received its training and had reached stardom initially in St. Petersburg slipped away. Although the company continued to be known as Russian, it became more international in flavor and make-up. Gradually, the company decayed artistically; the music became increasingly trivial, the dancing more and more capricious and fragmentary. What had been his hallmark—parody, irony, sardonic sophistication, and an irreverent spirit which Kisselgoff suggested had descended from the seventeenth-century *commedia dell'arte*—ultimately ran dry. A number of Diaghileff's leading dancers and choreographers had left the company long before he died in 1929. At his death, the company dissolved, although attempts were made to carry on its tradition under a number of competing sponsors.

Nijinsky and Pavlova

Diaghileff's two greatest stars were Vaslav Nijinsky and Anna Pavlova; their reputations are legendary.

Nijinsky is reputed to have been the greatest male ballet dancer of all time, although his dancing career lasted for only nine years, during two of which (1914–1916) he danced little. Of Polish extraction, but born in the Ukraine in 1890, Nijinsky attended the St. Petersburg Imperial School of Ballet, where he was considered to be a brilliant performer although weak in his general studies. Shortly after his graduation in 1908 and his debut in Fokine's *Don Juan,* he accepted Diaghileff's proposal to go to Paris for his first season there. Nijinsky was an overwhelming success in several of Fokine's ballets and, two years later, in 1911, resigned formally from the St. Petersburg Company to become a permanent member of Diaghileff's company. There, he continued as a *premier danseur* until 1913, dancing such great roles as *Le Spectre de la Rose* and *Petrouchka.* He temporarily left the Diaghileff company because of the impresario's anger at his marriage; although he later returned to it in 1916 for a tour of the United States and performed briefly after that in South America, Nijinsky's career came to a tragic end. He was mentally ill and was confined to sanitariums for the remainder of his life.

Vaslav Nijinsky in *Afternoon of a Faun.* Photograph by de Meyer, Paris, 1911. Reprinted with permission of the Dance Collection of the Library and Museum of the Performing Arts at Lincoln Center in New York City.

What was the basis of the Nijinsky legend? First, it stemmed from his great ability as a classic dancer; he was famed for his tremendous technique, his elevation, leaps, and pirouettes. He was believed to be the greatest jumper of all time and could accomplish an *entrechat douze* (six full crossings of the feet in mid-air).

But Nijinsky was not just a classic dancer. He explored the possibilities of movement in a way that was akin to the beginning modern dancers of the 1920s. He was a remarkable choreographer who created four works: *Afternoon of a Faun, Le Sacre du Printemps, Jeux,* and *Till Eulenspiegel.* The first two of these aroused great controversy because of their radical break with traditional movement and what some saw as a too frank depiction of sexual behavior on the stage. Nijinsky created movement that had never been seen before on the stage: ". . . instead of tension, extension, elevation, feet turned-out, Nijinsky used relaxation, hugged-in shivers, jerky shakes, sub-human vibrations and feet turned-in . . . the grotesque, ugly, brutal and the strong he wielded like a weapon. . . ."[7]

Millicent Hodson, a dance scholar who helped to reconstruct the choreography of *Le Sacre du Printemps* (*The Rite of Spring*) for a 1987 Joffrey Ballet revival, concluded that Nijinsky's work was a precursor of modern dance. It was the first time, for example, that the dancer's fall to the ground became an integral part of a dance idiom; many of his other movements resembled early modern dance far more than they did traditional ballet.

Even at his most experimental, Nijinsky did not reject the classic ballet technique; indeed, his unique choreography was based on technical skills that could be performed only by a highly trained artist. To it, he added a remarkable gift for dramatic portrayal. Finally, Philp pointed out that his magnetic performances and

Anna Pavlova in *The Dying Swan*. Reprinted with permission of the Dance Collection of the Library and Museum of the Performing Arts at Lincoln Center in New York City.

Anna Pavlova and Vaslav Nijinsky in *Le Pavillon d'Armide*, about 1909. Reprinted with permission of the Dance Collection of the Library and Museum of the Performing Arts at Lincoln Center in New York City.

his personal brilliance helped to "secure for the male dancer a dignity which had not been present for generations" and drew huge audiences of nonballetomanes to see Diaghileff's touring company.[8] Thus, he made a great contribution to the world of ballet.

In contrast was the role played by Anna Pavlova. Like Nijinsky, her name is legendary as the greatest female dancer in ballet history, although it is hard to compare her abilities accurately with those of present-day ballerinas. She was born in 1881, studied as a girl at the Maryinsky Theater's Imperial School, and was a featured performer in St. Petersburg for ten years. With Adolph Bolm, she toured Scandinavia in 1905, thus becoming the first great Russian ballerina to perform outside her country. She joined Diaghileff in Paris in 1909, but then left him and, forming her own company with Mikhail Mordkin, toured independently through-out the world for twenty years, until her death.

To millions, Pavlova was the embodiment of ballet. Chujoy commented that she took what had been an aristocratic, imperial art found in the theaters and opera houses of Russia and Western Europe and gave it to the common people in towns and villages throughout America: "She played her great art in theaters and music halls, high school auditoriums and movie houses. She made available to the people an art form that before her had belonged to a chosen few, and thus elevated the people to an understanding, appreciation and enjoyment of it."[9]

Particularly in America, Pavlova's influence was tremendous. As Elssler had done during the Golden Age of ballet, she toured the country to tumultuous acclaim, making almost annual coast-to-coast tours between 1912 and 1925. Thanks to her, a generation of Americans became exposed to ballet as worthy art. What they saw was nothing like the revolutionary choreography or dancing of Nijinsky. Instead, Pavlova was a conservative and traditional dancer. Her performances on tour were not embellished by a sumptuous corps of dancers, but featured herself and a leading male partner. Her dancing was "distinguished by its grace, airiness, and absence of visible effort. It was sincere, refined, marked by a vivid sense of style-atmosphere, and a genuine and deeply felt reverence for the poetry of movement. . . ."[10]

Other leading figures during the Diaghileff period included Leonide Massine, Bronislava Nijinska, and George Balanchine.

Leonide Massine

Massine, known both as an outstanding character dancer and as one of the leading choreographers of the twentieth century, was born in Moscow in 1894. He graduated from the Moscow Imperial Ballet School and was selected by Diaghileff in 1912 to join his company as a dancer. In 1915, he was assigned the task of ballet master and then that of choreographer to replace Nijinsky. From that time to the late 1940s, Massine produced some fifty ballets for the Diaghileff Company, for the Roxy Theater in New York, Colonel de Basil's Ballet Russe de Monte Carlo, La Scala in Milan, and Ballet Theater in America.

Massine was known for two ballet styles. The first was the so-called symphonic ballet, in which he composed major works to the symphonies of Tchaikovsky, Berlioz, Beethoven, and Shostakovitch. Essentially, these were abstract dance works. His other metier involved story ballets, often with a high degree of comedy, satire, and character dancing; typical of these were *The Good-Humored Ladies, La Boutique Fantastique, The Three-Cornered Hat,* and *Capriccio Espagnol.* Throughout his work, Massine achieved a reputation for a high degree of musicianship and for great color, inventiveness, and choreographic soundness.

Bronislava Nijinska

Bronislava Nijinska was also a leading dancer and choreographer for the Diaghileff Company. Born in Warsaw in 1891, the sister of Vaslav Nijinsky, she studied at the

St. Petersburg School, joined the Maryinsky Theater, and, in 1909, went to Paris with Diaghileff. With some interruptions, she continued to choreograph for Diaghileff through the 1920s. She revived a number of works for him and for several years, was his chief choreographer, creating such major works as *Le Renard, Le Train Bleu, Les Biches,* and *Les Noces,* the most striking. Set to Stravinsky's revolutionary music scored for pianos, percussion, and voices, the latter:

> . . . was a primitive Russian wedding ceremonial, with starkly simple scenery . . . and an unornamented, architectural use of movement, mostly by solid groups of dancers. There was a marked kinship here to her brother's use of purely invented movement for expressive purposes, though in a more ordered and less violent form . . . [the work displayed] a kind of inarticulate, archaic passion . . . [it remains] one of the outstanding modern masterpieces.[11]

During the decades after the death of Diaghileff, Nijinska continued to choreograph for the Ballets Russes de Monte Carlo, the Markova-Dolin Company, Ballet Theater, and other opera and ballet companies throughout the world. Nijinska respected the classical ballet grammar of movement but also, like her brother, was a prolific inventor of new dance movement.

George Balanchine

Without question, the member of Diaghileff's choreographic team who had the greatest influence on ballet in America was George Balanchine. Born in St. Petersburg in 1904, he entered the Imperial School of Ballet at the age of ten. After graduating in 1921, having appeared in many student performances drawn from the established nineteenth-century Imperial repertory, he began to choreograph a number of experimental works with a small group of young dancers in what was now Leningrad. However, there was much opposition to his work, and in 1924, Balanchine was permitted to leave Russia for a tour of Germany with a small group of young artists known as the Soviet State Dancers. Traveling on to Paris, they were auditioned by Diaghileff and absorbed into his company. At the age of twenty, Balanchine became ballet master, replacing Nijinska. He served in this role for four and a half years, creating ten new works, restaging many others, and producing ballets during the opera seasons at Monte Carlo.

When Diaghileff died in 1929, the members of his company scattered. When Balanchine had joined the company, he was a young man of remarkable gifts but immature in his judgment. Now, he had become a fully developed choreographer. Due to a severe knee injury in 1927, he was no longer able to dance in demanding roles. What was he to do? Two of his works, *Apollo* and *The Prodigal Son,* had aroused much interest, but thus far he had not achieved a major reputation.

He was invited to the Paris Opéra to stage a new version of *Prometheus,* a two-act work to music by Beethoven. However, illness intervened; he had contracted tuberculosis and could not go on. After several months, he recovered, but the Paris assignment was gone. The period that followed was a rootless one for Balanchine. He concocted minor ballets and entertainments in revues in Paris and

London. He served as guest ballet master in 1930 and 1931 for the Royal Danish Ballet in Copenhagen. He acted as ballet master for a new company under the direction of René Blum in Monte Carlo. He organized another new company at the Champs-Élysées in Paris. And then he was invited by a wealthy young American, Lincoln Kirstein, to come to the United States. With the cooperation of Edward Warburg, Kirstein had plans for the ballet in America. Taper wrote: "He was not content to have some Russian . . . company come here on tour, but, rather, it was his idea to have ballet take root and prosper as a vital, indigenous art in the United States—to establish a ballet company, a ballet repertoire, and a ballet audience."[12]

Russian Ballet in America

It was not an auspicious time to begin a ballet venture in the United States. While there had been a number of tours by foreign companies, such as the one-year tour by the Diaghileff Company in 1916, or Nijinsky's performances in 1916 and 1917, these had not served to arouse a permanent interest. Pavlova had appeared here first with Mikhail Mordkin at the Metropolitan Opera House, in 1910, and later had toured regularly until 1925. However, the Metropolitan itself, which might well have been the sponsor of a leading ballet company, never took sufficient interest to develop native talent, and relied heavily on European stars.

Adolph Bolm, who had been one of the leading stars of the Diaghileff Company, had remained in the United States and had formed a school and company. Later he was to work with the Chicago Civic Opera, to found Chicago Allied Arts, and to choreograph in Hollywood and with the San Francisco Opera. Michel Fokine came to the United States at the invitation of the impresario Morris Gest; he staged musicals and also founded a school and company here. A third major European dancer was Mikhail Mordkin, who had been Pavlova's partner at the Paris Opéra and in her early American tours. He toured the country, taught ballet in New York and Philadelphia, and formed the Mordkin Ballet (later to be assimilated into Ballet Theater) in 1937.

But in 1933, the picture was not promising. It was a time of depression in the United States—hardly a good moment to introduce an art which was usually viewed as exotic, aristocratic, and certainly costly.

The first ballet company to break the ice was the Ballet Russe de Monte Carlo, for which Balanchine had choreographed in 1932. Now Leonide Massine was the choreographer. Alexandra Danilova was the leading ballerina, and there were several fine young Russian ballerinas in the company. The repertoire was drawn largely from the Diaghileff period, with emphasis on works by Fokine. The 1933 season, consisting of a brief series of performances in New York and then a tour of the country, was a critical success but a financial loss. Sol Hurok, who had arranged the visit, was convinced, however, that America was ready for ballet. He brought the company back year after year, and it gradually became a widely accepted and profitable enterprise.

This was still essentially Russian ballet; it remained for Balanchine and Kirstein to provide the foundation for what was to become an American art. Their plans were to begin a new academy, to be called the School of American Ballet, and a performing company, to be called the American Ballet. The school began on a small scale in New York City, in 1934, and the first season for the company was in March, 1935. It presented a small repertory of Balanchine works: *Serenade, Dreams, Transcendence, Alma Mater, Errante,* and *Reminiscence.* Critical reaction was mildly negative, and the comment was voiced frequently that Balanchine was not an appropriate choice if the intent was to develop a truly American school and style of ballet. The company set out on a short-lived tour in the fall of 1935; shortly after, it disbanded as an independent performing group and joined the Metropolitan Opera as a resident ballet company, with Balanchine as ballet master. Conflict rapidly developed between Balanchine and the opera management. Critic Virgil Thomson pointed out that the clash lay in part between the Russian style that Balanchine had brought to America, ". . . dynamic, explosive, sharply precise . . . full of enormous tension and vigor," and the Franco-Italian stage movement employed by singers on the opera stage, which was slow, broad, and much softer.

A second and even more serious difficulty arose when it became clear that the Metropolitan had no intention of scheduling regular separate ballet performances, which was the custom in great opera houses in Europe. Most of Balanchine's work for the Metropolitan was mutually dissatisfying, with the exception of his choreography of a new production of Gluck's *Orpheus and Eurydice.*

In 1938, Balanchine and the Metropolitan dissolved their relationship. For several years, Balanchine turned to the Broadway stage and choreographed the most popular musicals to appear during this era, including *On Your Toes, I Married an Angel, Babes in Arms, The Boys from Syracuse,* and a number of other hits, as well as several movies.

In this same period, in 1939, Kirstein made a second attempt at developing a performing company. This was named Ballet Caravan, and it included a number of the original dancers from the American Ballet Company as well as others who had been trained by the School of American Ballet. Indeed, its avowed purpose was to promote dance as an indigenous art; it presented no ballets by Balanchine but concentrated on the works of such choreographers as William Dollar, Lew Christensen, and Eugene Loring. Christensen's *Filling Station,* and Eugene Loring's *Billy the Kid,* to music by Aaron Copland, were among the first major ballets to deal successfully with American themes.

In 1946, after a hiatus caused by World War II, Kirstein returned to the United States and, with Balanchine, formed the Ballet Society. Leon Barzin was musical director and Lew Christensen ballet master. This membership organization gave performances of a number of Balanchine's works, including *The Spellbound Child* and *The Four Temperaments,* and later, *Symphonie Concertante* and *Symphony in C,* as well as works by Todd Bolender, Merce Cunningham, William Dollar, and Lew Christensen.

The New York City Ballet

In 1948, the Ballet Society joined forces with the newly established New York City Center of Music and Drama under the title of the New York City Ballet. During the first years, the company performed in the New York City Center. Although it lacked a subsidy as such, the city's sponsorship and the low admission scale helped to build a large new audience for ballet. During the following decade, the company, under the artistic domination of Balanchine, achieved its reputation as one of the outstanding ballet companies in the world. A key factor in this growth was that the School of American Ballet had continued, during the twelve years since the demise of the original company, to train a number of outstanding young dancers who were now ready to join the company. Among these were Tanaquil LeClercq, Jacques d'Amboise, and Edward Villella. Other principal dancers included Maria Tallchief, Nicholas Magallanes, Francisco Moncion, and Todd Bolender.

The first season was brief, consisting of only fourteen performances. Artistically, it was considered successful. However, financially it was poor because of the competition of the Ballet Russe de Monte Carlo, which had just concluded a smash four-week season at the Metropolitan Opera House. In a second season, beginning in January 1949, the company was joined by Jerome Robbins and Antony Tudor as guest choreographers. The American public began to respond favorably to the new artistic directions, and financially the season was a greater success.

At the outset, however, it appeared as if the New York City Ballet would perform in the City Center only twice a year, for a total of about four or five weeks. This would mean that, even with rehearsal time, the dancers would be occupied for only thirteen weeks per year. Could many of the ranking dancers in the company remain committed under these conditions? Many of them had to go into musical shows, Ballet Theater, and other companies. However, under determined management and with the support of the City Center directors, the company continued; in the fall of 1949, attendance was larger and the deficit decreased. Then, remarkable recognition came for such a young company when Ninette de Valois, director of the famed British Sadler's Wells Ballet, which was on its first American tour at the time, indicated that she was extremely impressed with the New York City Ballet Company. Balanchine was invited to come to London in the following spring to stage his *Ballet Imperial,* and shortly thereafter, the entire New York company was invited to perform for a season at Covent Garden.

This season, in July 1950, was under the auspices of the Arts Council of Great Britain and was considered a quasi-official exchange visit for the Sadler's Wells Ballet season in New York in 1949. Sixty of America's leading dancers were in the company; it was the first international recognition of the United States in the field of ballet. The literary, art, and music worlds were well represented; all the London and Paris periodicals sent their leading dance critics. And the reviews were highly favorable. One critic wrote:

> . . . they danced with such vigour and athletic enthusiasm that they had the audience in this hallowed theater whistling its enthusiasm long before the end came. . . .
>
> These fresh young Americans bring no mystery or sentiment to their dancing. . . . The men attack feats of grace as a sport and the girls make almost a miracle of their execution of the classical routine. That is the strangest thing about their visit. They are not so much interested in the folksy style. They are pure classicists absorbed by the perfection of the old Imperial Russian Ballet.[13]

New York City Ballet in the party scene from *The Nutcracker*. Choreography by George Balanchine. Photograph by Martha Swope.

Although there was some criticism of Balanchine's revival of the Stravinsky-Fokine *Firebird,* and of Balanchine's "cold and undramatic" abstract ballet, in general the reception was highly enthusiastic. Chujoy commented that, despite some critical "coolness," the London audience was greatly impressed; indeed, much of the criticism served as excellent publicity: "Controversial ballets like *Illuminations, Age of Anxiety, Orpheus,* and *Firebird* attracted wide attention. Technically difficult ballets, the so-called abstracts, never failed to bring out cheers."[14]

The visit of Great Britain, which included a tour of other cities, was a triumph and focused international attention on the New York City Ballet. The artistic prestige of the United States was enhanced. Increasingly, leading dancers who had not formerly been with the company joined it, including Jerome Robbins, Janet Reed, Melissa Hayden, Hugh Laing, and Diana Adams. The next seasons brought widespread acclaim, and now the company was augmented by André Eglevsky and Nora Kaye. Through the 1950s, and then as it moved into its sumptuous new home, the New York State Theater in the Lincoln Center arts complex, it gradually assumed the status of being one of the world's few great ballet companies.

Under Balanchine, during the period from the 1950s through the 1970s, the New York City Ballet developed an enormous and brilliant repertoire; its dancers performed superbly, and its productions were handsomely staged. If it had a major problem in the view of some critics, it was that the company was so strongly dominated by Balanchine. Although it presented works by other leading choreographers, such as Todd Bolender, Antony Tudor, Frederick Ashton, and Jerome Robbins and a few ballets by members of the company, such as Jacques d'Amboise, it was always primarily a showcase for Balanchine's choreography. To some, his highly disciplined and unemotional neoclassic approach was too restrictive, lacking the color and variety that a great ballet company should have. Agnes de Mille gave a balanced view of Balanchine's work, commenting that, although he was highly musical, he demanded of his dancers only that they "hear a downbeat" and stay in time with the music. He sought to suppress all show of emotion and saw the dancer as anonymous, essentially a tool for the choreographer.

Ballet Theater

A second major thread that is traced through the development of ballet in the United States is that of Ballet Theater. This company developed more native American performers than any other; its repertoire was broad and diverse; it mounted the works of all the great modern ballet choreographers; and it presented superb ballet for half a century to audiences throughout the United States and abroad.

Ballet Theater developed as an outgrowth of the Mordkin Ballet, which had been founded in 1937 to provide a performing outlet for the students of Mordkin's New York school. In this little company, Lucia Chase and Leon Danielian were among the leading dancers, and the program consisted chiefly of older romantic works which Mordkin had restaged. In the following year, the Mordkin Ballet was expanded by a number of leading dancers and by additions to the repertoire.

As the company began to gain an audience and a sense of artistic direction, it decided in 1939 to expand. Lucia Chase, who was not only a dancer but also an extremely wealthy patron of the ballet, and Richard Pleasant, who had become general manager of the company, determined to form a full-fledged ballet company to be known as Ballet Theater. It was to be under Pleasant's direction, and Mordkin's role was subordinated. During the first season of the new company, four weeks in the winter of 1940, works were presented by Michel Fokine, Adolph Bolm, Anton Dolin, Antony Tudor, Agnes de Mille, Eugene Loring, and Bronislava Nijinska. The company included a considerable number of leading dancers, many of whom had been active in the Diaghileff Company in the 1920s, or in its successor organizations.

In its second year, 1941, the company displayed a new and unusual structure. Anton Dolin was choreographer-in-residence and stage manager of the Classic Wing, Eugene Loring of the American Wing, and Antony Tudor of the New English Wing. This was part of Pleasant's much broader plan, which was to develop not a single ballet company but rather a producing organization which would perform existing works of all periods and national sources as well as assist in the creation of new ballets from many contemporary viewpoints. Thus, Pleasant intended to develop a classical wing, a Fokine-Diaghileff Russian Wing, and contemporary American, British, black and Spanish Wings; there even was the intention of including modern dance in the company's repertoire.

Unfortunately, the plan was too ambitious and the financial hazards too great. Despite excellent reviews and enthusiastic audiences, Pleasant's plans could not be carried further, and he was forced to resign at the end of 1941. At the end of that year, Sol Hurok undertook to book Ballet Theater. In the years that followed, the company traveled widely, performing in all of Europe, the Near East, and South America. Particularly until the 1950s, it offered a roll call of the leading dancers to have appeared on the American scene: Diana Adams, Alicia Alonso, Agnes de Mille, André Eglevsky, Melissa Hayden, Nora Kaye, Michael Kidd, John Kriza, Harold Lang, Alicia Markova, Janet Reed, Jerome Robbins, and many others. Similarly, it provided a vehicle for the most talented choreographers of the time to present their works, either for the first time, or in revival.

Financial difficulties plagued Ballet Theater throughout its existence. The original plan to have a company in which there would be no star system, no subdivision of dancers in a complex classification of levels, but rather simply principals and company, was forfeited in order to develop glamour and encourage ticket sales. Similarly, during the years in which Hurok was in charge of Ballet Theater's touring schedule, its desire to be an American company was subordinated to the need for audience appeal. Instead, it was widely advertised as Russian ballet in an effort to capitalize on the reputation that had been established by Ballet Russe in years past. The company suffered from a lack of clear-cut artistic direction and, particularly during the 1950s, lost many of its leading dancers to other companies.

Nonetheless, it continued to perform throughout America and in many other countries and has made a major contribution to the world of ballet since 1957 under the name American Ballet Theater.[15]

Other Russian Ballet Influences

The third major development in American ballet represented the continuation, particularly during the 1930s and 1940s, of the Russian ballet tradition that Diaghileff had first brought to the United States. As described earlier, René Blum and Colonel de Basil had founded the Ballet Russe de Monte Carlo in 1932, assembling many of the leading dancers from the original Diaghileff company. At first, the company was under the direction of Balanchine, then under Leonide Massine.

The first season in New York and London, in 1933, chiefly involved works by the two Russian choreographers; it was regarded as an artistic success but a financial failure. However, Sol Hurok promoted the Ballet Russe de Monte Carlo (the title had been changed to the singular) strongly, and with each succeeding year, the tours and seasons grew longer and the audiences fuller and more appreciative. By 1935, the Ballet Russe de Monte Carlo was booked into the Metropolitan Opera House in New York; it had become an accepted part of the city's cultural life.

René Blum retired as codirector of Ballet Russe in 1936, with Colonel de Basil assuming full control. However, friction split the company, and in 1938 Leonide Massine left it, returning to Europe, where he founded a new company with Blum. The history from this point is one of tangled relationships, rapidly shifting titles, and lawsuits over the use of ballets. The major company to retain the name and tradition, however, was the company which came here under Massine's direction in 1938.

At the outset, the company was clearly Russian in its origin and style; those Americans who joined it often changed their names in order to sound foreign. During the late 1930s, Ballet Russe ventured into Americana with such works as Massine's *Saratoga* and *Union Pacific.* However, these were not truly in the American genre, and not until Agnes de Mille's *Rodeo* was created did the company produce a work that was really native in spirit and style. Cut off from Europe by World War II, Ballet Russe gradually became American in character and more and more American in its membership.

American Choreographers in This Period

A final important development of the period prior to 1950 in the United States was that a number of American dancers and choreographers had emerged who, in turn, began to develop regional ballet companies and schools in cities other than New York. Three of the leading examples of such home-grown talent were Catherine Littlefield, Ruth Page, and Lew Christensen.

Catherine Littlefield

Catherine Littlefield, a recognized American choreographer and ballerina, studied first in her mother's school in Philadelphia and then under Albertieri at the Metropolitan in New York and under Egorova in Paris. On her return to the United States, she danced in Broadway musicals and was for several years a *première danseuse* for the Philadelphia Grand Opera Company. In 1935, she founded the Littlefield Ballet, which later became known as the Philadelphia Ballet—the first of its kind to be organized and staffed entirely by Americans. The company toured the United States and also performed in Europe in 1937, where it was well received; it continued to be active under Littlefield's direction until 1942. She also served for several seasons as the director of the Chicago Opera Ballet.

During her years as a teacher and ballet director, Littlefield helped train a considerable number of fine young dancers who later performed on Broadway or in the major ballet companies in New York. Among these were Joan McCracken and Zachary Solov. Solov danced for both the American Ballet and Ballet Theater and served for seven years as choreographer at the Metropolitan Opera. Littlefield restaged a number of classical ballets, including *The Fairy Doll* and *Daphnis and Chloe.* Her own best-known work was *Barn Dance,* which became part of the repertoire of Ballet Theater.

Ruth Page

Another American-born dancer and choreographer was Ruth Page, whose career centered in Chicago, although she danced throughout the United States and on a number of international tours.

Page studied with Adolph Bolm and Cecchetti; at an early age she accompanied Anna Pavlova on a South American tour and appeared in the Broadway show, *Music Box Revue.* She was a leading dancer for Bolm in the Chicago Opera, for

Diaghileff's Ballets Russes, and was the first American prima ballerina of the Metropolitan during the late 1920s. She toured widely through the United States and the Orient with Harald Kreutzberg and was a guest performer with the Federal Theater Project. In 1938, she formed the Page-Stone Ballet Company with Bentley Stone. Among her best-known works were *Frankie and Johnny, The Bells,* and *Billy Sunday,* all choreographed during the period of 1945 to 1948 and produced by Ballet Russe.

Ruth Page was a choreographer of opera-ballet and converted into ballet form such works as *Carmen, Salomé, The Barber of Seville,* and *The Merry Widow.* After the middle 1950s, her company, titled the Ruth Page Chicago Opera Ballet, made major annual tours, with outstanding guest artists such as George Skibine and Marjorie Tallchief.

Lew Christensen

Lew Christensen, who was born in Brigham City, Utah, in 1908, was one of the leading American male dancers and choreographers. Like Littlefield and Page, he did much to develop regional interest in ballet—in his case, in San Francisco. Christensen came of a musical and dancing family; his brothers, Harold and William, were also distinguished dancers and teachers. He received his training with an uncle and at the School of American Ballet in New York. He danced in vaudeville and was a member of the American Ballet Company in 1934, taking the title roles of *Orpheus* and *Apollo* in performances at the Metropolitan Opera House. He also was a soloist, choreographer, and ballet master for Ballet Caravan during the period of 1936 to 1940. It was at this time that he choreographed *Filling Station, Pocahontas,* and *Encounter*—all part of Kirstein's effort to develop young native choreographers. His choreography was marked by clean lines and a fine sense of clarity and design. His most famous dancing role was that of Pat Garret in Loring's *Billy the Kid.*

After serving as ballet master of Ballet Society in 1946–1948 and as a faculty member of the School of American Ballet, he joined the San Francisco Ballet, which had been founded by Adolph Bolm in 1933 and was therefore the oldest extant company in America. Though originally formed as an auxiliary to the Opera, the San Francisco Ballet is now an independent organization, but it continues to dance the ballets that are part of the San Francisco Opera. In 1951, Lew Christensen succeeded his brother William as director of the San Francisco Ballet and held this post for many years. There is a close tie between this company and the New York City Ballet Company. Kirstein has served as the artistic director of the West Coast company, and Christensen was a director of the New York City Ballet.

In addition to these dancers and choreographers, who played a strong part in developing regional ballet enterprises throughout the United States, several other choreographers of major stature were attached to the leading New York companies; they will be described in chapter 9, which presents an overview of recent trends in American and world ballet.

In summary, what was the effect of the first fifty years of the twentieth century in terms of the development of ballet as a theater art? It broke through the traditional ties that had imposed artistic sterility on it in Europe and that had weakened it as an expressive theatrical form through the radical reforms of Fokine and the brilliant productions of Diaghileff. During the 1920s, ballet became truly an international art of high esteem.

In America, the scene was marked, beginning in 1933, by an increasing amount of performing activity, which was to culminate in the establishment of several major companies. By 1950, there was little doubt that ballet had gained acceptance as an American art form, with native dancers, choreographers, and schools of high standards. There was now a large, vitally interested audience, both for American and for foreign companies. This did not mean that the art was now on a thoroughly solid footing. Although great progress had been made in the artistic quality of American ballet performance, and although a measure of stability had been achieved in audience support, there was still much work to be done in terms of expanding the audience and achieving a real measure of financial security for ballet schools and performing companies.

Notes

1 Jack Anderson, "The Joffrey Ballet Restores Nijinsky's 'Rite of Spring'," *New York Times,* October 25, 1987, p. 12-H.

2 Jennifer Dunning, "Honoring a Modern Dance Pioneer," *New York Times,* June 3, 1984, p. 14-H.

3 Michel Fokine, quoted in Agnes de Mille, *The Book of the Dance* (New York: Golden Press, 1963), p. 138.

4 For a fuller discussion of Fokine's principles, see Lincoln Kirstein, *Dance: A Short History of Classic Theatrical Dancing* (New York: G. P. Putnam's Sons, 1935), 272–79.

5 Fokine, quoted in de Mille, *Book of the Dance,* p. 143.

6 Kirstein, *Dance: A Short History,* p. 289.

7 Ibid.

8 Richard Philp, *New York Times,* October 26, 1975, p. 6-D.

9 Anatole Chujoy, *The Dance Encyclopedia* (New York: A. S. Barnes and Co., 1949), p. 358.

10 Cyril Beaumont, quoted in Chujoy, *Dance Encyclopedia,* p. 356.

11 John Martin, *John Martin's Book of the Dance* (New York: Tudor Publishing Co., 1963), p. 57.

12 Bernard Taper, *Balanchine* (New York: Harper and Row, 1963), p. 161.

13 Paul Holt, quoted in Anatole Chujoy, *The New York City Ballet* (New York: Alfred A. Knopf, 1953), p. 254.

14 Chujoy, *New York City Ballet,* p. 261.

15 For a fuller discussion of Ballet Theater, see *Dictionary of Modern Ballet,* ed. Selma Jeanne Cohen (New York: Tudor Publishing Co., 1959), pp. 51–54.

CHAPTER 9

Ballet Today

Has the look of ballet companies changed in the last 30 years? Where are the glamorous stars of old? What has become of corps dancers with dramatic impact? Has individual personality and temperament been sacrificed for a uniformity of look and a better technique? There are days of heated discussions among balletomanes about the new look of ballet companies and the glories of the way things used to be.[1]

THE BRIGHT PROMISE THAT SHONE FOR BALLET in the United States in 1950 was not an illusion. At that time, George Amberg commented that while there had been some form of ballet in America for over a century and a half, ballet as a native form of art was barely fifteen years old. It appeared as a consequence of the stimulus provided by the Ballet Russe and was aided by expert training in the classical idiom provided by leading Russian teachers: "Native talent emerged and an appreciative audience has developed and been consolidated. Recent attendances throughout the country have exceeded an estimated million and a half, not counting the enormous audience of the musical comedy."[2]

And, three years later, choreographer Agnes de Mille was to say, at a luncheon celebrating her best-selling *Dance to the Piper,* that dance in America had finally come of age. It was, at last, "stimulating, indigenous, and important" to the country; it offered a career that was respectable. More men would be going into the profession, able to expect a "normal, happy life. There will be copyright laws for choreography. There will be literature for dancing, and a real school of choreography. I as a dancer rejoice in all this."[3]

When the New York City Ballet offered its first season at the City Center, it was barely able to justify a two-week season. By 1955, its season had expanded to eight weeks; in the same season, Ballet Theater performed at the Metropolitan Opera House for three weeks. The Sadler's Wells Company filled the Metropolitan for five weeks, and a host of other companies from abroad had seasons in New York during the fall and winter months.

By 1967, the number of indigenous and visiting ballet companies had strikingly expanded. During the months of April and May alone, in New York City, balletgoers were able to see performances by five major companies. The British Royal Ballet, starring Rudolf Nureyev and Margot Fonteyn, was to give its longest season yet in New York City. Simultaneously, in the New York State Theater, also located in the Lincoln Center complex, the New York City Ballet Company was completing a highly successful New York season before going on an extended six-month tour. In May, the American Ballet Theater moved into the New York State Theater for four weeks. During the same season, two comparatively new but highly regarded companies, the Joffrey Ballet and the National Ballet of Washington, appeared at the City Center.

All this indicated that the audience for ballet had grown tremendously. It reflected the national interest which had given rise to a number of other major companies—in Boston, Philadelphia, San Francisco, Houston, and other cities—as well as dozens of surprisingly competent regional ballet companies throughout the country.

Throughout the 1970s and 1980s, ballet's popularity continued to grow dramatically. Established American companies broadened their audiences, lengthened their seasons, and toured widely. Glamorous foreign companies—from Holland, Denmark, Great Britain, Canada, the Soviet Union, and Germany—toured the United States regularly. Regional ballet was thriving as never before, and ballet superstars had captured new audiences for their art through popular films and major television ballet broadcasts.

As an indication of the popularity of ballet in the nation's leading cultural center, when the New York City Ballet reached its fortieth anniversary in May 1988, it marked the event with a gala three-week American Music Festival. The company presented twenty-one world premières by fourteen choreographers, two company premières by two other choreographers, and twelve ballets by Jerome Robbins and George Balanchine that were already in the repertoire. In addition, illustrating the close link between ballet and music, the festival included works of more than forty American composers ranging from Charles Ives to Ray Charles.[4] In the same year, the first New York International Festival of the Arts, a month-long celebration of international music, dance, theater, film, and television of the twentieth century, included eleven premières and some of the world's leading dancers from the companies of American Ballet Theater, Dance Theater of Harlem, Frankfurt Ballet, and the New York City Ballet, in addition to works by Merce Cunningham, Jean-Pierre Perreault, Pina Bausch Tanztheater, and Kazuo Ohno, among others.[5]

Yet, although ballet companies proliferated and audiences swelled as part of the nation's cultural explosion, the whole financial base for the art remained fragile and insecure. More than one company was forced to curtail its season, and strikes of musicians paralyzed major performing contracts. As the role of government and foundations grew increasingly significant in the early 1970s, Siegel summarized the trend:

> The fortunes of ballet's private benefactors became insufficient to cover its growing needs. Government and quasi-public agencies have taken over more and more of its huge deficits, with a corresponding pressure for more egalitarian artistic policies. Companies became institutions, totems. Whether they do good ballets or not seems to have little more effect on their survival than the whims of fashion and habit, politics, and civic virtue. Big ballet's role has quietly shifted from serving the artist to serving society.[6]

During the 1980s, although many ballet companies continued to flourish, others faced severe fiscal problems and were compelled to find new sources of income and new administrative strategies. Chapter 13 describes a number of these approaches.

New York City Ballet

Without question, the highest-ranking ballet company in the United States, and one which rates as a co-equal with the best in the world, is the New York City Ballet, formerly directed by George Balanchine and now under the artistic leadership of Peter Martins. Its early promise, described in the preceding chapter, has been amply fulfilled. It is a handsomely mounted, vigorous, and exciting company, with superb dancing skills, and impeccably directed. Both in its extensive home seasons at the New York City Center and, since 1964, the New York State Theater at Lincoln Center, and in its many tours abroad, it has been acclaimed by critics and public alike.

In a sense, the New York City Ballet's great strength—the brilliant direction it was given by Balanchine—was also regarded as its weakness. For a number of years, critics protested that the repertoire of the company was so dominated by Balanchine's extraordinary body of work that the ballets of other major choreographers were rarely included in the company's programs.

The feeling was frequently expressed that Balanchine and the company management disregarded the wishes of the ballet's patrons for more diversified programming. This was coupled with resentment at the company's refusal to announce in advance the names of those who would be dancing in specific ballets. In a sense, this represented Balanchine's unwillingness to embrace the star system and his belief that the dancing was more important than any single performer. Hughes wrote:

> Up to now the public has allowed the company to ignore worthy works by choreographers outside the New York City Ballet in favor of second-rate items by Mr. Balanchine and choreographers of his choice. But how long will the regular public pay to see *Western Symphony, Con Amore* and *Fanfare?* How long will it be willing to buy repetitions of pieces like these when the best works of Sir Frederick Ashton, Antony Tudor, and Agnes de Mille, to mention a few of Mr. Balanchine's contemporaries . . . are being ignored?[7]

The implication of such criticism was that the New York City Ballet company had flourished since its inception under a benevolent dictatorship. During the 1970s, this situation eased somewhat, with a substantial offering of works by such leading choreographers as Frederick Ashton, Antony Tudor, and Jerome Robbins. By the 1977–1978 season at Lincoln Center, of the forty-nine ballets offered during the fall-winter season, ten were choreographed by Robbins alone.

In 1978, a number of special programs offered by the New City Ballet were devoted solely to such Robbins works as *Afternoon of a Faun, The Concert, Dances at a Gathering,* and *The Cage.* Generally considered to be the ballet world's finest American-born choreographer, Robbins had also been immensely successful on the Broadway stage as director-choreographer of *West Side Story, Gypsy,* and *Fiddler on the Roof.* Later, Peter Martins, a Danish-born dancer who had joined the company during the 1970s as part of an invasion by several outstanding Danes (including Ib Andersen, Helgi Tomasson, and Adam Luders) was encouraged to choreograph several works. His work, *Lille Suite,* set to music by the Danish composer Carl Nielsen, was well received; in addition, Balanchine presented ballets by younger choreographers, such as Edward Villella's *Narkissos, La Guilande de Campra* of John Taras, or the *Irish Fantasy* and *Prologue* of Jacques d'Amboise.

Another area of concern was Balanchine's tendency always to feature the ballerina in his works. He had a series of female protegées and through the years guided such performers as Patricia McBride, Allegra Kent, Suzanne Farrell, and Gelsey Kirkland to stardom. He consistently justified the dominance of women in

New York City Ballet in *Raymonda Variations.* Choreography by George Balanchine.

ballet. In contrast to the earlier Russian period in which such stars as Nijinsky, Massine, or Lifar were featured, Balanchine frankly avowed that:

> The principle of classical ballet is woman. The woman is queen . . . The man is prince consort. . . . If the woman were less important, it would not be ballet. The woman's body is more flexible, there is more technique. Why? Why is Venus the goddess of love, not a man? That's the way it is. Woman is like that. They don't have to fight, go to war. Men can be generals if they want, or doctors, or whatever. But the woman's function is to fascinate men. . . .[8]

Despite this sexist view, so great was the public and critical appreciation of Balanchine's choreography and artistic direction of the company that he continued to perform in both roles well into his seventies. One of his unique contributions was to emphasize the *corps de ballet*. In his company, this ensemble, which formerly was seen almost as a muted background for the featured dancers, was given great emphasis. He employed in it only dancers with soloist capability, and he choreographed works that gave the members of the corps challenging and dynamic movement equal to the action and appeal of soloists. Another aspect of his brilliance was his musicality. A thirty-year member of the New York City Ballet's orchestra wrote, after Balanchine's death in 1983:

> . . . Mr. Balanchine used to urge people to come to the ballet to listen to the music and to regard the ballet as a concert. Music was the core, not only of Balanchine's ballets, but of his very life. He had studied at both music and ballet academies in Russia, and was both composer and choreographer of some early ballets there. He was a thorough musician able to make his own piano reductions of orchestra scores.[9]

After Balanchine: A New Era

Given his remarkable gifts and the degree to which the New York City Ballet was identified with Balanchine, when he died there was great apprehension about the future. *Time* commented:

> . . . Balanchine . . . was possibly the greatest choreographer of the century. He brilliantly synthesized ballet's elegant classical heritage with the explosive athletic energy of modern dance and the show-biz turns of jazz and tap. . . . Despite the size of its activities today, the City Ballet remains very much what it was at the beginning: a 104-member instrument of one man's artistic vision; in that, it is unique among the world's major companies.[10]

In a review of a book on his choreography published shortly before his death at age seventy-nine, Saal concluded that the Russian-born choreographer had made a "real revolution." He challenged the complacency of such powerful organizations as the Kirov and Bolshoi companies in Russia and the Royal Ballet in England, which had

. . . conserved an admirable tradition of theatrical dance and a handful of romantic fairy tales that are called classics since they constitute virtually the only legacy ballet has. But Balanchine whetted the appetite of audiences for more than diversity. Over 200 companies, including the Royal Ballet and the Kirov, dance Balanchine ballets now. Most of the new generation of choreographers are his (descendants). He is the fixed star by which all measure their positions and plot their progress.[11]

In the mid- and late 1980s, under the leadership of Jerome Robbins and Peter Martins (as co-ballet masters-in-chief, with Martins in charge of day-to-day operations), the New York City Ballet has continued to flourish, with much greater diversity in terms of work performed and with strong funding support and attendance. In terms of music, particularly, there has been an unusual breakthrough. While Martins prefers classical scores for his compositions, choreographing to music by Mozart, Bach, Rossini, and Handel, Robbins has been far more experimental and has choreographed works to music by Philip Glass and Steve Reich, both leading composers of the minimalist school. A second important change in the company has been Peter Martins's decision to encourage a much greater infusion of modern dance choreographers.

There has been criticism in some quarters of Martins's leadership of the company, including sharply divided assessments of the works performed at the American Music Festival. Schiff summarized the negative views, referring to the City Ballet's "artistic and moral" disarray and citing the firing of the company's managing director and withdrawal of a distinguished board member, as well as poor morale among many dancers. He argued that Balanchine's rigorous artistic and personal standards have been replaced by favoritism, sloppiness, and "vulgarity" in many new works in the repertoire and in daily rehearsal and performance.[12]

Schiff's attack was disputed by the *New York Times'* influential critic, Anna Kisselgoff, who drew up a detailed "tally sheet" of the post-Balanchine era and concluded that the legacy still lives: ". . . the house that Balanchine built still rests upon its original foundations."[13]

American Ballet Theater

Meanwhile, America's second great ballet company, American Ballet Theater, continued through the decades following mid-century with mixed triumphs and defeats. If anything, this company's major weakness has been the reverse of the criticism of the New York City Ballet—that throughout its history it *lacked* the consistently strong hand of a powerful artistic director.

After its period of greatest success in the 1940s and early 1950s, the American Ballet Theater experienced a time of great financial difficulty, with a gradual decline in the quality of its performances. Nonetheless, under the leadership of Lucia Chase, its codirector, it continued to tour widely and to perform some of the major ballet works of the modern era. Fortunately, it received substantial grants in the late 1960s from the National Council for the Arts on a matching-funds basis. This assistance was instrumental in helping the company maintain its extremely varied and expensive repertoire, including both classical and new, specially commissioned works.

Lacking a home of its own, American Ballet Theater has in recent years held seasons at the Lincoln Center's New York State Theater and Metropolitan Opera House, the New York City Center, and the Kennedy Center in Washington, where it has been the official company. In addition, it has toured widely both in the United States and Canada and has had frequent seasons abroad. It has always had a reputation for having a group of internationally renowned dancers in its company. In the 1970s, Ballet Theater continued this reputation, starring among others the great Danish dancer, Erik Bruhn, such outstanding ex-Soviet artists as Rudolf Nureyev, Mikhail Baryshnikov, and Natalia Makarova, and a number of leading American dancers, including Cynthia Gregory, Gelsey Kirkland, and Fernando Bujones.

Both Antony Tudor and Nora Kaye served during this period as associate artistic directors and continued the policy of choreographic eclecticism that has always characterized Ballet Theater. In the late 1970s, programs ranged from continuous weeks of such classics as *The Nutcracker, Giselle,* and *Swan Lake,* to programs featuring José Limón's *The Moor's Pavane,* Eliot Feld's *At Midnight,* and Twyla Tharp's *Push Comes to Shove.*

Despite financial adversity—which it has met in a variety of ways, including fund-raising galas in cities throughout the United States used to match challenge grants from the National Endowment for the Arts—American Ballet Theater has continued to thrive and tour. The company remains a repository of works by

American Ballet Theater in *Les Noces,* with choreography by Jerome Robbins to Igor Stravinsky's dance-cantata.

American Ballet Theater in *Helen of Troy*, choreographed by David Lichine to music by Offenbach. Photograph by Fred Fehl.

de Mille, Tudor, Robbins, Feld, Fokine, and other choreographers. In addition, it has sponsored a unique smaller touring company, Ballet Repertory Company, under the direction of George Englund. This group, founded with the assistance of the Touring Residency program of the National Endowment for the Arts, has toured widely, performing in many cities throughout the United States that had not seen professional ballet of high quality in many years.

A major change in direction for Ballet Theater came when Mikhail Baryshnikov became artistic director of the company in 1980. Having been trained and performed as a leading dancer in the Kirov Ballet, Baryshnikov left in 1974 for the West and became an instant star at Ballet Theater. Following an interlude in which he danced with the New York City Ballet for eighteen months, he returned to American Ballet Theater, succeeding Lucia Chase and Oliver Smith in the administrative role and also serving for a time as principal dancer.

Recognizing that while the New York City Ballet was known as a choreographer's company, American Ballet Theater was famed primarily for its dancing, Baryshnikov made *this* his primary concern from the outset. He rejected the guest star system and cast young corps members in leading roles. Reorganizing the company's school to take on a number of additional scholarship students, he initiated a choreographers' workshop and more rigorous rehearsals, which led to a visible improvement of the company's discipline, vitality, and precision, particularly among a number of the male soloists. Far from being simply a glamorous dancer who took on the assignment of a figurehead, Baryshnikov proved to be a strong and demanding administrator.

Through the 1980s, the company had extended seasons at the Metropolitan Opera House in New York and in other major cities in the United States and abroad. It survived recurrent crises, such as labor conflicts, financial problems, and contract disputes with principal dancers. Baryshnikov continued to dance through the mid-1980s, despite serious injuries, although he performed less with Ballet Theater itself than with his own small touring unit.

A number of the newer works have been critically acclaimed, such as Kenneth MacMillan's 1986 work, *Requiem,* a stunning theater piece choreographed to an Andrew Lloyd Webber score, with twenty-eight dancers, an orchestra, a forty-voice choir in the pit, and three vocalists onstage. Typically, in a recent nine-week season in New York, Ballet Theater presented four new ballets, one by David Gordon (primarily a modern dancer), and two successful gala evenings. In 1988, it unveiled a new work, *The Informer,* by Agnes de Mille, who had suffered a debilitating stroke thirteen years before but who had indomitably fought back to resume an active creative life. Thus, it continued under Baryshnikov's leadership to be one of the premiere ballet companies in the world, although it was announced in June 1989 that Baryshnikov would be leaving the company within a year to move more fully into an acting career.

Smaller Ballet Companies

On a much smaller scale, there has always been a need for more modest ballet companies. Walter Terry commented that small-scale companies are able to tour both in the United States and abroad with relative ease:

> For years and years in America, there has always been a need for small ballet units, for inexpensive ensembles which could bring classical ballet at budget prices to towns, high school auditoriums, women's clubs. So there is nothing really new about the small-size ballet groups—what is new is what they used to dance and what they dance now. . . .[14]

In the past, Terry wrote, such companies built their programs around abridged versions of the Russian classics, extracts from famous works, all sorts of *grands pas de deux,* and sometimes a novelty version of a dramatic or operatic work. Today, however, the small-scale companies are embarking on fresh, creative choreographic works that are particularly appropriate for their personnel and skills. Obviously, the huge ballet companies of the world—such as the New York City Ballet, the Royal Danish Ballet, the Royal Ballet of Britain, or the Bolshoi Ballet, do the "great old classics or the new spectacle ballets" better than the smaller groups. However, these are extremely expensive, and the larger companies are less likely to risk commissioning new works than the small-scale companies.

Joffrey and Harkness Ballets

Two such companies, founded in the 1950s and 1960s, were the Joffrey Ballet (formerly known as the City Center Joffrey Ballet), and the Harkness Ballet, sponsored by the Rebekah Harkness Foundation. Curiously, these two companies, each with fewer than forty dancers, had a closely intertwined past.

Robert Joffrey, a gifted young dancer who had studied at the School of American Ballet and performed with Roland Petit's Ballets de Paris during its New York engagement, began his own school, the American Ballet Center, in New York in 1952. In 1956, he set out with six dancers in a rented station wagon as the Robert Joffrey Ballet. They performed in twenty-three different locations in eleven states; after ten consecutive tours, they appeared in more than 400 cities in forty-eight states. The company also toured the Near and Far East for the State Department, appeared at the Kirov Theater in Leningrad as part of a ten-week tour of Soviet Russia, and gave a command performance at the White House.

In 1964, the Harkness Foundation, which had given financial support to the company for two years, wished to give its name to the company. When Joffrey refused this arrangement, the Foundation set up a separate Harkness Ballet, which drew away not only many of Joffrey's better dancers, but also the rights to many of the ballets that had been produced by the company. Fortunately, Joffrey was able to rebuild his company quickly, using many of the talented dancers in his Ballet School, and he was given assistance by the Ford Foundation in reestablishing the company.

In 1966, the New York City Center formally affiliated itself with the Joffrey Ballet; this young, experimental company now had a permanent home and the promise of a rich future. Joffrey's chief choreographer became Gerald Arpino, a fresh and exciting talent whose major works included *Viva Vivaldi, Sea Shadow, Secret Places, The Clowns,* and *Trinity.*

Meanwhile, the newly named Harkness Ballet, which consisted largely of Joffrey's original dancers and repertoire, began in 1964 with the assistance of a grant of $1 million from the Harkness Foundation to be spread over a ten-year period. The company was noted for its brilliant productions, with colorful and handsomely designed costumes, decor, and lighting. For a period of time, it received favorable critical reviews, but during the 1970s, it appeared to reach a point of artistic sterility, declined in reputation as a leading ballet company, and ultimately disbanded. The Harkness Foundation also established a school of ballet at Harkness House in New York City, under the direction of Patricia Wilde and with leading artist-teachers on the faculty. The elaborately remodeled and decorated mansion which housed the school also held an exhibition gallery for dance documents, art, scenery, and costume designs. It served as the base for the Harkness Training and Research Center, concerned with scientific analysis of movement in classical ballet training.

Joffrey's Success in the 1970s and 1980s

In contrast, the Joffrey Ballet continued to be an artistically vital and successful organization, noted in particular for the variety of its choreography. As Robert Joffrey withdrew from choreographing original ballets, Gerald Arpino assumed the role of resident choreographer during the 1970s. His approach at this time was regarded as typical of the Joffrey spirit—vital, trendy, breezy, and committed to classical dance movement. In terms of repertoire, the company ranged from reviving major works of past centuries, to serving as a repository for the great

City Center Joffrey Ballet in the multimedia production of *Astarte*, with choreography by Robert Joffrey, score by the rock group, The Crome Syrcus, kinetic scenery by Thomas Skelton, and projected photography by Gardner Compton. Tinette Singleton and Maximiliano Zomosa are featured. Photograph by Herbert Migdoll.

modern ballets of the twentieth century, to commissioning new ballets by the most avant-garde modern dance choreographers.

In the late 1970s, for example, the company sponsored an all-American season at the New York City Center, with thirty ballets by such American choreographers as Jerome Robbins, Agnes de Mille, Arpino, and modern dancers Twyla Tharp and Anna Sokolow. However, it also presented revivals of Leonide Massine's *Parade, The Green Table* by Kurt Jooss, and numerous other works by Frederick Ashton, Antony Tudor, John Cranko and other leading international choreographers. In

City Center Joffrey Ballet in *The Clowns*, choreographed by Gerald Arpino. Photograph by James Howell.

contrast to the larger companies, the Joffrey Ballet emphasized a no-star policy, with dancers listed in the programs alphabetically.

By the early 1980s, behind American Ballet Theater and the New York City Ballet, the Joffrey Company gained widespread recognition as America's third major ballet company. Without secure funding initially and with no master plan, it had evolved and survived through the years, maintaining a high level of artistic quality and popular support. In 1982, it acquired a new base of operations at the Los Angeles Music Center, with substantial financial backing from a new California board of trustees. Arpino continued to grow as a choreographer, with numerous new ballets ranging from pure dance and classical works to ballets fitted to music with a pop veneer and often sensual, erotic appeal. In addition, the Joffrey Company has continued to feature ballets by Frederic Ashton, including such works as *Fille Mal Gardée, Facade, Les Patineurs,* and *A Wedding Bouquet* in the late 1980s. When Joffrey died in 1988, Arpino succeeded him as artistic director.

Dance Theater of Harlem

A unique, outstanding American ballet company based in New York City is the Dance Theater of Harlem. Founded in 1968 by Arthur Mitchell, a leading black solo dancer with the New York City Ballet, Dance Theater was initially a school designed to encourage gifted young blacks to enter the ballet field. Working closely

City Center Joffrey Ballet performs in Agnes de Mille's famous work, *Rodeo*, to music by Aaron Copland. Courtesy Shubert Theater, Philadelphia.

with Mitchell was Karel Shook, an American-born teacher and ballet master who had performed with the Ballet Russe de Monte Carlo and the Dutch National Ballet and had also taught ballet at the Katherine Dunham School. Shook was one of the few white ballet teachers to instruct and encourage blacks in the 1950s, a period when American ballet was almost exclusively the province of white dancers.[15]

Classes were held at first in a barren, cold garage in Harlem, but with a grant from the Ford Foundation, the school moved to better quarters, ultimately becoming a fully accredited professional training school. Three years later, the performing company itself was formed and, following a period of struggle to gain acceptance and support, became recognized as a leading contemporary ballet troupe. Under Mitchell's artistic direction, the company's repertoire was initially heavily based on the works of George Balanchine, who encouraged and assisted it. Over the years, its programs diversified to include classic ballets (including excerpts of *Paquita* and *Swan Lake,* and a Creole version of *Giselle*); John Taras's new version of *Firebird;* Geoffrey Holder's *Banda,* based on voodoo ritual; Valerie Bettis's *A Streetcar Named Desire;* John Butler's *Othello;* Agnes de Mille's *Fall River Legend;* and numerous other revivals and new works by leading ballet and modern dance choreographers.

Having weathered fiscal crises and even a temporary suspension of its performing activities in the late 1970s, with the help of grants from the National

Endowment for the Arts, the New York State Council on the Arts, and other corporations and foundations, the Dance Theater of Harlem regained financial stability and continues to be a recognized and respected ballet company. Initially composed predominantly of black dancers, today the company has several white dancers as well; a number of its graduates have moved on to perform with other companies. Apart from its own artistic success, the Harlem group has demonstrated the point that motivated Mitchell and Shook at its inception—that blacks are fully capable of performing classical ballet at its highest level.

The Feld Ballet

Another outstanding American company, the Feld Ballet, was founded by dancer–choreographer Elliot Feld in New York in 1974. It made its debut in the New York Shakespeare Festival's Newman Theater and has since used the Joyce Theater, a former motion-picture theater rebuilt expressly for dance, as its permanent home. A veteran choreographer who has composed over fifty ballets, many of them for American Ballet Theater, Feld favors a youthful, athletic company of dancers and is extremely innovative in terms of stage design, music, and even costuming. Some

Feld Ballet performance of Elliot Feld's work, *Half-Time*, to music by Morton Gould. Courtesy Shubert Theater, Philadelphia. Photograph by Lois Greenfield.

critics regard him as closer to the experimental modern dance tradition than to ballet, citing his use of sneakers in some works rather than ballet slippers, or of elbow and knee pads, and his frequent use of music by the minimalist composer, Steve Reich, as well as movement taken from outside the ballet tradition.

However, Feld has stressed his intention to remain within the classical ballet idiom, and his ballets require classically trained dancers. His own choreography includes work that is brilliant, clean-cut, highly imaginative, and audience-pleasing, set to music by such diversified composers as Ives, Hindemith, Mahler, Bach, and Copland. Among the Feld company's accomplishments has been the founding of the New Ballet School, a tuition-free professional ballet training program that draws most of its talent from the New York City public schools.

Other American Ballet Companies

In addition to these companies, there are several other important ballet organizations in cities throughout the United States. Among these are the San Francisco Ballet, the Boston Ballet, the Pennsylvania Ballet in Philadelphia (briefly linked to the Milwaukee Ballet), the Ohio Ballet, the Los Angeles Ballet, the San José-Cleveland Ballet, and others.

San Francisco Ballet

The early development of the San Francisco Ballet was discussed in chapter 8. While Lew Christensen retained artistic direction of the company for over twenty years, he was joined in 1973 by Michael Smuin, former principal dancer and choreographer with American Ballet Theater, as associate director. The San Francisco Ballet performs the works of many choreographers, including a number of ballets created originally for the New York City Ballet. It has gone on a number of federally sponsored tours in the United States, which, together with a repertory season of several weeks in San Francisco and a commitment to its Opera, means that the company has had regular employment for as much as forty weeks during the year. Even without foreign tours—which many companies rely on to provide more performing time and income—this has given the San Francisco Ballet dancers and staff substantial income and security during the year.

Artistically, the company is highly regarded. Clive Barnes wrote:

> The impression the company gives is one of joyous youth. They are beautifully trained dancers. The men have a buoyant elegance, with big broad jumps and an attractive stylistic openness. The women have something of the same directness and power. . . . These San Franciscans are such fun. When they dance they put their hearts and muscles into it. They care. It shows.[16]

The company's eclectic choreographic works have been widely applauded, ranging from full-length revivals of *Swan Lake* and *The Nutcracker* to twentieth-century classics by Ashton, Balanchine, and other leading choreographers and newer works by its own composers, including Smuin. Like the Joffrey, the San Francisco company does not rely on a star system; instead, it has attempted to build a true ensemble company, with marked success.

Evidence of the company's success at home was the San Francisco Ballet's ability to raise funds to construct a new company center and school building, at a cost of $11.5 million, next to the Opera House in the city's downtown Performing Arts Center. Civic leaders, foundations, and wealthy patrons joined together to raise the funds in record time, with substantial amounts set aside for building maintenance expenses and plans in the works to seek endowment funds through a challenge grant from the National Endowment for the Arts.

Boston Ballet

A more recently formed company is the Boston Ballet, founded by E. Virginia Williams. Originally known as the New England Civic Ballet, this company received several major Ford Foundation grants and developed a strong list of subscribers and a number of bookings that enabled it to employ its dancers regularly from October through April.

One of the major problems of new ballet companies is the task of building up a repertoire for performance. Unlike the situation facing a new opera company, symphony orchestra, or drama group, there is no convenient supply of ballet works as part of a standard repertoire which may readily be performed by such fledgling ballet organizations. The problem is twofold: acquiring rights to the ballet, and also being able to mount it properly. In the case of the Boston, Philadelphia, and Washington companies, Balanchine made a large number of his own ballets available and, in some cases, arranged to have leading dancers of the New York City Ballet visit them as guest performers.

Thus, the Boston Ballet has performed Balanchine's *Symphony in C* and *Apollo,* with Edward Villella and Patricia McBride of the New York company as guest artists. Other works presented by the Boston Ballet have included Talley Beatty's *Phoebe Snow,* August Bournonville's classic *Flower Festival at Genzano (Pas de Deux),* and new works that were specially choreographed by John Butler, Anna Sokolow, and Joyce Trisler. Over the years, the company developed a special relationship with Agnes de Mille; in 1977, it gave a special program devoted solely to her works.

In the late 1970s, the identity of the Boston Ballet was sharply altered under the cosmopolitan influence of a French codirector, Violette Verdy, who had been a leading dancer with the New York City Ballet for almost twenty years. Having toured the Far East, Mideast, and Europe, the company had an extended New York debut and initiated plans to expand its budget and the number of its dancers. However, the costs of touring and a decline in subscription renewals at home led to turmoil in the company's administration. Bruce Marks, who had spent nine years as director of Ballet West in Utah, was appointed artistic director in 1985. Since then, reorganization of the School of the Boston Ballet and its syllabus, appointment of Bruce Wells as associate director, and a thorough reordering of company members have led to renewed audience enthusiasm and financial stability.

A five-year plan developed by Marks and Wells included increased community involvement and service to neighborhood children, providing rehearsal space for other Boston dance companies, a capital gifts campaign to renovate studios in the Boston Center for the Arts, and

> . . . plans for an international choreography competition for the 1987–1988 season; the addition of works to the repertoire by Balanchine, Béjart, Cullberg, Kylián, Landers, and Tudor, and a twenty-fifth anniversary memorial to E. Virginia Williams, in the form of an evening-length ballet version of Der Rosenkavalier, to be choreographed by Marks and Wells.[17]

Pennsylvania Ballet

The Pennsylvania Ballet was founded in Philadelphia in 1962 under the direction of Barbara Linshes Weisberger, with George Balanchine as artistic consultant. After only three years, it was providing more continuous employment for its dancers than all but one United States company—the San Francisco Ballet. Its Philadelphia performances were staged at the Academy of Music, and in the 1970s it also assumed the unique position of being New York City's unofficial fourth major ballet company by becoming the resident ballet company of the Brooklyn Academy of Music.

A small company, with only about thirty dancers, the Pennsylvania Ballet nonetheless earned a reputation for versatility. Its repertoire included many ballets by Balanchine, important contemporary works that have been performed by other companies, and a number of original dances specifically choreographed for the Pennsylvania group itself—including works by the company's artistic director, Benjamin Harkavy, and ballets by Gene Hill Sagan, Margo Sappington, and others. The Pennsylvania Ballet had considerable funding support at the outset from the Ford Foundation, which permitted it to develop at its own pace and not be pressured into fast money, guest-artist promotions.

In the early 1980s, Harkavy, who had founded the Netherlands Dance Theater and had been artistic director of the Royal Winnipeg Ballet and the Harkness Ballet, was joined by Lupe Serrano, formerly a prima ballerina with American Ballet Theater, to head the company's school and apprentice program. Like a number of other companies at this time, the Pennsylvania Ballet went through a severe financial crisis, with an intermission of three months during which all personnel were released and the 1982 spring season was canceled. Since then, the company has been reorganized on a sound financial basis. In 1987, it was formally joined with the Milwaukee Ballet, forming a merged performing group to present seasons in both cities as well as other activities in their home cities on an independent basis. However, this experimental arrangement did not prove successful and was ended in March 1989.

Ohio Ballet

Founded in 1968 as an ensemble of eight part-time dancers, called the Chamber Ballet, this company has expanded to sixteen fully professional performers under the artistic direction of Heinz Poll, a German-born dancer and choreographer. Its repertoire consisted mostly of Poll's work, although it also included varied ballets by Gerald Arpino, Ruthanna Boris, Paul Taylor, and other contemporary choreographers.

What is unusual about the Ohio Ballet is its relationship with the University of Akron's Dance Institute. At first, all company members were students in this program or the university itself, and many of the dancers hold Bachelor of Fine Arts degrees from it. By the late 1970s, the programs were closely integrated. Although the university gives the Ohio Ballet no direct funding, it provides rent-free space, a portion of the artistic director's salary, and services such as utilities, maintenance, and storage, all valued at about $50,000 a year. In addition, the company is able to use Thomas Hall, a spectacular university theater built in 1973 at a cost of $13.9 million, for its rehearsals and performances at the lowest possible rate. In return, Salisbury pointed out, the ballet company enhances the cultural image of Akron University by carrying its name on tour and in all promotional materials.[18] Clearly, the Ohio Ballet provides a model of cooperation between the university and the performing arts that other companies and universities might do well to examine.

The Ohio Ballet has toured widely. In New York, for example, it has performed at various universities, the Brooklyn Academy of Music, the Joyce Theater in Manhattan, and nearby Jacob's Pillow. In the mid- and late 1980s, it made increasing use of works choreographed by modern dancers, including Paul Taylor, Merce Cunningham, Anna Sokolow, Kathryn Posin, and, more recently, Laura Dean and Molissa Fenley.

Los Angeles Ballet

Another relatively new company founded in the early 1970s, the Los Angeles Ballet has toured widely, with the assistance of the Dance Touring Program of the National Endowment for the Arts. However, it also provides substantial seasons in Los Angeles as a residential company, with financial support from the City and County of Los Angeles. Under the artistic direction of John Clifford, formerly a leading dancer with the New York City Ballet, it has a considerable number of Balanchine works in its repertoire of approximately fifty-five ballets. In addition, Clifford has choreographed a number of new works for the company, including several which represent updated versions of older ballets, such as Balanchine's *Apollo,* Nijinsky and Robbins ballets of *Afternoon of a Faun,* and Ashton's *Illuminations.*

San José-Cleveland Ballet

Founded in 1976 by Ian Horvath, artistic director, and Dennis Nahat, associate director and resident choreographer, both best known as leading dancers with American Ballet Theater, the Cleveland Ballet joined forces with the city of San José, California, several years later. This coventure between the California and Ohio cities represents a strategy borrowed from the business world—the corporate merger. Through it, the Cleveland company, which continues to use that name when performing in its home territory, sought to combat such problems as rising costs of touring, diminishing production values stemming from too much time on the road, and similar concerns.

With additional support in the San José area (a region rich in the arts and home to California's oldest symphony orchestra as well as opera and theater companies), the Cleveland company was able to add audiences and financial resources and extend the guaranteed performing season for its dancers. Now under Nahat's leadership as artistic director, the company encompasses work by both classical and modern choreographers and has plans to expand its annual budget to over $6 million and its number of dancers from thirty-seven to forty-three. Hardy pointed out that while other companies have developed second-home partnerships, the San José–Cleveland pairing has several distinguishing features:

> The two boards of trustees maintain independent funding activities and serve very different cities. They share an artistic product and Andrew Bales, president of the company, who is a gifted administrator. Long-range plans percolate with the stimulating dynamics that are evolving between the two complementary boards. The Clevelanders have gained know-how through years of overcoming obstacles. The Californians bring a freshness and dash that spark new possibilities. . . .[19]

Washington Ballet

Another relatively small ballet company, the Washington Ballet was founded in 1976 with a small group of talented dancers who had been trained in the Washington School of Ballet by Mary Day and her teacher Lisa Gardner. After a decade of performing, the company expanded in terms of numbers of dancers and budget, with thirty-eight contract weeks during the year. It was the first American ballet company to tour the People's Republic of China and has operated without financial loss for its entire existence. It also has toured throughout the Far East and in Central and South America, and in 1986 it announced plans to open a branch of its school in Baltimore and to include twelve performances a year in that city. The repertoire consists of a number of works by Choo San Goh, a resident choreographer, along with several ballets by Balanchine, and emphasizes a classical approach to ballet with a contemporary flavor.

Metropolitan Opera Ballet

The Metropolitan management has made an effort, through the years, to strengthen its ballet component so that it would be reasonably comparable to the ballet of leading European opera houses. During the 1930s, George Balanchine's and Lincoln Kirstein's American Ballet was the opera's ballet unit and offered separate all-ballet evenings at the Metropolitan. In the early 1950s, as part of an effort to have ballet become an increasingly important part of its staged performances, Janet Collins, a leading black choreographer, assumed leadership of the dance component. Then, for several years, Zachary Solov was responsible for ballet at the opera and succeeded in mounting exciting ballets as part of such operas as *Eugen Onegin, Samson and Delilah,*

Carmen, Rigoletto, La Perichole, La Traviata, and *Faust.* Leading ballerinas of the New York City Ballet or Ballet Theater, such as Mary Ellen Moylan, Carmen de Lavallade, Alicia Markova, and Melissa Hayden, appeared in these productions.

In 1963, Markova became director of the Metropolitan Opera Ballet and succeeded in strengthening its artistic quality. In the late 1970s, Norbert Vesak, a Canadian-born choreographer attached to the Royal Winnipeg Ballet who had also worked with the San Francisco Opera Ballet, was made artistic director. One of his projects was to develop a smaller Opera Ballet Ensemble which would tour as an independent performing unit, thus providing additional employment for the dancers and additional revenue for the ballet operation. However, through the years, dancing at the Metropolitan has generally suffered from the lack of a consistent management policy that would support the building of a strong permanent company and that would encourage separate ballet performances in the opera house as a regular feature. In general, this has been true of other opera companies throughout the United States, such as those in Chicago and San Francisco, which, although they have given a degree of support to ballet, have seen it essentially as part of the total opera complex rather than an independent art form.

Ballet West. This company began as the Utah Civic Ballet, with many of its first dancers having been trained in the Department of Ballet at the University of Utah. With the assistance of a Ford Foundation grant, it made the transition to professional status in the 1960s. Influenced heavily by the Christensen brothers, it tours widely throughout the West and Southwest from its home base in Salt Lake City. It has also made a successful European tour and performed on national television; it is regarded as the classical ballet company of the Rocky Mountain States. In addition to reviving major works of the past, Ballet West is developing a body of new contemporary choreography in its repertoire. It also offers an intensive summer training program in Aspen/Snowmass, Colorado, where the company gives a summer performance season.

Atlanta Ballet. A young and growing company in the southern region of the United States, the Atlanta Ballet held its first full season in 1977–1978, featuring a production of *Carmina Burana, Swan Lake Act II, The Nutcracker,* and other classic works. In addition, the company has been augmented by other Atlanta dance and musical performing groups and has sponsored performances by premier dancers of American Ballet Theater and the Pennsylvania Ballet.

While it is not possible to describe all other American companies in detail, several should be briefly mentioned: the Houston Ballet, a widely touring company under the direction of Ben Stevenson, formerly of the Sadler's Wells Ballet; the Miami City Ballet, directed by Edward Villella, which had its first season in 1987; Pittsburgh Ballet Theater, a veteran company under the artistic direction of Patricia Wilde which expanded recently through a dual-city residency with Savannah, Georgia, as well as through the acquisition of a $2 million studio/office complex and a subsequent move into a new performance space; the Tulsa Ballet Theater, directed by Roman Jasinski and Moscelyne Larkin, former members of the original Ballet

Russe and Ballet Russe de Monte Carlo, and which has maintained revivals of works by Fokine, Massine, Lichine, and Lifar in its repertoire; and the Pacific Northwest Ballet, a respected company directed by Kent Stowell and Francia Russell, formerly dancers with the New York City Ballet, and with a repertoire drawn heavily from Balanchine ballets and other works by contemporary choreographers.

Regional Ballet

To gain a full picture of the growth of ballet in the United States, it is necessary to look at what appears to be a uniquely American phenomeon—the development of an extensive network of highly successful regional ballet companies.

The term *regional ballet* is usually applied to those companies scattered throughout the United States which consist largely of nonsalaried dancers and directors, although their directors may occasionally perform professionally and may indeed have had extensive performing experience. They often are supported by organizations of local community residents who are interested in the arts and who contribute their services. They provide performance opportunities to local dancers and help to promote local interest in ballet. They do not tour nationally, although there is often interchange among regions.

In general, two types of regional ballet companies exist: those whose members come from a single school, and those whose members may come from several schools. Invariably, they are incorporated as nonprofit organizations, and whatever income may be received through performance does not go back to the school but goes to production expenses—costuming, scenery, rent for rehearsal space, and similar costs. Usually, such companies require their members to pay annual dues, to sign a contract guaranteeing their commitment to the group, and to observe a rigorous schedule of classes and performances.

The regional ballet movement began with the formation of the Atlanta Civic Ballet in 1929 by a dedicated teacher and choreographer, Dorothy Alexander. Since then, the movement has swept the country. In 1955 there were 30 such companies, and by 1965 there were over 200 regional ballet groups. The growth continues steadily; in 1966, for example, the Southeastern Regional Ballet Association numbered 22 member companies. In the following year the number climbed to 25; the new groups were the City Center Ballet of Tampa, Florida; the Huntsville, Alabama, Civic Ballet; and the Savannah, Georgia, Civic Ballet.

Most regional ballet companies offer a series of public performances during the year; sometimes their directors give lectures or demonstrations throughout their region to heighten interest in ballet. Other activities of regional ballet companies include publishing newsletters or newspapers, making scenery, and being involved with all the business aspects of scheduling performances. Often, nondancers in the community, such as lawyers, businesspeople, and other professionals, are extremely helpful in filling committee positions involving publicity, fund raising, transportation, printing of programs and tickets, stage crew tasks, set design and construction, and the like.

One of the highlights each year for regional ballet companies is participation in festivals sponsored by regional ballet associations. The Southeast Regional Ballet

Association was the first of these to be formed, and it has held an annual festival since 1956. Since then, four other associations have been established—the Northeast, Southwest, Southeast, and Pacific and Mid-States Regional Ballet Associations.

In 1963, the National Association for Regional Ballet (NARB) was founded, and in 1972 it received its first major grant from the National Endowment for the Arts. By the late 1970s, the NARB had 120 member companies; Doris Hering described their criteria for affiliation:

> [Each member company] consists of at least 12 dancers, had been incorporated for at least one year before applying for membership, and had given at least one performance for a paying public prior to membership. A company may be admitted as a performing member or as an intern member, which means it needs to gain strength.
>
> [To promote professionalism], the NARB has a Professional Wing consisting of those companies that maintain at least 12 paid dancers under contract for 30 weeks or more and that give between 10 and 20 performances a year (theater size being a factor) in their home communities. They also maintain a minimum budget of $120,000 per year and have three people (artistic director, business manager, and technical director) under annual contract.[20]

Customarily, yearly fees are paid by member companies to support annual festivals, which represent a climax for the total year's activity. Master classes, rehearsals, symposiums, and workshops are held, with, of course, the main event being performances by member companies. Works are selected through adjudication by experts, and customarily the general public is admitted to gala performances, while only association members view workshop or showcase performances.

Large audiences, often numbering several thousand, usually view regional ballet festivals, particularly the gala events. In addition, such events frequently offer workshops and special classes for teachers and students. Often, these are in areas other than traditional ballet technique; they may include modern dance, jazz, Oriental, and character dancing. The interchange that takes place among directors and teachers provides an important stimulus to the work they carry on in their own regions.

In addition, each year the NARB sponsors two Craft of Choreography conferences. Emphasis is given to dance technique and improvisation, music, lighting, costume design, and choreographic problem solving within a workshop setting and with lecture-demonstrations by leading experts.

The goals of regional ballet companies are varied. However, a fairly representative statement of purpose is that of the Richmond, Virginia, Ballet Impromptu:

1. To establish a regional ballet company which shall be adjudicated in festival competition.
2. To present ballet programs of the highest quality for adults and children.
3. To elevate the art of the regional performing dancer to the highest degree possible.
4. To provide a medium of expression for regional choreographers, designers, musicians, and dancers.

5. To stimulate interest and support of ballet and ballet schools.

6. To solicit and raise funds to further these purposes.

Probably the fifth purpose, that of stimulating interest and support of ballet, is of greatest importance to those concerned with the expansion of dance as a performing art today. The growth of larger, professional companies around the United States must in large measure be supported by the existence of knowledgeable and enthusiastic audiences, young and old, throughout the country. Without question, a major contribution of the regional ballet movement has been to develop such audiences—and in this effort they have been highly successful.

Outstanding Foreign Ballet Companies

In addition to the aforementioned American ballet companies, any review of the contemporary ballet scene must include a number of important ballet companies in other countries.

In the highest rank are such companies as the Leningrad Kirov Ballet and the Bolshoi Ballet of Moscow, the Royal Ballet of England, and the Royal Danish Ballet. Close behind them are three strong Canadian companies—the National Ballet of Canada, Les Grands Ballets Canadiens, and the Winnipeg Royal Ballet— the Paris Opéra Ballet, Ballet National de Marseilles, the Netherlands Dance Theater and Dutch National Ballet, Ballet Rambert and Sadler's Wells Royal Ballet, and a number of other smaller or newer companies in Europe, Australia, Latin America, and the Orient.

In a second category of companies with a strong ethnic or folk orientation are such groups as the Hungarian National Ballet; Kolo, the Yugoslav company; the Ballet Folklorico of Mexico; the Moiseyev Dance Company of Russia; Antonio and his Ballets de Madrid; the Philippine Folk Dance company, Bayanihan; and many smaller companies or solo performers, particularly of Oriental and Eastern dance forms.

Russian Ballet

Apart from their leading role in nineteenth and early twentieth-century ballet and the fact that for many years ballet in this country was regarded as synonymous with Russia, Soviet dancers have had another unusual impact on American ballet through their defectors. Rudolf Nureyev's leap into the Western world at Paris's Le Bourget Airport in 1961 was the first in a series of departures by great Russian dancers who sought greater personal and artistic freedom in the West. Others included Natalia Makarova, Mikhail Baryshnikov, and Galina and Valery Panov of the Kirov Ballet, and Alexander Godunov and Leonid and Valentina Koslov of the Bolshoi company. Despite these defections, the two major Russian ballet organizations remain in the top flight of international dance institutions.

Bolshoi Ballet

For most of its history, the Bolshoi Ballet of Moscow was regarded as second to the more celebrated Maryinsky Ballet in St. Petersburg. Even today, there is a strong feeling of competition between the Bolshoi and Leningrad's Kirov Ballet, as the Maryinsky is now called. Yet most regard the Bolshoi as preeminent today. It is a huge company; when it first came to America, it brought over 135 dancers and sent its famous ballet master, Asaf Messerer, six weeks in advance of the rest of the group to train an additional 65 American dancers for lesser roles in such giant spectacles as the full-length *Spartacus*.

It is brilliantly trained in the classical ballet technique; with their better-subsidized schools, the Russians have a tremendous advantage in the development of sheer dancing ability. The general level of Russian performance is superb; the men in particular are capable of dancing with great zest and vigor—in an almost flamboyant style, and with unbelievable athleticism. The ballerinas of the Bolshoi, Galina Ulanova (as legendary for her time as Pavlova) and, in more recent years, Raissa Struchkova and the magnificent Maya Plisetskaya, are among the very top rank of world dancers. The productions are splendid and the entire effect highly theatrical.

Yet, for years, those visitors who saw the Bolshoi perform in Moscow or who saw it when it visited Western Europe in 1956 or embarked on its first tour to the United States in 1959 were highly critical of its choreography. Of all the nations of the world, Russia, which underwent a national revolution in 1917, has been the most determinedly conservative in its approach to the arts. This has had two effects on its ballet choreography. First, the Bolshoi has continued until recently to base its repertoire very heavily on the great works of the Romantic era—such ballets as *Giselle, The Sleeping Beauty, Raymonda, Swan Lake,* and *Don Quixote.* Even when works have been choreographed in fairly recent times, they have dealt heavily with bird-maidens, gnomes, goblins, fairy princesses and godmothers, and pastoral romances.

A second preoccupation in more recent choreography has been dramatic subject matter that served the point of view of the Soviet state. Just as in Russian painting, literature, and sculpture, the ballets are expected to contribute in some way to Socialist ideology; Russians are serious about their art and usually expect that it present a recognizable image or narrative. The leading choreographer of the Bolshoi, Yuri Grigorovich, commented that while he regarded pure classical ballet as the "highest form of dance," for him this did not mean plotless ballet: "While I feel there can exist, must exist, dance form without subject matter, for myself I am interested in the total theatrical aspect, in a ballet theater that has a literary as well as a dance component."[21]

And, whenever possible, this literary component must be made to support Soviet doctrine. Thus, *Romeo and Juliet,* choreographed in 1946 by Lavrovsky, has been interpreted as an aspect of the class struggle; the Soviet ballet version of *Othello,* produced by Chabukiani, has similarly been seen as an example of racial conflict.

The initial impression many had of the Bolshoi's choreography was that it was ponderous, tedious, and, while technically excellent, so stodgy and traditional that it represented a throwback to the nineteenth century. Hering commented in 1959:

Sometimes we felt as though we were returning to a neglected and worthy esthetic—the esthetic of realism. Sometimes that very realism seemed to be nothing more than a repository for outmoded sets, costumes and gestures . . . their reliance upon narrative mime seemed uncomfortably melodramatic . . . sometimes their approach to pure dance passages was merely athletic, with no sense of character revelation or dramatic furtherance. . . .[22]

Gradually, however, as the Bolshoi dancers and choreographers have been exposed to the performances of British and American companies—including the Jerome Robbins State Department tour of Russia in the early 1960s—they appear to have broadened their view of choreographic possibilities. While they still mount huge spectacles and present revivals of classical works as a major feature of their repertoire, they are demonstrating a greater level of inventiveness, adventurousness, and humor.

In the 1980s, the Bolshoi was transformed by the addition of many exciting younger dancers, including the brilliant Irek Mukhamedov, and by greater experimentation in choreographic approaches under the direction of Yuri Grigorovich. However, it continues to maintain a policy of reviving older works or mounting only those new ballets that have realistic themes and recognizable plots. For example, when asked whether plotless ballets would ever be shown at the Bolshoi Theater (which includes both opera and ballet companies), Stanislav Lushin, its overall administrator, indicated that they would not be. Kisselgoff concluded: "The implication was that the Bolshoi Theater, with its 3,000 employees (including 1,000 performers) was a national theater and that its tradition could be upheld only by staging narrative works on an opera-house scale."[23]

Kirov Ballet

In many ways, the Kirov Ballet in Leningrad is comparable to the Bolshoi; the dancers are equally superb and the productions equally lavish. The major difference is that the Kirov is less flamboyant and more reserved than the Bolshoi and is characterized by an air of elegant style—a "pure line, musicality, and a restrained and aristocratic bearing." It has produced many of Russia's leading choreographers, including Vachtang Chabukiani, Rotislav Zakharov, and Grigorovich.

Among its leading dancers in recent years have been Natalia Dudinskaya, Alla Sizova, Yuri Soloviev, and Konstantin Sergeyev—as well as the four outstanding performers, Nureyev, Makarova, Baryshnikov, and Panov, who came to America in the early and mid-1970s.

There is little question that the Soviet ballet system has been successful in creating a number of the world's most magnificent dancers. The reason lies in the Russian system of ballet instruction. This is carried on through state-supported, controlled schools throughout the member republics of the Soviet Union. Often, those pupils who are most talented find their way to the major centers of dance, such as Moscow or Leningrad, to complete their training and to join the Soviet's top companies. Rudolf Nureyev, in his autobiography, told of his training in the Kirov

School before he joined the company, achieved stardom, and ultimately fled to the West. It was a highly conservative establishment in which students worked between eight and eleven hours a day, starting early in the morning. There were usually two hours of instruction in art history and aesthetics each day, and then two hours of literature. This was followed by two hours of classical dance instruction which, in Nureyev's words, was "so concentrated, so well prepared, and so absorbing that one session there was worth four hours' instruction anywhere else in Europe."[24] In the afternoon, students were given two hours on the history of the ballet and the history of music and then another two hours of dancing, this time character work. In addition, academic courses were also scheduled during the week in physics, chemistry, geography, and similar subjects, as well as regular lessons in fencing. In the evenings, students would often observe rehearsals of the Kirov company or see actual performances in the theater next door.

The competition was severe and the discipline rigid. The sense of uncertainty or lack of societal approval that affects many dance students in the West (in the sense that they recognize that the career they have chosen lacks widely accepted status) never affected Nureyev. He wrote:

> The fact that ballet teaching in Russia is such a scrupulously regulated profession is, I believe, the main reason for our ballet's consistent high standard. Many European dancers (I don't know yet about the American ones) go endlessly from one studio to another in a misguided search for innovations and amplifications of their technique—and not always to teachers fully qualified for their work. The end result of amateur teachers in charge of shaping amateur dancers is that ballet gradually loses its purity and splendid traditions.
>
> How different in Russia! How severely controlled, how strongly rooted in tradition is the profession of the ballet teacher![25]

Over the past ten years, there has been a degree of change in the policies governing the Kirov's presentations. Since 1977, the company's artistic director has been Oleg Vinogradov, a contemporary and classmate of Nureyev at the Kirov's Vaganov School. Given a period of demoralization marked by creative stagnation and the defections and even suicide of some leading dancers, Vinogradov was apparently given the freedom to seek new directions. In the 1980s, he has gone ahead to produce ballets by contemporary French choreographers like Roland Petit, Maurice Béjart, and Pierre Lacotte and has even presented a number of Balanchine's works.

Ballet in Great Britain

Of all the great foreign ballet companies, perhaps the most familiar to most Americans has been the Royal Ballet, both under its present name and as the Sadler's Wells Theater Ballet, the name under which it first came to the United States.

Royal Ballet

Although it was not founded until just after World War II, this company had its roots in 1926 when Ninette de Valois established a ballet school in London shortly after leaving the Diaghileff Company. For a period of years, she staged the ballets which were produced at the Old Vic Theater, and, when the new Sadler's Wells Theater was built, de Valois was asked to found a school there. She did so in 1931. The students of the Sadler's Wells Ballet School, known as the Vic-Wells Ballet, continued to dance at the Old Vic and in operas given at the Sadler's Wells. This continued into the 1940s; during the war, the company performed at the New Theater under the worst bombing raids, and so helped to maintain the morale of Londoners.

After the war, in 1946, the company began to perform at the Covent Garden Royal Opera House, rapidly gaining in public and critical esteem. It was the wartime service of the Sadler's Wells Theater Ballet that won the affection of the British public and a later government subsidy (under the Arts Council of Great Britain) and, finally, the Royal Charter in 1956. During the late 1940s and early 1950s, the company performed over thirty ballets by Ninette de Valois, Frederick Ashton, Robert Helpmann, and others.

When, in 1951, the Sadler's Wells Theater Ballet toured the United States for the third time, it consisted of an extremely young company—the average age of the dancers was eighteen. A new choreographer, John Cranko, had created works that were now highlights of the repertoire: *Sea Change, Harlequin in April, The Fairy Queen,* and *Pineapple Poll.* Ashton's works, including musical abstractions such as *Symphonic Variations* and *Scènes de Ballet,* the superb coronation ballet, *Homage to the Queen,* and *Birthday Offering,* created in celebration of the twenty-fifth anniversary of the ballet company, had become masterpieces of the British company's repertoire.

Now known as the Royal Ballet, the company continued through the 1960s with an outstanding cast of superbly skilled dancers and an extremely diverse repertoire. Thus, in 1967, it revived Nijinska's powerful *Les Noces* (first performed four decades before by the Diaghileff ballet); it continues to have new works by Antony Tudor (*Shadowplay*) and Ashton (*The Dream,* a one-act version of Shakespeare's *A Midsummer Night's Dream*); Kenneth MacMillan's *Song of the Earth;* a new production by Ashton of *Cinderella; Paradise Lost* by Roland Petit; and many other works both classic and modern.

In the 1970s, the Royal Ballet made a number of extensive tours of the United States. Perhaps its major effect was in the introduction of full-evening spectacle ballets. At first, Americans, who were accustomed to having three short, separate works in a program, found this difficult to accept. However, after exposure to the Royal Ballet, with its full-evening *Sleeping Beauty, Swan Lake,* and *Cinderella,* as well as similar long works by the two Russian companies, the New York City Ballet and American Ballet Theater have also began to produce full-evening works.

In 1981, the Royal Ballet celebrated its fiftieth anniversary at its Covent Garden home, performing extracts from some thirty-eight ballets over a four-hour period. At the end of numerous curtain calls, the orchestra played a waltz and the curtains parted once more to reveal Ninette de Valois dancing with choreographer Kenneth MacMillan, Frederick Ashton with Margot Fonteyn, and Norman Morrice, then company director, with Alicia Markova. This milestone celebration was followed in the early and mid-1980s, however, by a sense of decline in the Royal Ballet. With fewer and less glittering stars and a dearth of strong new choreographers, critics claimed that the company had become too tradition-bound and that its dancing was sloppy and its productions dull. In 1985, Anthony Dowell was named to succeed Morrice as director of the Royal Ballet, and he embarked on an effort to help it regain its former stature.

Sadler's Wells Royal Ballet

When it began in 1931, the Royal Ballet had 6 dancers and a school of 20 students. By the early 1980s, it had two companies totaling 120 dancers and two schools averaging 200 pupils. The second company came into being in 1946, when part of the overall Royal Ballet moved to Covent Garden while the remaining group stayed at Sadler's Wells to work with its aspiring opera company. Both groups are approximately the same size, although the Sadler's Wells company (known colloquially as "the second company") usually has a younger group of dancers and is said to represent the spirit of de Valois's original company. Among the Sadler's Wells directors have been Peggy van Praagh, who left in 1955 to found the Australian Ballet, and two leading choreographers, John Cranko and Kenneth Macmillan.

Throughout its history, the Sadler's Wells Royal Ballet has been viewed primarily as a touring company, giving performances throughout the provinces, in Europe, and occasionally in Covent Garden. Over time, it developed a number of outstanding dancers, including Lynn Seymour, Christopher Gable, and David Wall, with Peter Wright as artistic director. Today, it is regarded as an attractive, youthful, and enthusiastic company.

Ballet Rambert

A third important English company is Ballet Rambert, a newly invigorated group that combines a classical tradition with a fresh new choreographic repertoire. Recently, under Norman Morrice's direction, the company cut many of its older works, reduced the number of dancers, and undertook a number of highly contemporary new works by choreographers like Richard Alston, Michael Clark, and Ashley Page. Influenced heavily by such modern dance choreographers as Merce Cunningham, Ballet Rambert recently toured the United States and Canada with a program that featured several of Alston's ballets.

Other Major European Companies

Two other major European companies that have maintained a strong classical tradition while at the same time being open to new choreographic influences are the Royal Danish Ballet and the Paris Opéra Ballet.

Royal Danish Ballet

This internationally famous company has an ancient history; it was founded in 1748 and has been under royal patronage since that time. The school in which its young

Stars of the Royal Danish Ballet. Courtesy Shubert Theater, Philadelphia.

dancers are trained was founded in 1829 by August Bournonville, who was responsible for the initial development of the company, whose repertoire of classic ballets is still performed by the company, and whose system of dance training still gives the graduates of the Royal Danish Ballet School a unique character.

Since the middle of the nineteenth century, the Royal Danish Ballet has continued to perform such Bournonville works as *Napoli, Konservatoriet, Far from Denmark,* and *Valdemar.* While it had produced a number of outstanding dancers and excellent new works under the direction of its ballet master during the 1940s, Harald Lander, the company was not widely known. Then, after the first annual ballet festival in Copenhagen in 1950, it began to tour more widely. When it visited the United States for the first time in 1956, it received high praise from American critics. Hering wrote:

> Their pure dance passages are meticulously hewn. And their acting is a human experience. Americans are known for their realistic acting in modern works. But the Danes have found a way of extending this style into the traditional ballets, so that even the oldest ones like *La Sylphide* and *Napoli* (both more than a century old) emerge curiously alive and convincing. And from an acting point of view the Danes are equally at home in contemporary works like Frederick Ashton's *Romeo and Juliet* and Balanchine's *La Sonnambula.* . . .[26]

In summarizing the strengths and weaknesses of the Royal Danish Ballet, the question of its repertoire has often been raised. Chiefly, it has consisted of the Bournonville works, a number of other classic ballets, and several modern ballets drawn from choreographers of other nations. While the Royal Danish Ballet has a curious gift for endowing the works of other companies, periods, and national origins with a uniquely different style and manner, its problem clearly will be to establish a modern Danish repertoire to accompany the Bournonville works that are its unique trademark.

In terms of dancing, the Danish dancers reflect their Bournonville heritage: It is a style that requires both stamina and strong technique. Leaps have extra bounce and spring, and the footwork is brilliant and precise. Probably the best-known Danish dancer of the modern era has been Erik Bruhn, who performed with a number of major companies throughout the world. Other leading dancers have been Henning Kronstam, Niels Larsen, Peter Martins, and Helgi Tomasson among the men, and Anna Laerkesen, Viveka Segerskog, and Ruth Andersen among the women.

Under Flemming Flindt's direction during the late 1970s, the Danish Ballet has given seasons at New York's Metropolitan Opera House and in Washington, D.C. and has been featured in ensemble form at Jacob's Pillow in Massachusetts. In more recent programs during the 1980s at the Metropolitan Opera House in New York, the company demonstrated a return to the Bournonville tradition, with dances that make use of exotic foreign color and with revivals of popular nineteenth-century works. At the same time, it has acquired ballets by such varied choreographers as Alvin Ailey, Glen Tetley, and the Russian Yuri Grigorovitch.

Paris Opéra Ballet

The historic Paris Opéra Ballet continued to present dance through the years, both as part of operas themselves and as independent productions. For almost thirty years, Serge Lifar, who had been a leading dancer with Diaghileff, was director of the Opéra Ballet and choreographed many of its works. One interpretation of the failure of French ballet to achieve a greater reputation in the modern era is that the close connection between ballet and opera has tended to encourage choreographic novelty and sensationalism for its own sake—almost a frivolous and dilettantish attitude toward the production of new works.

In such a situation, ballet has not flourished as an independent art, and works of choreographers of the stature of Balanchine or Ashton have rarely been performed. In the late 1960s, George Skibine joined the Opéra Ballet as a leading dancer and choreographer, and greater emphasis was put on diversifying the company's works. However, ballet at the Opéra continued to be poorly supported and viewed as an artistic fifth wheel through the 1970s. In 1977, Violette Verdy, a French-born ballerina and star of the New York City Ballet, was appointed artistic director in an attempt to upgrade the Opéra's ballet component.

However, the company's efforts continued to be frustrated by artistic confusion and political interference. Horosko pointed out that, although its dancers have enjoyed good salaries and a high degree of security as government employees, its directors have been subject to "the political tides of the country," rarely holding their posts for more than three years.[27] In 1983, Rudolf Nureyev inherited the position as artistic director, taking over from Rosella Hightower, who had succeeded Violette Verdy three years before.

Nureyev's plan was to reduce the size of the 140-member company, strengthen its school and studio facilities, and diversify its repertoire markedly. By 1986, he had made radical changes, giving the Paris Opéra Ballet a much more international image. In January 1984, he invited the Martha Graham Company to perform on the stage of the Palais Garnier, the first foreign troupe to do this since Diaghileff. He has actively cultivated the leading contemporary choreographers, commissioning William Forsythe, Michael Clarke, Lucinda Childs, and Karole Armitage, among others, to create works for the Opéra Ballet.

Following a tour of Japan, Nureyev brought the full company to the Metropolitan Opera House in New York, where it was received with great critical and public enthusiasm. In addition to such classical works as *Swan Lake* and *Raymonda,* the company performed ballets by Serge Lifar and Balanchine and was praised for its superb classical style, with such dancers as Michael Denard, Ghislaine Thesmar, and Patrick Dupond. John Gruen concluded: ". . . in the short years of his tenure, Nureyev has transformed the Paris Opéra into a technically brilliant and forward-looking ensemble. Today, Rudolf Nureyev has emerged as more than a legendary dancer, more than a visionary company director, more than a world-renowned figure in the arts. He is history personified."[28]

Other French Companies

A number of other important French Ballet companies have flourished in recent years, including the Ballet National de Marseille and the Lyon Opéra Ballet. Roland Petit, in charge of the Marseille company, is a master of the story ballet who has collaborated in the past with leading designers, composers, and writers. During the 1980s, the Ballet National has typically been a company of fifty-five dancers that gives forty performances a year in its home and tours for six months in Europe and around the world. The Lyon Opéra Ballet is a smaller, younger company, trained in both classical ballet and modern dance technique. In a recent tour of the United States, including two weeks at the City Center in New York, critics commented on its imaginative staging and costuming and its overall contemporary approach.

Other European Companies

Other companies are to be found in most of the larger European cities, as well as in many smaller ones. Typically, they are attached to the local opera house, performing during the opera season (which may last as long as ten or eleven months) and also producing evenings of ballet performance or scheduling ballet seasons of their own. Two such companies are to be found at the Bavarian Staatsoper in Munich and La Scala in Milan. Both companies maintain schools from which dancers enter the corps de ballet. They are fairly sizable; the Munich Staatsoper has seventy dancers, and La Scala company forty-six.

In Holland, ballet companies include the Dutch National Ballet, directed by Rudi van Dantzig, which performs both the traditional classics and a number of early European modern dance works (like Kurt Jooss's *The Green Table*), and the Netherlands Dance Theater, whose Czech-born artistic director, Jiri Kylian, presents powerful choreography in a wide range of moods from the somber to the farcical. In nearby Brussels, the Ballet of the 20th Century, directed by Maurice Béjart, tours frequently, with a number of highly innovative contemporary ballets by Béjart and others; its works are often seen as controversial, emotionally gripping, and theatrical.

In West Germany, the Frankfurt Ballet is headed by William Forsythe, whose compositional method has employed Cunningham-like involvement of dancers in creating their own movement, and even computer input. Forsythe for a time was a strong exponent of expressionist, issue-based ballets and more recently has returned to a more classical, formalist approach to choreography. The Stuttgart Ballet also performs and tours successfully in West Germany. In Sweden, the Royal Swedish Ballet and the Cullberg Ballet have both developed sound reputations.

Ballet in Other Countries

Still other ballet companies are sponsored by the member republics of the Soviet Union and other European and South American countries. The Australian Ballet has flourished in recent years under Maina Gielgud's direction; its production of *The Sleeping Beauty* was used to inaugurate the State Theater in Melbourne's new $225 million Victorian Arts Center, and it has gained support also through regular seasons at Sydney's famous Opera House as well as through successful foreign tours. Israel, Cuba, Spain, Mexico, Brazil, and Venezuela have all become active in hosting touring ballet companies and developing their own dance theaters.

Ballet in Canada

There are three strong companies at present in Canada: the National Ballet of Canada in Toronto (the largest and most firmly established), the Royal Winnipeg Ballet (the oldest company in the country, about the size of the Joffrey Ballet), and Les Grands Ballets Canadiens from the Province of Quebec. All three companies are subsidized by the Canada Council, a program for support of the arts that is modeled after the Arts Council of Great Britain. The National Ballet, which is viewed as one of Canada's leading arts institutions, receives 38 percent of its annual budget from the government; in return, it is regarded as a "diplomatic service with a national obligation" for touring and giving performances from Halifax to Vancouver. In addition, the companies receive funding from provincial governments and are able to raise substantial contributions from private industry.

The National Ballet in particular has been heavily influenced by the Royal Ballet of Britain; it was formed after a visit of the Royal Ballet to Toronto and was directed for a number of years by Celia Franca, formerly a dancer with the British company. Gradually, it grew in professional stature, and today, under the artistic direction of Alexander Grant—also with strong Royal Ballet connections—it is regarded as an excellent company, on par with Stuttgart, Joffrey, Paris Opéra, and Dutch National Ballet. It has featured such outstanding stars as Rudolf Nureyev and Erik Bruhn as guest artists on tour. One of its weaknesses is that it has been required to tour so heavily in order to maintain itself. Both the demands of a heavy travel schedule and the fact that it must often perform before audiences with little knowledge of ballet and with a preference for the older, classic full-evening ballets have limited its choreographic development.

In 1983, Erik Bruhn was appointed artistic director of the National Ballet with a twofold purpose: to strengthen the company's classical repertoire in terms of dancing and presentation, and to vitalize it by introducing each year several new, specially choreographed works with a modern influence. The company made major strides in the next three years and is today highly regarded, although Bruhn died in 1986. One of the key elements in its success has been the outstanding National Ballet School, regarded as one of the world's leading training centers, directed by Betty Oliphant.

Les Grands Ballet Canadiens, Canada's second company, has a much more innovative repertoire and functions uniquely under a troika of directors: Linda Stearns in charge of the classical works, Daniel Jackson in charge of the contemporary wing, and Colin McIntyre responsible for the administrative functions. Although it has dancers of many nationalities, the company's members are primarily graduates of its own school and have a strong French-Canadian style—vivacious and sophisticated. Its repertoire of ballets has ranged widely from the rock ballet *Tommy* to works like Paul Taylor's *Aureole,* the Doris Humphrey/Ruth St. Denis *Soaring,* and others by its own gifted young choreographer, James Kudelka.

The Royal Winnipeg Ballet, like the National Ballet, was established by British dancers and choreographers; today it focuses on twentieth-century classics and dance dramas, with an occasional revival of older works like *Giselle.* A final, smaller Canadian company is the Toronto-based Desrosiers Dance Theater, founded in 1980 by Robert Desrosiers, an internationally acclaimed and highly controversial choreographer known for his surrealist works often performed with incredible speed and frenetic energy.

International Festivals and Competitions

A relatively new influence on ballet throughout the world, reflecting the growth of popular interest in it, has been the emergence of international festivals and competitions that attract great numbers of performers and balletomanes. For example, the International Ballet Competition held in the ancient city and modern resort of Varna, Bulgaria, on the Black Sea, has been called the "Olympics of dance." Hundreds of dancers in separate age categories perform before a panel of jurors from twenty nations, headed by outstanding choreographers. As evidence of the quality of such competitions, winners in the past have included stars like Mikhail Baryshnikov, the Bolshoi's Ekaterina Maximova and Vladimir Vasiliev; Hungary's Ivan Nagy; Canada's Martine van Hamel; and America's Fernando Bujones, all of whom became leading dancers with major world companies.

Other important competitions are held in Moscow and Japan; the World Ballet Concours held every two years in Tokyo has the pomp and circumstance of a national event, attended by royalty and leading government figures. Contestants perform solos and *pas de deux,* with excerpts taken both from the classical repertoire and from major contemporary ballet works. In the late 1970s, International Ballet Festivals were established in the United States, in Chicago and Jackson, Mississippi, and it seems likely that such events will continue to grow in number.

International competitions sometimes are designed to encourage promising young dancers. For example, the prestigious Prix de Lausanne is an elimination contest among about eighty outstanding teenage performers who compete for scholarships to nine of the world's leading ballet schools. Normally held in Lausanne, Switzerland, in 1985 its closing rounds were held in the United States.

In 1987, the National Ballet of Canada announced the first annual Erik Bruhn prize—designed exclusively for young dancers from one of the four companies that Bruhn had been most closely associated with: the Royal Danish Ballet, the Royal Ballet (British), the National Ballet of Canada, and American Ballet Theater. Two other recently announced competitions include the Boston International Choreography Competition, sponsored by the Boston Ballet, and the Lausanne Competition: The New Choreographers, Philip Morris Prize. Kisselgoff noted that, although such contests have obvious pitfalls, their ". . . popularity with audiences and the career benefits to the winners seem to balance out the fact that ballet as art form needs no such official consecration—that public-relations and prestige benefits to the organizers might be as important as furthering excellence."[29]

Internationalism in Ballet

The nomadism of dance companies, performers, and choreographers, and the sharing of an increasingly common contemporary repertoire, has meant that a new sort of international ballet has come into being. Superstars like Baryshnikov, Makarova, Nureyev, Gregory, and others have traveled from country to country, doing a special performance here or a brief season there. Often, they tend to influence the style and standards of the indigenous company with whom they perform. Choreographers are commissioned to create works across national lines, often incorporating modern dance approaches and techniques.

However, it has become increasingly clear that ballet art is one which—while it may arouse widespread interest and attendance—has great difficulty in supporting itself properly in a financial sense. It is unlike the legitimate theater, which may have as few as a handful of actors and a single set or two. Instead, a ballet company with an extensive repertoire must have a large number of dancers, plus different sets and costumes for each work that is to be performed and an orchestra that in some cases is a full-scale symphony orchestra. Under these circumstances, even granted a full house or a close-to-capacity audience throughout its home and touring season, ballet must operate at a considerable deficit. The alternatives of charging admission prices that are so high that much of the potential audience is excluded, or of having subscription series that insure a regular, capacity attendance, are at least partially self-defeating.

In part, the problem has been met by some companies through offering special seasons or performances which highlight international stars; these may be specially priced and usually attract capacity audiences. However, this approach tends to undermine the artistic integrity of the company itself, which serves chiefly as a backdrop for the visiting artist and which is pressured to offer works which the public at large will readily accept rather than to explore new choreographic directions which may be less popular at the box office.

The alternative of having foundation grants or governmental support for specific dance projects, or of receiving grants to support special aspects of touring, training, or production, is becoming increasingly recognized as a desirable solution for the support of the performing arts. Later chapters describe this pattern of foundation and government support for dance—both modern dance and ballet—as it has evolved in recent years.

Notes

1 Gwin Chin, "Balletomanes Debate the Style of Today's Dancers," *New York Times,* August 7, 1983, p. 24-H.

2 George Amberg, *Ballet in America* (New York: Duell, Sloan and Pearce, 1949), p. viii.

3 Agnes de Mille, quoted in *The New York Herald-Tribune,* January 16, 1952, p. 13.

4 Diane Solway, "City Ballet Moves to an American Beat," *New York Times,* April 24, 1988, p. 1-H.

5 "Critics Look at the First New York International Festival," *New York Times,* July 10, 1988, pp. 1-H, 36-H.

6 Marcia B. Siegel, *At the Vanishing Point, A Critic Looks at Dance* (New York: Saturday Review Press, 1972), p. 9.

7 Allen Hughes, *New York Times, Theater Section,* January 26, 1964, p. 18-X.

8 Flora Lewis, "To Balanchine, Dance is Woman," *New York Times,* October 6, 1976, p. 45.

9 Leon Goldstein, "A Ballet Musician Recalls Balanchine," *New York Times,* May 6, 1984, p. 30-H.

10 Michael Walsh, "The Joy of Pure Movement: George Balanchine: 1904–1983," *Time,* May 9, 1983, p. 91.

11 Hubert Saal, "He Made a Revolution," *New York Times Book Review,* May 22, 1983, p. 9.

12 Stephen Schiff, "Life After Balanchine," *Vanity Fair,* December 1988, pp. 200–205.

13 Anna Kisselgoff, "City Ballet at 40: Balanchine's Legacy Lives," *New York Times,* November 20, 1988, pp. 1-H, 25-H.

14 Walter Terry, "The Not-So-Little Little Ballet," *The New York Herald-Tribune Magazine,* April 24, 1966, p. 40.

15 Jennifer Dunning, "A Man Who Championed Blacks in Ballet," *New York Times,* August 11, 1985, p. H-14.

16 Clive Barnes, "Up and Coming San Franciscans," *New York Times,* February 27, 1977, p. 15.

17 Iris Fanger, "Brucing up Boston Ballet," *Dance Magazine,* December 1986, pp. 42–47.

18 Wilma Salisbury, "Akron's Treasure: The Ohio Ballet," *Dance Magazine,* October 1978, pp. 50–53.

19 Camille Hardy, "On a Roll with Cleveland and San Jose," *Dance Magazine,* October 1986, pp. 56–59.

20 Doris Hering, "Regional Ballet in on the March," *New York Times,* April 24, 1977, p. 10-D.

21 Yuri Grigorovich, quoted in Clive Barnes, "The Fresh New Look of the Bolshoi," *New York Times,* May 15, 1966, p. D-5.

22 Doris Hering, "First Impressions of the Bolshoi Ballet," *Dance Magazine,* June 1959, p. 38.

23 Anna Kisselgoff, "Where is Yuri Grigorovich Leading the Bolshoi," *New York Times,* August 2, 1987, p. H-4.

24 Rudolf Nureyev, "Nureyev: An Autobiography," *Dance Magazine,* May 1966, p. 40.

25 Ibid., p. 42.

26 Doris Hering, "The Danes: An American Debut," *Dance Magazine,* November 1956, p. 14.

27 Marian Horosko, "Nureyev Takes the Helm of the Paris Opéra Ballet," *New York Times,* September 4, 1983, p. 1-H.

28 John Gruen, "The Force Still With Us," *Dance Magazine,* July 1986, p. 51.

29 Anna Kisselgoff, "Should Ballet Be a Competitive Event," *New York Times,* September 27, 1987, p. H-9.

CHAPTER 10

Modern Dance Today

"Total theater" also seems to appeal to many of today's younger choreographers, who are returning to heightened theatricality after the sparse, post-modernist exercises of the last decade.[1]

As Chapter 9 showed, ballet has acquired an extremely broad audience in the United States since mid-century. Many professional companies and organizations have been formed throughout the country—often with major public subsidies or foundation grants—and a broad network of regional performing ballet companies has been established. A number of these companies now can assure their dancers thirty or more weeks of paid employment through the year in addition to special tours and other performances.

Modern dance has not yet achieved this level of public acceptance and support. Even so, there are many more modern dance companies today than there were four decades ago, and there is certainly an expanded number of performances, particularly in larger cities and on university campuses. In terms of worldwide influence, American modern dance companies have toured successfully throughout Europe, the Far East, and in other regions to enthusiastic acclaim.

However, it is clear that, when compared to ballet, interest in modern dance is relatively much narrower throughout the United States. The public—with the exception of those exposed to this aspect of dance in colleges and universities, or those who are generally interested in the arts—tends to be much less informed about modern dance than ballet. There are no companies with the stability and support of the major ballet companies; nor have any companies, lacking strong support from citizens' groups, been identified with the communities that support them. The typical pattern of having a ballet company that represents a city and that bears that city's name—the Boston Ballet, the Houston Ballet, the Pittsburgh Ballet, for example—is simply not found in modern dance.

Yet, despite these reservations, modern dance has had an immense impact over the past four decades on all forms of contemporary art—and it has infused ballet with new approaches to choreography and staging that have been heavily responsible for ballet's expanded appeal.

Trends in Modern Dance

Certain changes have taken place in the field itself. First, in terms of approaches to choreography, there appear to be three distinct groups active today. The first consists of those artists or companies who were active and successful before mid-century and who have continued to maintain their companies and to develop as creative artists. The second consists of those dancer-choreographers who gained recognition in the post-World War II period and who have continued to move ahead in exciting new directions. The third group is an extremely diverse collection of younger artists who, particularly during the 1960s and 1970s, developed radical new approaches to dance. Like their counterparts in other avant-garde art forms, they tended to create works that were so spontaneous, unpredictable, and unlike what had gone before in dance that many considered them to be almost antidance or nondance.

The general tenor of modern dance purpose or philosophy seems also to have changed through the years. The early modern dancers were in a sense crusaders who sought to create a new, vital, uniquely American form of dance. This purpose does not seem to exist today. Nor has the psychoanalytically oriented view of dance as a means of emotional catharsis or release continued as a primary motivation. Many choreographers, particularly the more experimental ones, have been concerned chiefly with developing new forms of movement or ways of using sound and visual effects, objects, and events from everyday life as the basis for creating dance. Marcia Siegel wrote in the early 1970s:

> Some of the most interesting dance of our time is classifiable as dance only because it doesn't fit anywhere else. . . . Today's experimental dancers frequently do not dance. They seldom employ music, and when they do, they don't use it as accompaniment for their dancing or non-dancing. They hardly ever dance, or non-dance, in theaters. Their structures, content, methods, and means not only exist outside the usual channels of dance production but call into question the nature of dance itself. Yet this is not a destructive revolution. . . . Experimental dance today is affirmative and challenging.[2]

In the 1980s, other changes were apparent in modern dance—including the use of the term itself. So diverse are the creations of the younger choreographers of the past decade that no single adjective applies to them. Such terms as *postmodern, minimalist, avant-garde, next wave,* and *experimental* are used to describe the work of different groups of choreographers. As this chapter shows, there has been a trend toward theatricalized dance, in the sense of dance that is no longer minimalist, without music, plot, dance-like movement, or props. Many newer works are marked by grotesque imagery, complex settings, emotional content, and suggested relationships or roles. In some cases, the linkage with other art forms seems to have resulted in a new form which some critics have labeled *performance art*.

Rapprochement with Ballet

What other shifts have occurred over the most recent two or three decades? The most striking is that modern dance and ballet have had a marked influence on each other and have grown closer in many respects. Modern dancers are rarely as opposed to training in ballet technique as they were at the beginning of the modern dance period. Instead, many recognize the fundamental value of classic dance technique. In a number of other ways, the gulf that existed between modern dance and ballet has now been bridged; ballet choreography has been markedly influenced by modern dance approaches, and a number of leading modern dancers have been commissioned to design works for major ballet companies.

It would be a mistake to suggest that because modern dance has not been as successful in gaining popular support and understanding as ballet, it has failed in its mission. Any art form that is at the cutting edge of creative discovery tends to limit its audience by definition. At the same time, much of what is being done by the more experimental modern dancers today is universal in its appeal and has potential meaning for all those open to aesthetic experience—whether or not they have had previous exposure to dance.

International Exchanges

As chapter 8 showed, in its inception modern dance was almost totally an American phenomenon—with the exception of Mary Wigman's pre-World War II expressionist dance and some elements of Laban's work, along with choreography by Kurt Jooss and Nijinsky. Certainly, all the great figures of early modern dance were American. However, over the last two decades, more and more Europeans have become interested in modern dance as a result of tours by American companies or American artists teaching or holding residencies abroad. And, over the last decade, several companies from Germany, France, and other European or Asian countries have gained recognition in modern dance and have toured America to critical praise.

To understand what has occurred in modern dance, it is helpful to examine each of the three major groups of dancers and choreographers in turn, beginning with the preeminent figure in American modern dance, Martha Graham.

Martha Graham

Through the 1960s and 1970s, Graham's company continued to represent a major influence among modern dancers—almost like that of George Balanchine in the professional ballet field. Graham's prestige and identity have been so well established that among audiences that would otherwise not see modern dance, she is accepted and appreciated.

Martha Graham and Company in *Clytemnestra*. Photograph by Martha Swope.

What changes occurred in Graham's approach to choreography and performance through the years? In her last years of creative original work, she was concerned only with creating major dance-dramas made, in Doris Hering's words, "to last."[3] But a number of her dances choreographed in the 1960s tended to be less weighty or serious than the earlier works. While not to be regarded as fillers or pleasant trifles, they tended to be abstract in mood or to reveal a satirical bite. Some, like *Acrobats of God,* a lively and joyful comedy piece about herself and dance, were of this category. Others, notably *Part Dream, Part Real; Circe;* and *Phaedra,* had a marked erotic quality justified by the dramatic content of the work. Overall, her works continued to be impressively staged, superbly choreographed, and danced by a company of unmatched dancing skill and physical attractiveness.

The Graham Company continued to receive impressive financial support from varied sources. For example, in the late 1960s, a substantial grant from the Lila Acheson Wallace Foundation made possible her three-week season in New York; two new works presented at this time, *Dancing-Ground* and *Cortège of Eagles,* were

Martha Graham and Company in *The Lady of the House of Sleep*. Photograph by Martha Swope.

financed by a grant from the National Council on the Arts. Graham's school and company have continued to be financed through the years by the de Rothschild Foundation.

In her mid-seventies, Graham went through a two-year period of illness and disassociation from her work. Then, in 1972, she returned to her company, having made two major decisions—she would not perform again (although she would continue to choreograph and appear on stage as commentator), and she would help her company reconstruct her old works.

Graham continued to direct her company successfully through the 1980s, reviving a number of her earlier works and creating new dances well into her nineties. In some cases, such as the company's performance of *Clytemnestra,* the original choreography was repeated. In others, as in *Frescoes,* she choreographed a new version of *Judith* with a score by Varèse. In *Andromache's Lament,* premiered in the early 1980s, she returned to her interest in the ancient Greeks; and in 1984, she created a major new work to Stravinsky's ecstatic hymn, *The Rite of Spring.*

In 1988, at the age of ninety-four, this phenomenon of the American art world continued to direct her company and school and to rehearse the company for its new season at the New York City Center. Reflecting on her life in dance, she had commented three years earlier that she never discussed the idea of genius in reference to herself. Instead, she said: ". . . it's the animal quality, it's the sense of wonder, it's the curiosity, the avidity for experience, for life. And you have to eat it all the time; sometimes it's bitter, sometimes it's very sweet."[4]

José Limón

A second major figure whose reputation was established long before mid-century, and who continued to perform, choreograph, and teach for a period after it, was José Limón. Though lacking the stability afforded by a major school and permanently established company, he had a number of important affiliations through the years. He was a director of the Juilliard Dance Theater, where his company performed both his own works and those by Doris Humphrey. He continued to be head of the faculty and a leading performer at the Connecticut College of the Dance in New London where, summer after summer, many of his new works received their premieres.

Through the years, the Limón Company carried out a number of highly successful tours of Europe, the Orient, and Latin America under State Department sponsorship. In 1964, when the New York State Council on the Arts agreed to underwrite two performances of the American Dance Theater at Lincoln Center in New York, José Limón acted as artistic director, bringing together the works of Donald McKayle, Anna Sokolow, and Doris Humphrey on a single program and performing in a premiere of his own *A Choreographic Offering*.

José Limón and Lucas Hoving in *The Traitor*. Photograph by Matthew Wysocki.

However, it was difficult for Limón to discover a consistent audience for his works. In 1966, for example, his dance company was able to arrange only one appearance in New York City, at the Brooklyn Academy of Music, where he performed two of his most recent works, *A Choreographic Offering* and *Missa Brevis.* Clive Barnes commented on this occasion that the inability of the Limón company to have more than a "meager one-night stand" in New York City, despite its distinguished reputation, was "scandalous."[5]

Although no longer in his prime as a dancer in the later years of his career, Limón continued to be an impressive and moving figure. His choreography was consistently serene and powerful; unfortunately, there was too little opportunity for it to be seen during his lifetime. After his death in 1972, it was expected that his company would dissolve. However, under the artistic direction of Ruth Currier, later succeeded by Carla Maxwell, the José Limón Company continued to perform.

Since 1984, the company's associate artistic director, with Maxwell, has been Lutz Forster, a German dancer who had trained in the Folkwang School in Essen, founded by Kurt Jooss. In a two-week season at the Joyce Theater in 1986, the Limón company performed a number of works by choreographers who had been strongly influenced by German modern dance, including Susanne Linke, Carlos Orta, Heinz Poll, Lucas Hoving, Anna Sokolow, and Meredith Monk. Thus, although it continues to do major works by Limón, it also is involved in a process of artistic change and growth.

Merce Cunningham

Another dancer-choreographer whose career has bridged the last half-century is Merce Cunningham. During the years from 1940 to 1945, Cunningham was a soloist with the Martha Graham Company, creating such roles as the Acrobat in *Every Soul Is a Circus,* the Christ Figure in *El Penitente,* March in *Letter to the World,* and the Revivalist in *Appalachian Spring.* While with Graham he also studied ballet at the School of American Ballet where, during the late 1940s, he taught a class in modern dance.

Since the 1940s, Cunningham has been extremely successful as a choreographer with his own company. He has used the works of a number of contemporary composers but has collaborated most intensively with the avant-garde pianist-composer John Cage. His work has varied greatly and invariably stirs up a strong audience reaction. He is known for his experiments with "choreography by chance," as illustrated in a 1953 work titled *Suite by Chance.* For this long dance in four movements, a large series of charts was made. One gave body movements, phrases, and positions; another chart gave numbered lengths of time; and another gave directions in space. These charts, which defined the physical limits within which the continuity would take place, were not made by chance. But from them, the actual continuity was determined as by a lottery:

> . . . a sequence of movements for a single dancer was determined by means of chance from the numbered movements in the chart; space, direction and lengths of

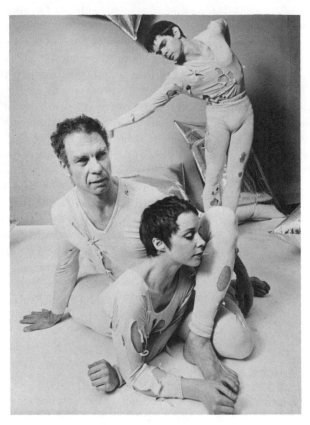

Merce Cunningham, Barbara Lloyd, and Albert Reid in *Riverwind*, with décor by Andy Warhol. Photograph by Jack Mitchell.

time were found in the other charts. At important structural points in the music, the number of dancers on stage, exits and entrances, unison or individual movements of dancers were all decided by tossing coins. . . .[6]

Often, Cunningham's choreography has been jarring and unpleasant:

The sound score by Gordon Mumma relentlessly blares the hideous noises of our modern life. . . . For *Place* sets us down in one spot and shows us with pitiless inexorability the shrinking of the world until there is no space left. There is only this tiny plot of ground into which the dancers huddle. Cunningham is sometimes in sole possession of it, but the others crowd in and he is reduced to cringing in a corner. They inch their way into a vacant place but, with foot in midair, they find that the space is no longer free. Only the air is still without boundary and they flail their arms, creating an illusion of freedom in which to move. . . .[7]

Consistently, Cunningham has been a gadfly; in Don McDonagh's words, intent on "baffling the unwary," or "deriving some personal satisfaction from practicing a unique audiovisual torture technique." At one point, when presenting four programs at the Brooklyn Academy of Music as a resident company, he deliberately scheduled all four programs as events, with hour-and-a-half-long dances, with whole dances, parts of dances, and excerpts thrown together in no particular order and without an intermission. The audience staged a near-riot. Twelve years later, in 1974, when Cunningham had become a respected elder statesman of the dance world, a Boston Ballet performance of *Winterbranch,* with lighting by Robert Rauschenberg that left the dancers dancing mostly in the dark but beamed a blinding white light directly at the audience, caused half the audience to respond by leaving the theater.

Cunningham has a great range of moods; in *How to Pass, Kick, Fall, and Run,* his dancers caper about in the gayest of spirits. In general, his choreography is an imaginative, no-holds-barred commentary on life, visually exciting and often highly demanding of the audience.

Of all modern dance choreographers, Cunningham probably comes closest to ballet in his movement approach. His dancers have typically had extensive ballet training, and his movement vocabulary makes use of the complicated and articulate footwork of ballet combined with an upright, open torso and expressive arm and hand gestures. It is always clear to the audience that if what the dancers are doing does not *look* like dance as it is popularly conceived, at least it is by the choreographer's choice rather than the performers' inability to dance.

Just as Cunningham was a featured dancer with the Graham Company early in his career, so today a number of members of his company have become well-known choreographers in their own right. Probably more than any other established artist, he has influenced the young generation of avant-garde performers in their movement experimentation.

Cunningham has continued to choreograph, to teach, and to influence the dance world through the 1980s; in the view of many, his company has become the premier modern dance troupe in the world. In vivid contrast to his early, struggling days, he is so firmly established that his four-week season at the Joyce Theater in New York in March 1988 was an artistic and financial triumph. A number of his new works, including *Roaratorio, an Irish Circus on Finnegan's Wake* (1986), *Fabrications* (1987), and *Eleven* (1988) show constant change and experimentation—as well as an increasing emphasis on dance technique, with "exceptional shapes, line and intricate rhythmic phrasing."[8]

As an indication of his acceptance within the overall art world, in 1986 this one-time renegade of American modern dance was awarded the five-year, $300,000 MacArthur Foundation Fellowship, the so-called genius grant. Many of his former students or dancers, including Gus Solomons, Jr., Meg Harper, Douglass Dunn, Karole Armitage, and Charles Moulton—among dozens of others—have gained independent recognition as contemporary choreographers.

Anna Sokolow

Another major modern dance choreographer whose career was well under way before mid-century and who has continued to teach and create important new works has been Anna Sokolow. One of the most unusual choreographers of the past several decades in terms of her background and the scope of her work, Sokolow spans the period from Martha Graham's early days at the Neighborhood Playhouse on the lower East Side, through the present.

Sokolow performed in the Graham company during the 1930s; she also appeared in workers' clubs with her Dance Unit, performing works with anti-Fascist themes and other themes of social significance. She worked and performed in Russia in the mid-1930s and in 1939 was invited to Mexico by the Fine Arts Ministry to appear for a six-week season with a company she had formed there years before. She remained in Mexico, teaching young Mexican dancers, who called themselves "Las Sokolovas" and who later became the nucleus of a large group called "La Paloma Azul." From this group came several leading Mexican choreographers, including Raquel Gutierrez and Ana Mérida. For nine years after this, Anna Sokolow commuted between New York and Mexico City. There, the largest and most impressive theater was hers, and she choreographed a number of important works with the collaboration of Mexico's leading composers and designers. Mexican themes have since pervaded a number of her works, such as *Mexican Retablo* and *Lament for the Death of a Bullfighter*.

Drawn back to New York City as a center for her creative work, Sokolow was again involved in another land when, in 1953, she went to Israel to teach movement to the Inbal group, a company of Yemenite dancers. Over a period of years, she then divided her activities between Israel and the United States, spending between four and six months in Israel each year, staging theater works. In the early 1960s, she served as director-teacher-choreographer for the Lyric Theater there, a unique form of experimental theater: "It is in the truest sense of the word a dance theater fusing dance and drama. . . . Essentially, I want to experiment with the spoken word and movement as I have done with Kafka's *Metamorphosis.* Kafkaesque images particularly lend themselves to the style of dance theatre I conceive."[9]

Since that time, Anna Sokolow has become extremely active once again in the United States, teaching the actors of the Lincoln Center Repertory Theater dramatic movement, just as years before she taught choreography to ballet students in New York's School of American Ballet. This crossing of traditional lines is typical of Sokolow's career. In 1967, the National Ballet of Washington performed the Broadway premiere of her work, *Night,* a grim and ominous study to electronic music by Luciano Berio. At the same time, her jazz ballet *Opus 65* was being performed by the City Center Joffrey Ballet in New York. Her work *Rooms* was performed by the Alvin Ailey Company and the Netherlands Dance Theater.

In these works, as in others which she performs with her own company (such as *Dreams, Déserts, Lyric Suite,* or *Time +7*), Sokolow shows a deep concern with modern people's existential state. Her view of life is a bleak and painful one, and her dances are bitter, frightening, tragic—and yet somehow compassionate and moving. The choreography of *Night* is described as "[a] madhouse delirium of weird night-shapes . . . and compulsive night fears . . . terrified and lost, full of half formulated gestures and dances either shaking with tension or limp with despair. . . ."[10]

In *Dreams,* there is the shattering imagery of humans imprisoned in an imaginary concentration camp; people running hopelessly in place; falling, despairing; an unbearable message of misery. In *Déserts,* a world of mystery and loneliness is exposed. It begins and ends with the same image: A dozen individuals are seated on the floor, heads bowed, their postures defenseless and exhausted.

In the mid-1980s, summing up a choreographic career that had already spanned four continents and over fifty years, Sokolow commented, "I started very young and just kept going." In her seventies, she had just created a new work in Mexico City in honor of the famous Mexican painter, Siqueiros, was teaching at the Juilliard School, and preparing her company, Players' Project, for New York performances. Later in the season, she would travel to Ireland, Holland, and Israel to stage and supervise other dances from her past repertoire. As late as 1988, her company performed successfully in New York City, although some critics objected to the pessimism that now seemed to dominate and even to "deaden" much of her work.[11]

We now turn to a group of several choreographers who became widely known and successful in the decades immediately after mid-century and who are today recognized as outstanding creative artists.

Alwin Nikolais

Alwin Nikolais, who for a number of years was director of the Henry Street Playhouse Dance Company in New York City, is an accomplished musician who worked closely with Hanya Holm for a number of years and who composes his own musical scores, which are usually electronic. He has, since the late 1950s, become noted for a new kind of dance theater which is almost completely abstract in terms of dramatic content but which represents a unique and imaginative fusing of sound, color, light, bizarre props, shapes, and movement to create a remarkably theatrical set of illusions on the stage.

The first of his works to be widely seen was *Totem,* choreographed in 1960. This is a full-evening work, consisting of fifteen episodes in which abstract props seem to extend the performers' bodies. In one episode, *Shadow Totem,* dancers appear to be headless; in another, *Banshee,* dancers create a weird effect as they wave lights about under their huge, shapeless costumes; in still another, titled *Clowns,* figures clad in felt of bright color move heavily, their feet and arms suggesting bells. It is a work that has been described as deriving from "mysticism, fetishism and fanaticism." Choreographer-designer Nikolais said of it:

> Ritual and ceremony are like a formula in that certain ingredients, proportioned and mixed, cause a magical result. *Totem* comprises a number of such imagined rituals and ceremonies. I can conceive ritual in the growth of a flower, the kaleidoscopic interplay of geometrical design, the intermingling of people, the flickering of colored lights. Some of *Totem* is fun and foolish ritual, some macabre, and some frightening. To me it shows some of the fanciful moods of nature as it transpires through some of its earthly instruments, including man.[12]

Imago, dance theater-piece by Alwin Nikolais. Photographs by Robert Sosenko.

A second major work of Nikolais's has been *Imago,* a full-evening dance theater piece premiered in 1963. It consists of twelve episodes involving solos, small groups, or the entire company. Choreography, lighting, and costumes are by Nikolais, and he created the electronic score in collaboration with James Seawright. *Imago* has been variously described by critics as weird, fantastic, and delightful. Like *Totem,* it combines dance movement, color, lighting, and electronic music. Its ten dancers are depersonalized through remarkable costuming, the use of white make-up, and stylized headdresses. It contains both humor and menace as well as sequences of great visual beauty.

Other important works of Nikolais have included *Sanctum* (1964), *Galaxy* (commissioned by the John Simon Guggenheim Foundation in 1965), and *Vaudeville of the Elements,* first performed in New York in 1966 and described as a "shifting science-fiction world."

Works created in the late 1970s include: *Gallery,* based on the idea of a moving shooting gallery, with multimasked, hydra-like figures; *Castings,* a variation on his many works using dancers encased in stretch fabric; and *Sanctum,* often considered his most dance-like work.

As he became increasingly successful, Nikolais moved from the tiny Henry Street Playhouse to larger halls in New York, such as the Brooklyn Academy of Music, the City Center, and the Beacon Theater, where he had fuller scope for his environmental works. As much as any other dance choreographer, Nikolais has succeeded in reaching both an audience of dancers and dance enthusiasts (including those influential in the other modern arts) and the public at large.

Throughout the 1980s, the Nikolais company has continued to perform widely. In 1984, for example, it gave programs at twelve cities in Spain, ten of which had never seen modern dance before, as well as at the first Australian Spoleto Festival. It also performed at other festivals in Berlin and Lyons that honored Mary Wigman, whose style had influenced Nikolais in the 1930s. Nikolais's programs typically include works created during the 1950s and 1960s, as well as other, more recently conceived pieces, such as *Crucible* (1984), *Velocities* (1986), and *Contact* (1985).

The single major criticism that is frequently made of Nikolais's work is that it is dehumanized, impersonal—simply a visual and auditory design in which the performers are not dancers as such, but rather movable props, and in which people are not the concern of the dance. To this, Nikolais has replied eloquently, pointing out that all the arts have today become freed from the need to portray literal subject matter and are able to directly translate the "abstract elements that characterize and underline an art object":

> I look upon this polygamy of motion, shape, color, and sound as the basic art of the theater. To me, the art of drama is one thing; the art of theater is another. In the latter, a magical panorama of things, sounds, colors, shapes, lights, illusions, and events happen before your eyes and your ears. I find my needs cannot be wholly satisfied by one art. I like to mix my magics. We are now in a new period of modern dance, and it is a period of new freedom.[13]

Nikolais went on to comment that, while the early modern dance explored the human psyche and was almost a form of psychological drama, today character is no longer dominant. In his view, dance figures speak through motion, shape, time, and space. He pointed out that people's ability to communicate in nonverbal ways, and to sense meaning beyond literal and materialistic language or visual symbols, is their greatest distinction from the lower animals. Finally, Nikolais defended his work against the charge that it is cold, unemotional, and dehumanized by claiming that it is the very reverse; that it has the power to depict people as no literal image could.

Among Nikolais's leading dancers have been Gladys Bailin, Bill Frank, Phyllis Lamhut, Carolyn Carlson, and Murray Louis—several of whom have emerged as successful choreographers in their own right.

Murray Louis

Of this group, Murray Louis in particular has gained recognition as a remarkable choreographer-dancer. Performing first at the Henry Street Playhouse with a small company drawn chiefly from the overall group of Nikolais dancers, Louis has since appeared in other dance series and in tours of the major cities in the United States. He is widely regarded as a brilliant dancer and a highly creative choreographer whose stage works display a great range of inventive movement, humor, pathos, a suggestion of mimetic meaning, remarkable sensitivity, and choreographic author-ity. The mood is often mysterious, and while dramatic relationships may be suggested, the overall characteristic of Louis's work is abstraction.

Among his better-known works have been *Interims,* to music by Lucas Foss; *Chimera,* a solo which offers what seems to be a pop-art parody of electronic music; *Illume,* danced to a score by Toshiro Mayuzumi, suggesting strange creatures of the sea; *Facets,* a duet with Gladys Bailin; and *Calligraph for Martyrs,* an impressive piece which reaches great heights of emotion. He has shared programs at the Brooklyn Academy with Alwin Nikolais and has also choreographed works in the mid- and late 1970s for major international ballet companies. While his choreography has undoubtedly been influenced by Nikolais, Murray Louis makes much less use of elaborate sets, props, and visual effects and is much more directly concerned with the recognizable and comparatively unadorned dancer.

Writing in 1988, Acocella commented that, as seen in his famous work, *Junk Dances,* Louis is interested in "unnatural" movement, ". . . in robotism, frozen tableaus, clowning, acrobatics, eccentric dances. And at his very best, he is able to carve out, in this material, a territory of true and poetic strangeness."[14]

For himself, Louis denied having a consistent, deliberate personal style. Instead, he wrote: "My creative philosophy of the modern dance has always been that each work achieve its own vocabulary of movement style and structure. I never worked to create a personal style or become identified with a singular creative approach . . . This is how I was taught, and I was always a good student. . . ."[15]

Paul Taylor

Among the most successful American dancer-choreographers, in terms of having reached a broad international audience in recent years, has been Paul Taylor.

Paul Taylor and Company in *Orbs*. Photograph by Jack Mitchell.

Originally a painter, Taylor danced first with Merce Cunningham and then with Martha Graham. Since 1956, when he formed his own small company—now consisting of eleven dancers—he has choreographed many works, has toured widely, and has earned a reputation as one of the world's leading modern dance choreographers. The Paul Taylor Dance Company appeared at the 1960 Spoleto Festival, toured Italy in 1961, danced at the Festival of Nations in Paris in 1962 (where Taylor received an international critics' award as best choreographer), and performed in 1963 in performances in Mexico sponsored by the Mexican Government. In 1964, his company toured throughout the United States and then through Europe (Italy, France, Belgium, Holland, England, Iceland). In the following years, he has continued to travel widely.

Taylor, unpretentious about his own work, has written amusingly on the theme, "Down with choreographers!" Nonetheless, his work is painstakingly developed and permits his excellent dancers to show their strengths in well-mounted pieces. It is both complex and simple, serene and exciting, stylish and witty. Taylor is not afraid to repeat himself to build an effect, and sometimes deliberately limits the amount of invention in his dances, repeating and changing basic movement patterns and setting them to music with contrasting tempi in order to develop them fully. His vocabulary of movement tended to be extremely simple at one point;

instead of formal dance movement, he often made use of such ordinary movements as walking, running, falling, or even standing still. Recently, his work has tended to be more action-packed, often at breakneck speed and with ebullient energy. McDonagh described Taylor's typical movement as "modified balletic with free swinging arms for gestural comment." His work is also orderly and highly musical, and he has choreographed pieces to works by Bach and Handel.

For the most part, Taylor's work is abstract, although the viewer may perceive dramatic content if he or she wishes to do so. Among his dances have been *Party Mix,* a parody on party-going; *Scudorama,* concerned with the grim life of cities; *Aureole,* a bouncing, poetically musical work to a setting by Handel; *From Sea to Shining Sea,* a satirical appraisal of American culture; and *Orbs,* an examination of humankind and the universe, which was premiered in New York in 1966 and was hailed by critics and the public as a masterpiece of choreography. Taylor has choreographed for major ballet companies and has featured Rudolf Nureyev as a guest artist with his own company.

Despite his increased success and public acceptance in the 1970s, Taylor had difficulty in maintaining his company on a sound financial base. For years, he found it necessary to tour abroad in order to support his company, and in 1976, steps were taken to dissolve the group until an emergency grant from the National Endowment for the Arts made it possible to continue. Of the earlier period, Taylor commented:

> We're homebodies and we like to perform our work for American audiences. And for dancers, the constant traveling is disruptive and exhausting. But it's financially impossible to put on a big-city show in the United States. The expenses always exceed what we take in at the box office. Actually, we're very lucky to be one of the few companies that can exist by performing abroad.[16]

Through the 1980s, Taylor continued to choreograph new works and at the same time present many of his older dances. In his four-week season at New York's City Center in 1985, for example, twenty of the eighty ballets he had created over a thirty-year period were featured. Among his best-known pieces during the early 1980s were: *Arden Court* (1981), *Lost, Found and Lost* (1982), *Byzantium* and *Equinox* (both 1984), and *Last Look* (1985).

Alvin Ailey

Another American dancer-choreographer who enjoyed remarkable success both abroad and in the United States was Alvin Ailey. Originally trained as a dancer on the West Coast, Ailey assembled a company of strong dancers who perform both his own works and those of a number of other modern choreographers. One of the highlights of the Alvin Ailey Dance Theater is that it was the first black company to be sent abroad by the President's International Exchange Program, administered by ANTA under the auspices of the U.S. State Department. During this 1962 tour, the company presented sixty performances for 146,791 people in twenty-five cities in ten countries. Rich praise was heaped on them; in Hong Kong a dance critic wrote: "These dancers spin, jackknife, twist, swivel, leap, prance, ripple, flutter, slide, contract, recoil, spring, shiver and quake in a way that makes any other dancing look jaded, wooden and stiff."[17]

One important effect of this tour was that it conveyed an understanding of creative dance in America to large groups of artists and intellectuals throughout the East as well as a more varied and positive view of the role of the American black. Edwin Reischauer, American Ambassador to Japan, commented:

> In many fields of art and culture we of the United States have much to learn from the culture of Japan, but in other fields—and here I would especially single out the field of modern dance—we believe that we have something of value to contribute. . . . In the entire range of the performing arts, I know of no art form more uniquely American than the music of the American Negro. This music, and the dances which derive from it . . . have about them something of the originality of expression and the vitality that I like to think of as characteristic to the United States.[18]

Actually, the Ailey company does not perform works that are restricted to black themes or musical sources. In the Far Eastern tour, for example, the following works were performed: John Butler's drama of New England, *Letter to a Lady;* Glen Tetley's *Mountain Way Chant,* an archaic ritual of the Navajo Indian with music by Carlos Chavez; and *Hermit Songs,* a series of solo dances by Ailey set to ancient poems written by Irish monks and to music by Samuel Barber. Only in the final forty-minute section of the two-hour program were black materials used exclusively. This section included one of Ailey's major works, *Revelations,* a deeply felt work based on the black experience in America—full of anger, compassion and, ultimately, a moving spirit of celebration. Among the most popular works performed by the Ailey Dance Company have been *Congo Tango Palace* and *The Road of the Phoebe Snow,* both by Talley Beatty; *Caravan,* by Louis Falco; and *Rainbow Round My Shoulder,* by Donald McKayle.

The Ailey company has continued to offer works not only by himself but by a wide variety of other choreographers, young and old, white and black, men and women. On this policy, Ailey commented: "I think it's much more important in a program of dance to see many people's ideas, rather than just one person's. This also keeps the public interested; the catholicity of what we do keeps the audiences coming, to see lots of different kinds of work."[19]

Inspired in his youth by the California modern dance pioneer, Lester Horton, a white man who maintained the first major interracial dance company in the United States—long before the Civil Rights era—Ailey was determined to do the same in his own company. Kisselgoff pointed out that he stood his ground when he came under pressure to eliminate nonblack dancers from some of his pieces drawn from the black heritage. She described him as a man who insisted on celebrating the human spirit, ". . . artist and humanist rolled into one."[20]

Among the works of other choreographers performed by the Alvin Ailey American Dance Theater during the mid-1980s were Elisa Monte's *Pigs and Fishes,*

Bill T. Jones's *Fever Swamp,* and numerous others. Ailey revived the works of Katherine Dunham, with a highly successful evening-length retrospective of her work in the late 1980s. He also choreographed a number of works dedicated to leading jazz musicians, such as *For Bird—With Love,* inspired by the life and music of Charlie "Bird" Parker, the late jazz saxophonist, and *Mingus Dances,* in honor of the great jazz musician, Charles Mingus. An important 1985 work was a program titled *In the Black Tradition,* consisting of four works derived from black American history, with Judith Jamison, a former leading dancer in the company, as commentator.

Alvin Ailey was the first choreographer to be awarded the City University of New York's Distinguished Professorship, and he became "adopted" by his home town, Kansas City, Missouri, where he had a number of residencies and seasons and where funds were raised to support his choreography. Over the years, he choreographed ballets for such companies as the Joffrey Ballet, the Harkness Ballet, and American Ballet Theater and for opera productions, including Virgil Thomson's *Lord Byron.* Yet, it is a reflection of the economic difficulties faced by modern dance choreographers that in 1988 he was forced to reduce the size of his company and faced eviction from his Manhattan dance studio because of a substantial company debt. Despite such problems, Ailey continued to tour widely. It is clear that, far from being a choreographer who dealt only with folk materials—in this case dance and music of the American black—Alvin Ailey must be recognized as a major creative artist of our time. Like Paul Taylor, he was a superb ambassador for America abroad, as well as for dance itself in his own land. When he died in 1989, Judith Jamison became artistic director of the Ailey company.

Erick Hawkins

Another gifted and original choreographer is Erick Hawkins, a leading dancer with the Graham Company for a number of years. Working to music composed by Lucia Dlugoszewski, musical director of the Hawkins Dance Company, he has performed with a small group of dancers in major modern dance series, has toured the college circuit for decades with much success, and has taught as a guest artist in public schools. Through lectures, discussions, and printed materials, he seeks to broaden the audience's understanding of his art. Hawkins's work is highly experimental and abstract and stresses the use of unusual music or "choreographic sound," created during the performance on sculpturally designed instruments. Indeed, the totality of dance, music, and stage design has always been a key element in his choreography; whether the music is performed by symphony orchestra, chamber music groups, or Dlugoszewski, it is critical to his work, and he insists on it being live rather than played on tapes, records, or electronic devices.

Hawkins is also unique in that he has deeply probed the roots of dance in a variety of ethnic cultures; he has studied the Greeks, the ritual dances of Southwestern American Indians, and Oriental religion and aesthetics. Among his best-known works have been *Early Floating, Geography of Noon, Naked Leopard,* and *Lord of Persia.*

Erick Hawkins (right) with Nancy Meehan and James Tyler in *Early Floating*. Photograph by Jack Mitchell.

A highly intellectual and thoughtful choreographer, Hawkins began his career in the 1930s studying under George Balanchine at the School of American Ballet. A star pupil, he taught at the school and danced with the American Ballet and Ballet Caravan before joining the Graham company. Fifty years later, he has continued to choreograph a number of powerful works concerned with American history and literature, including *Ahab,* a rendering of Melville's novel, *Moby Dick; The Joshua Tree,* an allegorical Wild West tale; and *God's Angry Man,* the story of John Brown. Still dancing at the age of seventy-eight, he received the 1988 Samuel H. Scripps American Dance Festival Award of $25,000 in recognition of his work.

Other Established Choreographers

A number of other modern dancers who continued or developed successful careers as choreographers during the period after mid-century include Glen Tetley, Daniel Nagrin, Donald McKayle, and Bella Lewitsky.

Tetley is particularly noteworthy for having successfully bridged the gap between modern dance and ballet. He had extensive ballet training with Margaret

Craske and Antony Tudor but also studied and performed with Martha Graham and Hanya Holm; he has frequently appeared with his own company as part of modern dance series. He has also been a soloist with American Ballet Theater and has choreographed works for that company. He choreographed for the Netherlands Dance Theater, resident company of The Hague, eventually becoming its codirector. After John Cranko's death in 1973, he briefly held the post of artistic director for the Stuttgart Ballet, and during the 1970s he also mounted works for the Hamburg State Opera Ballet and the British Royal Ballet.

Regarded as an extremely inventive and subtle choreographer and performer, Tetley's works include *Ricercare,* created for the American Ballet Theater; *Pierrot Lunaire,* danced by the Netherlands Company; and *The Mythical Hunters,* commissioned for the *Batsheva Company* of Israel.

Daniel Nagrin, for many years codirector of the Tamiris-Nagrin Dance Company with his wife Helen Tamiris, studied dance with Martha Graham, Hanya Holm, and Anna Sololow. In 1946, he was given the lead dance role in *Annie Get Your Gun,* choreographed by Tamiris; he continued to perform on Broadway, receiving the Donaldson Award for Best Male Dancer in 1955 for his performance in *Plain and Fancy.* His dance style is rooted in jazz, which always has been an important element of his choreography.

At the age of forty, Nagrin presented his first solo concert; two of his most acclaimed works were *Spanish Dance* and *Pelopennesian War,* a commentary on the social and political aspects of the human condition. In 1970, Nagrin organized an improvisational dance company, the Workgroup, and during the 1970s continued to tour the United States, Europe, and the Pacific as a solo performer, teacher, and lecturer. An extremely intense and vigorous dancer, Nagrin is known for such other works as *A Gratitude; Not Me, But Him;* and *Indeterminate Figure*—a view of humankind, whose commanding self-image is contradicted by its irrepressible foibles and weaknesses of character.

A leading black dancer who has performed with the Martha Graham Company, the New Dance Group, the Anna Sokolow Dance Theater, and the New York City Center Opera Ballet is Donald McKayle. He has appeared on Broadway in a number of musicals and has choreographed several successful shows, including *Golden Boy,* as well as many television productions. On the concert stage, his best-known early works were *District Storyville, Rainbow Round My Shoulder,* and *Games,* based on such themes as Southern chain gangs, jazz in a New Orleans brothel years ago, and street games played in the urban ghetto. His later work, such as *Barrio* or *Songs of the Disinherited,* is a less literal treatment of the black experience and is more fully concerned with movement exploration as such.

Another leading choreographer is Bella Lewitsky, who has been referred to as the "West Coast modern dance guru." Her initial training was in ballet, but early in her career she studied and performed with Lester Horton in California. They had fifteen years of intense collaboration, and they jointly founded Dance Theater, a combined school of dance and theater. After breaking with Horton, Lewitsky organized Dance Associates in 1950, which led to the Bella Lewitsky Dance

Company. This group has toured widely and successfully, giving performances and lecture demonstrations.

The Lewitsky Company is well established, traveling around the country in a sleek gray bus donated by CBS, complete with a dance barre and other refinements. In 1988, ground was broken for the construction of a $14 million Dance Gallery, to serve as the company's resident Los Angeles theater. While the company has generally been regarded the leading modern dance group on the West Coast, its most unique feature has probably been Bella Lewitsky herself. Rubinstein quoted the *New York Times* review of her 1971 New York debut:

> Lewitsky is one of America's great dancers, but you won't find her name in the Dance Encyclopedia. What makes her remarkable is her presence. She has the animal presence of Graham, but also a kind of Dionysiac presence, wild, brooding, very womanly, earth mother, strongly physical and compulsively hypnotic. When she dances, it is impossible to watch anyone else. . . .[21]

Other dancers active during this period included Pauline Koner, Pearl Lang, Katherine Litz, Paul Sanasardo, Sybil Shearer, Bertram Ross, Ruth Currier, Stuart Hodes, Lucas Hoving, Helen McGehee, and May O'Donnell. In many cases, they had been leading dancers with one or more of the companies or choreographers described earlier and have since ventured into independent careers heading their own performing groups.

The New Experimentalists

A group of new, younger choreographers emerged, chiefly during the 1960s and 1970s, who might best be described as the new experimentalists—or far avant-garde. In many ways, these individuals differed from their predecessors. Their performances, or presentations, often had little that was dance-like about them in a conventional sense. They seemed to be improvised and unstructured, and often consisted of pedestrian movements drawn from daily life. Often they were performed casually, in impromptu settings—lofts, remodeled warehouses, church basements, streets, and parks—rather than in proscenium theaters or concert halls. Usually, their costumes were casual; often, they consisted of jeans and T-shirts or exercise clothes, and frequently they were shed as the dance continued. Instead of using formal music as accompaniment, the dancers performed in silence, or to the spoken word.

With this nondance or antidance approach, they tended to appeal to new kinds of audiences—people not necessarily interested in or knowledgeable about the arts but open to new kinds of human expression. Similar things were happening in the other arts, and the modern dance experimentalists were part of an important new trend. Often, the groups were fluid in nature; sometimes they formed cooperative organizations which made it possible for different individuals to organize and present concerts through a mutual assistance plan. Instead of the companies being known by the name of the director-choreographer, they had such titles as *Acme*

Dance Co. (James Cunningham), *The Farm* (Deborah Hay), *Grand Union* (Yvonne Rainer), and *The House* (Meredith Monk), reminiscent of the titles of rock bands.

Although one cannot say that any single event or group was responsible for the avant-garde dance that emerged at this time, certainly the Judson Dance Theater in New York City provided a major stimulus. Housed in a Baptist church at the edge of Greenwich Village, members of an experimental composition workshop led by Robert Dunn initiated a series of concerts beginning in July 1962. Before long, the theater became known as the center of unique, exciting, and highly controversial choreography. Such choreographers as Yvonne Rainer, Deborah Hay, Trisha Brown, Steve Paxton, James Waring, David Gordon, Judith Dunn, and Lucinda Childs presented works there regularly in an atmosphere that encouraged freewheeling experimentation in all the arts. Anderson commented that no single choreographic style predominated, but that the work could generally be classified either as "Judson-plain" or "Judson-fancy." He wrote: "The Judson-plain choreographers celebrated human physicality without frills and borrowed dance ideas from pedestrian activities, work movements, games and athletics. . . ."[22] In contrast, the Judson-fancy approach was often extravagant and flamboyant, or occasionally mixed dance styles wildly, as in James Waring's choreography, which often incorporated classical ballet or made whimsical use of props and costumes. Although the Judson Dance Theater only presented two years of its own members' work (other groups continued to offer concerts there until the late 1970s), its influence continued through the 1980s.

In considering the work of the newer choreographers who emerged at this time, it must be recognized first that experimentalism has always flourished in modern dance, as in all contemporary art. The essence of modern dance is that it challenges old traditions and must represent a seeking for the new rather than a replaying of old tunes.

The notion of dance being abstract—in the sense of not having a literal message—is not at all shocking or controversial. While historically ballet represented a form of drama in that it told recognizable stories, most of the choreography of George Balanchine (to select the most solidly entrenched choreographer in that field) was completely nonliteral. What if dance movement is not familiar to the audience (as the ballet *danse d'ecole* would be) or does not fit its expectation in other ways? Throughout the history of dance, new techniques and movements have constantly been developed by innovative performers and choreographers.

In terms of having dancers disguised as objects, or making use of properties that tend to make the dance something of an engineering phenomenon—these too have counterparts in history (such as the lighting and staging techniques of Loie Fuller) and in the other arts (for example, op art, which makes use of objects that are moved by magnetism and built-in motors). Even the sound that is used to accompany avant-garde dance is paralleled by what is happening widely in the music field itself—the use of "fixed" instruments, electronic sound, or even silence as a form of "sound."

Happenings in Avant-Garde Dance

The real stumbling block for many audiences and dance critics appeared during the late 1960s and early 1970s in the realm of dances that were essentially "happenings." One writer defined the term as follows:

> A Happening is simply anything that happens to more than one person in a sort of half-planned, half-spontaneous way. It is an experience shared, and each individual takes from it what he will. Sometimes there are performers and an audience; sometimes the audience are themselves the participants; sometimes there are participants and no audience. A Happening usually consists of several Events which are totally unrelated—a kaleidoscope of impressions, as it were. Performers do not portray characters in specific environments; they are always themselves in precisely the environment in which the Happening is taking place.[23]

The following are examples of possible happenings:

> Tortoises with flashlights tied onto their backs are set loose to "race" toward the finish line in a dark armory space.

> Dancers crawl about on an overhead rope grid, getting into and out of the clothing threaded onto the grid, while an actual rummage sale takes place below them.

> On park benches, dancers perform phrases of movement for a random audience of passersby. Two men move the dancers one by one into other locations as they continue doing their phrases.

There is something intriguing about all of this. A good part of it has to do with the unlikely nature of the situation and with humans involved in a sometimes confrontational process of self-discovery and social contact. When a dance "happening" was staged, it usually involved a degree of preplanning and structure. Thus, in one work, a solo dancer moved around the stage in a dance of five sections. For each section, the audience was asked to participate in a different way. In the first, they rattled paper. In the next, they shouted out numbers at random. In another, they scraped their feet on the floor or cleared their throats. Presumably, the dance was influenced by the sounds they made. After a period of time, the dance was over.

In another dance on the same program, a jazz musician played a series of unconnected, spontaneous phrases on a horn; the sounds were evocative, original, and drew forth a series of vocal sounds from the dancer who sat next to the musician for the first part of the work. Finally, the dancer began to move about the floor as the musician explored the possibilities of his instrument with short bursts of sound. The dancer's movement had no strict beginning or end; it seemed to be a cross-section of unrelated gestures and locomotor movement chosen at random and stopped abruptly.

All of this, as indicated, has a base in the other arts—particularly in trends in the graphic and plastic arts. There, the surrealist, abstract expressionist, and action schools of painting prepared the way, through the 1960s, for the pop and op movements. Characteristic of the latter are that they frequently are based on, or make use of, commonplace objects. Sometimes these may be found objects which most would regard as little more than junk. When it is not the actual object itself, it may be the photograph-like painting of it, as in the painting of giant soup cans, comic strips, or posters. The concept of using such objects in art and performance relates to the French artist Duchamps's idea of the ready-made. It is actually a celebration of the mundane and a challenge to theatrical convention, which insists that to be worthy of presentation work must be polished, technically superior, and certainly not ordinary.

Over a period of time, a number of leading choreographers have reflected these approaches. In Merce Cunningham's chance dances, the idea of improvisation, based on certain stimuli being chosen at random, results in what might be called found movement. In almost all of the avant-garde works, there is a tendency to avoid literal thematic material and also to avoid the appearance of dance that is organized, fitted to instrumental musical accompaniment, and consistently danced in the same way.

Consider the work of one of the major experimenters in avant-garde dance, Ann Halprin. Her company, the Dancers' Workshop of San Francisco, performed an extensive piece titled *Parades and Changes* in New York in 1967. Hering described their work as intended to be fluid and semi-improvisational yet quite intense in mood. The curtain was raised as the audience assembled; the dancers, dressed in trousers and skirts, moved down the aisles and lined up neatly on stage. Then they turned to face the audience and began to disrobe.

> . . . one's interest shifted to the cleverly timed device of having some dancers dressing while others were undressing; by having some dancers suddenly contemplate each other or give the impression that they were competing over each other. All of this was understated, almost ritualistic. Endless carpets of brown wrapping paper were stretched across the stage. The dancers, by now all nude, became entangled in the paper. Some punched at it furiously. Some crawled or stood beneath it. . . . By degrees all gathered up huge armfuls of the paper and began jumping into the pit. . . .[24]

At a later point, the company, dressed now in white, crawled down the aisles, ran down, descended from rope ladders which were attached from the balcony, or just stood and swayed epileptically. They trembled, shouted at the audience and flopped to the floor, now and then rearing up like a "mass of beached fish." The dancers embraced wildly but sexlessly. They stamped on little platforms, yelled like jungle beasts, laughed hysterically, and threw themselves about with no concern for their physical safety.

Environmental Events

In another series of experiments in California, Halprin's dancers joined together with a group of architects exploring the possibility of kinetic environments. The purpose of this collaboration was to enable members of each group to become aware of the nature and possibilities of the other art. As part of it, they constructed a driftwood village on the beach, each person or small team developing environments that suited their needs. Another involved a tower-and-paper event in which dancers told stories, either physically or verbally, and the architects designed and immediately put up light-and-paper constructions based on the repeated telling of the story in different locations. Anderson recounted a major event which illustrates the approach to developing the kinetic environment. It took place in Union Square in San Francisco and was designed to constitute simultaneously a dance composition, an architectural investigation, and, finally, a theater event. At noon on a July day, forty young people entered the square. They sat about, ate lunch, casually napped, or fed pigeons. At three o'clock, chimes from a nearby building struck the hour.

> The 40 young people immediately stopped whatever they were doing and solemnly rose to their feet, as though for a ceremony in church. Each person scanned the square, attempting to establish eye contact with at least 20 other people from the group. That done, they slowly began walking to the center of the square. As though they were magnets or modern-day Pied Pipers, their simple act of walking to a common meeting-point drew a crowd of curious followers behind them. Now in the center where all the paths converged, each of the 40 inflated a balloon and either let it fly off into the air or gave it to a child. Then the 40 mysterious strangers walked away.[25]

In the late 1970s, Charles Reinhart, director of the American Dance Festival, commented that when the Festival was held at Connecticut College, all the younger choreographers were creating environmental pieces and performing outdoors. As an example, he cited Twyla Tharp's *Medley,* in which her dancers performed slow arabesques in a field through the night, although after a while no one was watching. Another example—and a more dramatic one—was Meredith Monk's use of motorcycles and horses "thundering over the campus hills," which led to problems with the college authorities.[26]

Other Trends and Influences in Avant-Garde Dance

Linked to these experimental approaches were several other influences that helped to shape modern dance in the 1960s and 1970s. The first of these was shared with other art forms during the same period—*minimalism*. This consisted of paring the creative expression away to its ultimate core. In fine art, it might have consisted of the use of mundane objects, as described earlier, or of paintings which were solid all-black or all-white-panels. In music, some composers offered works in which a pianist, or several pianists, simply played the same thirty-two bars of music in endless repetitions, while audiences came and went. Fitzgerald described a work by Douglass Dunn, ". . . who proposed in 1974 that stillness could constitute a dance. In *101,* a piece that lasted four hours a day, six days a week, for two weeks at a time, Dunn perched, inert, on the top of a huge maze constructed in his loft."[27]

Contact Improvisation

Another important influence during this period was contact improvisation, a form of movement expression in which dancers (some questioned whether it was really a form of dance) took part in an improvised and unstructured interactive process. Laine described it as the spontaneous interaction, physical and emotional, between two dancers moving together: rolling and tumbling along the floor, sliding over each other's bodies, and leaping into each other's arms. "Sensitivity to touch, balance, momentum, center of gravity and personal dynamics yields a continuous flow of activity involving the giving and taking of weight and the exchange of active and passive roles."[28]

For a period of several years, contact improvisation became a popular form of dance performance, involving both actual demonstrations and participant workshops and festivals. It has been taught at a number of universities and has a national magazine, *The Contact Quarterly,* and an international network of enthusiasts. Although it has the appearance of being totally unrestricted, both partners in a contact improvisation experience are subject to physical laws, similar to those linked to martial arts such as aikido or tai chi' chuan.

Still another trend at this time was based on the use of nonnarrative, associative forms of organization—for example, creating *collage works*—a format borrowed from the 1960s avant-garde theater movement.

Throughout the United States, a number of cooperative or collective dance groups were formed, chiefly during the 1970s, that evolved and used these creative dance approaches. An important example was Grand Union, whose members included Trisha Brown, Yvonne Rainer, David Gordon, Steve Paxton, and Douglass Dunn, among others. This group, while highly improvisational in its approach to dance, was relatively stable in that its members worked closely together over a ten-year period, helping to build what came to be known as Next Wave dance in the United States. Still other well-known choreographers during the 1970s and 1980s included James Cunningham, Laura Dean, Lucinda Childs, Meredith Monk, Rudy Perez, and Twyla Tharp. While it is not possible to describe them all in full detail, profiles of several of them are presented in the following sections.

Trisha Brown

Trisha Brown's early work focused on improvisation and the use of human figures within a massive environment of structures and planes. Improvisation was typically used as a means of having dancers work together to develop a dance structure and jointly create a group work before performing it. In the more contemporary sense, it involves dancers actually creating new movement solutions or relationships while in the process of performing before an audience.

The group of dancers is given a problem and then, based on an awareness of each other's movement styles and responding to signals, moves ahead to develop a choreographic solution to it. The problem may relate to a relationship or other situation within the group, a prop, costumes, or movement phrase; as the dancers explore it over time, they develop a facility for dealing with it in an entertaining and creative way. In one dance, called *Sticks* (part of a larger work titled *Line Up*), five women lie on their backs in a head-to-toe line, with long sticks lined up above and parallel to their bodies. Maintaining contact with the sticks in a straight line, they

Trisha Brown Dance Company in *Glacial Decoy,* with visual presentation and costumes by Robert Rauschenberg. Courtesy of Performing Artservices, Inc. Photograph by Babette Mangolte.

crawl out from under them, step over them, and get under them again from the other side. In another piece from the same work, titled *Mistitled (5'Clacker),* they repetitively run forward and back from a starting line, with more steps each time, to the accompaniment of a tape of a wooden stick hitting a glass at ten-second intervals.

In another series of works presented by the Trisha Brown group, dancers stood on the roofs of fifteen buildings, relaying movement in a steady stream to the one member of a group in a position to see all of them. One of Brown's best-known pieces consisted of having dancers walk vertically up and down the walls of the Whitney Museum of American Art, assisted by suction-soled shoes and cables attached to an overhead trolley. Siegel commented about her work:

> Brown has a special quality of plainness and unexcitability that always makes her work seem extraordinary to me. . . . Brown's work is concerned first with the subjective experience of the dancer, then with the vicarious experience of the audience. Presentation, or how it looks as a theatrical show, comes pretty low in her priorities. . . .[29]

In the 1980s, Brown developed more complex and elaborate works, with designs and costumes by Robert Rauschenberg, Nancy Graves, and Beverly

Emmons, and scores by Laurie Anderson and Peter Zummo. Her dances have become less dependent on "cartoon jokes" (in her own words) and more theatrical, using all the resources of the theater—after years of performing chiefly in alternative spaces such as art galleries, studies, and open-air spaces.[30]

Laura Dean

Laura Dean's work is characterized by simple dance structures (often geometrical in nature) and minimal movement elements, such as stepping, kicking, clapping, jumping, or turning, performed to a steady, driving rhythm set by the choreographer. In *Circle Dance,* for example, performed in the mid-1970s, ten performers, dressed in simple white pants and shirts, moved in four concentric circles for thirty-five minutes. There was no variation, except for occasional reversals of direction. At the end of the dance, each performer broke away into five minutes of rapid spinning. In *Jumping Dance,* twelve people arranged in a three-by-four pattern jumped steadily in unison, until exhausted, grunting "ha" as they landed.

One critic has called Dean's work "overly possessed by the rudimentary"; another described it as "extremely monotonous." Yet, somehow, it radiates a sense of vitality and clockwork precision; a single new gesture or change of direction carries a strong impact. Toby Tobias summed up the audience's typical reaction as one of disarmed pleasure: "Drawn into the work by its hypnotic qualities, they are . . . seduced by the forthright simplicity and the vigor of Miss Dean's compositions into seeing exactly what she intends them to see: the freshness and enormous interest of the simple elements of dancing."[31]

Beyond this, like Trisha Brown, Laura Dean is also deeply concerned about the dancers themselves; she sees the work as a means of unifying the group, strengthening its sense of kinship and minimizing its differences. Music is a critical part of Dean's work; the company itself is called *Laura Dean Dancers and Musicians*. Through the 1980s, they have toured widely and have had seasons at the Joyce Theater in New York. Gradually, their movement has become somewhat more varied, with fuller use of the upper body and arms. A number of critics have commented that Dean's work has a strong Near Eastern or American Indian ritual quality.

Lucinda Childs

Another member of the Judson Theater group of experimental choreographers, Lucinda Childs tired in the late 1960s of the extremely spare dance technique and the use of nondance movement that had been the vogue, and she left dance for a time. Returning with her own small company in the early 1970s, she began choreographing solos and small pieces that focused on the exploration of space and spatial relationships. In 1976, she spent a year working on and performing in the Robert Wilson/Philip Glass avant-garde opera, *Einstein on the Beach*. This radically affected her work. Until this time, she had not used music but had relied on spoken monologues or no sound at all. Now she began to collaborate with Philip Glass,

Steve Reich, and other composers as well as with architects and lighting designers in choreographing much more elaborate works for the Paris Opéra Ballet, the Pacific Northwest Ballet, and the Los Angeles Museum of Contemporary Art.

In her more recent works, such as *Portraits in Reflection,* presented at the Joyce Theater in 1986, Childs has made use of photography and complex lighting schemes and classical dance movements. In addition, like a number of other formerly freewheeling performers, she has become much more business-minded in her approach to production, with a management group and intensive fund-raising efforts.

Meredith Monk

Another uniquely different avant-garde creator and performer is Meredith Monk. Although she began her career as a dancer and is customarily reviewed by dance critics, her work is a unique blend of music, dance, and theater which she herself has described as opera-epics, theater cantatas, nonverbal opera, visual poetry, image dance, and mosaic theater.

"The Rally," a section from Meredith Monk's *Quarry.*

Her pieces are not improvised on the spot; instead, they are carefully structured and staged, with elaborate musical accompaniment, and often with extensive trappings or in planned environments. For example, in a major work, *Juice,* sections of the dance were presented along the spiraling ramp of New York's Guggenheim Museum, with spectators taking an elevator to the top and walking down along the ramp to view the exhibits.

Much of Monk's work has a mystical, symbolic, and child-like quality. In another piece, *Education of the Girlchild,* several dancers perform what appear to be a series of rites, visions, and morality plays; at one point, Monk is dressed as an old crone by the others and left to sit alone and immobile on a cloth-shrouded throne during intermission, while the audience mills around her. In a later section of the work, Monk does a forty-five-minute solo, retracing the stages of life back to childhood. In these and other pieces, Monk uses music which consists of singing, chanting, her own creation of nonliteral, yelp-like sounds, and simple but evocative keyboard music. Her movement consists, in John Rockwell's words, of "quick stylizations of natural motion, funny, oddly flowing, puppetlike jerkiness and sudden ritual poses."[32]

Critical reaction to Monk's work has been mixed. Clive Barnes dismissed her as "mildly tedious" and later as "a disgrace to the name of dancing." Yet other critics have called her "spectacularly original" or "the most significant intermedia artist of our time." In the mid-1980s, her theater piece, *The Games,* a multimedia collaboration with Ping Chong, was a spectacular combination of a futuristic set, almost magical lighting effects, and an usually rich score that made use of chanting and vocal sounds with effects created by varied exotic instruments. The movement of the dancers, presided over by Monk as the Gamemaster, was mystical and puzzling and had the overall quality of a science fiction piece about life in the future after some event that destroyed contemporary civilization.[33] The dream-like quality of much of her work was found again in a 1986 piece, *Acts From Under and Above,* which one critic said ". . . [expresses] the unvoiced parts of human experience. . . . Monk's originality and precision, her almost uncanny ability to tap into veins of experience, make her *Acts* not merely a riff on the human condition but a chamber epic."[34]

Steve Paxton

For years a leading dancer in the Merce Cunningham company, Steve Paxton has been deeply concerned with discovering the sources of dance movement. He has used varied devices to suggest movement forms and sequences and has, like other avant-garde choreographers, sought to develop performers as people, rather than technicians. To facilitate this, he has simplified movement to the basic actions of walking, standing, turning, and jumping, and has at times used nondancers because they were more natural and personal in their approach to movement than dancers. Indeed, he has incorporated animals such as dogs and chickens in his work, seeking to express the casual untidiness of everyday life. Once, after a duet with a chicken, he commented, "The performance was bad but we had a good rehearsal."

In his attempt to help audiences view dance in new ways, Paxton has used nudity as a choreographic element—a vogue that became accepted on the Broadway stage with *Oh, Calcutta* and *Hair* and in the much more radical presentations of the Environmental Theater Company directed by Richard Schechner.

At one point, when invited to perform in a dance series sponsored by New York University, Paxton notified the directors of the series that his concert included having forty-two nude redheaded people walking across the stage of the theater. When the university ruled that it would not permit this, he canceled his scheduled performance; however, since there was no way of notifying the prospective audience of the change, he substituted a piece titled *Intravenous Lecture*. This consisted of Paxton's delivering a lecture on performing situations and sponsors while having a doctor plunge a needle in his arm and having an unidentified liquid drip into his vein for twenty minutes—as a bitter protest against the university's action. Siegel asked:

> Why do college administrators fail to see that the difference between art and pornography turns on something besides the amount of human flesh exposed? And why, having exercised their right of uncomprehending censorship, are they surprised when the artist doesn't spew out his anger . . . around the debating table, but instead restates the issue in a harsher and more obscene way than anyone had intended?[35]

One of the originators of contact improvisation, Paxton has given much of his time through the 1980s to conducting workshops and presentations in this area of movement exploration.

Twyla Tharp

Twyla Tharp is inexhaustible in invention and dynamic performance. The dances she creates are rich in musicality, underlying structure, and a casual, loose-jointed, quickly shifting energy which often presents a nonchalant, meandering view of the dancer. Born in Indiana, her family moved to California when she was a young child, and she remained there until attending Barnard College. While a student in New York, she studied a great deal of dance. Upon graduating in 1963 with a degree in art history, she joined Paul Taylor's Company for two years. In the mid-1960s she began to choreograph extensively, completing twenty-two works between 1965 and 1970.

The *Bix Pieces* was premiered in 1971 and has become one of the best known of her works. A group of dances interspersed with dialogue appears casually serious yet as an extremely personal statement. The dances have a strong relation to music by Bix Beiderbeck, Joseph Haydn, and Thelonius Monk; she conveys her ideas and reactions in a variety of dance styles.

In addition to continued extensive choreography for her company, Tharp also has created dances for Joffrey Ballet Company and American Ballet Theater; and her *Push Comes to Shove,* choreographed for Mikhail Baryshnikov, was hailed by ballet and modern supporters alike. In the late 1970s, she choreographed a dance for Olympic medalist John Curry, contributing to the broadening concept of ice dancing. She has been the recipient of numerous awards, including the respected Guggenheim Fellowship, which she received twice.

In the 1980s, Tharp continued to choreograph new works, including *The Catherine Wheel* (1981), *Nine Sinatra Songs* (1984), and *In the Upper Room* (1987). She has choreographed dances for a number of films, including *Hair* (1979), *Ragtime* (1981), *Amadeus* (1984), *White Nights* (1985), and *Singing in the Rain* (1985). Tharp carefully differentiates between commerce and art: "Commercially when I work, I serve my audiences. . . . When I'm working for my company and for myself, I'm an artist and I do what I feel is necessary. . . ."[36]

In a 1987 four-week engagement at the Brooklyn Academy of Music, Twyla Tharp demonstrated versatility in her range of dance movements; in one piece, the dancers wore pointe shoes and sneakers (which she refers to as "stompers" and "squatters"), and in another they were entirely on pointe. In 1988, in a major career decision that she described as a "shakedown," Twarp disbanded the modern dance company that she had begun in 1965 and joined American Ballet Theater as artistic associate and resident choreographer, a billing shared with Kenneth MacMillan.

Pilobolus

A uniquely entertaining modern dance company, Pilobolus is known for its offbeat humor, inventive use of the body, and the illusions that it has created through sculptural combinations of its dancers. Founded in 1971 by four male athletes as an outgrowth of a dance class taught by Alison Chase at Dartmouth, it had the aura of a college humor magazine, along with vaudeville-like routines and occasionally moving psychological works.

Pilobolus Dance Theatre in *I'm Left, You're Right, She's Gone*. Photograph by Michael O'Neill.

Pilobolus's leading spirit has been Moses Pendleton, although the other dancers in the group (including Chase, Robby Barnett, Jonathan Walken, and Michael Tracy) have played key roles in creating pieces. The original members have left the company through the years to become independent choreographer-dancers or to pursue other performing arts projects, and they have been replaced. At the outset, most Pilobolus dances were group works, often with the dancers disguised to create magical illusions. Goldner described the effect: "Six bodies intertwine so that it's impossible to figure out whose arm is attached to whose shoulder is attached to whose neck. And just how many bodies are up there on the stage, anyway?"[37]

Originally abstract and gymnastic in nature, the company's dances have become more thematic and, as women joined the group, more dramatic and emotionally suggestive, although their meaning is always ambiguous. The name *Pilobolus* is taken from a vigorous genus of fungi that thrives on horse manure. Commenting on the name, Jonathan Wolken said: "Pilobolus doesn't leap forward, it ectoplasms its way along. True to our biologic nature, we grow amoeba-like. We don't solve problems, we engulf them."[38]

Bill T. Jones/Arnie Zane and Company

Another American modern dance group that rose rapidly in public popularity and critical acclaim during the 1980s was the Bill T. Jones/Arnie Zane and Company. Jones and Zane were close professional and personal associates for seventeen years, until Zane's death in 1988. Their work, marked by collaboration with innovative rock composers, designers, and theater people, has invariably been inventive and highly theatrical. In the mid-1980s, the ten-member company, with both Jones and Zane dancing in their collaborative programs, had several two-week seasons at the City Center in New York, as well as numerous performances on tour.

One major piece has been *Secret Pastures* (1984), which consists of a high-tech fantasy epic with seven episodes set to an inventive rock score by Peter Gordon. In Kisselgoff's words, it presents "a plain moral tale about the corrupting influence of civilization on natural man."[39] In 1985, Jones and Zane choreographed a new work, *How to Walk an Elephant,* for the Alvin Ailey American Dance Theater, and also a New York premiere of *Freedom of Information,* a three-part piece which Laine described as ". . . a melange of spoken text, visual design, unusual musical accompaniment and a dance vocabulary that comprises classical, modern, jazz, mime, gymnastic and everyday movement [making use] of a computer-generated film design . . . and a tape sound collage. . . ."[40]

In a later work, *The History of Collage,* performed at the City Center in 1988 after Zane's illness and death, the dance progresses from scattered, quiet movement of solitary figures into what Dunning described as a "powerful and almost painfully resonant evocation" of the political history of homosexuals during the past few decades in America.[41] Like a number of other Jones-Zane works during the preceding years which had dealt with issues of black consciousness, this piece is compelling and highly emotional.

Foreign Modern Dance Companies

One of the unique aspects of the 1980s has been the emergence of a number of outstanding avant-garde modern dance companies in several European countries and Japan.

Pina Bausch Tanztheater Wuppertal

Pina Bausch is a West German choreographer who is regarded as the leading exponent of the Neo-Expressionist movement that has become widely popular in Europe and is known as Dance Theater. Bausch's early training was with Kurt Jooss at the Folkwang School in Essen, Germany; in 1959 she went to New York as a special student at the Juilliard School of Dance and also studied with Paul Taylor, José Limón, and several of Graham's followers. After performing with the New American Ballet and the Metropolitan Opera, Bausch returned to Europe as a soloist in the Folkwang Ballet Company, later becoming director of the Wuppertal Opera Ballet.

Since then, she has directed and choreographed works for opera and film and has evolved a "total theater" approach that is highly emotional and disturbing. Galloway described her theater dance as blending tenderness with savagery, celebration with despair. He wrote: "Her choreography, with its uninhibited gestural style and distinctive, often disturbing imagery heavily laced with eroticism and male-female violence, has been a subject of controversy wherever the Dance Theater has appeared."[42]

In a number of her works, relations between the sexes are explored. *Kantakthof* equates male-female encounters in a dance hall with episodes in a house of prostitution; in *Bluebeard,* the wife killer is savagely depicted; in *Seven Deadly Sins,* based on the musical theater of Kurt Weill and Bertolt Brecht in the 1920s and 1930s, she deals with the issue of women treated as commodities. Her works are not explicit, but rather imagist, and are usually performed in everyday dress, often with a minimum of actual dance movement. They are created through a sustained process of improvisation and exploration which all the dancers of the company share. Bausch has been an extremely popular choreographer in Europe over the past ten years. Her company has performed at a number of major festivals, has been acclaimed in South America, Israel, and Australia, and came to North America in 1985 to perform in New York, California, and Canada.

Compagnie Maguy Marin

This French avant-garde modern dance company, formerly the Ballet Theatre de l'Arche, was renamed in 1984 for its new director, the young, Spanish-born Maguy Marin. Marin's initial training, like many other European dancers, was in ballet. She danced with the Strasbourgh Opera Ballet and then with Maurice Béjart's Ballet of the Twentieth Century.

Her first important dance work to be seen in the United States was *May B,* inspired by the English playwright Samuel Beckett and performed at the American

Dance Festival in North Carolina in 1983. It is an understated work of shabby figures in gray make-up and poorly fitting gray clothing who move in a cramped, shuffling way. In later works, shown at the Brooklyn Academy of Music's Next Wave Festival in 1987, Maguy Marin's choreography became far more theatrical and exciting in works like *Babel, Babel* and *Eden*. She creates vivid images dealing with complex questions—often making use of multimedia effects, nudity, wigs and masks, and almost cartoon-like movement episodes. Hardy commented: "While Marin's pictorialism can be moving, the tendency to sensationalize sex, violence and pop culture delivers cheap thrills more often than cosmic truths. . . . Given time and rigorous editing, her work may become seasoned to a point where its impact is as powerful as its imagery."[43]

Other foreign avant-garde dancers or companies that have appeared in the United States over the last several years have included the Japanese Butoh groups, Sankai Juku and Muteki-Sha; and several Belgian dance groups, including those directed by Anne Teresa de Keersmaeker, Wim Vandekeybus, and Michèle-Anne de Mey.

Major Changes in the 1980s

Summing up, what are the major changes that have occurred in modern dance over the past decade? Essentially, there were at least five of these, including new choreographic approaches, different kinds of settings for performance, the evolving relationship with ballet, innovative methods of fiscal management and promotion of dance companies and programs, and growing geographic diversity.

Changing Choreographic Approaches

During the 1980s, the Minimalist approach, which had characterized dance during the previous decades, gave way to a much fuller and more theatrical and dance-like style. A growing number of choreographers began exploring new movement themes, presenting narratives or at least dances with hints of relationships and conflicts. Gradually, they made use of much fuller staging and costumes, decor, and varied forms of musical accompaniment.

This trend was not unique to dance. In music, art, sculpture, and other areas of creative expression, the Minimalism of the 1960s and 1970s had rejected traditional modes of expression, formal and complex presentations, and sought to pare down work to its absolute core. Writing about musical composition, Rockwell said that Minimalism reached its peak in the late 1960s as ". . . a movement—never formally organized but still a tangible linking of like-minded artists—[that] embraced all the arts, starting with painting and sculpture and quickly spreading to dance and music and beyond."[44]

In music, the Minimalists of the 1960s struck out against what they saw as the ornate complexity and compositional virtuosity of late-Modernist composers. In sculpture, the Minimalist vogue had resulted in an esthetic that "boxed and walled in every alternative" with its hard edges, seamless surfaces, and primary forms. But, by 1986, Brenson wrote that the stranglehold of Minimalism had ended and that sculpture has become much freer, with a "dizzying diversity of materials and the freedom to know how to use them."[45] In 1983, a noted art critic commented that "painting is once again provocative" and was becoming again what it had been for centuries—"the locus of some of the deepest and most tenacious of human feelings."[46]

In the mid-1980s, Anna Kisselgoff discussed the changes that were occurring in modern dance. Increasingly, she concluded, avant-garde choreographers were concerned about their "meaning" reaching the public and no longer considered communication to be irrelevant. More and more, she wrote, the newest generation of choreographers were rediscovering words such as *emotion* and *narrative* and were dealing with significant social themes.[47]

Beyond this, avant-garde dance was becoming far more concerned with using varied media to create vivid, high-impact stage effects.[48] More and more, dance was becoming part of a multimedia approach using light, sound, movement, painting, poetry, mime, and other forms of expression to create what some have described as performance art. Rockwell commented that this genre might seem both strange and unclassifiable:

> Strange, because it takes a "non-narrative" theatrical form, full of imagery that must be intuitively appreciated rather than "understood" in the way that a conventional plot can be grasped. Unclassifiable, because to the uninitiated, a performance work might look like theater or dance or poetry or music or mime, yet be considered "performance art."[49]

Physical Settings for Dance

Another major change that occurred during this period had to do with the places where dance was presented. Although the major modern dance companies had traditionally performed in concert halls or theaters, many of the more experimental dancers in the 1960s and 1970s sought different performance settings, for both aesthetic and economic reasons. Richard Schechner wrote:

> The first scenic principle of environmental theater is to create and use whole spaces. Literally spheres of spaces, spaces within spaces, spaces which contain, or envelop, or relate, or touch all the areas where the audience is and/or the performers perform. All the spaces are actively involved in all the aspects of the performance. . . . And the theater itself is part of larger environments outside the theater. These larger out-of-the-theater spaces are the life of the city; and also temporal-historical spaces—modalities of time/space.[50]

Often, interior spaces were redesigned to permit a fluid use of different kinds of space and to enable the actors or dancers to become involved with the audience. Environmental theater was greatly concerned with the ways in which space could be transformed and animated. Its performers sought to communicate with space and with each other through space by learning to locate" . . . centers of energy and boundaries, areas of inter-penetration, exchange, and isolation, 'auras' and 'lines of energy'."[51]

Avant-garde dancers were influenced by this approach. McDonagh, for example, commented that one of Twyla Tharp's main purposes in choreography was "to throw lines of movement across and through space and thereby establish a zone of human mastery over the real estate that is our environment."[52]

Loft Dance. An inevitable outcome of this concern with controlled space, as well as of the economics of modern dance performance, resulted in a growing number of experimental modern dancers developing remodeled loft, garage, or warehouse areas where they lived, rehearsed, choreographed, and performed for audiences. Often living in run-down industrial and manufacturing areas, side by side with other artists, such arrangements made it unnecessary to rent space in expensive theaters or concert halls and provided an intimate setting for informal dance presentations. Often, too, since rehearsal space was also performance space, the line between groups improvising and creating dances, and presenting them, tended to disappear. Audiences came to see process, as well as product, and in many cases became involved in the work themselves. At the same time, the works tended to be so casual, informal, and modest in presentation that the dance critics ignored them and, without public attention, they came to constitute a sort of dance underground. In some measure, this tendency was counteracted by festivals which brought together a variety of smaller avant-garde companies in joint presentations designed to attract larger audiences and public attention.

Modern Dance Cooperatives

In the early decades of modern dance, a number of smaller halls were made available for performance in many cities. In New York, for example, the 92nd Street Young Men's and Young Women's Hebrew Association, the Judson Memorial Church in Greenwich Village, and Riverside Church, near Columbia University, provided such settings.

During the 1960s and 1970s, avant-garde choreographers and smaller companies began to join together in cooperative producing groups with their own rehearsal and performing halls. In New York City, one of the first such organizations was the Dance Theater Workshop, headed by David White, which sought to assist small modern dance companies with problems of promotion, scheduling, rehearsal and performance space, publicity, and similar administrative concerns. Operating at first in a loft in the Chelsea area of Manhattan, the workshop encouraged member groups to exchange services with each other. In time it became known as the American Theater Laboratory, operating in a larger facility leased from Jerome Robbins and presenting a rich forty-five-week performance season with assistance from the National Endowment for the Arts and other nonprofit foundations. It has continued through the 1980s as a vital center of creative dance activity and is described more fully in chapter 13.

Similarly, in the mid-1970s, a modern dance cooperative known as the Dance Umbrella was formed to provide a permanent and economically viable performing space for dance in New York. Twelve established groups, including the Viola Farber, Cliff Keuter, James Cunningham, Lar Lubovitch, Merce Cunningham,

Kathryn Posin, Elizabeth Keen, Dan Wagoner, Margaret Beals, and Kazuko Hirabayashi dance companies, joined together to sponsor separate dance evenings for each of the groups at the Roundabout Theater in New York. The theater itself, with a large stage and 300-seat hall, provided box office and administrative services, technical functions, and equipment; a subscription series relieved many of the companies of the need to promote their own performances. With funding by the National Endowment for the Arts Dance Panel, the New York State Council on the Arts, and grants by the Mellon and Ford Foundations, the Dance Umbrella concept flourished, projecting a clearer and more forceful professional image of modern dance than the companies' separate seasons would have done individually.

By the 1980s in New York, as in other large cities with sustained real estate booms, the formerly cheap lofts in run-down neighborhoods were frequently purchased, gentrified, and made economically inaccessible to struggling young painters, musicians, or dancers. Although new centers for dance continue to emerge, such as The Kitchen and St. Marks-in-the-Bowery in New York, the tendency of small dance groups to form cooperatives has declined.

Instead, Zimmer described the trend in downtown dance involving a shift from loft concerts to club performances. Artists, she wrote, who several years ago might have taken several months to prepare an hour-long performance, have been superseded by younger artists who "book dates to do ten-minute pieces in scruffy East Village rooms," scarcely distinguishable from stand-up comedians.[53] At the same time, in the 1980s, there continued to be a great number of performances by more established companies in halls ranging from large centers, such as the New York State Theater or the Joyce Theater, to theaters in various colleges and universities and in hundreds of community arts centers throughout the nation. Without question, the sheer volume of modern dance in the late 1980s far exceeded that of the preceding decades.

Geographic Diversity and New Management Approaches

While New York City has continued to be the recognized center of modern dance activity in the United States, there are growing numbers of performance groups and modern dance centers or cooperatives in other cities. Among the most active sponsors of new performing groups are colleges and universities. Many of them host special dance workshops, institutes, student groups, and dance series in which leading companies perform on tour.

In the San Francisco Bay Area of California, for example, modern dancers have forged a solid organizational foundation for mutual support and sharing. Numerous dance groups cooperate in sponsoring professional-level classes and workshops, sharing rehearsal and performing space, and promoting each others' efforts. A considerable number of groups involved in contact improvisation, such as Mangrove, Metropolitan Quartet, Reunion, and West Wing, make up the Bay Area Contact Coalition. The San Francisco Dancers' Workshop, led by Ann Halprin, has encouraged creative development in modern dance and sponsored year-long series of free concerts for the public at large in cooperation with the San Francisco

Museum of Modern Art. Other groups, including the San Francisco Bay Area Dance Coalition, have joined in efforts to hold dance film festivals, establish an archives system for the performing arts, and assist performing groups with legal and other administrative needs. A nonprofit corporation, Performing Arts Services, Inc., was established to help modern dance and other performing arts companies in the Bay Area promote attendance and make low-cost tickets available to a wider segment of the general public.

The Colorado Contemporary Dance is a nonprofit organization of volunteers in Denver established to heighten awareness of modern dance and develop enthusiastic dance audiences. Recently, it began a well-received performance series of professional companies, including the Alwin Nikolais Dance Theater, the Utah Repertory Dance Company, the Pilobolus Company, and others.

Winnipeg's Contemporary Dancers is promoting modern dance throughout Western Canada, with a repertory subscription series and extensive touring funded by the Canada Council. Because of the shortage of trained dancers in the region, auditions are held in Winnipeg, Toronto, Montreal, and occasionally in New York.

The Bureau for Cultural Affairs in Atlanta, Georgia, has actively promoted modern dance festivals and performances by a large number of local and regional contemporary dance groups. In addition, the Metropolitan Atlanta Dance Coalition, a cooperative effort of local modern dance companies, has been formed to assist its members as an information-clearinghouse, to publish a dance newsletter, and to conduct seminars on grant strategies and proposal writing.

The Utah Repertory Dance Theater, a democratically run modern dance collective established originally by Virginia Tanner, has toured widely, sponsored a number of dance workshops in collaboration with colleges in the Rocky Mountain region, and offered regional summer dance festivals in Salt Lake City.

The Detroit Metropolitan Dance Project, in cooperation with the Michigan Dance Association, has sponsored statewide conferences to explore varied aspects of dance aesthetics, criticism, management, and production.

Numerous other examples might be cited of local or state organizations formed to assist modern dance or to join the efforts of smaller, struggling companies in collaborative productions, seasons, or other promotional efforts. Such coalitions have typically sponsored professional concert series, regional dance festivals, dance event calendars, master classes, and choreographic workshops; have served as resource centers for the dance community; and have encouraged expansion of dance awareness in the public at large.

Changing Relationship with Ballet

In examining the relationship between modern dance and ballet, it is important to recognize that they tend to appeal to markedly different audiences. The ballet audience tends to be somewhat more conservative and tradition-oriented, while the modern dance enthusiast is usually somewhat more open to innovation and probably more liberal in terms of social and artistic attitudes.

There is an obvious contrast between the two forms of dance with respect to technique and the ability to judge it. Even the relatively inexperienced ballet enthusiast can usually recognize the difference between amateurish, poor dancing and the crisp, forceful, and controlled movement of the skilled ballet artist. That ballet is based on traditional training and vocabulary of movement provides a consistent basis for judging its performance. In modern dance, while a skilled spectator may be able to make comparable judgments, often an avant-garde work may actually have little recognizable dance content in it or may be based on deliberately awkward, clumsy, or distorted movement.

A related problem is that, unlike ballet, where it is assumed that an individual must have a substantial background of training and performance before becoming a choreographer, often in modern dance it is assumed that anyone may become a choreographer. Since one of the purposes of modern dance in education is to encourage creativity and self-expression, students with almost no background in dance may be asked to create dances.

As a consequence, many individuals with relatively little training, skill, or talent have established themselves as choreographers and have presented works through which audiences have judged the field of modern dance. The result has frequently been that the product is poor and the audience response negative. The temptation of avant-garde dance is that it creates a situation in which there are few standards which an audience or choreographer can apply.

The premises on which avant-garde dance are based sacrifice certain strengths inherent in a more traditional approach to choreography. Self-expression, naive as it may be, at least provides an impulse for the composer and the possibility of meaningful communication with an audience. The selection of thematic material which is dramatic, or which is perceptibly concerned with social content or psychological insights, again offers the possibility of holding an audience or providing the piece with structure. The use of music which has its own form, mood, rhythms, and aesthetic content lends another kind of strength to dance. The approach to choreography which values the application of traditional principles of artistic construction—balance, contrast, sequence, climax, dynamics—offers a system in which the composer may learn a craft and through which he or she may be judged.

Much avant-garde dance has tended to lack these elements. It stands or falls strictly on the basis of superficial and transitory audience appeal. And, based on many of the works that have been presented thus far, many of the most experimental pieces have little to offer once the novelty of improvisational freedom, or the surprise of seeing dancers in uncustomary activities or states of dress (or undress), has passed away.

This, of course, represents a personal judgment. Each artist, as well as each spectator, must make his or her own decisions in matters of artistic taste. However, many teachers and choreographers fear that if an increasing number of choreographers—particularly those who lack real conviction in this area, or whose basic skills are limited—adopt this approach because it is fashionable and easy and cannot be judged with rigor, the risk is that modern dance will be judged as a strange and mysterious "put on." Instead of being regarded as a significant art form, it will be threatened, even more than in the recent past, with rejection or disinterest.

Therefore, an atmosphere somehow must be maintained—both in dance academies and in colleges where beginning choreography is done—that permits young artists to evaluate the trend critically, to see it in comparison to other styles of choreography, and, if they wish, to reject it rather than accept it blindly. During the 1980s, it has become clear that a growing number of choreographers *have* moved away from the more extreme forms of Minimalist, content-less dance, in the direction of more theatrical, richer works. At the same time, continued experimentation must be encouraged if modern dance, like any other art, is to be healthy.

Finally, it is necessary to examine the changing relationship between modern dance and ballet. During the early decades of modern dance's development, there was much hostility between the two. Modern dancers for the most part rejected ballet strenuously as a foreign, decadent, and mechanical art form. In their view, it was so committed to an obsolete movement vocabulary and to themes of a distant past that it no longer was significant to those who wished to view dance as part of the contemporary cultural scene.

Margaret H'Doubler, the leading pioneer of modern dance in higher education, wrote:

> The ballet is a form of theater dance that continues to be popular in the more urban centers of this country, although as an art form it has never taken root in American soil. Its earliest importations were taught by foreign dance masters, and in essence they were dances of an aristocratic Europe. . . . If ballet were denied its spectacular settings, costumes and orchestra, and were forced to rely upon its movements for conveyance of meaning, it is doubtful if it would carry as much significance as drama or dance. Both the technique and the themes seem to have lost touch with life, with common human impulses from which all the arts spring.[54]

On the other hand, Lincoln Kirstein, writing in the mid-1930s, characterized the way in which many of the proponents of ballet thought about modern dance. He described those who create "in spite of and outside tradition" as almost invariably suffering from lack of information, competence, or accomplishment. Ultimately, he saw what they created as becoming a rigid "school of formulated dilettantism."

Even more critically, the English ballet critic Arnold Haskell wrote about an early stage of what was to become modern dance:

> Dancing that gets its inspiration from ancient Greece is also popular today, and doubtless it is of distinct benefits as physical education. So is hockey. (Both have a thickening effect on the ankles.) Its artistic pedigree will not bear close examination. . . . The dancing rebels do provide one fine ingredient—thought. There is a close parallel here with the unlicensed medical practitioner.[55]

Thus, there was a mutual hostility between modern dancers and ballet performers; it extended to audiences, teachers, and choreographers. Most modern dancers, although they might have had a degree of ballet training in their youth, regarded it as a separate and unrelated art and one in which they had little interest—certainly one which had no part in their own systems of technical training. Most ballet dancers and choreographers saw modern dance as a somewhat obscure cult of enthusiasts who concealed with mystic statements of purpose their lack of ability to dance. Or, in contrast, they viewed it, as Haskell did, as a fairly vigorous but certainly not artistic form of physical education.

However, even in the early years there were some exceptions. Ted Shawn, who had been trained in ballet, regarded it as a valuable ingredient in the development of a dancer:

> So much has been said and written against the ballet that I feel it is wise to emphasize some of its positive virtues. Nothing has ever taken its place for disciplinary training. There is no technique in any other style of dancing that is so valuable for producing exactitude, precision, sense of form, and sense of line. I do not think that it should be used as the sole type of training, just as I would not advocate in an academic curriculum that a student should have nothing but mathematics. . . . It must be taught wisely and with discrimination. . . . [56]

An increasing number of ballet choreographers came to be influenced by modern dance. In a number of cases, their works became hardly distinguishable from modern dance itself. Kurt Jooss, in Germany during the 1920s and 1930s, was strongly influenced by the work of Mary Wigman and Rudolf von Laban; many of his important ballet works, including the famous *The Green Table,* clearly show the influence of early modern dance. In England, which has never had a strong modern dance movement (in spite of Laban's influence there), Susan Lester commented:

> The visit of Martha Graham and her company from the U.S.A. in 1954 was a significant introduction to Britain of a unique form, combining highly trained artists, an artistic director and principal choreographer of great ability, and intensely theatrical ballets with finely conceived modern musical scores and décors. The chief barrier between Graham and her public in Britain has been unfamiliarity with her medium and hence, some prejudice and a general hesitation in acceptance. [57]

Others were to follow Graham; by the middle 1960s, the companies of Merce Cunningham, Alvin Ailey, and Paul Taylor all enjoyed extended seasons in Great Britain. In 1964, Francis Mason, Deputy Cultural Attaché of the United States Embassy in London, described their great success: ". . . audiences were fervent, faithful, and articulate. . . . If there ever was a prejudice here against dance that is not strictly ballet, it is now strictly on the wane." [58]

Both in the United States and abroad, the barrier between modern dance and ballet has been breached in two ways. First, modern dancers have increasingly recognized the value of ballet training. More and more, they are incorporating fundamental ballet terms and movements into their systems of modern dance training. It is becoming increasingly necessary for a skilled modern dancer to take separate classes in ballet as part of his or her training. This is reflected both in the schools that are attached to professional modern dance companies, and in curricula devoted to dance as a performing art in American colleges and universities. As this chapter has shown, some of the leading modern dancers today had their first training and performing experiences in ballet.

On the other hand, ballet has chiefly been influenced by modern dance in terms of choreographic ideas and approaches. Many of the great choreographers of the past three or four decades, including Tudor, de Mille, Robbins, and Ashton, have selected the kinds of themes that modern dance broke new ground exploring— in symbolic works involving psychological insights of human behavior. They have also clearly been influenced by the leading modern dancers in terms of their use of dancers and dance groups, in their selection of music and decor, and in their extension of the range of dance movement.

As a consequence of this breakdown of the barriers between the two forms, in recent years modern dance choreographers have been called on frequently to develop works for major ballet companies. One of the recurring problems of the ballet world is its lack of gifted young choreographers. Thus, company directors have felt free to cross the line. American Ballet Theater has premiered new works by Glen Tetley, known as a modern dance choreographer. The Joffrey Ballet presents works by Anna Sokolow and Norman Walker. Martha Graham and Balanchine collaborated on a two-part work, *Episodes,* with music by Anton Webern. Other examples are numerous. In 1966, Merce Cunningham created a new work, *Summerspace,* on commission for the New York City Ballet. John Butler, whose primary background is in modern dance, composed many works for the Harkness Ballet, the Netherlands Dance Theater, the Pennsylvania Ballet, and the Metropolitan Opera Ballet, as well as nationwide television dance programs. James Waring, a highly experimental and creative choreographer, merged the two forms so fully in both his teaching and composition that it was not possible to identify him definitely with either modern dance or ballet. McDonagh wrote:

> [Waring] never believed in the distinctions that people drew between the performance of modern dances and ballets and thought that the generic name, ballet, should be applied to both forms of serious theater dancing. At one point, he referred to his own works as "choreographies" so as not to skew them into one camp or the other. . . .[59]

More recently, modern dance choreographers who have been commissioned to create works for major ballet companies include Murray Louis, Twyla Tharp, Paul Taylor, William Forsythe, David Gordon, and Molissa Fenley.

Much of the work of such choreographers as Glen Tetley, John Butler, Gerald Arpino, Norman Walker, and John Cranko is really a synthesis of both forms and is not clearly distinguishable as either. Arpino is an interesting case in point. In his early career, he studied dance with two former Graham dancers, May O'Donnell and Gertrude Shurr, and danced in performances with Anna Sokolow and Sophie Maslow. Such backgrounds on the part of American dancers and choreographers have helped to make ballet more of a native art. Arpino commented that he and Robert Joffrey were always concerned with a vision of American dance: "We were of our own country and of our own time. I think in American rhythms, motifs and sensibilities . . . Bob and I came from the true grit of American background. We know our own society. Ballet is still a foreign term to my brothers. . . ."[60]

In contrast to the directors of the two major American ballet companies (Mikhail Baryshnikov of American Ballet Theater and Peter Martins of the New York City Ballet), who were trained in state-supported dance academies, Arpino and Joffrey were American-trained and fought for years to gain acceptance for ballet in this country. Certainly, the exposure of many ballet dancers and choreographers to modern dance in their early years has given them a uniquely American outlook and artistic style.

In many ways, then, the barriers that formerly existed between ballet and modern dance have broken down. Yet will they disappear completely? It seems unlikely. There will be, for the foreseeable future, a group of modern dancers and choreographers who will reject ballet training, or at least be unwilling to accept it as a primary source of technique. They will be determined to pursue such irrevocably experimental directions that they will continue to be recognized as modern dancers. On the other hand, certain companies will continue to base their repertoire heavily on classic dances of the Romantic period, or on modern works which have a strong classic flavor about them; these companies will be easily identifiable as ballet companies. Somewhere in the middle, there will probably be an increasing number of modern dance companies that look as if they are performing ballet—and vice versa.

This process of cross-fertilization is undoubtedly good for theater dance in America. It does not, for the immediate future, however, solve the pressing problems of professional dance companies—particularly those of modern dance artists. For them, as suggested earlier, there continues to be a minimal degree of support and acceptance by the public at large.

Without question, for both modern dance and ballet, the key is audience readiness for dance and the approaches that are used to bring dance more effectively before the public. The roles of educational institutions and of government and foundation programs in doing so are explored in later chapters.

Notes

1 Barry Laine, "Theatricality in Dance," *New York Times,* February 2, 1984, p. 21.

2 Marcia B. Siegel, *At The Vanishing Point, A Critic Looks at Dance* (New York: Saturday Review Press, 1972), p. 247.

3 Doris Hering, "What Sorrow Is There That Is Not Mine?" *Dance Magazine,* May 1967, p. 55.

4 "Martha Graham Reflects on Her Art and a Life in Dance" (Conversation with dance critics of *New York Times*), March 31, 1985, p. H-1.

5 Clive Barnes, "A Master's One-Night Stand," *New York Times,* February 14, 1966, p. 33.

6 Remy Charlip, "Composing by Chance," *Dance Magazine,* January 1954, p. 19.

7 "Merce Cunningham Dance Company," *Dance News,* January 19, 1967, p. 9.

8 Anna Kisselgoff, "Merce Cunningham—Still Taking Chances," *New York Times,* March 20, 1988, p. 6-H.

9 Walter Sorell, "We Work Toward Freedom," *Dance Magazine,* January 1964, p. 53.

10 Clive Barnes, "A Sombre 'Night' Unfolds," *New York Times,* May 7, 1966, p. 8.

11 Doris Hering, "Anna Sokolow's Players' Project," *Dance Magazine,* April 1988, p. 36.

12 Alwin Nikolais, quoted in *Dance Magazine,* February 1962, p. 43.

13 Alwin Nikolais, "No Man from Mars," in *The Modern Dance: Seven Statements of Belief,* ed. Selma Jeanne Cohen (Middletown, Conn.: Wesleyan University Press, 1966), pp. 63–64.

14 Joan Acocella, "Review: Murray Louis Dance Co.," *Dance Magazine,* April 1988, p. 26.

15 Murray Louis, "Modern Dance's Continuing Search for Identity," *New York Times,* October 5, 1980, p. 14-D.

16 Paul Taylor, quoted in "Have Troupe, Will Travel," *New York Times,* July 3, 1966, p. 16-D.

17 Arthur Todd, "Two Way Passage for Dance," *Dance Magazine,* July 1962, p. 39.

18 Edwin Reischauer, quoted in Todd, "Two Way Passage," p. 39.

19 Richard Philp, "Twenty Years Later: The Alvin Ailey Dance Theater," *Dance Magazine,* October 1978, p. 73.

20 Anna Kisselgoff, "Ailey: Dancing the Dream," *New York Times,* December 4, 1988, p. 1-H.

21 Leslie Rubinstein, "Earth, Wind and Sun," *Ballet News,* January 1986, pp. 22–26.

22 Jack Anderson, "How the Judson Theater Changed American Dance," *New York Times,* January 31, 1982, p. 24-D.

23 Jerome Rockwood, "What's Happening," Letter to the Editor, *New York Times,* January 16, 1966, p. X-7.

24 Doris Hering, "Dancer's Workshop of San Francisco in 'Parades and Changes'," *Dance Magazine,* June 1967, p. 37.

25 Jack Anderson, "Dancers and Architects Build Kinetic Environment," *Dance Magazine,* November 1966, p. 52.

26 For a full discussion of Minimalism as a movement, see John Rockwell, "The Death and Life of Minimalism," *New York Times,* December 21, 1986, pp. 1-H, 29-H.

27 Nora Fitzgerald, "Douglas Dunn to Play the Kitchen," *Dance Magazine,* March 1988, p. 10.

28 Barry Laine, "Is Contact Improvisation Really Dance?" *New York Times,* July 3, 1983, p. H-7.

29 Marcia Siegel, *Watching the Dance Go By* (Boston: Houghton Mifflin Co., 1977), p. 298.

30 Allen Robertson, "Gravity's Rainbow," *Ballet News,* September 1988, p. 28.

31 Toby Tobias, "Step, Kick, Jump—Back-to-Basics Dance," *New York Times,* November 6, 1977, p. 6.

32 John Rockwell, *New York Times,* March 28, 1976, p. D-8.

33 Eileen Blumenthal, "Singable Practices, Natural Acts," *New York Village Voice,* April 15, 1986, p. 95.

34 Ibid.

35 Siegel, *At the Vanishing Point,* p. 266.

36 Diane Solway, "Twyla Tharp: Turning Sharp Corners," *New York Times,* January 1, 1989, p. 8-H.

37 Nancy Goldner, "Illusion Experts on the Dance Stage," *Philadelphia Inquirer,* March 18, 1984, p. 1-M.

38 Barry Laine, "Pilobolus Expands Its Dramatic Forms," *New York Times,* February 3, 1985, p. H-18.

39 Anna Kisselgoff, "When the Tale Gets Lost in the Telling," *New York Times,* November 25, 1984, p. 6-H.

40 Barry Laine, "Dance Troupe with Multimedia Flair," *New York Times,* December 8, 1985, p. 18-H.

41 Jennifer Dunning, "Bill T. Jones/Arnie Zane and Company," *New York Times,* May 15, 1988, p. 86.

42 David Galloway, "Visionary Dance or Total Theater?" *New York Times,* June 10, 1984, p. 26-H.

43 Camille Hardy, "Review: Compagnie Maguy Marin," *Dance Magazine,* February 1988, p. 44.

44 Rockwell, *op. cit.*

45 Michael Brenson, "Sculpture Breaks the Mold of Minimalism," *New York Times,* November 23, 1986, p. H-1.

46 John Russell, "Painting is Once Again Provocative," *New York Times,* April 17, 1983, p. H-1.

47 Anna Kisselgoff, "How Emotion Is Being Dealt with in 80's Dances," *New York Times,* November 11, 1984, p. 19-H.

48 See Barry Laine, "Theatricality in Dance," for a discussion of this trend.

49 John Rockwell, "Is Performance a New Form of Art?" *New York Times,* August 14, 1983, p. 1-H.

50 Richard Schechner, *Environmental Theater* (New York: Hawthorn Books, 1973), p. 2.

51 Ibid., p. 12.

52 Interview with Trisha Brown, in *Contemporary Dance: An Anthology,* ed. Anne Livet (New York: Abbeville Press, 1978), p. 51.

53 Elizabeth Zimmer, "Waiting for the End of the World," *Dance Magazine,* February 1987, p. 67.

54 Margaret H'Doubler, *Dance: A Creative Art Experience* (New York: F. S. Crofts and Co., 1940), p. 38.

55 Arnold Haskell, *Ballet* (Harmondsworth, Middlesex, England: Pergamon Books, 1951), p. 45.

56 Ted Shawn, *Dance We Must* (London: Dennis Dobson, Ltd., 1946), p. 88.

57 Susan Lester, *Ballet Here and Now* (London: Dennis Dobson, Ltd., 1961), p. 25.

58 Francis Mason, "London Likes American Dancer," *New York Times,* December 27, 1964, p. X-19.

59 Don McDonagh, "Keeping James Waring's Choreography Alive," *New York Times,* March 6, 1977, p. D-16.

60 Anna Kisselgoff, "At the Joffrey, The Curtain Rises on Act 2," *New York Times,* October 23, 1988, p. 10-H.

CHAPTER 11

Black Dance
in America

When I think about the Dance Theater of Harlem . . . I begin to reminisce against a flood of images that lead back to that dreadful moment in 1968 when a bullet ended the life of Martin Luther King, Jr. . . .

It was his tragic and untimely death that sparked Arthur's decision to start a ballet school, to build a ballet company *in* Harlem and *from* Harlem, one with Harlem minds and Harlem bodies. It was to be a school whose purpose was not to create an entire Harlem of dancers, but one to stimulate in its people a sense of what can be achieved through dedication and hard work. Ideally, the school was to provide role models and professional goals for aspiring dancers.[1]

Dance Theater of Harlem has become one of the nation's most successful international arts ambassadors and a leading American ballet company with a new, strong profile. . . .[2]

WHY SHOULD A SEPARATE TEXTBOOK CHAPTER BE DEVOTED TO the subject of black dance when no other ethnic group is singled out for special analysis? What *is* black dance, and what can we learn from investigating it in detail?

Although the influence of American blacks on dance in popular culture has been cited briefly in earlier chapters of this book, this chapter describes the overall impact of African and Afro-American dance and music on the performing arts in America. Since the mid-nineteenth century, African-based dance and music have made major contributions to the field of popular entertainment. During slavery, blacks combined African dance forms with the social dances of European origin that they saw performed by plantation owners. The minstrel stage preserved these song and dance styles and disseminated them to the general American public.

Many twentieth-century dance fads owe their origins to black dance. Crazes such as the turn-of-the-century Turkey Trot, and later fads such as the Charleston, Big Apple, and other social dances stemmed from African-based dance and music. Musicologists have traced the influence of blacks on American popular music from the jazz and swing eras through the more recent rock-and-roll period.

In addition, a number of leading black dancers and choreographers have contributed significantly to the development of dance as a concert form in the United States. Several of these have been described in preceding chapters, including Alvin Ailey, Arthur Mitchell, Donald McKayle, and Bill T. Jones. To understand fully the development of dance in American society, it is necessary to examine their role—both as dancer-choreographers and as blacks.

Since the 1960s, Afro-American studies have become a recognized academic discipline in American higher education. There has been increased interest in researching the role of blacks within the arts. Pace wrote:

> Blacks have scored a number of notable successes in the performing and dramatic arts in recent weeks and months, prompting discussion in artistic, academic and other circles of a question: Do these triumphs reflect real advances for blacks in American culture and society as a whole?[3]

Thus, over the past several years, there has been growing recognition of the impact of blacks on American dance forms. In 1983, for example, the Brooklyn Academy of Music staged *Dance Black America,* a four-day event that gathered together virtually every living figure in the history of black dance and combined performances with a variety of films, lectures, and seminars. Three years later, the heritage of black dance was featured in a summer pilot project at the American Dance Festival in Durham, North Carolina. The project's intent was to preserve and reconstruct the work of leading black choreographers.[4]

Without question, black dance has been recognized as a significant scholarly subject within the spectrum of American culture and dance history. However, it also provides a prism through which to examine American society at large. That there were no leading black choreographers during the first several decades of American modern dance, and that even today blacks are largely unrepresented within the mainstream of major ballet companies, reflects harsh realities about racial exclusion in the United States. For this reason, black dance is treated here as a separate and important concern.

Defining Black Dance

What is black dance? To define this term, one must distinguish between black dance and dancers who are black. Although often the two terms are used interchangeably, they have distinctly different meanings. For the purpose of this text, *black dance* is defined as dance forms indigeneous to and developed by specific African, Caribbean, or Afro-American cultural groups. Like ballet or modern dance, black dance should be considered a generic dance form. Just as ballet and modern dance embrace a variety of dance idioms (such as the Cecchetti and Vaganova ballet techniques, or the Graham and Cunningham styles of modern dance), so black dance encompasses a variety of techniques and vocabularies. In some cases, it may involve movement or themes that are drawn directly from African dance sources. In others, it may be based on African dance movements that have filtered through generations of religious and social practices among blacks on Caribbean islands. In still others, it has been transformed into creative dance works that use traditional black dance movements and rhythms, or that deal with themes drawn from the lives of black people in America.

Obviously, dancers who are black may perform in different dance styles—ballet, modern dance, jazz, or black dance. When they are part of a modern dance company performing abstract or avant-garde works to contemporary music or other accompaniment, they are simply dancers and are not distinguished in any way by their color. Similarly, if they are part of a ballet company performing *Giselle* or *Les Sylphides,* their color and ethnic background should be irrelevant; they are just dancers who happen to be black. Garth Fagan, a well-known black dancer-choreographer, said:

> Although I'm proud of who I am . . . I think the idea of a form of dance that's specifically called 'black' is a double-edged sword. . . . I see Jewish choreographers with strong Yemenite influences—they don't necessarily get labeled 'Jewish choreographers.' The same with Asian choreographers. . . . I think I, and other black choreographers, deserve the right to change, grow and explore without being forced into categories.[5]

Alvin Ailey with Carmen de Lavallade in *Roots of the Blues.* Photograph by Jack Mitchell.

To clarify this distinction, the phrase *black dance forms* is used through much of this chapter, rather than the ambiguous term *black dance*. Obviously, it covers a wide range of possibilities. On the one hand, there are a number of black concert dance companies which present traditional African-based movement forms within a theatricalized concert dance framework. Such groups are comparable to well-known companies, like the Russian Moiseyev troupe, that use folk steps, music, and themes in elaborately choreographed stage presentations.

On the other hand, there are concert dance companies, such as the Alvin Ailey American Dance Theater or the Dance Theater of Harlem, which are racially integrated (although predominantly black) and whose repertoire is in the modern dance or ballet idiom. In some cases, there have been black dancer-choreographers, such as Pearl Primus, who have based their work much more directly on African-related sources (such as observed dance rituals) or on the lives of American blacks. Still others have combined a variety of dance forms performed by American blacks over several historical periods.

Overview of Black Dance in America

Societies throughout the world have used dance extensively in varied settings—as worship, celebration, education, and simply as social pastime. Nowhere has there been a fuller or richer illustration of this than in Africa, where dance has been an integral part of community life for many centuries. Robertson wrote:

> In traditional African society, there is no one who does not dance. For Africans, dance is much more than an art; dance is at the center of the rituals and relationships that define African society. While Africans use dance as recreation—South African mine workers dance during their lunch breaks—every African village has a repertory of sacred dances that mark the most important events in the life of the community (harvest, religious ceremony) and of the individual (puberty, marriage, death).[6]

Too often, the conventional American perception of African dance has been based on totally inaccurate Hollywood film versions of half-clothed natives leaping about in a savage ceremony in a jungle clearing. The reality is that often African dance is highly complex, elaborate in costuming and accompaniment, and with a great range of skilled movement and rhythm, far from the crude "ooga-booga-booga" dances depicted in Tarzan movies. For example, a dance performed by Charles Moore shows the *Takai,* a festival dance of the court nobility of the Hausa tribe. It is an exuberant dance, rhythmically intricate and visually exciting, with the swirling robes of the dancers embellishing their movements. In another striking dance, *Awassa Astrige,* Moore shows how African art often depicts nature by imitating ". . . an ostrich, wearing only huge ostrich tail feathers. He [the dancer] walks with the immense selfless pride of a large animal, his head jutting, birdlike, back and forth, his rippling arms suggesting the motion of vestigial wings."[7]

Although enslaved blacks in the American colonies and later in the Southern United States were stripped of their African religions and converted to Christianity, they kept elements of earlier religious practice in their new worship forms. In the Caribbean, Catholic saints were merged with African deities and were embraced as single entities; African music and dance forms were integrated into worship in Protestant churches as well. Thus, although the social structure of their lives was radically altered, slaves managed to retain much of their inherited African culture. Centuries later, anthropologist-dancer Pearl Primus noted the clear similarities between African sacred dance rituals and movement in religious worship in Southern Baptist churches in the United States.

The range and variety of movement in black churches was limited because dancing was considered sinful by many fundamentalist preachers. However, slaves developed ways of meshing their dance heritage with their adopted faith. It was not considered sinful—it was not even regarded as dancing—if the feet did not cross or leave the floor. Given this limitation, blacks were able to develop new ways of tapping their feet—shifting their weight and alternating emphasis from heel to toe, bending their knees and changing the direction and articulation of the torso—with the feet never crossing or leaving the ground.[8]

These new shuffling movements ironically became a new form of dance and were the basis for "buck" dancing and later tap dancing and ballroom dance forms. Because African drumming was often prohibited by slave owners (with some exceptions, as described in chapter 6), dances evolved in which the beat was kept by foot tapping and by clapping, patting, or slapping other parts of the body to produce drum-like rhythms. One such dance was the "pattin" Juba, characterized by patting and slapping of arms, chest, and thighs. Originally an African dance of skill, the Juba became the basis for hambone variations, which served as a game for Afro-American children and an occasional variation in minstrel and vaudeville routines.

Other plantation dances evolved into new social dances, such as the Cakewalk (originally a plantation challenge dance in which dancers would take turns doing spectacular, difficult, and original moves); the Turkey Trot, Grizzly Bear, Black Bottom, Ballin' the Jack, Shimmy and the Mooch—to name some of the best-known dances of black origin. The Cakewalk had a particularly interesting history; it progressed from the plantation amusement of slaves to minstrel shows and ultimately to turn-of-the-century Afro-American musicals produced by performers such as Bert Williams, George Walker, and Will Marion Cook. Gaining popularity among both blacks and whites, its strut step was the forerunner of a variation, called simply the strut, and the jazz walk familiar to musical comedy.

In addition to creating such appealing social dance forms, after the Civil War blacks also influenced the minstrel stage and other performance outlets, such as tent shows, carnivals, and traveling road shows. Refined and developed, Afro-American plantation dance forms became the basis for many minstrel show routines—although, ironically, blacks were widely barred from performing in minstrel shows. Instead, the comic actors, singers, and dancers in these popular stage presentations were usually white—but made up in exaggerated blackface to maintain the fiction of being black performers. Indeed, minstrel shows were often demeaning presentations of the lazy, ignorant, and superstitious "darky" stereotype that dominated many forms of entertainment and periodicals at the time. When blacks were permitted to perform in the minstrel shows, they too were required to blacken their faces with burnt cork, to paint on huge lips, and to depict a cadre of stock characters, such as the shuffling rural oaf or the humble, servile Uncle Tom. Although they were skilled performers, most white audiences believed that blacks were ignorant primitives who were realistically portraying an inferior culture, and that their talents were inborn and uncultivated rather than learned and technically adept.[9]

During the late 1800s, blacks often appeared in the variety shows which were offered by white burlesque houses; at this time, burlesque was a form of song, dance, and comic entertainment considered the lowest rung on the show-business ladder of success. Other black entertainers performed in segregated theaters on Afro-American vaudeville circuits during the early decades of the twentieth century; and by the 1920s and 1930s, a small number of successful black artists were featured in white vaudeville and on Broadway. Ultimately, this led to greater acceptance of popular black singers and dancers, jazz orchestras, and comedians and to a number of all-black musical revues and Broadway shows, such as *Green Pastures* and *Carmen Jones*. Gradually, too, the identity of the black entertainer shifted from the banjo-strumming, clown-like plantation "darkies" sentimentalized by performers like Al Jolson, to more mature and honest roles in which black performers, such as Paul Robeson and Ethel Waters, gained worldwide recognition.

Meanwhile, there was a continuing interchange between social dance and stage dance as expressions of Afro-American culture. During the late nineteenth and early twentieth centuries, many segregated public dance halls were established throughout the South. Stemming from these settings, along with the growth of black-influenced popular music, came many new dance steps. These were popularized in all-black Broadway musicals with names like *Shuffle Along* and *Chocolate Dandies* (both composed by the team of Eubie Blake and Noble Sissle) which flourished until the 1930s, as well as in nightclubs that featured black entertainers and were limited to white audiences. Adopted and toned down by the white public, they evolved into so-called ballroom dances and were the basis of dance fads like the Charleston or Turkey Trot, described earlier. Later examples of this process were the *Big Apple* and the *Lindy Hop,* popular crazes of the 1930s and 1940s.

Social dances frequently found their way to the popular stage and, in turn, dances from theaters and nightclubs often filtered back to the social realm. Throughout, dances originating in Afro-American communities were incorporated into vaudeville and Broadway routines, after which they gained popularity as white social dances. Choreographer Buddy Bradley, of the famous black Cotton Club in New York, described the shuffling, shaking, shimmying, and other improvised steps that continued to catch the public's taste: "We thought nothing of the fact that everybody in and out of colored show business seemed to know a million old jive steps. . . . We all knew these movements as kids. . . . They were a part of our life that we took for granted. . . ."[10]

During the Swing era of the 1930s and 1940s, growing numbers of whites began to frequent such night spots in Harlem and other black communities as the famous Savoy, Renaissance, and Alhambra ballrooms. Often, when Europeans came to the United States, these were among the first places they wanted to visit—as a uniquely American form of popular culture. And, as motion pictures and touring companies of nightclub revues and black musicals, including the famous Blackbirds shows, visited Europe and other foreign lands, black music and dance gained a truly international audience. After the 1960s, with increased racial militance and hostility in many American cities, whites did not feel as free to visit black nightclubs and ballrooms as in the past. However, during the 1970s and 1980s, with the accessibility of television and video cassettes, black-based entertainment forms have become a truly global language. The dances and songs of superstar Michael Jackson and other major black entertainers have become as well known in countries like Turkey or Japan as they have in the United States.

Black Concert Dance Forms

We now examine black concert dance forms. What is concert dance? The term is used here to describe movement learned by study in a dance school or studio, intended for performance before a nonparticipating audience in a space in which performers and audience are separated—typically with performers on a stage and spectators seated before them.

Companies which have transformed traditional black dance movements and themes into theatricalized, staged dance works are referred to here as black concert dance groups. The term does not apply to those black dancers whose work is based exclusively on ballet or modern dance forms, although there are a number of leading dance artists, such as Alvin Ailey, Eleo Pomare, Rod Rodgers, and Garth Fagan, who frequently use black dance forms and themes in their choreography.

Black concert dance may be roughly subdivided into two broad categories: African-based, and American-based, although even here many choreographers may use more than one source of material. It is important to recognize that the forms presented in concert versions are often *not* the original dances. Once a dance form has been removed from its authentic sociocultural context, adapted for performance, and placed in theatrical environment for a viewing audience, it represents a new artistic expression.

Black concert dance received a major impetus in the 1930s, when researchers and dancer-choreographers began to bring dance works based on authentic African and Afro-Caribbean sources before the American public. At first, their presentations were sponsored by local organizations such as clubs, brotherhoods, and friendly societies—institutions which often were based on African cultural and social traditions. Black churches and colleges soon became interested in presenting dance and music drawn from authentic backgrounds. It was recognized that during the passage from Africa and the centuries of slavery that many blacks had endured, they had been cut off from their history and traditions, and there was a hunger to learn the truth of their cultural past.

As an example, the Hampton Institute Creative Dance Group was a student concert dance ensemble directed by two teachers at Hampton Institute, a Virginia college. In the 1930s, they performed works based on their African and Afro-American heritage during tours of schools and colleges around the United States.

One of the first performers to take authentic African material and use it to create an artistic concert dance was Asadata Dafora. In 1934, Dafora, a native of Sierra Leone, produced a work called *Kykunkor,* which premiered in New York and was billed as an opera. It consisted of a full evening's spectacle based on an African legend in which both native Africans and American blacks performed.

Dafora continued to teach and perform in the United States until his death in the mid-1960s. His work was extended by other pioneers, notably Katherine Dunham and Pearl Primus, who used extensive research as the basis for reconstructing and adapting African and Afro-Caribbean dances for the concert stage.

Katherine Dunham, who earned a degree in anthropology from the University of Chicago, gathered numerous dances from Africa, the Caribbean, and Central and South America, putting them within a stage dance format. She gained recognition first as a choreographer for the Federal Theater Project in the mid- to late 1930s, and then she choreographed works for the concert stage, films, cabarets, and Broadway shows. Beyond this, she developed her own modern dance system—Dunham technique—that included barre work, center-floor work, and movement across the floor. Dunham was a remarkable pioneer in that she encompassed many careers—as scholar, teacher, dancer, choreographer, author, and humanitarian, with her company productions under varied names—Bal Négre, New Tropical Revue, A Caribbean Rhapsody—gaining immense popularity abroad as a spectacular mixture of show business and art.[11]

Dunham trained a generation of professional dancers, some of whom starred in her company, including Talley Beatty, Lavinia Williams, and Charles Moore. She also trained a number of actors who studied with her, including Marlon Brando and James Dean. In the 1960s, she withdrew from the professional stage to work with disadvantaged youth in ghetto neighborhoods in East St. Louis, Illinois, where she established a dance academy. In 1986, she was awarded the $25,000 American Dance Festival Award in acknowledgment of her many achievements.

A second outstanding black dancer-choreographer whose work was first seen in the 1940s was Pearl Primus, an anthropology graduate of Hunter College in New York City. Her early works included protest dances such as *Strange Fruit, Hard Time Blues,* and *The Negro Speaks of Rivers,* which depicted the harsh realities of black life in America, such as lynching, poverty, and the sharecropper's barren existence. Later, she traveled and studied authentic dance forms in Africa and developed theatrical dance versions of such dances as the Fanga dance of the Rwanda Burundi Watusi, and West African dances from the Congo and other sources.

Chronology of Black Dance

To give a more detailed picture of the development of black concert dance during the period from the 1930s through the 1950s, the following section presents highlights of the period. It is drawn from a chronology prepared by several researchers (Joe Nash, William Moore, and Zita Allen)[12] and identifies a number of the outstanding events and individuals who contributed to black dance during these three decades. Artists and events from the 1960s to the present are then listed but are not discussed in detail.

1931: Dancer-choreographers Hemsley Winfield and Edna Guy gave what was identified as the "first Negro dance recital in America"; Guy subsequently focused on dancing to Negro spirituals.

1933: Hensley Winfield danced in the Metropolitan Opera's production of Emperor Jones; he was the first black to appear with that organization.

1934: Asadata Dafora of Sierra Leone created an African dance-drama entitled *Kykunkor* (Witch Woman); it was the first concert work based on authentic African sources, and it stimulated others to follow.

1935: The Hampton University Creative Dance Group, a student troupe directed by Charles Williams and Charlotte Kennedy, performed concert versions of African and Afro-American dances. Other touring black concert dance troupes were formed at such Southern black institutions as Spelman College, Fisk University, Howard University, and Tuskegee Institute.

1937: A Negro Dance Evening was held at the New York YM-YWHA, similar to programs sponsored by modern dance troupes led by Martha Graham, Doris Humphrey, and Charles Weidman. Dafora, Dunham, and Guy performed, and Talley Beatty made his New York debut in the Dunham company.

1937: A German dancer-choreographer, Eugene Von Grona, formed the Von Grona American Negro Ballet, to present blacks in modern dance concerts.

1937: Bernice Brown, a modern dancer encouraged by Gertrude Lippincott, a leading dance educator, organized the first racially integrated dance company, in Minneapolis.

1938: Katherine Dunham created her first full-length ballet, *L'Ag'Ya,* for the Federal Theater Project. As various federal arts programs sponsored Negro music and dance performances, white audiences were exposed to serious black artists for the first time. Shortly after, plans were initiated to develop a separate Negro group as a wing of the evolving Ballet Theater; however, this never developed fully.

1942: Belle Rosette (also known as Beryl McBurnie), who taught at the New Dance Group studio in New York, directed *Antilliana,* a Coffee Concerts Series offering at the New York YM-YWHA. The program included dances from Martinique, Cuba, Trinidad, Bermuda, Haiti, and Grenada. Pearl Primus was on the program, along with Boscoe and Geoffrey Holder and Percival Borde.

1943: Pearl Primus's reputation as an outstanding dancer-choreographer grew rapidly; she was acclaimed as Dance Debutante for 1943 by John Martin, dance critic for the *New York Times.*

1943: Wilson Williams premiered a new group, the Negro Dance Company, in New York City; he also taught and lectured on dance at the Harlem Branch of the YMCA.

1947: Talley Beatty, who had begun with the Dunham company in Chicago in the 1930s and continued to dance with her through the 1940s, choreographed *Southern Landscape,* receiving critical praise. His later works included *The Road of the Phoebe Snow* (1959), *Come and Get the Beauty of It Hot* (1960), and numerous other works for Alvin Ailey and other dance companies.

1949: Ballerina Janet Collins made her debut with the Metropolitan Opera Ballet Company as the first black dancer to be contracted with the group.

1951: Donald McKayle's *Games* premiered. McKayle had performed on tour with the Martha Graham company, as guest artist with Merce Cunningham, Anna Sokolow, and Jean Erdman, and in Broadway musicals. Other signature works included *Rainbow 'Round My Shoulder* (1959) and *District Storyville* (1962). McKayle has choreographed extensively since for Broadway, Hollywood, and television productions and for modern dance troupes nationwide.

1952: Ballet-trained Louis Johnson performed with the New York City Ballet Company in Jerome Robbins' *Ballade.* Although he had been granted a scholarship at the School of American Ballet and was a capable dancer, he was never able to become a regular member of the company. Johnson choreographed and performed for the Broadway stage, and his works have been in the repertory of concert dance companies such as the Ailey troupe and the Philadelphia Dance Company (Philadanco).

1956: Arthur Mitchell became the first black ballet dancer to be engaged under permanent contract by a major white company. After study as a scholarship student at the School of American Ballet, he joined the New York City Ballet. As late as the 1970s, Mitchell remained the only black dancer in the company.

The decade of the 1950s saw the advent of many new black concert dance companies, including those directed by Louis Johnson, Donald McKayle, Carmen de Lavallade, Walter Nicks, Jean Léon Destiné, Talley Beatty, Geoffrey Holder, Janet Collins, and Alvin Ailey. In the 1960s, other black dancers, including Eleo Pomare, Rod Rodgers, Fred Benjamin, and Arthur Hall, established troupes which have survived through the 1980s. In the 1970s, emerging black choreographers included George Faison, Dianne McIntyre, Gus Solomons, Chuck Davis, Gene Hill Sagan, and Billy Wilson. Other significant black dancers in the late 1970s and 1980s included Bill T. Jones, Blondell Cummings, Garth Fagan, Milton Myers, Ishmael Houston-Jones, Bebe Miller, Harry Sheppard, and Jawole Willa Jo Zollar, artistic director of the Urban Bush Women company.

Without question, blacks have entered vigorously into the field of concert dance, both in terms of their involvement in modern dance companies generally and in groups concerned with black dance themes. However, as the foregoing chronology demonstrates, there has been far less acceptance of blacks in ballet.

Exclusion of Blacks from Ballet

The long exclusion of black dancers from classical ballet companies has been thoroughly documented. It reflected the persistent pattern of segregation by race in American society within such major areas as social and fraternal organizations, the church, business, education, and sports organizations. In the dance field, ballet remained the most stubborn obstacle to blacks' achieving recognition. Arthur Mitchell knew this, and he achieved the remarkable goal of capturing the position of principal dancer with the New York City Ballet, being the first and—thus far—the only black male to achieve that pinnacle. Cicely Tyson described Mitchell's motivation in establishing the Dance Theater of Harlem School and performing company in 1968, to offer training and performance outlets for blacks in ballet:

He knew . . . what it meant to him. The joy of release of physical power, the communion with audiences, the spiritual healing and, lastly, salvation from what might have become an impoverished spirit. It was this that he wanted to impart to black children steeped in the smells of poverty and despair. He agreed that the company should not carry his name. And it was his decision to call it the Dance Theater of Harlem.[13]

One of the rationalizations used to defend the rejection of blacks by major ballet companies was that the highly disciplined technique of classical ballet was unsuited to them, and that it would be inappropriate for them to appear in the older romantic and classical ballets. It was presumably felt that they would disrupt the uniformity of the company's appearance; that often black bodies did not fit prevailing white aesthetic standards; even that black bodies and white tutus would provide a jarring visual effect for audiences. Part of Arthur Mitchell's purpose was to disprove these contentions by training young blacks rigorously in academic ballet technique, which he did with marked success. Indeed, among the Dance Theater of Harlem's most acclaimed ballets were *Swan Lake* and *Giselle,* as well as many of Balanchine's neoclassical works.

Despite this record, few major ballet companies have engaged blacks as permanent company members. After starring with the Dance Theater of Harlem, Mel Tomlinson joined the New York City Ballet, retiring from dance in 1987. Debra Austin also danced with the New York company, later joining the Pennsylvania Ballet as a principal dancer. But few other blacks have been accepted. As of 1987, Barillo wrote:

> Among the three major New York-based ballet companies, black dancers are rare or absent. The New York City Ballet has three dancers in a company of 100. Mikhail Baryshnikov's American Ballet Theater has one black dancer out of 90 and the Joffrey Ballet Company currently has none.
>
> In the New England area, the Boston Ballet has one black dancer out of 36; the Hartford Ballet has one black dancer in its company out of 22; and [the Connecticut Ballet Theater], though it has had black members in the past, has none at present. . . .[14]

Some have attempted to explain the exclusion of blacks from major performing companies in sociological terms—either that ballet, as an upper-class, or elite activity, is unsuitable for many young blacks coming from lower socioeconomic class homes, or that it simply clashes with their accepted lifestyles. However, neither of these rationalizations is justified. Many lower-class whites regularly achieve success in ballet without difficulty. In fact, as Americans, we are all removed in terms of cultural tradition from the classical world of European ballet.[15]

Indeed, research shows that there have been as many blacks trained in ballet since the 1940s and 1950s as there were blacks trained in other forms of dance. Since the Von Grona days of the 1930s, blacks have been regularly trained in ballet as part of preparation for a professional dance career. Ballet was an integral part of the training of Katherine Dunham dancers, beginning in the 1940s, and was actually a part of black performance tradition since the 1920s.

Given the recognized achievements of the Dance Theater of Harlem and the striking success of blacks in many other forms of dance and popular entertainment, it seems clear that racial prejudice has been the culprit—and that it continues to prevent many young blacks from entering and building careers in ballet. In part, that discrimination persists in ballet may have to do with the nature of ballet itself. Ballet tends to be an elite and generally conservative art form—supported and controlled by wealthy and powerful groups in American society and regarded as appropriate training for young children of upper-class backgrounds. While racial integration in sports has been widely accepted, dance, with its sexual connotations, may provoke special resistance to close physical contact. The intimate linkage between the ballerina and her partner in older, romantic ballets, or the relationships of dancers in newer, psychologically oriented works, may continue to excite lingering prejudices that should have disappeared in American society.

In any case, many young black dancers have frequently attested to what they perceived as prejudice against them. They have felt that they were not encouraged in ballet studios, and that they were not given individual attention in classes, like other students. Some have claimed that they were rarely recommended for roles, and that there appeared to be an unspoken bias among artistic directors, who sought to keep ballet as a "lily-white" art form.[16]

An even more unmistakable example of racial discrimination in dance that has affected blacks through the years is the Rockettes, a famed constellation of thirty-six dancers at Radio City Music Hall in New York City. Over a period of several decades, during which 5,000 Rockettes were members of the troupe, there had never been a single black Rockette as of the mid-1980s. Peterson commented that, although in some types of dance one could make a case for the need for racial authenticity, thus excluding certain groups, this could not be a rational assertion for the Rockettes. They portray, he wrote:

> . . . no recognizable public figures, ethnic groups or racially coherent families. Most often they dance as objects—wooden soldiers, bon-bons, cigars—and winsome fauna—baby chicks, penguins, bunnies—when they're not simply Rockettes. For the Rockettes, racial authenticity is irrelevant.[17]

The mere notion that black dancers lack the skills or other qualities needed to be part of the high-kicking Rockettes is absurd. From the time of Juba, regarded as the greatest of all minstrel dancers, through the period of Josephine Baker, the immensely popular singer and dancer who was the toast of Europe during the Jazz Age, to the more recent successes of entertainers like Sammy Davis, Jr. and Ben Vereen, blacks have been preeminent musical comedy and stage dancers. There can be no justification for their exclusion from any form of professional dance in contemporary America.

One of the ways to facilitate better understanding of the contributions of blacks to popular American culture is through school and college courses. Karen Hubbard described an excellent example of a college course in ethnic dance history offered at Ohio State University. The course traced the evolution of jazz dance from its African origins to the plantation dances of slaves and through the popular dances of the 1940s. Hubbard wrote:

> Informal conversations with dance scholars, dance historians and jazz artists specializing in jazz provided valuable insights into American dance history as well as valuable sources of research information. Because the course was intended to communicate aspects of black life in America, literature which dealt with other related areas of black life were also very useful.[18]

Although this course included a healthy component of jazz movement, a major part of its value lay in its scholarly examination of historical and social influences in American culture. It provided convincing documentation that dance can be a valuable academic subject in terms of meeting established educational goals. More detailed exploration of this point, and examination of current programs of dance in education, are provided in later chapters of this text.

Notes

1 Cicely Tyson, "It's Homecoming Time for Harlem's Ballet Company," *New York Times,* March 23, 1986, p. H-27.

2 Jennifer Dunning, "A Dance Troupe Rebounds," *New York Times,* n.d., n.p., 1982.

3 Eric Pace, "Blacks in the Arts: Evaluating Recent Successes," *New York Times,* June 14, 1987, p. 1.

4 Anna Kisselgoff, "Heritage of Black Dance Gets a Boost in Durham," *New York Times,* July 4, 1986, p. H-13.

5 Eric Taub, "I Want My Dancers to Keep that Wildflower Feeling," *New York Times,* July 1, 1984, p. 16-H.

6 Michael Robertson, "Dancing the African Way," *New York Times,* September 23, 1979, p. 21.

7 Ibid., p. 48.

8 Marshall and Jean Stearns, *Jazz Dance* (New York: Schirmer Books, 1979), pp. 27–29.

9 See Lynne Fauley Emery, *Black Dance* (Palo Alto, Calif.: National Press Books, 1972), chap. 6 and 7.

10 Stearns, *Jazz Dance,* p. 165.

11 Anna Kisselgoff, "Dunham Has Been a Controversial Pioneer," *New York Times,* June 8, 1986, p. 18-H.

12 Zita Allen, William Moore, Joe Nash, *The Black Tradition in American Modern Dance* (unpublished manuscript). See also Anna Kisselgoff, "Limning the Role of the Black Dancer in America," *New York Times,* May 16, 1982, p. 10-D.

13 Tyson, "Homecoming Time," pp. H-1, H-27.

14 See Jack Anderson, "The Time Was Right to Try the Classics," *New York Times,* January 6, 1980, p. 14-D.

15 Madeline Barillo, "White Face of Ballet: Blacks Hurt by Artistic Directors' Desire for Uniformity," *Baltimore Sun,* June 28, 1987, p. 5-N.

16 Curiously, this resistance continued at a time when blacks were making great strides in the arts generally in American life. See Pace, "Blacks in the Arts," p. 1.

17 Gregory J. Peterson, "What's All White and Dances in New York?" *New York Times,* May 31, 1985, p. A-27.

18 Karen Hubbard, "Ethnic Dance: The Origins of Jazz; A Curriculum Design for Dance," *Journal of Physical Education, Recreation and Dance,* May-June 1988, pp. 58–61.

CHAPTER 12

Vernacular Dance Forms:
Ethnic, Folk,
Ballroom, Jazz, and Tap

When the Argentine tango was introduced to the United States by Vernon and Irene Castle in 1913, it became the rage in ballrooms, theaters and films, as popular as rock and roll is today. It even caused scandals for its blatant sensuality. But the story of this riveting dance didn't begin in 1913, and it didn't end when the style faded from fashion in the 50's. The tango is part of a rich and ongoing 100-year Argentine tradition of rhythmic music, gutsy songs and dynamic couples dancing.[1]

Last June [1985] Argentine tango erupted onto the New York scene for a week's run at the City Center sporting laurels won in Paris, Venice, Vienna and throughout Germany and France. With rapturous reviews in the daily press, the short season quickly sold out and emboldened the U.S. presenters [to] arrange a return engagement, this time for five weeks.... Audiences, including a sizable Hispanic turnout, are still filling the theater months later and are not about to allow this exotic, yet familiar, entertainment to depart.[2]

THE TERM *VERNACULAR* IS DEFINED AS "belonging to, developed in, and spoken or used by the people of a particular place, region or country."[3] While it usually applies to the use of language, it may also refer to customs, art forms, or other characteristics of a given people or nation. In this book, it is used to describe varied forms of dance which are typically performed or enjoyed as popular and ceremonial forms, rather than as entertainment for the concert stage, and which are transmitted from generation to generation.

The preceding chapters have dealt in detail with the artistic or theatrical forms of dance that are most familiar to the Western world—ballet and modern dance. In addition to these, there are several other types of dance which are found around the world. These forms are *ethnic, folk, ballroom, jazz,* and *tap* dance. While related to each other, each has a distinct character and function in society. They serve as a means of retaining and reenacting customs and traditions of a nation or cultural group, and as a popular form of community sociability. They also are frequently found in education and are used, in a theatricalized form, in ballet or other dance entertainment.

Ethnic Dance

Ethnic dance describes the traditional dances performed by the people of a given nation or region, as part of their cultural heritage. They may be primarily ritual in nature, with serious religious meaning or overtones, primarily social, or a blend of the two. La Meri, a leading dancer, teacher, and scholar in this dance form who was particularly expert in Spanish and Indian dance, wrote:

> The term *ethnic* dance designates all those indigeneous dance arts that have grown from popular or typical dance expressions of a particular race. The term came into general usage during the 1940s as a way to differentiate among ballet, modern and ethnic in theater-dance presentations.[4]

A number of contemporary dance scholars, including Joanne Kealiino-homoku, have argued that *all* dance should be regarded as ethnic, in the sense that each form of dance stems from a particular social group with its own cultural and social traditions. In their view, ballet should be considered a form of Western European ethnic dance. However, this view has not been generally accepted, and so the more specialized concept of ethnic dance is presented in this chapter.

Ethnic dances have close ties to national history, social customs, religion, or other cultural elements. The term itself is derived from the Greek *ethnos,* meaning "people." While ethnic dances are usually performed by lay people with limited dance training, they may also be difficult or complex dances which are presented by highly skilled performers to large audiences.

We tend also to apply the term *ethnic* to the dance of non–Western cultures in Asia, Africa, or Latin America. These dance forms tend to be somewhat less familiar to us and more exotic than the traditional dances of Western nations; in addition, they are generally more closely attached to their original cultural sources or ceremonial functions. However, the authentic dances of Spain, Yugoslavia, or other European nations which have retained a peasant way of life in rural areas and have treasured their historic customs are also often referred to as ethnic dances.

Among the most unique and interesting ethnic dance traditions are those of Indonesia, Japan, India, and Spain.

Indonesian Dance

Dance is an integral part of life throughout the Indonesian archipelago, and particularly on the island of Bali. According to Beryl de Zoete and Walter Spies, it accompanies every stage of life from infancy to the grave and is an essential element in an endless series of public and private festivals, temple services, and processions:

". . . it is as members of age groups that unmarried boys and girls perform ceremonial dances of offering and dedication in the temple, where also old women renew the religious dances of their youth."[5]

In nonreligious dances, people of every age, caste, or occupation may perform, and most dancers or actors (the same word applies to both) have other occupations as craftsmen, agricultural workers, or fishermen. Only for a few highly skilled dancers or teachers does dance become an exclusive way of life. The Balinese people are physically extremely graceful and sensitive; their daily movement appears to have an almost choreographic quality. In addition, music pervades the atmosphere, with even the youngest children sitting between their fathers' knees in the *gamelan* orchestra, or learning the melodies and complicated rhythms of the gongs, drums, cymbals, and other percussive instruments at an extremely early age.

Dance appears everywhere, not only in temples or other religious ceremonials, but throughout the Balinese village. De Zoete and Spies wrote: ". . . wherever there is a space to dance, to mount a play, there is the Balinese stage. It may be the village street, the graveyard, the temple-court, the ground outside the temple, the courtyard of a Balinese house. . . . Its floor is the bare earth . . . its roof the sky or an overhanging tree. . . ."[6]

Dances are of many traditional types and may be carried on as dramatic spectacles for extended periods of time while villagers sit in the audience and at the same time eat, drink, chat, or play with their children. Many dances are performed in spectacular costumes and masks, often of monkeys, birds, or other animals. Other dances, such as the *Pentjak,* are war-like spectacles, dramatic plays, known as *Legong,* or sung dance-dramas called *Ardja.* Perhaps the most spectacular Balinese dances are the so-called trance dances, in which performers go into an apparent state of hypnosis or religious possession, handling red-hot coals or striking themselves with the Malay kris (a long, sharp dagger) so forcefully that the weapon may bend against their chests but apparently does not wound them. From time to time, troupes of highly skilled Balinese dancers tour the world and are acclaimed by sophisticated dance audiences and critics for the remarkable virtuosity of their performance. When this happens, obviously, the dance has been removed from its natural setting and is presented in a concert art form; yet it gives a vivid impression of the unique quality, grace, and mood of Indonesian dance.

Japanese Dance

Somewhat more formalized in its style, presentation, and organization is the ethnic dance art of Japan. This may be described under several categories: the theatrical, classic dance known as *Bugaku,* the famous *Kabuki* dance-theater, or such peasant dances as the *Bon* dances, linked to countryside festivals and celebrations.[7]

Dance in Japan has an ancient and well-documented history. *Gagaku* is the term used to describe noble or elegant music stemming from a period from the ninth to tenth century A.D. which drew elements from many Asian nations and cultures and was established as a traditional form of entertainment in the Imperial Japanese household. *Gagaku* incorporated music and dance of both sacred and secular origin as part of Buddhist services, at Shinto shrines, and as entertainment at the Imperial Court. A dance performance in *Gagaku* is known as *Bugaku*. *Bugaku* dance is relatively simple and symmetrical, lacking in rapid or complex movement and with dramatic elements subordinated to pure dance form. Extremely subtle in its impact, and generally done in old court costumes, *Bugaku* is not a dead art. New dances continue to be composed within the traditional style for presentation at major ceremonies or national events, such as the marriage of a crown prince.

In contrast, the *Kabuki* dance theater is a relatively new form of dance art, having originated during the nineteenth century. However, it was clearly influenced by older and more traditional elements of the Japanese theater. Much of its content, in terms of dramatic themes, costuming, and other conventions of dance, is descended from ancient sources. However, *Kabuki* also continues to change, as new plays are created to fit contemporary themes. *Kabuki* blends music, acting, and dance in a highly stylized performance. Men enact all the roles, both male and female. Many of the poses and movements are influenced by an earlier period of puppet theater, and the performers wear extremely heavy make-up, which gives them a fixed facial expression, like puppets. *Kabuki* is performed in several styles or types: the *Kyogen Zyoruri,* which is related to the puppet drama and has much dramatic content; dances drawn from the traditional *Noh* drama, which are performed only at special times of the year; so-called transfiguration dances, in

Japanese Butoh Company, Sankai Juku's work, *Jomon Sho.* Photograph by Martha Swope.

which there is little story or plot but in which dancers change roles and characters; comic *Zyoruri* dances; and others.

In addition, dances are also characterized by the style and range of movement. *Odori* is a form of stage dance marked by swift movements of the feet and lower part of the body; while *Mai* involves movement of the upper half of the body, including the head, arms, and shoulders; and *Shosa* dance is generally mimetic and realistic imitative movement. Like the dance of Bali, Japanese stage dance is deeply rooted in cultural tradition and may be difficult for Westerners to understand and appreciate. Nevertheless, outstanding *Kabuki* or *Bugaku* companies occasionally visit the United States and are generally well received as emissaries of a unique and fascinating dance tradition.

An example of more recent Japanese theatrical dancing is *Butoh,* a post–World War II Japanese dance style performed by a five-man troupe that has visited the United States, Sankai Juku. It is noted for its harsh and ugly images and grotesque and acrobatic movements and has occasionally been mistakenly reviewed as a form of ethnic dance. However, it simply represents a unique avant-garde dance movement.[8]

Indian Dance

Indian dance represents probably the most varied and highly developed ethnic dance form of the Orient. There are several major schools of Indian dance, related to the varied regions and ethnic or religious subgroups of this nation, with the predominant form being Hindu dance. Since the Hindus believe that the universe was created by Lord Shiva, a dancing god, dance is intricately attached to their religion and is found in many ceremonies, rituals, and in varied temple decorations and carvings. In India, dance has been highly developed as a form of communication, with stylized movements and gestures of many parts of the body—hands, fingers, arms, eyes, nose, mouth, head, and neck, among others—used to convey literal meaning. While the upper part of the body is the most active in dance, there are also definite foot positions and movements both on the ground and in the air.

Bharata Natya is one of the major Hindu dance styles or schools of Southern India and is believed to date back as far as 1500 B.C. It is practiced by temple dancers and originated in and around Madras, where it was found as part of the royal court. *Bharata Natya* programs, with both dancers and musicians on stage, continue without pause for three hours or more and range from abstract, lyric dances to more literally expressive or pantomimic works. *Kathakali* is a separate dance form (actually a dance-drama) which originated at a much later time in the region of Malabar and is used to illustrate the broad range of Hindu literature.

In a recent review of a Kathakali performance sponsored in New York City by the Asia Society, Bialor described the eight actor-dancers, whose "rigorous training cannot be equalled in the West":

> They were accompanied by drummers and vocalists who sing and recite text and dialogue—the actors of Kathakali do not speak but utter grunts . . . while miming,

employing mudras and dancing. There is no more splendid sight than fully madeup, costumed and caparisoned Kathakali actor-dancers prancing, stamping, twirling, glittering and grunting.[9]

Dances of the North tend to be less ornate and structured. *Kathak* dance, for example, was originally done by Brahmin priests known as Kathaks, who used dance movement to illustrate religious fables or anecdotes of the gods. Today it is performed by both men and women as a form of entertainment and is marked by heavy, rhythmic beating of feet on the ground, chanting of syllables to the drummer to convey rhythms, and pantomimic episodes drawn from religious lore. *Manipuri* dance represents still another important dance form of the Northeast region; it also deals with religious themes, has relatively little gesture language, and tends to be more flowing and quiet than other Indian dance styles.

Spanish Dance

Spanish dance is one of the most exciting and varied of ethnic dance forms. It has traditionally been a highly popular form of stage dance, with many touring companies and star dancers who perform in night clubs and theaters around the world. Spaniards have a deep love for their native dances; for them it is almost a cult. Within the nation's forty-nine regions, there are over one hundred accepted, unchanging, traditional dances of several major styles. The mood of Spanish dance ranges widely from the fiery, explosive flamenco to quieter, subtler, and even languorous dance styles which are somewhat Oriental in their flavor. Typically, Spanish dancing is accompanied by the guitar and singing, although it may also be performed to the orchestral music of leading Spanish composers. It represents both a popular, even peasant, art form which is seen everywhere—at village festivals, processionals, and varied social events—and, in more developed presentations, a dance art that approaches ballet in its technical demands and virtuosity.

Historically, a number of popular Spanish dances have come into being throughout the centuries—each one arousing a great wave of national interest and then becoming part of the body of national dance. Examples of these have been the *Fandango, Bolero, Zarabanda, Chacona,* and *Seguidillas.* Some dances were typically found in the popular lyric theater, while others are attached to the major regions of Spain, such as Andalucia, Catalonia, or the region surrounding Seville. A distinctly different style is the flamenco, a flirtatious, fiery dance of gypsy origin using castanets, much heel work on the floor, and staccato, explosive guitar playing and singing.

Spanish dancing has typically been done to the music of such composers as de Falla, Granados, and Albeniz and has been a popular element in operas like *Carmen* or folk ballets like *The Three-Cornered Hat.* It has also been an important element in the repertoires of such early ballerinas as Taglioni or Fanny Elssler; in more recent years, leading Spanish dance idols have been Argentina, Argentinita, Pilar Lopez, José Greco, or Rosario and Antonio, who have toured extensively with their own companies of dancers, singers, and musicians to popular acclaim. Within the past two decades, Spanish dance has undergone an ebb in popularity, as far as public interest is concerned. In part, this is due to changing modes of popular entertainment. The kinds of night clubs or theaters that featured Spanish dance and similar forms of musical entertainment have declined sharply, possibly because of the growth of television as a form of home-based amusement.

However, there is no question that it will persist as an important national dance art and that, as companies continue to present Spanish dance, it will grow again in popularity. Indeed, in 1986, Kisselgoff commented that just when it seemed time to lament that Spain's great flamenco dancers had all died out, a "completely superb" company of singers, dancers, and guitarists known as *Flamenco Puro* put on an outstanding program at New York's Hellinger Theater. Kisselgoff pointed out that while flamenco is essentially a folk form and accessible to all as entertainment, its depths ". . . seem to be plumbed only by those who are initiated into its mysteries—into its complex rhythms, structures and more important, the distilled cries of joy and pain that lie at its base. That foundation is clearly an esthetic one. For all its popular roots, flamenco is an art."[10]

Spanish dance has influenced the dance of other nations which were colonized by Spain, including the Philippines and several countries in Central and South America. In many cases, they blend the original traditions of the tribal groups that had existed at the time of the Spanish invasions with dance styles learned from their conquerors. *Ballet Folklorico,* for example, an outstanding company that performs throughout the year in Mexico and on tour, includes both dances derived from pre-Cortés Aztec Indian traditions and others transported from Spain in theatricalized versions.

Numerous other examples might be cited of how ethnic dance has been transformed into a spectacular and appealing stage art. Probably the leading example is the *Moiseyev Dance Company,* a popular Soviet group that was formed in the 1930s and has toured the world—including the United States—frequently over the past three decades. Based on solid ballet technique, but with numerous pyrotechnics and characteristic dance movements drawn from traditional dance forms, the ninety-five Moiseyev dancers, accompanied by singers and musicians, perform a repertoire of humorous, sad, patriotic, and other dances. Walsh described a drill team dance in Moldavian mufti as raising ". . . folk dancing to a highly regimented, breathtakingly athletic art form. Drawing inspiration from the more than 100 different ethnic groups in the Soviet Union, but predominantly Russian in personnel and outlook, the company remains the personal expression of its founder, Choreographer Igor Moiseyev, 80."[11]

Folk Dance

The term *folk dance* is often used interchangeably with *ethnic dance* and indeed may be used to describe the same kinds of traditional national dances. In a scholarly analysis of European folk dance, Joan Lawson showed clearly how the historical development, geography, social customs, religion, and occupations found in various regions of Europe have directly influenced the folk dances that emerged through the centuries.[12]

Today the term *folk dance* tends to be applied to dances which are related more closely to social customs and recreational events than to ancient religious and ceremonial sources. Typically, many folk dances are based on such ballroom dance steps as the waltz, schottische, mazurka, and polka, and thus are of relatively recent origin with little or no ritual or other cultural significance.

Folk dancing is particularly popular as a recreational pastime in the United States. Since World War II, there has been a thriving international folk dance movement, with thousands of clubs or community groups that practice traditional dances of many nations. Dances from the Balkan countries, such as Rumania, Bulgaria, and Yugoslavia, along with Greek, Israeli, and other Middle-Eastern dances, are performed in many college and university dance groups.

The very nature of the folk process, in which dances, songs, or stories are changed as they are passed along from teacher to teacher or performer to performer, means that the cultural heritage inevitably is transformed over time. Sometimes dances of the common people are deliberately stylized for performance or put together in new forms in published collections or phonograph record descriptions. Not infrequently, new dances are created by folk leaders. If these are widely accepted and continue to be performed over a period of time, eventually they come to be regarded as folk dances.

An organization that is highly regarded within the folk arts field is the Country Dance and Song Society of America. Early in this century, a leading British folklorist, Cecil Sharp, revived interest in the traditional Morris, sword, country, and court dances of England and explored the lingering heritage of English dancing in the American Appalachian Mountain region. He established an English folk dance and song society; its American counterpart was formed by an outstanding English teacher of folk dancing who came to the United States, May Gadd. Today, the Society has several branches throughout the United States which offer courses, workshops, festivals, publications, and leader-training courses in traditional English and American country dancing and music. Yet, even this organization, which greatly values authentic presentation of old materials, does not hesitate to include newer American square dances, contra dances, mixers, and English dances as well in its repertoire.

Perhaps the most interesting example of how a literature of folk dance may deliberately be created is found in Israel. Here, when Jews came together from all over the world after Israel was declared a nation, it became necessary to weld a new, unified culture based on many old traditions. Dance was seen as one of the ways of doing this. Judith Ingber wrote:

> The dance creators took their inspiration from the rich characteristics of the various communities outside of Israel in the Diaspora; from the traditions and rituals of Judaism; from the colorful life-styles of those who had continued to live in Israel. . . . The folk dance creators forged all these factors in their individual yet Jewish experience, creating dances that spoke to the kibbutzim, the villages, the cities, and the immigrants. The dances gathered a swift momentum and the result has been a spirited dance, Mid-Eastern yet reflective of the experience of the Diaspora.[13]

The new Israeli folk dances had many roots: the traditional dances of North African or Oriental Jews who settled Israel, or the exciting Slavic dances of Russia or Poland, from which many other pioneers came. Often, dances were created to celebrate first harvests or the discovery of water wells in the desert; typically, too, dances were choreographed for national festivals or to commemorate historical events or major festivals of biblical times.

Square and Contra Dancing

Although people of many nations have brought their folk arts to the United States—immigrants from the British Isles, Scandinavia, Italy, Germany, Poland, and a host of other countries—the one uniquely American form of folk dance is the square dance.

This form is descended from the quadrille, a four-sided set dance performed as a type of social or ballroom dance throughout the Western world during the nineteenth century. It also was influenced by the movement patterns and steps of English and other European folk dances; in American cities and rural areas, these tended to be combined into a form of lively, robust, informal dance which emphasized a play-like, humorous spirit and was marked by the role of the caller. Traditionally, the square dance caller either chants, sings, or prompts the dances and may improvise the sequence of the action to challenge the dancers or catch them unawares. His or her humor and ingenious "patter" calling tends to make square dancing a rhythmic, highly entertaining activity.

Interest in square dancing died out during the early decades of this century and then was revived by Lloyd Shaw in Colorado and by a number of other callers and teachers after World War II. It became extremely popular, with millions of dancers and thousands of clubs, particularly in small towns and suburban areas. Square dancing appeared on television and in the movies and attracted widespread interest; however, as the fad spread, it became highly competitive. Companies published square dance books and magazines and manufactured records of new dances, costumes, loudspeaker systems, and other forms of square dance paraphernalia. The movement itself became extremely complex, with high-level callers constantly creating new dances and movements to the point that square dance clubs required that dancers take extended beginners' courses before being considered for membership. This overemphasis on complicated dancing—which often resembled close-order drills more than dancing—resulted in the movement narrowing down to a much smaller number of enthusiasts doing advanced dances in tightly knit, exclusive square dance clubs.

Contra Dancing. Recently, there has been a new wave of interest in contra dancing, the traditional line dance form of New England. Today, there are hundreds of contra dance groups around the country serving participants of all ages. Often, contra dancing is combined with square dancing in groups in university towns; students and faculty members dance to live fiddle and banjo music and practice informal clogging and relaxed, easy-going, traditional square, circle, and line dances of authentic regional backgrounds. In this sense, country dance interest is closely tied to a revival of interest in folk music. John Wilson wrote of folk music festivals throughout the United States and Canada with swelling attendance, in which emphasis is placed on authentic styles rather than the synthetic music created during the folk music boom of the 1960s. Dancing plays an important part in these folk events. There is less emphasis on the words of the songs and more on the danceable rhythms of British and Irish-inspired melodies; often, dancers do impulsive solo clogging or other improvised dancing along with structured set dances.[14]

Ballroom Dancing

This represents a purely social form of dance originally done in the royal court or by polite society and today practiced as a popular, recreational activity. In past generations, it tended to include such set or group dances as cotillions, quadrilles, contra dances, or circle progressive dances, which are today regarded as part of the country dance movement. In contrast, ballroom dancing today is generally enjoyed by couples and includes both the foxtrot, waltz, jitterbug, or Latin-American dances (which have been popular for the past few decades) as well as the newer dances, which represent offshoots of disco and rock-and-roll dancing.

Ballroom dancing is truly international in scope; the same dances tend to be done in discotheques, night clubs, adult resorts, and as part of social recreation in similar settings around the world. It is performed to popular music of the present day, in which the music determines the type of dance that is to be done. The disco dance craze of the late 1970s and early 1980s emerged as a $4 billion-a-year industry, with immense sales of records and tapes and thousands of popular dance halls or discotheques, catering primarily to young people and offering nonstop recorded music of the latest hits, skillfully blended to create a hypnotic, exciting effect on the dancers—often in a highly stylized setting with dramatic strobe lighting effects. The movement itself, as seen in such hit films as *Saturday Night Fever* or on popular television teenage dance shows, is a blend of older dance forms, with elements of rock and roll, Latin dance, the jitterbug, and much sexually expressive movement.

Overall, social dancing is certainly the most popular dance form in terms of public awareness and direct participation. Many thousands of dance teachers are employed in commercial dance studios in cities and towns throughout the country, either as part of large chains or as independent enterprises. Particularly for children of socially elite or upward striving families, the "right" dancing class or assembly has traditionally been one of the rites of passage approved by society. In Philadelphia, for example, Anne Lorimer commented that for the upper classes, dancing class was the first step along the road that ended at the altar. Well-bred boys and girls met and mingled and learned the waltz and the manners of ladies and gentlemen. Lorimer wrote:

> For years, upper-crust mothers have ignored the tempos of the times, dressed their unwilling offspring in lace-collared, velvet party dresses, Mary Janes and white gloves or gray trousers and blazers, and trotted them off to dancing class. They know it's the fox trot, not the frug, that Lester Lanin and Meyer Davis play at the hundreds of charity balls that grease society's wheels each winter season.[15]

Although youngsters at this age may resent dancing classes that force them to mingle with the opposite sex, dance during the teen years becomes closely linked with adolescent musical crazes, with parties and school dances, and with that fundamental function of dance in many societies—courtship. So, each generation tends to have favorite songs and dances that linger as sentimental memories of youth as they continue through the middle and later years of life.

Ballroom dancing is linked to other types of dance in several ways. In the studios found throughout big-city and small-town neighborhoods, it is usually taught side by side with ballet, tap, and jazz dance. There are also high-level ballroom dance contests in which amateur enthusiasts compete for regional, national, and even international awards, much like major ice-skating competitions. Ballroom dancing is a popular form of entertaining on cruise ships or at resorts, with skilled ballroom dance couples doing exhibitions and, in some cases, giving dance lessons as a second form of entertainment. The spectacular dancing of Fred Astaire, Ginger Rogers, Gene Kelly, and similar stage musical or motion picture stars was in part tap and jazz and in part exhibition ballroom dancing.

Finally, ballroom dancing has frequently been featured on Broadway stages or in concert halls, as in *Tango Argentina,* described earlier. In some cases, it has been the basis for ballet or modern dance choreography, as in George Balanchine's *Liebeslieder Waltzer* or Twyla Tharp's *Nine Sinatra Songs.* And, surprisingly, in the mid-1980s, a performing company of six couples named the American Ballroom Theater sold out the Joyce Theater in New York and the Academy of Music in Philadelphia and garnered admiring reviews from such disparate journals as the *London Times* and *Wall Street Journal.*

Jazz Dance

Jazz dance evolved in the early twentieth century as a natural accompaniment to jazz music—a highly syncopated, rhythmic, and uniquely American form of popular music. Jazz got its start in the South, particularly in New Orleans, and was first played by small black bands which provided music for funeral marches, parades, honkey-tonks, and brothels. The nation first became fully aware of it during the 1920s when, as part of the new freedom and vibrancy in national life after World War I (a period known as the Jazz Age), dances like the Bunny Hug, Charleston, and Varsity Drag became widely popular. Jazz moved North and gave rise to the era of swing music, with large bands, both white and black, that played popular music heavily influenced by the rhythm and style of the earlier jazz pioneers. Swing represented a watered-down, popularized form of jazz; a smaller and more specialized group of musicians continued to perform what was often called Dixieland music, closer to the original jazz in spirit and appealing to a much smaller group of jazz aficionados.

Jazz dance emerged as a hybrid form during this period. It took many of the movements that had been created as part of the popular new dances of the 1920s and combined them with elements of African dance, as well as other steps or movements that were used in the musical stage dance. All these were blended into a varied and eclectic form of theater dance. Heavily influenced by black sources, jazz has become a popular movement art which is used as an important area of dance training for those who seek to become professional stage or television dancers, regardless of race.

As a dance form, jazz has an exciting, vibrant, and dynamic quality that makes it a natural for popular stage performances. Students of jazz learn to use their bodies in new ways. In describing a class for performers of the American Dance Machine, a company devoted to exploring past jazz traditions and presenting them for modern audiences, John Gruen commented that much of the movement resembles ritualistic steps and gestures out of deepest Africa, with vigorous, rhythmic movement of the torso and pelvis carried on to an insistent, staccato rhythm:

> For an hour-and-a-half, the on-going dance movements are carefully dissected and analyzed. Head, neck, shoulders, torso, arms, hips, and pelvis are given difficult and highly specialized isolated movements. When the group is ready, the movements are all put together, and, two by two, the dancers execute a perfectly coordinated variation that translates into an exhilarating '60s frug.[16]

The same company has reconstructed and performed such other historic dances as the Charleston or tango of the 1920s, a Lindy or rumba of the 1940s, a 1950s jitterbug or samba, and other dances which have been part of the continuing social dance tradition. Other teachers or choreographers do not concern themselves with specific dances of the past but simply use jazz dance steps and movements as a key element in dance training and performance. Among the leading choreographers who have used jazz in this way have been Jerome Robbins, Jack Cole, Michael Kidd, and Bob Fosse.

Tap Dance

Closely linked to jazz dance is tap dance, a more intricate and sophisticated form of clog dance. Tap and clog both are believed to have descended from traditional Irish step dances, from Spanish flamenco dancing, and from the footwork of many African dances. In tap, the fluid body articulation of African dance is easily recognized, rather than the ramrod-stiff spine of Irish jigs, reels, and hornpipes.

Long popular in vaudeville and on the musical stage, tap dance experienced a period of decline in which, although it was still taught and performed, it was rarely seen as a separate entertainment dance form. In the early and mid-1980s, it began to enjoy a new wave of popularity, with tap dancers performing in revivals of old Broadway shows like *My One and Only* and *42nd St.* Tap dance sequences were incorporated in some ballets, small tap dance companies performed on tour, and some of the outstanding dancers of past generations were given a chance to show their art. Although tap dancing is customarily thought of as a lighthearted display of technical virtuosity or even acrobatics, as in the dancing of the famous Bill "Bojangles" Robinson, it has been performed to classical music by Bach or Rimsky-Korsakoff by such artists as Paul Draper or Danny Daniels and has been given emotional content and dramatic impact.

In more recent work by artists like Gail Conrad, tap is incorporated into a total theater dance form, with all the theatrical trappings of sets, props, costumes, and lighting—and with a mood that may range from comic to serious or surrealistic. Draegin commented about Conrad's work:

> Turning tap into theater might seem almost antithetical to what traditional tap has been about: a jazz-based form that is highly individual, idiosyncratic and improvisatory. But then, Miss Conrad is not interested in being a tap purist. In her choreography she draws from all sorts of movement styles—everything from flamenco to ballet—and musical forms—from salsa to rock to Tchaikovsky to jazz.[17]

Each of the dance forms described in this chapter continues to play an important role within the overall dance scene in the United States. Ethnic dance, for example, comprises hundreds of stage performances in major cities each year. In a review of a single season in New York City, Linda Small described performances by a leading Scottish group, the Regimental Band of Her Majesty's Grenadier Guards and the Pipes, Drums, and Dancers of Her Majesty's Scots Guards, appearing in honor of the Silver Jubilee of Queen Elizabeth II; the Yatran Ukrainian Dance Company; the Soviet Georgian Dancers; the Ballet Nacional Festivales de España, Spain's official representative company formed to preserve historic dances of the nineteenth-century bolera school and neoclassical dance; the Mariano Parra Spanish Dance Company; the Ibrahim Farrach Near East Dance Group; the Dancers and Musicians of Bali and Penca and Topeng Babakan of West Java; and numerous other performing groups, including Indian and Japanese dance companies.[18] Similar performances are scheduled each year in major cities throughout the country, and outstanding new ethnic or folk dance companies continue to emerge from time to time.

Notes

1 Lois Draegin, "Tango Traces a Society," *New York Times,* June 23, 1985, p. 8-H.

2 Perry Bialor, "Tango," *Ballet News,* January 1986, p. 11.

3 William Neilson, ed., *Webster's New International Dictionary of the English Language* (Springfield, Mass.: G. and C. Merriam Co., 1956), p. 2833.

4 La Meri, *Total Education in Ethnic Dance* (New York: Marcel Dekker, 1977), p. 1.

5 Beryl de Zoete and Walter Spies, *Dance and Drama in Bali* (New York: Thomas Yoseloff, 1958), p. 7.

6 Ibid., p. 11.

7 See Gladys Michaelis, "The Kabuki—A Dance-Drama Art Form of Japan," *Dance Magazine,* May 1977, pp. 83–86.

8 See Terry Trucco, "Dancers Who Probe the Dark Corners of the Mind," *New York Times,* October 28, 1984, p. H-1.

9 Perry Bialor, "Ethnic Update," *Ballet News,* February 1985, pp. 30–31.

10 Anna Kisselgoff, "Savoring the Art and Mystery of Flamenco," *New York Times,* November 2, 1986, p. 14-H.

11 Michael Walsh, "Spit and Polish, Braids and Boots," *Time,* September 15, 1986, p. 100.

12 Joan Lawson, *European Folk Dance* (London: Sir Isaac Pitman, Ltd., 1955), chapter 1.

13 Judith B. Ingber, "The Roots of Israeli Folk Dance," *Dance Perspectives,* no. 59 (Autumn 1974).

14 John S. Wilson, "Today's Folk Music: It Goes to Your Feet," *New York Times,* September 7, 1975, p. D-1.

15 Anne Lorimer, "Ballroom Dance Still Holds Sway in Young Society," *Philadelphia Inquirer,* November 29, 1981, p. 1-N.

16 John Gruen, "American Dance Machine: The Era of Reconstruction," *Dance Magazine,* February 1978, p. 48.

17 Lois Draegin, "Turning Tap Dance into Total Theater," *New York Times,* February 13, 1983, p. 12-H.

18 Linda Small, "Reflections on a Season of Ethnic Dance," *Dance Magazine,* April 1978, p. 79.

CHAPTER 13

Dance as a Public Art: Prospects and Strategies

He [David White] is doing his best. His systems are spreading. In 1985, with funding from the Ford Foundation and NEA, he inaugurated the National Performance Network, whereby, every year, alternative presenting organizations in various American cities—the Walker Art Center in Minneapolis, MoMing in Chicago, Dance Umbrella in Boston, the Colorado Dance Festival in Boulder, and so on—will each bring in two to four out-of-state artists of their own choosing for one- or two-week residencies, the costs to be covered half [roughly] by NPN and half by the host organization.[1]

HAVING DOCUMENTED THE CHANGES THAT HAVE TAKEN PLACE IN ballet, modern dance, and other important dance forms over the past several decades, we now turn to a consideration of dance as a public art. What is the level of public support, understanding, and interest in dance? What roles have government and the business community played in supporting the performing arts, including dance? What strategies have performing companies and sponsoring organizations developed to stimulate public awareness and support and provide financial stability for dance as a vital art form?

Chapter 1 summarized the remarkable expansion of cultural institutions and programs that occurred in the United States during the post–World War II period, as well as the period of financial cutbacks and retrenchment that marked the late 1970s and early 1980s. This chapter examines these developments in more detail and then describes recent efforts that have been made to broaden public interest and involvement in dance.

The case for the cultural explosion was widely documented. What brought it about? Gertrude Lippincott outlined a number of key factors:

(1) an increase in the amount of . . . leisure time, (2) an increase in family and personal income, (3) an emphasis on urban living which promotes a climate for the arts, (4) America's continuing [growth] as a consumer . . . society, (5) the great stress laid on creativity in education and in daily living, (6) the tax-exempt status of many art objects and gifts presented by individuals and corporations to museums, educational institutions, etc., (7) the financially profitable state of the arts for many dealers and artists, particularly painters, (8) the financially profitable investment possibilities of the arts, and (9) the status symbol syndrome of owning works of art.[2]

Public Attitudes about the Arts

Perhaps more important than any of these factors was a change in American attitudes about art. In the past, it tended to be regarded as an activity suited only for highly gifted performers and a wealthy or intellectually elite audience. This was linked to an attitude that art was just not too important; that it was only a peripheral concern of life and certainly did not justify the serious attention of government, industry, foundations, or educational institutions.

In the decades following World War II, these attitudes changed markedly. No longer was art viewed as the exclusive province of a few wealthy patrons. Toffler suggested that a new middle class of well-educated persons, young and intelligent, numbering between 30 and 45 million, had become the backbone of artistic support and involvement.[3]

John D. Rockefeller III, president of the Lincoln Center for the Performing Arts, gave his view of the change in public attitudes, seeing the growth of popular interest and participation in the arts as:

. . . another evidence of our national maturity, a natural and predictable deepening of interest in artistic matters. . . . It is a clear call that we accept the arts as a new community responsibility, that we place them alongside our already accepted responsibilities for the health, welfare, and education of our community. . . .[4]

However, there also is evidence that the overall national picture has not been as positive as these statements would suggest. Two critical studies, conducted during the 1960s, suggest that reports of the cultural boom of the postwar period had been exaggerated.

Studies of the Performing Arts

Two Princeton University economics professors, William J. Baumol and William G. Bowen, spent several years studying the performing arts in America under a grant of the Twentieth Century Fund. Their report, *Performing Arts: The Economic Dilemma,* did much to dispute the view that there had been a widespread increase of actual attendance at artistic events, or that the explosion had truly cut across class and geographical lines to reach new audiences and grass roots regions of the country. They concluded that the cultural explosion:

. . . is shown to be an extremely spotty affair, with some levels of activity increasing, some declining, and the overall result amounting best to a small and patchy pattern of growth. . . . In sum, this analysis of the record entitles us to conclude neither that this nation has entered a great cultural renaissance nor that it is lost in an artistic wilderness. Rather . . . the overall progress of professional activity in the living arts has amounted to little more than a continuation of past trends.[5]

The Twentieth Century Fund report found that, although there had been an "air of excitement and growth" that augured well for the future, there had been in reality no sharp increase in the attendance statistics at professional performing arts events.

The audience for the performing arts, concluded Baumol and Bowen, was still drawn from an extremely narrow segment of the population, consisting chiefly of well-educated, professional people in their late youth and early middle age, amounting to no more than 5 million individuals, about 4 percent of the population.

The economic dilemma of the performing arts received the major portion of Baumol and Bowen's concern. With the salary level of "performers in many organizations . . . still scandalously low," Baumol and Bowen described the performer's lot as being a "nightmare world." Cutting through the impressive figures about the growth of performing groups (which they identified chiefly as amateur), they concluded:

> In no case is the number of professional organizations very large; they range [in 1965] from about 60 metropolitan and major orchestras and 40 to 50 permanent theatrical groups to perhaps 7 opera companies and a slightly larger number of dance groups. In number of performers they vary from a dance company of 6 to an orchestra with over 100 musicians and grand opera with a cast of over 200.[6]

The Twentieth Century Fund concluded that if the performing arts—theater, opera, music, and dance—were to survive and grow, government and foundation financial support would be absolutely essential.

Another report issued in the 1960s, *The Performing Arts: Problems and Prospects,* published by the Rockefeller Brothers Fund, was somewhat more positive about the cultural explosion in general. It confirmed that a marked expansion of the performing arts had taken place and concluded that the potential for the successful development of the performing arts was tremendous:

> There are millions of Americans who have never seen a live professional performance of any kind. There are untold numbers who might, with opportunity and training, become first-rate performing artists. There are electronic devices, still in a relatively early stage of development, to bring performances to vast audiences at modest expense. And the material resources to do all these things are available if we choose to do them.[7]

The Rockefeller Panel Report also made a significant comment—that almost all the expansion in the arts had been amateur. For example, it was shown that the professional commercial theater had declined sharply in recent years; that, of the large number of symphony orchestras, only fifty-four were composed predominantly of professional musicians; that only five or six dance companies met high professional standards and had a real degree of institutional stability; that, of the 754 opera groups, only 35 to 40 were fully professional, with not more than ten companies providing performances for more than fifteen days in the year. If it were not for amateur or semiprofessional companies, many communities far from the great urban centers would have no opportunity at all to view live performing arts. Nonetheless, the report argued strongly that

> . . . it is on the professional performing artists and arts organizations that ultimate responsibility for the highest levels of creative output and quality rests. Some of these organizations, particularly the orchestras, are expanding rapidly, some are actually in declining health, others are just barely holding their own, and others are growing at a rate much slower than might be. In general, there has been no significant improvement in the basic health of the professional arts organizations. There is much to be done.[8]

Status of Dance Companies

Exactly how did professional dance fit into this picture? What did the Twentieth Century Fund and the Rockefeller Report say of this art, in terms of its health and prospects for the future?

In general, they commented that it suffered from the same difficulties as all the performing arts: problems in finding regular employment and maintaining an adequate standard of living for the performer; with few exceptions, a lack of opportunities for first-class training throughout the country; the need for more theaters designed for dance and available to dance companies for seasons of the appropriate length; a lack of strong and stable sponsoring organizations, combined with a dependence on crisis financing; and, finally, insufficient long-range planning and research.

The Rockefeller Report concluded that not more than five or six dance companies had both a national reputation and a reasonably stable organizational structure. In addition, the Twentieth Century Fund study also pointed out that the largest and most enthusiastic audiences tended to flock to performances by glamourous foreign groups and troupes like the Bolshoi, Royal Ballet, Royal Danish Ballet, and other visiting companies. Only the New York City Ballet's audience compared favorably with those of the foreign companies.

Both studies presented a picture of dance as an area of artistic activity with considerable potential for the future, but one which would require the combined support of government, foundations, and universities in order to operate on a stronger base.

Government Support of the Arts

How promising were the prospects of such support for dance? It was clear that in many ways the United States had lagged far behind other nations in supporting the arts through government subsidy.

Examples of Other Nations

In England, for example, the Arts Council of Great Britain had been extremely effective since World War II in providing annual grants to support opera, ballet, and theater. In France, there are two national theaters (the Opéra Comique and the Comédie Française) which receive subsidies amounting to several millions of dollars annually, granted by the national Ministry of Beaux Arts. In the French provinces, opera is subsidized locally, and there are many national festivals which also receive governmental support.

In Italy, the famous La Scala Opera House in Milan is supported by municipal and state funds; such national festivals as the one at Spoleto each year are supported by the Italian government. In Austria, the government aids such undertakings as the Vienna State Opera, the Vienna Philharmonic, and the Salzburg Festival.

Past Efforts in the United States

In the United States, the first large-scale effort on the part of the federal government to assist the performing arts came during the depression of the 1930s. It was prompted not so much by a recognition of the special need of the arts as it was part of a total effort to provide employment during a period of national emergency. Thus, in the mid- and late 1930s, the Federal Theater included a dance unit which helped to promote a nationwide program of dance performance.

The Federal Dance Theater, founded in January, 1936, which included Doris Humphrey, Charles Weidman, and Helen Tamiris among its supervisors, sponsored many performances and tours which reflected the view of dance as part of "people's theater." Before long, along with the Federal Theater itself, dancers and dance came under political scrutiny and attack because of alleged left-wing influences. Ultimately, the program of support for the arts was discontinued.

This experience illustrated the fears shared by many individuals with respect to support of the arts by a national government. In their view, there are grave risks of government attempting to use the arts as a means of propaganda. It is feared that even if the attempt to control is not overt, some artists may, in their desire to retain support, unconsciously yield to a form of artistic censorship to avoid giving offense to the establishment. For these and other reasons, there has been hesitation, on the part of many legislators and some professionals in the arts, to support a full-fledged program of government support of the arts.

Justification for Subsidies

Apart from the question of whether government should subsidize the arts (in terms of potential dangers in this relationship), there is the even more basic question of *why* it should do so.

Some have made the point that if the arts cannot justify themselves through attendance and ticket sales, as commercial motion pictures, or stage shows, or ice shows, or the circus, or rodeo, or rock-and-roll shows do, then they have no right to ask for support.

The answer to this, of course, is that government is in a position to support whatever it considers important in national or community life. The provision of parks, health services, sanitation, police, and education are all usually mandated by law—but only because those who make the laws perceive these as essential functions of government which are not likely to be adequately provided in other ways. Throughout the history of the Western world, music, drama, painting, dance, and architecture have all been strongly supported in European countries. Today, it has become increasingly evident that the arts are essential to the fullest and richest life in both the community and the nation, that they express the highest ideals of a society, and that they provide a vital and necessary dimension of human existence.

In the United States during the 1940s and 1950s, there were a number of specific programs assisting the arts on a limited basis. For example, a number of dance companies, including those headed by José Limón, Martha Graham, Alvin Ailey, Ballet Caravan, and Ballet Theater, made "goodwill tours" of Europe, South America, and the Orient, with funding assistance by the U.S. State Department. Such grants by no means represented full-fledged subsidies. Emphasis was placed on assisting only those companies that were able to attract large audiences in the countries visited; State Department funds were used to supplement the tour's income and to make it possible.

Expanded Federal Support of the Arts

A broader program of federal support of the arts aimed at assisting domestic performance—rather than foreign tours—was initiated in 1964 when the National Arts and Cultural Development Act established a National Council on the Arts within the Executive Office of the President. A year later, the Arts and Humanities Act of 1965 established a National Foundation on the Arts and Humanities, with separate endowment programs and advisory bodies for the arts and the humanities. The National Council on the Arts was identified as the advisory body for the National Endowment for the Arts and made responsible for providing funds (chiefly on a matching-grant basis) to nonprofit organizations and to state and other public organizations and individuals for the following purposes:

> . . . To assist artistic and cultural productions which give "emphasis to American creativity" and encourage professional excellence; to help make available artistic programs of high merit in areas of the country which otherwise would be culturally barren; to encourage and assist individual artists; to promote a general appreciation and understanding of the arts; and to provide assistance for relevant projects related to surveys, research and planning in the arts.[9]

The Commissioner of Education of the United States Department of Health, Education, and Welfare was empowered to make grants and loans to strengthen instruction and establish teacher-training institutes in the arts and humanities.

Recognizing that one of the primary needs within the dance community was to have a permanent service organization which would encourage dancers and choreographers to work together in common causes, the National Endowment for the Arts funded a planning meeting to help establish such an organization. In 1966, the organization was formally launched, assisted by the National Endowment for the Arts, with promise of additional funds to be granted on a matching basis. Titled the Association of American Dance Companies, it was intended to serve as an umbrella organization, bringing together such other groups as the North American Association of Ballet Companies, the National Association for Regional Ballet, the Foundation for American Dance, and the American Dance Guild in the overall advancement of dance as a performing art.

Continuing Economic Pressures

Despite such efforts, and despite the growth of public interest in the performing arts through the 1960s and early 1970s, there continued to be severe economic pressures. In 1973, at the final hearing for the triennial reauthorization for the National Endowment for the Arts and the National Endowment for the Humanities, national arts leaders testified before Congress that the arts in America were facing a serious financial crisis.

In 1976, the Association of American Dance Companies concluded its tenth annual conference with a warning that the preceding decade of expansion in the dance field might well be followed by a severe "financial squeeze." A year later, arts critic Harold C. Schonberg wrote in the *New York Times:* "Inflation is killing off arts organizations left and right, and our biggest organizations—opera houses, museums, drama and dance groups, name it—are in desperate trouble, all of them, with an ever-widening gap between income and expenses."[10]

Deficits of Major Dance Companies

The problem, which was nationwide, was illustrated dramatically in 1977 in New York City, when the orchestra of the New York City Ballet walked out in a labor contract dispute that closed down more than half of the month-long run of *The Nutcracker,* the company's most popular, money-making work. The strike resulted from the demand of the musicians for pay parity with other major Lincoln Center orchestras and was only one example of the mounting financial pressures that threatened even the most successful and prestigious of dance organizations.

As another example of mounting financial costs of dance production, Alwin Nikolais reported that when his company and the Murray Louis Company performed for a four-week season at the Lyceum Theater in New York City in the mid-1970s, although the house was sold out, they lost $75,000. Similarly, Martha Graham lost $125,000 in a three-week run on Broadway. A major problem of professional performance arises from demands made by stagehands' and musicians' unions. (For example, in a later season, Nikolais was faced by union demands that he hire twenty-four musicians for a Broadway season, despite the fact that he uses electronic music and had no need for live musicians at all. As a result, the season was canceled. "What a great idea," said Nikolais. "Perhaps I should pay a dozen dancers not to dance.")[11]

Only that many companies throughout the United States operate in university theaters or publicly subsidized arts centers, with largely volunteer dancers, musicians, and support personnel (although increasingly dancers expect to be paid for rehearsal and performance time) has made it possible for them to survive economically.

National Endowment for the Arts Programs

The most positive aspect of the 1970s, in terms of economic assistance to the arts, was the expanded funding provided by the National Endowment for the Arts (NEA). Total funding under this program rose from $15.7 million in 1970 to a high of $188.1 million in 1980. These funds helped to support such projects as the following:

Coordinated Residency Touring Program. Under this program, sponsors of dance company residencies received, through their state arts councils, as much as one-third of the fee of the companies participating in the program. This program has enabled many schools and communities to sponsor professional companies for concerts as well as workshops in dance technique, improvisation, and choreography for periods generally ranging from a few days to a week.

Choreography Fellowships and Production Grants. There have been several categories for these grants, some including individual choreographers and others directed to companies.

Artists-in-the-Schools Program. This program, jointly supported by the U.S. Department of Health, Education, and Welfare and the National Endowment for the Arts, represented an exciting and innovative effort to bring the arts to elementary and secondary schools throughout the country. With respect to dance, it "was developed to use the best American dance artists . . . to bring to our public schools the discovery of dance as an art form and the experience of movement as a method of learning." Dance artists and companies typically went to schools or groups of schools for a period of two to four weeks to teach children directly or to work with teachers and parents, and perform in concerts.

Other Grants Programs

In addition, numerous cultural institutions—including museums, opera associations, and ballet companies—received direct subsidies from NEA to support their programs, on a challenge grant basis under which Federal funds had to be matched. The National Endowment for the Humanities assisted research projects in the arts, primarily those concerned with historical and theoretical studies and criticism of major significance.

Throughout the 1970s, the Dance Touring Program of the National Endowment for the Arts continued to expand; by 1975–1976, it had become a major income source for many dance companies.

In the late 1970s, the basis for subsidizing the dance touring program was restructured, with a limited number of companies chosen to divide $2.5 million in grants. Approval of companies and their subsequent listing in the Dance Touring Program Directory, which made them eligible for residency grants, shifted from purely quantitative criteria to a panel process in which companies were selected on qualitative measures as well.

CETA Support of the Arts. Another development in the late 1970s was the expansion of the federal Comprehensive Employment and Training Act (CETA) of the U.S. Department of Labor. In the most ambitious employment program operated by the federal government since the Federal Art Project and Works Progress Administration of the 1930s, a plan was set in motion to employ thousands of artists in communities throughout the nation, at salaries of $10,000 a year with additional fringe benefits. Hundreds of dancers were employed; typically, the Association of American Dance Companies, various state councils on the arts, and specific professional groups were able to employ dancers and choreographers under the CETA residency and income guidelines.

Grants from Foundations. Throughout this period, financial support of the performing arts by private foundations played an important role. Typically, the American Ballet Theater, which has produced more diversified works than any other American company and has spawned many brilliant choreographers and teachers, survived largely through the generosity of a single patron, Lucia Chase. Similarly, Martha Graham, through the years, has been assisted heavily by the gifts of a single individual, administered through the B. de Rothschild Foundation.

Through the years, the largest single contributor to the arts has been the Ford Foundation. During the period from 1957 to 1964, it gave $30 million to Lincoln Center and the National Cultural Center, and approximately $30 million more for other purposes.

The major Ford contribution to dance consisted of $7.7 million given in 1963 to eight ballet organizations. The New York City Ballet and its affiliated School of American Ballet, both administered by George Balanchine and Lincoln Kirstein, were given control of $5.9 million or more than 75 percent of the allotment, to strengthen the company and school over a ten-year period and to use in programs bringing ballet to communities and schools in the New York region. The remaining millions went in varying amounts to the San Francisco Ballet, the Pennsylvania Ballet of Philadelphia, the Utah Ballet in Salt Lake City, the Houston Ballet, and the Boston Ballet.

Other major foundations which have given substantially to the performing arts during the past two decades have been the Rockefeller Foundation, William Hale Harkness Foundation, the Avalon Foundation, the A. W. Mellon Educational and Charitable Trust, the E. and A. E. Mayer Foundation, and the Old Dominion Foundation.

Role of State Arts Councils

Another important factor in providing financial support and stability to dance organizations within the past two decades has been the emergence of active arts councils on the state level throughout the United States. State arts councils provided important assistance in channeling federal grants to appropriate community arts organizations. For example, a number of them developed panels for screening dance companies to determine their eligibility for different federal grants programs. In many cases, special emphasis was given to serving ethnic minority communities, such as blacks, Hispanics, Asian, native American, and European. In some cases, state arts councils offered technical assistance to companies to solve problems of fund raising, promotion, audience development, programming, community relations, accounting, budgeting, and legal affairs.

Concerns about Art Subsidies Practices

As many performing arts companies became increasingly dependent on government and foundation grants during the 1960s and 1970s, concerns were voiced about the nature and effect of the funding process. Obviously, any method that is used to grant support to certain performers, choreographers, or companies, while at the same time denying it to others, is likely to be controversial. Companies may be rejected for reasons not based on artistic merit, such as association with "in" factions, personal alliances or enmities, or political influence. When government is in a position to influence aesthetic choices, it may be destructive to free artistic expression. Walter Goodman pointed out that totalitarian leaders recognize the power of art to shape people's minds. The Athenian philosopher Plato, for example, was determined:

> . . . that his ideal society would not be undermined by the perverted display of "vice and intemperance and meanness and indecency." Musicians, sculptors, architects who did not express "the image of good in their works" would simply be prevented from practicing; better to expel them than allow them to corrupt the young.[12]

Even without the fear of repression, the mere existence of government subsidies has had important implications for performing arts groups. Marcia Siegel pointed out that with increased numbers of grants, arts funding gradually became part of the industry of arts consumerism, with dance companies' success in attracting grants increasingly based on their popular appeal, ability to sell tickets, and overall budget:

> Subsidy did not stimulate new artists, it encouraged safe ones. Novelty was more important than innovation. The star system flourished. In addition to putting our large ballet and dance companies into an almost unassailably prominent position in the public view, government funding has created a middle echelon of management and production organizations at every level of dance activity.[13]

In many cases, rather than make the kinds of difficult choices which are involved in dealing directly with choreographers and performing groups, funding agencies have preferred to assist festivals, touring programs, or other centralized booking agencies which in turn make the actual selections of groups to perform.

Major Cuts in Funding

Such problems were less critical than the dramatic decline in the level of support that occurred during the early 1980s. Cutbacks in federal funding for the arts actually began in the late 1970s, with severe reductions in funding for CETA programs, which had supported many dance projects. In February 1981, President Reagan alarmed the arts community when he announced to Congress that federal aid to the arts and humanities would have to suffer severe cutbacks:

> . . . instead of boosting the budget for the National Endowment for the Humanities to $176 million as had been proposed by President Carter, Mr. Reagan wanted Congress to chop that grant by $85 million. The Arts Endowment would be similarly dealt with. . . . It seemed to many stunned observers that the day was fast approaching when the Federal Government would cease to be the significant patron of the arts and humanities that it had gradually become over the past two decades.[14]

The changing policies toward the arts appeared to reflect a generally hostile attitude toward smaller, avant-garde companies as opposed to larger, more elite institutions. The regional theater movement was especially threatened. In the early 1960s, there were no more than a dozen such small theaters throughout the United States. However, by the early 1980s, this number had grown to 175, many of them of outstanding professional quality that provided a major source of new works for the Broadway stage. However, the regional theaters were dealt a severe blow by policies of the new administration, and many of them faced severe budgetary crises.[15] Similarly, during the period that followed, numerous art museums throughout the country found both their funding and their attendance lagging and were forced to cut back on their programs and acquisitions.[16] Following a wave of unprecedented expansion, opera companies and symphony orchestras faced similar difficulties and in some cases were forced to close or to suspend operations temporarily.[17]

Despite the intent of the administration to slash federal subsidies to the arts by half, the actual cuts were considerably less, thanks to the formation of a strong Congressional Arts Caucus, composed of 149 Senators and Representatives. Nonetheless, the budget reductions that were enacted left major dance organizations uncertain about programs that had been already funded—and that were now faced with funding freezes.[18]

Crisis in Arts Support

Over the next several years, the touring and residency programs that had provided grants for many choreographers and smaller companies were terminated and other support elements reduced sharply. As a result, many ballet and modern dance companies were forced to reduce their seasons and their number of dancers or even suspend operations during this period. In 1988, Chicago's only resident ballet company, the Chicago City Ballet, was forced to disband—both for financial reasons and because of its inability to compete with the world-class ballet companies that regularly visit the city. In the same year, the Dance Theater of Harlem's planned tour of the Soviet Union was threatened by lack of financial support, despite the fact that it was invited to serve as an official emissary of the United States under the 1985 cultural exchange agreement with the Soviet Union. Hunt described the situation:

> . . . the Dance Theater of Harlem now does more international touring than any other company . . . and its members are very conscious of their role as ambassadors. Plans for the Soviet Union include open rehearsals and lecture-demonstrations for the public as well as for dance professionals. Finer and more elegant American Representatives don't exist. . . . The Soviet Union will pay about $680,000 in expenses in addition to performance fees of $240,000. Yet the U.S. government is providing not a cent. As a result, after months of company planning and negotiating, the tour is in jeopardy.[19]

The federal government's reluctance to support the Dance Theater of Harlem as a valued cultural ambassador was in sharp contrast to the Soviet Union, which had sent over the Kirov and Bolshoi Ballets, the Moiseyev Folk Dance Company, and other special contingents appearing at American arts festivals in the two preceding years. In contrast, the only American company to appear in the Soviet Union in this period was a children's theater group.

Positive Responses to the Fiscal Crisis

However, the mid- and late 1980s were also a period in which many dance companies were able to gather substantial new support. Earlier chapters of this text have described the success of the Houston Ballet, the San Francisco Ballet, the Boston Ballet, the Feld Ballet, and the Joffrey Ballet in terms of extending their seasons and, in several cases, building impressive new facilities. A number of dance companies developed new affiliations with cities at a geographical distance from their original homes—such as the San José and Cleveland linkage, the Alvin Ailey Company's connection with Kansas City, or the Joffrey Ballet's new base of operations in Los Angeles.

Such arrangements were not without their difficulties, however. In the case of the linkage of the Pennsylvania and Milwaukee Ballets, it was agreed by both parties that it was essential to maintain the civic identities and funding sources that each troupe had maintained over the years. Thus, both sides were adamant about calling the new arrangement a joint venture rather than a merger: "The boards in each city will remain fully operative and independent of each other; so will both troupes' ballet schools and orchestras. The financial arrangements also are designed to enhance the sovereignty of each city. Philadelphia will not be paying for the company's performances in Milwaukee, and vice versa."[20]

The arrangement was a complex one; and, as indicated earlier, due in part to the lack of support for the new company in Milwaukee, it was terminated in March 1989.

Role of Dance Organizations

Another important force in assisting dance companies in their struggle against financial adversity in the 1980s was the creation of a number of major dance organizations. Operating on national, regional, and state levels, these bodies have worked closely with other arts organizations and political groups, as well as with universities and educational organizations. In addition to the National Association of Regional Ballet Companies and the Association of American Dance Companies, a number of others have continued to play a critical role in the development of quality dance programs and in the increased awareness of dance as a significant art form.

One such organization was the National Council of the Arts in Education, a federation of national associations concerned with the arts at all educational levels and now known as the Assembly of National Arts Education Associations. It supports general education in the arts in elementary and secondary schools, in preprofessional and professional education, and in teacher education. Member organizations include many national groups concerned with theater, music, art education, ethnomusicology, architecture, and dance.

Another key organization has been the National Dance Association (NDA), a division of the American Alliance for Health, Physical Education, Recreation, and Dance. Today, the NDA is the largest dance education organization in the country, with a membership exceeding 3,000 teachers, students, community leaders, and performers. One of its primary goals is to provide leadership at a national level in order to encourage high-quality programs, materials, and methods of dance. Its structure includes a framework of national, district, and state officers, with a target of reaching every school and college throughout the United States.

As a member association of the American Alliance for Health, Physical Education, Recreation, and Dance (AAHPERD), NDA is able to use the Alliance's publications department and public information services in promoting dance by reaching nearly 50,000 readers through the *Dance Dynamics* insert in AAHPERD's professional magazine, *Journal of Physical Education, Recreation, and Dance,* as well as through the *Dance Information* column and feature articles in the AAHPERD monthly newspaper, *Update,* and other publications.

Commissions on children's dance, elementary and secondary dance in education, dance in higher education, and dance therapy work with the publications unit to prepare selected bibliographies, conference reports, records for dance, guides for curriculum building and program planning, career information, and creative films.

The American Dance Guild, founded in 1956 in New York City as the Dance Teachers Guild, is an organization designed to meet the needs of creative teachers of dance throughout the country. Its goals are to improve instruction in dance, to develop increased community awareness of dance and a higher level of aesthetic taste ("to combat the impact of commercialism and its corruption of taste through techniques of parent education"), and to further the progress of dance through support from a number of levels: community, state, and federal governments. The Guild, whose initial membership was primarily in the Northeast region of the country, has greatly spread its membership and range of influence. By the late 1970s it had members in fifty states, two territories, and seven foreign countries. It publishes a newspaper, sponsors workshops through local chapters, provides a placement bureau, and holds annual conferences.

In contrast to the American Dance Guild, which is essentially concerned with the teaching of creative dance on a noncommercial level, there are a number of powerful organizations which represent commercial dancing teachers throughout the United States.

Organizations of this type include the Dance Masters of America, a professional organization for certified dance teachers which holds large-scale regional and national conventions each year. The curriculum of such conventions includes: "ballet, tap, jazz, baby work, children's work, modern, acrobatic, baton, and ballroom dance." Faculty include leading dancers and choreographers—many of whom have been successful in movies and television.

The Dance Educators of America, Inc. is a similar organization, consisting of "qualified dance teachers" who are essentially connected with private and commercial studios and whose orientation is dance instruction or performance on a popular level.

Example of national convention of major dance organization: Eugene Loring conducts ballet workshop at annual conference of Dance Masters of America. Photograph by Romaine Photography, San Francisco, California.

There are numerous local and state chapters of the Dance Masters of America and Dance Educators of America, as well as of the American Society of Teachers of Dancing and a variety of similar organizations. Most of these organizations, both national and regional, are affiliated with the National Council of Dance Teacher Organizations, with offices in Elmira, New York.

Other Dance Organizations

A number of other important organizations have contributed to the development of dance from an academic perspective. These groups, which have promoted ongoing research and scholarship in dance, are described in chapter 18. A number of other groups have been formed which assist dance companies by arranging tours, providing rehearsal and performance space, coordinating schedules, and in their marketing and promotional efforts.

Dance Theater Workshop

An outstanding example of such an organization is the Dance Theater Workshop in New York City. It was founded in 1965 by three choreographers, Jeff Duncan, Art Bauman, and Jack Moore, to serve as a center for experimental dance. Since 1975, it has been directed by David White and has become a leading producer of performances by dozens of small, avant-garde companies of every description. White is a forceful and articulate spokesman for the performing arts and has developed ingenious new strategies for dance funding. Under his leadership, the organization:

> . . . offers its 500 members a computerized direct mail service, advertising and advertising discounts, a skills file that furnishes the names of everyone from chiropractors to composers, and the Poor Dancer's Almanac, a guide to survival in New York's dance world. And companies and artists presented by Dance Theater Workshop have their work copyrighted and videotaped. . . . Members also receive promotion for their events, the services of two lighting designers (and a system of 150 lights) and facilities that include a new custom-designed sound system.[21]

Beyond these practical accomplishments, Dance Theater Workshop has served as a vehicle for White's philosophy. White sees modern dance—particularly avant-garde dance—as essentially a countercultural, even revolutionary artistic force. In contrast to ballet, which has always identified itself with the power structure (with wealthy patrons and influential board members), modern dance has tended to be more down-scale in its support base. Thus, instead of seeking grants from high-society sponsors, although he has obtained them on occasion, White relies on subversive business tactics and has learned ". . . how to make a system that basically oppresses [creative] work in this country begin to support it. It's something like when you learn a martial art: you don't so much exert force as you use the forces exerted against you, to throw your partner off balance."[22]

What the dance world needed, White believed, were new structures and ways of organizing cooperatively, to take best advantages of everything from available spaces to bulk postal rates, and to build a larger and more receptive audience for all new dance. So successful has this been that Dance Theater Workshop has expanded enormously under White's leadership. In the mid-1970s, its annual budget was $80,000; by 1985, it was $1.6 million.

In 1985, with funding from the Ford Foundation and NEA, White established the National Performance Network. This structure enables sponsors in various American cities to bring in out-of-state artists during the year for one- or two-week residencies, with costs to be shared by the National Performance Network and the host organization. Acocella wrote: "The idea is to stabilize artistic communities in cities other than New York, by bringing in money to small presenters and above all by bringing in outside artists to share ideas with local experimental artists, thus curbing the latter's widespread tendency to take the first bus to New York."[23]

By the late 1980s, the Network was developing offshoots, with state arts councils increasingly coming up with grants for visiting artists to tour their states, and with sponsors in new pilot cities. More and more, White has provided encouragement and assistance to small, independent producers. In his view, the purpose is to provide a new "generation of leadership that is about to rip the entrails out of what is an old and hackneyed cultural warhorse . . . the way artistic culture is perceived in this country."[24] While Dance Theater Workshop is an outstanding example of such local dance-producing organizations, numerous others have appeared in cities and states throughout this country and Canada.

As an example, in Philadelphia, the Philadelphia Dance Council, representing a cross-section of active choreographers and dance companies, has presented numerous programs, workshops, and other dance events in recent years. Beyond this, the Philadelphia dance scene is enriched by Dance Celebration, a joint project of Dance Affiliates of American Ballet Competition and the Annenberg Center of the University of Pennsylvania. Directed by Randy Swartz, Dance Celebration each year presents a highly successful performance series featuring such companies as Pilobolus, the Bella Lewitzky Company, Alvin Ailey Dance Theater, the Feld Ballet, Paul Taylor, the Frankfurt Ballet, Ballet du Nord, Twyla Tharp, Dance Theater of Harlem, and other companies presenting jazz, tap, and ballroom dance. In addition, Group Motion, Philadanco, ZeroMoving Dance Company, Ann Vachon/Dance Conduit, the South Street Dance Company, and, of course, the Pennsylvania Ballet are other companies that contribute to dance in Philadelphia.

Beyond the shift to a grass roots, cooperative approach to sponsoring dance events through networking organizations, individual dancers and choreographers have had to develop a more aggressive and entrepreneurial approach involving effective promotional and marketing techniques. This suggests a critical concern that has always troubled the creative artist but that has become more pressing during the past two decades: Is it possible to reconcile the need to survive economically and to function as an efficient business manager with the need to create original, honest work? Can the dancer-choreographer do both, or does the pressure to be a public relations expert, personnel manager, budget planner, auditor, and tax accountant mean that the aesthetic impulse of the dance artist is inevitably diminished?

Dancer as Artist or Businessperson

Kisselgoff pointed out that along with the institutionalization of dance companies has come an increasing tendency for their managements to depict them as sound business enterprises:

> Boards of directors, once non-existent, have sprung up around dance companies as fund-raisers and at the demand of private foundations and government funding agencies—who require an accounting of monies disbursed. Many of these boards, understandably, encompass businessmen who are there for their fund-raising capacity and financial skills.[25]

Inevitably, then, the company's emphasis tends to be placed on its bottom line—the financial report, which documents its income and expenditures and, hopefully, its profit during the year. When Charles Rannells became president and chief executive officer of the Pennsylvania Ballet in 1982, he inherited a $2.4 million debt. Over a two-year period, he reduced the debt by two-thirds, using a professional marketing staff with daily cash flow forecasts and a totally computerized ticket sale operation. Leaving the company, Rannells reported:

> In 1981, *The Nutcracker* lost money; in 1982 it earned a modest surplus; in 1983 sales were 30 percent higher than in the preceding year. Our production budget has almost tripled . . . for 1984–1985 it's close to $400,000. We turned an annual operating loss of $600,000 into a surplus for next year.
> In the last two years we've tripled the number of corporations supporting the ballet, quintupled the number of individuals backing it and increased 12-fold the number of patrons.[26]

When financial goals become paramount, must they necessarily influence artistic policies and goals? Rannells was adamant that they should not, stressing that the board should make financial policy, frame budgets, hire administrative personnel, and determine how much touring can be done but should have no say in artistic policy. In contrast: ". . . the artistic director tells the board what his vision is. He defines the company's style and look, decides programming and casting. The board costs all of this and says yes or no. The board makes it possible for the artistic director to do what he wants to do, but it doesn't dabble in artistic decisions."[27]

However, it is not always possible to keep the two areas separate. When, in the early and mid-1980s, the administrators of the National Endowment for the Arts challenged a number of dance projects which had been approved by the screening panel, it was because the Endowment's chairman, Francis Hodsoll, was not convinced that they represented true art and that there was a "defined audience" for them. One work, for example, titled *Dance of Machines,* sponsored by the Snake Theater/Nightfire Division in Sausalito, California, proposed having cranes and heavy construction machines "dance" at a construction site, accompanied by video projections and original music.[28]

Whether or not such projects should be viewed as dance, the risks involved in having a choreographer's artistic purpose judged by a funding group composed essentially of businesspeople or government officials are serious. And, when a corporation-minded board makes key decisions regarding the framework in which dances are choreographed and produced, there is a strong likelihood that financial concerns will influence artistic ones.

A curious example of the possible linkage between artistic creation and funding strategies was evidenced in 1988 when, as part of a Next Wave Festival at the Brooklyn Academy of Music, avant-garde choreographer David Gordon presented a work called *United States*. Goldner wrote: "In this ongoing project, Gordon immortalizes those states and regions whose art presenters have bought into the project with grants and guarantees of touring venues. On Wednesday . . . Gordon and his Pick-Up Co. began a five-day run of the 'Minnesota,' 'New York City,' 'San Francisco,' and 'New England' sections of *United States*."

Unfortunately, the reviews of the actual dances were mediocre. However, Goldner concluded: "If a funding strategy could be transcribed into choreography, David Gordon's *United States* would be a great work of art."[29]

Historically, there have always been patrons for the arts—royal, church, or private. Yet, dance has tended to be less obsequious than the other arts. Kisselgoff commented that even when the choreographers of the royal opera houses in Europe

David Gordon/Pick Up Company in *What Happened*? Photograph by Lois Greenfield.

seemed most directly "under the thumb" of their patrons, they acquired a reputation as an unruly lot—many being punished for their stubbornness. Even in the present, she wrote: ". . . there is no doubt the great choreographers of our day have never been primarily concerned with the public. One has only to look at the entire career of George Balanchine to realize that he choreographed ballets for himself first, then his dancers and then the public."[30]

Balanchine's history of his own early companies collapsing, his dismissals from other companies, and his friction with administrators reveals not simply a tempestuous personality—but rather his vision of "art for the artist's sake" as an intensely personal credo. The creative work of numerous other choreographers, from Isadora Duncan to Merce Cunningham and beyond, has illustrated the need to produce work that one believes in, without regard for the audience. Yet, in an era in which the choreographer is expected to be an entrepreneur in order to survive and in which businesspeople make many of the key decisions, it is inevitable that conflicts will arise between the two sets of values.

Dance and the Mass Media

Another important factor in the growing acceptance of dance as a popular art form in the United States has been its increased presentation through the mass media. In the 1970s, for example, a number of major television series or specials brought ballet and modern dance to huge new audiences. Beginning in 1976, the Public Broadcasting Service (PBS) broadcast a "Dance in America" series, assisted by a $1.5 million grant from the National Endowment for the Arts, the Corporation for Public Broadcasting, and the Exxon Corporation. Among the programs featured in this outstanding series was an hour-long introduction to the City Center Joffrey Ballet. Other programs in the series presented Twyla Tharp and her company, Martha Graham and a number of her outstanding works, and the New York City Ballet.

Other presentations of modern dance and ballet on television included Alwin Nikolais and his company; the American Ballet Theater's production of Tchaikovsky's *The Nutcracker;* a "Live from Lincoln Center" broadcast of the New York City Ballet's *Coppelia;* a one-hour ABC-TV special of "Ben Vereen—His Roots"; and a one-hour performance by Mikhail Baryshnikov and Gelsey Kirkland in several ballet works in the Public Broadcasting Service series, "Performance at Wolf Trap." White commented about the "Dance in America"'s impact: "The series could not have come at a better time. . . . WNET estimates that between four and five million viewers will see the first hour of "Dance in America." That, in itself, is reason for applause".[31]

The "Dance in America" series continued through the 1980s, although with lessened financial support. Initially, dances had been filmed under controlled studio conditions; however, with limited funding, the series turned in the early 1980s to filming productions in theaters during actual performance. With limited camera angles and perspectives and other compromises imposed by taping live dances, the result was not altogether disappointing. Judy Kinberg, producer of the series, commented, "What you lose in precision, you gain in spontaneity and continuity of performance."[32]

Through the past several years, there have been a number of other major dance works on the leading networks. American Ballet Theater has been particularly successful in having a British company, National Video Corporation, tape its performances and package them for broadcasts and home viewing for a worldwide market. The New York City Ballet has been seen in a number of major television specials; in October 1983, for example, it presented a two-hour program on PBS in honor of Balanchine for a national audience. Three years later, the work of Jerome Robbins was presented over the NET Network by the New York City Ballet, in two pieces, *Fancy Free* and *Antique Epigraphs*.

With National Endowment for the Arts funding in the late 1980s, the Walker Arts Center in Minneapolis has produced *Alive From Off-Center,* a provocative series devoted to experimental dance, video, and performance art. As VCRs became increasingly popular, a wide variety of dance forms have been packaged. Major Russian works, such as the Bolshoi company's *Romeo and Juliet* and *Cinderella,* or the Kirov's *Swan Lake* and the Moiseyev's folk dance performances, have all been published in videocassettes, along with ballets by other leading British and American ballet companies. Similarly, many major modern dance companies have taped their works for the home viewing audience. A leading example is Merce Cunningham, who has taped a number of dances through the Cunningham Dance Foundation, and who has also published an extensive series of workshops, lectures, and technique demonstrations on tape.

Through the years, dance has made an increasingly strong impact on the public through the musical theater and in movies. Such works as *Oklahoma, Carrousel, Brigadoon,* and *West Side Story* have had dance of high quality—choreographed by such artists as Agnes de Mille and Jerome Robbins—as integral parts of their story lines and stage appeal. In a number of cases, choreographers like Michael Kidd and Bob Fosse went on to become extremely successful directors of musical productions themselves and created plots based on dance as the primary ingredient. Popular musicals of the late 1970s, *A Chorus Line,* and *Dancin',* illustrate this trend.

Such films as *The Turning Point* have had immense success. Featuring Mikhail Baryshnikov, Leslie Browne, Alexandra Danilova, and nearly the entire company of American Ballet Theater and directed by a former dancer and choreographer, Herbert Ross, with Nora Kaye, a well-known and successful dancer, this film fanned the nation's interest in ballet. A later work, *Dancers,* produced by Ross and starring Baryshnikov in the late 1980s, involved retelling the classic *Giselle* story with contemporary overtones. In terms of rock and roll or disco dancing, films like *Saturday Night Fever* and *Dirty Dancing* were smash hits during the 1970s and 1980s.

Effects of Mass Media Exposure

The effects of mass media exposure on the public's interest in and awareness of dance are obvious—it has helped to acquaint millions with dance as a performing art and to introduce outstanding companies and dancers to regions of the country that otherwise may never have had the opportunity to view them. At the same time, such exposure imposes some risks. Bringing top professional companies into such areas may undermine the efforts of smaller, struggling companies that perform on a much more rudimentary level. The sheer impact of television's availability, ease, and professionalism may discourage live local performance; one of the effects of phonographs becoming widely available was that there was much less employment for musicians in restaurants or night clubs that had formerly employed small orchestras.

Harris Poll Findings. There is growing evidence that the nation's rapid adoption of VCRs as a form of home entertainment has seriously cut into the public's attendance of live performing arts events. In the late 1980s, the Louis Harris polling organization reported a decline in attendance statistics for classical music concerts, opera, the professional theater, and dance—which it attributed to a reduction in leisure time that occurred over the past two decades and to the growing appeal of home video.[33]

While the reported decline in attendance for dance (14 percent) was considerably less than that reported for opera and musical theater (38 percent), classical music (36 percent), or dramatic theater (25 percent), it nonetheless represents a serious concern. At the same time, Harris reported that the public continues to maintain a high level of participation in arts-related activities and has increased its contributions to the arts. Harris concluded: "Clearly, the arts have won a place in American life that is well nigh indispensable. . . . [They] are going through a period of uncertainty now as to just how much expansion there will be in their future. But their role is beyond dispute."[34]

In his report, Harris emphasized the willingness of many respondents to rent tapes of dramatic plays, operas, orchestras, and ballet companies and suggested that arts leaders should explore such "alternative distribution channels" instead of simply fearing the competition presented by VCRs. However, this strategy has a dangerous potential in terms of its possible effect on audiences. If people can view the great dance companies of the world conveniently and inexpensively in their homes, will they be as likely to attend their live performances? It may be that viewing ballet and modern dance through VCRs will promote overall interest in dance and thus increase attendance in the long run. However, particularly for smaller dance companies that must struggle to find an audience and that inevitably compete with better known, glamourous major companies, the risk is that easy availability of dance through the mass media will seriously threaten their ability to survive.

Having explored the present status of dance as a performing art form, we turn to the second major focus of this text—its role in education. The following chapters outline its development as an accepted element of the curriculum in American schools and colleges, beginning with colonial dance and extending through the 1980s. They show that, just as dance became an important part of national culture during this period, it also gained recognition as significant means of personal growth.

Notes

1 Joan Acocella, "Programming the Revolution," *Dance Magazine,* February 1987, p. 73.

2 Gertrude Lippincott, "The Cultural Explosion and Its Implications for Dance," *Journal of Health, Physical Education and Recreation,* January 1965, pp. 83–84.

3 Alvin Toffler, *The Culture Consumers* (New York: St. Martin's Press, 1964), pp. 26–27.

4 John D. Rockefeller II, in Joseph Prendergast, "The National Cultural Center," *Recreation Magazine,* October 1960, pp. 363–64.

5 William Baumol and William Bowen, *Performing Arts: The Economic Dilemma* (New York: The Twentieth Century Fund, 1966), pp. 67–69.

6 Ibid., p. 32.

7 Rockefeller Panel Report, *The Performing Arts: Problems and Prospects* (New York: McGraw-Hill Co., 1965), p. 11.

8 Ibid., p. 15.

9 "National Foundation on the Arts and Humanities Act of 1965," *Health, Education and Welfare Indicator* (Washington, D.C.: U.S. Govt. Printing Office, November 1965), pp. 4–5.

10 Harold C. Schonberg, "A Bright Idea to Help Fund the Arts," *New York Times,* April 3, 1977, p. 2-1.

11 Alwin Nikolais, "Why Do I Go Through the Torture of New York?" *New York Times,* August 1, 1976, p. 6-D.

12 Walter Goodman, "The Artists and the Politician—Natural Antagonists," *New York Times,* April 24, 1977, p. 2-1.

13 Marcia B. Siegel, *Watching the Dance Go By* (Boston: Houghton Mifflin Co., 1977), p. xii.

14 Irvin Molotovsky, "The President, the Congress and the Arts—Can They Live Together in Happiness?" *New York Times,* August 9, 1981, p. 2-1.

15 William B. Collins, "A Time for the Theater to Re-Evaluate," *Philadelphia Inquirer,* June 27, 1982, pp. 1-H, 11-H.

16 Douglas McGill, "Troubled Museums Try to Master Fine Art of Survival," *New York Times,* August 28, 1988, p. 24-E.

17 "Let's Do the Time Warp Again: Economic and Spiritual Crisis Besets U.S. Orchestras and Opera Companies," *Time,* January 11, 1988, pp. 68–71.

18 Ginger Danto, "Dance Troupes Tighten Belts," *New York Times,* September 19, 1982, p. H-20.

19 Marilyn Hunt, "Whither Glasnost?" *Dance Magazine,* May 1988, p. 34.

20 Nancy Goldner, "Pennsylvania and Milwaukee Ballets Plan Joint Troupe," *Philadelphia Inquirer,* January 30, 1987, p. 7-C.

21 Jennifer Dunning, "A Laboratory for New Dances Marks a Milestone," *New York Times,* September 22, 1985, p. H-14.

22 Acocella, "Programming the Revolution," p. 71.

23 Ibid., p. 73.

24 Ibid.

25 Anna Kisselgoff, "The Danger of Trying to Equate Ballet with Business," *New York Times,* March 14, 1982, p. 20.

26 Nancy Goldner, "Ballet on Its Feet, He's Stepping Down," *Philadelphia Inquirer,* June 6, 1984, p. 4-D.

27 Ibid.

28 Robert Pear, "Reagan's Arts Chairman Brings Subtle Changes to the Endowment," *New York Times,* April 10, 1983, pp. H-1, H-26.

29 Nancy Goldner, "Next Wave Festival at Brooklyn Academy of Music," *Philadelphia Inquirer,* December 17, 1988, p. 3-D.

30 Anna Kisselgoff, "Art for the Artist's Sake Still Applies to Dance," *New York Times,* November 18, 1984, p. 8-H.

31 Wallace White, "Videodance—It May Be a Whole New Art Form," *New York Times,* January 18, 1976, p. D-10.

32 Judy Kinberg, quoted in Tullia Limarzi, "Squeezing Dance Onto the Tube," *Ballet News,* December 1985, pp. 22–23, 41.

33 Louis Harris Poll, cited in "Poll Shows Arts Attendance Decline," *Philadelphia Inquirer,* March 16, 1988, pp. 1-A, 4-A.

34 Richard Phelp, "New Harris Poll Shows Busy Americans Value the Arts," *Dance Magazine,* June 1988, pp. 8–9.

CHAPTER 14

Early Development of Dance Education

Hall [an early twentieth-century American educator and psychologist] recognized that dancing had been connected with all the profound experiences of life in traditional societies. He felt that educational dance should include religious dances, love dances, and war dances. . . .

Hall did not limit his recommendations to formalized and imitative dances. He also argued for free and unstructured dancing for emotional expression and physical and psychological release. Feelings that are not evoked or not permitted in ordinary life could by this means be experienced and expressed. This he felt would provide a safety valve for the emotions, lead to psychic health, and enrich the dancer's emotional life.[1]

WE NOW TURN TO THE SECOND MAJOR FOCUS OF THIS BOOK —an examination of dance as a vital form of education. Some critics of contemporary education in the United States have suggested that dance was introduced in school and college curricula through the progressive education movement of the early twentieth century. Clearly, this was not the case. Dance has held a long and honored place in the curriculum, both in earlier and lineage-based societies throughout the world and during the long evolution of Western civilization.

Margaret Mead wrote about the teaching of dance in Samoan village life. It takes place there as a highly individual activity, set in a social framework. Children learn to dance at small informal parties or entertainments, often in honor of visitors or wedding celebrations. Both visitors and hosts take turns providing music and dancing. The chief's wife, or one of the young men, calls out the names of children, who come out on the floor to perform in small groups. There is a minimum of preliminary instruction in dancing, and the form of the dance itself is highly varied: "No figures are prescribed except the half dozen formal little claps which open the dance and the use of one of a few set endings. There are twenty-five or thirty figures, two or three set transitional positions, and at least three definite styles. . . ."[2]

As the dancing goes on, the audience calls out praise, comments, and suggestions. Younger children are good-naturedly advised to move in certain ways, or to adjust their costumes, while the more expert older children receive a steady murmur of appreciative remarks: "Thank you, thank you for your dancing!" "Beautiful! Charming! Bravo!"

Within most lineage-based cultures, dance is thus learned—as a natural part of growing up, and through participation in everyday social occasions or in special festivities or rituals.

Historical Review of Dance Education

As indicated earlier, the purposes of dance education were well understood by the ancient Greeks. Socrates expressed high esteem for dance, recommending that it be taught more widely:

> . . . for health, for complete and harmonious physical development, for beauty, for the ability to give pleasure to others, for "reducing," for the acquisition of a good appetite, for the enjoyment of sound sleep. He confesses that he himself dances alone "at dawn," . . . and he openly expresses the wish that he may acquire greater skill in the graceful art.[3]

Aristotle also noted the place of dance in education. Although he did not favor requiring it as a formal educational activity before the age of fourteen, he saw it as affording intellectual and aesthetic gratification of the highest type. In his view, it was useful in purging the young student's soul of "unseemly emotions," and it helped to prepare the future citizen for worthy enjoyment of leisure.

Dance came to the fore as an important aspect of the education of the European nobility during the later Middle Ages and the Renaissance. Michel de Montaigne, the great French sixteenth-century essayist, wrote in his treatise, *The Education of Children,* that education should include training for character and for life; that it should strengthen the body and also cultivate the mind:

> Our very exercises and recreations, running, wrestling, dancing, hunting, riding and fencing will be a part of his study. I would have his manners, behavior, and bearing cultivated at the same time with his mind. It is not the mind, it is not the body we are training; it is the man and we must not divide him into two parts. . . .[4]

The arts of music and dance, along with the skills of warfare and hunting, were an integral part of the education of courtiers in all of the castles of Europe. A leading Italian schoolmaster, Vittorino da Feltre (1378-1446) made Latin, Greek, and classical archaeology the main body of instruction, but also made dance along with other physical skills part of knightly instruction. Dance was perceived both as an essential social skill and as a valuable means of physical training. Many historians suggest that the modern physical education movement began with the appearance of a text, *De Arte Gymnastica,* dated 1569 and written by Hieronymus Mercurialis, a famous physician who lived in Rome. In this book, Mercurialis sought to revive the gymnastic education of the ancient Greeks; among the activities he recommended was dancing. Another influential writer on education who lived in the following century, John Locke, published a text, *Some Thoughts on Education,* in 1693. In this, he dealt extensively with training not only the intellect, but also the constitution and health of the child. In addition to other forms of activity, he wrote specifically of dance:

> . . . besides what is to be had from study and books, there are other accomplishments necessary for a gentleman, to be got by exercise, and to which time is to be allowed, and for which masters must be had. Dancing being that which gives graceful motions all the life, and above all things, manliness and a becoming confidence to young children, I think it cannot be learned too early. . . .[5]

Johann Guts Muths, a leading pioneer in the development of German education, published *Gymnastics for Youth* in 1793, in which he advocated dancing as a means of physical exercise, writing, "Dancing is an exercise strongly deserving recommendation, as it tends to unite gracefulness and regularity of motion with strength and agility." He was perhaps the first author to use the term *gymnastic dance:* "A good gymnastic dance for the open air, approaching the heroic ballet for young men or boys, calculated to exercise their strength and ability, excite innocent mirth and youthful heroism and cherish their love of country through the accompaniment of song, is an extremely desirable object. . . ."[6]

Other educators who were active in the beginning Turnverein (German gymnastic clubs) movement introduced the so-called folk roundel, which consisted of simple marching, hopping, skipping, and running movements and patterns. These were always accompanied by singing and sometimes by music and were apparently the forerunners of what later came to be considered gymnastic dance in American physical education. At the same time, there were many private teachers of dancing throughout Europe who taught it as an art in schools of ballet, or as a social grace in the homes of wealthy or royal families.

Dance Education in America

Meanwhile, what of America? As mentioned earlier, as religious attitudes condemning dance grew less severe in the American colonies during the pre-Revolutionary period, a great wave of interest in dancing developed. The purpose of such education was seen as the very opposite of frivolity; indeed, an example of dancing not learned entirely for pleasure is suggested by an incident at the Philadelphia Assembly in 1781: " 'Come, miss, have a care what you are doing,' shouted the Master of Ceremonies to a damsel who was permitting a bit of gossip to interrupt her turn in a contradance. 'Do you think you are here for your own pleasure?' "[7]

Treatises on education by European authorities became increasingly available in the United States. In particular, the works of Froebel, the German founder of kindergartens and champion of education for girls and women, began to affect educational philosophy here. Increasingly, the conviction developed that the schools were responsible for physical as well as academic growth of children, and that activities other than the purely academic should be included in the curriculum.

During the first years of the new century, an increasing number of state colleges or church-supported colleges were founded, as well as the first women's colleges (which were founded originally as seminaries) at Mount Holyoke and elsewhere in New England. In all of these settings, dance was taught. Some women educators, including Emma Willard and Mary Lyon, attempted to provide some form of physical education for their students. Emma Willard taught during the winter of 1807–1808 at Middlebury College in Vermont. It was an extremely bitter and snowy winter and, according to Marks, Willard later wrote: ". . . and while those who could sing would strike up some stirring tune, I, with one of the girls for a partner would lead down the dance, and soon have them all in rapid motion. After which we went to our school exercises again."[8]

While dancing was, as a rule, found more frequently in programs for girls and women than for male students, one of the first recorded examples of dance as part of the required program for men was in the military academy at West Point. It was included in the course of instruction which was submitted to President Washington in 1783. Its rationale, of course, was that each officer had to be able to conduct himself as a gentleman and that instruction in dancing would help him do this and would provide poise and social competence. However, it was not actually taught until 1817 when Pierre Thomas, the Academy's first fencing master, was permitted to organize a voluntary dancing class for cadets who requested it. In 1823, dancing was made a required subject in the summer encampment, with daily lessons for the third and fourth class taught by Papanti, a famous Boston dancing master of the period.

Dance as Social Training

During the first quarter of the nineteenth century, dancing began to be found in schools for young children. An educational writer of the time, the Reverend John L. Blake, wrote in *The Farmer's Every-Day Book* that dance should be provided in every country school under the direction of the schoolmaster.

> In the middle of the day, or prior to the commencement of the afternoon studies, let half an hour be spent in this fascinating exercise, as a reward of good conduct as scholars, and the prediction is made with confidence, that neither girls or boys will ever be tardy. The design is by no means to fit them for the ballroom. It is simply to give them a healthful exercise; for boys, instead of playing ball—and the girls, instead of romping.[9]

Dance tended to be found more widely in private academies than public schools, where it was occasionally challenged on the grounds of utility or morality. In some cases, when dance was taught it was in fact disguised as a form of musical gymnastics or as calisthenics. Thus, when Mary Lyon published a book of exercises at Mount Holyoke College in about 1853, teachers were warned that the exercises, done to music, should not be performed in a dance-like fashion—or they would arouse opposition. However, in Lyon's teaching, and also in the calisthenics taught by Catherine Beecher during the 1840s and 1850s in a girls' school in Cincinnati and at Mount Holyoke, the activity resembled dance greatly. The exercises involved simple movements to be accompanied by music to produce grace of motion and good carriage.

Dance as Exercise

Between the time of the Civil War and the close of the nineteenth century, dance became a more fully accepted part of physical education and thus of general education. Dio Lewis, a popular temperance and health lecturer, developed a system of graceful exercises using light dumbells and accompanied by music or drum beats for rhythm. In his book, *The New Gymnastics,* published in 1862, he wrote:

> . . . persons of both sexes unite in all the exercises with great social enjoyment, thus adding indefinitely to the attractions of the place. . . . In the New Gymnasium, everything is set to music. Marches, free movement, dumbells, wands, rings, mutual-help exercises. No apathy can resist the delightful stimulus. The one hundred persons on the floor join in the evolutions inspired by one common impulse. Under the old system each person works by himself, deprived of the sympathy and energy evoked by music and the associated movement.[10]

Lewis did not regard his system of "new Gymnastics" as dancing, commenting that the exercises "are arranged to music and . . . possess a charm superior to that of dancing and other social amusements." However, they clearly resembled a modified form of dance, involving marching, leaping, and skipping actions, with partners traveling around the floor together.

There was an increasing readiness to accept dancing in education during the latter decades of the nineteenth century. This was in part due to the fact that it was a popularly accepted social pastime among all classes in society. Indeed, when it was introduced at Vassar, a leading women's college, and opposition was expressed, the trustees and officers of the college supported it strongly. Matthew Vassar, the founder of the college, said to the trustees in 1869:

> Years ago I made up my judgment on these great questions in the religious point of view, and came to the decision favorable to amusements. I have never practiced public dancing in my life, and yet in view of its being a healthful and graceful exercise, I heartily approve of it, and now recommend it being taught in the college to all pupils whose parents or guardians recommend it.[11]

Similarly, years later, the president of Harvard University, Charles W. Eliot, wrote in a letter to Charles Francis Adams, "I have often said that if I were compelled to have one required subject in Harvard College, I would make it dancing if I could. West Point has been very wise in this respect. . . ."

Aesthetic and Gymnastic Dance

A major influence in helping to bring dance as art into schools and colleges was the work of the French dramatic teacher, François Delsarte. His American followers developed a Delsartian system of exercise which attempted to relate outer movements to inner states of feeling. This method, widely used in the 1890s, was introduced at Chautauqua, the famous adult education camp in upstate New York which began a nationwide movement during the later years of the nineteenth century. The Delsartian system stressed freedom and harmony of movement and had a vague rationale about making the body "a temple for the indwelling soul." Some called it "aesthetic gymnastics"; it included a great many dance movements and maneuvers.

The Delsartian system in turn led to the introduction of a method which was termed "aesthetic calisthenics." This approach was formulated by Melvin Ballou Gilbert, a Portland dance teacher, who developed it as a substitute for regular gymnastic work for women. The method was introduced to physical educators in 1894 by Dr. Dudley A. Sargent, a pioneer in this field and professor of physical training at Harvard, who organized what later became the Sargent School of Physical Education. Gilbert's method was based on:

> . . . the long-established five positions of the feet and the five positions of the arms, together with the positions of the whole body known as attitudes, arabesques, poses, elevations, groupings, etc. From these precepts are established, whereby the steps, attitudes and motions are systematic and in strict harmony with time and music.[12]

The Gilbert method gradually became known as *aesthetic dance*. During the early years of the twentieth century, its practitioners were influenced by the work of Isadora Duncan and sought to make it a highly expressive and artistic form. While aesthetic dance made considerable use of ballet movements as well as such ballroom dance steps as the polka, schottische, waltz, and mazurka—all fitted into series of exercises or routines that might then be performed—it was modified in its level of difficulty so that it might be taught to large classes without difficulty.

Sargent had hoped that the Gilbert method might be used with both men and women. However, as it became increasingly artistic and expressive, men and boys resisted it. Thus, "it became necessary to modify the dancing so as to give opportunity for a heavier kind of work. . . ."[13]

This "heavier" and more masculine kind of work became known as *gymnastic dancing*. It rejected the balletic orientation of aesthetic dance; Staley and Lowery wrote of it as "any balance exercise that is free, serial, rhythmical," with coordinated simple movements, strenuous enough to be good exercise, and of a genuinely masculine make-up. The fundamental foot and arm positions, and the terminology of steps found in the aesthetic dance, were discarded, along with the turnout, the difficult technical steps and the expressive emphasis.

Gymnastic dance made use of the terminology of gymnastics. It could be taught by the "physical director and not by a dancing master." The subject matter of gymnastic dance was drawn from various fields of physical activity: "folk dancing, aesthetic dancing, gymnasium exercises, athletic exercises, play and work." Men, in performing it, wore gym costumes: shorts, athletic shirts, high stockings, and basketball sneakers. Thus, in the early years of the twentieth century, two forms of dance became established in college and secondary school physical education—gymnastic dance for boys and men, and aesthetic dance for girls and women.

Folk and National Dance

A third form of dance that rapidly became popular in the early part of the twentieth century was folk or national dance (the term *national* usually referred to those folk dances that were characteristic of a nation and which were found within its borders, such as the *Irish Jig,* the *Italian Tarantella,* or the *Scottish Highland Fling*).

At the same time that much of the folk dance material became incorporated into gymnastic dance, it also developed as a separate stream of activity in physical education and in the early recreational or playground movement throughout the country. Two collectors of traditional folk dances, Elizabeth Burchenal and C. Ward Crampton, did much original research in European countries. They published extensive collections of traditional folk dances which were still being performed in such countries as Germany, Denmark, Sweden, Finland, and the British Isles—as well as traditional American country dances. These became widely adopted in physical education syllabi and in community recreation programs throughout the country. They were seen as having important recreational values and also as yielding intercultural benefits in a society whose citizens had come from many nations.

By the beginning years of the twentieth century, dance had become widely adopted in schools and colleges throughout the United States. Before long, physical educators developed an impressive litany of its benefits. Dr. Luther Halsey Gulick, an early physical educator who, like many of his counterparts, was initially a medical doctor, wrote rather mystically of the background of folk and national dances:

> The movements of folk and national dances . . . are . . . an epitome of many of the neuro-muscular coordinations which have been necessary to the life of the race. They have grown up very slowly through centuries until they have come to fit and express the very soul of the people, embodying its memories, expressing its psycho-physical traits and aspirations. Upon the basic neuro-muscular coordinations have been embroidered, for esthetic purposes, certain finer movements. The movements themselves, however . . . follow long-inherited tendencies toward neuro-muscular coordinations which arose under the selective influence of survival.[14]

The physiological outcomes of dance were further described in great detail:

> . . . dancing . . . exercise removes excess accumulations of fat, replacing the same with healthy muscle tissue, thereby transforming a body that was soft, inactive, and soggy into one that is tonic and elastic. As a means of organic stimulation, dancing can be made vigorous enough to satisfy the most hardy nature. . . . The dancer prosecutes the most vigorous steps with no thought for the work he is doing. He is aware only of his pleasure.[15]

Dance was now widely established as part of the teacher training program for both men and women in many departments of physical education throughout the country. It took many and varied forms, as illustrated by this description of end-of-summer performances at Chautauqua in the 1890s:

> The exhibitions by students of the School of Physical Education were the highlight of each Chautauqua season for years. . . . In 1892, "1,000 pupils participated in the exercises closing the course, at which a vast audience was amazed as well as delighted at the feats of strength and agility shown." Old pictures show gymnasts, small dance groups, and large mixed classes of several hundred—including foreign pupils—doing wand drills and dances. Tumblers, Bolin's Swedish class, high bar work, Indian club drills, and the flambeaus (hoops of fire) set the pace with band music to fill any gaps. Minuets by tiny girls, Delsarte Health exercises, and dances—Swedish folk, English Morris, and clog—done to piano accompaniment, excited audiences.[16]

Roots of Modern Dance in Education

Despite these varied approaches to the introduction of dance in American education, it was inevitable that sooner or later it would emerge as an expressive art form. Modern dance was to be the leading creative dance form in American schools. Three educators were particularly instrumental in the early decades of the twentieth century in this development. They were Gertrude Colby, Bird Larson, and Margaret H'Doubler.

Dance at Teachers College, Columbia University

In 1913, Colby joined the staff of the Speyer School, the demonstration school of Teachers College, Columbia University, in New York City. A graduate of the Sargent School of Gymnastics, she was asked to develop a physical education program that would be natural and free and that would permit self-expression. Gradually, she began to experiment with creative dance based on natural movement and on children's interests, a form that could be integrated with other curricular experiences in the school. Colby later joined the staff of Teachers College, where she taught a number of students who became leading American dance educators, including Martha Hill, Mary O'Donnell, Martha Deane, and Ruth Murray.

Colby gave the name of *natural dance* to her new method. In a sense, it was the forerunner of what was to become modern dance in schools and colleges. Before this was to happen, her method was to be influenced by the leading professional dancers of the 1920s and 1930s and also by other educators who were to provide it with a scientific rationale.

Closely associated with Gertrude Colby was Bird Larson, who was in charge of dance at Barnard College on the Columbia University campus. While Larson recognized the value in Colby's natural dance, she also felt that there was a need for dance technique that would be based on the laws of anatomy, kinesiology, and physics. Having an extensive background in corrective physical education, Larson experimented with a system of movement which would have its origin in the torso of the body and which would in effect represent not a preconceived system of technique and dance patterns but a science of movement.[17]

H'Doubler at University of Wisconsin

In 1916, Margaret H'Doubler, who had taught physical education at the University of Wisconsin, came to Teachers College to study for her Master's degree. As a part-time teacher at Columbia University between 1916 and 1918, H'Doubler carefully observed the experimental work of Colby and Larson.

H'Doubler succeeded in establishing a major in dance at the University of Wisconsin in 1926, thus achieving formal recognition for the dance in university education and bringing into existence a major center in the Midwest for the creation of a large dance audience. In addition, many teachers were brought into meaningful contact with dance education. H'Doubler wrote extensively, and her texts became influential in the professional preparation of dance educators and physical educators. She also founded *Orchesis,* the University of Wisconsin dance club which served as a model for many college and university performing groups.

New Forms of Dance in Schools

During the 1930s, three streams of dance activity were evident: folk and social dance; tap, clog, and character dance; and, most important, the new modern dance.

Proponents of folk and national dance such as Louis Chalif, Mary Wood Hinman, and Elizabeth Burchenal had succeeded in widely promoting this activity in schools and colleges throughout the United States. Burchenal, who was organizer and chairperson of the folk dance committee of the Playground and Recreational Association of America, brought a wealth of material to the movement from original sources, and through her authoritative lectures and publications she trained many teachers over a period of several decades. Louis Chalif, through his special courses for teachers and a variety of publications, also spurred this activity forward. Mary Wood Hinman was active in the development of all kinds of dancing: gymnastic, Morris, Maypole, folk, national, and clog dance.

Clog and tap dancing attained considerable success in schools and colleges during the 1920s and early 1930s. In its earlier development, the term *clog dance* was used, based on the original use of shoes with wooden soles which created rather crude and heavy rhythmic patterns. Tap dancing, which made use of leather soles with aluminum heel and toe taps, and of modern, popular music, with faster and syncopated tempo and rhythms, gradually replaced clog on the musical stage and, ultimately, in dance education. Duggan commented:

> Clog is to tap dancing, therefore, what natural is to modern dance—an immediate predecessor to designate this type of rhythmic work in educational institutions. The term *clog* persisted in education long after it had been replaced by *tap* in professional circles. This was due in part to the school's hesitancy to sponsor an activity associated with the theater. The name persists now partly due to habit and partly due to the fact that much published material was brought out during the period when *clog,* not *tap* dance, was the correct term for school teachers. . . .[18]

Creative Dance

At the beginning of the 1930s, much of the creative dance which was taught in the schools stemmed from the natural dance which had been taught by Colby. It tended to emphasize free and unstructured movement, self-discovery, and spontaneous response to music. Teachers were encouraged to undertake the activity with younger children—whether or not they had dance skills themselves. In fact, one influential author thought that dance skills could be a handicap:

> . . . dancing, like children's art, is not dependent on background. In fact, as in their art, it can be a good thing if the teacher is unencumbered with old ideas on the subject. What the teacher needs is faith and understanding. Faith that there is the capacity within the child to do surprisingly beautiful things when encouraged and freed by the teacher—understanding that children's dancing is not a thing of steps, of artificial movements to be learned by rote. The moment we concern a child with steps, we tie him up, inhibit his free movement, make him fearful, put false emphasis.[19]

Even for students on the high school or college level, many teachers encouraged an extremely free approach based on Colby's natural dance theories. Betty Lynd Thompson wrote of creative dancing at this time:

> This form is taught in most large colleges and universities and in many high schools. It is developed along the lines of education and aims at developing personalities rather than dancers. . . . All of the movements are based on natural movements of the body, movements which we normally can do, but which are studied and practiced until they can be done with ease, perfect balance and coordination. . . .[20]

When the dancer has developed a degree of skill in the control of the body and becomes able to "sense the rhythm and the emotion of music," then, according to Thompson, he or she is ready to create dances. Essentially, the emphasis throughout this period was placed on personal creativity and aesthetic expressiveness—without the conviction that the body had to be trained as a tool, or instrument, before it could perform effectively. The influence, however, of concert dancers was to create a much greater interest in technical mastery, in expanding the range of dance movement, and in developing a recognition of dance as an art form—rather than a means of catharsis or naive self-expression.

During the middle and late 1920s, two movements existed side by side. On the one hand, educators—primarily physical educators—were teaching creative dance under a variety of names in the schools and colleges of the nation. On the other hand, professional dancers were presenting their first recitals and concert tours throughout the land.

It soon became apparent that they needed each other. The dance educators in schools and colleges needed the professionals to provide a body of technique and to explore the artistic potentialities of the new medium; in addition, many of them began to study dance in the studios or special workshops directed by concert dancers. In turn, the professionals needed the school and college people both to *attend* their classes and to provide an audience for them, particularly on national tours with concert groups.

Notes

1 Discussion of G. Stanley Hall, in Nancy Lee Chalfa Ruyter, *Reformers and Visionaries: The Americanization of the Art of Dance* (New York: Dance Horizons, 1979), p. 98.

2 Margaret Mead, *From the South Seas* (New York: William Morrow and Co., 1939), p. 112.

3 Lillian B. Lawler, *The Dance in Ancient Greece* (Middletown, Conn.: Wesleyan University Press, 1964), p. 125.

4 Michel de Montaigne, *The Education of Children,* quoted in Emmet Rice, John Hutchinson, and Mabel Lee, *A Brief History of Physical Education* (New York: Ronald Press Co., 1958), p. 73.

5 John Locke, *Some Thoughts on Education,* quoted in Fred Leonard, *A Guide to the History of Physical Education* (Philadelphia: Lea and Febiger, 1923), p. 60.

6 Johann Guts Muths, *Gymnastics for Youth,* quoted in S. C. Staley and D. M. Lowery, *Gymnastic Dancing* (New York: Association Press, 1920), p. 6.

7 Joseph Marks, *America Learns to Dance* (New York: Exposition Press, 1957), p. 51.

8 Alma Lutz and Emma Willard, *Daughter of Democracy* (Boston: Houghton Mifflin Co., 1929), p. 37:

9 John L. Blake, *The Farmer's Every-Day Book* (Auburn, N.H.: Derby, Miller Co., 1850), p. 165.

10 Dio Lewis, quoted in Leonard, *History of Physical Education,* p. 261.

11 Matthew Vassar, quoted in Marks, *America Learns,* p. 97.

12 Melvin Ballou Gilbert, "Classic Dancing," *American Physical Education Review,* June 1905, p. 153.

13 Dudley A. Sargent, quoted in Marks, *America Learns,* p. 102.

14 Luther Halsey Gulick, quoted in Staley and Lowery, *Gymnastic Dancing,* pp. 22–23.

15 Ibid., p. 24.

16 Harold L. Ray, "Chautauqua, Early Showcase for Physical Education," *Journal of Health, Physical Education and Recreation,* November 1962, p. 39.

17 Mildred Spiesman, "Dance Education Pioneers: Colby, Larson, H'Doubler," *Journal of Health, Physical Education and Recreation,* January 1960, pp. 25–27.

18 Anne Schley Duggan, "The Evolution of Tap Dancing," *Educational Dance,* February 1940, p. 2.

19 Natalie Robinson Cole, *The Arts in the Classroom* (New York: The John Day Co., 1940), p. 69.

20 Betty Lynd Thompson, *Fundamentals of Rhythm and Dance* (New York: A. S. Barnes and Co., 1933), p. xviii.

CHAPTER 15

Dance
and the Goals
of Contemporary Education

George Leonard used the term "ultimate athlete" as "one who joins body, mind and spirit in the dance of existence".... Seeking personal well-being and harmony through physical activity is a lifelong pursuit. Leonard referred to the search for the ultimate athlete. The preferred phrase "inner athlete" enables one to focus on centering, balance and self-awareness. The inner athlete seeks personal integration, synthesis, and transcendance of limitations. The concept emphasizes that each student has unsuspected human potential and the educator's job is to effectively aid the personal search.[1]

THE HISTORICAL DEVELOPMENT OF DANCE AS A CULTURAL FORM in American society has been marked by the increasing inclusion of dance as a medium of education in American schools and colleges. On all levels—elementary, secondary, and in higher education—some form of dance instruction is provided today. What is the contemporary rationale for such programs, and what are the actual practices? These questions are considered in this chapter and in the following chapters.

As chapter 14 showed, such pioneer dance educators as Gertrude Colby, Bird Larson, and Margaret H'Doubler had been successful in arousing widespread interest in creative dance in education during the first three decades of the twentieth century. However, a curricular framework was needed through which dance might be more widely offered in American schools and colleges. This was to become physical education, which had gained broad acceptance and departmental status by the early 1930s.

Relationship with Physical Education

By 1930, many female physical educators had developed a considerable interest in dance education—and particularly in modern dance, as creative dance had become known. The National Society of Directors of Physical Education for Women devoted an entire meeting to dance at its national convention in Boston in 1930. In 1931, the American Physical Education Association established a separate Section on Dance. This became a leading force in promoting dance education throughout the United States; it sponsored major dance events and workshops, issued publications, provided advisory services, and stimulated research.

A number of women's colleges or women's physical education departments in larger universities, including Smith, Vassar, Wellesley, Barnard, New York University, and the University of Michigan, sponsored symposiums on dance education during the 1930s. Increasingly, professional dance artists were drawn into educational programs and workshops:

> In the . . . 1930s the concert dance artists and their groups were on tour in specific areas and at times on transcontinental trek. . . . Into almost every state came the top American dancers to appear in concert, to give lecture-demonstrations, to spend a day or two on a college campus, or to present a program at a national or district association convention.
>
> One could see Martha Graham in solo performance or with her group; Doris Humphrey and Charles Weidman in duo, or with their company, which then included José Limón; Hanya Holm and company; Ruth St. Denis and Ted Shawn; and a bit later, Ted Shawn and his group of men.[2]

Programs at Bennington and Connecticut College

In the summer of 1934, the Bennington School of the Dance was established at Bennington College in Vermont; Martha Hill, director of dance at New York University, was made director of programs, and Mary Josephine Shelley, dance and physical education teacher at New College, Teachers College, Columbia University, became administrative director. In 1936, Margaret Lloyd wrote:

> The Bennington Festival of the Bennington School of the Dance is unlike any other summer festival in Europe or America. It is the only one devoted exclusively to the dance and to the dance in its newest, experimental forms. It is a festival that is making rather than commemorating art . . . I think it can truthfully be said that the Bennington School of Dance has gathered the modern dance up in its conglomerate arms and swept it several paces forward.[3]

By the end of the 1930s, the professional point of view toward modern dance had become highly influential in educational dance circles. This posed a problem. Were the goals and needs of college or secondary school students the same as those of aspiring dance artists? Should the teaching techniques used by dance educators be the same as those who taught in professional studios?

In 1937, Eugene C. Howe summarized what he considered to be the "most recent event of major importance in physical education"—the extraordinary rise of the modern dance—and asked some searching questions about the relationship between the two fields:

> It can hardly be denied that the recent adoption by the profession of the leading concert dancers, critics, and counselors as *professors extraordinaire* has been a truly

remarkable phenomenon. The dance of the 1920s in physical education, though the seed came from the world of art, grew up *in* and *for* physical education; the dance of the 1930s in physical education is for and by the concert artist in that he now virtually heads up this activity in a field foreign to his primary interests. . . . The situation obviously has possibilities for both good and evil.[4]

Howe went on to suggest that serious difficulties might develop in the years ahead in terms of the compatibility of dance as a serious art form with physical education as a sponsoring department. Before this could happen, however, World War II forced a hiatus on all kinds of educational innovation and growth. The grim necessity was to win the war, and education went on an austerity basis. Dance, where it continued to be offered in secondary schools or colleges, was frequently given a body conditioning emphasis, in accord with the national concern about physical fitness. In community life, dance was widely used as a form of social recreation (folk and square dancing became popular in service centers and community clubs during this period). But in schools and colleges, dance education went on hold.

Post-World War II Era: The American Dance Festival

World War II ended the Bennington epoch, but its vision of dance as a potentially vital force in American education persisted in the energy and planning drive of Martha Hill. As a result, the Connecticut College Summer Dance Program, which came to be known as the American Dance Festival, was established, with Ruth Bloomer, a former Bennington student and teacher of dance at Connecticut, and Martha Hill, as codirectors. By 1950, choreographers-in-residence at New London included José Limón, Jane Dudley, Sophie Maslow, William Bales, Merce Cunningham, Katherine Litz, and Pearl Primus. Preclassic and modern dance forms were taught by Louis Horst, and Doris Humphrey guided students through intermediate and advanced composition.

By 1957, a decade since the founding of the Connecticut College American Dance Festival, 60 works had been premiered and 189 dances had been performed. In the summer of 1957, more than 150 summer students attended, representing thirty states and seven foreign countries. The summer program in 1969 had 319 students and employed a full-time faculty of thirty-five. In 1978, the Festival moved to Duke University in Durham, North Carolina where, in addition to the summer school program with leading dancer-choreographers, it sponsored an annual Critics Conference; an annual Dance Television Workshop; Dance Therapy Workshops; a Dance Educators' Weekend; and a community outreach program.

Throughout this period of rapid expansion of activity after World War II, it was necessary for dance educators to come to grips with their basic objectives. What was the theoretical rationale for dance in education? At a time of considerable ferment in educational philosophy, this became a critical issue.

Early Rationales for Dance in Education

Certainly, it was not an entirely new question. During the earlier periods of its history, dance had been supported in very specific terms as an activity area within physical education intended to achieve certain outcomes important to that field. Also, it had been praised for its cultural and aesthetic values. Frederick Rogers wrote in 1941:

> . . . our major thesis is that dance, earliest of the arts and pedagogies, should become once more a basic educational technique, because it may serve, and probably more rapidly than any other single kind of pupil activity teachers now utilize, to transform children into more healthy, graceful, sensitive, courteous, courageous, cooperative, cultured, and charitable citizens. The classic Greeks knew this, and made practice conform to knowledge, as have more ancient and primitive peoples everywhere. But contemporary English and American pedagogy, beclouded by heritages of asceticism, scholasticism, and puritanism, has, until very recently, ignored or even proscribed dancing in schools.[5]

Margaret H'Doubler had a vision of dance education as a liberating and civilizing force that would contribute to a healthy philosophy of life and an integrated sense of self for all:

> . . . every child has a right to know how to achieve control of his body in order that he may use it to the limit of his ability for the expression of his own reactions to life. Even if he can never carry his efforts far enough to realize dance in its highest forms, he may experience the sheer joy of the rhythmic sense of free, controlled, and expressive movement, and through this know an addition to life to which every human being is entitled.[6]

In the late 1940s, it became evident that this sort of statement of purpose, inspiring though it might be to dance educators, would not hold much currency in the marketplace of educational philosophy and curriculum development. There were many other special subjects in the curriculum, all of whose adherents were equally convinced of the merit of what they were teaching. Why were the writings of dance enthusiasts to be considered of any greater value than theirs?

Attacks on Nonacademic School Subjects

The need to develop a more convincing and objective rationale for dance as an important element in modern education became increasingly apparent as a number of highly regarded critics launched a vigorous attack on the pervasive influence of "progressive educationists" on the American educational system during the 1950s and early 1960s. Paul Woodring, Arthur Bestor, H. G. Rickover, and others were critical of curricula that had proliferated far beyond the "three Rs" to include a host of activities that Rickover, for example, described as having ". . . little resemblance to traditional programs and intellectual disciplines but . . . making the school a sort of gigantic social-service agency aimed not at education but adjustment."

Woodring characterized the period of the 1930s and 1940s in these terms:

> The high schools tried in a hundred ways to keep the student interested: easier courses, more "practical" courses, more varied offerings, individual guidance,

dances, parties, and other social activities supervised by the school, including extensive athletic programs and allowing high school credit for everything from social dancing to camping and fishing.[7]

It was proposed that greater stress be placed on the fundamental academic disciplines, such as the sciences and social sciences, mathematics, and the language arts. In the face of these attacks and their influence on the taxpaying public and on school administrators, many educators found themselves under extreme pressure.

Life-Adjustment Curriculum Emphasis. Many educators had accepted the goal of improving social adjustment as a primary objective. To illustrate, Ruth Radir justified dance because it gave students group democratic experiences:

> Dance fulfills its function in the curricula of democracy's schools only if group work is so conducted that it is a little laboratory in democratic living. Students, working in groups, should be, in effect, self-directing, with the teacher acting only as a guide in helping them solve the problems of construction. . . . In . . . group composition there is a constant interchange of ideas, opportunity to lead, and to follow, and a kind of informal majority rule . . . the core of the learning experience in a democracy. . . .[8]

By the late 1950s, this emphasis on the life-adjustment goals of education was decidedly out of style.

Those who had sought to pursue dance primarily as an aesthetic experience also were experiencing difficulty. Following the first Russian Sputnik and the disclosure of the advanced level of Soviet education in mathematics, science, and engineering, there was a crash program of strengthening these areas of education. Greater academic pressure in the schools meant that many students who might formerly have been involved in school music, theater, or dance activities now found it difficult to fit them into their schedules.

Physical educators seized on recent research findings that demonstrated the poor physical fitness of American youth as a basis for embarking on crash programs of testing and conditioning for fitness. Surely in a period of continuing national emergency, the fitness of youth was an important concern.

Renewed Emphasis on the Arts in Education

But dance educators could not accept this as a focal point for their efforts. If anything, those who were leaders in the field pressed even more strongly for the recognition of dance as an area separate from physical education and one which was essentially an art form.

The growth of public interest and involvement in the arts provided justification for a fuller place for the performing arts at the educational table. The American Association of School Administrators adopted the following resolution at its annual conference in 1959:

> The American Association of School Administrators commends the president, the Executive Committee, and the staff for selecting the *Creative Arts* as the general

theme for the 1959 convention. We believe in a well-balanced school curriculum in which music, drama, painting, poetry, sculpture, architecture, and the like are included side by side with other important subjects such as mathematics, history, and science. It is important that pupils, as a part of general education, learn to appreciate, to understand, to create, and to criticize with discrimination those products of the mind, the voice, the hand, and the body which give dignity to the person and exalt the spirit of man.[9]

Nor was support for the arts lacking among many of the leading educational philosophers of the period. In a sharp rejoinder to the mid-century critics of modern education, Sidney Hook wrote:

An unfailing mark of philistinism in education is reference to the study of art and music as "the frills and fads" of schooling. . . . A sufficient justification for making some study of art and music required in modern education is that it provides an unfailing source of delight in personal experience, a certain grace in living, and a variety of dimensions of meaning by which to interpret the world around us.[10]

Increasingly, there was recognition of the need for educational experiences which would provide a sense of personal involvement to counteract the growing tendency toward depersonalization in a mechanized society dominated by mass media communication. Philip Phenix commented:

People feel isolated and estranged from nature, from themselves, from one another, and from the ultimate sources of their being. . . . Man has become assimilated to the machine, and in the process has lost his identity as a person. He has merged with the mass in the anonymity of impersonal organization.[11]

Within this climate, there was increasing need for education to provide experiences which would help students become aware of their own uniqueness and that would help them become capable of making meaningful personal judgments within all areas of life. Thus, there developed support for the arts as a form of highly personalized creative experience.

Creativity is believed to be fostered in education when students are permitted or encouraged to exhibit spontaneity and individuality; when they are not regimented or repressed by imposed restraints or required conformity; and when they have the freedom to initiate purposeful behavior, to communicate freely, and to make their own choices of activity or learning experiences.

Most educators in the arts—including dance educators—believe that their position in education today is strengthened because of the current need for creative development of students. But this is only one aspect of a total rationale supporting dance in the curriculum. Viewed broadly, how are educators to define the values and objectives of dance in the curriculum?

Conflicting Philosophies of Education

In the United States, educational philosophers have developed two prevailing orientations, broadly described as "traditionalist" and "experimentalist." The traditionalist position has generally been concerned with the development of the intellect; all other values related to morality, civic or social development, creative involvement, or preprofessional career training have been viewed as secondary.

In contrast, the view of the experimentalist is that education must meet the needs of modern people by helping them adjust to their environment and helping them remodel or reshape it. John Dewey, who was the most influential of modern experimentalist philosophers, held that the study of the past must be made relevant to the needs and demands of the present; that the curriculum must be broad and of great variety, respecting individual needs, interests, and capacities; and that the study of society is at the heart of the school's effort. Stated succinctly, Dewey's view of education was as follows: "Education is that reconstruction of experience which adds to the meaning of experience, and which increases ability to direct the course of subsequent experience."[12]

Throughout the period between the 1930s and the 1950s, the view of education as a dynamic process of change that both improved society and enabled individuals to live most effectively within society was established. The well-educated person was described as one who had the basic academic skills needed to function effectively in various personal and communal contexts. It was considered that the well-educated person had an understanding of the cultural heritage of the past, had an intelligent, inquiring mind, and was—as far as his or her capabilities permitted—a creative individual.

During this period, dance was generally conceived of as a skill or activity area within physical education. As such, it was expected to contribute to widely cited goals of organic development, neuromuscular development, interpretive development, and personal-social development. None of these goals implied any great stress on creative or aesthetic expression. Nor, in the great majority of situations in which dance was taught, was it really approached as an art form.

In the 1950s and early 1960s, no new overall philosophy of education emerged. There continued to be strong pressure to emphasize the basic academic disciplines, with two justifications. The first was the "great books" approach, which sought to narrow the focus of education to traditional areas of scholarship. The second involved a utilitarian approach to meeting the practical needs of the individual and society. With an increasing number of students completing high school and going on to some form of higher education, a strong effort was made to help this larger population achieve more advanced levels of vocational competence and understanding.

Humanistic Influences and Student Pressures

During the late 1960s and early 1970s, students, including many of the most gifted, began to question and reject the values that were imposed on them. The increasing specialization of learning in particular disciplines and their subfields had resulted in an "academic pressure cooker" which many students resisted. There was a widespread demand for a relaxation of rigid academic standards and required curricula. Many secondary schools initiated more diverse elective courses or alternative programs; colleges relaxed their curriculum requirements, in some cases giving students considerable flexibility in planning their course programs. Courses concerned with humanistic lifestyles, ethnic history and identification, women's needs, and similar contemporary interests were introduced into the curriculum.

What did all this have to do with the arts? Clearly, one way for secondary school and college students to achieve a more meaningful personal involvement in life is through participation in the creative arts. Increasingly, educational authorities spoke out in recognition of the contribution of the arts. C. Robert Pace, for example, suggested that there was a need for another kind of learning—one which is essentially nonverbal, creative, and open. He urged that we give fuller emphasis to:

> . . . the languages of movement and form, of color, and sequence, and sound, the languages of direct expression and feeling. Throughout history these have been powerful and significant avenues by which man has expressed his knowledge, his aspirations, his beliefs, his insights, and his wisdom. . . . If we must require competence in two languages for graduation from college, why not the languages of painting and sculpture, of drama and dance or of music?[13]

One major stumbling block preventing a fuller acceptance of the arts within American education has been the sharp distinction made between art and science in the public mind—in an era in which science is viewed as increasingly essential to our survival. Harold Taylor noted that scientists are seen as rational, objective, abstract, concerned with the intellect and with reducing everything to a formula, while artists, on the other hand, are seen as temperamental, subjective, irrational, and chiefly concerned with the expression of the emotions. He wrote:

> One of the most unfortunate results of this misunderstanding of the nature of the intellect is that the practice of the arts and the creative arts themselves are too often excluded from the regular curriculum of school and college or given such a minor role in the educational process that they are unable to make the intellectual contribution of which they are supremely capable.[14]

The Science-Art Dichotomy

There is greater awareness today that the barrier that has been erected between science and art is a false one. More and more, the dichotomy between "the two cultures" is being challenged by thoughtful educators and philosophers. Taylor suggested that there is a need to recognize that dance, music, painting, design, and sculpture are all forms of knowledge even though they do not express themselves in words. Further, he protested against adding "more blocks of science and mathematics while we allow the arts and the humanities to languish." He wrote:

> Do we not need scientists and engineers who combine with knowledge and skill of a practical kind a sensitivity to human values, a sense of social responsibility, an understanding and appreciation of the arts? The widest sweep of imagination, the deepest level of intuition, the greatest command of insight are as necessary to the true scientist as to the poet or to the philosopher.[15]

The needs to educate feeling, to inculcate sensitivity, and to provide a testing ground for values and personal growth and change are all related to the search for educational experiences which can counter the stultifying effect of the "high-pressure knowledge industry" of the present. It is within this philosophical context that all forms of creative and artistic experience in education, including dance, find their support.

Pressures in the 1980s

The 1980s continued to be a time in which education was the focus of national concern. The National Commission on Excellence in Education report, *A Nation at Risk,* stressed the need to upgrade standards in education on all levels and to strengthen performance in subjects related to the nation's economic viability, such as science and mathematics.[16] The Carnegie Task Force on Teaching as a Profession urged that a national board for professional teaching standards be created and that schools be restructured to provide a professional environment for teachers. It did not, however, make major recommendations for the content of education on elementary or secondary levels.[17] A number of reports supported the arts in education. For example, a research report of the Rand Corporation, *Beyond Creating: The Place for Art in America's Schools,* stressed that students should be engaged both in the study and the making of art products. Published by the Getty Center for Education in the Arts, this report showed how school programs could include productive, critical and critical modes of art education. In it, Andrew Heiskell, chairman of the President's Committee on Arts and the Humanities and chairman of the board of Time Incorporated, stated that:

> The teaching of the arts and the humanities in our schools is essential to all of us. Our ability to communicate effectively, the growth and vitality of our cultural institutions, and the preservation of our cultural heritage, all depend upon understanding and appreciating the pivotal role of the arts and the humanities in developing a truly literate society.[18]

The influential College Board issued publications in 1983 and 1985 stressing the need for high-quality education in the arts as preparation for college study.[19] At the same time, the strong movement for educational reform and upgrading stressed the need to develop more explicit goals and objectives in education in the arts, and ways of testing these in order to assure accountability.

Values of Dance in Education

Meanwhile, what of the specific area of the curriculum to which dance has traditionally been attached over the past several decades—physical education? What shifts occurred in this field, particularly in its philosophical undergirding?

Following the period in which primary emphasis was given to achieving physical fitness as a goal of physical education, there was a pronounced move toward identifying physical education as an academic discipline. Franklin Henry described the field in these terms:

There is indeed a scholarly field of knowledge basic to physical education. It is constituted of certain portions of such diverse fields as anatomy, physics and physiology, cultural anthropology, history and sociology, as well as psychology. The focus of attention is on the study of man as an individual, engaging in the motor performances required by his daily life and in other motor performances yielding aesthetic values or serving as expressions of his physical and competitive nature. . . .[20]

Far from being concerned solely with sports and games, physical educators in the 1960s and 1970s saw all of the following as important aspects of their discipline: kinesiology and body mechanics; the physiology of exercise, training, and environment; neuromotor coordination, the kinesthetic senses, motor learning, and transfers; emotional and personality factors in physical performance; and the history and sociology of sports and related physical activities. During the 1980s, many physical educators once again joined the bandwagon of promoting physical fitness as a primary thrust. Particularly with the growing evidence that American youth was performing poorly on standardized fitness tests, this became a high-priority goal for the profession.

As these concepts of physical education as an academic discipline and a vehicle for improving national fitness gained currency, dance educators were compelled to examine their essential values and purposes. Although an impressive number of dance departments in colleges and universities were housed in programs or departments of the performing arts—often linked to drama, music, or liberal arts—the majority were still part of physical education programs.

However, dance obviously has a character and identity of its own and cannot simply be regarded as another sport or a form of gymnastics. Its long history as an independent art in human society, and the unique roles that it plays in cultures throughout the world, mean that it must be examined and understood in its own right.

Statement of National Dance Association

In a policy statement on dance as education, formulated through a National Dance Association Project on *Issues and Concerns in Dance Education,* the following justifications for dance within the curriculum were cited: (a) dance is basic education, intensifying and clarifying the human experience; (b) dance reinforces all learning, relating to and enhancing other academic areas; (c) dance provides an alternative to the usual modes of education and is valuable in reaching children who may not respond to more formal modes of teaching; (d) dance promotes self- and social awareness, helping students confront and understand themselves and cooperate effectively with others; (e) dance promotes good health and may be of particular value to students with physical or mental disabilities; and (f) dance promotes fuller understanding of one's own culture and that of other peoples.[21]

Extending this statement, eight different goals of dance in education are identified and discussed in the concluding section of this chapter.

1. Movement Education. As indicated earlier, movement education has become an important thrust of physical education, particularly on the elementary level. What is the special contribution to be made by dance in this area? Elizabeth Hayes suggested that its particular appeal lies in the satisfaction or enjoyment that it provides the participant; it is pleasure in the kinesthetic sensation of movement that impels the dancer to move as he or she does. Hayes wrote:

> The key to its distinction lies in that the dancer's immediate concern is not with lifting weights, transporting himself through water, balancing on skates or skis, or winning a game, but rather with movement per se—movement that has consciously been given form and rhythmic structure to provide physical, emotional or aesthetic satisfaction. If dance happens also to promote good physical condition or otherwise contribute to the welfare of the dancer, so much the better; but the derivation of such benefits is not the essential reason for the existence of dance.[22]

Movement education has been given particular emphasis on the elementary level, where it has been seen as a vital element in the overall personality development of the child. Research by Kephart and others has shown the child's motor performance to be closely linked to emotional development, intellectual, and cognitive functioning, and indeed all aspects of personal growth. Obviously, dance provides a medium for experimentation and creative performance in movement that is rich with potential. Gladys Andrews Fleming wrote:

> *Movement is not dance, but all dance involves movement.* . . . Dance . . . is not concerned with developing movement in a vacuum but rather with developing, inventing, and controlling movement simultaneously with thinking, sensing, responding, feeling, and inquiring. . . . The development of the imagination is ignited and creativity is uncorked as inventiveness and selection of movement are used abundantly.[23]

Although movement education is usually thought of primarily as a needed experience for young children, it also may have important values for people of all ages. Dance, as a pleasurable physical activity, offers a unique alternative to other forms of physical exercise in which adults may participate. Even among retired adults in senior centers, more and more dance is being offered today as a form of exercise.

Many physical educators have made the case that dance should be regarded as an integral part of the total educational experience concerned with movement and not as a narrowly conceived, performance-oriented art. Ulrich wrote: "It will also be necessary for the new band of dance educators to acknowledge the artistry and expression found in gymnastics, sport, and aquatics. The dancers' world can not be apart from these movement forms; it must be a part of the whole world of human movement."[24]

The linkage between dance and sport may be seen in several ways, such as the use of dance to expand the movement capabilities of varsity athletes, or the use of sports as a theme in dance choreography. Some activities, such as rhythmic gymnastics, are almost indistinguishable from dance. Silverman pointed out that dance classes have cross-over potential for numerous other school activities. She wrote:

The choir, band, and theater instructors, the gymnastics coach, and the cheerleading, pom-pom, and dance club sponsors were all concerned with timing, grace, precision, and rhythm in their students. The many elements of dance—kinesthetic sense, strength, agility, rhythmic ability, flexibility, and audience manipulation—are used in one way or another in any physical activity.[25]

2. Development of Personal Creativity. Dance, like all the arts, offers the opportunity for teaching and learning that is designed to enhance and encourage the personal creativity of students. Through the posing of compositional problems, as well as tasks related to performance and staging, the student is encouraged to produce imaginative and inventive thinking and movement solutions. Such experience, at any age, makes a vital contribution to the growth of the individual. Taylor wrote:

> The essence of the modern movement in education is the idea of creativity and its liberating effects on the individual. The modern movement . . . refuses to accept the conventional forms in which life is presented to us and looks for fresh ways of interpreting facts, for new forms of art, of architecture, of scientific discovery, of literature, of science. . . .[26]

Creative modern dance in particular may be taught as a problem-solving experience in which students seek solutions to assigned movement tasks involving the elements of energy, time, and space; or combinations of movement directions and levels; or uses of different parts of the body. Such experiences, Ellen Moore wrote enhance the learner's creative development and enrich technical development, which may otherwise become a dry or boring routine.[27]

In the past, the creative thrust was considered to be a free and spontaneous effort not to be limited by the instructor's expectations or standards. Today, within all forms of art, it is assumed that there are fundamental principles which provide the foundation for a general arts curriculum. Roucher suggested that meaningful creative performance must be based on:

> . . . students learning concepts and vocabulary in the arts and developing perceptual skills. This provides a systematic structure for understanding visual art, music, drama, and dance by examining each art form for:
>
> *Sensory Elements*—qualities of art work perceived through the senses;
>
> *Formal Elements*—structure and organization of the art work;
>
> *Technical Elements*—skill of execution; technique and materials used in the art work;
>
> *Expressive Elements*—mood, emotional qualities, character states, and energy qualities of the art work.[28]

3. Aesthetic Experience. At the same time that it develops personal creativity for students, dance provides a focused aesthetic experience for them. The purpose of such experience is not narrowly confined to specially gifted individuals. Robert Henri, the art critic, wrote several decades ago:

> Art, when really understood, is the province of every human being. . . . When the artist is alive in any person . . . he becomes an inventive, searching, daring,

self-expressive creature. He becomes interesting to other people. The world would stagnate without him—and the world would be beautiful with him. He does not have to be a painter or a sculptor to be an artist. He can work in any medium.[29]

The uniqueness, of course, of dance as a form of aesthetic experience is that the dancer's body, intellect, and emotions are all *directly* involved in a unified expressive experience. Unlike other art forms, in which the poem, painting, or piece of sculpture may exist as a product *apart* from its creator, the dancer in action *is* the work of art. A second remarkable aspect of dance is that its presentation lends itself to a fusion of all the arts. It may involve music, literary expression, sculptural design, or painting (in both costumes and sets), and other forms of artistic expression used either as the inspiration or accompaniment for dance or as an integral part of the dance work itself.

Gelbard pointed out that aesthetic theory encompasses three possible points of view: (a) art as *imitation* of life; (b) art as *personal* expression, often with a strong emotional emphasis; or (c) art as *form,* with its structure being the key concern. No single approach may be used to analyze dance as a form of aesthetic expression; ideally, it encompasses all of them: "Dance inevitably includes an element of imitation in that it evokes images of the human body, an element of expression in that it elicits a human response, and an element of form in that movement is selected and structured by the choreographer. . . . There is no pure imitation, pure expression, or pure form. . . ."[30]

Beyond this, recognizing the strong pressure in education today to establish defined goals and to demonstrate accountability, dance represents an art form that *can* be assessed as an aesthetic expression. LeBlanc wrote:

> . . . the evaluation of student achievement in this domain has . . . become an institutionalized ritual of arts education. Either the product, the process, or both facets of psychomotor achievement are regularly presented to the public or evaluated by expert critics. Consider, as examples of this traditional public presentation, the dance recital, the school band festival, the juried art exhibit, or the school play.[31]

4. Intercultural and Integrative Experience. Dance provides a rich medium for exploring the customs, attitudes, history, and living circumstances of people of other lands. Through the study of folk and ethnic dance, carried on under skilled instructors or sometimes as field assignments, students may venture deep into ethnology and anthropology. Similarly, in terms of the integration of various subject areas, dance has strong links with such fields as the fine and graphic arts, music, the language arts, and theater.

Often, dance may provide a medium in which the spirit and philosophy of people of other lands may be meaningfully experienced. Sondra Fraleigh, for example, pointed out that in the Western world we have sought to integrate the arts into the general fabric of life in a "self-conscious" way, and that, in so doing, we have focused on competition, speed, and productivity—typical characteristics of the Western way of life. In contrast, Fraleigh suggested that Eastern dance represents a more unifying and humanizing force, stemming from a deep philosophy based on humankind's essential "oneness" in harmony with nature. Instead of being active, athletic, and outgoing, as in the Western world, Eastern dance leads to a fuller sense of unity and internal harmony and self-awareness.[32]

When fully understood and intelligently presented, then, dance may provide a valuable medium for transmitting in-depth awareness of the philosophy and lifestyles of other people of the world. It may be as literal and direct as a performance of the folk dances of other nations, or an exploration of their religious or national customs through ethnic dance forms. Creative dance may also be used to depict the lives of other peoples, or themes drawn from their history or current existence.

5. Social Involvement. Recognizing that *social adjustment* and *life adjustment* have become archaic terms in today's educational glossary, it is clear that many of the most serious concerns of adults about young people over the past decades have had to do with their rebellion against traditional societal values in such areas as work orientation, sexual behavior, or the use of drugs.

Within the field of sports, many physical educators are concerned about the degree to which the traditional character-building values that were associated with athletics have been subverted in recent years. Frey and Massengale pointed out that values such as "striving for excellence, achievement, humility, loyalty, self-control, respect for authority, self-discipline, democracy, hard work and deferred gratification" have largely disappeared in school and college athletics. Instead, they argued: ". . . the desire for profit, power, prestige, notoriety, visibility, community support, and organizational survival has replaced character building as a guiding value of school sport."[33]

As a challenging and personally rewarding form of personal expression, dance is not subject to such pressures. Instead, it provides a unique opportunity for meaningful and constructive group involvement. It encourages intensive, cooperative social interaction and interpersonal relationships in small working groups. The range of social participation in dance activities, and the necessity for both providing and accepting critical judgment, is rarely equalled in other courses or student activities.

Even at the youngest ages, working on problems of group or individual composition or developing simple performance projects may assist children in setting goals and following through on them. Group planning and decision making help children develop useful interpersonal skills, as well as other important components of psychosocial development.

On more advanced levels, dance provides a medium through which participants may examine their own values and come to grips with new ideas and challenges. Edrie Ferdun, for example, suggested that many of our most stereotypic views—in such areas as appropriate sexual identification and behavior, bodily display and attitudes toward pleasure, or worthy forms of achievement in life—may be reexamined as part of the process of dance involvement.[34]

6. Carry-over Values. Clearly, a major purpose of education today must be to prepare for the enjoyable and enriching use of future leisure. Dance—as well as experiences in the other arts—must be viewed as such preparation. Through it, students may gain favorable attitudes and performing skills for active participation in modern dance or ballet, or recreational dance forms that combine physical, social, and creative values.

Without question, one of the major reasons for the tremendous growth of interest in the arts has been the expansion of leisure during the past several decades. It is essential, therefore, that school and college programs in the arts help to equip students to use their present and future leisure most creatively and constructively. Dance, because of its varied values—aesthetic, physical, social, and intellectual—is uniquely useful in this regard and may be enjoyed at any age. Indeed, a number of special projects involving dance with senior adults have been initiated. Liz Lerman, director of the Dance Exchange in Washington, D.C., has successfully developed a senior adult performing group, Dancers of the Third Age. In addition to this group, which has members ranging in age from sixty to eighty-eight, Lerman also teaches dance classes in the community—in nursing homes and in senior centers.[35]

7. Dance as Exercise. Increasingly, we have become aware of the unique values of dance as a form of exercise. While some types of dance, such as aerobic dancing or Jazzercise, have been developed specifically for this purpose, modern dance and ballet also are both valuable forms of exercise leading to improved physical fitness. In addition to promoting cardiovascular fitness, they provide neuromuscular activity that improves endurance, helps to shape muscles and eliminate fat, extends flexibility and coordination, and has other important fitness-related outcomes.

When compared to repetitive forms of exercise, such as the use of exercise machines, dance is worth doing as recreation for its own sake—and not just for fitness purposes. Thus, it is much more likely that adults will continue to take part in dance classes, rather than drop out, which often happens in other fitness programs.[36] Given the growth of interest in women's fitness—as an outcome of the women's movement—dance also can play a vital part in such fitness programs.

Aerobic dance may also be modified easily to suit the fitness needs of senior adults.[37] When it is presented for health purposes, participants should become familiar with fitness principles and other health and safety factors. In the University of New Mexico's aerobic dance program, for example, Carleton and Marsh pointed out that:

> . . . in addition to progressive in-class workouts during the first eight weeks, students are given material that relates fitness principles to cardiovascular conditioning and dance. Class lectures focus on safe exercise technique, the essentials of aerobic class design (warm-up, workout, cool-down, and toning), and the application of frequency, intensity, and duration.[38]

8. Career Goals in Dance. A final value of dance in education is the potential it offers for future careers in dance. Obviously, a number of young people who have had early training and shown promise in modern dance, ballet, tap, jazz, and related forms are likely to have a dance career as a personal goal. At an early point, they may have to make a difficult decision—whether to continue through a program of education in high school and college which will provide a broad general education as well as a specialization in dance, or to move directly into specialized dance schools, studios, dance conservatories, or academies that emphasize dance as a performing art.

While it is a legitimate goal of dance education to prepare individuals for careers in this field, it is essential also that they be given honest and detailed career counseling that will make their planning as realistic as possible. Frances-Fischer pointed out that dance teachers in private studios, high schools, and colleges or universities are likely to meet numbers of "hopefuls—the serious and the starry-eyed, the planners and the dreamers" who are considering careers in dance and who need information and advice. Often, they dream of becoming professional dancers. Frances-Fischer wrote:

> But how realistic are these ambitions for the majority of dance students? In the fast-paced, highly competitive, everchanging world of professional dance, how many of your students stand even a chance of "making it"? How many of them possess the fierce drive and dedication, and the rare talent? Do any of them have the physical and psychological make-up, the appropriate body type, and the years of excellent training needed in order to be considered for professional performing careers?[39]

On the other hand, it is entirely possible to build satisfying and rewarding careers in dance in fields that are not as competitive or demanding as the top professional dance companies would be. These include a number of diverse roles: (a) as performer, in a range of smaller companies or diversified settings; (b) as teacher, in public schools, colleges, private studios, adult education or recreation classes, children's dance programs, drama departments, and other settings; (c) as choreographer, in dance, opera, or musical comedy companies, or on television programming; (d) as dance therapist in hospitals, mental health settings, or other rehabilitation programs; or (e) in other roles as dance critic, historian, writer, or movement notator.[40] Often, students have limited awareness of such possibilities and should learn about them through individual or group counseling sessions and personal exploration.

Goals of Dance in Education

The goals of educational dance encompass all the values that have been presented in this chapter—ranging from creative and artistic values to other social or health-related purposes. In programs that limit themselves to teaching dance simply as technique, it is likely that many of these outcomes will not be achieved. In a diversified, well-planned, and supervised program of dance education, all of them should be achieved to some degree. A decade ago, Bruce King made a convincing case that education had not yet fully committed itself to supporting the varied creative arts fields, and that it was particularly necessary to train and require certification for dance specialists and to provide an adequate core of competence in movement education for all elementary school teachers.[41] The American Council for the Arts in Education concluded, in a comprehensive report titled *Coming to Our Senses: The Significance of the Arts for American Education,* that a massive contradiction exists concerning the arts in our national life. On the one hand, popular interest in the arts has grown steadily over the past three decades. On the other hand, arts education has continued to lack adequate support, and when national crises or budgetary cutbacks have occurred, fields such as art, music, theater, or dance have suffered in the schools—rather than science, mathematics, and other academic disciplines.

Given this paradox, exactly what *is* the state of dance education in the United States today? The following chapters outline actual practices and programs on all three levels of education: elementary, secondary, and college. They show the remarkable diversity of offerings in the dance, ranging from nonexistent or inadequate to curricula of extremely high quality.

Notes

1 Ann E. Jewett, "Excellence or Obsolescence: Goals for Physical Education in Higher Education," *Journal of Physical Education, Recreation and Dance,* September 1985, p. 39.

2 Barbara Page Beiswanger, "National Section on Dance, Its First Ten Years," *Journal of Health, Physical Education, and Recreation,* May–June 1960, p. 23.

3 Margaret Lloyd, quoted in Tom Rorek, "The Connecticut College American Dance Festival," *Dance Perspectives,* no. 50 (Summer 1972), p. 10.

4 E. C. Howe, "What Business Has Modern Dance in Physical Education?" *Journal of Health and Physical Education,* March 1937, p. 132.

5 Frederick Rand Rogers, *Dance: A Basic Educational Technique* (New York: The Macmillan Co., 1941), p. viii.

6 Margaret H'Doubler, *Dance: A Creative Art Experience* (New York: F. S. Crofts and Co., 1940), p. 66.

7 Paul Woodring, *A Fourth of a Nation* (New York: McGraw-Hill Book Co., 1957), p. 3.

8 Ruth Radir, *Modern Dance for the Youth of America* (New York: A. S. Barnes and Co., 1944), p. 4.

9 Resolution adopted by the American Association of School Administrators, Atlantic City, N.J., February 1959.

10 Sidney Hook, *Education for Modern Man* (New York: Alfred A. Knopf, 1963), p. 154.

11 Philip M. Phenix, *Realms of Meaning, A Philosophy of the Curriculum for General Education* (New York: McGraw-Hill Book Co., 1964), p. 34.

12 John Dewey, *Democracy and Education* (New York: The Macmillan Co., 1938), pp. 89–90.

13 C. Robert Pace, in *The College and the Student,* eds. Lawrence F. Dennis and Joseph F. Kauffman (Washington, D.C.: American Council on Education, 1966), p. 99.

14 Harold Taylor, *Art and the Intellect* (New York: Museum of Modern Art, 1960), p. 9.

15 Ibid., p. 27.

16 Ernest L. Boyer, "The Need for School-College Collaboration," *Higher Education and National Affairs,* September 2, 1985, p. 1.

17 "A Nation Prepared: Teachers for the 21st Century," *Chronicle of Higher Education*, May 21, 1986, pp. 43–55.

18 Research Report of Rand Corporation, Santa Monica, Calif., 1985, p. 8.

19 See Charles M. Dorn, "An Integrative Model for Art Curriculum Conception," in *Design for Arts in Education* (Washington, D.C.: Heldref Publications, March–April 1986, pp. 6–7.

20 Franklin Henry, "Physical Education as an Academic Discipline," *Journal of Health, Physical Education and Recreation*, September 1964, p. 32.

21 Charles B. Fowler and Araminta Little, *Dance as Education* (Washington, D.C.: National Dance Association and Alliance for Arts Education, 1977), pp. 10–13.

22 Elizabeth R. Hayes, *An Introduction to the Teaching of Dance* (New York: Ronald Press Co., 1964), p. 3.

23 Gladys Andrews Fleming, "Helping Children Discover Dance," *Journal of Physical Education and Recreation*, October 1971, pp. 38–39.

24 Cèleste Ulrich, "Education for a Dynamic Life Style," *Journal of Physical Education and Recreation*, May 1977, p. 48.

25 Paula Silverman, "Dancing Bridges: Connecting Dance to Other High School Disciplines," *Journal of Physical Education, Recreation and Dance*, May–June 1986, p. 32.

26 Harold Taylor, "Individualism and the Liberal Tradition," in *The Goals of Higher Education*, ed. Willis D. Weatherford, Jr. (Cambridge, Mass.: Harvard University Press, 1960), p. 12.

27 Ellen Moore, "Dance Technique Through Problem-Solving," *Journal of Physical Education and Recreation*, January 1974, p. 53.

28 Nancy Roucher, "Perceptual Skills: Foundation for an Arts Curriculum," in *Design for Arts in Education*, p. 38.

29 Robert Henri, *The Art Spirit* (Philadelphia, Pa.: J. B. Lippincott Co., 1923), p. 5.

30 Elaine Fruchter Gelbard, "Dance: An Aesthetic Pie," *Journal of Physical Education, Recreation and Dance*, May–June 1988, p. 33.

31 Albert LeBlanc, "Measurement of Attitude Goals in Arts Education," in *Design for Arts in Education*, September–October 1986, p. 37.

32 Sondra Fraleigh, "Humanizing Dance Education: Eastern Acquisitions," *Journal of Physical Education and Recreation*, May 1975, pp. 51–52.

33 James H. Frey and John D. Massengale, "American School Sports: Enhancing Social Values Through Restructuring," *Journal of Physical Education, Recreation and Dance*, August 1988, p. 40.

34 Edrie Ferdun, "Dance Power," *Journal of Physical Education and Recreation*, April 1975, p. 35.

35 Cynthia Ensign, "An Interview with Liz Lerman," *Journal of Physical Education, Recreation and Dance*, January 1986, p. 46.

36 See Leonard M. Wankel, "Personal and Situational Factors Affecting Exercise Involvement: The Importance of Enjoyment," *Research Quarterly for Exercise and Sport*, 56, no. 3 (1985), 275–82.

37 Marianne M. Shea, "Senior Aerobics: Improving Cardiovascular Fitness," *Journal of Physical Education, Recreation and Dance*, January 1986, pp. 48–49.

38 Nancy L. Carleton and Marjory J. Marsh, "Lifetime Fitness Through Dance," *Journal of Physical Education, Recreation and Dance,* September 1986, p. 31.

39 Jana E. Frances-Fischer, "Career Counseling for Dance Students," *Dance Teacher Now,* September 1987, p. 27.

40 See special issue of *Journal of Physical Education, Recreation and Dance* on dance careers, May–June 1984.

41 Bruce King, "Will Education Discover Dance?" *Dance Magazine,* March 1978, pp. 56–58.

CHAPTER 16

Dance in Elementary and Secondary Schools

Dance is a discipline having an organized set of theories, concepts, principles and skills. It consists of a distinct body of knowledge that needs to be studied in order to be understood. The study of dance as a discipline involves the acquisition of concepts, facts, and skills related to developing an understanding of the nature of dance, how dance functions in culture, the making of rational decisions and informed value judgments about dance, as well as actual dance performance. . . .

Dance is experience. It involves the physical, mental, and emotional aspects of the individual and is experienced through dancing, creating dance, and responding to dance.[1]

INSTRUCTION IN VARIED FORMS OF DANCE IS PROVIDED in many different settings in the United States today. First, it is part of general education, in the sense that the elementary and secondary schools of the nation, as well as colleges and universities of all types, often provide some form of dance education. Second, dance is offered in a variety of professional or specialized settings, in thousands of privately owned studios, academies, conservatories, or schools associated with ballet companies or other performing groups. Third, a number of community organizations or associations of dance professionals sponsor classes, teachers' workshops, and conferences in dance education. Community recreation centers, Ys, and similar nonprofit organizations also offer varied dance classes.

No comprehensive studies of dance education in the United States have been published in recent years, although one of the authors of this text carried out surveys of dance on various education levels during the 1960s and 1970s. In one such survey, a random sample of 510 schools and colleges throughout the United States was examined. The survey showed that a majority of responding institutions offered dance instruction in their curricula, as follows: junior high school (63.9 percent); senior high school (62.0 percent); junior college (58.6 percent); and senior college (82.4 percent).[2]

Dance Education in Elementary Schools

What forms of dance are offered in elementary schools? A 1977 report on the arts in American education gave the following brief description of typical programs on this level:

> An elementary school dance program usually consists of dancing games, folk, and square dances. Activities such as gymnastics and calisthenics are often included as part of the dance program.
>
> Fundamental movement, rhythm games and activities, and folk dance are common at the kindergarten through third grade level.
>
> Rhythmic activities (for example, skipping rope), and folk and square dance are common at the fourth through sixth grade level.
>
> Movement exercises with an emphasis on problem solving can be found in some schools. . . . There is greater acceptance for creative movement as a separate subject, and increased use of the movement specialist.
>
> Dance is becoming part of interrelated arts and interdisciplinary approaches.[3]

In a more detailed analysis, two physical education authorities, Arthur Miller and Virginia Whitcomb, suggested that there should be three components to the dance education offering in elementary schools:

> *Movement Fundamentals and Variations.* This consists of the necessary tools for dance, including such fundamental locomotor and nonlocomotor skills as walking, running, hopping, jumping, leaping, galloping, skipping, bending, pushing, twisting, falling—or combinations of these—all learned and practiced in various rhythms, tempos, and floor patterns or groupings.
>
> *Creative Rhythms and Dance.* This extends the fundamental movements into creative expression, by having children create dance movement or actual dance, through response to such stimuli as music, percussion accompaniment, stories, songs, pictures, poems, suggestions for pantomime (i.e., sports movements, work movements, familiar characters), moods, colors, textures, etc.
>
> *Folk Dance.* This includes singing games and folk dances of America and other lands, performed in various formations: circles, lines, squares, threesomes, and as mixers and icebreakers.[4]

Ruth Murray, whose text *Dance in Elementary Education* has been considered one of the most authoritative on this subject, suggested that there are four major categories of experience: *creative movement and movement skills, rhythmic skills* (related primarily to musical understandings and rhythmic competence), the development of *original individual or group dances,* and *learning dances,* such as singing games, play parties, folk, and square dances. She suggested that the emphasis in each of these categories should vary according to the age level of children being taught.[5] In general, the emphasis shifts from freer and less structured movement experiences in the early elementary grades to more formal and structured activity in the later grades. At the same time, dance may be related in a more complex way to problems of space, force, meter and dynamics, or linked to other curricular subjects.[6]

Teaching Responsibilities in Dance

In the lower elementary grades, it is usually the classroom teacher who is responsible for "rhythms," as the activity is often termed. This teacher is expected to be competent in a wide range of learning skills—with the priority usually given to the more academic skills of arithmetic and reading instruction. He or she may have had a course or two in physical activities for elementary school. Usually, this course will have emphasized the use of traditional singing games and folk dances, as well as other forms of physical activity such as group games, self-testing, and fitness exercises.

Most teachers in the elementary grades who provide such movement activities use phonograph records which have different rhythmic sequences (and sometimes verbal instruction or songs which provide cues for movement) as accompaniment. Occasionally, in the lower elementary grades, a music or physical education specialist may provide movement activities; such teachers, however, rarely work directly with children in the lower grades.

It is usually at about the fourth grade level that curriculum specialists in the fields of art, music, physical education, and sometimes science are introduced to elementary school classes. A common practice is for such specialists to work with individual classes once or twice a week and have the classroom teacher take responsibility for other teaching sessions. The specialist is also expected to provide consultation assistance to classroom teachers and, in many schools, to offer in-service training sessions for teachers.

At this point, in many elementary schools, boys and girls are separated in physical education classes. When this occurs, the boys are usually assigned a male teacher and the girls a female teacher. The boys' program then focuses on active games and sports, tumbling, gymnastics, conditioning exercises, and similar activities. If they have any involvement at all in dance, it usually consists of special coeducational classes (usually in folk and square dancing), often under the direction of the female physical education instructor. More frequently, boys have no involvement at all in creative dance forms after the third or fourth grade, unlike the English approach to movement education, in which both boys and girls participate extensively in creative movement experiences throughout the grades.

Status of Dance Instruction

While the literature contains impressive guidelines for children's dance, and while there have been a number of positive reports about "weaving" dance into public education at this level,[7] recent research studies suggest that its impact has been minimal. The 1985 National Children and Youth Fitness Study found that a full third of American children and youth do *not* take part regularly in any sort of vigorous physical activity. They watch more television, score lower on health-related fitness measures, weigh more, and have more body fat than children did twenty years before.[8]

A survey of over 10,000 students in public and private schools throughout the United States found that the average student was exposed to 11.8 different activities in a physical education class during the year, with girls experiencing slightly more variety than boys and with the range of different activities growing smaller from year to year:

> The typical student spends the largest portion of physical education class time on five activities listed in descending rank order: basketball, calisthenics/exercises, volleyball, baseball/softball, and jogging (distance running). The next 10 top activities, again in descending order, are kickball, running sprints, relays, dodgeball/bombardment, weight-training or weight-lifting, gymnastics (tumbling), aerobic dance, field or street hockey, gymnastics (free exercise), and swimming.[9]

Based on this report, it is clear that dance—other than aerobic dance—is not even mentioned in the top fifteen physical education activities and has therefore a relatively low priority. This finding is supported by an examination of physical education texts published in the 1970s. In popular texts by Bucher and Koenig and by Nixon and Jewett, dance hardly is mentioned.[10] In other elementary school physical education texts, dance is presented under headings such as "creative play" or "rhythmic activities."[11] Rarely is there reference to dance as a meaningful, independent form of creative experience.

Despite this, there have been a number of positive trends affecting dance education in elementary schools during the late 1970s and 1980s, including the following: (a) a strong thrust toward enriched programs of movement education which incorporate dance-like activities; (b) an expansion of arts education throughout the entire country with an emphasis on both visual and performing arts, including dance; and (c) the development of many "magnet schools" or other experimental programs designed to provide creative learning experiences.

Movement Education Approach. In a number of textbooks published during this period such as *The New Physical Education for Elementary School Children* by Elsie Carter Burton, movement education is highlighted as the most important recent development in American physical education. Burton presented the following definition of movement education:

> . . . that phase of the total education program which has as its contribution the development of effective, efficient, and expressive movement responses in a thinking, feeling, and sharing human being. . . .
>
> Emphasis is placed on *self-* and *body awareness, basic skill development, creative satisfaction, and a sense of total involvement in the learning experience*. . . . Exploration is the principal teaching method employed in movement education . . . a 'child-centered' approach or method of teaching which allows for individuality, creativity, spontaneity, and self-discovery.[12]

In some applications of Laban's approach, movement education may be closely linked to dance education as such, with emphasis on using movement to further aesthetic awareness or to promote personal expression or communication. Movement exploration may lead to the actual creation of individual or group dances by children. Indeed, in a discussion of educational dance based on Laban's work, Kate Barrett identified a progressive sequence of themes which are inherent in movement education as well: (a) awareness of the body; (b) awareness of weight and time; (c) awareness of space; (d) awareness of the flow of movement; (e) awareness of adaptation to partners and small groups; (f) awareness of the body; and (g) awareness of the basic effort actions.[13]

Curriculum Guidelines

A number of curricula have been designed to assist all teachers, whatever their background, to provide more effective movement education for the elementary grades. In one such effort designed for grades three through five, Carlisle developed sequential activities based on fundamental movement skills and concepts, and scientific biomechanical principles designed to develop both physical and motor fitness.[14] Numerous other teachers have contributed similar approaches which specify precise program objectives and progressive patterns of instruction and clearly define evaluative techniques for measuring course outcomes.

Culminating such efforts, the National Dance Association has published a set of dance curriculum guidelines for grades kindergarten through twelve. This manual defines the nature of the dance education experience and describes its major components, including the following: (a) movement skills and underlying principles; (b) movement elements; (c) aesthetic principles; (d) social-cultural-historical elements of dance; and (e) dance processes.[15]

Strengthening the Arts in Education

Increasingly, national organizations have sought to develop greater support for arts programs in elementary and secondary schools. The American Council for the Arts has made a vigorous effort to promote awareness of the need for more highly trained arts specialists and for upgrading curriculum designs to include more creative experiences for children. In many school districts, the Council argued, arts education:

> . . . has been neglected. . . . Arts specialists are not being trained in education or even recruited to the school system. Instead, schools are relying upon classroom teachers to teach these subjects about which they know little and therefore frequently feel intimidated. Budgets for instruments, equipment, and supplies have been slashed.[16]

To remedy this situation, the American Council for the Arts has played a leadership role in mobilizing twenty-eight national arts and arts education organizations to fight to improve the quality of arts education in the schools. Through a number of regional and national conferences, it has identified basic concepts and strategies toward achieving this goal.[17] Similarly, eight national organizations representing the fields of music, art, dance, and theater education joined together to publish a briefing paper for the arts education community. This publication, *K–12 Arts Education in the United States: Present Context, Future Needs,*[18] presents a realistic look at the place of the arts in American culture and education and suggests goals and advocacy techniques to help achieve greater support of quality programs in the arts.

The national cultural center, the John F. Kennedy Center for the Performing Arts, has sponsored major children's arts festivals—including dance as an important component—throughout the nation since the mid-1970s. In addition, the Kennedy Center has each year honored dozens of elementary and secondary school principals and school district superintendents who have encouraged exemplary programs of arts education.[19]

Magnet Schools and Other Experimental Programs

One of the most promising approaches that evolved in the 1970s and 1980s was the concept of the "magnet school," a special school designated to provide intensive exposure to the arts and to serve children drawn from throughout a city or school district because of their special interest or ability. In Eugene, Oregon, for example, the Condon School provides an alternative program of arts education, originally funded by a federal IMPACT grant. In this program, dance is one of the key curriculum areas; all students take dance classes, and fifth and sixth grades have the opportunity to perform with the Magnet Arts Dance Company. Since staffing is so critical in such programs, this school's staff includes: ". . . six teachers with master's degrees [and] two pianists, a potter, a calligrapher, two dancers, a singer, a computer graphic artist, and a folk musician."[20]

In numerous other school districts, similar programs have been developed on the elementary level. Often, they involve all schools, rather than a single center for the arts. For example, in Richmond, Virginia, an interdisciplinary program of arts and humanities has given strong emphasis to dance, both as a form of movement education and in its relation to other arts, including drama, music, painting, and poetry. Thousands of children have attended citywide performances of Arthur Mitchell's Dance Theater of Harlem; the Duquesne University Tamburitzans; the Richmond Ballet; Ezibu Muntu, an African dance group from Virginia Commonwealth University; and the Virginia Dance Theater, from Madison College.

In some cases, elementary school programs have involved special linkages with university dance groups, leading performers, or other community agencies. To illustrate, the South Miami, Florida, Elementary School has been involved in a two-week residency program of The Dancers' Company, the modern dance performing group of Brigham Young University in Utah. This residency involved lecture-demonstrations, concert performances, parent-teacher evenings, teacher in-service classes, dance classes on all grade levels, and a culminating performance which the children shared with the company.[21]

Jacques D'Amboise, for over thirty years a leading dancer with the New York City Ballet, initiated a program in the early 1980s that drew as many as 1,000 children from public and parochial schools in New York and New Jersey—many from slum areas and of black, Oriental, and Hispanic background—with striking results. In some states, such as Michigan, the state dance association has been active in promoting residencies and intensive programs in the arts in elementary schools. In Oklahoma, thirty-two different "demonstration" schools have been used to provide leadership in a statewide Arts in Education program. In New York City, the central school board provides "cluster" teachers—who are specialists in various subjects—to assist local schools in developing intensive programs in the arts. One such school has worked with the Alvin Ailey Dance Company to provide special classes and program events as part of an intensive dance project.[22]

Thus, while dance continues to be a relatively minor element in most grade school curricula, there is a growing awareness of its potential as a valuable educational experience.

Dance Education in Secondary Schools

In public secondary schools throughout the United States, dance is customarily taught in departments of physical education. A typical statement of its purposes in secondary education includes the following objectives:

1. To develop a perception of rhythm for greater efficiency and pleasure in the performance of all motor skills.
2. To develop a knowledge of the fundamentals of music and other accompaniments as they relate to dance.
3. To develop an awareness and appreciation of dance as presented in concert and theater.
4. To develop a vocabulary of movement and a knowledge of the factors which influence movement.
5. To develop strength, endurance, flexibility, and coordination.
6. To develop a feeling of pride in the body as an instrument of expression, not only in dance, but in life situations as well.
7. To provide greater enjoyment of dance as a recreational activity both in school and later in adult life.
8. To provide satisfactory socializing experiences through the use of group activity.

However, the reality of what is offered in high school physical education programs has often been at variance with such objectives. The texts on physical education that were published in the 1960s and 1970s illustrate this point. For example, in a popular text on secondary school physical education published in this period, the authors recommend that such forms of dance as "rhythms," "gymnastic," and "tap dancing" be presented—ignoring any discussion of dance as a creative art form.[23] In other guides for secondary school physical education curricula, only a minimal amount of class time was assigned to dance—with primary emphasis given to gymnastics, athletic sports, and related activities.[24]

In a 1976 survey of secondary schools sponsored by the National Dance Association, Nancy Schuman reported the following findings:

Modern dance is the most widely found form of dance.

Students are typically required to enroll in dance classes, and receive credit for them.

Dance is offered at several skill levels, but advanced classes are rarely provided.

Dance units are relatively brief, consisting of classes meeting twice a week, for three or four week units once a year, as a typical pattern.

Phonograph records are the most frequently found form of accompaniment for all forms of dance.

Classes tend to be large, sometimes extending up into the hundreds, and with few male students enrolled.

Teachers are generally trained in physical education, with some course work in dance; they express a strong need for workshop experiences in such areas as composition and dance technique.

Most respondents indicate that there are few dance programs or other resources in their communities.[25]

As in elementary schools, there are rarely special teachers of dance. With few exceptions (see page 338), in order to teach dance in secondary schools one must meet state certification requirements in physical education. Typically, this would include two or three courses in modern dance and/or recreational dance forms. Only rarely on the secondary level is a teacher hired as a full-time dance specialist (with physical education credentials, of course).

Posey provided a realistic picture of practices in many secondary schools:

> A term or two out of a four-year high school physical education program may offer modern dance or jazz dancing. This is generally provided as an elective and chosen by girls; boys usually are not encouraged to study dance even when they have expressed an interest. Students cannot be expected to attain a basic dance education under these circumstances, even in the hands of experienced and knowledgeable teachers.[26]

More Advanced Secondary School Programs

Despite this generally negative picture, in some areas of the country there has been a considerable amount of dance interest on the secondary school level. In states like Michigan and California, for example, enthusiastic leadership and support by physical educators have resulted in a fairly high level of dance activity in the schools. In such areas, professional organizations hold conferences and meetings and provide in-service training classes for teachers. Dance festivals are held, and high school students and teachers attend concerts by leading companies at nearby colleges, sometimes taking part in dance clinics and workshops.

In a number of situations, teachers have been successful in involving boys in modern dance activities. One technique that has been used to promote male involvement in dance has been to encourage members of athletic teams to join dance classes. It has long been recognized that dance training can be extremely helpful to athletes in developing coordination, grace, and related qualities; and a number of college coaches have actually required their basketball or football players to take courses in modern dance or ballet. In a Dade County, Florida, high school, teacher Diane Pruett has persuaded numerous male athletes to take dance classes and join the performing dance group.[27]

In other cases, dance instructors build interest in their programs by connecting dance to other high school activities. Silverman, for example, pointed out that the dance teacher may volunteer to work with the school's choir, band, theater groups, gymnastics team, and cheerleading squad, using dance to develop timing, grace, precision, and rhythm and to develop routines for performance.[28] Taylor and Chiogioji stressed that whenever possible, physical education should be linked to other high school educational disciplines. This can readily be done with creative or folk forms of dance in school programs that deal with art, music, theater, or social studies—through festivals and similar programs.[29]

Sometimes, secondary school dance programs are strengthened by input from nearby colleges offering dance majors. Jefferson Junior High School in Champaign, Illinois, has had a cooperative arrangement with the Dance Department of the University of Illinois, under which junior or senior dance majors at the University regularly work at the junior high school as part of a methods course. Such experiences have a two-way effect; the college dance program focused heavily on dance as a theater experience, but exposure to the active dance program in the Junior High School showed many college students the value of folk, ethnic, jazz, and social dance forms as well.

In some circumstances, dance lacks strong administrative support because students initially have little interest in it. Jean Sabatine wrote that jazz dance can be useful in overcoming such obstacles:

> . . . jazz dance [stimulates] and [broadens] the students' interest in dance. Students identify with jazz. It draws from their jazz and rock music, and they can use their rock dance as a source of movement. . . . The male student finds, in jazz, an opportunity to move in a masculine manner. There is nothing ethereal, bloodless, or sexless in jazz. Some students respect jazz as the only native American concert dance form.[30]

In a few cases, entire school systems have developed strong support for dance as an educational medium. In Salt Lake City, for example, eighteen high schools have full-time dance teachers, some with as many as three. Dance classes, which can be substituted for physical education, are extremely popular; in recent years boys have shown growing interest in dance, and in several high schools there are all-male or coeducational classes.

In other schools, special arrangements may be made to enable specially gifted students to pursue their dance interests more fully. The Nassau County, New York, Board of Cooperative Educational Services operates a Cultural Arts Center for forty-four school districts. Through this, talented public high school students may spend half a day in their home schools doing academic studies and the other half at the Center doing intensive work in music, drama, dance, or art. In another situation, the Teaneck, New Jersey, high school has permitted a talented student to spend her mornings taking regular academic courses at the high school and her afternoons taking classes at the School of American Ballet in New York City—for academic credit.

While other examples of successful secondary school dance programs might be cited, they are the exception rather than the rule. In part, this is because dance is usually regarded as a minor part of the physical education program, which itself is not fully accepted and supported in many communities. In the late 1980s, for example, Griffey wrote: "Secondary school physical education is suffering from reduced support, resource cutbacks, lack of understanding by administrators and teachers in other subject areas, misunderstanding by the public about our mission, and reduced time requirements for physical education in America's schools."[31]

As a consequence, Griffey concluded, effective programs in physical education tend to be rare and are usually found within a single school rather than throughout an entire district. In addition to the kinds of experimental programs just described, one way in which a number of larger cities have dealt with this problem is by establishing special secondary schools devoted to the fine and/or performing arts.

Dance in Special Secondary Schools

Such schools usually offer advanced programs in music, art, theater, and dance along with a solid academic study component. Their purpose is to give students professional-level skills in selected performing arts areas while at the same time giving them the option to continue academic study after graduation.

The first public secondary school to initiate a curriculum providing professional preparation in the performing arts was the High School of Performing Arts in New York City. Founded in 1947, this public school was designed to provide talented boys and girls in New York City with the opportunity to specialize intensively in music, drama, or dance, and at the same time to obtain an academic education of high quality. The premise for its existence was that New York City, as a major artistic and cultural center and, in effect, the entertainment capital of the nation, offered a considerable amount of employment to professionals in the theater arts, the concert field, television, radio, and night club fields. However, any student who wished to gain intensive professional development in his or her high school years found it almost impossible to obtain a rounded academic education at the same time. John Martin commented in the *New York Times:*

> Professional dance education . . . has always had to be obtained in spare time and chiefly after the normal high school years have been completed. Since dancing is a profession demanding youth, this means just that many years lost out of the income producing career. The advantage of getting the professional training along with a standard high school education can hardly be overestimated.[32]

The approach to instruction is extremely realistic and practical; the attempt is made to equip students with real skills and knowledge that will make them as professionally competent as possible upon graduation. Many graduates have

Two students in High School of Performing Arts ballet class. Photograph by Victoria Beller.

achieved success in the performing arts. Several of those actually attending the school are members of Actor's Equity; some have performed in summer stock, danced in musical shows on Broadway, played with major symphony orchestras, or performed in concerts. In dance, a number of graduates have joined the New York City Ballet or leading modern dance companies or have performed on television.

The dance curriculum includes both theory and practice in the broad range of ballet, modern dance, musical comedy, and other theater dance forms as well as various types of ethnological dance—African, Spanish, and Oriental.

A number of outstanding dancers have been employed as teachers of dance by the High School of Performing Arts. The New York Board of Education has made it possible for noncertified teachers to be employed by the school, in order to insure a high caliber of professional instruction.

Another example of a professionally oriented secondary school offering high-level instruction in the performing arts is the North Carolina School of the Arts in Winston-Salem. This school was established by an act of the North Carolina Legislature in 1963 and is open by audition to junior high school, high school, and college students throughout the nation who are considered to have outstanding talent in music, drama, or dance. Professional training in the arts constitutes the major emphasis of the course of study, supplemented by an intensive academic curriculum. The thirty-acre campus includes dormitories, dance studios, rehearsal halls, theater, and classrooms; it has served students from over thirty states plus such foreign countries as Bolivia, Brazil, Japan, Mexico, and Hungary. For a number of years, Pauline Koner, formerly a leading performer, choreographer, teacher, and guest soloist with the José Limón Company, directed modern dance instruction at the School. Ballet students worked under the direction of Robert Lindgren, formerly a featured artist with Ballet Theater, the Ballet Russe de Monte Carlo, and the New York City Ballet, and his wife, Sonia Tyven. At a later point, Lindgren became dean of the entire program. In addition to varied courses dealing with modern dance, ballet, choreography, and production, students take courses in repertory, mime, and acting for dancers and have the opportunity to perform with the North Carolina Dance Theater.

Growing Support for Arts in Education

In addition to such special schools, probably the most important trend with respect to strengthening dance as an academic discipline in the secondary schools has been the development of overall principles for arts education and specific guidelines for dance. A number of the strategic policy goals developed in 1986 by a consortium of representatives of national organizations in the arts illustrate the broader principles. These goals include the following:

> To establish and maintain sufficient programs, personnel and resources for teaching the arts as disciplines to all K–12 students.
>
> To advance the philosophical and operational concept that arts instruction must be a regular and basic part of the curriculum in all elementary and secondary schools.
>
> To increase, over time, the level of artistic literacy and comprehension in the nation as a whole, and thus develop an increasingly significant role for arts education in cultural formation.
>
> To maintain and enhance national capabilities for the preparation of individuals with high levels of artistic skills who are dedicated and effective full-time teachers. This includes appropriate arts content in state certification requirements throughout the nation, as well as appropriate resources for teacher education. . . .[33]

Curriculum Requirements

To achieve these goals, a number of states are establishing new curriculum requirements to strengthen the arts in their secondary schools. For example, in the mid-1980s, the Maryland State Department of Education imposed a new secondary school graduation requirement for all matriculating students in the fine arts, defined as music, dance, theater, and the visual arts. Following this new requirement, the University of Maryland sponsored a series of summer institutes on the fine arts in 1987 and 1988 to accomplish the following three aims:

> . . . to provide secondary school teachers with a strong intellectual background in the fine arts; to consolidate ties between university and secondary school faculty in Maryland; and to make the resources of the University of Maryland available on a regular basis in helping teachers to implement the new fine arts requirement.[34]

In the late 1980s, the Minnesota Department of Education initiated Comprehensive Arts Planning Programs (CAPP) designed to assist thirty school districts throughout the state. Through the Minnesota Alliance for Arts in Education, professional artists in varied media—music, dance, creative writing, theater, visual, and film/video arts—work closely with students and teachers. A number of other states have recently undertaken similar efforts.

Michigan Dance Education Guidelines

Outstanding curriculum guidelines may be found in a 1987 publication of the Michigan State Board of Education, which stipulates specific goals for the arts. It makes clear that dance education may be structured in alternative ways:

> The dance education program may exist as a component of the physical education program, activities integrated into a classroom program, or as a discrete instructional program that specifically addresses the art form. Dance education at all levels should examine the unique contributions provided by this form of movement education and allow students to participate in dance activities appropriate to their skill and age level.[35]

The Michigan K–12 curriculum program standards present the following guidelines for dance and suggest professional organizations in the dance field that can assist in program development.

Desirable Components of a Dance Education Program

A. At the elementary level, students are taught:

1. The basic vocabulary of dance.
2. Basic technical skills common to different dance forms.
3. The role of dance in our culture and in the cultures of other people.
4. The process of producing unique, creative, and expressive personal dance studies.
5. Skills in developing their own criteria for making aesthetic judgments.

B. At the elementary level, students will have opportunities to:

1. Apply the knowledge and skills learned in the making of dance.
2. Utilize creative problem-solving processes.
3. Sharpen their perceptive, imaginative, and creative abilities through dance experiences.
4. Observe professional dancers and discuss their work.

C. At the middle/junior high and high school levels, students are taught:

1. Specific technical skills in different dance forms.
2. Specific knowledge about dance, including a historical context and the impact of dance on our culture and the cultures of others.

3. Skills in interpreting different forms of expression in dance.

4. To respect their own unique ideas and visions, and those of others.

D. At the middle/junior high and high school levels, students will have opportunities to:

1. Create their own dance using the skills and knowledge taught.

2. Analyze, discuss, and critically examine student and professional dance performances.

3. Explore dance as a vocational and avocational pursuit.

Unique Instructional Resources and Facilities for a Program in Dance

A. Instructional Resources

1. A collection of recordings and sound systems are available for instruction.

2. A listing of professional dancers is available for consultant work.

B. Facilities

Large, open space with adequate flooring is available.[36]

The May–June 1989 issue of the *Journal of Physical Education, Recreation and Dance* featured a twenty-eight-page series of articles documenting new and comprehensive guidelines for K–12 education in dance in the following states: California, Florida, Georgia, Idaho, Illinois, Indiana, Michigan, North Carolina, North Dakota, South Carolina, Texas, Utah, and Wisconsin. While only the North Carolina dance education guidelines had been put fully into practice at this time, this report is clear evidence of the growing acceptance of dance in the elementary and secondary schools.

Other Sources of Dance Education

Another important source of dance education in the United States is private schools, studios, or academies which are devoted exclusively to the performing arts or to dance. Such private schools range from small operations that teach a variety of tap, children's dance, modern dance, and ballet along with adult ballroom dancing classes, to impressive dance academies with high-caliber instructors that attract talented and motivated students who are determined to pursue dance as a profession.

Many private schools are of extremely high quality and have impressive traditions and teaching staffs. For example, the Orcutt/Botsford School, founded in 1922 in Rochester, New York, offers an outstanding curriculum, chiefly in ballet and jazz dance, for children, youth, and adults. Its faculty includes Jurgen Schneider, a veteran of the Kirov Ballet School and the Moscow Bolshoi Theater and presently Ballet Master with American Ballet Theater; Luba Gulyaeva, a graduate of the Vaganova School in Leningrad and a long-time soloist with the Kirov Ballet; and other teachers who have had extensive backgrounds in dance. Graduates of the

Orcutt/Botsford have become members of numerous professional companies, including the Joffrey Ballet, American Ballet Theater, the Cleveland Ballet, Ballet Oklahoma, and other performing groups.

In addition to such programs, there are many arts centers, YWCAs and YM-YWHAs, performing arts councils, and similar sponsoring groups throughout the country which offer a high level of dance instruction. Often, they are connected to civic arts organizations or dance alliances, and in some cases they are directly sponsored by public (municipal, township, or county) recreation departments. Occasionally, independent dance schools may be linked administratively to nearby colleges or universities, with an interchange of staff and facilities.

Numerous examples of such community-based programs may be cited. The Walker Art Center in Minneapolis, Minnesota, offers a variety of dance courses and has sponsored major summer dance workshops. The Salt Lake City Children's Dance Theater was directed by Virginia Tanner for a number of years, as part of the Conservatory of Creative Dance, which is linked to the McCune School of Music and Art of Brigham Young University. In Cleveland, a famous settlement, Karamu House, has for years offered a variety of courses in all the arts and has been the center of outstanding dance instruction and performance.

Public recreation and parks departments frequently sponsor a range of different dance classes for children and adults and in some cases combine these with performances, special workshops, dance camps, and similar projects. For example, Joyce described the Recreation Department in San Mateo, California, which enrolls a wide range of participants, from age four or five through adulthood, in children's dance, tap, ballet, jazz, and choreography classes. The San Mateo program also offers an annual summer dance week in the Santa Cruz Mountains and has a group of young performers who tour regularly, presenting dance dramas in regional public schools.[37]

Summer Dance Schools

Similarly, there has been an increasing number of special summer workshops in dance. One of the best known of these was the annual Interlochen, Michigan, National Music Camp, which included a strong performing arts and dance component. This has been transformed into a year-round Arts Academy sponsored by the Interlochen Center for the Arts, which includes highly professional study and rehearsal schedules with a strong precollege academic program. Probably the best-known summer dance school has been Jacob's Pillow in Lee, Massachusetts, founded and directed for many years by Ted Shawn. In addition to courses in modern, ballet, and ethnic dance presented by well-known instructors, Jacob's Pillow offers a series of summer performances by visiting artists and companies and has contributed greatly to interest in creative dance in America. While it attracts many students of college age and has offered college credit through Springfield College, it also has had many high-school-age students enrolled through the years.

Other summer camps and schools include the Mt. Pinnacle Dance Camp in Hendersonville, North Carolina; the Southern Vermont Art Center in Manchester,

Vermont; Stonegate Music and Arts Camp in Long Lake, New York; and many other such camps in New England and throughout the country, some of which are devoted to all the performing arts and some exclusively to dance. In the area of recreational dance, annual summer dance camps are held in square, folk, and country dancing in many states. Among the best-known programs of this type have been the folk dance camp of the College of the Pacific, in Stockton, California; the Maine Folk Dance Camp conducted by Michael and Mary Ann Herman; the Pinewoods Camp in country dancing and folk music sponsored by the Country Dance and Song Society of America in Plymouth, Massachusetts.

Status of Dance Instruction

Despite the progress that has been made, it is clear that the teaching of dance in elementary and secondary schools throughout the United States is at best scattered and superficial. If it is to be used to its fullest as a significant educational experience, and if all students are to be exposed to this vital form of artistic expression during their formative years, certain steps must be taken. These fall within several areas of concern: (a) developing and gaining support for more effective dance education within the established school curriculum; (b) improving the quality of instruction in dance; (c) involving boys and male teachers more fully in dance education; and (d) achieving more awareness and support of dance within the community at large in order to develop a climate in which dance in education can flourish.

Strengthening Dance within the Established School Curriculum

If dance is to become a more respected and meaningful part of the curriculum, it will be necessary to develop and introduce units of instruction at appropriate levels that expose students to movement skills, creative experiences, and general understanding of dance as an art form. The Michigan K–12 program outlined on page 334 provides an example of such a sequentially developed curriculum, and a number of states or big-city school systems have developed comparable approaches. McLaughlin cited several examples of state or urban school systems that have successfully integrated dance within their overall curricula, including New York City, San Francisco, Boston, and Utah.[38]

Within the schools themselves, efforts must be made to give dance greater visibility and to make it a recognized activity. If performance—as part of assembly programs, parents' day, arts festivals, or other special events—can be a culminating activity of a particular focus in dance instruction, it will reinforce the interest of children. Obviously, such performances should not be the sole goal of dance instruction and should not be permitted to dominate the actual process of learning to move and to create dance for its own sake. However, they provide visible goals for classes as well as a means of demonstrating the outcomes of dance instruction. If such performances are vital and exciting rather than stilted and mechanical, they will provide interest and enthusiasm for dance classes. Further, such experiences reinforce the concept of dance as a performing art as well as an educational medium.

Other resources must be drawn on if dance is to become a more established part of the school curriculum. McLaughlin pointed out that partnerships with community dance groups, artists, and college or university dance departments can provide the advocacy needed to promote dance in the schools, as well as the technical expertise needed to develop outstanding programs. He wrote:

> These collaborative ventures, involving schools, arts specialists, artists, cultural institutions, institutions of higher education, and arts provider organizations, have yielded significant results in communities where they have occurred. These communities have garnered increased advocacy for the arts in school, have enacted arts education policies leading to curriculum development, and have witnessed increased number of artist residencies and relationships with cultural facilities.[39]

Value of Demonstration Programs. Given the limited resources available in many school systems and the competition among many different curriculum areas for greater fiscal support, a logical strategy for the present is to focus on carrying out special demonstration programs in selected schools, to show the potential of well-conceived and directed dance activities. Such programs should gradually build support for dance within the elementary and secondary school curriculum.

Improving the Quality of Dance Instruction

As this chapter has shown, one of the key problems of improving dance instruction in the schools is the lack of qualified dance teachers. Classroom teachers must recognize the value of creative rhythmic and structured dance activities and should receive training to improve their teaching skills in these areas. This can be accomplished both in their preservice training in undergraduate colleges and also through in-service education and graduate study. Those in allied fields, such as music or art education on the elementary level, must also become more knowledgeable about dance and creative movement if they are to assist classroom teachers.

As a rule, those who teach dance in elementary schools must be certified in another area, such as physical education. While some such teachers have a strong background and interest in dance, too often dance is presented in an extremely limited way. Although efforts have been made to approve separate certification in dance so that well-qualified dance specialists might obtain teaching licenses without having to meet requirements in another field, these have been approved in only a few states. In addition, in such states as New York, New Jersey, Colorado, and Hawaii, special dance instructors have been placed in schools without separate certification, on projects funded by the Elementary and Secondary Education Act (Title III/IV), by the Artists in the Schools program, or by special state or arts council funding.

Dance Teaching on the Secondary Level. How can dance instruction be strengthened in high schools? Elizabeth Hayes pointed out that many physical education teachers who are required to teach dance have had only a minimum of training in it and, in addition, often lack the temperament or creative interest to be successful in it. Many of them recognize their own lack of ability in dance and are therefore extremely reluctant to teach it.

Not only should a stronger core of basic dance courses be provided in college physical education major departments, but there should be a wider provision of dance concentrations, or minors, for physical education majors with a special interest and skill in dance. Thus, such students could become identified at an early point as dance specialists and could build their competence in a sustained way throughout their college programs. Beyond this, it would be extremely helpful if state education departments could develop a special physical education certification requirement which gives credit to a large block of courses in dance and which keeps other skills areas to a minimum.

The well-developed dance specialist is badly needed in many schools, and a modified certification requirement (still under the heading of physical education) would encourage more students interested specifically in dance education to enter this field. A number of states, notably Utah and Idaho,[40] have developed such special certification options; and many others, including several cited in this chapter, have made special arrangements for dance specialists to teach in pilot school programs in the arts.

More Involvement of Boys in Dance

As this chapter has shown, sex stereotyping continues to play an important role in most school systems today in terms of assigning female students to dance and male students to sports, within the overall physical education curriculum. While a number of dance teachers have been effective in attracting and involving boys in modern dance classes (see page 330), in general such efforts have been limited. This means that not only are boys excluded from the benefits of dance education, but the image of dance as essentially feminine is maintained.

In part, the exclusion of boys from dance—particularly in junior and senior high schools—reflects their own attitudes toward it, which in turn reflect community stereotypes of dance. How *can* secondary school dance be made more attractive for boys?

If it is not possible to involve boys directly in creative forms of dance as a school requirement, one approach would be to establish coeducational classes in modern dance or recreational dance forms (square, folk, social, and tap) on an elective basis. Once boys became interested and challenged, many of them would gain a more favorable attitude about dance as an appropriate masculine activity.

Beyond this, the successful programs that have involved male athletes with dance have shown that boys can be impressed by the physical demands that dance can make and the challenge that it offers. If it is not feasible to offer dance classes for boys, then every effort should be made to develop club programs which include boys on the secondary school level. Many boys would welcome such a program if it were effectively presented and did not prove embarrassing to them. It might be offered as part of a music program, a conditioning program, or in connection with school dramatic presentations. If the staff itself did not have qualified teachers to guide such club or special programs on an extracurricular basis, capable instructors might be brought in from the community on a special-teacher basis.

In terms of promoting the overall prominence of dance, many techniques can be used to arouse interest in it in secondary schools. Recreational dance activities—square and folk dance festivals, jamborees, clubs, and clinics—can all be developed. Students may attend master classes, seminars, and concerts at nearby colleges, or regional dance events. Student choreography may be presented in assemblies and concert programs. Often, unified programs of the arts, such as special week-long festivals presenting plays, poetry readings, art exhibitions, concerts, and dance events, arouse student interest.

Developing Community Awareness and Support of Dance

If such steps are taken to promote dance in the school program both as part of the curriculum and in allied activities, it will contribute much to the aesthetic environment of the schools—as well as to a general awareness and support of dance. The school does not exist in a vacuum, and school programs, film series, demonstrations, performances, and similar ventures reach and influence many parents.

Much can be done to promote dance within the community at large, in order to create a more favorable audience for dance and more support for its role in the schools. Over the past twenty years, federal and state arts and humanities programs have assisted touring companies, provided subsidies for performance and special workshops in schools and colleges, and supported major conferences concerned with the arts in community life and in education. Many dancers and choreographers have struggled to create a more favorable audience for dance. In some communities, arts centers have been established where art exhibits, poetry readings, concerts, and dance series have promoted overall public interest in the arts. Such efforts must be continued—and redoubled—if dance in education is to become more widely accepted and supported.

Notes

1 Beverly Allen, "Teaching Training and Discipline-Based Dance Education," *Journal of Physical Education, Recreation and Dance,* November–December 1988, pp. 65–66.

2 For more details, see Richard Kraus and Sarah Chapman, *History of the Dance in Art and Education,* 2d ed. (Englewood Cliffs, N.J.: Prentice-Hall, 1981), pp. 275–76, 284.

3 David Rockefeller, *Coming to Our Senses: The Significance of the Arts for American Education* (New York: McGraw-Hill Co., and the Arts, Education and Americans Panel, 1977), p. 74.

4 Arthur G. Miller and Virginia Whitcomb, *Physical Education in the Elementary School Curriculum,* 3rd ed. (Englewood Cliffs, N.J.: Prentice-Hall, 1969), pp. 228–79.

5 Ruth Murray, *Dance in Elementary Education* (New York: Harper and Row, 1960), p. 23.

6 Helen V. Wagner, "A Dance Lesson Based on Geometric Shapes," *Journal of Physical Education and Recreation,* January 1975, p. 67, and Gertrude Blanchard, "Alphabet Dance," *Journal of Physical Education and Recreation,* February 1975, p. 65.

7 See "Dance Dynamics: Weaving Dance into Public Education," *Journal of Physical Education, Recreation and Dance,* May 1982, pp. 15–22.

8 James G. Ross and Glen G. Gilbert, "The National Children and Youth Fitness Study: A Summary of Findings," *Journal of Physical Education, Recreation and Dance,* January 1985, pp. 45–50. See also JOPERD, November–December 1987, pp. 51–56.

9 Ross and Gilbert, "National Children and Youth Fitness Study," p. 48.

10 Charles A. Bucher and Constance R. Koenig, *Methods and Materials in Secondary School Physical Education* (St. Louis: C. V. Mosby, 1978), and John E. Nixon and Ann E. Jewett, *An Introduction to Physical Education* (Philadelphia: W. B. Saunders, 1974).

11 Victor P. Dauer and Robert P. Pangrazi, *Dynamic Physical Education for Elementary School Children* (Minneapolis: Burgess, 1976).

12 Elsie Carter Burton, *The New Physical Education for Elementary School Children* (Boston: Houghton-Mifflin Co., 1977), p. 11.

13 Kate R. Barrett, in Bette J. Logsdon et al., *Physical Education for Children* (Philadelphia: Lea and Febiger, 1977), p. 125.

14 Cynthia Carlisle, "Dance Curriculum for Elementary Children," *Journal of Physical Education, Recreation and Dance,* May–June 1986, p. 31.

15 *Dance Curriculum Guidelines, K–12* (Reston, Va.: National Dance Association, 1988).

16 Fred Lazarus, "Retracing Our Steps: Teaching the Arts—Again," *Vantage Point,* no. 14 (1987), p. 3.

17 Ibid.

18 *K–12 Arts Education in the United States: Present Context, Future Needs* (Reston, Va.: National Assoc. for the Arts in Education, January 1986).

19 See *Interchange* (Washington, D.C.: Alliance for Arts Education and J. F. Kennedy Center for the Performing Arts, Spring 1986), pp. 1, 6.

20 Gwen Curran, "Weaving Dance Through a Magnet School," *Journal of Physical Education, Recreation and Dance,* May 1982, pp. 25–26.

21 Diane Milhan Pruett, "Interactions: Elementary Schools with University Dance Companies," *Journal of Physical Education, Recreation and Dance,* November–December 1982, p. 40.

22 Mary C. Daley, "Weaving Dancing Through a School District," *Journal of Physical Education, Recreation and Dance,* May 1982, pp. 23–24, 28.

23 Charles A. Bucher, Constance R. Koenig, and Milton Barnhard, *Methods and Materials for Secondary School Physical Education* (St. Louis: C. V. Mosby Co., 1965), pp. 192–93.

24 Karl W. Bookwalter, *Physical Education in the Secondary Schools* (Washington, D.C.: The Center for Applied Research in Education, 1964), p. 52.

25 Nancy Schuman, "Secondary School Commission Report," *Spotlight on Dance,* May 1976.

26 Elsa Posey, *"Discipline-Based Arts Education—Developing a Dance Curriculum,"* November–December 1988, p. 63.

27 Diane Milhan Pruett, "Male High School Athletes in Dance Classes: An Interview with Nancy K. Perez," *Journal of Physical Education, Recreation and Dance,* May 1981, pp. 43–45.

28 Paula Silverman, "Dancing Bridges . . ." see pg. 313.

29 John L. Taylor and Eleanor N. Chiogioji, "Implications of Educational Reform on High School Programs," *Journal of Physical Education, Recreation and Dance,* February 1987, pp. 22–23.

30 Jean Sabatine, "Jazz Dance in the Secondary Schools," *Journal of Health, Physical Education and Recreation,* February 1972, pp. 69–70.

31 David C. Griffey, "Trouble for Sure; A Crisis—Perhaps: Secondary School Physical Education Today," *Journal of Physical Education, Recreation and Dance,* February 1987, p. 21.

32 John Martin, "The Dance: Training," *New York Times,* November 2, 1947; see also David Boroff, "High School with a Flair," *Dance Magazine,"* February 1962, pp. 29–33. *Note:* In 1984, the High School for Performing Arts was merged with the High School of Music and Art, in the new F. H. La Guardia High School of Music and the Arts. With a combined enrollment of 2,400, the school occupies a nine-story building close to Lincoln Center, the Metropolitan Opera, the School of American Ballet, and the Juilliard School.

33 See *K–12 Arts Education in the United States,* p. 29.

34 *Humanistic Perspectives on the Fine Arts* (College Park, Md.: Special Institute at University of Maryland, Summer 1987).

35 "The Dance Education Program," in *1987 Michigan K–12 Program Standards of Quality,* Michigan State Board of Education, 1987, pp. 31–32.

36 Ibid.

37 Mary Joyce, "Community Dance, A Program for Children," *Journal of Physical Education, Recreation and Dance,* May–June 1986, pp. 29–30.

38 John McLaughlin, "A Stepchild Comes of Age," *Journal of Physical Education, Recreation and Dance,* December 1988, pp. 58–60.

39 Ibid.

40 See Diane B. Walker, "The Idaho Model for Certification," *Journal of Physical Education, Recreation and Dance,* November–December 1981, pp. 64–65.

CHAPTER 17

Dance in Higher Education

... the goals of dance in higher education today ... will vary according to the institution and the role of dance in that institution. In some places, dance may be available only as a general experience and not as a major program. In this case dance offers a broad experience concerned with discovering movement; finding the potential for creating; and knowing dance as an art experience.

When a concentrated dance major is offered, then dance must meet the equivalent kind of goals as those held in any other discipline within the university ... in English, history, science, or any other field. That implies that we must be clear about our body of knowledge, and find ways to provide appropriate experiences. In a more direct way, our goal is related to that of the university's concern with research and creativity, and with helping people prepare themselves to move in whatever direction they want to move—as a performer/choreographer, teacher, researcher, or whatever.[1]

WHILE IT IS TRUE THAT IN THE PAST most leading dancers and choreographers received their training in private studios or company schools of ballet or modern dance, in recent years a growing number of young men and women have combined specialized dance training with the goal of achieving a broad, liberal arts education. They have done this by taking degree programs in colleges or universities; as a result, dance has become a much more widely accepted field of major study in American higher education.

Through the years, a number of surveys have examined dance programs in colleges and universities. During the 1940s, Walter Terry conducted such surveys, reporting in his book, *Invitation to the Dance,* and in the *New York Herald-Tribune,* that dance in higher education was expanding rapidly. In the decades that followed, surveys of dance in higher education conducted by *Dance Magazine* documented this growth. In the late 1970s, the *Dance Directory of Programs of Professional Preparation in American Colleges and Universities,* published by the National Dance Association, gave details of programs ranging from the baccalaureate through the master's degree and doctorate. It identified three major types of curricula:

> *Dance Education:* a major curriculum in dance designed to prepare teachers of dance.
>
> *Performing Arts:* a major curriculum in dance designed to prepare performing dance artists.
>
> *Dance Concentration:* a selection of dance courses required in professional preparation for a major in a related field, such as Physical Education or Fine Arts.[2]

In 1979, two of the authors of this text carried out a survey of 165 college and university programs drawn from the *Dance Magazine Directory* or listed in that magazine's columns on dance education.[3] Of the 95 responding institutions, 67 had major undergraduate programs and 44 had graduate curricula. The majority of dance education programs had been established during the period between the mid-1960s and the mid-1970s, and were housed administratively in departments or schools of physical education. The titles of responding programs varied, with the largest single group being Department or Program of Dance. Other frequently used titles included Dance Education, Dance in Theater Arts, or Dance Concentration in Physical Education. The states in which the largest number of dance curricula were found included California, Michigan, New York, and Ohio.

Among the most frequently offered courses were those in modern dance and ballet, usually at several skill levels, along with courses in choreography and production (see Table 17-1).

Sources of current information on dance in higher education may be found in the annual *Dance Directory* published by *Dance Magazine,* which also lists local dance schools and centers, academies and conservatories, and performing companies,[4] and in annual reports issued by the National Association of Schools of Dance.[5] While no recent survey findings of the total number of higher education dance curricula have been reported, Norwood and Worthy stated in 1986 that: ". . . two hundred forty-two American colleges and universities now offer undergraduate degree programs in dance, with 25 percent offering both undergraduate and graduate degrees."[6]

Role of National Association of Schools of Dance

Beyond this quantitative increase, college and university dance curricula have become much more sophisticated in presenting dance as a strong academic discipline than was the case during the 1960s and 1970s. In large measure, this has been due to the influence of the National Association of Schools of Dance (NASD). This organization was established to develop a closer relationship among schools and programs of dance and to examine and improve practices and professional standards in dance education and training.[7]

Table 17-1   Kraus/Chapman Survey of Dance in Higher Education★

Courses Offered in Dance Curricula

Types of Courses	Frequency	Types of Courses	Frequency
Modern Dance		Dance Teaching Methods	56
Elementary	88	Music for Dance	52
Intermediate	88	Movement Fundamentals	50
Advanced	76	Jazz/Musical Comedy Dance	47
Ballet		Folk Dance	46
Elementary	74	Dance Notation	40
Intermediate	66		
Advanced	55	Square/Country Dance	37
		Ballroom Dance	35
Choreography		Ethnic Dance	34
Elementary	74	Effort–Shape	26
Intermediate	76	Dance Therapy	27
Advanced	63	Dance Research Methods	22
Dance Production	68	Improvisation	6
Dance History/Philosophy	63	Dance for Children	3

Additional scattered references to: Adagio, Anatomy for Dancers, Character Dance, Lighting Design and Stagecraft, Repertory, Rhythmic Analysis, Sacred Dance, Special Ethnic Forms, Tap Dance, Anatomy, and Kinesiology for Dance.

★Temple University, 1979.

Beyond these goals, the National Association of Schools of Dance has also been active in developing a strong code of ethics, curriculum guidelines for degree-granting institutions, and operational standards for proprietary (privately owned, profit-making) dance schools. It has worked closely with several other organizations (the National Association of Schools of Art and Design, the National Association of Schools of Music, and the National Association of Schools of Theater) in developing guidelines and in planning for joint evaluation of institutions' arts programs.

Types of Undergraduate Degree Programs

NASD has identified two principal types of undergraduate dance curricula. It has defined these as "professional" and "liberal arts" degrees and has given examples of the kinds of majors offered, as follows:

A. **"Professional" Degrees.** Degrees in this category include the Associate of Fine Arts and the Bachelor of Fine Arts, and require that at least 65% of the course credit be in studio work and related areas.

B. **"Liberal Arts" Degrees.** Degrees in this category include Associate of Arts or Bachelor of Arts with a major in dance and Associate of Science or Bachelor of Science with a major in dance. These degrees usually require that one-third to one-half of the total course credit be in dance.

C. **Majors/Areas of Emphasis.** The term "major" is used to indicate the field of study constituting the focus of a particular degree program, the name of this field normally being appended to the generic degree title. For example, in the titles "Bachelor of Fine Arts in Dance Performance," "Bachelor of Arts in Dance History," and "Bachelor of Science in Dance Education," Dance Performance, Dance History, and Dance Education are requisite majors.

In order to be designated a "major" in a B.F.A. or studio program, a field of specialization must be accorded no less than 25% of the total credits required for the B.F.A. degree. In order to be designated a "major" in a liberal arts program, a comprehensive field such as dance or dance history must be accorded no less than 35% of the total credits required for the liberal arts degree.[8]

Examples of College and University Dance Curricula

To illustrate the types of dance curricula found today, Table 17-2 presents profiles of eleven leading programs found in different types of colleges and universities. Following the table, a number of additional descriptions of leading higher education dance curricula are provided. Taken together, these charts and summaries present a diverse picture of programs in institutions large and small, both public and private, and with varied departmental affiliations.

Characteristics of Curricula

These profiles suggest certain differences between the programs of private and public (usually state-supported) colleges and universities. As a rule, private colleges tend to be smaller in enrollment and to give primary emphasis to dance as a performing art. In contrast, the public institutions have larger enrollments and have traditionally located dance within departments or divisions of health, physical education, and recreation.

Of the individual colleges listed, Butler University and Juilliard are excellent examples of private institutions with a professional approach to the preparation of dance performers. Their curricula emphasize both modern dance and ballet and offer extensive experience in performance and production. Stephens College and Mills College are more typically liberal arts institutions with a performing arts orientation but without the strong professional emphasis in the other programs described.

Of the state universities, Ohio State University and the University of Illinois, along with Texas Woman's University, have traditionally offered strong modern dance programs to which ballet has been added in recent years. In these programs,

Table 17-2 *Dance Education in U.S. Colleges*

	1. Butler University Indianapolis, Ind.	2. Mills College Oakland, Cal.	3. Stephens College Columbia, Mo.
Enrollment	4,000	1,000	1,200
Type of Institution	Private, Coeducational	Private, Women; Coeducational	Private, Women's
Department Sponsoring Dance	Dance Department in College of Fine Arts	Dance Department	Performing Arts/ Dance
Dance Degrees	B.A. in Pedagogy B.A. in Arts Admin. B.F.A. in Performance M.A.	B.A. in Fine Arts; Performing Dance, Dance Education; M.A.	B.A., B.F.A., Performing Dance Major, Concentration, Dance Education B.F.A., Musical Theater
Courses Offered★			
Modern Dance			
Elementary	X	X	X
Intermediate	X	X	X
Advanced	X	X	X
Ballet			
Elementary	X	X	X
Intermediate	X	X	X
Advanced	X	X	X
Choreography	X	X	X
Improvisation	X	–	–
Production	X	X	X
Performing Group	X	X	X
Stagecraft		X	X
Other forms			
Folk	–	–	–
Square	–	–	–
Ballroom	–	–	–
Ethnic	–	–	X
Tap	X	–	X
Jazz/Musical Comedy	X	–	X
Dance History/ Philosophy	X	X	X
Dance Teaching Methods	X	X	X
Dance Practice Teaching	X	X	X
Music for Dance	X	X	X
Dance Therapy	–	X	–
Labanotation	–	X	X
Number of Dance Majors			
Undergraduate	65	35	30
Graduate	4	35	–

★Courses listed here include only undergraduate courses.

Table 17-2   *(cont.)*

	4. *Juilliard School New York, N.Y.*	5. *Ohio State University Columbus, Oh.*	6. *Brigham Young University Provo, Ut.*
Enrollment	850	59,000	Over 20,000
Type of Institution	Private Coeducational	State, Coeducational	Private, Coeducational
Department Sponsoring Dance	Dance Division	Department of Dance, College of Art	Dance Department, College of Physical Education
Dance Degrees	B.F.A., Performing Arts	B.A., M.A., B.F.A., M.F.A., all in Performance/Choreography, Education	B.A., Performing Arts Dance Education; B.F.A. in Musical Dance Theater; M.A.
Courses Offered★			
Modern Dance			
Elementary	X	X	X
Intermediate	X	X	X
Advanced	X	X	X
Ballet			
Elementary	X	X	X
Intermediate	X	X	X
Advanced	X	X	X
Choreography	X	X	X
Improvisation	–	–	–
Production	X	X	X
Performing Group	X	X	X
Stagecraft	X	–	–
Other forms			
Folk	–	X	X
Square	–	–	X
Ballroom	–	–	X
Ethnic	–	X	X
Tap	–	X	X
Jazz/Musical Comedy	–	X	X
Dance History/ Philosophy	X	X	X
Dance Teaching Methods	–	X	X
Dance Practice Teaching	–	X	X
Music for Dance	X	X	X
Dance Therapy	–	–	–
Labanotation	X	X	–
Number of Dance Majors			
Undergraduate	80	64	160
Graduate	–	26	20

★Courses listed here include only undergraduate courses.

Table 17-2 *(cont.)*

	7. University of Illinois, Urbana, Ill.	8. University of California, Los Angeles, Cal.	9. Texas Woman's University, Denton
Enrollment	36,000	Over 30,000	9,000
Type of Institution	State, Coeducational	State, Coeducational	State, Women, State, Coeducational (Graduate)
Department Sponsoring Dance	Department of Dance, College of Fine and Applied Arts	Dance Department, Interdisciplinary Degree with World Arts and Culture	Department of Dance College of HPERD
Dance Degrees	B.F.A., M.F.A., Performing Arts	B.A.	B.A., B.S., M.A., M.F.A. Ph.D., Performing Arts Dance Education, Dance and Related Arts, Choreography and Performance

Courses Offered★

Modern Dance			
Elementary	X	X	X
Intermediate	X	X	X
Advanced	X	X	X
Ballet			
Elementary	X	X	X
Intermediate	X	X	X
Advanced	X	X	X
Choreography	X	X	X
Improvisation	X	–	–
Production	–	X	X
Performing Group	X	X	X
Stagecraft	–	X	–
Other forms			
Folk	X	–	X
Square	–	–	X
Ballroom	X	–	X
Ethnic	X	–	X
Tap	X	–	X
Jazz/Musical Comedy	X	X	X
Dance History/ Philosophy	X	X	X
Dance Teaching Methods	X	X	X
Dance Practice Teaching	X	X	X
Music for Dance	X	X	X
Dance Therapy	–	X	–
Labanotation	X	X	X
Number of Dance Majors			
Undergraduate	35	78	50
Graduate	12	75	50

★Courses listed here include only undergraduate courses.

Table 17-2   *(cont.)*

	10. *Arizona State University* *Tempe, Az.*	11. *Temple University* *Philadelphia, Pa.*
Enrollment	43,000	33,000
Type of Institution	State, Coeducational	State, Coeducational
Department Sponsoring Dance	Dance Program, College of Fine Arts	Dance Department, College of Health, Physical Education, Recreation and Dance
Dance Degrees	B.A., B.F.A., Dance Education, Performance, Choreography, Teacher Certification; M.F.A.	B.F.A., M.F.A., Ed.D., Performance, Choreography, Dance Education; Somatics
Courses Offered★		
Modern Dance		
Elementary	X	X
Intermediate	X	X
Advanced	X	X
Ballet		
Elementary	X	X
Intermediate	X	X
Advanced	X	X
Choreography	X	X
Improvisation	–	X
Production	X	X
Performing Group	X	X
Stagecraft	–	–
Other Forms		
Folk	–	–
Square	–	–
Ballroom	–	–
Ethnic	–	–
Tap	X	X
Jazz/Musical Comedy	X	X
Dance History/ Philosophy	X	X
Dance Teaching Methods	X	X
Dance Practice Teaching	X	–
Music for Dance	X	X
Dance Therapy	–	–
Labanotation	X	X
Number of Dance Majors		
Undergraduate	93	42
Graduate	12	49

★Courses listed here include only undergraduate courses.

as in the curriculum of Arizona State University, students may choose between a performing arts option and a teacher-certification, dance-education option.

Of the programs described, the University of California at Los Angeles has the strongest graduate curriculum, both in terms of numbers of students and the variety of course options.

Other Examples of Dance Curriculum Emphases

Many state colleges and universities continue to offer dance minors or concentrations that are essentially part of a Bachelor of Science degree in physical education. Two state universities in Indiana, at Terre Haute, and Ball State, in Muncie, provide examples of such curricula designed to prepare teachers of physical education with public school certification but with a strong component of dance education skills. Ball State also offers a Bachelor of Arts degree with a heavy emphasis on ballet and performance.

Colleges with Separate Dance Departments

The University of Indiana in Bloomington has had two completely separate dance majors for a number of years. The physical education department has sponsored an undergraduate Dance Education major emphasizing modern dance and recreational dance forms and teaching methods, while there has been a strong separate ballet department in the School of Music.

Similarly, the University of Oklahoma at Norman offers an Educational Dance major and minor in the physical education department which stresses modern dance, folk dance, and teaching methods. Also, at the University of Oklahoma there is a dance department in the School of Drama with an extensive instruction in ballet and modern dance, choreography, and production.

For a number of years, perhaps the most interesting example of such separate departments was found at the University of Utah in Salt Lake City. There, Professor Elizabeth Hayes was in charge of a strong modern dance program within the department of physical education, assisted by such specialists as Virginia Tanner, known for outstanding work in children's dance. At the same time, there was a strong ballet program with an attached ballet theater company in the College of Fine Arts under the direction of William Christensen and Gordon Paxman. Relationships between the two departments were good. Eventually, the modern dance educators sought their independence from physical education; in this case, they joined the ballet program in a separate department of ballet and modern dance in the College of Fine Arts. Although the physical education department wished to retain service classes (classes used to fulfill part of the physical education requirement in general education) in modern dance, all these were assigned as a teaching responsibility to the new department. Folk, square, and social dancing continued to be offered by the physical education department.

There was considerable resistance to this move on the part of physical education administrators at the University of Utah. Thus, although the new department continued to offer a teacher education program in dance with the full

Kathryn Karipides and Kelly Holt, of Dance Training Program at Case Western Reserve University, Cleveland, Ohio.

support of the University's College of Education, the Utah State Office of Education refused to approve state accreditation for dance as an area distinct from physical education. For a time, this meant that the best-prepared teachers of dance were not permitted to teach in all-dance positions in the state's major high schools. In time, the certification policy was changed, and now dance specialists are employed in many secondary schools in Utah. Today, there are separate ballet and modern dance departments, with the ballet program in particular being recognized as one of the leading university-connected ballet curricula in the country.

Another example of a university dance program with several different major curricula and emphases is New York University. For many years this private institution has had a degree program in education connected with the physical education department. This has evolved into a Department of Dance and Dance Education, which offers degrees on the bachelor's, master's, and doctoral levels, with a variety of career options—including dance teaching, dance criticism and writing, studio and dance company management, choreography, and dance company management. In addition, New York University has a separate Department of Dance within the Tisch School of the Arts which emphasizes dance as a performing art.

Performing Arts Emphasis

Many higher education dance curricula have developed strong performing arts emphases, including intensive concentrations in ballet. One of the first such programs was Texas Christian University, which for years has had a Department of Ballet and Modern Dance offering both B.F.A. and M.F.A. degrees.

Similarly, Florida State University in Tallahassee has a Department of Dance with a strong emphasis on ballet and modern dance technique, choreography, and performance. It is administratively located in the University's School of Visual Arts. Students must take course sequences in both ballet and contemporary dance, as well as courses in the musical foundations of dance, history and philosophy, Labanotation, movement analysis, and body alignment.

The dance program at the University of Nevada at Las Vegas is influenced by the numerous hotels and casinos in its area that provide professional entertainment. Many of its students are already professional dancers, and others are either beginning to work in the entertainment industry or planning on that as a goal. All students must take four years of ballet, modern dance, and jazz, as well as other specialized dance forms, including Spanish Flamenco and Broadway Show Dancing.[9]

Other Special Emphases

A different special emphasis is found at Brigham Young University, in Provo, Utah, which features recreational and ethnic dance forms; its International and American Folk Dance Groups have regularly toured the United States, Canada, and Europe. Other performing groups at Brigham Young include a touring and performing Ballroom Dance Team with 450 members, a Theater Ballet Company, Orchesis (a modern dance group), and the Cougarettes, a "pep and precision-dance drill team."

The dance department at Teachers College, Columbia University in New York City, has long offered a special emphasis in Laban Movement Analysis, "effort-shape" theory, and movement for special needs. The University of Hawaii has bachelor's and master's degree curricula in dance ethnology and offers specialized instruction in a wide range of Eastern dance forms, including Chinese, Japanese, Korean, Javanese, and Philippine. The Naropa Institute in Boulder, Colorado, offers both bachelor's and master's programs in dance therapy, with numerous courses in psychology and psychopathology, nonverbal expression, methods in dance therapy, and social systems in group dynamics. York University in Ontario, Canada, offers a professional program in dance therapy linked to Laban "effort-shape" training as part of its four-year Honours B.A. program in its Faculty of Fine Arts. In some cases, dance courses are adapted to meet special needs, as in special ballet classes for women who have had mastectomies at the University of Santa Clara in California.

Visiting Artists and Performing Companies

The strongest single emphasis among college and university dance departments is on developing a high level of performing skill among students and on providing an intensive and sustained contact with dance as an art form. To achieve these goals, many curricula bring in leading dancers, choreographers, and companies for performances, residencies, and workshops.

Woman the Pioneer, choreographed by Virginia Tanner, performed by Brigham Young University dance company, Provo, Utah.

For example, at Randolph-Macon College in Lynchburg, Virginia, Helen McGehee has been director of a Visiting Artists program which has brought leading artists from the Martha Graham, José Limón, and Anna Sokolow Companies and the London School of Contemporary Dance. These guest instructors have given workshops and master classes, taught sections of repertory works, and performed in concerts.

The University of Montana at Missoula has hosted the Alvin Ailey Repertory Ensemble, the Nikolais Dance Theater, Steve Paxton and the Grand Union Company, and numerous other individual performers or groups as visiting artists. In addition, it has cooperated with the Cecchetti Council of America in sponsoring workshops in the Cecchetti ballet instruction method for the Rocky Mountain and Northwest regions of the United States and maintains an active children's theater-

Example of use of dance in therapeutic programs: special ballet class for women who have had mastectomies is offered at University of Santa Clara, Santa Clara, California.

dance company, the Magic Movers, which gives frequent community performances.

Towson State University in Maryland sponsors a University Dance Company which gives as many as thirty lecture-demonstrations or performances and residencies each year in schools and colleges throughout its region. The Towson State Company's work is enhanced by professional choreographers, such as Gus Giordano, William Hug, and Jo Rowan, and it has sponsored residencies by the Ohio Ballet, José Limón Company, and Pilobolus Dance Theater.

A relatively small curriculum at Stockton State College in Pomona, New Jersey, sponsors its own resident dance company and has hosted numerous master classes and performances by well-known professional dance companies and dancers. The Ohio State University Department of Dance has regularly presented such companies or choreographers as the Alvin Ailey Dance Theater, Paul Taylor Company, and Bill Evans in concerts, master classes, and lecture-demonstrations. At Temple University in Philadelphia, there are no fewer than three professional dance companies (Sybil, ZeroMoving Dance Company, and Ann Vachon/Dance Conduit) that are directed by Temple faculty members.

Student dance company at Randolph-Macon Women's College, Lynchburg, Virginia. Photograph by Aubrey Wiley.

In some cases, college and university dance companies perform only works by their department's faculty and student majors. In others, they may reconstruct and perform dances by major choreographers. For example, in a 1987 concert by the Dance Corps of the State University College at Purchase, New York, the following works were presented: *Serenade,* George Balanchine's first American ballet; Lester Horton's *The Beloved,* with staging by Carmen de Lavallade; Merce Cunningham's *Changing Steps;* and Paul Taylor's *Cloven Kingdom.*

In a number of cases, universities have developed outstanding facilities for the performing arts and have become regional cultural centers, with dance as a major component along with music and theater. A leading example is the Krannert Center for the Performing Arts at the University of Illinois. Built in 1969, this campus landmark is an impressive complex of five theaters and concert halls with remarkable support facilities for costume design, lighting, scenery, make-up, and other technical production needs. The Krannert Center hosts as many as 450 performances a year by major symphonies, dance companies, chamber groups, and soloists from the United States and abroad. Increasingly, higher education dance departments have developed expertise in sponsoring such events and in presenting dance companies; Kassing and Wolff, Nunn and Sandback, and Straits have written useful articles on the management of touring dance companies in colleges and universities.[10]

Cooperative College Programs

In some cases, neighboring colleges join together to share their resources or to cooperate in sponsoring dance events or special programs. For example, through a five-college Dance Department which links dance curricula at the University of Massachusetts, Smith College, Mount Holyoke, Hampshire, and Amherst, it has been possible to sponsor courses in dance notation and "effort-shape" with adequate enrollment to justify these classes. In addition, the cooperation approach makes it possible to offer three levels of dance history courses and to sponsor various other seminars taught according to the needs of dance majors on the five campuses. With each of the participating colleges providing dance specialists from its faculty, the overall curriculum is extremely diverse, ranging from extensive ballet and modern dance technique classes to tap dance, contact improvisation, Baroque and Renaissance dance, and methods of dance therapy.

Graduate Degree Programs in Dance

In general, graduate degree programs tend to focus on more theoretical and highly specialized aspects of dance education than undergraduate curricula. For example, the University of North Carolina at Greensboro offers a Master of Fine Arts degree in dance with a thirty-six-point requirement, including a written Comprehensive Examination and a Master's Thesis. Core courses include work in choreography on several levels, and students may elect other courses which survey contemporary dance, dance criticism, dance education, anthropological aspects of dance, dance notation, and music for dance.

The extensive graduate dance curriculum at UCLA offers separate specializations on the Master of Arts level in the following areas: Choreography, Dance Criticism, Dance Ethnology, Dance Kinesiology, Dance Performance, Dance Therapy, and Dance Teaching. For example, the Dance Therapy option offers courses in movement dynamics and personality growth, dance in rehabilitation, seminar in movement therapy, and directed study or research in a hospital or clinic, along with related courses in the behavioral sciences.

One effect of the growing number of graduate programs in dance education is that more and more academically trained professionals are now moving into teaching roles at other colleges and universities. For example, approximately 80 of UCLA's 400 dance alumni are now members or chairpersons of dance programs at other institutions.[11]

Conflict Between Studio and Theoretical Courses

Within the arts, there has always been disagreement between those who stress so-called studio or performing courses on the graduate levels and those who believe that graduate education should be purely theoretical—consisting of courses in history or aesthetics rather than performance. Many dance curricula continue to

Performance by dance company at Texas Woman's University, Denton, Texas. Photograph by Buddy Myers.

emphasize performance on the graduate level, much as a department of theater or music might stress advanced creative work. A considerable number of those who are in graduate programs are interested in developing performing careers, and such programs encourage more advanced levels of technique and increased choreographic understandings, as well as an expanded view of dance as a creative and expressive medium within society.

On the other hand, in some graduate programs—particularly in teachers colleges or schools of education with strong physical education departments—the emphasis is on advanced studies and research of a scientific or theoretical nature. Typically, graduate students are advised to take courses in physiology and kinesiology, motor learning and performance, or psychological and sociological aspects of human movement as reflected in dance and sport.

Whatever the emphasis of individual programs, scholarly investigations of dance as an art form and as an important aspect of cultural life in general need to be encouraged. Over the past fifteen years, there has been considerable growth of interest in dance research in relation to the social and behavioral sciences. Dance history in particular has been the subject of numerous well-attended conferences, and growing numbers of specialists in this area have been developed and are contributing to its professional literature.

Traditionally, the arts have often been regarded as less worthy of scholarly interest than the humanities or the social and physical sciences. To the degree that dance aesthetics and criticism are refined and developed as academic disciplines, dance will gain respect as a serious aspect of university life. It is also important that dance curricula not be dominated solely by professional dancers, active or retired, who are skilled in teaching and directing techniques and performance but who may not be prepared to organize and direct a college or university dance program. There is an important place in dance education for the talents of those who have earned academic degrees and for the courses they offer. The faculty selection process must be sensitive to the need to provide balanced forms of expertise appropriate to the philosophical and applied aspects of each dance curriculum.

Doctoral Programs in Dance

Ebenstein summarized the progress that has been made in an article titled, "A Ph.D. in *What? A Survey of Doctoral Programs in Dance.*"[12] She described a conversation with an individual who, on being told of doctoral degree programs in dance, replied, "Well, I can't believe you can get a Ph.D. in dancing. Do you write your dissertation or perform it?" The comment displays ignorance of trends that have occurred over the past several decades in higher education. In a number of leading university departments in the creative arts, it has long been possible to meet master's or doctoral degree requirements by making a film, composing a symphony or concerto, writing a novel or novella, or accomplishing other major creative projects.

Ebenstein described several Ph.D. and Ed.D. programs in dance, including those at New York University, Temple University, Texas Woman's University, and the University of Wisconsin at Madison. In addition to these curricula, where the doctoral degree is offered by the dance department, other universities make it possible to take a doctoral degree focusing on dance within associated departments, such as music, theater, aesthetics, or ethnology. Ebenstein concluded:

> Although dance research has been conducted for many years, dance has not . . . been widely recognized as a subject of scholarship by the general public. The continuing productivity of these doctoral programs and of their graduates should insure a future upgrading of the academic status of dance. . . . The need is tremendous for additional programs to conduct further research and to train future dance leaders.[13]

(Chapter 18 provides a more detailed discussion of dance research and criticism, including descriptions of leading scholars and organizations in this field.)

Dance Education for Nonmajor Students

Thus far, this chapter has focused exclusively on the role of dance in higher education with respect to the dance major. While this individual is important, there are millions of college students who take dance courses who are *not* dance majors.

The largest single group consists of general education students who may take dance to meet degree requirements for credits in the arts or in physical education. Griffith pointed out that such students are likely to have widely varying motivations and expectations. A student registering for a modern dance class may expect to gain movement skills, receive a whole-body workout, or experience dance as an emotional release or creative outlet. Students in a social dancing class may expect to gain skills, to meet people, or even to learn social etiquette. Griffith wrote:

> If general education students register for a ballet class, they may expect to achieve technical skills, poise, and grace, or may aspire toward performance. If a student registers for a folk dance class, expectations may include acquiring skill in performing dances from a specific country, acquiring knowledge of various cultures of the world, or having fun. Students registering for aerobic dance classes are expecting to improve aspects of their physical fitness. . . .[14]

Whatever their expectations, the college or university dance instructor should not view the nonmajor student as trivial or of secondary importance. Having substantial numbers of general education students in so-called service courses frequently helps department heads or college deans justify their more specialized or advanced dance major courses, which are likely to have a smaller student/instructor ratio and to generate fewer tuition credits.

Contribution to Personal Growth

Of greater importance is that dance may contribute significantly to nonmajor students' personal growth. Hankin described the experience of teaching beginning

University of Utah Dance Company in *Sculpture Garden*, choreographed by Joan Woodbury. Dancers are Edd Pelsmaeker, Robert Beswick, and Rich Rowsell.

modern dancers, college students who had virtually no previous dance training. She commented:

> Faced with a classroom of hyperextended lower backs and apprehensively raised shoulders, I was struck by how uncomfortable these young adults appeared inside of their own bodies. I realized that these students had not heard of a plié, let alone the possibility of experiencing energy streaming through their bodies. They had little foundation on which to build, no store of previously acquired knowledge, no assumptions about how to conduct themselves in a dance class.[15]

Beyond the goals of learning to move more freely and confidently with greater poise and control, students may also learn for the first time to create something that is uniquely theirs. Improvisation, or the development of simple dance compositions (often done as part of beginning modern dance classes) may contribute significantly to this process. Sandback pointed out that beginning students are often terrified by the challenge of simple choreographic tasks and feel great satisfaction when they have met the challenge successfully. In part, Sandback wrote, this is because: ". . . choreography exposes the self. Students are asked to create something that is uniquely theirs. Furthermore, this creation cannot then be set apart from themselves and viewed as an object but usually must be presented on their own bodies—a further revelation of self."[16]

Understanding and Appreciation of Dance. A related outcome is that nonmajor dance students may become more aware of the value of dance as an educational or aesthetic experience. When great numbers of college students take courses in dance, they become more familiar with it as an art form, more enthusiastic, and—hopefully—part of the growing audience for dance in community life.

Dance and Other Special Fields

In addition to its value for major students and for general students, dance also may prove to be a rich area of training and experience for students in other specialized fields, such as theater, music, kinesiology and motor learning, childhood education, or aesthetics.

A common complaint of many dance faculty members in higher education is that their field is not understood or respected by other professors or university administrators. The surest way to improve this is for the dance program to become an integral part of university life through linkages with other academic areas, well-publicized and attended performances by their own companies and by visiting troupes, seminars and festivals and publications, and other strategies designed to familiarize the campus community with dance and to build support for it.

Dance in Physical Education

Dance educators often view the role of a dance major, minor, or concentration within a department of physical education with hostility and disdain. They feel that dance is too often regarded as a small, specialized area in physical education comparable to gymnastics or volleyball and surely not as important as aquatics. Often, it is taught by individuals with limited dance skills forced to use poorly equipped and designed gymnasiums as studios, and it is treated, in effect, as an area of physical skill or social activity of limited importance.

Potential Role for Dance

Dance, even when it is a specialized activity area within physical education, can play a meaningful and important role. The physical education field has been under considerable pressure for a number of years to justify itself and its academic role and purpose. Particularly in higher education, where the requirement of physical education credits for graduation has been abandoned in many institutions, a number of physical education departments have had poor enrollments or have come under attack.

In the mid-1980s, Jewett concluded that physical education in colleges and universities needed to go on the offensive and to work harder at communicating the message that physical education is an essential component of a liberal education. She stated that the basic goals of physical education in colleges and universities include the following:

1. Achievement and maintenance of long-term health-related fitness, including the abilities to be self-directing, physically independent, and capable of minimizing unavoidable deterioration in physical abilities and capacities.
2. Development of motor performance skills that facilitate regular and continuing participation in physical activity and are appropriate to the maintenance of a personally active adult lifestyle.
3. Development of the adult "inner athlete" who seeks active recreation and enhancement of the quality of life through personal fulfillment in challenging and satisfying achievement in physical activities.[17]

Given the emphasis on excellence in today's achievement-oriented society, Jewett stressed the need to demonstrate the highest possible quality of performance within each of these areas of purpose. Clearly, dance can contribute significantly to these goals. Rather than view themselves as underprivileged orphans in departments of physical education, dance educators should make every effort to become part of the mainstream of their departments and to contribute to their fullest effectiveness.

Issue of Administrative Location

Many dance educators are likely to make the case that the only logical place for dance in higher education is in an arts-related administrative location. Therefore, we explore the pros and cons of dance's past and present relationship with physical education in colleges and universities.

Historically, dance education in the United States came into being under the sponsorship of physical educators and has long been viewed as an important activity area in that field. Many physical educators have strongly supported dance as the "aesthetic side of physical education" or for its social and physical values. Without question, that it has been part of the physical education *requirement* has meant that vast numbers of students have been exposed to dance through the years.

However, those who are dissatisfied with the place of dance in physical education point out that in most physical education departments, dance is treated primarily as a form of exercise rather than as a creative or artistic experience. When it is sponsored by physical education, dance seldom assumes a role in school or college programs comparable to that of music or fine art. Indeed, dance educators claim that the size of classes and other administrative circumstances surrounding the provision of dance in physical education make it impossible for it to function effectively as aesthetic education.

The point has already been made that dance is often taught by physical education teachers who are poorly equipped in this field (with foreseeably disappointing, and often disastrous, results), while individuals who have excellent training in dance may not be permitted to teach it—unless they have physical education credentials. It is claimed that physical educators rarely see dance as a vital concern or promote its interests as strongly as they do sports and other aspects of the physical education program. In college programs, while they support courses in basic dance skills, they are often reluctant to introduce more advanced technique courses or courses in dance composition, production, history, or notation. Teachers of dance are often compelled to teach courses in other physical education activities in which they have been inadequately prepared.

Finally, as mentioned earlier, the argument is advanced that having dance sponsored by women's physical education departments perpetuates the separation of men and women in this field, whereas having it as a separate department would mean that both sexes would be able to study it with less difficulty.

Essentially, many dance educators feel that these reasons justify taking dance—particularly dance as an art form—out of the administrative sponsorship of physical education. On the other hand, the majority of physical educators continue to affirm the relationship, seeing dance as a valid aspect of physical education and stressing that in this setting it has administrative support that it would not readily gain if independent. Other authorities argue that dance is an essential part of the discipline of physical education, which is the "science and art of movement." Celeste Ulrich made a strong case for this argument:

> . . . movement is our unique means of education. Certainly dance has been recognized for a long time as the purest of all movement expression. It is an activity which fosters the complete utilization of the total body in order to express meaning and interpret feelings. In a sense, dance permits and encourages the sort of body expression that sports activities only allow in rigid and stratified patterns.[18]

Ulrich expressed the views of many physical education leaders:

> . . . it seems inappropriate for dance educators to seek organizational formats which cater to the fine arts and drama. The logical place to administer and organize

dance is as a viable entity of . . . physical education. Both dance educators and sport educators can touch hands in the arena of human movement. To ensure that this is an honest interface, it will be necessary for departments and schools of health and physical education to add dance to their titles—a phenomenon already under way.

It will also be necessary for the new band of dance educators to acknowledge the artistry and expression found in gymnastics, sports, and aquatics. The dancers' world cannot be apart from these movement forms; it must be a part of the whole world of human movement.[19]

These arguments represent the viewpoint of many influential physical educators and college administrators today. It seems unlikely that they will consent to a severing of the relationship between dance and physical education. Therefore, for the foreseeable future, there will probably continue to be three different models of dance sponsorship in colleges and universities: (a) departments which are located in schools or administrative units of theater arts, music, or fine arts, which emphasize ballet and modern dance, choreography, and performance; (b) arrangements in which there are separate curricula in the same institution (one a department of dance as a performing art, and one located within or attached to a department of physical education, with an emphasis on teacher education); and (c) programs in which dance plays a limited role as part of the service program for all students, or is at most a minor area of specialization for physical education majors.

University Dance Programs as Preprofessional Training

One must ask whether college-level preprofessional training in dance is really feasible. Is it possible to bring a dancer to the required level of professional performing competence in a college or university program? In the past, few institutions have had programs of the required intensity and standard of instruction. Because of all the other requirements of the college curriculum, the dance major may not be able to give enough energy and time to work in dance. A physical educator, Eleanor Metheny, questioned whether the serious artist should be in college at all:

> . . . at best, it can only lay the foundation for the later development of the student artist's talents; at worst, it may encourage him to dissipate talents in diversity and quasi-artistic performances at the dilettante level. For the dancer, whose life-span as a performer is limited by the effects of age on the body, this delay in accepting the rigorous requirements of preparation for full use of talent and creativity may well be disastrous. . . .[20]

This concern is more critical today than it might have been two or three decades ago because of the higher expectations that are placed on young dancers who seek to break into the professional world. In the past, many modern dance companies had a relatively low standard as far as the training and technique of their members was concerned. Similarly, on the musical stage or other fields of dance entertainment, it was possible to get by with a moderate degree of dance skill.

The Texas Christian University Ballet Company, with Zac Ward, Barbara Macklen, and Julie Rigler, in *Aurora*.

Today, such companies have become far more demanding. Modern dance groups often require that their members have extensive training in ballet, and dancers in television, night clubs, or other popular entertainment settings must normally be skilled in modern, ballet, jazz, tap, and other dance forms.

Many of the students who enter college as performing arts dance majors today have not had the kind of intensive training that they should have had during adolescence if they are to mature into highly skilled performing artists. The real professional dancer—particularly in ballet—will already have had several years of intensive training and, at the age of eighteen or nineteen, may well be serving his or her apprenticeship in a professional or semiprofessional ballet company or on the musical stage. Too often, dance majors in college have little idea of the commitment required to become a professional dancer. Murray Louis wrote:

> . . . the art of dance must be approached as seriously as any art or science. It would never dawn on anyone that pre-med students would study without an enormous dedication to their art. Law or science in general could not be studied without dedication. Our art is plagued with dilettantism; I don't know why. There is something very polite that has been associated with the word *dance,* and this generally turns out a very well-placed young lady who knows how to carry herself and to sit well.[21]

To some degree, this problem is mitigated by the higher standards that many college and university dance departments are now beginning to impose. Today, a number of such departments hold competitive auditions around the country for those who seek admission to them as dance majors. Many departments today offer greater emphasis on technique development than in the past, and their graduates reflect this higher level of training.

Other Advanced Forms of Dance Education

Advanced training in dance as an art form does not only take place in colleges and universities. The highest level of performing skill is usually developed in the professional studios associated with leading performers or dance companies, or the outstanding dance conservatories or academies that serve both youth and adults.

Their work is supplemented by special master classes, workshops, short-term courses, and similar programs sponsored by the leading professional organizations in the field, such as the Dance Masters of America, Inc., the Cecchetti Council of America, the National Dance Association, and similar groups. Such organizations not only provide ongoing training for adult teachers and performers, but they also examine the business techniques involved in operating studios and schools or in managing dance companies. As in other professions, dance teachers, performers, choreographers, and entrepreneurs and managers must continue to grow and develop throughout their careers if they are to be successful. Thus, continuing higher education in dance is essential for those who are seriously committed to it as a professional endeavor.

Notes

1 Alma Hawkins, cited in Sandra Minton, "Alma Hawkins: An Academic Perspective," *Journal of Physical Education, Recreation and Dance*, May–June 1986, p. 40.

2 Vera Lundahl, ed., *Dance Directory: Programs of Professional Preparation in American Colleges and Universities* (Reston, Va.: National Dance Association, American Alliance for Health, Physical Education, and Recreation, 1986).

3 See Richard Kraus and Sarah Chapman, *History of the Dance in Art and Education*, 2d ed. (Englewood Cliffs, N.J.: Prentice-Hall, 1981), pp. 292–95.

4 See, for example, Dance Directory in *Dance Magazine*, September 1988, pp. 105–13.

5 See *Data Summary: Higher Education Arts Data Services (HEADS)* (Reston, Va.: National Association of Schools of Dance, 1985–1986).

6 Louanne Norwood and Terry Worthy, "Dance Teacher Evaluation," *Journal of Physical Education, Recreation and Dance*, February 1986, p. 85, and "Job Classifications— Writers, Artists and Entertainers," in *Occupational Outlook Handbook* (Washington, D.C.: U.S. Dept. of Labor, 1988), p. 197.

7 The Association has also monitored the field and gathered total statistics of dance in higher education, including data summaries of dance degrees, enrollments, faculty members, etc. See *Data Summary, Higher Education Arts Data Services*.

8 Ibid.

9 Carole Rae, "From Scratch: A Dance Program Emerges," *Journal of Physical Education, Recreation and Dance,* May–June 1986, pp. 37, 55. See also Jan Wilkens, "Landing a Job in Las Vegas," *Dance Teacher Now,* October 1986, pp. 15–16.

10 See Gayle Kassing and Bernard Wolff, "A Guide to University Dance Company Touring," *Journal of Physical Education, Recreation and Dance,* November–December 1982, pp. 35–36, 41; also articles by Melissa Nunn and Patricia Sandback and Sue Ann Straits in same issue.

11 Carol Scot Horn, "Dance in Higher Education: UCLA Department of Dance," *Dance Teacher Now,* January–February 1988, p. 35.

12 Barbara J. Ebenstein, "A Ph.D. in *What?* A Survey of Doctoral Programs in Dance," *Journal of Physical Education, Recreation and Dance,* October 1986, pp. 18–21.

13 Ibid., p. 20.

14 Betty Rose Griffiths, "New Approaches: Dance for General Education Students," *Journal of Physical Education, Recreation and Dance,* May–June 1986, p. 36. See also Carole Sokolow-Casten, "Aerobics in College: What Do the Students Want?", *Dance Teacher Now,* February 1986, p. 28.

15 Toby Hankin, "The Technique Class: How Can We Help Students to Dance?" *Journal of Physical Education, Recreation and Dance,* November–December 1986, p. 36.

16 Patricia R. Sandback, "Structuring Beginning Choreographic Experiences," *Journal of Physical Education, Recreation and Dance,* November–December 1986, p. 38.

17 Ann E. Jewett, "Excellence or Obsolescence: Goals for Physical Education in Higher Education," *Journal of Physical Education, Recreation and Dance,* September 1985, p. 39.

18 Celeste Ulrich, "Dance as an Art Form in Physical Education, A Symposium by Selected Educators," *Journal of Health, Physical Education and Recreation,* January 1964, p. 55.

19 Celeste Ulrich, "Education for a Dynamic Lifestyle," *Journal of Physical Education and Recreation,* May 1977, p. 48.

20 Eleanor Metheny, "Dance as an Art Form in Physical Education," p. 19.

21 Murray Louis, in *Dance as a Discipline, Focus on Dance IV,* ed. Nancy W. Smith (Washington, D.C.: American Association for Health, Physical Education, and Recreation, 1967), p. 35.

CHAPTER 18

Dance Research
and Criticism

. . . the dance field [is] an art form that is inextricably related to the science of the body. No matter what area of inquiry is chosen—with the possible exception of dance history which has begun to accumulate a body of literature—there is a need for basic theory building, the posing and testing of relevant research questions and hypotheses, the generation of data, and the publication of results so that knowledge can be disseminated and serve as a catalyst for continuing and more sophisticated research.[1]

Dance criticism is a misunderstood art. Everyone has a version of what a dance critic should be: publicist, cheerleader, litterateur, adviser, consumer guide. Everyone has his own favorite myth: dance critics are frustrated dancers; dance critics are power brokers; dance critics are parasites on the dance community. Even dance critics misunderstand themselves. Theirs is a profession in search of an identity, an art form that is constantly redefining itself.[2]

ACCOMPANYING THE GROWTH OF DANCE AS A RESPECTED ART FORM has been the emergence of an impressive body of scholarly studies in dance. These studies attest to the recognition of dance as a significant aspect of human culture, and they contribute to our understanding of dance's role in society. They include a wide range of published writings, from newspaper reviews of dance performances or popular books about famous dance artists, to much more abstruse articles or texts dealing with the aesthetics of dance or specialized periods of dance history.

A key factor in the development of dance scholarship over the past twenty years has been the establishment of numerous university graduate programs that require master's degree or doctoral candidates to write theses or dissertations. In addition, several national organizations have been founded that promote research and criticism in dance as an academic discipline and that publish journals serving scholars in the field.

Meaning of Research and Criticism

Exactly what do the terms *research* and *criticism* mean? Leedy commented that the word *research* has been so loosely used in everyday conversation that few of us understand its real meaning. It has become common jargon, used to describe everything from casual observation or skimming through magazines and books, to rigorous sociological studies or experiments in scientific laboratories. Typically, we think of research as the process of gathering knowledge. However, Leedy wrote: ". . . no matter how elaborate the collection of data, the mere accumulation of fact is not research. It is, rather, an exercise in information-gathering, in library-orientation, in ferreting out relevant bits of factual data, in self-enlightenment—but it is not *research*."[3]

Research extends far beyond the familiar course assignment which involves looking up a number of facts in bibliographic sources and writing them down in a documented paper—or even beyond carrying out a simple survey or conducting a set of interviews. Instead, research should involve *systematic inquiry,* which is purposeful and carefully directed, using scientifically designed data-gathering methods and controls to arrive at valid and trustworthy results. It is concerned not only with gathering facts, but also with identifying patterns of behavior and events. These may lead to hypotheses to be tested, or to theories which help to explain or interpret human behavior or other natural phenomena. Summing up, research is defined in *Webster's New International Dictionary* as: "Studious inquiry or examination . . . critical and exhaustive investigation or experimentation having for its aim the discovery of new facts and their correct interpretation, the revision of accepted conclusions, theories, or laws, in the light of newly discovered facts, or the practical application of such new or revised conclusions."[4]

Selma Jeanne Cohen, a leading dance historian, wrote that history is concerned with discovering what has been called the "configuration of continuums"—meaning that within any sphere of human culture, there are trends or sequences of activity which can readily be identified: "Everything is constantly moving and changing, and the historian must arrest the momentary configuration, or pattern, which he discovers within all of his facts. Although a simple chronology has tremendous value, particularly in dance where we have really recovered so little as yet, chronology is not history. . . ."[5] Cohen wrote that the dance historian must be able to place the subject under review within the context of the period in which it occurred. In referring to the "climate of ideas" at a given time, she stressed that not only ideas about dancing are important; instead, the historian must consider all the cultural, social, and political influences of the period: "These ideas affect what the choreographer does and how the dancer interprets it. No great choreographer ever lived in an ivory tower; a choreographer is a part of his time and reflects that time, and we can understand him only in relation to his time."[6]

Use of Varied Research Methods

While history represents one major research method that is employed in dance scholarship—as in the other performing arts—it is not the only method used.

Instead, research may involve any of the following techniques: (a) *anthropological* study, in which the popular dance forms of a given culture or social group are observed and analyzed; (b) *psychological* analysis, in which the motivations and values of dance may be explored, or in which the creative process itself may be studied; (c) *sociological* examinations of dance, in relation to such variables as social class, age, gender, economic, or other factors; (d) *philosophical* reviews, which analyze the aesthetics of dance choreography and performance, or which examine dance itself in the light of different philosophical theories; or (e) *kinesiological* or *physiological* methods, which are concerned primarily with the physical performance of dance as an aspect of human movement subject to basic scientific laws.

The Nature of Criticism

How does criticism relate to dance research? Both processes have much in common. What distinguishes criticism from research is that it tends to be a highly personal process, rather than one which relies on rigorous research techniques or methods of analysis. A major thrust of dance criticism concerns making judgments, in that dance critics typically review and appraise dance performances and present their reactions for the public at large in newspapers or magazines. Shelton defined dance criticism as follows: "Fundamentally, dance criticism is a blend of perception, analysis, and expression. It requires equal parts seeing, understanding, and communicating. Above all, it is a participatory art in which the seer interacts with the seen."[7]

Shelton pointed out that the skilled critic must have an acute and lively eye, able to determine subtle shifts in space, time, and dynamics—and must also possess powers of analysis, a rich background in dance history and personalities, and awareness of technical elements of dance.

The professional role of the dance critic may vary greatly. Shelton wrote that some critics seek to serve as a second pair of eyes for their readers, acting as "consumer guides" who advise readers on how to spend their entertainment dollars. Others wish to serve the dance community, or envision themselves as "power brokers" who can make or unmake careers, influence the policies of dance companies or organizations, or attach themselves to the economic structures that surround the performing arts.[8]

Relevance of Dance Research and Criticism

Why is it important for dance students and educators to be aware of current trends in dance research and criticism? One crucial reason is that dance has rarely been regarded as an art comparable to the other performing or literary arts. Anderson, for example, commented that we have historically taken a cavalier attitude toward choreography because, despite pious protestations to the contrary, dance has not been considered a serious art form. Anderson wrote: "We have been so brainwashed by prudes, who call dance immoral, and pedants, who call it trivial, that we find it difficult to regard dance as potentially equal to poetry or music."[9]

Other factors aside, one reason for this failure to recognize the artistic significance of dance has been its ephemeral quality. Dance happens—and then it disappears. Only during the past few decades, with the invention of Labanotation and filming or videotaping techniques, has it been possible to capture a dance work and reconstruct authentic versions of it after a considerable lapse of time. As a result, Anderson wrote:

> Dance may be an art of magnificent spectacle, but it is an art surprisingly lacking in any sizable and coherently organized body of choreographic literature that can be compared with the extant bodies of musical or dramatic literature. Precious few examples of historically important choreography can be seen anywhere. The creations of the 18th- and early 19th-century reformers—including those of Jean-Georges Noverre, Gasparo Angiolini and Salvatore Vigano—are totally lost. No complete ballet exists by Jules Perrot. Not many exist by the prolific Marius Petipa [or the great 19th-century Danish] choreographer, August Bournonville.[10]

Preservation and Reconstruction of Dances

As chapter 13 pointed out, many important works of leading twentieth-century choreographers and dance companies are now preserved on film or videotape. Beyond this, there has been a growing effort to reconstruct dances of earlier periods. In 1988, the International Dance Biennale in Lyons, France, featured live performances and public balls, films, and video showings which depicted four centuries of dance in France, ranging from Renaissance court dances to the latest experimental dance works. Some dance films have been revived and made available in recent years, from existing footage, to show the work of leading dance pioneers—among them Mary Wigman, Ruth St. Denis, Ted Shawn, Harald Kreutzberg, and others. More and more, the work of today's choreographers and companies will be preserved through film for future generations to enjoy and learn from.

However, merely reconstructing dances of the past is not enough. A primary goal of scholarly research is to recapture and interpret the complete history of dance in terms of its major influences, choreographers, social functions, and traditions. If we are to understand the varied roles dance has played in human culture or in relation to religion, therapy, education, or entertainment, such research is essential.

Beyond these needs, Brennan pointed out that, if dance is to be established and respected as a valued art form in our society, we must have evidence that confirms its purposes and values. Commenting that the National Dance Association has sought to gain support for dance education as a means of enhancing the quality of life for children, youth, and adults, Brennan wrote:

> However, there is little research to show that dance really does develop aesthetic values, foster self-confidence and self-awareness, promote appropriate socialization skills, enhance creative thinking, or provide any of the other values we feel and write about so strongly. Research in this area would begin to tell us if what we claim about the importance of dance can be verified. . . .[11]

Finally, there are many unanswered questions about the processes of dance training and performance that cry out for greater exploration and understanding.

Juana de Laban commented that dancers in the past were rarely concerned with dance research and tended to rely on highly subjective or intuitive approaches to explaining their art. She wrote that many dancers still give credence to "traditional notions of beauty, the sublime in art, and to conventional modes of expression," rather than come to grips with other theories or approaches to aesthetic analysis that would be more useful in today's world.[12]

History of Dance Research and Criticism

A number of leading dance authors during the Renaissance made important contributions to this art form and should be viewed as pioneers in dance criticism and analysis. One of the first of these was Guglielmo Ebreo, the so-called Jewish dancing master of the Renaissance, who taught dance in the Italian courts of the late 1400s and who wrote extensively about the dances themselves and their execution. The most important record of sixteenth-century dancing was the *Orchesographie* of Thoinot Arbeau, a Catholic priest with varied scholarly interests who published an extensive history and description of the dances performed in the French and Italian courts of this period.

Pierre Beauchamps, regarded as the first great French dancer and ballet master to King Louis XIV of France in the late seventeenth century, was a leading authority on dance who codified the fundamentals of ballet movement and developed the first system of dance notation. Following him, Jean Georges Noverre was an eighteenth-century reformer of ballet whose book, *Letters on Dancing and Ballet,* expressed a radical philosophy of dance as a dramatic art. Other writers in this period contributed to the growing body of dance literature; in England, John Playford published an immense collection of country dances performed in the late seventeenth and early eighteenth centuries.

Gradually, critics of dance who were not themselves performers or choreographers emerged. In nineteenth-century France, for example, Théophile Gautier was a leading journalist and dramatic critic who helped shape popular interest in the ballet; other influential writers of this period were Stephane Mallarmé and Jules Lemaître. With growing interest in dance as an art form, a number of dance historians explored classical sources and began to develop a comprehensive history of dance in Europe. Gaston Vuillier wrote *A History of Dance,* which described the major epochs of dance's development in Europe and the Middle East.[13]

In the United States, there were few writers who specialized in dance. Indeed, for the first few decades of the twentieth century, it was common practice for newspapers to have their music or drama critics—and sometimes even sports reporters—review dance performances. However, gradually a number of writers who specialized in dance were employed by leading newspapers, and dance criticism as a field of special expertise came into being.

Early American Dance Critics

One of the first of these American dance critics was Carl Van Vechten, a journalist and photographer who was assistant music critic for the *New York Times* during the period from 1906 to 1913 and who reviewed ballet performances as well as such premodern dancers as Isadora Duncan, Maud Allen, and Loie Fuller. Another important dance critic was H. T. Parker, music, drama, and dance reviewer for the *Boston Evening Transcript,* who wrote reviews of Anna Pavlova, Mary Wigman, and the Denishawn company, among others, during the first three decades of this century. Edwin Denby was a dancer-choreographer and poet before becoming a dance critic in the 1930s. His viewpoint strongly influenced the field of dance criticism; he made it clear that the reviewer should be highly knowledgeable in the history and theory of dance styles, eras, and performers.

During the post-World War I period, a number of writers emerged in Europe as influential dance critics, including the Russian-born Parisian, André Levinson and the widely published British ballet authority, Cyril Beaumont. In mid-century America, several leading critics gained reputations as dance authorities, including John Martin, reviewer for the *New York Times* for several decades; Walter Terry, reviewer for the *New York Herald-Tribune;* and Walter Sorell, who wrote for a number of publications. In addition to their regular reviews, they also wrote a number of highly successful books dealing with dance history and the current dance scene in America, including John Martin's *Book of the Dance,*[14] Terry's *The Dance in America,*[15] and Sorell's *The Dance Has Many Faces.*[16] Other books published during this period included Ted Shawn's *Dance We Must,*[17] George Amberg's *Ballet, The Emergence of An American Art,*[18] Agnes de Mille's *The Book of the Dance,*[19] and Lincoln Kirstein's *Dance: A Short History of Classical Theatrical Dancing.*[20]

Scholarly Research in Dance

Although these authors obviously carried out research as preparation for their writing, with the exception of Kirstein they relied heavily on secondary sources and on their own subjective appraisal of the dance scene.

Curt Sachs's book, *World History of the Dance,* was viewed for several decades as an authoritative account of the development of dance in earlier historical periods and in non-Western societies.[21] Recent critics have concluded that many of the sources that Sachs used were ethnocentrically biased, reflecting the "colonialist" misconception that Western European culture was the highest form of human civilization.[22] Although he dealt seriously with non-Western, ancient, and other traditional dance forms, Sachs saw them not so much as autonomous cultural expressions with their own value systems and symbolic meanings, but rather as primitive stages or elementary building blocks in the vertical development of Western art dance.

During the decades that followed World War II, a number of individual researchers began to make significant contributions to the field of dance scholarship. Among the leading scholars to emerge at this time were Lillian Lawler, Lillian Moore, Katherine Dunham, and Gertrude Kurath.

As an example of growing specialization in dance research, Lawler's *The Dance in Ancient Greece*[23] consisted of a comprehensive study of relevant passages in Greek literature, archaeological findings, surviving notation of early Greek music, and other anthropological and comparative sources of data. Based on her personal expertise in Greek classical literature and culture, Lawler was able to synthesize and interpret materials in order to arrive at a systematic, accurate picture of dance in this early period of history.

Researcher Lillian Moore has been described as ". . . an experienced dance historian and social historian who is equipped with high-powered ingenuity as a detective, a global navigator, a person able to sift apparently meaningless material in search of meaning."[24] She began as a ballet dancer in the American Ballet, Metropolitan Opera Ballet, and other companies in the 1930s and 1940s, and she retired from the stage in the mid-1950s to become a teacher, principally at Robert Joffrey's American Ballet Center, and a writer.[25] Moore did dance reviews and feature articles for London's *Dancing Times* and the *New York Times* and *New York Herald-Tribune,* and, in time, for scholarly dance journals like the *Dance Index* and *Dance Perspectives.* Her area of special expertise was the history of theatrical dancing in America, from its beginnings in the early 1700s to the late nineteenth century.[26]

Katherine Dunham, whose performing career was summarized in chapter 12, was far more than a producer of popular dance revues in the ethnic genre. Instead, she was a recognized dance anthropologist whose work bridged the gap between two categories of dance scholarship described by anthropologist Alan Merriam: the humanities-oriented, art-aesthetic point of view, and the social science approach, which examines dance from an anthropological or sociocultural perspective. Both in her teaching and in her choreographic work, Katherine Dunham fused anthropological research in traditional dance forms with performance-oriented goals. Dunham also wrote extensively on subjects including Caribbean dance forms, as in *Journey to Accompong.*[27]

Gertrude Kurath was trained in modern dance in Germany and the United States. Having taught dance from the 1920s through the mid-1940s, she shifted her professional focus to dance ethnology and ethnomusicology, carrying out extensive research on North and Central American Indian folklore. She published widely, both in dance magazines and such scholarly journals as *Current Anthropology,* and she also wrote a number of respected books, including *Dances of Anahuac.*[28] In 1961, she founded the Dance Research Center at Ann Arbor, Michigan, which is affiliated with the Society for Ethnomusicology and was created to serve as a research resource center for dance ethnologists. Kurath was particularly influential in encouraging and developing the careers of a number of individuals who have become leading dance ethnologists over the past two decades, including Joanne Kealiinohomoku, Judith Lynne Hanna, and Anya Peterson Royce.

During the 1970s and 1980s, dance scholarship expanded rapidly both in terms of its scope and variety and the quality of investigative and analytical techniques used. Conferences of dance scholars are held regularly, and various research centers have been established both in the United States and abroad.

Major Types of Research Designs

Research in dance—as in the physical or social sciences—may take several different forms. Typically, these are classified under the following headings: (a) descriptive

research; (b) experimental research; (c) historical research; and (d) philosophical/
analytical.

Descriptive Research. This involves any type of study which examines current
practices or other phenomena by gathering data, analyzing, and interpreting it in
order to provide an accurate picture of the subject. Best defined descriptive research
in the following terms:

> A descriptive study describes and interprets what is. It is concerned with
> conditions or relationships that exist, opinions that are held, processes that are
> going on, effects that are evident, or trends that are developing. It is primarily
> concerned with the present, although it often considers past events and influences
> as they relate to current conditions.[29]

Descriptive research may make use of a variety of investigative techniques,
including direct observation; surveys through the use of questionnaires or interviews; case studies of individuals or organizations; or longitudinal studies, which
examine practices over a period of time.

Customarily, descriptive research is done in field situations. Anthropological
observation of authentic dance practices is a typical example of its application.
However, if it is to be effective, it must involve more than simply describing the
outward manifestation of the dance; instead, it must relate the dance to social
customs, religious beliefs, and gender roles, and may trace its relationship to other
practices or place it within the context of overall anthropological theory.

Numerous studies of this type have been reported at Congress on Research in
Dance (CORD) conferences, including Elsie Dunin's *Lindo in the Context of Village
Life in the Dubrovnik Area of Yugoslavia;*[30] Sandra Green's *The Sacred Dances of
Ladakh;*[31] and Candi de Alaiza's *The Evolution of the Basque Jota as a Competitive
Form.*[32]

Another type of descriptive study is an analysis of the mechanics of dance
movement based on anatomical and kinesiological research. Here, principles of
physical science are applied to identify, describe, and compare different elements in
dance performance. Two examples of such studies are: Margaret Gray and Margaret
Skrinar's *Support Base Use in Two Dance Idioms;*[33] and Priscilla Clarkson, Theresa
Kennedy, and Jeanne Flanagan's *A Study of Three Movements in Classical Ballet.*[34]

Still other descriptive dance studies may be concerned with current practices in
dance education, the economics of dance performance, public attitudes regarding
dance, government policy and the arts, employment in dance, or business practices
in dance schools and studios.[35]

Experimental Research. Experimental research is generally considered to be
the most rigorous and trustworthy type of research and is used extensively within
the physical sciences, where it is possible to control various elements in the research
and to measure outcomes precisely. It is essentially a form of action research, in that
the researcher structures actual situations and controls certain variables in order to
measure their effect. While experiments may take different forms, the key elements
in the classical type of experimental study include the following:

(a) presentation of a formal hypothesis, in which the investigator states clearly the proposition that the research is intended to test; (b) random selection or formation of two or more groups of subjects, including "control" and "experimental" groups; (c) pretesting of both groups on measures of the quality or performance element that the study is investigating; (d) application of one or more experimental procedures or "interventions"; and (e) posttesting of both groups.[36]

In dance, experimental studies have been conducted which examine the physiological effects of various types of dance. Examples include Luc Léger's *Energy Cost of Disco Dancing,*[37] Dowdy, Cureton, DuVal, and Outzts's *Effects of Aerobic Dance on Physical Work Capacity, Cardiovascular Function and Body Composition of Middle-Aged Woman,*[38] and Clarkson, Freedson, Keller, and Skrinar's *Maximal Oxygen Uptake, Nutritional Patterns and Body Composition of Adolescent Female Ballet Dancers.*[39] Other examples of recently published research include Lesté and Rust's *Effects of Dance on Anxiety,*[40] and Crain, Eisenhart, and McLaughlin's *Application of a Multiple Measurement Approach to Investigate the Effects of a Dance Program on Educable Mentally Retarded Adolescents.*[41] Still other studies have examined the cardiovascular fitness, flexibility, and strength of dancers, or such variables as age, gender, and the number of years in dance training in relation to the development of technical dance skill.[42]

Historical Research. This has been the most widely found type of research in dance, with literally hundreds of books and articles dealing with specific periods of dance history or with leading dancers and companies. Historical research too often has dealt superficially with earlier events, with names, dates, chronologies, and a dry recounting of discovered facts. A more meaningful approach to historical research is social history, which weaves together the complex lives of people in past societies, showing the interaction of religion, government, daily living patterns, economic factors, and social customs. Best wrote: "History . . . is not merely a list of chronological events, but a truthful integrated account of the relationships between persons, events, times, and places. We use history to understand the past, and to try to understand the present in light of past events and developments."[43]

Historical research makes use of two types of data: (a) information drawn from *primary sources,* which are eyewitness accounts or firsthand reports of events and trends as reported by actual observers or participants, including letters, diaries, autobiographies, transcriptions of oral history, and official documents and records; and (b) *secondary sources,* which are secondhand accounts in which word of mouth, translated, or interpreted information is presented. Obviously, primary sources are regarded as more valid. Ideally, historical research in dance, as in other fields, is conducted within a theoretical framework and involves interpretation that gives meaning to the source material.

Most of the dance history texts that have been written—including this one—depend heavily on bibliographical research of existing sources, including both primary and secondary citations. However, many shorter research articles and monographs involve in-depth historical analysis and original critical interpretation. As an example of the range and diversity of published research in dance history, the

Dance Research Journal for spring 1984 presented an international bibliography of dance history articles and books published in a single year, with 180 separate entries.

Philosophical/Analytical Research. In direct contrast to the other types of research designs, which usually gather and analyze factual data, this form of research is primarily concerned with ideas or concepts. For example, philosophers such as Susanne Langer, Monroe Beardsley, and Nelson Goodman, although not primarily concerned with dance, have examined it as a form of communication. Folklorists, art historians, and ethnomusicologists such as Robert Farris Thompson and Alan Lomax have dealt with dance as an important element in lineage-based cultures. Dance-trained anthropologists such as Jeanne Kealiinohomoku and Judith Lynne Hanna, and sociologists such as Katrina Hazzard-Gordon, have documented dance's role as a societal function. Other dance-trained scholars with a strong philosophical orientation include Maxine Sheets-Johnstone and Susan Foster. Sheets-Johnstone's area of expertise is phenomenology, a specialized contemporary branch of philosophy; while Foster focuses on semiotics, a branch of linguistics which Maya Pines described as a relatively new "fashionable academic discipline" concerned with decoding the meaning of messages that surround us in modern life.[44] In some cases, dance scholars probe deeply into the philosophies of leading dancers or choreographers, as in Dianne Howe's study of mysticism in the philosophy and choreography of Mary Wigman.[45]

Finally, there are numerous newspaper writers and critics whose primary function has been to review current performances but who have extended their writings to articles and sometimes books which examine dance from a broader and more scholarly perspective. Such writers include Arline Croce, Don McDonagh, Jack Anderson, Anna Kisselgoff, Deborah Jowitt, and Marcia Siegel. Of the contemporary researchers, writers, and critics (in many cases, the roles are interchangeable), a number are employed as university faculty members—either in dance departments or in departments of philosophy, drama, communications, American culture, or related fields.

Organizations Promoting Scholarship in Dance

Dance has developed a cadre of scholarly societies which promote research and publication both for the dance field itself and for a broader academic audience. These groups usually cooperate in sharing resources, encouraging admission to each other's conferences at member rates, and cosponsoring major seminars and workshops. Such cooperation is essential to the overall development of dance scholarship at this time. Rosen, Souriau, and Rubin wrote: "Today's bleak economic picture has helped to make cooperative effort more attractive than in the past, when organizations were fearful of losing their identities."[46]

Among the organizations sponsoring, promoting, or publishing dance research and criticism today in the United States are: American Dance Guild (ADG); American Dance Therapy Association (ADTA); Congress on Research in Dance (CORD); Cross Cultural Dance Resources (CCDR); Dance Notation Bureau (DNB); Dance Research Center; Laban Institute of Movement Studies (LIMS); and Society of Dance History Scholars (SDHS).

American Dance Guild. This organization has made publication a major focus of its activities, and it publishes books and bibliographies on dance and dance pedagogy. The *ADG Newsletter* is published bimonthly; *Dance Scope* was published as a quarterly for sixteen years; and *American Dance,* an annual publication, was established in 1986. ADG also conducts workshops, seminars, special events (such as a major dance film series), and sponsors an annual conference on dance.

American Dance Therapy Association. This organization promotes the development of dance therapy in several ways. It has established the Marian Chace Memorial Fund to encourage educational, literary, or scientific studies involving dance and mental health. Its publications include the quarterly *Newsletter;* the annual *American Journal of Dance Therapy;* the annual *Membership Directory;* the *Dance Therapy Bibliography;* and numerous monographs and conference proceedings. ADTA holds an annual conference each June.

Congress on Research in Dance (CORD). This professional group has been described as:

> An interdisciplinary open membership, nonprofit organization dedicated to encouraging research in all aspects of dance and related fields; fostering the exchange of ideas, resources and research methods in dance and related areas through publications, conferences, symposia, institutes and other media; and promoting the accessibility of research materials.[47]

CORD's publications include the semiannual *Dance Research Journal* and *Newsletter* and the *Dance Research Annual;* its annual conference is held each October.

Cross Cultural Dance Resources. Established to promote cultural pluralism and intercultural understanding, this organization houses literature archives, audiovisual materials, instruments and costumes, and other materials vital to researching dance as a force in different societies and cultures. Housed in Flagstaff, Arizona, close to the campus of Northern Arizona University, CCDR publishes a quarterly newsletter and sponsors workshops, lectures, and seminars.

Dance Notation Bureau. An outgrowth of the work of Rudolf von Laban (see page 129), the Dance Notation Bureau was established to develop improved dance notation systems and to document and preserve major dance works through collecting notation scores. DNB's Ohio State University extension is an accredited school using the method which trains dance notators, reconstructors, and teachers. Its library holds over 3,000 notation scores, as well as theses, dissertations, books, and articles, and its publications include the semiannual *Dance Notation Journal* and *Newsletter;* the annual *School Catalog;* and texts on Labanotation and effort-shape.

Dance Research Center. Founded in 1961 by Gertrude Kurath, this facility was established to meet the needs of scholars in the specialized field of dance ethnology and is affiliated with the Society for Ethnomusicology. The Center functions as an international clearinghouse in this field and publishes dance-related reports and reviews in the *Journal of Ethnomusicality.*

Laban Institute of Movement Studies. This organization supports research, training, and practical application of the study of human movement through the Laban movement analysis system. It offers workshops, seminars, and a certificate program and maintains a library of literature on movement, psychology, and art. LIMS publishes a quarterly *Newsletter;* an annual *Membership Directory;* the *Laban Movement Analysis Bibliography;* and proceedings of its biennial conferences.

Society of Dance History Scholars. Historical research in dance is the main focus of this organization, although related subjects, such as aesthetics or other critical studies, are included in its scholarly meetings and presentations. Its publications include annual conference proceedings, a membership list, and a newsletter. An annual conference is held in February.

Sacred Dance Guild. Established in 1956 as the Eastern Regional Sacred Dance Association and consisting largely of directors of sacred dance choirs in New England, today the Sacred Dance Guild has a membership of 600 choreographers, teachers, students, and religious leaders of all denominations throughout the United States and in several other countries. It explores varied forms of religious dance; disseminates information about it; publishes a journal and calendar of sacred dance events and an annotated bibliography and directory of specialists in the field; and sponsors workshops and festivals.[48]

Other national organizations which serve the needs of dance researchers include the Dance Critics Association, the American Dance Festival, the National Dance Association (see page 281), and the American College Dance Festival Association.

Research Resources

In addition to the work of such groups, dance researchers and critics are able to find considerable assistance through the collected materials and bibliographic services of several different types of libraries and resource archives.

College and University Libraries. When students or faculty members undertake research projects, the first source of information they usually consult is the college or university library. Many such facilities have a librarian assigned to the arts, if not specifically to dance. In addition, many college libraries can search for needed research material on specialized computer databases.

An important step in dance research is to consult source materials in related disciplines such as music, theater, and anthropology in addition to dance. These may include bibliographical aids such as the *Music Index; RILM Abstracts* of music literature; *Psychological* and *Sociological Abstracts;* the *Education Index;* early compilations of dance research published by the National Section on Dance of AAHPER, forerunner of the National Dance Association; and other indexes and listings in the performing arts. Among the best-known of such collections are the Harvard Theater Collection in Cambridge and the Katherine Dunham Archives at the Morris Library, Southern Illinois University at Carbondale.

Most college libraries belong to nationwide consortia, such as the Library Research Group, which share computerized services and interlibrary loans. Dissertations and theses, although usually not published today in book or monograph form, are available through most college interlibrary loan systems and expand the potential resource value of a college library beyond its actual holdings.

Municipal Libraries. Public library facilities vary greatly from city to city, but some municipal libraries have extensive performance-related collections in their public holdings. The main branch of the Philadelphia Free Library, for example, has dance, theater, and music collections including clipping files, photographs, and scores. Frequently, such collections emphasize local dance endeavors; the Philadelphia Library includes much material on Catherine Littlefield, artistic director of the first major American ballet company.

Some municipal libraries house special collections. One of the best of these is the New York Public Library, which has not only several collections in the performing arts but also two branches, the Main Branch on Fifth Avenue and the Donnell Branch on 53rd Street, which have special dance collections. Also in New York City is the Lincoln Center Dance Collection, housed at Lincoln Center for the Performing Arts, in a special building that includes a circulation branch of the New York Public Library, an exhibition gallery, a theater-auditorium, and special dance, music, and theater research collections. Under the direction of curator Genevieve Oswald, a *Dictionary Catalog of the Dance Collection* has been compiled with 8,000 subject listings cross-referencing every phase of dance.

Private Collections and Sources. There have also been numerous privately sponsored collections of books, periodicals, prints, photographs, playbills, films, videos, and oral interviews in dance and the other performing arts. In some cases, these have been donated by their owners to public or universities libraries; in others, they are housed independently and are often accessible to scholars. For example, the Newberry Library in Chicago has an extensive collection of materials dealing with history, musicology, cartography, and genealogy, including many first editions of books concerned with social dance and ballet from the late Renaissance period into the second half of the nineteenth century.[49]

Several such special collections deal with a particular form of dance or a dance-related subject. For example, a researcher in the field of black dance will find extensive resources in New York City at the Hatch-Billops Collection of varied materials in Afro-American theater and visual art, including programs, posters, clipping files, oral interview records, doctoral dissertations, and unpublished manuscripts.[50] The Schomburg Center for Research in Black Culture, a special branch of the New York Public Library, has a wealth of dance-related resources, including the contents of two unique collections donated by private individuals: a collection of vintage film shorts on black popular dance forms, donated by Ernie Smith, and a varied archive of materials on black concert dance gathered by Joe Nash during his lengthy performing and teaching career in the United States and abroad.

In addition to such resources, many newspapers across the nation maintain their own archives, including clipping and photograph files unavailable elsewhere. These are likely to be of considerable value to the dance researcher who seeks information about particular performers, companies, or events not covered in books or magazines.

From a relative paucity of meaningful scholarship on dance at mid-century, we have moved to a vigorous period of research, criticism, and publication that undergirds dance instruction in colleges and universities and that helps to build public understanding and support for dance.

Notes

1 Juana de Laban, "Dance Research: Inherent Approaches," *Dance Research Monograph I* (New York: Congress on Research in Dance, 1971–1972), pp. 193–94.

2 Suzanne Shelton, "A Definition of Dance Criticism," *Journal of Physical Education, Recreation and Dance,* March 1987, p. 60.

3 Paul D. Leedy, *Practical Research* (New York: Macmillan, 1985), p. 3.

4 *Webster's New International Dictionary* (Springfield, Mass.: G. and C. Merriam Co., 1956), p. 2118.

5 Selma Jeanne Cohen, "How Does the Researcher Get the Facts?" *CORD Journal,* n.d., p. 67.

6 Ibid., p. 70.

7 Shelton, "Definition of Dance Criticism," p. 60.

8 Ibid., p. 61. See also Wendy Oliver, "Demystifying Dance as an Art Form—Teaching College Students to Critique Dance," *Journal of Physical Education, Recreation and Dance,* February 1989, pp. 47–50.

9 Jack Anderson, "Will Choreography Ever Be Respected as an Art Form?" *New York Times,* September 5, 1982, p. 6-H.

10 Ibid.

11 Mary A. Brennan, "A Look Ahead: Dance Research Needed," *Journal of Physical Education, Recreation and Dance,* May–June 1986, pp. 49, 53.

12 de Laban, "Dance Research," p. 194.

13 Gaston Vuillier, *A History of Dance* (New York: D. Appleton and Co., 1897).

14 John Martin, *John Martin's Book of the Dance* (New York: Tudor Publishing Co., 1963).

15 Walter Terry, *The Dance in America,* (New York: Harper and Bros., 1956).

16 Walter Sorell, *The Dance Has Many Faces* (New York: World Publishing Co., 1951).

17 Ted Shawn, *Dance We Must* (London: Dennis Dobson, Ltd., 1946).

18 George Amberg, *Ballet in America* (New York: Duell, Sloan and Pearce, 1949).

19 Agnes de Mille, *Book of the Dance* (New York: Golden Press, 1963).

20 Lincoln Kirstein, *Dance: A Short History of Classic Theatrical Dancing* (New York: G. P. Putnam's Sons, 1935).

21 Curt Sachs, *World History of the Dance* (New York: W. W. Norton and Co., 1937).

22 Suzanne Youngerman, for example, argued that Sachs's work was questionable because he had not directly observed the dance forms he described, and the English edition of his book lacked full documentation.

23 Lillian B. Lawler, *The Dance in Ancient Greece* (Middletown, Conn.: Wesleyan University Press, 1964).

24 David V. Erdman, "Historical Research," *CORD Dance Research Annual I,* 1967, p. 48.

25 For a more detailed discussion of Moore's background, see *The Dance Encyclopedia,* ed. Anatole Chujoy (New York: A. S. Barnes, Inc., 1948), p. 640.

26 For her approach to dance history, see Lillian Moore, "How Does a Researcher Get the Facts?" *CORD Dance Research Annual I,* 1967, p. 55.

27 Katherine Dunham, *Journey to Accompong* (New York: Henry Holt and Co., 1946).

28 Gertrude Kurath (with Samuel Martí), *Dances of Anáhuac* (Chicago: Aldine Publishing Co., 1964).

29 John W. Best, *Research in Education* (Englewood Cliffs, N.J.: Prentice-Hall, 1981), p. 93.

30 Elsie Ivancich Dunin, "Lindo in the Context of Village Life in the Dubrovnick Area of Yugoslavia," in Lynn Wallen and Joan Acocella, *A Spectrum of World Dance* (New York: Congress on Research in Dance [CORD], 1987), p. 1.

31 Sandra Green, "Sacred Dances of Ladakh," in Wallen and Acocella, *Spectrum of World Dance,* p. 18.

32 Candi de Alaiza, "The Evolution of the Basque Jota as a Competitive Form," in Wallen and Acocella, *Spectrum of World Dance,* p. 36.

33 Margaret Gray and Margaret Head Skrinar, "Support Base Use in Two Dance Idioms," *Research Quarterly for Exercise and Sport,* no. 2 (1984), pp. 184–87.

34 Priscilla Clarkson, Theresa Kennedy, and Joanne Flanagan, "A Study of Three Movements in Classical Ballet," *Research Quarterly for Exercise and Sport,* no. 2 (1984), pp. 175–79.

35 Such research is usually not reported in scholarly dance journals devoted primarily to scientific research, but rather in publications directed to practitioners, such as *Dance Teacher Now* or *Journal of Physical Education, Recreation and Dance.*

36 Richard Kraus and Lawrence Allen, *Research and Evaluation in Recreation, Parks and Leisure Studies* (Columbus, Ohio: Publishing Horizons, Inc., 1987), p. 61.

37 Luc A. Léger, "Energy Cost of Disco Dancing," *Research Quarterly for Exercise and Sport,* March 1982, p. 49.

38 Deborah Dowdy, Kirk Cureton, Harry DuVal, and Harvey Ouzts, "Effects of Aerobic Dance and Physical Work Capacity, Cardiovascular Function and Body Function on Composition of Middle-Aged Women," *Research Quarterly for Exercise and Sport,* September 1985, pp. 227–33.

39 Priscilla Clarkson, Patty Freedson, Betsy Keller, and Margaret Skrinar, "Maximal Oxygen Uptake, Nutritional Patterns and Body Composition of Female Ballet Dancers," *Research Quarterly for Exercise and Sport,* June 1985, pp. 180–84.

40 A. Lesté and J. Rust, "Effects of Dance on Anxiety," *Perceptual and Motor Skills,* 58 (1984), 767–72.

41 Cindy Crain, Margaret Eisenhart, and John McLaughlin, "The Application of a Multiple Measure Approach to Investigate the Effects of a Dance Program on Educable Mentally Retarded Adolescents," *Research Quarterly for Exercise and Sport*, no. 3 (1984), pp. 231–36.

42 Generally, these appear in publications concerned with physiology of exercise, motor learning and performance, or other scientific aspects of sport, movement, or physical education.

43 Best, *Research in Education*, p. 131.

44 Maya Pines, "What's the Real Message of 'Casablanca'? Or of a Rose?" *New York Times*, September 28, 1982, no. p.

45 Dianne Howe, "The Notion of Mysticism in the Philosophy and Choreography of Mary Wigman, 1914–1931," *Dance Research Journal*, 19, no. 1, p. 19–23.

46 Bernice Rosen, Manon Souriau, and Grace Rubin, "History of the American Dance Guild," *American Dance Guild Conference Program*, 1987, p. 6.

47 See *Dance Magazine Annual*, 1985, p. 259.

48 Constance Garcia-Barrio, "Spirituality and Dance: The Sacred Dance Guild," *Dance Teacher Now*, April 1986, pp. 35–38.

49 Edward Pease, "The Newberry Library: Some Rare Primary Sources on Dancing, 1581–1868," *Dance Research Journal*, no. 13/1 and 2 (1981–1982), p. 77.

50 Brenda Dixon-Stowell, "The Hatch-Billops Collection," *Dance Research Journal*, 2, no. 15 (1983), p. 49.

CHAPTER 19

Careers in Dance Today

The educational requirements and special training for careers in dance vary greatly. A professional dancer, for example, requires considerable special training but little formal education. The special training often begins at an early age in a dance studio and continues there throughout, even after, the performing years. The dancer's formal education may end with a high school diploma or may continue through a college degree. On the other hand, to administer a university dance department usually requires a graduate degree.[1]

WHILE DANCE MAY BE THOUGHT OF IN MANY WAYS— as an art form, an area of personal expression, a popular entertainment, or enjoyable exercise—it also represents a diversified career field for many thousands of men and women in modern society. Typically, those who consider dance as a possible occupation do so because of a personal interest in dance performance. Often, they have excelled in ballet, modern dance, or jazz dance classes, have been part of school or studio productions, and have admired the work and careers of famous dancers. While it is true that a career in dance, as in other performing arts, represents for many a harsh struggle for economic survival, it *does* represent a diversified field of employment with many career possibilities for gifted and determined young people.

Range of Career Opportunities in Dance

Career opportunities occur in several aspects of dance, including: (a) dance performance and management; (b) dance teaching; (c) dance therapy; and (d) dance research and criticism.

Dance Performance and Management

Jobs involving dance performance include not only work as a dancer in ballet or modern dance companies, but also work in Broadway or regional or touring musical theater companies. Many dancers with strong jazz, tap, and ballet background are employed in resorts or on cruise ships, in Las Vegas and Atlantic City casino hotels, at theme parks, on television shows, and in industrial trade shows and similar settings.

Indeed, the U.S. Employment Service lists the following dance-related terms in its *Dictionary of Occupational Titles* in the section dealing with amusement and recreation: *acrobatic dancer, ballet dancer, ballroom dancer, belly dancer, choreographer, chorus dancer, dancer, dance director, host/hostess, dance hall, interpretative dancer, show girl, strip-tease dancer,* and *tap dancer.* Surprisingly, it does not include the title, *modern dancer.*[2] U.S. Department of Labor reports give more details of performing dance careers, indicating that while the number of positions is expected to continue to grow, competition will be keen and only the most talented will find regular employment.[3]

The *Occupational Outlook Handbook* points out that the earnings of most professional dancers are governed by union contracts, with those in the major opera ballet, classical ballet, and modern dance companies belonging to the American Guild of Musical Artists. Those who perform on live or videotaped television belong to the American Federation of Television and Radio Artists; those in films, to the Screen Actors Guild or the Screen Extras Guild; and those in musical comedies to the Actors' Equity Association. As of 1987, minimum salary for dancers in opera and stage productions was $72 per performance. Single performances in ballet paid $183, with additional allowances for touring expenses. The fee for a one-hour television show was set at approximately $550, including rehearsal time.[4]

Performing in professional dance companies is just one aspect of dance as a career field. In many large ballet or modern dance groups, a number of individuals are involved in various aspects of production or company management. Lee wrote that the role of dance administrator represents an expanding employment area both for those seeking to enter the field and for men and women who are approaching the end of their active involvement as performers: "Dancers should capitalize on their professional strengths of fund raising, promotion, management, and administrative skills, while integrating their knowledge of dance in such careers in dance company management as artistic director, managing director, development officer, public relations officer, and booking agent."[5]

Given the limited number of openings that occur each year in the established professional companies, many young dancers seek other, less prestigious performance opportunities. These may involve being part of, or founding, smaller and less professional dance groups often connected to colleges and universities, dance schools, or community arts centers.

Dance Teaching

Since such career roles rarely yield substantial incomes, they often are combined with teaching jobs that do provide a secure livelihood. Minton summarized these opportunities: "In terms of teaching, the greatest employment potential exists with dance studios, high schools, or colleges. The possibility of offering dance classes through recreation departments, health spas, and the YMCA should be explored by contacting the directors of these institutions."[6]

Qualifications for dance teaching positions vary greatly. In private studios and schools, the individual's personality, appearance, and teaching skills are usually the primary concerns of employers, and formal credentials are rarely required. In public elementary and secondary schools, certification by the state department of education is required, with physical education degrees usually being the specialized teaching area on the secondary level. However, in recent years, a number of school systems have established independent certification requirements in dance.

On the college level, customarily a teacher is expected to have at least a master's degree, and in many cases a doctorate, to be qualified to teach dance as a professor and to gain tenure. However, in some universities, teachers in the arts are considered qualified without these formal academic credentials, provided that they have distinguished themselves as creative artists. Thus, in dance, as in music, theater, or fine arts, it is not unusual for individuals with only a bachelor's degree, and sometimes not even that, to gain faculty status. In conservatories, arts academies, and schools attached to dance companies, it is customary for teachers to be drawn from the ranks of performing artists, without concern for academic credentials. Dance teaching may also provide a broad range of opportunities for teaching skills in other dance forms, including folk and square dancing, ballroom dancing, aerobic dancing, jazz and tap dancing, and varied ethnic forms.

Diverse Audience for Dance Education. While we tend to think of dance instruction as directed only to children and youth, many middle-aged and older individuals today take part in dance. There is growing evidence that regular exercise helps to maintain fitness and health, and geriatric specialists increasingly recommend that the elderly continue such activities through the later decades of life. Frequently, dance instruction is combined with other health-related class experiences.

For example, Carleton and March have described the University of New Mexico's aerobic dance program as an educational experience that includes both progressive exercise sessions and the learning of fitness principles. Class lectures deal with cardiovascular conditioning, safe exercise techniques, and appropriate sequencing of aerobic dance activities.[7] At other universities, similar classes are offered for students, faculty, and staff members, both with and without academic credit.

At the University of Nebraska at Omaha, intergenerational classes have been conducted for students and older adults; similar programs have been organized in nursing homes and worship settings.[8] Sometimes, these dance activities have been geared to achieve social and fitness goals, but in some cases they have involved creative dance performance. For example, an unusual group, Dancers of the Third Age, has consisted of senior adults, from age sixty through the late eighties, who rehearse and perform regularly at the Dance Exchange in Washington, D.C.[9]

Dance teaching opportunities may also be found in varied treatment settings and in work with other special populations. One of the authors of this text, for example, worked regularly as a folk and square dance leader with psychiatric patients in a large, private hospital, with elderly residents in a nursing home, and from time to time with deaf adolescents and mentally retarded young adults. The Alvin Ailey American Dance Center in New York City has conducted a pilot project to teach dance movement and music to blind and visually impaired youth. Carried out in cooperation with the Very Special Arts, a Washington, D.C.-based nonprofit organization concerned with sponsoring arts program for the disabled, this program, known as New Visions Dance Project, has been highly successful. Using the Pilates Method of mind and body conditioning, its instructor, Wendy Amos, has also presented numerous workshops on dance for the blind at teacher-training workshops in the United States and abroad over the past several years.[10]

In part, such programs have been stimulated as a response to Public Law 94-142, which requires that handicapped children be mainstreamed wherever possible—that is, integrated and educated with nonhandicapped children to the maximum degree possible and in the "least restrictive" environment. This law has particular applications for the fields of physical education and recreation, and mandates forms of participation by the disabled in activities that are educational, recreational, and therapeutic in nature—including dance. (A special issue of *Focus on Dance,* published by the National Dance Association in 1980, deals with dance for the handicapped.)

Dance Therapy

A specialized approach to using dance with such populations is known as dance therapy. Levy pointed out that the use of dance and movement as a psychotherapeutic or healing tool is based on the premise that body movement reflects inner emotional states and that changes in movement behavior can lead to changes in the psyche, thus promoting health and growth. She wrote: "Helping individuals—those who are generally healthy as well as those who are emotionally or mentally disturbed, physically or mentally disabled—to regain a sense of wholeness by experiencing the fundamental unity of body, mind, and spirit, is the ultimate goal of dance therapy."[11]

Kathlyn Hendricks pointed out that the core of the dance therapy process is about regaining feeling and awareness; people often come to dance therapy because they are out of touch with their bodies. She wrote: "Dance therapists work with every conceivable population, including geriatric, forensic, autistic, neurotic, psychotic, rehabilitation, chronic pain, retarded, deaf, and blind. All of these dance therapists have in common a commitment to the life of the body, the importance of reclaiming lost parts of ourselves, and the meaning in the dance."[12]

Partly as a consequence of the emphasis on personal expression and self-exploration of many early modern dancers, the writings of such leading psychoanalysts as Freud, Adler, and Jung led to widespread experimentation of the use of dance with psychiatric patients. By the 1940s, a considerable number of dance therapy programs had been initiated in mental hospitals throughout the United States, and by the following decade, as Levy pointed out, a number of dancers and dance educators had established themselves as independent therapists using dance in their own studios. Gradually, through the work of such pioneers as Claire Schmais,

Marian Chace, and Blanche Evan in New York, and Trudi Schoop and Mary Whitehouse in California, the field became more professionalized and developed a stronger scientific base.

The American Dance Therapy Association was established in 1966, and a number of colleges and universities initiated undergraduate programs in the 1960s and graduate degree programs in the 1970s. Over the past fifteen years, more progress has been made in professionalizing dance therapy as a field of practice, including the development of curriculum standards for graduate degree programs and guidelines for determining the professional competence of individuals working in this field. Levy wrote:

> Dance therapy is currently being used in medical and mental hospitals, clinics, rehabilitation centers, schools, and in private practice. Today's dance therapists function as primary therapists, as ancillary therapists, and as family and couples counselors. They serve a wide spectrum of patients of all ages, from individuals with severe emotional and physical problems and handicaps to normal individuals seeking in-depth self-exploration through expressive movement. In short, dance therapy is moving into countless areas of mental health and continues to expand its education, practice, and organizational alliances.[13]

Dance Research and Criticism

A new discipline of dance research and criticism has emerged in recent years. As described in chapter 18, it involves a wide range of academic and journalistic roles. As Lappe wrote, in addition to newspaper or magazine reporting on dance events: "Research writing in dance is also worth investigation [as a career], especially as it relates to physiology, history, aesthetics, and psychology. The dance researcher and allies, the dance historian and dance archivist, contribute to preservation of dance as an art form."[14]

There are relatively few jobs available at any given time for the journalistic dance critic or reporter. However, not infrequently, such assignments may be part of the overall professional work of college or university dance faculty members, or others involved professionally in dance. Research published in professional journals, scholarly reports, or books, along with presentations at academic conferences and symposiums, becomes an important part of the individual faculty member's advancement.

Strategies for Career Success

How does one plan for and achieve success within a given area of dance activity? Obviously, there is no single formula. A number of highly successful dancers and choreographers did not have an initial interest in dance and only began to study it at a relatively late age. Not infrequently, a dancer may pursue a performing career with only minor success, but then may become a successful school or college teacher, or manager-operator of a private dance studio. Often, those who develop a strong interest in dance therapy do so because of a prior interest in psychology or psychotherapy. Leading dance critics or scholars may have had earlier career experiences or education in philosophy, theater, history, anthropology, or other disciplines.

In many cases, the individual's interest in dance begins as a student in a community-based, private dance studio, where he or she may study ballet, modern dance, tap, jazz, or a combination of these forms. Typically, it continues over a period of years as the most talented and highly motivated individuals move on to more highly qualified teachers or schools, take summer camps or intensive workshops, and in some cases enroll in special arts-oriented secondary schools.

Usually, at this point the young dance student must make a choice. If he or she is to continue with dance after high school, how should it be done? For the individual who hopes to perform in a recognized ballet company, the training most frequently recommended in the past has been in a ballet company school, conservatory, or other institution providing an intensive curriculum in the various elements of ballet and music. Today, as growing numbers of universities have developed strong ballet programs, it is possible to obtain a higher level of training, as well as a broader college education, in a degree-granting institution.

In general, those interested in modern dance as a career have tended to enroll in college or university dance majors, particularly those that offer bachelor's and master's degree programs in dance as a fine art. Over the past two decades, such curricula have become more sophisticated, with selective admissions standards, well-qualified faculty members, and strong course sequences linked to performing opportunities in department-sponsored companies.

Alma Hawkins pointed out that there are distinct differences in focus and purpose between studio and university-based dance programs. Studio training, she commented, does not have a responsibility to cover many of the areas of the discipline, such as history, aesthetics, philosophy, notation, and music. In contrast, a good university dance curriculum not only deals with these elements but also is concerned with the overall growth of the student:

> Dance education is not just training in technical proficiency. Some people would say that our goal is to prepare people to take on certain kinds of jobs. I think we do have a concern about what they are going to do, but personally, I don't think that's the first priority. We try to see possible kinds of outcomes for our students, so that those who are interested will be able to move into the professional dance world, or into research and scholarly work . . . [but] the first priority is an education that provides a broad experience in dance. . . .[15]

In deciding what type of institution would be most appropriate, questions of cost, regional availability, quality of faculty, diversity of curriculum, and availability of knowledgeable counseling all come into play. Beyond this, as Erick Hawkins stressed, teaching should be on a mature and conscientious level. In ballet, he pointed out, the problem is less critical than in modern dance:

> . . . ballet training . . . has been standardized so that even though the individual teacher might not be adequately experienced, the starting point is so crystallized

and universalized that the teacher might not make such bad mistakes, whereas a more idiosyncratic approach by someone who just might not have had enough theoretical and practical training may mislead or narrow the experience of a young dancer. . . .[16]

The implication is that because of much greater variations in teaching modern dance and structuring it within a curriculum, there is greater risk for the young student of selecting a program unsuited to his or her needs. One college program may emphasize developing the individual student's creativity at an early point, while another may focus on learning technique with little choreographic or performing involvement.

In many of the established college dance curricula today, students are given a balance of both ballet and modern dance, along with other courses dealing with choreography, production, dance history, and theory. Courses should also be provided that offer a solid, scientific understanding of the body and how it moves. Erick Hawkins pointed out that too often dance teachers do not have sufficient background themselves in dance or in the basis of movement to be able to teach it properly: "You cannot have a technique that is not based on the science of kinesiology any more than you can design an airplane that is not based on the laws of aerodynamics. There are certain things that work and you just can't have a whimsical airplane. Neither can you train the body in a whimsical way."[17]

Erick Hawkins rejected the idea of teaching a single, specialized approach to dance, such as Graham, Limón, or Cunningham technique, as too partial and limited. Instead, what is needed, he wrote, is a more general theory that teaches principles of movement rather than idiosyncratic approaches based on a single dancer or choreographer's style and philosophy. Lesio supported this position, arguing that an understanding of efficient movement principles and correct body alignment makes the "difference between comfort or pain" to the dance student and leads to freer artistic expression.[18]

In some college or university dance programs, students may also obtain the specific courses and teaching experiences needed to meet dance certification requirements. Within such programs, there should be realistic and knowledgeable advisement that will help the student make some early, intelligent career choices and establish a sound foundation for them in college study.

For example, a college faculty advisor may feel justified in encouraging a student who has a rare degree of talent and dedication, as well as the appropriate physical and psychological make-up, to pursue the goal of becoming a professional dancer. However, the advisor also has the responsibility of telling other, less qualified students that a performing goal may be unrealistic for them and that they should consider other career possibilities.

Ideally, by the time a student has graduated, he or she should have a clear understanding of the career possibilities that lie ahead and should have gained a core of basic competencies and experiences that will be helpful in entering an appropriate field.

Strategies for Entering the Field

When formal training in college or university is over, how does the young dancer enter the field? Kassing raised a typical problem: "You can't get the job without experience, and you can't get experience without the job!"

Many colleges offer professional practice programs in terms of required field work or internship, co-op leaves for paid work, alternative semesters of work and study, and similar plans. In the field of dance, such assignments should be tailored to the individual student's career goals and may include positions as dance teacher, choreographer, rehearsal assistant, production assistant, or arts manager in a variety of settings ranging from community-based programs to commercial or professional companies.

Kassing described the approach used at Illinois State University at Normal, which established a Dance Laboratory to provide an experiential education site for undergraduate and graduate dance majors. The ISU Dance Laboratory offers students practical exposure to the varied roles described earlier, accompanied by requirements for extensive reports and evaluation.[19] The curriculum also developed linkages with local dance studios, community dance groups, a civic ballet school, and other dance companies in the region in order to provide internships for professional practice.

In addition to seeking employment with better-known ballet or modern dance companies, young dancers may audition for regional dance opportunities. In the mid-1980s, over 320 companies in the United States and Canada were listed in the *Dance Annual,* with the National Association for Regional Ballet listing 103 member companies. In contrast to the fiercely selective nationally and internationally known companies, Glazer suggested that the sheer number of these smaller companies means that there are numerous job openings each year for dancers:

> Small ballet ensembles provide some performing opportunities for literally thousands of dancers (including in the corps de ballet as well as for soloists and guest dancers) across our nation. These groups come and go, some lasting only a season, but the ephemeral nature of the groups does not necessarily spell failure. Booking agencies like to send these small companies to places which cannot underwrite the cost of a large company. Many regionally-based ballet companies travel outside the United States, and some groups even specialize in overseas engagements.[20]

Jazz dance has grown steadily as a source of jobs in dance, with generous rewards for dancers willing to leave the United States to perform in Europe, Asia, and Africa. With new concert jazz companies being formed, and varied opportunities for jazz dancers in television variety shows, commercials, and industrial shows, this represents another important area of potential employment. In describing the work of professional show dancers at Las Vegas casinos and resorts, Wilkens disputed the popular notion that Las Vegas shows consist only of "sex, feathers, naked girls and tall, good-looking guys." Solid dance training in ballet and jazz are essential, and gymnastic and acrobatic skills are also useful. As an example of the job possibilities in this field, the Bally Grand Casino show employs nine lead dancers, seven principal singers, fourteen chorus singers, twenty-eight girl dancers, plus twenty-eight topless girl dancers, fourteen boy dancers, and ten "ethnic" dancers.[21] Obviously, many would-be dancers would not be willing to perform topless (although nudity has become increasingly accepted as an element in serious theater and dance performance), and others might object to being classified as a "boy" or "girl" dancer. Nonetheless, many dancers enjoy the glamour and excitement of this type of performing role, and some college programs provide specialized training emphasizing the skills needed for show dancing.

Many young dancers get their initial professional experience working at theme parks. Almost all such parks use dance as an element in their popular entertainment programs. For example, Wise described the show at Wild World Amusement Park in Mitchellville, Maryland, a relatively small operation: "A total of 15 dancers perform two shows five times a day, six days a week. In addition to 'Broadway Magic,' they put on a country-western show called 'Pickin' 'n Lickin'.' The dancers begin work in April and continue through the end of September, working only on weekends in the early and late part of the season."[22]

On a larger scale, Walt Disney World in Florida usually employs about two hundred dancers on a full-time, year-round basis, with about eighty positions opening up each year. In addition to solid dancing skills and the ability to fill stage show, character, and parade parts, Disney's hiring seeks clean-cut, all-American-style performers who are lively, animated, and enthusiastic—with the men having a strong, athletic appearance. Ballet, jazz, and tap skills are required, and singing ability is also helpful.

Within the modern dance field, there tends to be a constant shifting of personnel in many of the larger companies, with older dancers leaving companies or shifting to teaching or choreographing roles and newer dancers joining the groups. However, the overall number of such positions is limited, and even the more established companies often cannot guarantee full-time, year-round employment for their dancers. As a result, many young modern dancers supplement their performing income with teaching, modeling, and other part-time or seasonal jobs.

In contrast to ballet, jazz, or musical show dance, where performers accept the idea of being part of a company and performing work choreographed by others, many modern dancers seek to choreograph their own work. Traditionally, modern dance has been regarded as a creative art form which serves as a vehicle for self-expression. From their earliest dance experiences, through school and college, modern dancers are often encouraged to improvise and to choreograph original dances. As a result, many young modern dancers form their own small companies, either independently or in cooperation with other dancers.

The Dancer as Entrepreneur

Taken literally, the term *entrepreneur* suggests that one is a businessperson, who assumes risks and hopes for the rewards of establishing a successful, independent economic venture. During the late 1960s and early 1970s, growing numbers of young and middle-aged Americans grew cynical about establishment values and the constraints of work within bureaucratic organizations, and they sought to develop independent businesses. In part, it was the idea of risk and reward that was so challenging; being an entrepreneur meant also being imaginative, creative, and risk-taking.

In the arts, it became evident that, as grants and other forms of government support declined, dancers and other performing artists would have to become far more creative in developing and holding audiences, acquiring appropriate spaces for rehearsal and performance, gaining community support, and similar tasks. The specialized professional role of arts administrator became fully recognized at this time, and more and more degree programs and special workshops were established to help train such individuals.

Dance Studio Management

In terms of dance, an obvious example of entrepreneurship is the traditional dance studio established by one or two teachers to serve a community, with classes that may range from ballet, tap, and creative dance for children to ballroom, jazz, and aerobic dancing for adults. In recent years, through conferences and training programs sponsored by national dance teacher associations and through publications serving their memberships, strategies for entrepreneurial success of such businesses have been widely publicized.

For example, in *Dance Teacher Now,* numerous successful community dance studios have been profiled. Some dance studio managers have initiated ballroom outreach programs, in which they take their teaching out of the studio to attract new students. The Starlight Studio in San Diego, California, typically provides a series of free lessons at a nearby upscale restaurant that attracts large numbers of new potential patrons: ". . . they exude the high spirit of aerobics classes and running festivals. Many of them are rock and rollers who grew up listening to new age radio; part of the generations that were passed by in the learning cycle that would have included social dancing."[23] In forty-five-minute lessons, rapidly paced with steady repetition of basic steps as well as appealing stylistic elements, the participants quickly learn to dance to music—and many sign up for classes at the studio itself. As a related outreach strategy, the Starlight Studio manager conducts courses consisting of ten weekly lessons for the Convair Aeronautics Company of San Diego through their employee recreation association. At the end of the series, videos of students practicing the steps they have learned are made available to them at minimal cost, for self-instruction and home practice.

Similarly, at the King Center for the Performing Arts in Wanaque, New Jersey, the school's director, Nancy King, has explored varied strategies for making the school a successful business enterprise. At one point, she was teaching four days a week in rented locations at nearby clubs or storefronts, but now she operates a spacious and well-equipped school, with five studios, some of which divide into smaller spaces, as well as dressing rooms, offices, a celebrity gift shop, and a setting for performances. The King Center is a customer-oriented business, with eighty classes a week, September through June, and a six-week summer session with a total enrollment of 500 students.

King's range of classes includes ballet, jazz, tap, modern dance, and acrobatics and gymnastics; acting and voice lessons have also been added to the curriculum. The school has achieved strong external recognition; its students have won highest awards in jazz performance from Dance Masters of America, Dance Educators of America, and numerous other competitions; they have appeared professionally in numerous companies and on radio and television; and its five performing units, grouped by age, have toured abroad several times.[24]

Tactics for Performing Artists

For those determined to break into the world of performing dance, succeeding as a dancer requires a range of skills involving getting and keeping jobs, maintaining health, fiscal management, grantsmanship, tax laws, and the use of modern technology in dance programs and promotion. During the 1980s, the California Institute of the Arts developed a manual titled, *For the Working Artist: A Survival Guide for Artists*. This publication pointed out that in the past, it was assumed that artists were not expected to be knowledgeable about financial matters, but that this has changed dramatically:

> Today an artist who markets his paintings or successfully negotiates a contract is no longer viewed as an oddity or a traitor to his profession.
>
> All artists are arts managers. Some manage better than others but every artist who pays rent, has a phone and buys food is an arts manager on a basic level. . . . The same discipline and creativity that goes into writing a play or choreographing a new work will also serve an arts manager well. Preparing a grant proposal or booking a tour requires research and planning and the same organizational skills all competent artists employ on a daily basis.[25]

Another publication designed specifically for choreographers, managers, and dancers was published in 1983 by Dance Theater Workshop in New York City. Titled *Poor Dancer's Almanac,* this manual evolved from earlier survival manuals that had been developed during the period of student uprisings in the late 1960s and early 1970s, and it covers a detailed set of strategies geared to helping the young dance artist maintain himself or herself in the urban environment. While it is specifically directed to dancers in New York City, many of its guidelines apply to other large cities, as in the following areas:

1. *Getting established*—includes telephone resources and services; dance referrals sources; libraries; transit systems; dance publications; entertainment needs.
2. *Health*—involves medical services, clinics, and hotlines; insurance, emergencies, and referrals; dance injuries and related health problems.
3. *Space for living and working*—finding living spaces; loft living; finding a working space; evaluating a dance floor; tenant loft organizations.
4. *Making ends meet*—employment options: waiting tables, office work, manual labor, teaching; arts management and technical production.

5. *Government financial services*—unemployment insurance, food stamps, welfare, and Supplementary Security Income (SSI); taxes and record keeping.

6. *Structure of operations*—private and business selves; sole proprietorship, partnership, unincorporated association, corporation; nonprofit, tax-exempt corporation.

7. *Publicity and promotion*—press releases, photographs, public service announcements, inviting the critics; direct mail, posters, advertising, graphic design methods.

8. *Production*—finding performing space; box office, ticket printing and reservations, vouchers and programs; staging, lighting, sound and scenery; video, film, and notation documentation; legal considerations, unions, royalties, building codes.[26]

The arts management process has become increasingly complex and sophisticated in recent years—particularly with respect to promotion and public relations, maintaining audience lists, networking for mutual assistance among dancers and choreographers, and similar needs. For example, a computerized dance network called Dansource has been established, which assists companies in finding dancers on short notice to meet specific needs.[27] Computers are becoming invaluable in fund raising, creating promotional pieces, designing and controlling budgets, maintaining needed databases, scheduling programs and rehearsals, and similar tasks through the use of popular software packages like WordPerfect.[28] Indeed, dance technology has grown rapidly as an area of special expertise, including the use of software for composing dances; video techniques in scoring and recording, choreography and animation, and production effects; and other production-related roles. For example, Gray pointed out that computer-controlled lighting systems can effectively cut in half the amount of time spent on writing lighting cues: "It is no longer necessary to literally write anything down. . . . Gone are the days when it took two or three stage hands to manipulate the dimmer switches. Today, at the touch of a few keys, the lighting cue information is stored as electronically encoded data and, as such, can be instantly retrieved and modified."[29]

The Dancer's Life

As a career field, dance has long had a number of negative stereotypes attached to it. Certainly, it suffered from the overall lack of interest and support that affected all the arts in America for many years. However, as earlier chapters have shown, this situation has changed radically, and the arts have become a respected and valued part of American life over the past several decades.

Critical Perceptions of Dance

Other negative stereotypes apply more directly to dance than to the other arts. Often, dance is viewed as an elitist activity, particularly in the case of ballet, or as a difficult-to-understand art form, in the case of modern dance. For this reason, continuing efforts must be made to help the public understand dance and respect it, both as a significant art form and as a meaningful educational experience. In the past, there has also been considerable distrust of dance as an "immoral" activity. A number of fundamentalist religions in particular, such as present-day conservative Protestant groups, continue to condemn it—along with rock and roll music, popular television or movie entertainment, and similar expressions of popular culture.

Dance as Feminine Activity. Another problem is that dance has traditionally been perceived as a feminine activity—a stereotype which has discouraged many educators from supporting it as an appropriate subject for boys and young men in schools and colleges. What accounts for this attitude? Surely history tells us that throughout the ages man has always danced. José Limón wrote: "The male of the human species has always been a dancer. Whether as a savage or civilized man, whether warrior, monarch, hunter, priest, philosopher, or tiller of the soil, the atavistic urge to dance was in him and he gave it full expression. . . ."[30]

The roots of the feminine stereotype of dance lie in the past. During the early history of ballet, when boys and young men dressed as women to play feminine roles in the French court, the sexual identification of the male dancer was clearly weakened. Later, during the nineteenth century, when the ballerina was glorified and the male dancer denigrated, dance as a profession lost its appeal for many men—except as choreographers, ballet masters, or producers. Marcia Siegel commented that for 200 years, ballet has been a woman's art; and through this period:

> . . . the ballet stage has been inhabited by beautiful females with uncanny skills of speed, balance, accuracy, and elevation—women whose virtuosity gave tangible support to their stage roles as princesses or leaders, often endowed with supernatural powers. Countless ballet heroes have fallen helplessly in love with these splendid creatures. . . . the ballerina is what you go to the ballet to see. A male dancer hoping for stardom in this world learns to incline his head and step backward with regal deference.[31]

By the time the Golden Age of ballet in Europe had run its course, few men were willing to embark on a career in which they could find little prestige or economic reward. Dance became a field in which the female performer was preeminent, although men continued to be the leading teachers, choreographers, and impresarios.

In modern times, other factors have contributed to the stereotype. Because dance, as all the stage arts, has been a competitive and economically precarious field, many young men who had the intention of marrying and raising families hesitated to enter it or, in some cases, were forced to leave it because of economic pressures. In contrast, the unmarried male dancer or homosexual dancer with fewer ties or responsibilities has been better able to withstand the economic stresses and the demands of touring and performance.

The stereotype has not attached itself to men in the more commercial phases of dance; performers like Fred Astaire, Ray Bolger, and Bill Robinson have not suffered from it. What is there about ballet in particular that arouses prejudice? Some of the adverse reputation undoubtedly has been due to the reaction of the untutored and artistically unsophisticated American to the very appearance of ballet. The exaggerated and flamboyant gestures, the walk which was perceived as mincing, the tight-fitting and revealing costume of the male dancer—all these aroused disapproval and suspicion of this ornate, aristocratic, and graceful art.

In addition, the view of dance as an essentially feminine activity has been strengthened by the way it has been presented in schools and colleges. During the late 1800s, when aesthetic dance was developed for women and gymnastic dance for men, the male role was defined as vigorous, strong, and essentially nonartistic. As sports became increasingly important in the program of physical education for boys and men, they tended to displace dance activity. The fact that, almost invariably in secondary schools and often in colleges, physical education classes were divided into separate departments, with men teaching classes for boys and men and women teaching girls and women, made it extremely difficult to involve males in dance programs. Sports were inevitably regarded as the most appropriate and prestigious activity for males, while dance was considered the most suitable movement domain for females.

Many dancers and dance educators have striven to overcome the prejudice against males in dance. Ted Shawn, through his all-male touring group and his teaching and writing, was one of the early dance pioneers who had strong influence in supporting male dancing during the 1930s and 1940s. Today, an increasing number of boys and men appear to be entering dance; certainly, in colleges and community programs, more male dance teachers are employed. There is a growing respect for the sheer physical and athletic demands of performing dance; one leading physical educator described his experience in seeing an outstanding male dancer:

> Never before had I witnessed such a display of sheer power, quickness, and body control. . . . his . . . presence on stage captured my complete attention while raising disturbing simple questions. Who is this dancer? Why is he the only male performer in the company? And why is such a superb athletelike male pursuing a career in dance? His performance made me uneasy.[32]

More and more, educators are realizing that boys can actually *like* dancing and take part in it enthusiastically when it is approached seriously as a fine art and when it involves a significant creative and physical challenge. With increased acceptance of homosexuality (both in a legal sense and also as an alternative lifestyle—rather than a form of mental illness), the stereotype was no longer as damaging as it had once been. When Walter Terry revealed, after his death, that Ted Shawn had actually been a bisexual despite his lifelong effort to maintain a virile heterosexual identity, the disclosure received little public attention.[33] Increasingly, dance has gained acceptance as a useful method of training male athletes in such team sports as basketball and even football.[34] Today, the public is aware of many examples of leading male dancers living traditional heterosexual lives with wives and children. At the same time, a growing number of prominent male dancers and choreographers who have died recently of AIDS-related disease reminds the public that there *has* been considerable truth to the stereotype.

And, despite the progress that has been made, women continue to dominate the modern dance field in particular. Copeland pointed out that, although there have been a number of leading male choreographers, the central figures have been "founding mothers." Copeland asked: "Why *are* modern and post-modern dance the only major art forms in which the creators, the consolidators, the second and third generation innovators have almost all been women?"[35]

Copeland credited the powerful influence of Isadora Duncan, Ruth St. Denis, and Martha Graham as a force that encouraged women to play a leading role in this art form. They represented an early thrust of what was to become the forceful feminist movement in the later decades of the twentieth century. With respect to postmodern choreographers, Copeland described the work of women like Yvonne Rainer, Trisha Brown, and Lucinda Childs as an effort to desexualize dance by creating works in which the dancers' sexual identity was barely visible.

In this sense, then, dance has been one of the arenas in which battles of sexual politics have been fought in recent decades. Manning saw the continuing female domination of German modern dance as an expression of artistic feminism.[36] In the late 1980s, a number of major dance events have stressed the role of women in dance; for example, in January, 1989, a two-week program titled *Womanworks* at the Joyce Theater in New York City featured ". . . an exposition of the remarkable invention of women dancemakers—eleven soloists and companies that span four generations . . . in shared programs [that] contrast and complement their distinct and extraordinary points of view. . . ."[37]

At the same time, continued efforts are made to strengthen the acceptance and understanding of men in dance. In an outstanding four-part British Television series called "Dancer," produced by Peter Schaufuss, the Danish ballet star who directs the London Festival Ballet, the world of the male ballet dancer is explored. Illustrating his case with sequences of outstanding men dancers in bravura and partnering roles, Schaufuss points out that male stars have always been revered in Danish and Russian ballet, and that increasingly they have become accepted on a level equal to that of women in today's leading ballet companies. Yet, elsewhere in the Western world, dancers must continue to combat the stereotype of dance as a feminine art, as illustrated in Balanchine's proclamation: ". . . the ballet is a purely female thing; it is a woman—a garden of beautiful flowers, and the man is the gardener."[38]

The Reluctant Body

A final aspect of the dancer's life is that ballet or modern dance performance is an immensely demanding activity, requiring intense commitment and self-mastery, and often imposing pain or injury. Solway pointed out that all dancers, during their performing careers, wage a losing battle against gravity and time. Although, with daunting offstage labor and a compulsive passion for physical perfection, the dancer may gain "airborne grace and quicksilver technique," ultimately the body rebels. Solway wrote:

> With the years, the dancer's artistry gains nuance and depth, yet, paradoxically, speed, power and flexibility begin to wane. In due course, the body simply refuses to perform as the mind wills it to. No wonder that careers in ballet assume a certain urgency: a dancer can expect about 10 years of peak performance; if recognition

and fulfillment of one's goals don't come by 30, they may not come, for most dancers are professionally finished by 40, at a point when those called to other vocations are just making their mark.[39]

Obviously, there are exceptions in both modern dance and ballet. In ballet, a handful of dancers, like Galina Ulanova, Alicia Markova, and Margot Fonteyn have continued to dance well into their fifties, and it is always possible to dance in more limited roles. In modern dance, Martha Graham, Merce Cunningham, Lucas Hoving, and Erick Hawkins are only a few of the many dancers who have continued to perform well into middle age and beyond. Yet, for most, an active performing career is inevitably brought to a halt by passing time. As physical capabilities decline and energetic, brilliant, younger dancers emerge from studios and schools, the time to stop active dancing comes all too soon.

Often, the end is accelerated by injuries that might have been prevented with appropriate treatment. Clippinger-Robertson pointed out that in the past, many dancers have "danced through" physical problems rather than understand and deal with the sensations of pain and inflamation. As a result, many injuries lead to more serious conditions, longer recovery periods, and perhaps even additional injuries. Today, according to Clippinger-Robertson:

> . . . dancers are becoming more concerned with the high incidence of injury in dance and the long-term consequences of the inadequate treatment of injuries. Kinesiology, the science of human movement, offers one important means of understanding how the dancer's body works and how injuries can be prevented.[40]

Through systematic, progressive training of the body, it is possible to strengthen specific muscle groups, improve strength, flexibility, and coordination, and prevent many injuries that stem from chronic overuse. In addition, experts in principles of body mechanics as applied to dance can help correct typical inaccuracies in technique which lead to excessive strain on muscles and joints and thus cause injuries.

Career Changes for the Older Dancer

While such methods may be used to minimize injuries or to heal trauma, sooner or later dancers must face the reality that their performing careers will end. Anderson commented that, while dancers may continue to make contributions to their art as teachers or choreographers all of their lives, they cannot expect to dance forever. Older dancers must be honest enough to admit that they will not be able to dance some of the roles in which they dazzled and audiences when they were twenty or thirty. Anderson wrote:

> Fortunately, it may still be possible for dancers to appear in other types of roles. But audiences must be willing to countenance such a thing. If certain dancers should be chided for attempting virtuoso parts when they are past their prime, some dancegoers could also mend their ways: for instance, the incurably star-

struck who fanatically cheer on their old favorites even in bad performances of unsuitable roles. Such adulation simply carries loyalty and sentiment to grotesque extremes.[41]

It is at this stage that many dancers shift from a performer's role to all of the other career possibilities described earlier in this chapter. If an individual has prepared for this transition over a period of years, both psychologically and through needed training or professional exposure, it need not be a difficult shift. For those who have not, counseling may be helpful. What to do after a performing career ends has been the subject of a special project carried out by career consultant Ellen Wallach, who directs a major research and information effort called *Life After Performing—Career Transitions for Dancers*. This project has worked with more than twenty-five ballet and modern dance companies in identifying appropriate new career roles for dancers which will make use of the skills they have learned during their performing careers.[42]

Of all the possible choices that dancers might make for a second career, including numerous business-related fields in which their knowledge of promotion, project organization, marketing, and similar skills can be useful, teaching should have strong appeal. Only if the quality and number of dance teachers on all levels of education throughout the United States are increased is there likely to be the kind of mass audience for dance that is still lacking today. This, of course, is an essential goal of dance education: the development of a literate, sensitive, and enthusiastic audience, as well as greater participation on all age levels.

When dance becomes recognized as a creative and academic discipline and is included more fully as a part of education on every level, the prophecy of Isadora Duncan will at last be fulfilled: "I see America dancing."

Notes

1   Sandra Weeks, "Dance Careers in the 80s," *Journal of Physical Education, Recreation and Dance,"* May–June 1984, p. 73.

2   *Dictionary of Occupational Titles* (Washington, D.C.: U.S. Employment Service, Department of Labor, 1977), pp. 1165–68.

3   *Occupational Outlook Handbook* (Washington, D.C.: U.S. Department of Labor, 1988).

4   Ibid., p. 198.

5   Susan Lee, "Dance Administrative Opportunities," *Journal of Physical Education, Recreation and Dance,* May–June 1984, p. 74.

6   Sandra Minton, "An Entrepreneur's Opportunity in Dance," *Journal of Physical Education, Recreation and Dance,* February 1987, p. 74.

7   Nancy L. Carleton and Marjory J. Marsh, "Lifetime Fitness Through Dance. Consumer Awareness and Education," *Journal of Physical Education, Recreation and Dance,* September 1986, p. 31.

8   Josie Metal-Corbin, "Shared Movement Programs: College Students and Older Adults," *Journal of Physical Education, Recreation and Dance,* May 1983, pp. 46, 50.

9   Cynthia Ensign, "An Interview with Liz Lerman," *Journal of Physical Education, Recreation and Dance,* January 1986, p. 46.

10 Constance Garcia-Barrio, "Wendy Amos: Teaching the Visually Impaired," *Dance Teacher Now,* April 1988, pp. 19–22.

11 Fran Levy, "The Evolution of Modern Dance Therapy," *Journal of Physical Education, Recreation and Dance,* May–June 1988, p. 36.

12 Kathlyn Hendricks, "Dance Therapy: The Shape and Content," *Journal of Physical Education, Recreation and Dance,* August 1986, p. 72.

13 Levy, "Evolution of Modern Dance Therapy," p. 41.

14 Mary Martha Lappe, "Dance Careers for the Next Decade," *Journal of Physical Education, Recreation and Dance,* May–June 1984, p. 76.

15 Alma Hawkins, cited in Sandra Minton, "Alma Hawkins: An Academic Perspective," *Journal of Physical Education, Recreation and Dance,* May–June 1986, p. 40.

16 Joan Hays, "Erick Hawkins: The Studio Perspective," *Journal of Physical Education, Recreation and Dance,* May–June 1986, p. 43.

17 Ibid.

18 Laura Lesio, "Toward Efficient Alignment: Dance Teachers Can Help," *Journal of Physical Education, Recreation and Dance,* April 1986, pp. 73–76.

19 Gayle Kassing, "Professional Practice: A First Step into a Dance Career," *Journal of Physical Education, Recreation and Dance,* May–June 1986, pp. 38–39.

20 Susan Glazer, "Performing Opportunities in Regional Dance Companies," *Journal of Physical Education, Recreation and Dance,* May–June 1984, p. 28.

21 Jan Wilkens, "Landing a Job in Las Vegas," *Dance Teacher Now,* October 1986, pp. 15–16.

22 Christy Wise, "Theme Park Auditions," *Dance Teacher Now,* January–February 1988, pp. 37–38.

23 Richard Bray, "Ballroom Outreach is Good Business," *Dance Teacher Now,* April 1988, pp. 32–33.

24 Valerie Sudol, "Nancy King Opens the World to Her Students," *Dance Teacher Now,* January–February 1988, pp. 14–17.

25 *For the Working Artist: A Survival Guide for Artists* (Valencia, Calif.: California Institute for the Arts, 1986).

26 Mindy Levine, ed. *Poor Dancer's Almanac: A Survival Manual for Choreographers, Managers and Dancers* (New York: Dance Theater Workshop, 1983).

27 Nancy Sullivan, "Job Networking with a Computer Service," *Dance Teacher Now,* September 1986, pp. 20–24.

28 Beatrice Hamblett, "Computerography," *Dance Magazine,* January 1987, pp. 86–87.

29 Judith A. Gray, "Dance Technology in Our Lives and Work," *Journal of Physical Education, Recreation and Dance,* May–June 1988, p. 53.

30 José Limón, "The Virile Dancer," in Walter Sorell, *The Dance Has Many Faces* (New York: World Publishing Co., 1951), p. 192.

31 Marcia B. Siegel, *Watching the Dance Go By* (Boston: Houghton Mifflin Co., 1977), pp. 103–4.

32 Dennis Fallon, "A Man Unchained," *Journal of Physical Education and Recreation,* May 1977, p. 43.

33 See Jack Anderson, "When Men Dancers Pioneered," *New York Times,* September 21,

1986, pp. 8, 26. See also Seymour Kleinman, ed., *Sexuality and the Dance* (Reston, Va.: National Dance Association, n.d.). On a related issue affecting many male dancers, see articles on AIDS in December 1985 and January 1986 issues of *Dance Magazine.*

34 Diane Milhan Pruett, "Athletes and Dancers: Training and Moving Together," *Journal of Physical Education, Recreation and Dance,* May 1981, pp. 27–28.

35 Roger Copeland, "Why Women Dominate Modern Dance," *New York Times,* April 18, 1982, p. H-1.

36 Susan Manning, "The Feminine Mystique," *Ballet News,* October 1985, pp. 11–17.

37 See "Women Works at the Joyce," advertisement in *New York Times,* January 8, 1989, p. 7-H. In some cases, as in performances of Wallflower Order, a San Francisco women's dance collective, political perspectives of the feminist movement are expressed in a mix of dance, theater, song, martial arts, humor, and sign language. Feminist and racial themes are blended in works of another contemporary group, Urban Bush Women.

38 See Martha Duffy, "Three Who Capture the Magic," *Time,* June 23, 1986, p. 87.

39 Diane Solway, "In a Dancer's World, the Inexorable Foe Is Time," *New York Times,* June 6, 1986, p. 1-H.

40 Karen Clippinger-Robertson, "Kinesiology and Injury Prevention: Every Dancer's Guide," *Journal of Physical Education, Recreation and Dance,* May–June 1986, p. 50.

41 Jack Anderson, "Older Dancers Should Have a Place in the Theater," *New York Times,* March 23, 1986, p. 8-H.

42 Renee Renouf and Martin David, "Performing Stops But Life Goes On," *Dance Teacher Now,* January–February 1987, pp. 39–41.

Bibliography

This is a selected bibliography of books on dance in several categories: history and theory of dance; ballet; modern dance; ethnic dance; and dance in education. A number of the books listed are no longer in print but may be available in university libraries or other dance collections.

Alovert, Nina, *Baryshnikov in Russia* (New York: Holt, Rinehart and Winston, 1984).

Amberg, George, *Ballet in America* (New York: Duell, Sloan and Pearce, 1949).

Anderson, Jack, *Dance* (New York: Newsweek Books, 1974).

Backman, E. Louis, *Religious Dances* (London: George Allen and Unwin Ltd., 1952).

Bellew, Helene, *Ballet in Moscow Today* (Greenwich, Conn.: New York Graphic Society, n.d.).

Bland, Alexander, *A History of Ballet and Dance in the Western World* (New York: Praeger, 1976).

Bland, Alexander, and John Percival, *Men Dancing* (New York: Macmillan Co., 1984).

Bruce, V., *Dance and Dance Drama in Education* (London: Pergamon Press, 1965).

Chujoy, Anatole, *The New York City Ballet* (New York: Knopf/Borzoi, 1953).

Chujoy, Anatole, and P. W. Manchester, *The Dance Encyclopedia* (New York: Simon and Schuster, 1967).

Clarkson, Priscilla, and Margaret Skrinar, *Science of Dance Training* (Champaign, Ill.: Human Kinetics Publishers, 1988).

Coast, John, *Dancers of Bali* (New York: G. P. Putnam's Sons, 1953).

Cohen, Marshall, and Roger Copeland, *What Is Dance? Readings in Theory and Criticism* (New York: Oxford University Press, 1983).

Cohen, Selma Jean, (American Editor), *Dictionary of Modern Ballet* (New York: Tudor Publishing Co., 1959).

———, *The Modern Dance: Seven Statements of Belief* (Middletown, Conn.: Wesleyan University Press, 1965).

de Mille, Agnes, *The Book of the Dance* (New York: Golden Press, 1963).

———, *America Dances* (New York: Macmillan, 1980).

de Zoete, Beryl, and Walter Spies, *Dance and Drama in Bali* (New York: Thomas Yoseloff, 1958).

Dunham, Katherine, *Journey to Accompong* (New York: Henry Holt and Co., 1946).

Emery, Lynn F., *Black Dance: From 1619 to Today* (Pennington, N.J.: Princeton Book Co., 2d ed., 1989).

Espenak, Liljan, *Dance Therapy: Theory and Application* (Springfield, Ill.: Charles C. Thomas, 1981).

Fitt, Sally S., *Dance Kinesiology* (Pennington, N.J.: Princeton Book Co., 1988).

Gregory, John, and Alexander Ukladnikov, *Leningrad's Ballet: Maryinsky to Kirov* (New York: Universe Books, 1980).

Gruen, John, *Erik Bruhn: Danseur Noble* (New York: Viking Press, 1979).

Guest, Ann Hutchinson, *Dance Notation: The Process of Recording Movement On Paper* (Brooklyn, N.Y.: Dance Horizons, 1984).

Hanna, Judith Lynne, *To Dance is Human: A Theory of Non-Verbal Communication* (Austin, Tex.: University of Texas Press, 1979).

———, *The Performer-Audience Connection: Emotion to Metaphor in Dance and Society* (Austin, Tex.: University of Texas Press, 1983).

———, *Dance, Sex and Gender* (Chicago, Ill.: University of Chicago Press, 1988).

Haskell, Arnold, *Ballet* (Harmondsworth, Sussex, England: Pergamon Books, 1951).

Hastings, Baird, *Choreographer and Composer: Theatrical Dance and Music in Western Culture* (Boston: Twayne Publishers, 1984).

Hayes, Elizabeth R., *An Introduction to the Teaching of Dance* (New York: Ronald Press, 1964).

H'Doubler, Margaret, *Dance: A Creative Art Experience* (New York: F. S. Crofts and Co., 1940).

Joyce, Mary, *Dance Technique for Children* (Palo Alto, Calif.: Mayfield Publishing Co., 1984).

Kendall, Elizabeth, *Where She Danced: The Birth of American Dance* (Berkeley, Calif.: University of California Press, 1984).

Kirstein, Lincoln, *Dance: A Short History of Classic Theatrical Dancing* (New York: Dance Horizons, 1935, 1962).

———, *Movement and Metaphor* (New York: Praeger, 1970).

———, *Thirty Years: The New York City Ballet* (New York: Alfred A. Knopf, 1978).

Kriegsman, Sali Ann, *Modern Dance in America: The Bennington Years* (Boston: G. K. Hall and Co., 1981).

Krokover, Rosalyn, *The New Borzoi Book of Ballets* (New York: Alfred A. Knopf, 1956).

Kurath, Gertrude, and Samuel Martí, *Dances of Anáhuac* (Chicago: Aldine Publishing Co., 1964).

LaFosse, Robert, *Nothing to Hide* (Pennington, N.J.: Princeton Book Co., 1987).

La Meri, *Spanish Dancing* (New York: A. S. Barnes and Co., 1948).

————, *The Dance in India* (New York: Columbia University Press, 1953).

————, *Total Education in Ethnic Dance* (New York: Marcel Dekker, 1977).

Lawler, Lillian B., *The Dance in Ancient Greece* (Middletown, Conn.: Wesleyan University Press, 1964).

Lawson, Joan, *European Folk Dance* (London: Sir Isaac Pitman, Ltd., 1955).

Leatherman, Leroy, *Martha Graham: Portrait of the Lady as an Artist* (New York: Alfred A. Knopf, 1966).

Lerman, Liz, *Teaching Dance to Senior Adults* (Springfield, Ill.: Charles C. Thomas, 1984).

Livet, Anne, ed., *Contemporary Dance* (New York: Abbeville Press, 1978).

Lloyd, Margaret, *The Borzoi Book of Modern Dance* (New York: Dance Horizons, 1949, 1970).

Magriel, Paul, ed., *Chronicles of the American Dance* (New York: Da Capo, 1949, 1970).

Martin, John, *Modern Dance* (New York: Dance Horizons, 1933, 1965).

————, *Introduction to the Dance* (New York: Dance Horizons, 1939, 1965).

————, *John Martin's Book of the Dance* (New York: Tudor Publishing Co., 1963).

Maynard, Olga, *The American Ballet* (Philadelphia: Macrae Smith Co., 1959).

McDonagh, Don, *The Rise and Fall and Rise of Modern Dance* (New York: Mentor Books, 1970).

————, *The Complete Guide to Modern Dance* (New York: Popular Library, 1977).

————, *George Balanchine* (Boston: Twayne Publishers, 1984).

Minton, Sandra Cerny, *Choreography: A Basic Approach Using Improvisation* (Champaign, Ill.: Human Kinetics Publishers, 1986).

Morgenroth, Joyce, *Dance Improvisations* (Pittsburgh, Pa.: University of Pittsburgh Press, 1987).

Nadel, Myron H., and Constance G. Nadel, *The Dance Experience* (New York: Praeger Books, 1970).

Newman, Barbara, *Striking a Balance: Dancers Talk About Dance* (Boston: Houghton Mifflin, 1982).

Nielsen, Eric B., *Dance Auditions* (Pennington, N.J.: Princeton Book Co., 1984).

Radir, Ruth, *Modern Dance for the Youth of America* (New York: A. S. Barnes, 1944).

Robbins, Jane, *Classical Dance: The Balletgoer's Guide to Technique and Performance* (New York: Holt, Rinehart and Winston, 1981).

Rogers, Frederick Rand, *Dance: A Basic Educational Technique* (New York: Macmillan Co., 1941).

Royce, Anya Peterson, *Movement and Meaning: Creativity and Interpretation in Ballet and Mime* (Bloomington, Ind.: University of Indiana Press, 1984).

Ruyter, Nancy Lee Chalfa, *Reformers and Visionaries: The Americanization of the Art of Dance* (New York: Dance Horizons, 1979).

Sachs, Curt, *World History of the Dance* (New York: W. W. Norton and Co., 1937).

Shafranski, Paulette, *Modern Dance: Twelve Creative Problem-Solving Experiments* (Glenview, Ill.: Scott Foresman and Co., 1984).

Shawn, Ted, *Dance We Must* (London: Dennis Dobson, Ltd., 1946).

Sherman, Jane, *Denishawn: The Enduring Influence* (Boston: Twayne Publishers, 1984).

Siegel, Marcia B., *At the Vanishing Point, A Critic Looks at Dance* (New York: Saturday Review Press, 1972).

———, *Watching the Dance Go By* (Boston: Houghton Mifflin Co., 1977).

———, *Shapes of Change: Images of American Dance* (Berkeley, Calif.: University of California Press, 1985).

Sorell, Walter, *The Dance Has Many Faces* (New York: World Publishing Co., 1951).

———, *Dance In Its Time* (Garden City, N.Y.: Anchor Press, 1981).

Stearns, Marshall, and Jean Stearns, *Jazz Dance* (New York: Schirmer Books, 1979).

Taper, Bernard, *Balanchine: A Biography* (Berkeley, Calif.: University of California Press, 1987).

Terry, Walter, *Invitation to Dance* (New York: A. S. Barnes and Co., 1942).

———, *The Dance in America* (New York: Harper and Bros., 1956).

Appendix

Dance Periodicals

The following list includes journals intended for a scholarly or professional audience and magazines intended for a more general readership. In addition to ballet and modern dance, these publications deal with dance research, dance therapy, folk and square dance, and dance education. The addresses are correct as of the late 1980s.

American Dance Scene, published bimonthly by American Dance Teachers Association, P.O. Box 85, Vienna, VA 22180.

American Journal of Dance Therapy, published annually by American Dance Therapy Association, Suite 230, 2000 Century Plaza, Columbia, MD 21044.

American Square Dance, published monthly, P.O. Box 488, Huron, OH 44839.

Arabesque, A Magazine of International Dance, published bimonthly, 1 Sherman Sq., Suite 22F, New York, NY 10023.

Attitude: The Dancers Monthly, published monthly, 1040 Park Place, Brooklyn, NY 11213.

Ballet News, published monthly by Metropolitan Opera Guild, 1865 Broadway, New York, NY 10023.

Ballet Review, published quarterly by Dance Research Foundation, 46 Morton St., New York, NY 10014.

Country Dance and Song, published annually, Country Dance and Song Society of America, 505 Eighth Ave., New York, NY 10018.

Dance and Dancers, published monthly by Brevet Publishing, Ltd., 445 Brighton Rd., South Croydon, Surrey, England.

Dance Chronicle, published quarterly by Marcel Dekker, Inc., 270 Madison Ave., New York, NY 10016.

Dance Gazette, published semiannually by Royal Academy of Dance, 48 Vicarage Crescent, London, SW113 LT, England.

Dance Herald: A Journal of Black Dance, published quarterly, Box 686 Ansonia Station, New York, NY 10023.

Dance in Canada, published quarterly by Dance in Canada Association, 38 Charles St. E., Toronto, Ontario M4Y 1T1 Canada.

Dance Magazine, published monthly, 33 West 60th St., New York, NY 10023.

Dance Medicine-Health Newsletter, published quarterly by International Center for Dance Orthopedics and Dance Therapy, 9201 Sunset Blvd., Suite 317, Los Angeles, CA 90069.

Dance Notation Journal, published semiannually by Dance Notation Bureau, 33 W. 21st St., New York, NY 10010.

Dance Research Journal, published semiannually by Congress on Research in Dance, Dance Dept., Education 675 D., New York Univ., 35 W. 4th St., New York, NY 10003.

Dance Scope, published quarterly by American Dance Guild, 1133 Broadway, Rm. 1427, New York, NY 10010.

Dance Teacher Now, published monthly by SMU Communications, Inc., Univ. Mall Suite, 805 Russell Blvd., Davis, CA 95616.

Dance Theatre Journal, Laban Centre for Movement and Dance, Laurie Grove, New Cross, London, SE 14, England.

Folk Dance Scene, published monthly by Folk Dance Federation of California, 12350 Ida Ave., Los Angeles, CA 90066.

Journal of Physical Education, Recreation and Dance, published monthly by American Alliance for Physical Education, Recreation and Dance, 1900 Association Dr., Reston, VA 22091.

Performing Arts in Canada, published quarterly, P.O. Box 517, Station 7, Toronto, Ontario M4Y 2L8 Canada.

National Dance Organizations

American College Dance Festival Association, 82 Livingston St., Brooklyn, NY 11201.

American Dance Guild, 570 Seventh Ave., 20th Floor, New York, NY 10018.

American Dance Therapy Association, 2000 Century Plaza, Suite 230, Columbia, MD 21044.

Choreographers Theatre (Dance Division of Composers and Choreographers Theatre, Inc.), 225 Lafayette St., New York, NY 10012.

Congress on Research in Dance, New York University, Education 675D, 35 West Fourth St., New York, NY 10003.

Country Dance and Song Society of America, 505 Eighth Ave., New York, NY 10018.

Dance Critics Association, P.O. Box 47, Planetarium Station, New York, NY 10010.

Dance Films Association, 241 East 34th St., Rm. 301, New York, NY 10010.

Dance/USA, 633 E St., NW, Washington, DC 20004.

International Association of Black and African Choreographers, P.O. Box 49199, Chicago, IL, 60649.

International Network for Therapeutic Use of Dance/Movement, P.O. Box 20064, Montclair Station, Denver, CO, 80220.

Laban/Bartenieff Institute of Movement Studies, 133 W. 21 St., New York, NY 10011.

Laban Guild, Yew Tree Cottage, Hardham, Pulborough, Sussex, RH20, England.

National Association for Regional Ballet, 1860 Broadway, New York, NY 10023.

National Corporate Fund for Dance, 130 W. 56 St., New York, NY, 10019.

National Dance Association (AAHPERD), 1900 Association Dr., Reston, VA 22091.

National Square Dance Convention, 2936 Bella Vista, Midwest City, OK 73110.

Sacred Dance Guild, 411 West Lemon St., Lancaster, PA 17603.

Society of Dance History Scholars, 79 State St., Brooklyn, NY 11201.

Dance Teacher Organizations

American Dance Teachers Association, P.O. Box 85, Vienna, VA 22180.

Canadian Dance Teachers Association, P.O. Box 5185, Vancouver, British Columbia V6b 4B3 Canada.

Cecchetti Council of America, 35904 Lyndon, Livonia, MI 48154.

Dance Masters of America, P.O. Box 1117, Wauchula, FL 33873.

National Association of Dance and Affiliated Artists, Inc., 50 Victoria Ave., Millbrae, CA 94030.

National Dance Council of America, 107-43 106th St., Ozone Park, NY 11417.

Professional Dance Teachers Association, Inc., 159 Franklin Turnpike, Waldwick, NJ 07463.

Royal Academy of Dancing, Canadian Branch, 209/3050 Yonge St., Toronto, Ontario, M4N 2K4 Canada.

Royal Academy of Dancing, U.S.A., 8 College Ave., Upper Montclair, NJ 07043.

In addition to the foregoing, there are numerous state and regional associations in the United States and Canada which are branches of the national organizations or are affiliated with private ballroom dance chains.

Name Index

Subject Index